FAMILY LAW

Fifth Edition

FAMILY LAW

Fifth Edition

D. Kelly Weisberg

Professor of Law

Hastings College of the Law

University of California

The *Emanuel® Law Outlines* Series

 Wolters Kluwer

Published by Wolters Kluwer in New York.

Wolters Kluwer Legal & Regulatory U.S. serves customers worldwide with CCH, Aspen Publishers, and Kluwer Law International products. (www.WKLegaledu.com)

To contact Customer Service, e-mail customer.service@wolterskluwer.com, call 1-800-234-1660, fax 1-800-901-9075, or mail correspondence to:

Wolters Kluwer
Attn: Order Department
PO Box 990
Frederick, MD21705

Printed in the United States of America.

1 2 3 4 5 6 7 8 9 0

ISBN 978-1-5438-0752-3

Library of Congress Cataloging-in-Publication Data

Names: Weisberg, D. Kelly, author author.
Title: Family law / D. Kelly Weisberg, Professor of Law, Hastings College
 of the Law, University of California.
Description: Fifth edition. | New York : Wolters Kluwer, [2021] | Series:
 The Emanuel law outlines series | Includes index.
Identifiers: LCCN 2020056313 | ISBN 9781543807523 (paperback) | ISBN
 9781543823509 (ebook)
Subjects: LCSH: Domestic relations—United States—Outlines, syllabi, etc.
 | LCGFT: Study guides.
Classification: LCC KF505 .W45 2021 | DDC 346.7301/5—dc23
LC record available at https://lccn.loc.gov/2020056313

About Wolters Kluwer Legal & Regulatory U.S.

Wolters Kluwer Legal & Regulatory U.S. delivers expert content and solutions in the areas of law, corporate compliance, health compliance, reimbursement, and legal education. Its practical solutions help customers successfully navigate the demands of a changing environment to drive their daily activities, enhance decision quality and inspire confident outcomes.

Serving customers worldwide, its legal and regulatory portfolio includes products under the Aspen Publishers, CCH Incorporated, Kluwer Law International, ftwilliam.com and MediRegs names. They are regarded as exceptional and trusted resources for general legal and practice- specific knowledge, compliance and risk management, dynamic workflow solutions, and expert commentary.

Abbreviations Used in Text

FEDERAL STATUTES

Adoption and Safe Families Act (ASFA)

Adoption Assistance and Child Welfare Act (AACWA)

Americans with Disabilities Act (ADA)

Bankruptcy Abuse Prevention and Consumer Protection Act (BAPCPA)

Bankruptcy Reform Act (BRA)

Child Abuse and Neglect Treatment Act (CAPTA)

Child Support Recovery Act (CSRA)

Deadbeat Parents Punishment Act (DPPA)

Defense of Marriage Act (DOMA)

Employee Retirement Income Security Act (ERISA)

Fair Housing Act (FHA)

Fairness for Breastfeeding Mothers Act (FBMA)

Family and Medical Leave Act (FMLA)

Family Support Act (FSA)

Freedom of Access to Clinic Entrances Act (FACE)

Full Faith and Credit for Child Support Orders Act (FFCSOA)

Illegal Immigration Reform and Immigrant Responsibility Act (IIRIRA)

Indian Child Welfare Act (ICWA)

International Child Abduction Remedies Act (ICARA)

International Parental Kidnapping Crime Act (IPKCA)

Lautenberg Amendment

Parental Kidnapping Prevention Act (PKPA)

Partial-Birth Abortion Ban Act (PBABA)

Patient Protection and Affordable Care Act (PPACA or ACA)

Personal Responsibility and Work Opportunity Reconciliation Act (PRWORA)

Pregnancy Discrimination Act (PDA)

Religious Freedom Restoration Act (RFRA)

Retirement Equity Act (REA or REAct)

Targeted Regulation of Abortion Providers (TRAP)

Tax Cuts and Jobs Act (TCJA)

Title VII of the Civil Rights Act of 1964

Unborn Victims of Violence Act (UVVA)

Uniting American Families Act (UAFA)

Violence Against Women Act (VAWA)

UNIFORM ACTS

Revised Uniform Reciprocal Enforcement of Support Act (RURESA)

Uniform Child Abduction Prevention Act (UCAPA)

Uniform Child Custody Jurisdiction Act (UCCJA)

Uniform Child Custody Jurisdiction and Enforcement Act (UCCJEA)

Uniform Collaborative Law Act (UCLA)

Uniform Interstate Enforcement of Domestic Violence Protection Orders Act (UIEDVPOA)

Uniform Interstate Family Support Act (UIFSA)

Uniform Marital Property Act (UMPA)

Uniform Marriage and Divorce Act (UMDA)

Uniform Nonparent Custody and Visitation Act (UNCVA)

Uniform Parentage Act (UPA)

Uniform Premarital Agreement Act (UPAA)

Uniform Premarital and Marital Agreements Act (UPMAA)

Uniform Probate Code (UPC)

Uniform Reciprocal Enforcement of Support Act (URESA)

Uniform Services Former Spouses Protection Act (USFSPA)

Summary of Contents

Table of Contents xi

Preface. xxxi

Casebook Correlation Chart xxxiii

Capsule Summary C-1

Chapter 1.   Introduction 1

Chapter 2.   Preparing to Marry 11

Chapter 3.   Being Married. 57

Chapter 4.   Nontraditional Families 95

Chapter 5.   Divorce. 119

Chapter 6.   Financial Consequences of Dissolution. 147

Chapter 7.   Child Custody 185

Chapter 8.   Procreation 215

Chapter 9.   The Parent-Child-State Relationship in Special Contexts. 251

Chapter 10. Adoption 271

Essay Exam Questions. 295

Essay Exam Answers 299

Glossary of Terms. 307

Table of Cases 323

Table of Statutes 329

Subject Matter Index 335

Table of Contents

Preface xxxi

Casebook Correlation Chart xxxiii

Capsule Summary C-1

Chapter 1

INTRODUCTION

I. **Generally** 1
   A. Definition 1
   B. Central theme 1
   C. Dynamic nature of field 2
II. **Societal Influences on Family Law** 2
   A. Women's movement 2
   B. Rising incidence of divorce 3
   C. Dissatisfaction with the family 4
   D. Dissatisfaction with the traditional dispute resolution process 4
   E. Children's rights movement 4
   F. Gay rights movement and the advent of marriage equality 4
   G. The waxing and waning impact of morality and the accommodation of
      religious beliefs 5
   H. The curtailment of reproductive freedom 5
   I. The increasing use of assisted reproductive technologies 6
III. **Legal Trends** 6
   A. Federalization of family law: Increasing congressional role 6
   B. Constitutionalization of family law 7
   C. Movement toward uniform state laws 8

Chapter 2

PREPARING TO MARRY

I. **Premarital Controversies** 12
   A. Breach of promise to marry 12
      1. Generally 12
      2. Historical background 12
      3. Criticisms 12
      4. Judicial and legislative responses to criticisms 12
      5. Damages 12
      6. Defenses 12
      7. Conflict of laws 13
   B. Gifts in contemplation of marriage: Engagement rings 13

    1. Generally 13
    2. Legal theories 13
    3. Modern trend 13
    4. Other gifts 14
    5. Effect of abolition of heartbalm suits on the recovery of engagement gifts 14

   Quiz Yourself on PREMARITAL CONTROVERSIES 14

II. Premarital Agreements 15
  A. Traditional view 16
  B. Premarital agreements distinguished from other contracts 16
    1. Ordinary contracts 16
    2. Contracts during marriage 16
    3. Separation agreements distinguished 16
  C. Modern approach 16
    1. Trend 16
    2. Limitation 17
    3. Formalities 17
    4. Scope 17
  D. Requirements for validity 17
    1. Full disclosure 17
    2. Fair and reasonable 18
    3. Voluntariness 19
  E. Representation 19
  F. Spousal support 19
  G. Uniform Premarital Agreement Act 20
    1. Policy 20
    2. Reform 20
  H. ALI *Principles* 20

   Quiz Yourself on PREMARITAL AGREEMENTS 21

III. Restrictions on Entry into Marriage 22
  A. Constitutional limitations on regulation of the right to marry 22
    1. Race 23
    2. Poverty 23
    3. Special context: Prisons 24

   Quiz Yourself on CONSTITUTIONAL LIMITATIONS ON REGULATION OF THE
   RIGHT TO MARRY 24

  B. Substantive restrictions: Capacity 25
    1. Same sex 26

   Quiz Yourself on SUBSTANTIVE RESTRICTIONS: SAME-SEX MARRIAGE 31

    2. Substantive Restrictions: Bigamy 31
    3. Substantive Restrictions: Incest 35
    4. Substantive Restrictions: Age 37

   Quiz Yourself on SUBSTANTIVE RESTRICTIONS: INCEST, BIGAMY, AGE 39

    C. Substantive restrictions: State of mind 40
        1. Fraud 40
        2. Duress 41

Quiz Yourself on SUBSTANTIVE RESTRICTIONS: STATE OF MIND 42

    D. Procedural restrictions 43
        1. Licensure 43
        2. Physical examination and blood tests 43
        3. Solemnization 43
        4. Waiting period 44
        5. Recordation 44
        6. Failure to comply with the procedural formalities 44
        7. Abolition of marriage licenses 44
    E. Procedural variations 44
        1. Proxy marriages 44
        2. Confidential marriages 45
    F. Curative procedural doctrines 45
        1. Common-law marriage 45
        2. Putative spouse doctrine 47

Quiz Yourself on PROCEDURAL VARIATIONS AND CURATIVE
PROCEDURAL DOCTRINES 48

IV. Annulment 49
    A. Reasons to seek 49
    B. Void/Voidable distinction 49
        1. Void 49
        2. Voidable 49
        3. Grounds 50
        4. Relation back doctrine 50
        5. Effect of annulment on others' rights 50

Quiz Yourself on ANNULMENT 50

V. Conflict of Laws: Which Law Governs Marriage Validity? 51
    A. Generally 51
    B. Traditional rule: Law of place of celebration 51
    C. Restatement (Second) of Conflicts approach 51
    D. Restatement (Third) of Conflicts approach 52
    E. Uniform Marriage Evasion Act 52
    F. Divorce 52

Exam Tips on PREPARING TO MARRY 52

CHAPTER **3**

BEING MARRIED

I. Introduction 58
   A. Historical background: Ecclesiastic versus civil jurisdiction 58
   B. Contract versus status 58
      1. Marriage is a contract 58
      2. Marriage is a status 58
II. Regulation of Roles and Responsibilities 58
   A. Background: Married women's common-law disabilities 58
   B. Support rights and obligations during marriage 59
      1. Scope of spousal duty of support 59
      2. Limitation on spousal duty of support — family privacy doctrine 59
      3. Common-law necessaries doctrine 59
      4. Child's necessaries 60
      5. Modern statutory support obligations 60
      6. Criticisms of family privacy doctrine 60
   C. Names 60
      1. Married woman's surname change 60
      2. Married woman's resumption of maiden name 61
      3. Men's right to change their names upon marriage 61
      4. Same-sex partners' name change 61
      5. Transgender person's name change 61
      6. Name changes for victims of domestic violence 61
      7. Choice of children's names 61
      8. Constitutional protection for parental choice of child's name 63
      9. International perspective 63
   D. Married woman's domicile 63
      1. Definition 63
      2. Common-law rule 63
      3. Reform 63
   E. Employment 63
      1. Common-law disability 63
      2. Antinepotism (or no-spousal employment) policies 64
   F. Health care 65
      1. Common-law duty to provide medical care 65
      2. Spousal right to terminate life support 66
      3. Property rights in spousal remains 66

   Quiz Yourself on REGULATION OF ROLES AND RESPONSIBILITIES 66

III. Parenting 69
   A. Mandatory maternity leave policies 69
   B. No maternity leave policies 69

C.	Pregnancy Discrimination Act	69
	1. Generally	69
	2. PDA's preemption of state statutes	70
	3. Discrimination after the PDA	70
	4. Criticisms of the PDA	70
D.	Pregnancy accommodations	70
E.	Breastfeeding discrimination	71
	1. Constitutional protection	71
	2. Protection under the PDA and FMLA	71
	3. Federal protection	71
	4. State protection	72
F.	Parental and family leave policies	72
	1. Generally	72
	2. Judicial challenges	72
	3. Legislative reform: The Family and Medical Leave Act	72
G.	Work-family conflict and accommodating family needs in the workplace	73
H.	State paid leave legislation	73
I.	International perspectives	73
	Quiz Yourself on PARENTING	74
IV.	**Criminal Law and Tort Law**	74
A.	Crimes involving spouses	74
	1. Testimonial privileges	74
	2. Wiretapping	76
	3. Marital rape	77
	4. Crimes against spousal property	78
B.	Tort actions against third parties	78
	1. Generally	78
	2. Modern trend	78
	3. Reasons for abolition	78
	4. Problems posed by abolition	78
	5. Specific tort claims	78
C.	Interspousal tort actions	80
	1. Interspousal immunity doctrine	80
	2. Sexual torts	81
	3. Intentional infliction of emotional distress	81
	4. Intimate partner violence	82
	Quiz Yourself on CRIMINAL LAW AND TORT LAW	90
	Exam Tips on BEING MARRIED	92

CHAPTER 4

NONTRADITIONAL FAMILIES

I.	**Introduction**	95
	A. Background	95
	B. Types of nontraditional families	96
	C. Legal recognition	96
II.	**Functional Definition of Families**	96
	A. Formal versus functional	96
	B. Legal protection	97
III.	**Extended Families**	97
	A. Nature of the constitutional protection for the extended family	97
	B. Scope of the constitutional protection for the extended family	97
IV.	**Communal Family**	97
	A. Federal protection (or, lack thereof) for the communal family	97
	B. State protection for the communal family	98
	1. Generally	98
	2. Requirement: Familial-like	98
V.	**Unmarried Cohabitants (Opposite-Sex and Same-Sex Couples)**	99
	A. Criminal sanctions for sexual conduct: Traditional response	99
	B. Zoning: Zoning ordinances and the First Amendment	99
	C. Housing	99
	1. Occupancy rights to a rent-controlled apartment	99
	2. Occupancy rights under the Fair Housing Act (FHA)	100
	3. Occupancy rights under state nondiscrimination statutes in the face of a landlord's First Amendment claims	101
	D. Tort law	101
	E. Support and property rights of unmarried partners	102
	1. Traditional rule: Refusal to enforce agreements	102
	2. Minority view: Traditional rule	102
	3. Majority view: Modern judicial approaches	102
	4. Meretricious relationships in Washington state	106
	5. ALI *Principles*	106
	F. Employment	106
	1. Withdrawal of offer of employment or discharge	106
	2. Proposed federal legislation	107
	3. State laws	107
	4. Military discharge	107
	G. Inheritance law	107
	H. Parentage rights of unmarried fathers	107
	1. Constitutional rights	107
	2. Rebuttable presumptions of paternity	108
	3. Dual fatherhood	108
	4. Voluntary paternity establishment	109
	5. Extending paternity laws to unmarried same-sex partners	109

I. Citizenship by descent 110
J. Domestic violence 111
    1. Federal law 111
    2. Protection orders 111
    3. Obstacles for LGBT partners 111
K. Parentage 112
    1. Support rights of nonmarital children 112
    2. Uniform Parentage Act (UPA) 112

Quiz Yourself on NONTRADITIONAL FAMILIES 112

Exam Tips on NONTRADITIONAL FAMILIES 115

CHAPTER 5

DIVORCE

I. Background 120
II. Fault-Based Grounds 120
  A. Cruelty 120
    1. Elements 120
    2. Physical versus mental cruelty 120
  B. Adultery 121
    1. Elements 121
    2. Criminal versus civil overlap 121
  C. Desertion 121
    1. Elements 121
    2. Constructive desertion 121
  D. Other grounds 122
III. Fault-Based Defenses 122
  A. Recrimination 122
    1. Rule 122
    2. Policy rationale 122
    3. Criticism 122
    4. Limitations 122
  B. Connivance 123
  C. Condonation 123
  D. Collusion 124
    1. Rule 124
    2. Connivance distinguished 124
  E. Insanity 124

Quiz Yourself on FAULT-BASED GROUNDS AND DEFENSES 124

IV. No-Fault Divorce 125
  A. Early no-fault grounds 125
    1. Living separate and apart 125

2. Incompatibility 125
B. Modern no-fault legislation 125
1. Variations in no-fault regimes 126
2. California approach 126
3. UMDA approach 126
4. Problems accompanying the trend to no-fault 126
5. New York reform 126
6. Re-emergence of fault reform movement 126
7. Covenant marriage 127

Quiz Yourself on NO-FAULT DIVORCE 127

V. **Access to Divorce** 128
A. Religious limitations: The Get 128
1. Judicial redress for husband's denial of divorce 128
2. Legislative reform 128
B. Financial limitations: Filing fees 128
C. Right to counsel 129
D. Summary dissolution 129
E. Pro se divorce 129
F. Comparative perspective 129
VI. **Discrimination on the Basis of Divorce** 129
A. Constitutional protection 129
B. State civil rights protection 130
VII. **Role of Counsel** 130
A. Joint representation 130
1. Different approaches 130
2. Dispelling the aura of dual representation 131
3. Confidentiality issues 131
B. Representation of clients in different suits involving related matters 131
C. Sexual relations with clients 132
1. Different approaches 132
2. Background 133
3. Special case of coercion 133
4. ABA Rule 133
5. States without specific bans may still find ethical violations 133
D. Fees 133

Quiz Yourself on ROLE OF COUNSEL 133

VIII. **Divorce Jurisdiction** 134
A. Terminology 134
1. Jurisdiction in the divorce context 134
2. Definition of domicile 134
3. Ex parte versus bilateral divorce 134
4. Divisible divorce 134

   B.   Subject matter jurisdiction 134
     1.   Traditional rule: Domiciliary jurisdiction 134
     2.   Importance of domiciliary requirement 134
     3.   Restatement view: Divorce without domicile 135
     4.   Durational residency requirements 135
     5.   Full Faith and Credit Clause 135
   C.   Personal jurisdiction over the defendant 137
     1.   Proper notice 137
     2.   Long-arm statutes 138
     3.   Transitory presence 139
   D.   Foreign decrees 139
     1.   Comity doctrine: Recognition of divorce decrees rendered by a foreign country . . . 139
     2.   Full faith and credit distinguished 140
     3.   Estoppel 140
   E.   Domestic relations exception to federal jurisdiction: *Ankenbrandt v. Richards* 140
IX. Alternatives to Divorce: Annulments and Separations 141
   A.   Divorce, annulment, and separation distinguished 141
   B.   Reasons to seek 141
X. Alternative Dispute Resolution Processes 141
   A.   Arbitration, conciliation, and mediation distinguished 141
   B.   Enforceability of arbitration provisions 142
   C.   Mandatory mediation 142
   D.   Collaborative law procedure 142

   Quiz Yourself on DIVORCE JURISDICTION 143

   Exam Tips on DIVORCE 144

CHAPTER 6

FINANCIAL CONSEQUENCES OF DISSOLUTION

I. Standards for the Initial Award of Property, Spousal Support, and Child Support 147
   A.   Division of property 148
     1.   Marital property regimes defined 148
     2.   Equitable distribution generally 148
     3.   Traditional rationales 149
     4.   Modern rationale 150

   Quiz Yourself on DIVISION OF PROPERTY: RATIONALES 151

     5.   Property Distribution: Process 152
     6.   What is property? 152

   Quiz Yourself on WHAT IS PROPERTY? 158

   B.   Spousal support 160
     1.   Definition 160

      2.   Background 160
      3.   Rationale for spousal support 160
      4.   Spousal support and property division distinguished 162
      5.   Types of alimony 162

   Quiz Yourself on SPOUSAL SUPPORT 163

   C. Child support 163
      1.   Liability of both parents 163
      2.   Standards 163
      3.   Models of determining support 164
      4.   Deviation from guidelines 165
      5.   Liability of stepparents 165
      6.   Post-majority support 165
      7.   Support rights of nonmarital children 166
      8.   Support rights of children of same-sex couples 168

II. Modification of Spousal and Child Support Awards 168
   A. Standard 168
      1.   General rule 168
      2.   UMDA restrictive rule for modification of spousal support .. 168
      3.   Restrictive rule for retroactive modification of child support .. 168
   B. Relevant factors 168
      1.   Payor's changed circumstances 168
      2.   Recipient's changed circumstances 169

III. Jurisdiction and Enforcement of Child Support Awards 170
   A. Jurisdiction generally 170
   B. State long-arm statutes 171
      1.   Types of long-arm statutes 171
      2.   Constitutional limits of long-arm statutes 171
   C. Interstate enforcement: URESA, RURESA, and UIFSA 172
      1.   General procedure 172
      2.   Continuing problems led to UIFSA 172
      3.   UIFSA 172
   D. Federal legislation: Full Faith and Credit for Child Support Orders Act 172
      1.   UIFSA serves as model 173
      2.   Federal preemption 173
   E. Enforcement remedies 173
      1.   Traditional state remedies 173
      2.   Modern state remedies: License suspension 175
      3.   Federal remedies 175

   Quiz Yourself on CHILD SUPPORT 176

IV. Separation Agreements 177
   A. Premarital agreements distinguished 178
   B. Validity 178

    C. Policy 178

    D. Modification 178

    E. Enforcement of settlement agreement: Merger 178

V. Tax Considerations 178

    A. Traditional approach: Spousal support 178

        1. Taxable to the recipient 179

        2. Deductible by the payor 179

    B. Modern approach: Spousal support 179

    C. Transfers of property to spouse incident to divorce 179

    D. Child support 179

Quiz Yourself on SEPARATION AGREEMENTS 180

Exam Tips on FINANCIAL CONSEQUENCES OF DISSOLUTION 180

CHAPTER 7

CHILD CUSTODY

I. Introduction 186

    A. Definition of custody 186

    B. Functions of custody law 186

    C. Historical background 186

II. Standards for Selecting the Custodial Parent 187

    A. Presumptions 187

        1. Tender years doctrine (the maternal preference) 187

        2. Primary caretaker 187

        3. Other presumptions 188

    B. Best interests of the child 188

        1. Constitutional factors 188

        2. Fitness factors 189

    C. Joint custody 192

        1. Terminology 192

        2. Rationale 192

        3. Modern trend 192

        4. Different state approaches 193

        5. "Joint" custody does not mean equal time 193

        6. Parental agreement 193

        7. Joint custody reform 193

        8. Criticisms of the joint custody movement 193

    D. Pet custody disputes 193

    E. Parenting plans and parenting coordinators 193

Quiz Yourself on STANDARDS FOR SELECTING THE CUSTODIAL PARENT 194

III. Standards for Selecting the Noncustodial Parent: Visitation 196

    A. Denial of visitation 196

      1. General rule 196
      2. Visitation and support: Independent variables 196
  B. Conditions on visitation 196
      1. Domestic violence 196
      2. Sexual abuse 196
      3. Religious practices or beliefs 197
      4. Sexual conduct 197
      5. Substance abuse 198
  C. Interference with visitation rights 198
      1. Civil contempt 198
      2. Change of custody 198
      3. Tort actions 198

Quiz Yourself on STANDARDS FOR SELECTING THE NONCUSTODIAL
PARENT: VISITATION 199

IV. Standards: Parent versus Nonparent Disputes 199
  A. Biological parent presumption 199
  B. Custody and visitation rights of third parties 200
      1. Grandparents 200
      2. Stepparents 201
      3. Lesbian co-parents 201
      4. Uniform Nonparent Custody and Visitation Act 202
      5. ALI *Principles* 202

Quiz Yourself on STANDARDS: PARENT VERSUS NONPARENT DISPUTES 202

V. Role of Special Participants 203
  A. Child's preference 203
      1. Different statutory approaches 203
      2. Procedures to obtain child's preference 203
  B. Counsel for the child 204
  C. Expert testimony 204

VI. Modification 204
  A. Standard for modification 204
      1. Rationale for higher standard 204
      2. Traditional standard 204
      3. Strictest standard 205
      4. Most liberal standard 205
      5. Modification of joint custody 205
  B. Relocation controversies 205
      1. Generally 205
      2. Standards to resolve disputes 205
      3. ALI *Principles* standard 206
      4. Parental motives 206
      5. Infringement on the constitutional right to travel 206
      6. Domestic violence 206

Quiz Yourself on ROLE OF THIRD PARTIES AND MODIFICATION 206

VII. Jurisdiction and Enforcement 207
    A. Jurisdiction 207
        1. Traditional rule 207
        2. The UCCJEA 208
        3. Jurisdiction over Native American children: The Indian Child Welfare Act 208
    B. Enforcement of custody orders 208
        1. Contempt 209
        2. Habeas corpus 209
        3. Tort recovery 209
        4. Criminal sanctions 209
VIII. Child Abduction 209
    A. Uniform law 209
    B. Federal law 209
    C. International Treaty on International Child Abduction 209
IX. Process to Resolve Disputes 210
    A. Adversary process 210
    B. Mediation 210
        1. Voluntary vs. mandatory 210
        2. Waiver 210
        3. Qualifications of a mediator 210
        4. Domestic violence 211
        5. Ethics 211
    C. Collaborative law 211

    Quiz Yourself on JURISDICTION AND ENFORCEMENT 212

    Exam Tips on CHILD CUSTODY 213

Chapter 8

PROCREATION

I. Contraception 215
    A. Access to contraception generally 215
    B. Historical background 216
    C. Married persons' rights to contraception 216
        1. Case and holding 216
        2. *Griswold* concurrence 216
        3. *Griswold* dissent 216
        4. Rationale 216
        5. Source of the constitutional right to privacy 216
        6. The importance of marriage to *Griswold*'s holding 217
        7. Curtailment of police powers 217
        8. Fundamental right 217
        9. *Griswold* and the constitutionalization of family law 217
       10. Subsequent extension of the right to privacy 217

    D. Unmarried persons' rights to contraception 217
        1. Generally 217
        2. Background to *Eisenstadt* 218
        3. *Eisenstadt v. Baird* 218
    E. Minors' rights to contraception 219
        1. Access 219
        2. Parental notification for minors' access to contraceptives 220
        3. Minors' access to emergency contraception 220
    F. Misrepresentation of contraceptive use 221
    G. Right of refusal of health care providers and pharmacists 221
    H. Health insurance coverage of contraceptives 221
    I. Contraceptive Coverage: Recent developments 222
II. Abortion 222
    A. Generally 222
    B. Historical background 222
    C. A woman's right to an abortion 223
        1. *Roe v. Wade* 223
        2. Constitutional challenges to procedural requirements 224
    D. The abortion funding cases 228
        1. Background 228
        2. Restrictions on funding medically necessary abortions: *Harris v. McRae* 228
        3. Prohibition on use of public hospitals and public employees:
            Webster v. Reproductive Health Services 229
        4. Funding restrictions on abortions for military personnel 229
        5. Enhanced right to abortion funding under state constitutions 229
    E. Clinic access and FACE laws 229
    F. Partial-birth abortion bans 230
        1. State legislation on partial-birth abortions 230
        2. *Stenberg v. Carhart* 230
        3. Federal legislation on partial-birth abortions: *Gonzales v. Carhart*: 230
        4. Modern restrictions on late stage abortions 231
    G. Medication abortions 231
    H. State sanctions for abortion participants 232
        1. Providers 232
        2. Pregnant women 232
    I. Husband's rights in the abortion context 232
        1. Spousal consent 232
        2. Spousal notification 233
    J. Minor's right to an abortion 233
        1. Parental consent 233
        2. Parental notification 234
        3. Judicial bypass 234
        4. Undocumented minors' right to abortion 234

III. Fetal Protection Legislation 235
   A. Federal fetal homicide laws 235
      1. Federal legislation 235
      2. State laws 235
   B. Personhood laws and gestational limits 235
   C. Fetal heartbeat laws 235
   D. Fetal remains laws 235

   Quiz Yourself on ABORTION 236

IV. Assisted Reproductive Technology 238
   A. Early technique to address infertility: Artificial insemination 238
      1. Definition 238
      2. Legitimacy of children conceived thereby 238
      3. Role of husband's consent in child support obligation 238
      4. Sperm donor's right regarding anonymity 238
   B. Modern technique to address infertility: In vitro fertilization 238
      1. Definition 238
      2. Status of posthumously conceived children 238
      3. Sperm donor's rights regarding child support 239
      4. Parentage rights of same-sex partners 240
   C. Disposition of frozen embryos at divorce 240
   D. Surrogacy 241
      1. Definition 241
      2. Traditional view 241
      3. Modern view 241
      4. Theories to resolve disputes 242
      5. Obstacles to parentage determinations 243
      6. *Baby M.* 243
      7. Methods of fixing parental status 243
      8. Divorce during surrogacy process 244
      9. International law 245
   E. Three or More Parents 245
      1. Traditional view 245
      2. Modern approach 245
      3. State law reform 245
      4. Landmark California legislation 245
      5. Uniform law 246
   F. Legal Regulations of Sperm Banks 246
      1. Disclosure of medical information 246
      2. Federal law 246
      3. Model law 246
      4. State laws 247
      5. International regulation 247

   Quiz Yourself on ASSISTED REPRODUCTIVE TECHNOLOGY 247

   Exam Tips on PROCREATION 248

CHAPTER 9

THE PARENT-CHILD-STATE RELATIONSHIP IN SPECIAL CONTEXTS

I. Torts 251
   A. Children's liability: Traditional rule 251
      1. Standard of care 251
      2. Contributory negligence 252
   B. Exception to rule of liability: Children's conduct of adult activities 252
   C. Parents' liability for children's torts 252

Quiz Yourself on TORTS 253

II. Contracts 254
   A. Common-law rule 254
   B. Majority rule 254
   C. Policy 254
   D. Modern view: Special contexts 254
   E. Modern view: Restitution of benefits 254

Quiz Yourself on CONTRACTS 255

III. Property 255
   A. Earnings 255
      1. Common-law rule 255
      2. Emancipation 255
   B. Inheritance 255
      1. Traditional rule 255
      2. Guardianship and inheritance 256
      3. Inheritance rights of nonmarital children 256
      4. Inheritance rights of posthumously conceived children 257
      5. Methods of holding property for a minor 257

Quiz Yourself on PROPERTY 257

IV. Education 258
   A. Parents' right to control the upbringing of their children 258
   B. Minors' First Amendment rights 259
      1. Political speech 259
      2. Free speech in the context of school-sponsored and school-approved activities 259
      3. Minors' right to obtain sexually explicit and violent materials 260
      4. Schools' ability to punish students for their expressive activity 260
   C. Minors' Fourth Amendment rights 261
      1. Applicable standard 261
      2. Random drug testing 262
      3. Canine sniffing 262
      4. Locker searches 262
      5. Strip searches 262

6. Special needs doctrine 263

Quiz Yourself on EDUCATION 263

V. Medical Care 264
   A. Requirement of parental consent 264
   B. Minor's consent 264
      1. Specific circumstances 264
      2. Emancipated minors' ability to consent 264
      3. Mature minors' ability to consent 264
   C. Exceptions and limitations to parental consent requirements 264
      1. Emergency exception 264
      2. State-imposed health requirements 264
      3. Neglect limitation 264

Quiz Yourself on MEDICAL CARE 265

Exam Tips on THE PARENT-CHILD-STATE RELATIONSHIP IN
SPECIAL CONTEXTS 266

CHAPTER **10**

ADOPTION

I. Introduction 271
   A. Definition 271
   B. Best interests of the child 272
   C. Historical background 272
   D. Voluntary versus involuntary termination of parental rights 272
   E. Social reality 272
   E. Influence of the Internet 272
II. Selection Standards for Adoptive Parents 272
   A. Generally 272
   B. Relevant factors 272
      1. Preference for relatives 272
      2. Sexual orientation 273
      3. Race 275
      4. Religion 275
      5. Preference for the infertile 276
      6. Indian Child Welfare Act 276

Quiz Yourself on SELECTION STANDARDS FOR ADOPTIVE PARENTS 277

III. Consent 278
   A. Background 278
   B. Consent by the unmarried father 278
      1. Ramifications of *Stanley v. Illinois* 278
      2. Indicia of parenthood 278

3. Consent requirement where father never has opportunity
            to develop a relationship 279
    C. Noncustodial parent's consent in the face of a stepparent adoption 280

    Quiz Yourself on CONSENT 280

IV. **Placement Procedure** 281
    A. Background 281
    B. Agency's role: Disclosure requirements 281
    C. Independent placement: Intermediary's role 281
    D. Criticisms of independent adoption 282

V. **Subsidized Adoption** 282
    A. Background 282
    B. Federal legislation 282
        1. Adoption and Child Welfare Act 282
        2. Adoption and Safe Families Act 283

VI. **International Adoption** 283
    A. Background 283
    B. Criticisms 283
    C. Decline 283
    D. Applicable laws 283
    E. Hague Convention 283

VII. **The Legal Consequences of Adoption** 284
    A. Cutoff rule 284
    B. Marriage limitations 284
    C. Inheritance 284
        1. Intestate succession: By or from the adopted child 284
        2. Inheritance and stepparent adoption 284
        3. Stranger-to-the-adoption rule 284
    D. Custody and visitation 285

    Quiz Yourself on THE LEGAL CONSEQUENCES OF ADOPTION 285

VIII. **Open Adoption** 285
    A. Definition 285
    B. Modern trend 285
    C. Best interests standard 285

    Quiz Yourself on OPEN ADOPTION 286

IX. **Equitable Adoption** 286
    A. Definition 286
    B. Inheritance purposes 286
    C. Theories 287
        1. Contract theory 287
        2. Estoppel theory 287
        3. Equitable relief 287

    Quiz Yourself on EQUITABLE ADOPTION 288

X. Adoptee's Right to Know of Origins 289
    A. Traditional rule 289
    B. Modern view 289
    C. The Internet 289

    Quiz Yourself on ADOPTEE'S RIGHT TO KNOW OF ORIGINS 289

XI. Adult Adoption 290
    A. General rule 290
    B. Requirements 290
    C. Limitations 290
    D. Adoption of same-sex partners 290
    E. Modern view 290
XII. Adoption Failure: Revocation and Abrogation 290
    A. Revocation of consent 290
    B. Abrogation 291
        1. Definition 291
        2. Traditional view 291
        3. Wrongful adoption 291

    Quiz Yourself on ABROGATION 292

    Exam Tips on ADOPTION 292

Essay Exam Questions 295
Essay Exam Answers 299
Glossary of Terms 307
Table of Cases 323
Table of Statutes 329
Subject Matter Index 335

Preface

Welcome to the exciting and dynamic field of family law!

Family law is the body of law that regulates the family and its members. Historically, family law was regulated at the state level. Today, the federal government occupies an increasingly prominent role in family law. This book is designed to help you understand the importance of both state and federal regulation of this fascinating subject area.

This book is not intended as a substitute for class materials or class discussion. Rather, it provides a useful supplement that will help clarify and enhance your understanding of major issues.

Certain special features of this book will help you master this field. These include:

■ **Casebook Correlation Chart:** This chart (following this Preface) correlates each section of the *Outline* with the pages covering the same topic in each of the leading family law casebooks.

■ **Capsule Summary:** This section summarizes the black-letter law principles of family law.

■ **Quiz Yourself:** These short-answer questions, at the end of major sections in each chapter, help you test your knowledge on important concepts in family law.

■ **Exam Tips:** These suggestions, at the end of every chapter, alert you to issues that are likely to appear on family law exams to help you focus your studies in preparation for the exam.

■ **Glossary:** These definitions of key terms at the end of the book elucidate the meaning of words and phrases that appear in this study guide and in your casebook.

This book will be useful both throughout the semester and during exam preparation. Here are some suggestions about how best to use it:

1. Use this *Emanuel Law Outline* to prepare for each day's class. First, read the assigned material in your casebook. Then, use the *Casebook Correlation Chart* (following this Preface) to locate the corresponding subject matter in the *Outline*. Next, read the material in the *Outline* to help you better understand the casebook assignment. If you want to strengthen your knowledge about a particular case or statute, look up the case name in the Table of Cases or the statute in the Table of Statutes (at the back of this *Outline*), and read the discussion of the case or statute in this book.

2. At the end of each unit in your course, do the *Quiz Yourself* short-answer questions to see if you have grasped the assigned material.

3. At the end of the course, use the material in the *Capsule Summary* to help you structure and supplement your outline (if you choose to prepare a personal outline for the course).

4. When you begin studying for the exam, review the course material by reading the *Capsule Summary*. This overview will aid you in structuring your studying by helping you focus your attention on the areas you need to know for the exam.

5. Review some or all the *Quiz Yourself* short-answer questions. It is helpful to answer the *Quiz Yourself* questions both orally and in written form. In writing answers, prepare short essays addressing both sides of a question.

6. Review the course material by preparing answers (preferably, under exam conditions) to the full-length *Essay Exam Questions* at the end of this *Outline*. If the *Essay Exam Questions* identify any gaps in your knowledge, refresh your memory by reviewing relevant portions of the *Outline*.

7. On the day before the exam, quickly review the ***Capsule Summary*** and the ***Exam Tips*** sections at the end of each chapter.

I hope you will find the numerous study tools provided in this *Emanuel Law Outline* beneficial as you explore family law—an area of law that touches everyone. For research assistance, I would like to thank Jasmin Dimson for her invaluable help in the preparation of this manuscript.

Good luck and enjoy family law! If you would like any other publication of Wolters Kluwer Legal Education, you can find it at your bookstore, online, or at *www.WKLegaledu.com*.

D. Kelly Weisberg
Professor of Law
Hastings College of the Law
University of California
weisberg@uchastings.edu

Casebook Correlation Chart

(**Note:** General sections of the Outline are omitted for this chart.
NC = not directly covered by this casebook.)

Weisberg: *Family Law Emanuel Law Outline* (by chapter and section heading)	Areen, Spindelman, Tsoukala & Maldonado: *Family Law: Cases and Materials* (Seventh Edition, 2019) C: Concise Seventh Edition	Harris, Carbone, Teitelbaum & Rebouché: *Family Law* (Sixth Edition, 2018)	Abrams, Cahn, Ross & McClain, Contemporary Family Law (Fifth Edition, 2019)	Weisberg: *Modern Family Law: Cases and Materials* (Seventh, 2020)	Wadlington, O'Brien & Wilson: *Domestic Relations: Cases and Materials* (Eighth Edition, 2017)
CHAPTER 1 INTRODUCTION I. Generally II. Societal Influences on Family Law III. Legal Trends	1-12; C: 1-12 13-25; C: 13-25 NC	3-4 4-16 13-16, 139-63NC	1-4 4-9 9-22, 53-63	xxxiii-xxxviii xxxvii-xxxviii xxxviii	1-108, 475 NC 476, 521
CHAPTER 2 PREPARING TO MARRY I. Premarital Controversies II. Premarital Agreements III. Restrictions on Entry into Marriage IV. Annulment	140-41; C: 114-15 1362-1376; C: 934-43, 950-51 67-171; C: 62-138 115-19, 121-28, 138, 140, 143, 152-60, 171, 592, 1277-78, 1409; C: 93, 96-104, 113, 125-31, 137-38, 432, 875-76, 963-69	NC 624-51, 663, 691 139-200, 210-30 129-31, 133-38, 164-66, 169, 174	483-87 1064-1104 66-152, 156-78 152-56	104-26 113-27 128-201 195, 198-200	109-16 478-505 86-108, 116-84 148-62
V. Conflict of Laws: Which Law Governs?	162, 1277-1280; C: 875-78	200-08	136	214-15	123, 132
CHAPTER 3 BEING MARRIED I. Introduction II. Regulation of Roles and Responsibilities III. Parenting IV. Criminal Law and Tort Law	25-26, 78-79, 96-98,183-86, 1350-1356; C: 25-26, 68-70, 79-82, 145-48, 923-28 173-362; C: 139-270 56, 228-36, 258-77, 363-557, 771-774; C: 56, 183-88, 198-217, 271-408 101, 258-79, 297-362, 784, 822-38, 848, 854-57, 1434; C: 85, 198-219, 232-70, 558-59, 590-99, 604-07, 988	3-11, 125, 134, 145, 755 43-91, 145 NC 5, 45, 91-114, 129, 321, 581-90, 621	79-80, 1058 179-93, 204-34, 237-52 193-204 234-37, 415-92	219-22 223-90 251-90 290-301	185-89 189-213 NC 213-50

Weisberg: *Family Law Emanuel Law Outline* (by chapter and section heading)	Areen, Spindelman, Tsoukala & Maldonado: *Family Law: Cases and Materials* (Seventh Edition, 2019) C: Concise Seventh Edition	Harris, Carbone, Teitelbaum & Rebouché: *Family Law* (Sixth Edition, 2018)	Abrams, Cahn, Ross & McClain, Contemporary Family Law (Fifth Edition, 2019)	Weisberg: *Modern Family Law: Cases and Materials* (Seventh, 2020)	Wadlington, O'Brien & Wilson: *Domestic Relations: Cases and Materials* (Eighth Edition, 2017)
CHAPTER 4 NONTRADITIONAL FAMILIES					
I. Introduction	1-25; C: 1-25	3-4, 209-10	1-2, 4-9	373	NC
II. Functional Definition of Families	NC; C: NC	3, 32	19-20	1-7	
III. Extended Families	631-638; C: 455-62	30-32, 96	11-19	380-87	4-6, 28, 107, 197, 200, 910, 959, 969-76
IV. Communal Family	638-62; C: 462-75	32-39	19	374-80	4
V. Unmarried Cohabitants (Opposite-Sex and Same-Sex Couples)	5-6, 10-12, 109, 561-630, 665, 702-03, 709, 714-18, 726-28, 737, 1074, 1083, 1092; C: 5-6, 10-12, 91, 411-55, 479, 504-05, 510, 514-19, 527-28, 535, 729-30, 738-39, 747	11-13, 16-32, 225-51	255-306	387-465	1-31
CHAPTER 5 DIVORCE					
I. Background	28, 29, 31, 32-37, 775-80; C: 28, 29, 31, 32-37, 551-55	255-57, 282-94	493-500	467-72	259-61
II. Fault-Based Grounds	780-98; C: 555-68	257-62	504-21-	473-84	261-77
III. Fault-Based Defenses	798-807; C: 568-76	262-65	521-27	485-92, 501-02	277-80
IV. No-Fault Divorce	807-816, 850-57; C: 576-85, 601-07	265-79	500-03, 527-59	492-510	266-69, 280-92
V. Access to Divorce	5, 838-41; C: 599-601	280-82	994, 996-1001, 1008, 1011	511-22	502-04
VI. Discrimination on the Basis of Divorce	NC; C: NC	NC	NC	516-20	NC
VII. Role of Counsel	NC; C: NC	695-722	1003-07	523-38	329-33
VIII. Divorce Jurisdiction	1286-90; C: 880-83	754-67	1134-46	540-57	292-318
IX. Alternatives to Divorce: Annulments and Separations	152-60, 777-78, 797, 811-12, 1117-18, 1166, 1395-97; C: 125-31, 553-54, 568, 580-81, 769-70, 952-54	129-31, 133-38, 164-66, 169, 174, 256, 271-76, 664-94	148-56, 559-62	198-201, 653-58	148-62
X. Alternative Dispute Resolution Processes	1270-75, 1408-34; C: 869-74, 961-88	722-51	1017-58	752-62, 758	328-29

Weisberg: *Family Law Emanuel Law Outline* (by chapter and section heading)	Areen, Spindelman, Tsoukala & Maldonado: *Family Law: Cases and Materials* (Seventh Edition, 2019) C: Concise Seventh Edition	Harris, Carbone, Teitelbaum & Rebouché: *Family Law* (Sixth Edition, 2018)	Abrams, Cahn, Ross & McClain, Contemporary Family Law (Fifth Edition, 2019)	Weisberg: *Modern Family Law: Cases and Materials* (Seventh, 2020)	Wadlington, O'Brien & Wilson: *Domestic Relations: Cases and Materials* (Eighth Edition, 2017)
CHAPTER 6 **FINANCIAL CONSEQUENCES OF DISSOLUTION**					
I. Standards for the Initial Award of Property, Spousal Support, and Child Support	1111-79, 1185-1236, 1241-49; C: 763-818, 824-50, 854-61	295-462	565-682, 695-737	559-610	335-54, 385-478, 526-28
II. Modification of Spousal and Child Support Awards	1179-85, 1237-41; C: 818-24, 850-54	469-499	684-92, 737-50, 1183-87	621-27, 646-52	378-85
III. Jurisdiction and Enforcement of Child Support Awards	1107-09, 1249-70, 1323-47; C: 862-69, 904-21	499-517, 786-819	750-73, 1175-87	627-52	318-27, 528-41
IV. Separation Agreements	1356-62, 1394-1406; C: 928-34, 952-61	664-94	1117-29	653-58	505-24
V. Tax Considerations	NC	520-24	252, 692-94	610-11	524-526
CHAPTER 7 **CHILD CUSTODY**					
I. Introduction	859-940; C: 609	533-34	775-78	659-62, 665-68	853-54
II. Standards for Selecting the Custodial Parent	940-1031; C: 609-98	534-614	775-896	662-98	854-87
III. Standards for Selecting the Noncustodial Parent: Visitation	1032-39; C: 698-705	597-98, 614-621	913-20	698-708	887-99
IV. Standards: Parent Versus Nonparent Disputes	110, 448-57, 946-53, 1064-93; C: 92, 337-45, 615-20, 726-29	535-44, 833-41, 859-75, 889-916	921-41	709-26	899-948
V. Role of Special Participants	940-41, 974-78; C: 609-10, 641-43	541-42, 557, 590-97, 620-21	864-78	726-39	955-69
VI. Modification	1039-64; C: 705-26	782, 795-808	941-71	739-47	969-76
VII. Jurisdiction and Enforcement	1093-1109, 1290-1314; C: 748-62, 883-902	786-819	1154-75	748-52	948-54
VIII. Child Abduction	1299-1314; C: 889-902	796-808, 809-19	971-90, 1171, 1174-75	751-52	977-93
IX. Process to Resolve Disputes	1407-34; C: 961-88	721, 733-51	1001-14, 1028-58	752-62	NC
CHAPTER 8 **PROCREATION**					
I. Contraception	245-53; C: 193-98	114-15, 146, 148, 152	22-42	1-18	56-66
II. Abortion	57, 253-86; C: 57, 198-223	115-23	13, 44, 214-31, 316	24-87	67-86
III. Fetal Protection Legislation	NC; C: NC	NC	NC	24-87	NC
IV. Assisted Reproductive Technology	663-774; C: 477-549	953-72	341-53	763-79, 792-829	593-661

Weisberg: *Family Law Emanuel Law Outline* (by chapter and section heading)	Areen, Spindelman, Tsoukala & Maldonado: *Family Law: Cases and Materials* (Seventh Edition, 2019) C: Concise Seventh Edition	Harris, Carbone, Teitelbaum & Rebouché: *Family Law* (Sixth Edition, 2018)	Abrams, Cahn, Ross & McClain, Contemporary Family Law (Fifth Edition, 2019)	Weisberg: *Modern Family Law: Cases and Materials* (Seventh, 2020)	Wadlington, O'Brien & Wilson: *Domestic Relations: Cases and Materials* (Eighth Edition, 2017)
CHAPTER 9 **THE PARENT-CHILD-STATE RELATIONSHIP IN SPECIAL CONTEXTS**					
I. Torts	NC; C: NC	NC	467-72	842-48	
II. Contracts	NC; C: NC	NC	NC	NC	
III. Property	NC; C: NC	842-43	213-14	849-851, 1112-13	
IV. Education	363-68, 372-76; C: 271-76	15, 83, 452-61	NC	18-24	663-92
V. Medical Care	NC; C: NC	501	NC	70-85	770-842
CHAPTER 10 **ADOPTION**					
I. Introduction	457-59; C: 345-46	918-921	367-69, 372	763, 780-82	995-1054
II. Selection Standards for Adoptive Parents	504-37; C: 384-92	935-945, 948-53	377-87, 388-93	782-92	1080-1100
III. Consent	424-36, 459-67, 481-87, 520-31; C: 24-36, 345-53, 368-74, 397-408	859-75, 922-33	374-77	452-54, 836-44	554-75, 1105-10
IV. Placement Procedure	460-76; C: 346-63	933-35	370-73	788-89, 829-51	1048-73
V. Subsidized Adoption	476-81; C: 363-68	934	371-72	832-35	1101-05
VI. International Adoption	492-97; C: 378-84	945-48	393-96	848-50	1119-20
VII. The Legal Consequences of Adoption	457-58; C: 345-46	NC	369	787	NC
VIII. Open Adoption	487-92; C: 374-78	922-27	372, 394, 407-10	789, 791, 843	1018-41
IX. Equitable Adoption	NC; C: NC	921	387-88	NC	1111-18
X. Adoptee's Right to Know of Origins	491-92, 546-48; C: 377-78	922-27, 934-35	411-13	789, 791, 851	NC
XI. Jurisdiction	515-19; C: 392-97	808-09	370	782, 790-91, 851	NC
XII. Adult Adoption	NC; C: NC	NC	NC	NC	1120-26
XIII. Adoption Failure: Revocation and Abrogation	460-67, 541-46, 549-56; C: 346-53	925-26	376	844-51	1073-80

Capsule Summary

This Capsule Summary is useful for a quick review of the course in preparation for the exam. It is not intended as a substitute for mastering the material in the main outline.

CHAPTER 1

INTRODUCTION

I. DEFINITION

Family law explores the legal regulation of the family and its members.

II. SOCIETAL INFLUENCES ON FAMILY LAW

Family law reflects several important societal influences.

A. **Women's movement:** The women's movement led to a change in public policy toward women.

B. **Rising incidence of divorce:** No-fault divorce transformed rules of property distribution, spousal and child support, and custody.

C. **Dissatisfaction with the family:** Disillusionment with the nuclear family resulted in a reconceptualization of marriage and the family.

D. **Dissatisfaction with the traditional dispute resolution process:** Increased dissatisfaction with the adversarial process contributed to the growth of mediation and the recognition of parties' abilities to resolve their disputes without judicial intervention.

E. **Children's rights movement:** The civil rights movement and the women's movement contributed to the birth of the children's rights movement, which led to recognition of the child's increased role in decision making.

F. **Gay rights movement and the advent of marriage equality:** The gay rights movement began in the late 1960s. More recently, *Obergefell v. Hodges* recognized the freedom to marry for same-sex couples nationwide.

G. **The waxing and waning impact of morality and religious beliefs:** Beginning in the 1960s, family law reflected the decreasing influence of ideas about morality. Then, beginning in the 1970s, the rise of the religious right as a political movement brought renewed attention to the role of morality and religion in policy making about family-related issues.

H. **The curtailment of reproductive freedom:** In response to a dramatic rise in legal abortions after *Roe v. Wade* in the late 1970s, conservatives mobilized to elect politicians who would defend "Christian" values. After the election of President Donald Trump in 2016, religious rights were strengthened and fueled the raging battle over women's reproductive rights.

I. **The increasing use of assisted reproductive technologies:** Developments in reproductive technology have enhanced reproductive freedom, especially for members of the LGBT community.

III. TRENDS

Family law reflects three contemporary trends: (1) *federalization* (increasing congressional role), (2) *constitutionalization* (application of constitutional law), and (3) a movement toward *uniformity* of state law.

CHAPTER 2

PREPARING TO MARRY

I. PREMARITAL CONTROVERSIES

A. Breach of promise to marry

1. **Generally:** A few states permit an action for breach of promise to marry, which enables A to recover damages from B, if B terminates the engagement.

2. **Historical background:** The claim of breach of promise to marry has its origins in early English tort and contract law.

3. **Criticisms:** Criticisms have led many states to *abolish* the action.

4. **Judicial and legislative responses to criticisms:** Even in states that continue to recognize the action, state law *circumscribes* recovery.

5. **Damages:** The action is a *hybrid* (quasi-contract, quasi-tort), raising questions about the nature of damages, statutes of limitations, and abatement of the action upon death.

6. **Defenses:** Possible defenses include: fraudulent misrepresentation, nondisclosure of previous unchaste conduct, impaired physical or mental health, or the marital status of either party at the time of the engagement.

B. Gifts in contemplation of marriage: Engagement rings

1. **Generally:** The *majority rule* specifies that, if a ring is given in contemplation of marriage, the *party who breaks* the engagement without justification is *not* entitled to return or retention of the ring.

2. **Legal theories:** Several legal theories support recovery of the engagement ring: *conditional gift*, *fraud*, and *unjust enrichment*.

3. **Modern trend:** The *modern trend* disregards *the role of fault* in breaking an engagement.

II. PREMARITAL AGREEMENTS

A. Traditional view: Traditionally, premarital contracts that determined financial obligations in the event of dissolution were void, as *contrary to public policy*.

B. Premarital agreements distinguished from other contracts

1. **Ordinary contracts:** Premarital agreements *differ from ordinary contracts* because the parties are not at arm's length and premarital agreements are executory.

2. **Contracts during marriage:** According to the traditional rule, the parties *during the marriage* may not regulate by private contract their marital rights and responsibilities.

3. **Separation agreements:** Parties enter into a premarital agreement before marriage, and a separation agreement after they have decided to terminate their marriage.

C. **Modern approach**

1. **Trend:** Courts increasingly recognize premarital agreements.

   a. **Limitation:** Despite increasing recognition of premarital contracts, the parties may *not* enter into an enforceable agreement about *child support* or *child custody*.

   b. **Formalities:** The Statute of Frauds requires that premarital agreements be in *writing* and *signed* by the party to be charged.

   c. **Scope:** The trend is to *broaden the scope* of premarital agreements in terms of what property rights are affected.

2. **Requirements for validity:** A premarital agreement is valid if: (1) it provides full disclosure, (2) it is fair and reasonable, and (3) it is entered into voluntarily by both parties. Some courts reject the requirement that the agreement must be substantively fair.

   a. **Full disclosure:** Many courts impose an affirmative duty on the prospective spouses to disclose their financial status before execution of a premarital agreement.

   b. **Fair and reasonable**

      i. **Traditional rule:** Traditionally, courts required that the agreement be fair under all the relevant circumstances.

      ii. **Modern trend:** Under the **modern trend**, *courts will enforce agreements that are unfair* so long as the agreement accords with intent and is entered into voluntarily and with full disclosure.

         (a) **Factors relevant to determination of reasonableness:** Different factors enter into the determination of reasonableness.

         (b) **Time for determination of reasonableness:** Fairness can be evaluated at the time of either *execution* or *enforcement* of the agreement.

   c. **Voluntariness:** Parties must enter a contract without fraud or duress.

3. **Representation:** States generally do not require that the engaged parties be represented by independent counsel.

D. **Uniform Premarital Agreement Act:** The widely adopted Uniform Premarital Agreement Act (UPAA) and the less widely adopted Uniform Marital Property Act (UMPA) both address premarital agreements. The Uniform Premarital and Marital Agreements Act (UPMAA) was recently approved. It treats premarital and marital agreements similarly.

1. **Policy:** The policy of UPAA is to recognize contractual freedom.

2. **Reform:** The UPAA requires *a very high standard* (i.e., "unconscionability") to render a premarital agreement unenforceable.

III. RESTRICTIONS ON ENTRY INTO MARRIAGE

A. **Constitutional limitations on the right to marry:** State restrictions on the right to marry are subject to *strict scrutiny*. To survive constitutional challenge, the restrictions must be *necessary to a compelling state interest*.

1. **Race:** Racial restrictions on marriage are unconstitutional (*Loving v. Virginia*).

2. **Poverty:** Restrictions on the right to marry that are based on poverty are unconstitutional (*Zablocki v. Redhail*).

   a. **Some reasonable regulations will be upheld:** Reasonable regulations that do not significantly interfere with decisions to enter into marriage may be upheld (*Zablocki*).

   b. **Direct and substantial requirements:** Only those classifications that *directly* and *substantially* interfere with the right to marry will receive heightened scrutiny (*Zablocki*).

B. **Substantive restrictions:** States have substantive restrictions on who may marry.

   1. **Capacity**

      a. **Same sex:** Traditionally, states refused to recognize marriages of same-sex partners. State statutes expressly limited marriage to a man and a woman.

         i. **Early challenges:** Beginning in the 1970s, plaintiffs raised unsuccessful challenges to state marriage bans on both federal and state constitutional grounds. A Hawaii case in 1993 (*Baehr v. Lewin*), marked the beginning of change by invalidating a state ban.

         ii. **Congressional response:** Congress moved swiftly to stymie efforts to legalize same-sex marriage by enacting the Defense of Marriage Act (DOMA) permitting states not to recognize same-sex marriages.

         iii. **Constitutional right to privacy:** The U.S. Supreme Court's decision in *Lawrence v. Texas* (2003) (which overturned state sodomy laws based on the constitutional right to privacy) paved the way for recognition of same-sex marriage.

         iv. **Marriage equality:** The Supreme Court recognized same-sex marriage in *Obergefell v. Hodges* in 2015.

      b. **Substantive restrictions: Bigamy:** All states refuse to permit marriages that are bigamous or polygamous.

         i. **Civil restrictions and criminal sanctions:** Civil restrictions provide that a person may have only one spouse at a time. Criminal liability for bigamy also exists.

         ii. **Background:** Plural marriage is still practiced by some fundamentalist Mormon sects.

         iii. **Criminal requirements:** Modern courts require *intent* to commit bigamy or polygamy.

         iv. **Effect on validity of successive marriage:** If a party is still validly married to a prior spouse, any subsequent marriage is void. This rule is not applied in all cases.

         v. **Defenses**

            (a) **Freedom of religion:** Religious beliefs are not a valid defense to the crime of bigamy.

            (b) **Enoch Arden statutes:** Some statutes provide defenses to bigamy for spouses who remarry in good faith based on a belief that a prior spouse is dead.

         vi. **Conflict of laws:** Bigamous marriages may present issues of the conflict of laws.

         vii. **Presumptions:** Problems of proof have given rise to a presumption that the *most recent marriage is valid*.

        viii. Post-*Lawrence* challenge: Bigamy statutes do not violate the individual's right to privacy protected by *Lawrence v. Texas* because of the state interest in promoting marriage.

        ix. Modern developments: The Utah legislature recently enacted a law that *decreases* liability for bigamy/polygamy from a third-degree felony (with a penalty of up to five years in prison) to an infraction (subject to a $750 fine or community service).

   c. Substantive restrictions: Incest

      i. Civil restrictions: All states have civil restrictions requiring that parties who wish to marry must not be related within certain degrees of kinship.

        (a) Consanguinity: All states restrict marriages by those related by *blood*.

        (b) Affinity: A few states restrict marriages between those parties related by *affinity*.

      ii. Criminal sanctions: States also have criminal provisions punishing incest.

      iii. Rationale: Common rationale for incest provisions include genetic, religious, and sociological reasons.

      iv. Post-*Lawrence* challenge: State incest laws do not violate the constitutional right to privacy (based on *Lawrence v. Texas*) because *Lawrence* has not been interpreted so broadly as to create a fundamental right to engage in *all* forms of private sexual conduct.

   d. Substantive restrictions: Age: All state statutes establish *minimum ages* for marriage. Persons below those ages can marry with parental and/or judicial consent, depending on state statute.

      i. Rationale: The rationale for such restrictions is to promote marriage stability.

      ii. Effect: At common law, nonage rendered marriage void. Today, *such marriages are voidable*.

      iii. Constitutionality of parental consent requirements: Courts uphold the constitutionality of parental consent requirements.

      iv. Law reforms: The past few years have witnessed a trend towards increasing restrictions on teen marriages.

      v. Federal and international reforms: Many countries allow child marriages for economic reasons and the desire to control female sexuality. To address this issue, the Violence Against Women Reauthorization Act (VAWA) of 2013 requires the Secretary of State to develop and implement a strategy to prevent child marriage.

C. Substantive restrictions: State of mind: Fraud and duress furnish grounds for annulment.

  1. Fraud

   a. Requirements: Fraud must go to the ***essentials*** (*strictest test*), or be ***material*** (*more liberal test*).

   b. Significance of consummation: Some jurisdictions require the essentials test if the marriage has been *consummated*.

   c. Effect: The existence of fraud renders a marriage *voidable*, rather than void.

    d. Immigration fraud: Congress enacted the Marriage Fraud Amendments Act to curb problems of marriage fraud in immigration.

  2. Duress: Marriages are *voidable* for reasons of duress.

  3. Effects of voidable marriage for spousal benefits: Persons who enter marriages that are voidable for state of mind restrictions may be unable to collect spousal state benefits based on such marriages.

D. Procedural restrictions: States require that the parties *procure a marriage license*. All states require *solemnization* of marriage by an authorized person before witnesses. Many states impose a *waiting period*. Failure to comply with these procedural formalities will *not* invalidate the marriage unless the jurisdiction has a statute that expressly provides that issuance of a marriage license is a mandatory requirement for a valid marriage.

E. Procedural variations and curative devices: Parties may marry in some jurisdictions by means of **proxy marriages** or **confidential marriages**. Curative devices (*common-law marriage, putative spouse doctrine*) validate a marriage even though some procedural element may be absent.

  1. Proxy marriages: In a proxy marriage, a *substitute (a proxy) stands in* for an absent bride or groom.

  2. Confidential marriages: A "confidential" marriage may be recognized even though it fails to meet all of the statutory formalities (such as a marriage license and health certificate).

  3. Common-law marriage

    a. Generally: A few states recognize common-law marriage in which the parties presently *agree* to enter into a legal marital relationship, *cohabit*, and *hold themselves out as husband and wife*.

    b. Elements

      i. Present agreement: Although the parties must agree to enter into a legal marital relationship, *no specific words are required*.

      ii. Cohabitation: The couple must cohabit in a jurisdiction that recognizes common-law marriages.

      iii. Holding out: The couple must have the reputation in the community of being married.

    c. Conflict of laws: Common-law marriages present problems when the parties reside in multiple jurisdictions.

      i. Initial residence in a common-law jurisdiction: If the parties first reside in a jurisdiction that recognizes such marriages, but move to a jurisdiction that does not, the latter jurisdiction almost always recognizes the marriage.

      ii. Initial residence in a non-common-law jurisdiction: If the parties first reside in a jurisdiction that does not recognize such marriages, but later move to a jurisdiction that does, the latter jurisdiction usually recognizes the marriage.

    d. Common law marriage and same-sex couples: Following *Obergefell*, several states conferred common-law-marriage status *retroactively* on same-sex couples.

4. **Putative spouse doctrine:** The putative spouse doctrine protects a spouse who has a *good-faith belief* in the validity of the marriage.

   a. **Common-law marriage distinguished:** Parties to a common-law marriage are aware that they have not taken part in a marriage ceremony. A putative spouse has a good-faith belief that a valid marriage has occurred.

   b. **Conflicting claims:** Occasionally, both a putative spouse and a lawful spouse may assert claims to a benefit stemming from the marriage.

IV. ANNULMENT

An annulment declares a marriage void, whereas a divorce declares that a valid marriage has come to an end.

A. **Reasons to seek:** Today, parties may seek an annulment, rather than divorce, for religious or jurisdictional reasons (to avoid longer residency requirements for divorce).

B. **Void/voidable distinction:** An invalid marriage may be characterized as *void or voidable.*

   1. **Void:** A void marriage is invalid from inception and may be challenged by the parties themselves or by third parties, and may be collaterally attacked.

   2. **Voidable:** A voidable marriage is valid from inception and requires that one of the parties take judicial action to establish its invalidity. It may be attacked only by the parties, during the duration of the marriage, and cannot be collaterally attacked.

C. **Grounds:** Bigamy and incest provide grounds for a void marriage. Fraud, duress, and nonage provide grounds for a voidable marriage.

D. **Relation back doctrine:** The declaration of invalidity of an annulment "relates back" to the inception of the void marriage.

E. **Effect of annulment on other's rights:** Some statutes now permit spousal support awards following annulment. At common law, annulment resulted in bastardizing children born during the relationship. Statutes have modified this harsh result.

V. CONFLICT OF LAWS: WHICH LAW GOVERNS MARRIAGE VALIDITY?

A. **Traditional rule: Law of place of celebration:** Under the ***traditional rule***, marriage validity is determined by the law of the state *where the marriage was celebrated.*

B. **Restatement (Second) of Conflicts approach:** The Restatement (Second) of Conflict of Laws §283(1) has modified the general rule, holding that, in absence of statute, the validity of marriage is determined by the state that has the *most significant relationship to the spouses and the marriage.*

C. **Restatement (Third) of Conflicts approach:** The Restatement (Third) of Conflict of Laws §201.1 uses the term "domicile" to identify the "place where the person's life is centered for resolving choice-of-law issues" and emphasizes proof of intent by objective evidence.

CHAPTER 3

BEING MARRIED

I. INTRODUCTION

   A. **Historical background: Ecclesiastic versus civil jurisdiction:** In England, ecclesiastic courts maintained exclusive jurisdiction over marriage.

   B. **Contract versus status**

      1. **Marriage is a contract:** The colonists, rejecting the religious character of marriage, regarded marriage as a contract.

      2. **Marriage is a status:** Marriage is also a civil status.

II. REGULATION OF ROLES AND RESPONSIBILITIES

   A. **Married women's common-law disabilities:** At common law, the suspension of the wife's legal identity subjected women to significant legal *disabilities*. The Married Women's Property Acts eliminated these disabilities in the nineteenth century.

   B. **Support rights and obligations during marriage**

      1. **Scope of spousal duty of support:** At common law, the husband had a duty to support his wife. Today, the duty of support is gender neutral.

      2. **Limitation on spousal duty of support: Family privacy doctrine:** The spousal duty of support is limited by the doctrine of family privacy: courts are reluctant to interfere in an *ongoing* marriage to settle disputes.

      3. **Common-law necessaries doctrine:** A husband had a common-law duty to provide *necessaries* to his wife and children.

         a. **What constitutes a necessary:** Necessaries include: food, clothing, shelter, medical care, and sometimes other items.

         b. **Constitutional challenges:** Support obligations that are payable *only by the husband* are *unconstitutional*.

      4. **Criticisms of family privacy doctrine:** Criticisms of the doctrine include the following:

         ■ The doctrine does not preserve marital harmony.

         ■ Matters of spousal disagreements are not trivial.

         ■ Common-law rationales are outdated.

         ■ The doctrine inappropriately gives preference to third-party rights over those of an injured spouse.

         ■ The doctrine introduces needless circularity by enabling only creditors to sue.

   C. **Names**

      1. **Married woman's surname change:** At common law, a married woman assumed her husband's surname based on custom. Today, a married woman may retain her birth name so long as she has proven **consistent and non-fraudulent use**.

Upon divorce, many states authorize a married woman to resume her maiden name. A few states allow a man to assume his spouse's surname upon marriage.

  2. **Choice of children's names**

    a. **Generally:** Many modern statutes provide that the parents may choose, as the child's surname, (1) the husband's surname, (2) the wife's birth name, or (3) a combined surname.

    b. **Standard to resolve disputes:** Courts resolve disputes about *children's* surnames according to the *best interests of the child standard*.

    c. **Constitutional right:** Some cases raise constitutional challenges to statutes restricting parental choice in children's surname.

  3. **Same-sex spouses' rights:** Both same-sex spouses have the right to be listed on their child's birth certificate.

D. **Married woman's domicile**

  1. **Definition:** *Domicile* is important in determining *jurisdiction* for: the validity of a marriage, divorce, custody, legitimacy, and adoption.

  2. **Common-law rule:** At common law, a married woman lacked the capacity to establish, change, or retain the domicile of her choice.

  3. **Reform:** The Restatement (Second) of Conflict of Laws permitted a separate domicile for a wife who was living apart from her husband. Today, either spouse can establish a domicile.

E. **Employment: Antinepotism (or no-spousal employment) policies:** Antinepotism rules sometimes prevent one spouse from being employed by the other spouse's employer.

  1. **Rationale for policies:** Some business rationales support antinepotism policies.

  2. **Grounds of attack:** Plaintiffs have raised federal and state challenges to antinepotism policies based on the fundamental right to marry, Title VII, state civil rights statutes, and public policy.

  3. **Anti-fraternization rules:** Some employers have anti-fraternization rules, which ban all employees from dating co-workers or limit the prohibition to supervisor-subordinate relationships.

F. **Health care**

  1. **Common-law duty to provide medical care:** At common law, a spouse had a duty to provide medical attention to the other spouse.

  2. **Spousal right to terminate life support:** All states permit a person to express his or her wishes as to medical treatment in case of terminal illness or injury, and to appoint a proxy decisionmaker in the event the person cannot communicate for himself or herself.

III. PARENTING

A. **Mandatory maternity leave policies:** Many employers' mandatory maternity leave policies previously required employees to leave employment when they became pregnant.

B. **No maternity leave policies:** Plaintiffs unsuccessfully challenged, on equal protection grounds and Title VII, those employers' policies permitting disability, but not pregnancy, leave.

C. Pregnancy Discrimination Act

1. **Generally:** Congress responded to dissatisfaction with the lack of maternity leave policies by enacting the *Pregnancy Discrimination Act (PDA)* that amended Title VII.

2. **Did the PDA preempt state statutes?:** The Supreme Court held that the *PDA did not preempt state statutory schemes* that affirmatively provided for employment-related pregnancy benefits (*Cal. Fed. v. Guerra*).

3. **Criticisms:** The PDA treats pregnancy as a "disability" and permits employers to have no policy for pregnancy so long as they have no policy for disability.

4. **Parental and family leave policies: FMLA**

   a. **Constitutional challenges:** In response to constitutional concerns regarding equal protection, Congress liberalized leave policies. Congress enacted the *Family and Medical Leave Act* in 1993, requiring certain employers to provide eligible employees with *unpaid* leave.

   b. **Criticisms:** The FMLA has been criticized for providing only unpaid leave.

   c. **Reforms:** The U.S. Department of Labor liberalized the definition of *parent* in the FMLA to allow employees to have leave to care for children of a same-sex partner.

5. **Pregnancy accommodations:** Pregnant employees may need workplace accommodations enabling them to continue to work. Employers' failure to make *pregnancy accommodations* for pregnant workers with medical needs, while accommodating non-pregnant workers, violates the PDA.

6. **Breastfeeding discrimination:** Some employers have workplace policies that impose restrictions on breastfeeding mothers.

   a. **Federal protection:** Breastfeeding discrimination violates the PDA and the FMLA. The Affordable Care Act (Break Time for Nursing Mothers) requires employers to provide employees with reasonable break time to express breast milk for one year after birth in a private place other than a bathroom.

   b. **State protection:** State protections for breastfeeding include: exemptions of breastfeeding from public nudity and other criminal statutes, protection of breastfeeding mothers in any public or private location, protection of breastfeeding in civil rights remedies, encouragement or mandating employer accommodation of breastfeeding, and exemptions of breastfeeding women from jury duty.

D. State paid leave legislation: A few states now offer *paid* family leave programs.

IV. CRIMINAL LAW AND TORT LAW

In both criminal and tort law, courts and legislatures are abolishing special treatment for spouses.

A. Crimes involving spouses

1. **Testimonial privilege**

   a. **Common-law rule:** At common law, a spouse could not testify for or against the other spouse in criminal proceedings.

b. **Types of communications distinguished:** Adverse spousal testimony may consist of either *confidential marital communications* (made in the presence only of the other spouse) or *communications made to the spouse in the presence of third parties.*

c. **Adverse spousal testimony: Different state approaches:** States adopt one of *four* approaches to adverse spousal privilege:

■ some adhere to the common-law rule of disqualification;

■ some vest the privilege against adverse spousal testimony in the defendant, or in the husband and wife jointly;

■ some vest the privilege in the witness-spouse; and

■ some abolish the privilege.

d. **Federal approach:** The Supreme Court (*Trammel v. United States*) vests in the witness-spouse the privilege to *prohibit* testimony about communications made in the presence of third parties, while *leaving intact* the confidential marital communications privilege.

2. **Marital rape**

a. **Common-law rule:** At common law, a man *could not be guilty* of raping his wife.

b. **State approaches:** All states have **abolished or limited** the exemption.

c. **Modern trend:** Some states still provide preferential treatment to spousal rapists by making marital rape a lesser, separate offense to rape and/or providing some form of exemption for spouses who sexually assault their partners when the latter are drugged or otherwise incapacitated.

3. **Crimes against spousal property:** Modern case law permits spousal liability for a criminal act involving the other spouse's property.

B. **Tort actions against third parties**

1. **Generally:** At common law, the husband had a right to sue a third party in tort for interference with the marital relationship.

2. **Modern trend:** Many courts and legislatures *abolished* actions for alienation of affections and criminal conversation via *anti-heartbalm legislation.*

3. **Reasons for abolition:** Reasons for abolition include: divorce is not caused solely by a third party; awards are excessive; damages are difficult to assess and inappropriate; the law has no deterrent effect; and spousal affection is not a property right.

4. **Problems posed by abolition:** Problems sometimes arise in imposing civil liability on *psychologists and religious officials who engage in sexual misconduct* in the course of marital counseling.

5. **Specific tort claims**

a. **Alienation of affections**

i. **Generally:** At common law, a husband might bring an action against a third party for alienation of affections.

ii. **Elements:** A plaintiff must show:

■ a valid marriage;

- defendant's wrongful conduct;

- a loss of consortium; and

- a causal connection between defendant's conduct and plaintiff's loss.

    iii. Defenses: Consent on the part of the plaintiff's spouse is not a defense.

b. Criminal conversation

    i. Generally: This action was available only to the husband at common law.

    ii. Elements: A plaintiff had to show:

- a valid marriage; and

- the defendant's sexual intercourse with plaintiff's spouse.

    iii. Defenses: Criminal conversation was a strict liability offense.

    iv. Alienation of affections distinguished: A claim for alienation of affections might be brought *without* the need for proof of sexual intercourse.

c. Policy issue: Critics contend that the amatory torts are out-of-sync with the sexual attitudes of modern society and question whether the harm caused by adultery is actually alleviated by money damages.

C. Interspousal tort actions

1. Interspousal immunity doctrine

a. Historical background: The common-law doctrine of ***interspousal immunity*** barred tort actions between husbands and wives.

b. Rationale: Rationales supporting the interspousal immunity doctrine are that the bar:

- promotes marital harmony;

- prevents involving the judiciary in resolution of trivial matters; and

- prevents the spouses from collusion to defraud insurance companies.

c. Reform: Currently, the majority of jurisdictions have abolished the doctrine.

2. Sexual torts: Interspousal tort liability exists for ***negligent transmission of venereal disease***.

3. Intentional infliction of emotional distress: Several courts have allowed a spouse to recover damages for acts of extreme cruelty by the other.

a. Statutes of limitations: To avoid problems with statutes of limitations, some courts apply a "continuing tort theory" to permit a spouse to recover for acts of abuse during the entire duration of the intimate relationship.

b. Claim preclusion and joinder: Courts are split regarding whether an abused spouse's claim is barred in a post-divorce tort action because of the res judicata effect of the divorce decree. Most jurisdictions permit, but do not mandate, joinder.

4. Intimate partner violence: All states have legislation and case law that address intimate partner violence. Legal policy:

- liberalizes the admission of syndrome evidence;

- provides civil and criminal remedies against the abuser;

- addresses the issue of remedies against law enforcement personnel for failure to protect; and

- permits innovative federal and state reforms.

a. Role of age: Age plays a role in the law's response to intimate partner violence. Teens and elders experience intimate partner violence.

b. Other influential factors: Gender, sexual orientation, disability, race and ethnicity, and immigration status all play a role in the law's response to intimate partner violence.

   i. Gender: Women are significantly more likely than men to be victims of intimate partner violence and are more likely to suffer more severe injuries or be killed by intimate partner violence.

   ii. Sexual orientation: Intimate partner violence among same-sex couples occurs with the same or greater frequency as among opposite-sex couples.

   iii. Disability: Women with disabilities face a higher risk of IPV. They also suffer abuse by multiple partners, more severe abuse, more types of abuse, and abuse for longer durations.

   iv. Race and ethnicity: Native American women experience IPV largely at the hands of non-Native men. African-American women often hesitate to report abuse because of their fear that disclosure will subject their partners to a racist or violent response from the police.

   v. Immigration status: Immigrant women suffer high rates of domestic violence. They face language barriers, social isolation, and the lack of financial resources.

c. High lethality crimes: High lethality factors have been identified and are used to predict cases in which intimate partner violence is most likely to result in severe physical violence or homicide.

d. Admissibility of evidence of battered woman's syndrome: The *modern trend* is to permit admission of evidence of battered woman's syndrome. Battered woman's syndrome explains why women stay in an abusive relationship. Evidence of battered woman's syndrome addresses the reasonableness of the perception of imminence and the danger that a woman faces.

e. State remedies against the batterer: An abuser may incur criminal liability for assault. Most states have legislation providing for civil protective orders. Some states have mandatory arrest and/or "no-drop" policies.

f. Remedies against law enforcement for failure to protect

   i. Federal civil rights action under §1983: For a time, a few courts recognized a federal civil rights cause of action (under 42 U.S.C. §1983) against law enforcement and/or municipalities for the failure of public officials to protect abused women based on the "special relationship" doctrine (i.e., police assumed an affirmative duty to protect battered women who had protective orders).

   ii. Limitation on doctrine: The U.S. Supreme Court limited this doctrine in *DeShaney v. Winnebago,* thereby foreclosing claims based on substantive due process against government officials for failure to protect.

   iii. State-created danger doctrine: Another exception to *DeShaney* is the state-created danger doctrine, which provides that state actors may be liable under §1983 if they created or enhanced the danger of private violence.

  iv. No constitutional right to protection: The Supreme Court subsequently foreclosed claims based on *procedural* due process against government officials for failure to protect (*Town of Castle Rock v. Gonzales*).

 g. Difficulties for prosecutors: Problems arise for prosecutors because the Supreme Court limited the admissibility of hearsay evidence in *Crawford v. Washington*.

 h. *Crawford v. Washington*: The U.S. Supreme Court held that the Sixth Amendment requires actual confrontation for the admission of out-of-court testimonial statements.

 i. Federal legislative remedies: The federal legislative approach to intimate partner violence consists of funding for shelters, the Violence Against Women Act (VAWA), and regulation of firearms by perpetrators of domestic violence.

 j. Children's exposure to intimate partner violence: State laws are increasingly recognizing that children suffer harm resulting from witnessing domestic violence.

CHAPTER 4
NONTRADITIONAL FAMILIES

I. INTRODUCTION

The traditional nuclear family is on the decline. Many people now reside in nontraditional families, such as unmarried (opposite-sex or same-sex) couples, communal arrangements, and extended families. The law confers legal recognition on some nontraditional families for some purposes.

II. FUNCTIONAL DEFINTION OF FAMILIES

 A. Formal versus functional: The formal definition of family characterizes a "family" according to blood ties or legal ceremony (such as marriage or adoption). In contrast, the functional approach defines a family by virtue of its functions.

 B. Constitutional protection: Unmarried partners lack the automatic legal protections granted to formal families created through biology and legal ceremonies.

III. EXTENDED FAMILIES

 A. Nature of the constitutional protection for the extended family: To a limited extent, the Constitution protects the freedom of family members to choose to live together as an extended family.

 B. Scope of the constitutional protection for the extended family: The Constitution does not require a state to provide certain benefits to assist members of extended families to live together.

IV. COMMUNAL FAMILY

The U.S. Supreme Court *refuses* to provide legal protection, for zoning purposes, to the communal family. *Communal families* receive *more* favorable treatment in *zoning* challenges based on *state* constitutional law.

V. UNMARRIED COHABITANTS (OPPOSITE-SEX AND SAME-SEX COUPLES)

A. Criminal sanctions for sexual conduct: Traditional and modern response: The traditional legal response to unmarried couples is the imposition of ***criminal sanctions***. The U.S. Supreme Court decision in *Lawrence v. Texas* (which overturned state sodomy laws based on the constitutional right to privacy) signaled a major shift in the legal response to private consensual adult sexual conduct.

B. Zoning: Zoning ordinances and the First Amendment: State courts *have denied* constitutional protection to *unmarried* couples for *zoning* purposes.

C. Housing: States have made much progress in terms of remedying housing discrimination against unmarried couples.

   1. Occupancy rights to a rent-controlled apartment: A landmark case (*Braschi v. Stahl Assocs.*) recognized the *occupancy rights of same-sex partners* by adopting a broad functional definition of "family."

   2. Occupancy rights under the Fair Housing Act (FHA): The federal FHA prohibits discrimination on the basis of race, color, religion, national origin, gender, familial status (having children and pregnancy), and physical or mental disability. Marital status is not one of the protected categories.

   3. Occupancy rights under state nondiscrimination statutes: Landlords' refusals to rent to unmarried couples on religious grounds have met with varying success.

D. Tort law: Courts sometimes deny legal rights to cohabitants in the tort context that are available to members of traditional families.

E. Support and property rights of unmarried partners

   1. Minority view: Traditional rule: Under the ***traditional rule***, courts *refused to enforce contractual agreements* between members of unmarried couples as constituting a violation of *public policy*. A few courts still adhere to this rule.

   2. Majority view: Modern judicial approaches

      a. Express agreements: Under the ***majority view***, unmarried partners have the *same right as married partners* to enter into express contracts regarding the ownership of property.

      b. Express and implied agreements: Some courts (following *Marvin v. Marvin*) recognize both express and implied agreements between nonmarital cohabitants.

   3. *Marvin* and same-sex couples: Some courts extend *Marvin* to recognize cohabitation contracts between same-sex couples. However, other states prohibit enforcement of such contracts as a violation of public policy.

F. Employment: Unmarried cohabitants (same-sex and opposite sex) sometimes face discrimination from employers. Employment discrimination based on sexual orientation or gender identity violates Title VII.

G. Citizenship by descent: Rules governing citizenship by descent ("derivative citizenship") for foreign-born children of a U.S. citizen-parent violate the Equal Protection Clause if they are based on the citizen-parent's marital status and gender.

H. Domestic violence: All states have civil and criminal legislation addressing domestic violence, including protections for married, as well as unmarried, intimate partners.

1. **Federal law:** The Violence Against Women Act (VAWA) of 1994 applies to intimate partners whether married or unmarried. The VAWA Reauthorization Act of 2013 prohibits VAWA-funded programs from discriminating against domestic violence survivors on the basis of sex, sexual orientation, or gender identity.

2. **Protection orders:** All states have civil and criminal legislation addressing domestic violence, including provisions for protective orders.

I. **Parentage:** Nontraditional families experience limitations on the rights of nonmarital children as well as the rights of unwed parents

   1. **Support rights of nonmarital children:** Traditionally, the law regarded nonmarital children as *ilius nullius* and bastards ("illegitimate"), which affected their rights to support and inheritances. Today both parents must support the child regardless of their marital status.

   2. **Uniform Parentage Act (UPA):** The original UPA was promulgated in 1973 to address the unequal treatment of nonmarital children and to provide guidance to the states in response to U.S. Supreme Court decisions on the rights of nonmarital children. Since then, revised UPAs (2000, 2002, 2017) re-affirm the equal treatment of nonmarital children.

   3. **Constitutional rights of unmarried fathers:** The U.S. Supreme Court recognizes the constitutional rights of unmarried fathers in some circumstances: if the biological father manifests a substantial relationship with the child ("indicia of parenthood") his parent-child relationship will be accorded constitutional protection.

   4. **Conflict of fathers' rights:** The U.S. Supreme Court has held that, when an unmarried biological father's rights conflict with the rights of a married father, the married father will prevail if the child was born into an intact family.

   5. **Extending paternity laws to unmarried same-sex couples:** With the development of reproductive technology and the advent of marriage equality, courts face the issue of determining what role paternity laws should play in the establishment of parental rights of lesbian and gay couples.

   6. **Contrast with same-sex spouses' parental rights:** States cannot deny same-sex *spouses* the same benefits afforded to opposite-sex spouses (according to the Supreme Court in *Obergefell v. Hodges* and *Pavan v. Smith*).

Chapter 5

DIVORCE

I. BACKGROUND

American divorce law traditionally required fault-based grounds.

II. FAULT-BASED GROUNDS

A. **Cruelty:** Cruelty was the most common ground prior to the adoption of no-fault divorce.

   1. **Elements:** To prove cruelty, a plaintiff must show:

- a course of conduct that is so severe as to

- create an adverse effect on plaintiff's physical or mental well-being.

   2. Physical versus mental cruelty: Although early courts required physical violence, modern courts recognize mental cruelty.

B. Adultery

   1. Elements: To prove adultery for divorce purposes, a plaintiff must show:

- *opportunity* to commit the offense; and

- *disposition* to commit it.

   2. Criminal versus civil overlap: Adultery is both a crime and a ground for divorce.

C. Desertion

   1. Elements: Desertion requires:

- *a voluntary separation;*

- *with intent not to resume cohabitation;*

- *which is without the partner's consent or without justification.*

   2. Constructive desertion: Constructive desertion, an alternative ground for divorce and a defense, constitutes conduct that either causes a spouse to leave or justifies the spouse's departure.

III. FAULT-BASED DEFENSES

Fault-based defenses include *recrimination, connivance, condonation, and collusion.*

A. Recrimination

   1. Rule: Recrimination bars a divorce if both spouses are at fault.

   2. Policy rationale and criticism: Rationales include the clean hands doctrine, access to divorce only for an innocent spouse, preservation of marriage, and the need to provide economic protection to women. Commentators criticize the doctrine for its *harsh consequences.*

   3. Limitation: The doctrine of **comparative rectitude** permits a divorce to the party who was least at fault.

B. Connivance: *Connivance* is participation in, or consent to, a spouse's wrongful conduct.

C. Condonation: *Condonation* is forgiveness by a spouse, usually implying resumption of sexual relations.

D. Collusion

   1. Rule: *Collusion* occurs when the spouses agree to divorce by means of the commission of a marital offense.

   2. Connivance distinguished: Connivance is *consent* by one spouse whereas collusion is a spousal *agreement* to commit a marital wrong.

IV. NO-FAULT DIVORCE

A. Early no-fault grounds

1. Living separate and apart

a. **Elements:** Most states continue to provide for no-fault divorce based on physical separation.

b. **Meaning of "separate and apart":** The term *living separate and apart* may refer to both physical separation and an intention to dissolve the marriage. Spouses may live "separate and apart" even though they live in the same house.

2. Incompatibility: *Incompatibility* was one of the *earliest* no-fault grounds.

B. Modern no-fault legislation: All states now have some form of no-fault divorce. Some states are pure no-fault jurisdictions. Other states merely add no-fault grounds to their fault-based grounds.

1. **California approach:** California (the first jurisdiction to adopt no-fault divorce) permits divorce based on *"irreconcilable differences, which have caused the irremediable breakdown of the marriage."*

2. **UMDA approach:** UMDA permits divorce if the marriage is *"irretrievably broken"* or the parties have *lived separate and apart for six months.*

3. **New York reform:** New York became the last state to adopt no-fault divorce.

4. **Re-emergence of fault reform movement:** Some states still consider fault to be relevant in the division of marital property and determination of spousal support. A reform movement has resurrected the role of fault by means of *covenant marriages* that permit dissolution only on fault-based grounds or after a two-year separation.

V. ACCESS TO DIVORCE

A. Religious limitations: The "Get": Under Orthodox Jewish law, a wife whose husband civilly divorces her without granting her a *religious divorce* (*a "Get"*) is unable to remarry. Wives have challenged judicial refusals to enforce a "Get" on tort and contract principles. Religious divorce has constitutional implications.

B. Financial limitations: Filing fees: States cannot require an indigent to pay filing fees and court costs prior to filing for divorce (*Boddie v. Connecticut*).

C. Right to counsel: Indigent plaintiffs do *not* have a constitutional right to counsel in divorce proceedings. However, some states recognize an indigent's right to counsel based on state law. Pro se representation is common in family law litigation.

VI. DISCRIMINATION ON THE BASIS OF DIVORCE

Discrimination on the basis of divorce violates the Constitution and some states civil rights statutes.

VII. ROLE OF COUNSEL

A. Joint representation

1. **Different approaches:** Some states regard dual or joint representation in divorce as unethical. Other states permit it subject to restrictions.

2. **Dispelling the aura of dual representation:** An attorney may not give the *impression* of representation of both parties *when one party is unrepresented.*

3. **Confidentiality issues:** An attorney in a dual representation situation *may not reveal confidential information* or use such information to the disadvantage of a client or to the advantage of a third person.

B. **Representation of clients in different suits involving substantially related matters:** Representation of clients involved in different lawsuits that deal with "substantially related" matters can give rise to a prohibited conflict of interest.

C. **Sexual relations with clients:** An increasing number of jurisdictions regulate sexual relations between the attorney and client.

1. **Different approaches:** Some states prohibit all attorney-client sexual relationships. Others exempt sexual relationships predating the representation or those sexual relationships that adversely affect the practice of law.

2. **ABA:** An ABA Rule of Professional Conduct bans attorney-client sexual relationships absent a preexisting consensual relationship.

3. **States without express bans:** Even without a specific ban on attorney-client sexual relations, a state may nonetheless find that the attorney's conduct violates general conflict of interest rules.

D. **Fees:** A court may order one spouse in a divorce proceeding to pay the other's fees. Contingent fees in divorce actions are unethical.

VIII. DIVORCE JURISDICTION

A. **Subject matter jurisdiction: Traditional rule:** Traditionally, a state has jurisdiction to dissolve a marriage based on the petitioner's *domicile* in the forum state. Domicile signifies physical presence plus intention to remain permanently.

B. **Restatement view: Divorce without domicile:** The Restatement (Second) of Conflict of Laws relaxes the traditional domiciliary requirement.

C. **Terminology**

1. **Ex parte versus bilateral divorce:** In an ex parte (or unilateral) divorce, the court has personal jurisdiction over only one spouse. In a bilateral divorce, the court has personal jurisdiction over both spouses.

2. **Divisible divorce:** A court in an ex parte divorce has jurisdiction only over the marital status, and may not rule on the support and property rights of the absent spouse.

D. **Jurisdiction over the plaintiff**

1. **Full Faith and Credit Clause:** The Full Faith and Credit Clause of the Constitution (Article IV, §1) requires that a state give full faith and credit to a decree of a sister state provided that the sister state had personal jurisdiction. This requirement was applied to the divorce context by the U.S. Supreme Court in *Williams I* and *Williams II.*

2. **Durational residency requirements:** Durational residency requirements, imposed by some states, are constitutional (*Sosna v. Iowa*).

3. **The *Williams* cases**

a. *Williams I*: **Whether to give full faith and credit:** This case held that a state must recognize, under the Full Faith and Credit Clause, a divorce granted to a spouse who is domiciled in a sister state even though the stay-at-home spouse does not appear and is not served with process in the sister state.

b. *Williams II*: **When to give full faith and credit:** The decree-granting state's finding of domicile may be reexamined to determine the bona fides of a petitioner's domicile.

c. *Williams'* **limitation to the ex parte situation:** The *Williams* rules operate if the divorce was entered ex parte. The appearance of both parties confers jurisdiction on the court.

E. **Personal jurisdiction over the defendant**

1. **Proper notice:** Personal jurisdiction over the defendant is *not* required to terminate a marriage if the plaintiff is domiciled in the forum state. However, *notice* to the defendant in divorce actions *is required* in order to comport with due process.

2. **Transitory presence:** A state may acquire jurisdiction for divorce over a nonresident defendant who is physically present in the state even when the defendant lacks a substantial connection to the forum.

F. **Foreign decrees:** Under the ***comity doctrine***, states *may* recognize a judgment of another state or nation that comports with due process.

G. **Domestic relations exception to federal jurisdiction:** The U.S. Supreme Court *limits* the situations in which *federal courts can refuse jurisdiction* to adjudicate cases involving parties in different states who are involved in divorce, alimony, or custody matters (*Ankenbrandt v. Richards*).

IX. ALTERNATIVES TO DIVORCE: ANNULMENTS AND SEPARATIONS

Divorce terminates a valid marriage. An ***annulment*** is a judicial declaration that a marriage never took place. A ***legal separation*** is a judicial declaration that the parties are separated. A spouse might seek an annulment for religious reasons or to avoid durational residency requirements for divorce.

X. ALTERNATIVE DISPUTE RESOLUTION PROCESSES

A. **Arbitration, conciliation, and mediation distinguished:** Arbitration provisions in separation agreements require the parties to submit future disputes to an arbitrator prior to court action. In arbitration, a neutral third party makes a binding determination. Conciliation is counseling with an eye toward reconciliation. Divorce mediation is a process by which the parties make their own agreements with the mediator serving as a facilitator.

B. **Enforceability of arbitration provisions:** A few states maintain that arbitration of custody and visitation disputes is *violative of public policy*.

C. **Mandatory mediation:** A few states have ***mandatory mediation*** for divorcing parties in custody disputes. Some states exempt spouses if domestic violence is present.

D. **Collaborative law procedure:** *Collaborative law* procedure signifies an agreement by the parties and their attorneys to use cooperative techniques without resorting to judicial intervention. Collaborative law requires that, if the parties are unable to agree, the lawyers must withdraw.

CHAPTER 6

FINANCIAL CONSEQUENCES OF DISSOLUTION

I. STANDARDS FOR AWARDING PROPERTY, SPOUSAL SUPPORT, AND CHILD SUPPORT

At divorce, *absent an agreement*, the court divides the spouses' property and may also award spousal and child support.

A. Division of property

1. **Marital property regimes defined:** Two marital property regimes exist:

   - **common law**, and

   - **community property**.

   At **common law**, all property belonged to the *spouse who acquired it*. On the other hand, **community property** gives each spouse the right upon dissolution to an *equal* share of the community property.

2. **Equitable distribution generally:** At dissolution, the majority of states apply the doctrine of equitable distribution. Equitable distribution takes into account a number of statutory factors.

3. **Traditional rationales:** Different rationales traditionally characterize the distribution of property and spousal support.

   a. **Fault:** The most longstanding principle is to divide the property and award support so as to *punish* the spouse who caused the marital breakdown.

   b. **Need:** The need rationale, which replaced fault, divides property based on *a spouse's need for support*.

   c. **Status:** A court divides property based on the *status* that the parties *enjoyed during the marriage*.

4. **Modern rationale:** A new principle characterizes the distribution of property. According to the contribution theory, a court divides property based on the view that marriage is an economic partnership. Spousal earnings and resulting assets are subject to division.

   a. **Valuation of homemaker services:** Judicial and legislative reforms permit homemaker services to be taken into account.

   b. **Community property and the contribution approach:** The community property regime reflects the *partnership/contribution* rationale.

   c. **Limited role for fault:** Marital fault continues to play a limited role in equitable distribution.

5. **Property distribution process:** There are three basic steps in dividing property in a dissolution action: *characterization*, *valuation*, and *division*.

6. **What is property?**

   a. **Professional licenses and degrees:** Sometimes courts must determine whether a professional license or degree is an asset subject to distribution upon dissolution.

  i. Characterization: Majority versus minority approaches: Virtually all states *refuse* to treat professional licenses and degrees as marital property, although some jurisdictions take them into account in awards of spousal support.

  ii. Criticism of characterization as property: Courts have difficulty characterizing a license or degree as property because:

   ■ it lacks the attributes of property;

   ■ future earning capacity is too difficult and speculative;

   ■ it is a product of only one spouse's skills; and

   ■ it would result in indentured servitude.

  iii. Modern development: New York law reform: New York law provides that a spouse's enhanced earning capacity in the form of a professional license or advanced degree is no longer considered as marital property subject to equitable distribution upon divorce. Instead, the degree or license may *be one factor* in the determination of post-divorce *spousal support* and *equitable distribution*.

 b. Pensions and retirement benefits: Pension benefits constitute a significant part of the marital property for many couples.

  i. Definition: *Vested* pension rights are not subject to forfeiture by the employee if the employment terminates, in contrast to nonvested pension rights.

  ii. Characterization as marital property: Under the *majority rule*, *both vested and nonvested pension rights are marital property* subject to equitable distribution. Under the *minority rule*, only vested pension rights are marital property subject to equitable distribution.

  iii. Federal pension benefits and federalism principles: The distribution of federal pension benefits may involve a conflict between federal law versus state equitable distribution law.

7. Bankruptcy discharge

 a. Generally: The Bankruptcy Code permits a debtor-spouse to be discharged from certain divorce-related obligations.

 b. Rule: Nondischargeability from support obligations: According to the traditional rule, obligations attributable to a *property* division upon divorce were dischargeable but *spousal support and child support obligations were not*. The Bankruptcy Abuse Prevention and Consumer Protection Act (BAPCPA) changes the traditional rule to make property obligations nondischargeable in Chapter 7 bankruptcy in some circumstances.

B. Spousal support: Spousal support consists of the *award of future payments to one spouse from the future earnings of the other*.

 1. Rationale

  a. Traditional theories

   i. Need: At common law, the husband had a duty to support his wife. Because women were economically dependent on men, women "needed" support in the event of marital breakdown. Courts based awards on the plaintiff's *need* plus the defendant's *ability to pay*. The benchmark for need was the couple's standard of living during the marriage.

    ii. Fault: In a fault-based regime, only the innocent spouse is awarded spousal support. The guilty spouse is "punished" by denial of spousal support (and property). Theories of need and fault have been undermined by no-fault divorce and the transformation of gender roles brought about by the women's movement.

  b. Modern rationale

    i. Self-sufficiency: Many commentators urge that, because the original purposes of alimony awards (fault/need) are no longer relevant, spousal support should be abolished or, alternatively, awarded infrequently and for short periods of time. UMDA was influential in the adoption of self-sufficiency as the new rationale for awards of spousal support.

    ii. ALI's loss compensation: The ALI *Principles* proposes an innovative rationale of "loss compensation" for spousal support by which one spouse makes "compensatory spousal payments" to the other spouse to compensate for certain losses that the second spouse experienced during the marriage.

  c. Alimony reform

    i. Reform movement: An influential alimony reform movement began in Massachusetts by disgruntled divorced husbands and their second wives who were discontented about purportedly unjust long-term alimony awards to former wives.

    ii. Massachusetts reform movement: The alimony reform movement led to the Massachusetts Alimony Reform Act (2011) making alimony awards more predictable, linking the duration of alimony to the length of the marriage, and terminating awards of permanent alimony.

2. Spousal support and property division distinguished: Several differences exist between spousal support and property division.

  a. Modifiability: Unlike property awards, spousal support traditionally was modifiable upon proof of a change of circumstances.

  b. Terminability: Spousal support, unlike property payments, was terminable upon remarriage of the recipient-spouse.

  c. Enforcement by contempt power: Spousal support obligations, unlike property awards, are enforceable by means of contempt.

  d. Discharge in bankruptcy: Spousal support, unlike awards of property, traditionally was not a dischargeable obligation if the payor-spouse declares bankruptcy. Reforms limit the dischargeability of property awards in some cases.

  e. Tax consequences: Different tax consequences traditionally stemmed from the awards.

3. Types of alimony: Permanent alimony is rarely awarded today. Modern forms of spousal support include rehabilitative alimony and reimbursement alimony.

C. Child support

1. Liability of both parents: The ***modern trend*** considers *both* parents responsible for the support of their children.

2. Standards: Traditionally, vague statutory standards permitted courts *considerable discretion* in the award of child support. Modern law limits judicial discretion by the use of guidelines (i.e., mathematical formulae).

3. **Models of determining support:** States have implemented guidelines based on three different models: income shares model, percentage of income model, and the Melson Formula.

4. **Deviation from guidelines:** A court may order a *deviation* from the statutory guidelines in appropriate cases but should explain the reasoning for the deviation.

5. **Liability of stepparents:** Modern statutes and case law sometimes impose liability on stepparents.

6. **Postmajority support:** States adopt different approaches to a noncustodial parent's liability for postmajority support. Some states use a variety of legal doctrines to permit continuation of support.

7. **Support and inheritance rights of nonmarital children**

   a. **Traditional view:** Traditionally, nonmarital children had a right to support and inheritance only from their biological mother.

   b. **Modern view:** Both parents have a duty to support children regardless of legitimacy. The U.S. Supreme Court has held that some forms of discrimination against nonmarital children are unconstitutional. Modern law expands the inheritance rights of nonmarital children.

II. MODIFICATION OF SPOUSAL AND CHILD SUPPORT AWARDS

A. **Standard:** The most common standard for modification of spousal and child support is a *substantial and material change of circumstances* since the entry of the decree. UMDA requires that spousal support may be modified only if a change in circumstances has occurred that is *so substantial and continuing as to make the terms unconscionable.*

B. **Relevant factors:** Some circumstances may affect a spouse's support obligation. Changes in *either* former spouse's circumstances may warrant reduction or termination of spousal support, including the payor's changed circumstances, the payor's remarriage and subsequent family obligations, the payor's increased resources, and the payor's deteriorating health. The recipient's changed circumstances, such as remarriage or cohabitation, may also affect the payor-spouse's obligations.

III. JURISDICTION AND ENFORCEMENT OF CHILD SUPPORT AWARDS

Child support enforcement may be difficult when the parties reside in different states. To make or modify an award of child support or spousal support, a court must have *personal jurisdiction* over the obligor.

A. **Expansion of jurisdiction:** The trend is to expand the traditional methods of acquiring personal jurisdiction over nonresidents for support purposes. Many states authorize the assertion of personal jurisdiction in domestic relations cases by means of special long-arm statutes. This practice must comport with the requisites of due process.

B. **Interstate enforcement:** The Uniform Interstate Family Support Act (UIFSA) now addresses interstate enforcement of child support.

C. **Federal legislation: Full Faith and Credit for Child Support Orders Act:** To improve interstate enforcement, Congress also enacted the Full Faith and Credit for Child Support Orders Act.

D. **Enforcement remedies:** State and federal remedies exist to enforce child support obligations. Traditional state remedies include money judgments, criminal nonsupport proceedings, and the contempt power. Modern remedies include license suspension, wage withholding, tax refund intercepts, and passport revocations.

IV. SEPARATION AGREEMENTS

The validity of a separation agreement is determined by *contract law*. Such agreements may be set aside for fraud, duress, or overreaching. Courts can modify some provisions of a judicial decree (e.g., support provisions but not property divisions).

V. TAX CONSIDERATIONS

A. **Traditional approach: Spousal support**

1. **Taxable to the recipient:** Traditionally, spousal support was *taxable* to the recipient-spouse.

2. **Deductible by the payor:** Traditionally, spousal support was *deductible* by the payor-spouse.

B. **Modern approach: Spousal support**

1. **Alimony:** The Tax Cuts and Jobs Act (TCJA), Pub. L. No. 115-97, enacted by Congress in 2017, eliminates the tax deduction for payor-spouses for alimony payments and no longer requires the recipient-spouse to report alimony as income.

2. **Timing:** The TCJA provision is effective for divorce or separation agreements executed after December 31, 2018. The TCJA also applies to any divorce or separation instrument that was executed on or before December 31, 2018, and was *modified* after that date, if the modification expressly provides that the amendments made by this section apply to such modification.

C. **Child support:** Child support payments are *nontaxable* to the recipient and *nondeductible* by the payor. This rule remains unchanged by the TCJA.

CHAPTER 7

CHILD CUSTODY

I. INTRODUCTION

Prior to the nineteenth century, a rule of paternal preference prevailed. However, by the mid-to late nineteenth century, custody law began to reflect a maternal preference.

II. STANDARDS FOR SELECTING THE CUSTODIAL PARENT

A. **Presumptions:** Some states invoke presumptions to adjudicate custody disputes (such as the rebuttable presumption against custody for an abuser, and the biological parent presumption that favors custody to a biological parent over a nonparent).

B. Best interests of the child: The prevailing standard for resolution of custody is "the best interests of the child."

    1. Constitutional factors

        a. Race: The Supreme Court has determined that race may not serve as the *decisive* factor in custody decision making.

        b. Religion: The First Amendment serves as a limitation on judicial consideration of religion as a factor in awarding custody, but courts may consider the *effect* of a religion upon a child.

    2. Fitness factors

        a. Sexual conduct: According to the modern view, a parent's sexual conduct is only relevant if it has an adverse effect on the child. *Lawrence v. Texas* raises doubts about the constitutionality of custody restrictions on a parent's same-sex sexual conduct.

        b. Wealth: The relative wealth of the parties is not determinative *unless* one parent is unable to provide adequately for the child.

        c. Domestic violence: Some jurisdictions adopt a **rebuttable presumption** against custody to an abusive parent. "Friendly parent" provisions and joint custody presumptions serve to disadvantage abused spouses in custody determinations.

        d. Disability: Many statutes require consideration of the mental and physical health of the parties when applying the best interest standard.

C. Joint custody: Joint custody allows both parents to share legal responsibility for major childrearing decisions. Joint custody is based on the rationale that children benefit from *continued and frequent contact with both parents*.

    1. Different jurisdictions' approaches: Most jurisdictions now provide for joint custody. States regard joint custody as a presumption, preference, or a factor in the best interest determination. Most states follow the third approach.

    2. Joint custody does not mean equal time: A popular *misconception is that joint custody means equal time* with each parent.

    3. Parenting plans: Many states provide for *parenting plans* — written agreements by which parents specify caretaking and decision-making responsibility authority for their children (and often the manner for resolution of future disputes).

D. Pet custody cases: Increasingly, courts are addressing pet custody cases. The traditional analysis treats the pet as personal property and focuses on whether the pet is separate property and/or a gift. In contrast, a custody analysis focuses on the issue of the pet's "best interests" in terms of nurturing, emotional needs, and happiness.

III. STANDARDS FOR SELECTING THE NONCUSTODIAL PARENT: VISITATION

A. Denial of visitation

    1. General rule: Courts are reluctant to impose a total denial of visitation.

    2. Visitation and support: Independent variables: The right to visitation and the duty of support are not interdependent.

B. **Conditions on visitation:** Courts sometimes place conditions on visitation in cases of domestic violence, or physical or sexual abuse. A parent's sexual behavior may also lead to conditions on visitation. *Lawrence v. Texas* raises doubts about the constitutionality of restrictions on a parent's sexual conduct. Sometimes, First Amendment concerns *limit a court's power to settle religious disputes* about visitation.

C. **Interference with visitation rights:** Noncustodial parents may institute proceedings to enforce their visitation rights. Possible remedies for custodial interference include civil contempt, modification of custody, tort damages, and makeup parenting time.

IV. STANDARDS: PARENT VERSUS NONPARENT DISPUTES

A. **Natural parent presumption:** *A presumption* favors **biological parents** in *custody disputes* involving parents versus nonparents.

B. **Custody and visitation rights of third parties**

   1. **Grandparents:** At common law, grandparents had no right to visitation with their grandchildren. Many states now have visitation statutes that permit visitation to third parties (such as grandparents). The U.S. Supreme Court has held that a grandparent visitation statute infringes on family autonomy when it fails to give deference to a fit parent's wishes (*Troxel v. Granville*).

   2. **Stepparents:** Some statutes authorize courts to consider stepparents' rights in custody and visitation awards.

   3. **Same-sex co-parents:** Courts traditionally were not receptive to recognition of co-parenting rights after dissolution of a same-sex relationship. Increasingly, however, courts recognize the parental rights of the "second parent" (i.e., the non-biologically related parent) in LGBT families.

V. ROLE OF SPECIAL PARTICIPANTS

A. **Child's preference:** Most states, either by statute or case law, take into account a child's wishes when making custody determinations, but they accord that preference varying weight.

B. **Counsel for the child:** In most states, appointment of a child's legal representative is within the discretion of the court. However, statutory authority exists for the appointment of a guardian ad litem when allegations of abuse are raised in custody hearings.

C. **Expert testimony:** Experts frequently are asked to testify in custody determinations.

VI. MODIFICATION

A. **Standard for modification:** The *standard* for custody *modification* is *higher* than for an initial custody determination. The most commonly accepted standard requires proof of a *material or substantial change of circumstances*. Some states require *endangerment*. A few states require only that modification be *in the best interests* of the child regardless of any change in circumstances.

B. **Relocation controversies:** Relocation controversies often arise in the postdecree period. Courts employ different standards to resolve such disputes. The modern trend favors the best-interests balancing test taking into account many factors.

VII. JURISDICTION AND ENFORCEMENT

A. Jurisdiction

1. **Traditional rule:** The traditional rule permitted the assertion of jurisdiction if the *child was domiciled* in the state. Courts later permitted assertions of jurisdiction if another state had a *substantial interest* in the child's welfare. This led frequently to concurrent assertions of jurisdiction.

2. **UCCJEA:** The Uniform Child Custody Jurisdiction and Enforcement Act (UCCJEA) applies to initial custody awards as well as modifications. Virtually all states have adopted the UCCJEA.

VIII. CHILD ABDUCTION

Uniform law, federal law, and international treaties address international child abduction.

A. Uniform Child Abduction Prevention Act (UCAPA): UCAPA provides for abduction *prevention* measures.

B. The International Parental Kidnapping Crime Act (IPKCA): IPKCA makes it a *federal crime* for a parent to wrongfully remove or retain a child outside the United States.

C. The Hague Convention on the Civil Aspects of International Child Abduction: The Hague Convention provides for the *mandatory return* of children to their country of habitual residence for adjudication of custody disputes.

IX. PROCESS TO RESOLVE DISPUTES

Mediation and collaborative law are modern alternatives to the traditional dispute resolution process by which the parties resolve issues in dispute. Both processes are less expensive and less hostile than the adversarial process. Many statutes permit custody mediation, although a few states *mandate* it. Some mediation statutes exempt victims of domestic violence.

CHAPTER **8**

PROCREATION

I. CONTRACEPTION

A. Rights of married and unmarried persons: Access to contraception is protected by the constitutional right of privacy and does not depend on marital status (*Eisenstadt v. Baird*).

B. Minors' rights to contraception: The U.S. Supreme Court extends the constitutional right of privacy to minors' contraceptive choices (*Carey v. Population Services Int'l*).

C. Misrepresentation of contraceptive use: A father may not defend against imposition of his child support obligation based on the mother's misrepresentation about use of birth control.

D. Health insurance coverage of contraceptives: The Patient Protection and Affordable Care Act (ACA, also called "Obamacare") has a "contraceptive mandate," requiring employers of more than 50 employees to offer health care plans that cover free contraceptive services and FDA-approved contraceptives without out-of-pocket costs to patients. Federal regulations offer exemptions to religious employers (such as churches) and accommodations to nonprofit employers with religious *and moral* objections.

II. ABORTION

A. **Historical background:** Early American proscriptions against abortion date from the 1820s. Reform began in the 1960s when some states adopted the American Law Institute (ALI)'s Model Penal Code abortion provisions liberalizing abortion. The women's movement also contributed to reform.

B. **A woman's right to an abortion**

1. *Roe v. Wade*: The Supreme Court holds in *Roe v. Wade* (1973) that a woman has a constitutionally protected right to an abortion. The constitutional source for this right is the right of privacy. *Roe* holds that the right to an abortion is fundamental and requires strict scrutiny. In the first trimester, the woman has an unqualified right to an abortion that may not be infringed by the state. After the first trimester and until the point of viability, the state may regulate abortion in the interest of maternal health. After viability the state's interest in protecting potential life justifies the state in regulating, and even proscribing, abortion.

2. **Retrenchment on abortion right:** *Planned Parenthood v. Casey:* In *Planned Parenthood v. Casey*, the Supreme Court retreats from *Roe*'s guarantee of abortion freedom by allowing states to impose regulations provided that those regulations do not place an *undue burden* on the woman's right to an abortion. Rather than continuing to speak of abortion as a fundamental right, the court now refers to it only as a liberty interest. *Casey* weakens *Roe* further by abrogation of the trimester scheme and by the recognition "that there is a substantial state interest in potential life *throughout* pregnancy."

C. **The abortion funding cases:** The Supreme Court holds in *Harris v. McRae* that, although a woman has a protected right to an abortion, the government has no obligation to provide funds for that abortion.

D. **Other problems of access:**

1. **Abortion activists' tactics:** The *Freedom of Access to Clinic Entrances (FACE) Act* provides criminal and civil penalties for the use of force, threat of force, or physical obstruction aimed at injuring, intimidating, or interfering with abortion patients or providers.

2. **Informed consent laws:** Many states have abortion-specific informed consent laws that require a woman seeking an abortion to receive designated medical information about the fetus, procedure, and the availability of alternatives to abortion.

3. **TRAP laws**: Some states have enacted "targeted regulation of abortion providers" or "TRAP" laws that impose costly and burdensome requirements upon abortion clinics that are not imposed on other medical facilities. The Supreme Court has *invalidated* state laws requiring that physicians have admitting privileges at local hospitals and requiring abortion facilities to meet the strict standards of ambulatory surgical care centers.

E. **The husband's rights in the abortion context:** A husband has no constitutionally protected right to influence his wife's abortion decision (*Planned Parenthood v. Danforth, Planned Parenthood v. Casey*).

F. Minor's right to an abortion: parental consent: In *Bellotti v. Baird*, the Court holds that if a state requires one or both parents' consent, the state must provide an alternative judicial procedure (*judicial bypass*) whereby the minor can obtain authorization for the abortion.

G. Partial-birth abortion bans: Federal and state laws prohibit "partial-birth" (i.e., late-stage) abortions.

H. Medical or medication abortion: States have begun regulating medication abortions. Courts are split on the constitutionality of such restrictions.

I. State sanctions for abortion participants: Some states have enacted laws punishing abortion providers. Other states have laws punishing pregnant women who seek an abortion.

III. FETAL PROTECTION LEGISLATION

State and federal legislation (the Unborn Victims of Violence Act) have enacted laws that protect the fetus. These laws establish the crime of fetal homicide, restrict abortion based on the personhood of the fetus and its gestational age, restrict abortion based on the detection of a fetal heartbeat, and regulate the disposition of fetal remains.

IV. ASSISTED REPRODUCTIVE TECHNOLOGY

A. Artificial insemination

1. **Definition:** Artificial insemination is a reproductive technique to combat problems of, primarily, male infertility.

2. **Defense to child support:** The husband's *consent* to the artificial insemination of his wife *gives rise to obligations of child support*.

3. **Status of posthumous children:** Children conceived posthumously by in vitro insemination may share in a sperm donor's estate if he consented to the insemination and agreed to support the child.

4. **Status of posthumously conceived children:** Posthumously conceived children may be entitled to government benefits as dependents of a deceased insured wage earner, depending on their eligibility to inherit under state intestacy law.

5. **Sperm donor's rights:** Many statutes, including the original Uniform Parentage Act (UPA), provide that the *sperm donor has no rights* regarding a child born by artificial insemination.

6. **Disposition of frozen embryos at divorce:** Couples sometimes fight over frozen embryos created through in vitro fertilization (IVF). Courts use different approaches to decide these disputes.

B. Surrogacy

1. **Definition:** Surrogacy is a contractual arrangement whereby a woman agrees to be artificially inseminated with semen, and then to bear and surrender the ensuing child, or agrees to be a "gestational carrier" whereby she carries an embryo created from the intended parents' or others' genetic material.

2. **Traditional view:** The traditional view toward surrogacy is to treat surrogacy agreements as *void*. Increasingly, however, many states permit such arrangements subject to state regulation.

3. **Revised Uniform Parentage Act (UPA):** Many states rely on application of the Uniform Parentage Act to evaluate surrogacy agreements. UPA (2002) permitted surrogacy agreements (termed "gestational agreements") provided that the agreement was "validated" by procedures tantamount to a preconception adoption (including a home study and judicial approval) prior to making the intended parents the child's legal parents. UPA (2017) liberalizes enforcement of gestational surrogacy agreements by removing courts from parentage determinations.

4. **Adoption consent statutes:** An obstacle to surrogacy is adoption consent statutes. All states have laws prohibiting a mother from granting irrevocable consent to adoption *before* a child's birth.

5. *Baby M.:* The New Jersey Supreme Court ruled that the surrogacy contract is unenforceable because it violates babyselling laws and public policy. Despite holding the surrogacy agreement to be invalid and unenforceable, the court granted custody to the intended parents based on the best-interests-of-the-child standard. New Jersey law recently recognized surrogacy contracts.

6. **Surrogacy by same-sex partners:** Surrogacy is increasingly utilized by same-sex partners. The practice raises such issues as: what role paternity laws (such as the UPA) should play in the establishment of parental rights of children of lesbian couples, and whether states will permit pre-birth registration of same-sex parents. Courts increasingly are recognizing the parentage rights of same-sex former partners. UPA (2017) recognizes intended parents without regard to sex or sexual orientation (thereby facilitating surrogacy by same-sex couples).

7. **Pre-birth judgments**: Some states allow a pre-birth determination of the legal status of the intended parents of a child born pursuant to a gestational surrogacy agreement.

C. **Three or more parents:**

1. **Traditional view:** Traditionally, the law recognized only two parents for a child — one parent of each gender.

2. **Modern view:** Today, assisted reproductive technology makes possible multiple parenthood that separates biological parents from intended parents.

3. **State law reform:** Approximately a dozen states have laws that allow children to have more than two parents, although states take different approaches. California was the first state to pioneer landmark legislation in 2013 (dubbed the "third parent law") that allows children to have more than two legal parents.

4. **Uniform law:** UPA (2017) allows a state to choose in some circumstances to allow more than two parents. A court must find that the failure to recognize more than two parents would be detrimental to the child.

D. **Legal regulation of sperm banks:**

1. **Model law:** The ABA adopted a model act in 2019 that regulates fertility agencies (ABA Model Act Governing Assisted Reproductive Technology Agencies). The Act requires fertility agencies to obtain a license and sets forth affirmative duties to maintain that license.

2. **State laws:** Several states have criminalized *fertility fraud* by fertility physicians who fathered children with women who did not consent to being inseminated in this manner. The misconduct consists of medical malpractice and a violation of medical ethics.

CHAPTER 9
THE PARENT-CHILD STATE RELATIONSHIP IN SPECIAL CONTEXTS

I. TORTS

A. Traditional rule: Children are liable for their intentional and negligent torts.

1. **Standard of care:** Although children are liable for their torts, they are subject to a different standard of care than for adults. The *traditional rule* takes into account the minor's *age and experience*.

2. **Modern rule:** The modern rule still takes the child's age and experience into account but provides for exceptions for those children who are younger than five years old and children who are engaging in an adult activity.

3. **Contributory negligence**

   a. **Majority rule:** The *majority rule* adopts an *age-based standard of care* for a child's contributory negligence. The modern view, found in the Restatement (Third) of Torts, adopts an irrebuttable presumption that extreme youth (i.e., under five) precludes a finding of contributory negligence, although this is still the minority rule.

   b. **Minority rule:** A *minority* of jurisdictions adopt a presumption that children below a certain age cannot be held contributorily negligent.

B. Exception to rule of liability: Children's conduct of adult activities: The *modern trend* abrogates an age-based standard of care when a minor is performing an adult activity.

C. Parents' liability for children's torts: Parents may be liable today for their children's torts by statute, if they employ their child, permit a child to use a dangerous instrumentality, sanction or promote the wrongdoing, or know of their child's violent propensity.

II. CONTRACTS

A. Common-law rule: At common law, a minor could *disaffirm* a contract, i.e., assert a *defense of infancy*.

B. Majority rule: Most jurisdictions still follow the common-law rule.

C. Policy: The policy is to protect minors from immaturity and overreaching by adults.

D. Modern view: Special contexts: Some courts and legislatures have changed the common-law rule in limited situations (e.g., entertainment contracts).

III. PROPERTY

A. Earnings

1. **Common-law rule:** Many modern statutes incorporate the common-law rule that a *parent has the right to a child's services and earnings*.

2. **Emancipation:** *Emancipation* permits a child to acquire the right to dispose of his or her own earnings.

B. Inheritance

  1. Traditional rule: A child may inherit property; however, a guardian may have to be appointed to manage that property.

  2. Guardianship: Definition: At common law, if a child inherited property or was given property that required active management, a court appointed a ***guardian of the child's estate.*** The term "guardian" means both a guardian of the person and a guardian of the estate (property).

  3. Guardianship: Problems: Guardianship poses several problems: expense, limited powers, and automatic termination at a statutorily designated age.

  4. Inheritance rights of nonmarital children

  a. Traditional rule: Although both nonmarital and legitimate children could inherit by intestate succession from their mothers at common law, only legitimate children could inherit from their fathers by intestate succession.

  b. Modern trend: The modern trend minimizes differences in inheritance between legitimate and nonmarital children.

  5. Inheritance rights of posthumously conceived children: The U.S. Supreme Court has held that the right of posthumously conceived children to Social Security survivors' benefits depends on their eligibility to inherit under state intestacy law (*Astrue v. Caputo*).

  6. Trusts: A minor's property may be held in trust. The ***Uniform Transfers to Minors Act*** (UTMA) permits a minor's property to be registered in the name of a *custodian*.

IV. EDUCATION

  A. Parents' right to control the upbringing of their children: A trilogy of Supreme Court cases (*Meyer v. Nebraska, Pierce v. Soc'y of Sisters, Wisconsin v. Yoder*) announces a principle of enormous constitutional significance: Parents have a constitutionally protected right to control the upbringing of their children. The Court's decision in *Troxel v. Granville* affirmed this privilege of family privacy.

  B. Minors' First Amendment rights

  1. Political speech: Students have a right to freedom of expression in terms of political speech, although minors' exercise of that right must not *materially and substantially interfere with school discipline* or *invade the rights of others* (*Tinker v. Des Moines*).

  2. Free speech in the context of school-sponsored activities: Students' right to freedom of expression is restricted in *school-sponsored* and *school-approved* activities.

  3. Minors' right to obtain sexually explicit and violent materials: The U.S. Supreme Court has taken a seemingly paradoxical approach: upholding restrictions on sexually explicit materials but refusing to restrict minors' right to violent materials.

  C. Minors' Fourth Amendment rights: The U.S. Supreme Court holds that the Fourth Amendment's prohibition against unreasonable searches applies to juveniles. However, the standard for searches of juveniles ("reasonable suspicion") is lower than that for adults ("probable cause"). Thus, the law permits searches of juveniles that would be unconstitutional as applied to adults (e.g., random drug testing).

V. MEDICAL CARE

A. Requirement of parental consent: At common law, only a parent (not the child) could give consent to medical treatment for the child.

B. Minor's consent: Some statutes provide that an unemancipated minor may give consent to medical treatment for himself or herself in limited situations. Some states have statutes allowing unemancipated minors deemed "mature minors" to consent to medical care on the same basis as adults.

C. Exceptions to parental consent requirements

    1. Emergency exception: Under the common-law rule, a doctor may provide medical treatment to a child *without securing parental consent* in the event of an *emergency*.

    2. State-imposed health requirements: The state may mandate certain health requirements (e.g., newborn screening and testing, compulsory immunizations).

    3. Neglect limitation: At common law, parents have a duty to provide their child with necessary medical care. Parents who refuse may be subject to criminal or civil liability. The state may secure the necessary medical treatment for the child by declaring the child neglected in a juvenile court proceeding.

CHAPTER 10

ADOPTION

I. INTRODUCTION

A. Definition: Adoption terminates the legal rights and responsibilities of the biological parents and creates new legal rights and responsibilities in the adoptive parents.

B. Historical background: Adoption was not recognized by the English common law. As a result, American adoption law is entirely statutory.

C. Voluntary and involuntary termination of parental rights: Termination of the biological parents' rights prior to adoption may be *voluntary* or *involuntary*. Termination and adoption may take place in the same or separate proceedings.

D. Adoption statistics: The adoption rate in the United States has declined in the past few years. The decline is due, in large part, to the significant decrease in the number of intercountry adoptions. At the same time, the number of infant adoptions has remained constant, and the rate of special needs adoptions has increased.

E. Influence of the Internet: The Internet has dramatically changed the face of the adoption process. Social media compete with traditional adoption service providers to broaden the market for adoptable children.

II. SELECTION STANDARDS FOR ADOPTIVE PARENTS

A. Generally: The adoption process generally begins when a birth parent *voluntarily* relinquishes (or "surrenders") the child to a state-licensed or state-operated agency. The agency takes legal custody of the child and selects an adoptive family. Case law explores the factors (disability, marital status, race, sexual orientation) that agencies and the state can consider in choosing an adoptive placement.

B. Relevant factors

1. **Preference for relatives:** Some statutes incorporate a *presumption that adoptive placement with relatives is in the child's best interests*, absent good cause or detriment to the child.

2. **Sexual orientation:** State laws vary in their recognition of the rights of gays and lesbian parents to adoptive and foster care placements.

   a. **Traditional view:** Traditionally, some states restricted adoptions by same-sex partners.

   b. **Permissive jurisdictions:** Many states today permit adoption of children by LGBT adopters and foster parents. Some states *explicitly* prohibit such discrimination.

   c. **Modern *implicit* restrictions:** Several states continue to restrict adoptions and/or foster care placements by gay and lesbian parents. Such discrimination persists, despite *Obergefell*, based on service providers' constitutional claims of religious freedom and free speech. Various groups are challenging the constitutionality of states' protections or restrictions of faith-based adoption agencies that refuse to provide services to LGBT parents.

   d. **Proposed federal rule:** The Trump Administration proposed a rule in 2019 that would undo Obama-era protections for LGBT parents and allow foster care and adoption agencies to deny services to LGBT families on faith-based grounds. 84 Fed. Reg. 63831-01.

   e. **Full faith and credit:** Before *Obergefell*, some states declined to recognize adoption decrees issued to same-sex couples in other states. After *Obergefell*, the U.S. Supreme Court determined that a state must accord full faith and credit to another state's judgment so long as the court in the second forum had jurisdiction over the relevant parties.

3. **Race**

   a. **Historical background:** Traditionally, states allowed a policy of race matching in adoption.

   b. **Policy debate:** Racial matching became highly controversial.

   c. **Federal law:** In 1996, Congress legislated the "removal of barriers to interethnic adoption," and provided that no state receiving federal funds could "deny to any individual the opportunity to become an adoptive or a foster parent, on the basis of the race, color, or national origin of the individual, or of the child, involved." 42 U.S.C. §1996b (amending the earlier, less restrictive Multi-Ethnic Placement Act).

4. **Religion:** Religion may be relevant in the selection of adoptive parents. Some states have *religious matching policies*.

C. Indian Child Welfare Act (ICWA) of 1978:
ICWA dictates that Native-American origins are relevant in adoption. ICWA does not ban non-Native parents from adopting Native children but rather accords preferences to the tribe and the right to intervene in such adoptions. A legal challenge to the constitutionality of ICWA is pending in federal court.

III. CONSENT

Statutes generally require voluntary parental consent before an adoption may occur. For married parents, consent from *both* parents is generally required.

A. Consent by the unmarried father

1. **Ramifications of *Stanley v. Illinois*:** A statutory presumption that denies an unmarried father a fitness hearing before removal of his children violates due process (*Stanley v. Illinois*).

2. **Indicia of parenthood:** The Supreme Court has held, in a trilogy of cases (*Lehr v. Robertson, Caban v. Mohammed, Quilloin v. Walcott*), that an unmarried father is entitled to constitutional protection of his parental rights so long as he manifests certain "indicia of parenthood."

3. **Consent requirement where father never has opportunity to develop a relationship:** The most difficult cases occur when a father *never had an opportunity to develop a relationship* with his child.

B. Divorced noncustodial parent's consent in the face of a stepparent adoption: Some statutes facilitate stepparent adoptions by dispensing with a noncustodial parent's consent.

IV. PLACEMENT PROCEDURE

A biological parent (or parents) may relinquish a child to a licensed public or private *agency* or arrange for an *independent adoption* by which an intermediary facilitates the adoption.

A. Agency's role: Disclosure requirements: An agency that discloses information to prospective adoptive parents about the biological parents or medical history of the child or parents has a *duty not to mislead*.

B. Independent placement: Intermediary's role: Some state laws limit or prohibit the participation of independent agents in the placement process.

V. SUBSIDIZED ADOPTION

All states provide ***subsidized adoption programs*** to *facilitate adoption of those children who are difficult to place* for reasons of age, physical or mental disability, or racial or ethnic background.

VI. INTERNATIONAL ADOPTION

International adoption has generated considerable controversy.

A. Adoption rate: Intercountry adoptions have plummeted in recent years due to other countries' dislike of lax practices by U.S. adoption service providers, inadequate federal and state regulation, and politics.

B. International law: International adoptions are subject to international laws. The Hague Convention on Protection of Children and Cooperation in Respect of Intercountry Adoption facilitates international adoptions by requiring determinations that adoption serves the child's best interests. The legislation applies only when both countries involved are signatories to the Convention.

VII. THE LEGAL CONSEQUENCES OF ADOPTION

A. Cut off rule: An adoption decree terminates ("cuts off") the legal relationship between the adoptee and his or her biological relatives and replaces it with ties to the adoptive family.

B. Marriage limitations: Whether two people related by adoption may marry depends on statute.

C. **Inheritance:** Adoption into an adoptive family generally results in the child's loss of the right to inherit from a biological parent. Some jurisdictions correct this result by statute (especially regarding stepparent adoption).

VIII. OPEN ADOPTION

Open adoption, i.e., the continuation of contact between the biological parents and the adopted child, is growing in popularity.

IX. EQUITABLE ADOPTION

Equitable adoption is an equitable doctrine whereby courts effectuate an adoption (or effectuate the consequences of an adoption) in cases in which a legal adoption never occurred.

X. ADOPTEE'S RIGHT TO KNOW OF ORIGINS

A. **Traditional rule:** State adoption statutes traditionally required strict confidentiality.

B. **Modern view:** The modern trend facilitates the exchange of information between an adopted child and the biological parents.

C. **Internet:** The Internet enables adoptees to locate birth relatives with relative ease, thereby hastening the demise of the principle of the anonymous adoption.

XI. ADULT ADOPTION

A. **General rule:** Most states allow the adoption of an adult. However, some states have limitations on the practice.

B. **Requirements:** Adult adoption generally requires only the consent of the parties (unlike the adoption of a child which is predicated on the best-interests-of-the-child standard).

C. **Limitations:** Some jurisdictions inquire into the purpose of the adult adoption.

D. **Adoptions involving gays and lesbians:** The advent of the marriage equality movement reduces the need for adult adoptions by same-sex partners.

XII. ADOPTION FAILURE: REVOCATION AND ABROGATION

Adoptions may fail either because of the actions of a *biological parent who revokes his/her consent* or because of the desires of the *adoptive parent(s) to abrogate* the adoption.

A. **Revocation of consent:** Statutes confer the right to revoke consent to an adoption on grounds of fraud, duress, or coercion. Most jurisdictions now limit the period during which the birth mother may withdraw consent.

B. **Abrogation:** States are reluctant to allow abrogation, citing concerns about the best interests of the child and child support. Some states allow abrogation based only on evidence of fraud, misrepresentation, or a procedural defect by the agency.

CHAPTER 1

INTRODUCTION

ChapterScope ───────────────────────────────

This chapter provides an introduction to family law. First, it presents a definition of the field. Second, it examines societal influences that have contributed to dramatic changes in the field. Third, it explores important legal trends that characterize family law. Here are a few of the key principles covered in this chapter:

■ **Definition:** Family law explores the legal regulation of the family and its members.

■ **Societal influences:** Family law reflects several important societal influences that have contributed to dramatic changes in the field, including:

- the women's movement;

- the rising incidence of divorce and the "retreat from marriage";

- dissatisfaction with the traditional family, the growth of nontraditional family forms, and increasing fluidity between family types;

- dissatisfaction with the traditional dispute resolution process;

- the children's rights movement;

- the gay rights movement and the advent of marriage equality;

- the waxing and waning impact of morality and the accommodation of religious beliefs;

- the curtailment of reproductive freedom; and

- the increasing use of assisted reproductive technologies.

■ **Family law reflects three legal trends:** federalization, constitutionalization, and a movement toward uniformity of state law.

- *Federalization:* The federal government occupies an increasingly prominent role in the regulation of the family.

- *Constitutionalization:* A considerable body of federal constitutional law applies to the family, family relationships, and family members.

- *Uniformity:* Family law reflects a movement toward uniformity in the variety of state laws that apply to the family and its members.

I. GENERALLY

A. Definition: Family law explores the legal regulation of the family and its members. These members include: spouses, parents, children, as well as unrelated significant others.

B. Central theme: Family law is characterized by a conflict between individual and social interests. The individual interest is the desire to give consideration to family members' decisional autonomy in private matters. On the other hand, the state has various interests that precipitate its intervention in the family, including interests in the protection of family members and the promotion of marriage as an institution, among others.

C. **Dynamic nature of field:** Family law is a field in *transition*. This transformation is apparent even in nomenclature (for example, family law formerly was called the "law of domestic relations"). Change is apparent in terms of the roles and responsibilities of family members, the definition of *family* and *parent*, and the nature of legal regulation of the family and its members. The dynamic nature of the field is due, in large part, to societal influences that are explored below.

II. SOCIETAL INFLUENCES ON FAMILY LAW

Family law reflects several important societal influences (social developments and social movements) that have effectuated dramatic changes in the field over the past several decades.

A. **Women's movement:** In the early 1960s, the civil rights movement and the publication of Betty Friedan's *The Feminine Mystique* (1963) triggered the women's movement. The women's movement led to a change in public policy toward women by both Congress and the courts. Congress prohibited sexual discrimination in employment by Title VII of the Civil Rights Act of 1964. This legislation precipitated a change from a policy of paternalism toward women (e.g., the era of protective labor legislation) to a policy reflecting equality of opportunity. Women, and especially married women, flocked to the workplace as employment barriers came down.

During the same period, the U.S. Supreme Court significantly expanded women's legal protection by holding that sex discrimination is a violation of equal protection. In *Reed v. Reed*, 404 U.S. 71 (1971), the Court held that an Idaho statute was unconstitutional, and without a rational basis, for giving priority to men in the administration of estates. The Court followed with *Craig v. Boren*, 429 U.S. 190 (1976), ruling unconstitutional an Oklahoma law that permitted the sale of 3.2 beer to women over age 18, but to men only over age 21. *Craig v. Boren* requires that laws and practices that discriminate based on gender must meet the more exacting intermediate scrutiny test: A regulation or practice must be "substantially related to an important governmental interest."

The Supreme Court subsequently subtly heightened the level of scrutiny applicable to gender-based classifications. In *United States v. Virginia*, 518 U.S. 515 (1996), the Court held that a policy restricting admission to only men by a public military academy violated equal protection. Justice Ruth Bader Ginsburg thereby announced a revised standard of review for gender discrimination: The parties seeking to defend the classification must demonstrate "an exceedingly persuasive justification." Justice Scalia in a strongly worded dissent criticized that the Court was covertly applying "strict scrutiny."

Historically, some state courts have been more sympathetic than the Supreme Court to challenges regarding gender-based classifications. *See, e.g., Sail'er Inn v. Kirby*, 485 P.2d 529 (Cal. 1971) (applying strict scrutiny to invalidate a statute that prohibited women from working as bartenders). The strict scrutiny test requires that the regulation or practice must be necessary to a compelling state interest.

Women's entry into the public arena was accompanied by a transformation in gender roles. Women were no longer completely dependent upon men financially. Nor were women relegated to the private world of the family, with men in the public world of work. As women took on the role of providers, they called upon men to shoulder increasing responsibilities for child care and housework.

Family law reflects the ensuing degenderization of family roles. For example, the diminution in women's status as child caretakers led to the demise of the maternal presumption in awards of custody. The rise in men's participation in child care and housework led to the joint custody doctrine. And, women's enhanced financial position contributed to both men and women being financially responsible for child support, as well as to divorced women being regarded as less needy of spousal support.

B. Rising incidence of divorce: Until the nineteenth century, marriage tended to be a permanent commitment. Divorce was difficult and costly to obtain, and stigmatizing for the parties. Courts and legislators permitted divorce infrequently and only upon proof of serious marital misconduct.

California's enactment of no-fault divorce (with the Family Law Act of 1969, which became effective January 1, 1970) eliminated the need for the marital parties to claim fault-based grounds. Divorcing spouses no longer needed to show marital misconduct—only that "irreconcilable differences" caused the breakdown of the marriage. No longer was the "guilty" spouse punished at divorce by awards involving deprivation of property, denial of spousal support, or loss of child custody.

A few years later, in 1974, the National Conference of Commissioners on Uniform State Laws (NCCUSL) ratified the Uniform Marriage and Divorce Act (UMDA), which also permitted no-fault divorce but based on grounds of "irretrievable breakdown" or a six-month separation. Under UMDA, marital misconduct also is irrelevant to the determination of spousal support, property distribution, or custody.

Since then, states followed California's or UMDA's lead by adopting a no-fault system—either in whole (by replacing completely their fault-based systems with no-fault regimes) or in part (by superimposing no-fault onto fault-based grounds).

No-fault divorce transformed rules of property distribution, spousal support, and custody. The no-fault divorce doctrine reflects the evolution in women's status brought about by women's increased economic opportunities. The legal treatment of spousal support provides one example. The gender-based concept of "alimony" was replaced with the more neutral terms "spousal support" and "maintenance." Although spousal support is now available theoretically to either spouse after divorce, fewer courts today award spousal support than in the past and such awards tend to be limited in duration.

This development was accompanied by unanticipated adverse economic consequences for divorced women and their children. As sociologist Lenore Weitzman points out in *The Divorce Revolution* (1985), the standard of living for divorced women decreases after divorce, while men's standard of living increases. *Id.* at 382.

Beginning in 1970, a large increase occurred in the proportion of people who never married (from 5% of those aged 25-34 in 1970, to 50% by 2015, according to census data). The majority of adults now live outside of marriage—as single parents, as partners in cohabiting relationships, or as singles. This "retreat from marriage" (especially prominent among people of color and the poor) has been accompanied by a rise in nonmarital childbearing and an increase in "father absence" as more men live apart from their children. The "retreat from marriage" has profound socio-economic consequences in terms of adverse developmental outcomes for children and intergenerational transmission of inequality. This societal trend also highlights legal policies (e.g., child custody, child support) that are not well tailored to the emerging complexities of family life.

C. **Dissatisfaction with the family:** The 1960s witnessed increasing disillusionment with the nuclear family. Radical psychiatrists (e.g., R.D. Laing), as well as radical feminists (e.g., Shulamith Firestone, Kate Millett), highlighted the ills of the private nuclear family. Feminists challenged several beliefs: the nuclear family as a biological given with its sexual division of labor, the hierarchy of family relationships with women being subordinate to men, women's primary commitment to the home and children, and procreation as the central purpose of the family.

These criticisms contributed to the gradual reconceptualization of marriage and the family. Marriage became perceived as a means of personal fulfillment and a source of companionship. Rather than the concept of marriage as forever, a new idea took hold: When marriage failed to meet the parties' expectations, the parties could and should seek fulfillment elsewhere. Further, criticisms of the traditional family contributed to a growing awareness of, and acceptance of, the diversity of family forms (such as cohabiting couples). Nontraditional, as well as traditional, families provide intimacy and companionship.

Today, we are witnessing increasing fluidity among family forms. The majority of children born to unmarried parents experience multiple transitions in family structure as these children are exposed to different parental arrangements. Increasingly, nonmarital children spend time living with a parent to whom they are not biologically related. These diverse parental arrangements have profound implications for the custody and support of children.

D. **Dissatisfaction with the traditional dispute resolution process:** The 1960s witnessed increased dissatisfaction with traditional means of dispute resolution. Lawyers, judges, and scholars criticized the legal system and manifested a new interest in alternate dispute resolution. Critics recognized that the law was unwieldy and intrusive in the resolution of private disputes. This movement recognized "private ordering"—i.e., the ability of the parties to resolve their disputes without judicial intervention. We witness this development in the judicial recognition of premarital agreements, the growth of mediation of family disputes, and the development of the collaborative law movement.

E. **Children's rights movement:** Children now occupy a more central role in the family and society. Unlike in past centuries, families no longer value children solely for their economic contributions. Childhood has been reconceptualized as a prolonged period of economic and social dependency.

In the 1960s, the civil rights movement and the women's movement contributed to the birth of the children's rights movement. Family law began to reflect the idea of children having legally enforceable rights, including the right to a voice in decision making that affected them. The lowering of the age of majority in 1971 in the aftermath of the Vietnam War accelerated this movement. For example, children currently play a role in child custody decisions as well as abortion decision making.

F. **Gay rights movement and the advent of marriage equality:** The gay rights movement has its roots in the late 1960s. Influenced by the model of the civil rights movement, gay rights advocates began to organize politically. The Stonewall Riots at a Greenwich Village bar in New York City in 1969 led to a national outcry against discrimination directed at gays and lesbians. As an increasing number of gays and lesbians proclaimed their identity ("came out of the closet"), they ushered in a movement for social change.

The gay rights movement resulted in far-reaching law reform. Gay rights advocates first targeted employment discrimination and criminal sanctions against same-sex sexual conduct. Subsequent activism led to the marriage equality movement. In 2015, the U.S. Supreme Court recognized the freedom to marry for same-sex couples nationwide in *Obergefell v. Hodges*, 576 U.S. 644 (2015). The decision had major implications for all aspects of family law.

G. **The waxing and waning impact of morality and the accommodation of religious beliefs:** Beginning in the 1960s, family law reflected the decreasing influence of ideas about morality. The women's movement and the birth control movement liberalized sexual mores. Control over conception significantly decreased the number of nonmarital (formerly called "illegitimate") children. The women's movement cast a negative light on the sexual double standard that permitted premarital and extramarital sexual relationships for men but not women.

The waning of morality was reflected in family law in several ways. For example, no-fault divorce led to increasing acceptance of dissolution of marital relationships. Nonmarital children are no longer stigmatized and enjoy enhanced legal rights. Fault-based notions no longer play a significant role in determinations of spousal support, property, and custody. Same-sex couples enjoy enhanced rights in the areas of marriage, divorce, child support, child custody, adoption and assisted reproduction, to name a few.

The waning of morality was also reflected in changes in family law terminology. To eliminate strains of stigma, for example, we now speak of "dissolution" (rather than "divorce"), "spousal support" or "maintenance" (rather than "alimony"), "nonmarital children" (rather than "illegitimate" or "out-of-wedlock" children), and "unmarried couples" (rather than "persons living in sin" or persons involved in "meretricious" relationships").

Beginning in the 1970s, the rise of the religious right as a political movement brought renewed attention to the role of morality and religion in policymaking about family-related issues. This political movement was fueled by conservatives who were concerned about what they perceived to be moral decline engendered by threats to the family. They blamed this decline, in part, on the Supreme Court decision in *Roe v. Wade*, 410 U.S. 113 (1973) (affirming women's constitutional right to abortion). Their agenda included attempts to restrict abortion and prohibit state recognition of same-sex marriage. Recent efforts of the religious right led to state exemptions for religious officials and others (such as business owners) from having to solemnize gay marriages or provide services to LGBT people contrary to their religious beliefs. The resulting conflict pits the accommodation of religious liberty claims against the equality principle (e.g., non-discrimination in public accommodations laws).

H. **The curtailment of reproductive freedom:** Beginning in the late 1970s, many Americans were galvanized by the dramatic rise in legal abortions following the Supreme Court's decision in *Roe v. Wade*. Conservatives mobilized to elect politicians who would defend "Christian" values. A high water mark for the religious right came after the 2000 election of President George W. Bush whose evangelical sympathies led to his support for federal funding for faith-based charities and a federal constitutional amendment against same-sex marriage as well as his opposition to embryonic stem cell research, euthanasia, and abortion (resulting in the "partial-birth" abortion ban). The ensuing wave of state abortion restrictions made access to abortion more difficult, especially for poor women and women of color.

In 2014, the Supreme Court's decision in *Burwell v. Hobby Lobby Stores, Inc.,* 573 U.S. 682 (2014), significantly enlarged the scope of federal protection for claims of religious liberty by allowing closely held for-profit corporations to be exempt, on religious grounds, from the contraceptive mandate promulgated under the Patient Protection and Affordable Care Act (ACA). The election of President Donald Trump in 2016 strengthened the influence of the religious right and fueled the raging battle over women's reproductive rights. Subsequent federal regulations allowed broader refusal clauses, extending exemptions from the contraceptive mandate to some employers with nonreligious moral objections. Further, many state legislatures enacted religious refusal laws (also called "conscience clauses") that permit health care providers to refuse to provide certain medical procedures (such as abortion) on religious or moral grounds.

I. **The increasing use of assisted reproductive technologies:** Major developments in reproductive technology enhanced women's reproductive freedom. The discovery of the birth control pill in the 1960s led to decreased fear about preventing pregnancies. Subsequent concern focused on the means to *facilitate* reproduction.

Advances in medical technology made possible *assisted reproductive technologies (ARTs)* — methods to achieve pregnancy by artificial means (such as in vitro fertilization, embryo transplants, and surrogate motherhood) — and *collaborative reproduction* (the term used to describe fertility options that involve third parties, such as gamete donors and gestational surrogates). Several social conditions contributed to the development and use of these new reproductive alternatives, including an increase in infertility resulting from delayed childbearing, harmful contraceptive methods, and pelvic inflammatory disease, as well as the shortage of white infants for adoption.

Family law is now grappling with the delineation of the rights and responsibilities that flow from the development and utilization of these reproductive alternatives. The increasing use of these technologies has led to issues of access for members of nontraditional families, evolving definitions of parenthood, disputes between family members about ownership of genetic material, concerns about the rights of children conceived through these technologies, and the need for regulation of the health care industry that provides assisted reproductive technologies.

III. LEGAL TRENDS

Family law reflects three legal trends: (1) *federalization* (i.e., an increasing congressional role in family policy), (2) *constitutionalization* (i.e., the growing recognition of the constitutional dimensions of the regulation of intimate relationships), and (3) a movement toward *uniformity* of state law.

A. **Federalization of family law: Increasing congressional role:** The federal government occupies an increasingly prominent role in the regulation of family law. Formerly, family law was exclusively the domain of state regulation. However, in the past several decades, Congress has enacted considerable legislation on many issues of family life.

Federal legislation now addresses adoption, child support, child custody, child abuse and neglect, domestic violence, foster care, marriage validity, paternity establishment, and medical and parental leaves. The ever-increasing number of federal statutes includes (among others):

■ Adoption and Safe Families Act (ASFA) (promoting adoption of children with special needs and those in foster care), and Adoption Assistance and Child Welfare Act (AACWA) (addressing foster care reform);

■ Affordable Care Act (ACA) (requiring large employers that provide their employees with health insurance to cover some contraceptive costs in their health insurance plans (a "contraceptive mandate"));

■ Child Abuse Prevention and Treatment Act (CAPTA) (providing state programs and procedures to address the prevention and treatment of child abuse and neglect);

■ Child Support Enforcement Amendments (requiring states participating in the federal child support program to have procedures to establish paternity, to obtain child support awards, and to enforce child support obligations);

■ Family Support Act (FSA) (requiring states to adopt numerical guidelines); and the subsequent Full Faith and Credit for Child Support Orders Act (FFCCSOA) (requiring states to adopt procedures regarding recognition of other states' decrees of child support);

■ Family and Medical Leave Act (FMLA) (granting unpaid leave for birth, adoption, and illnesses of family members);

■ Foster Care Independence Act (FCIA) (helping youth who "age out of" foster care to achieve independent living skills) and Fostering Connection to Success and Increasing Adoptions Act (FCSIAA) (extending benefits to older foster youth and facilitating kinship guardianship assistance payments);

■ Indian Child Welfare Act (ICWA) (providing that the tribe has exclusive jurisdiction in matters concerning child custody, adoption, and foster care placements involving Indian children);

■ Parental Kidnapping Prevention Act (PKPA) (addressing parental abduction and jurisdictional conflicts between state courts regarding child custody);

■ Partial-Birth Abortion Ban Act (PBABA) (prohibiting a form of late-term abortion);

■ Pregnancy Discrimination Act (PDA) of Title VII of the Civil Rights Act (specifying that the term "sex discrimination" includes discrimination "on the basis of pregnancy" for purposes of employment discrimination);

■ Unborn Victims of Violence Act (UVVA) (recognizing unborn children as victims when they are injured or killed during the commission of federal crimes of violence); and

■ Violence Against Women Act (VAWA) (providing federal remedies for designated harm to a spouse or intimate partner and providing for interstate enforcement of protection orders).

These federal regulations usurp state supremacy over many issues of family law that were formerly regulated by the states.

B. **Constitutionalization of family law:** Beginning in the 1960s, the U.S. Supreme Court handed down numerous rulings on family issues. Before that time, the Court only occasionally regulated the family. A considerable body of federal constitutional law now applies to the family and supplements state regulation of family relationships. The Court's application of the principles of due process and equal protection have transformed family law.

For example, the Court expanded rights in the areas of (among others): abortion (*Roe v. Wade, Planned Parenthood v. Danforth*); contraception (*Griswold v. Conn., Eisenstadt v. Baird*); sexual conduct between consenting adults in the home (*Lawrence v. Texas*); the right to marry (*Loving v. Virginia, Zablocki v. Redhail*); the right to divorce (*Boddie v. Conn.*); parental rights (*Wisconsin v. Yoder, Santosky v. Kramer*); the rights of women (*Reed v. Reed, Craig v. Boren*); the rights of fathers in nonmarital families (*Stanley v. Illinois, Caban v. Mohammed*); and the rights of same-sex couples to marry (*Obergefell v. Hodges*) and to be recognized as parents (*Pavan v. Smith*) (all discussed *infra*). At the same time, the Court developed notions of marital privacy and family privacy based on liberal interpretations of the Fourteenth Amendment.

C. **Movement toward uniform state laws:** Family law, formerly, was a matter of state law and reflected state supremacy. That is, matters of marriage, divorce, custody, support, etc. were considered matters for exclusive state jurisdiction — matters regulated by the states and enforced by state courts. This resulted in considerable *variation* in the legal regulations applicable to the family and family members.

In an effort to impose some uniformity on family law, the Uniform Law Commission (formerly called the National Conference of Commissioners on Uniform State Laws) promulgated important model statutes. These include (among others):

■ the Uniform Child Abduction Prevention Act (addressing measures to prevent child abduction);

■ the Uniform Child Custody Jurisdiction and Enforcement Act (UCCJEA) (addressing interstate enforcement of custody decrees);

■ the Uniform Collaborative Law Act (UCLA) (regulating the use of collaborative law as a form of alternative dispute resolution);

■ the Uniform Deployed Parents Custody and Visitation Act (addressing issues of child custody and visitation that arise when parents are deployed in military or other national service);

■ the Uniform Interstate Enforcement of Domestic Violence Protection Orders Act (UIEDVPOA) (establishing uniform procedures to enable courts to enforce domestic violence protection orders issued in other jurisdictions);

■ the Uniform Interstate Family Support Act (UIFSA) (concerning the establishment, enforcement, and modification of child support obligations);

■ the Uniform Interstate Family Support Act Amendments (modifying UIFSA's international provisions to comport with the obligations of the United States under the 2007 Hague Convention on Maintenance);

■ the Uniform Marital Property Act (UMPA) (addressing marital property and premarital agreements);

■ the Uniform Marriage and Divorce Act (UMDA) (addressing marriage, divorce, and custody);

■ the Uniform Nonparent Custody and Visitation Act (UNCVA) (providing a framework for establishing child custody and visitation rights of nonparents);

■ the Uniform Parentage Act (UPA) and revised versions of the UPA (dealing with parentage establishment);

■ the Uniform Premarital Agreement Act (UPAA) (regulating premarital agreements);

■ the Uniform Premarital and Marital Agreements Act (addressing the different standards in premarital, as well as marital, agreements that have led to conflicting laws, judgments, and uncertainty about enforcement as couples move from state to state); and

■ the Uniform Representation of Children in Abuse, Neglect, and Custody Proceedings Act (addressing issues regarding counsel for children in various contexts).

In addition, the ***American Law Institute (ALI)*** completed a project that promotes uniformity in family law. (The American Law Institute is an influential group of lawyers, law professors, and judges who engage in law reform.) The product of that project is titled *Principles of the Law of Family Dissolution: Analysis and Recommendations* (2002) [hereinafter ALI *Principles*]. These *Principles* reformed family law by clarifying its underlying principles and making policy recommendations for implementation by courts and legislatures. The *Principles* cover such issues as the allocation of custodial and decision making responsibilities for children, child support, distribution of marital property, compensatory payments to former spouses, resolution of the economic claims of domestic partners, and the legal effect of various agreements between the parties.

PREPARING TO MARRY

ChapterScope

This chapter explores the law that governs the individual's *decision to marry*. First, the chapter examines the resolution of premarital controversies and the validity of premarital agreements. Second, it examines restrictions on entry into marriage. Third, it explores problems of marriage validity, such as annulment and conflict of laws. Here are a few of the key principles covered in this chapter:

- **Premarital controversies:** Two types of premarital controversies include actions for (1) *breach of promise to marry* and (2) *return of gifts in contemplation of marriage, such as engagement rings.*

  - A few states allow an action for a *breach of a promise to marry*, permitting A to recover damages from B, if B ends the engagement. However, the *modern trend* is toward *abolition* of the action.

  - *Gifts in contemplation of marriage* (such as engagement rings) are gifts that are conditioned on the occurrence of a marriage. These gifts may be recoverable in some circumstances. Pursuant to the *majority rule*, the party who is at fault in breaking the engagement is not entitled to the return or retention of the ring. According to the *modern trend*, the gift is recoverable without regard to fault.

- **Premarital agreements:** Under the *traditional view*, agreements between prospective spouses were void as contrary to public policy. Under the *modern view*, courts permit parties to regulate the financial aspects of the marriage. To be valid, such agreements must meet tests for procedural and/or substantive fairness.

- **Restrictions on entry into marriage:** Various restrictions exist concerning entry into marriage. Such restrictions consist of: (1) *constitutional limitations*, (2) *substantive restrictions*, and (3) *procedural restrictions*.

  - The U.S. Supreme Court has held that restrictions on marriage that are based on *race*, *poverty*, and *sex* are unconstitutional.

  - State substantive restrictions refer to *capacity* to marry and *state of mind*.

  - State procedural restrictions regulate *marriage procedure*.

- **Annulment:** An annulment declares a marriage *void ab initio*. In contrast, a divorce terminates a valid marriage. Grounds for annulment include **fraud, duress**, and **nonage**.

- **Conflict of laws:** Issues of conflict of laws concern which law governs marriage validity. Under the *traditional rule*, marriage validity is determined by the law of the place where the marriage was celebrated (the "place of celebration" rule). Under the *Restatement (Second) of Conflict of Laws*, the validity of marriage is determined by the state that has the "most significant relationship to the spouses and the marriage." The pending *Restatement (Third) of Conflict of Laws* defines "domicile" (for purposes of marriage validity) as "the place where the person's life is centered for reaching choice-of-law issues."

I. PREMARITAL CONTROVERSIES

A. Breach of promise to marry

1. **Generally:** A few states permit an action for breach of promise to marry. Under this cause of action, A can recover damages from B, if B breaches a promise to marry A (i.e., if B terminates the engagement).

2. **Historical background:** The claim of breach of promise to marry has its origins in early English common law. Although early cases resembled tort actions, the action gradually began to resemble contract claims.

   Recovery was premised on a view of marriage as a property transaction, and the belief that a woman was "sullied" by the broken engagement (i.e., stigmatized by the possible loss of virginity). The action came to be called a "heartbalm" suit because damages (i.e., the balm) soothed a plaintiff's broken heart.

3. **Criticisms:** Criticisms led most states to abolish the action via "anti-heartbalm legislation" (sometimes, confusingly, called "Heart Balm Acts"). These criticisms include:

   ■ the action is a form of blackmail;

   ■ persons should be permitted to break engagements without fear of legal damages;

   ■ the action is based on sexist and archaic stereotypes of women; and

   ■ damages are based on an outdated view of marriage as a property transaction (by compensating women for loss of social and economic position).

4. **Judicial and legislative responses to criticisms:** Even in the few states that continue to recognize the action, courts sometimes circumscribe recovery either by limiting damages or by strict adherence to statutory requirements.

   Example: Lori has an intimate relationship with David, a wealthy, married, recording producer. After David ends the relationship, he seeks partition of their jointly-owned property (a home that he quitclaimed from himself as sole owner to the couple as joint tenants) and the return of his personal property. Lori counterclaims for breach of promise to marry. Tennessee law recognizes the claim for breach of promise to marry but with limitations, requiring (1) a signed writing as evidence of the promise or (2) testimony of at least two disinterested witnesses. The court rejects Lori's argument that the quitclaim deed was a signed writing, reasoning that it lacks evidence of intent to marry. Further, the court holds that Lori's parents cannot be witnesses to the promise because parents are not "disinterested," especially if they are creditors (as here). *Rivkin v. Postal*, 2001 WL 1077952 (Tenn. Ct. App. 2001).

5. **Damages:** The breach-of-promise suit is a hybrid action (quasi-contract, quasi-tort). Its hybrid nature raises issues about the proper measure of damages, the applicability of the Statute of Limitations for contract or tort (many courts apply the longer statute), and the abatement of the action upon the death of either party (most courts hold that the action does abate in this event). Some states limit damages to economic loss.

6. **Defenses:** Traditional defenses include:

   ■ plaintiff's fraudulent misrepresentations;

   ■ nondisclosure of prior sexual conduct with a third party;

- impaired physical or mental health;

- the fact that either party was married at the time of the engagement;

- plaintiff's lack of love for the defendant; and

- mutuality of the decision to terminate the engagement.

7. **Conflict of laws:** Recovery for breach of promise to marry may present difficulties if the "promise" occurs in a jurisdiction that recognizes the cause of action but the "breach" occurs in a jurisdiction that does not.

   Example: Brian and Dana meet through an Internet dating service. Brian (who misrepresents that he is divorced) proposes marriage while the couple is visiting South Carolina. Subsequently, they live together in Brian's New York apartment. Dana breaks up when she suspects that Brian is dating other women. When Brian files suit in New York for the return of the engagement ring or its value, Dana counterclaims for breach of promise to marry (recognized by South Carolina but not New York). The New York court dismisses her counterclaim, based on a state statute banning suits for breach of promise to marry "whether such action arose within or without the state." N.Y. Civ. Rights L. §81. The court also rules that, because Brian was already married when he proposed, the agreement to marry was void as against public policy. *Callahan v. Parker*, 824 N.Y.S.2d 768 (Sup. Ct. 2006).

B. **Gifts in contemplation of marriage: Engagement rings**

1. **Generally:** During an engagement, the parties may give gifts to each other. Often, for example, the man gives an engagement ring to the woman. If the engagement is broken, whether the donee must return the gift may depend on who was responsible (at *fault*) for terminating the engagement.

   According to the majority rule, if a ring is given in contemplation of marriage, the party who breaks the engagement without justification is not entitled to either the return or retention of the ring.

   Example: Plaintiff and Defendant date for five months. A few days before Christmas, Plaintiff gives Defendant an engagement ring worth $13,500. Six weeks later, Plaintiff breaks off the relationship based on his belief that Defendant is not the "right" person and because his family opposes the match. He files suit for return of the ring or its value. Defendant argues that the ring was a Christmas gift or, alternatively, a conditional gift that she could retain because Plaintiff terminated the engagement. The court holds that the gift was an engagement present rather than a Christmas gift and that, in accordance with the state's fault-based approach, Defendant was entitled to keep the engagement ring (which the court characterizes as a conditional gift in contemplation of marriage) because her fiancé broke off the engagement through no fault of hers. *Clippard v. Pfefferkorn*, 168 S.W.3d 616 (Mo. Ct. App. 2005).

2. **Legal theories:** Several legal theories support the recovery of the engagement ring. Under the widespread conditional gift theory, A's gift to B of an engagement ring is conditioned on B's performance of an act (getting married). If the condition (the marriage) is not fulfilled, then A may recover the gift.

3. **Modern trend:** Under the minority rule (which is also the modern trend), the ring is recoverable without regard to fault (i.e., regardless of who broke the engagement).

   Example: Matthew proposes to his girlfriend Ashley. After they break up, Ashley claims that Matthew ended the engagement. He contends that the decision was mutual. Ashley also asserts that she twice offered to return the ring but Matthew refused. He contends that she refused to return the ring. The court adopts the no-fault view based on the impossibility of determining blame for a breakup, a desire not to penalize donors for preventing unhappy marriages, and the lack of any legislative intent (in the legislative abolition of fault-based divorce) to diminish protection of marriage. The court remands because of the need for a jury determination of credibility to assess Ashley's contention that the ring evolved into an absolute gift. *Campbell v. Robinson*, 726 S.E.2d 221 (S.C. Ct. App. 2012).

4. **Other gifts:** Engaged parties sometimes give each other tokens of affection in addition to an engagement ring. Whether these gifts must be returned depends on whether a gift is deemed to be conditioned on the marriage.

   Example: Layne proposes marriage to Jody and gives her an engagement ring. During their engagement, Jody asks Layne to pay for trips to Alaska and France, to buy a car for her son, and to have a vasectomy. Jody then breaks off the engagement and returns the ring. Layne sells the ring for half its purchase price. He then sues her based on theories of conditional gift and unjust enrichment, seeking reimbursement of $25,000 for the cost of the travel, car, vasectomy and a reversal procedure, and the difference between the ring's purchase and sale price. Rejecting his claims, the court holds that he did not allege that he expressly made the gifts conditional on the marriage and, in addition, the circumstances did not imply that the gifts were conditioned on the marriage when he gave them. The exception is the engagement ring, but the court found that Jody returned the ring, so Layne had received restitution. *Hess v. Johnson*, 163 P.3d 747 (Utah Ct. App. 2007).

5. **Effect of abolition of heartbalm suits on the recovery of engagement gifts:** In some jurisdictions that have abolished heartbalm suits (e.g., breach of promise to marry), the question arises as to the effect of the statutory abolition. That is, do such statutes similarly abolish the cause of action for return of an engagement ring?

   Example: Dennis gives Terry an engagement ring. Three months later, the engagement ends. Dennis sues Terry for return of the ring. Each party alleges that the other terminated the engagement. Dennis appeals from the dismissal of his claim for return of the engagement ring, contending that the trial court erred in holding that recovery was barred by the statutory abolition of actions for breach of promise to marry. The appellate court holds that abolition of breach of promise suits does *not* preclude suits for recovery of engagement rings, based on strict statutory construction (i.e., the statute contemplates abolition of "awards of damages for breach of contract to marry" and not abolition of restitutionary damages, such as return of the ring). *Brown v. Thomas*, 379 N.W.2d 868 (Wis. Ct. App. 1985).

Quiz Yourself on PREMARITAL CONTROVERSIES

1. Sally and Tom have been living together for several years. On Sally's birthday, Tom asks her to marry him, and she accepts. Three months later, after a fight, Tom breaks off the engagement. Can Sally recover from Tom for breach of promise to marry?_____

2. Alice and Bob have been living together for several years. During this time, Alice has never secured a divorce from her husband Carl. Bob asks Alice to marry him. She accepts, indicating that she would

marry him after she divorces Carl. Several months later, Bob breaks off the engagement. At the time, Alice is still not divorced from Carl. In a jurisdiction that recognizes a cause of action for breach of promise to marry, can Alice recover damages from Bob? _____

3. During his engagement to Linda, Martin purchases numerous items for Linda, including a diamond engagement ring, a car, a computer, and several horses. He also pays off her car loan and makes various improvements to her house. After a disagreement, Martin moves out of their apartment and breaks off the engagement. He then brings an action, seeking reimbursement for all his gifts. Will he be successful? _____

4. Same basic facts as above. Linda alleges that Martin is not entitled to the return of the engagement ring because he unjustifiably broke the engagement. Will her argument prevail? _____

5. Frank brings an action against his ex-fiancée, Frances, seeking recovery of his $20,000 engagement ring. The jurisdiction has an "anti-heartbalm" statute that bars all actions in contract law that arise from breaches of a promise to marry. Frances claims that Frank's action to recover the engagement ring is barred by the statute. Is his action barred? _____

Answers

1. It depends on the jurisdiction. A few jurisdictions still permit this cause of action, under the majority rule, Sally could recover from Tom because he ended the engagement without justification.

2. No. Courts have held that the fact that either party was **still married** at the time of the engagement **precludes recovery** for breach of promise to marry. (Alice was still married to Carl.) Some courts theorize that the party who is still married **lacks capacity** to enter into a subsequent marriage.

3. Yes, Martin's suit probably will be successful, but only for recovery of the engagement ring. The court will probably hold that the engagement ring is a conditional gift given in contemplation of marriage, but the other items were irrevocable inter vivos gifts that were not expressly conditioned on the subsequent marriage.

4. It depends on the jurisdiction. Under the majority view, Linda's argument (that Martin is not entitled to the return of the ring) would prevail because the party who is at fault in breaking the engagement (Martin) is not entitled to recovery of the ring or its value. Under the modern trend, however, the ring is recoverable by the donor without regard to fault (i.e., without regard to who broke the engagement).

5. No, probably not. A court would probably find that the anti-heartbalm statute is limited to precluding breach-of-promise suits and does not bar an action for return of an engagement ring.

II. PREMARITAL AGREEMENTS

Premarital agreements (sometimes termed "antenuptial agreements" or "prenuptial agreements") are agreements between prospective spouses that are made in contemplation of the marriage. Such agreements typically require a party to limit or relinquish certain rights (e.g., property rights, spousal support, inheritance rights) that the party would have acquired by reason of the marriage.

A. **Traditional view:** Traditionally, premarital contracts that determined financial obligations in the event of *dissolution* were void, as contrary to public policy. Such agreements were disfavored because it was thought they facilitated divorce by providing inducements to end the marriage and denigrating the status of marriage. However, premarital contracts that determined financial consequences upon *death* were permitted.

B. **Premarital agreements distinguished from other contracts**

1. **Ordinary contracts:** Premarital agreements differ from ordinary contracts in several ways:

■ The parties in ordinary commercial contracts are "at arm's length," i.e., the parties are bound without regard to whether they understand the terms or whether those terms are reasonable. Because of the state's heightened interest in marriage, premarital contracts traditionally have been governed by stricter requirements. Thus, for example, courts frequently inquire into the fairness of the premarital agreement, whereas courts expect the parties to ordinary contracts to look after their own interests.

■ Further, because premarital agreements are executory (performed in the future), the possibility is more likely that future circumstances may make these agreements unwise or unfair. Thus, a greater need arises for equitable intervention.

2. **Contracts during marriage**

a. **Traditional rule:** According to the traditional rule, the parties are not able to regulate, by means of their private contracts, state-imposed rights and responsibilities of the marriage (e.g., husband's duty of support, wife's duty to provide services).

Example: During their marriage, Margrethe agrees to pay Sidney $300 per month. In return, Sidney agrees to accompany Margrethe on her travels. Upon their divorce, Sidney sues to enforce the agreement. The court holds that because the agreement alters the essential obligations of the marriage contract (wife must follow husband's choice of domicile and husband has duty of support), it is void as contrary to public policy. *Graham v. Graham*, 33 F. Supp. 936 (E.D. Mich. 1940).

b. **Modern view:** Under the modern view, courts are more willing to permit the parties to regulate the financial aspects of the marriage. Public policy favors individuals' ordering of their interests through contractual arrangements.

Note: Community property jurisdictions have always permitted the spouses to enter into contracts that *transmute* (i.e., change the character of) separate property into community property or vice versa.

3. **Separation agreements distinguished:** Both separation agreements and premarital agreements address the financial consequences of dissolution. However, the parties enter into a premarital agreement before marriage, whereas they enter into a separation agreement (or a "marital settlement agreement") *after* they decide to terminate their marriage.

C. **Modern approach**

1. **Trend:** Courts increasingly recognize premarital agreements. A fivefold increase has occurred over the past 20 years in the number of couples obtaining prenuptial agreements. Five reasons

predominate for the rise in the use of such agreements: (1) millennials are marrying later, having more time to build wealth, and therefore are more desirous of protecting their wealth; (2) marital partners are more likely to include partners who were previously married (and who might have children from prior marriages) and therefore are more knowledgeable about the need for a prenuptial agreement; (3) marital partners are bringing more debt from student loans into their marriage and their prospective spouses want to be insulated from these debts; (4) an increasing number of couples have financial issues that they want to work out in advance; and (5) many millennials grew up with a divorced parent so they understand the need to be prepared for that eventuality.

2. **Limitation:** Despite increasing recognition of premarital contracts, prospective spouses may not enter into an enforceable agreement about *child support* or *child custody*. These limitations result from the state's countervailing interest in child welfare. *See, e.g.,* Uniform Premarital Agreement Act (UPAA) §3(b)(1983) ("the right of a child to support may not be adversely affected by a premarital agreement"). The Uniform Marital Property Act (UMPA) also precludes spousal agreements about child support.

3. **Formalities**

   a. **Writing:** The Statute of Frauds requires that premarital agreements must be in writing and signed by the party to be charged.

   b. **Consideration:** UPAA §2 provides that consideration is *not* required ("A premarital agreement must be in writing and signed by both parties. It is enforceable without consideration.").

4. **Scope:** The trend is to broaden the scope of premarital agreements in terms of property rights. For example, UPAA §3(a), which permits considerable latitude regarding contractual freedom, permits the parties to contract regarding the property of either or both spouses and "whenever and wherever acquired or located"; management and control of property; spousal support; making of a will or a trust; death benefits in life insurance policies; choice of law; and "any other matter, including their personal rights and obligations not in violation of public policy or a statute imposing a criminal penalty."

D. **Requirements for validity:** A premarital agreement is valid if: (1) it provides full disclosure; (2) it is fair and reasonable; and (3) it is entered into voluntarily by both parties. Procedural fairness refers to disclosure and the voluntariness with which each party enters into the agreement. Substantive fairness refers to the fairness of the substantive terms of the agreement.

Note: Some courts do not require all the preceding elements. That is, some courts enforce an unfair agreement provided that a party executed it voluntarily and with full disclosure.

1. **Full disclosure:** A valid premarital agreement requires full disclosure. However, full disclosure does not require *detailed* disclosure. Moreover, a spouse's independent knowledge of the other spouse's financial status can serve as a substitute for disclosure.

   Example: At divorce, Wife contends that Husband's failure to disclose his income at the time of the parties' premarital agreement renders the agreement unenforceable. The court rejects her argument. The court concludes that, although Husband's financial statement did not list his income, it did include the value of his CPA practice, investment accounts, home, and lake house. In short, it revealed that he was wealthy and had "significant income-producing assets." That disclosure, together with the fact that Wife lived with him for four years before marriage, supports the trial court ruling that the absence of Husband's income did not constitute nondisclosure of a material fact that would make the premarital agreement unenforceable. *Dove v. Dove*, 680 S.E.2d 839 (Ga. 2009).

Example: Teresa, a court reporter and bookkeeper, agrees to marry Randall, a personal injury attorney. Randall desires a premarital agreement to preserve his assets for the children of his prior marriage. He drafts the premarital agreement, to which he attaches a list of each party's assets. When the marriage ends, Teresa challenges the agreement as unconscionable, arguing that Randall failed to provide full and fair disclosure. The court rejects her claim, concluding that, because Teresa served as Randall's paralegal and secretary, she was sufficiently knowledgeable about his finances to satisfy the disclosure requirement. *In re Marriage of Shanks*, 758 N.W.2d 506 (Iowa 2008).

Note: The majority of jurisdictions now regard the engaged parties as being involved in a confidential relationship (thereby imposing heightened duties to each other). *Friezo v. Friezo*, 914 A.2d 533, 549 (Conn. 2007).

2. **Fair and reasonable:** Courts differ in their determination of the substantive fairness of the agreement.

   a. **Traditional rule:** Traditionally, courts required that the agreement be fair under all the relevant circumstances.

   b. **Modern trend:** Under the modern trend that reflects increasing respect for decisional autonomy and changing gender roles, some courts enforce agreements that are unfair so long as the agreement accords with intent, and also is entered into voluntarily and with full disclosure. This development renders premarital agreements more similar to ordinary contracts.

   Example: A 23-year-old unemployed nurse marries a 39-year-old neurosurgeon. Their prenuptial agreement limits her right to spousal support to $200 a week, subject to a maximum of $25,000. At divorce, she argues that the payments are not reasonable. The court upholds the agreement despite its unfairness because "there is no longer validity in the implicit assumption . . . that spouses are of unequal status [and] women are not knowledgeable enough to understand the nature of contracts. . . ." *Simeone v. Simeone*, 581 A.2d 162 (Pa. 1990).

   Example: A prospective bridegroom demands that his fiancée execute a premarital agreement. She signs an agreement that, upon divorce, precludes spousal support, a share in the marital home (which was the man's separate property), any portion of the man's retirement and investment assets, and attorney's fees. When the parties divorce 17 years later, the wife challenges the agreement as unconscionable based on the substantial increase in the husband's assets (i.e., appreciation due to his stock options and the value of the marital home). The court disagrees, finding that these financial circumstances were reasonably within the contemplation of the parties. *Crews v. Crews*, 989 A.2d 1060 (Conn. 2010).

   i. **Factors relevant to determination of reasonableness:** The following factors may enter into the judicial determination of reasonableness:

      ■ the parties' respective wealth;

      ■ respective ages;

      ■ respective intelligence, literacy, and business acumen; and

      ■ prior family ties.

    ii. **Time for determination of reasonableness:** Some courts determine fairness at the time of *execution* of the agreement. However, an increasing number of states evaluate fairness at the time of execution of the agreement *as well as at the time of* enforcement (at divorce). The former policy emphasizes contractual freedom; the latter, equitable principles.

        Note: UPAA §6(a)(2) requires *unconscionability* at the time of *execution*. The ALI *Principles* §7.05 assess fairness (requiring "substantial injustice" rather than unconscionability) at the time of *enforcement*.

3. **Voluntariness:** The parties must enter the contract voluntarily, i.e., without fraud or duress.

    a. **Meaning:** Although courts are not in accord with what constitutes duress, they tend to agree that a party's insistence on the premarital agreement as a condition of the marriage is not duress. In addition, courts increasingly hold that the presence of independent counsel militates against a finding of duress.

        Example: Wife argues that she signed a premarital agreement under duress because she discovered that she was pregnant and that Husband refused to marry her unless she signed. Although this situation presented Wife with "a difficult choice" according to the court, it is not sufficient to "divest[] the wife of her free will and judgment," especially considering that she was presented with the agreement one week before the wedding and had time to obtain the advice of counsel (that she rejected). The court adds that other jurisdictions reach the same result based on similar facts. *Biliouris v. Biliouris*, 852 N.E.2d 687 (Mass. App. Ct. 2006).

    b. **Timing of Execution of Agreement:** Some plaintiffs challenge premarital agreements by arguing that presentation of the agreement in close proximity to the day of the wedding constitutes duress. Most courts reject this view. Some statutes address the problem by requiring a designated amount of time between execution of the agreement and the marriage. See also the ALI *Principles* discussed *infra*.

E. **Representation:** States generally do not require that the engaged parties be represented by independent counsel. Some states specify that the parties must have an *opportunity* to consult counsel, but do not require that they *actually do so*, in order for the agreement to be valid.

Rationale: A requirement of representation would be paternalistic and interfere with contractual freedom.

Example: When baseball player Barry Bonds marries Sun at the beginning of his career, he insists that she sign a prenuptial agreement providing that each party's earnings and acquisitions remain separate property. When they separate, he is earning $8 million annually. She alleges that the agreement was not executed voluntarily because she did not understand it and was not represented by counsel. The California Supreme Court upholds the agreement, ruling that representation by counsel is only one of several factors to be considered and that substantial evidence supported the view that Sun understood the agreement and executed it voluntarily. *In re Marriage of Bonds*, 99 Cal. Rptr. 2d 252 (Cal. 2000).

F. **Spousal support:** Some state law reflects distaste for provisions in premarital agreements that preclude spousal support, stemming from the concern that the divorced spouse might become a public charge. As a result, some states prohibit such spousal support waivers. Other states provide that such waivers are not enforceable without safeguards. *See, e.g.,* Cal. Fam. Code §1612(c) (specifying that such waivers are not enforceable if the party against whom enforcement is sought was not represented by counsel or if the waiver is unconscionable at the time of enforcement). Still other states require that such waivers must be explicit.

Example: Husband, an attorney, marries Wife, an antique dealer. Before the marriage, Husband drafts, and Wife signs, a premarital agreement in which she waives her spousal property rights. Specifically, Wife agrees to "Waive and Renounce any and all Rights that, and to which, [she] would otherwise be entitled to because of such marriage, whether present or future rights, to any and all property which [plaintiff] has now, or which he may acquire in the future, whether the same be real, personal, [or] mixed property, or of any kind or nature and wherever situated." When Husband initiates divorce proceedings, Wife contests the validity of the premarital agreement. The court rules that the prenuptial agreement effectuated a waiver only of Wife's right to the distribution of property either then owned or later acquired but did not result in a waiver of Husband's support obligations because the waiver was not sufficiently explicit. *Bloomfield v. Bloomfield*, 764 N.E.2d 650 (N.Y. 2001).

G. **Uniform Premarital Agreement Act:** The Uniform Law Commission approved the Uniform Premarital Agreements Act (UPAA) in 1983. Currently, half of the states have adopted UPAA or some version thereof.

UPAA is one of two uniform acts that address premarital agreements. The other is the Uniform Marital Property Act (UMPA), also adopted in 1983, which was drafted with the much broader purpose of encouraging support for a system of shared property during the marriage. UPAA is far more widely followed. (UMPA is adopted only in Wisconsin.)

In 2012, the Uniform Law Commission approved a new act (the Uniform Premarital and Marital Agreements Act or UPMAA) that treats premarital and marital agreements under the same set of principles and requirements. Currently, only two states (Colorado and North Dakota) have adopted the UPMAA.

1. **Policy:** The policy behind UPAA is to recognize considerable contractual freedom so long as the ensuing agreements do not violate public policy.

2. **Reform:** UPAA requires a higher standard than previously in order to find a premarital agreement unenforceable. A party either must have executed the agreement involuntarily *or* the agreement must be "unconscionable." UPAA borrows the term "unconscionability" from commercial settings, thereby requiring more than mere lack of fairness.

   To constitute unconscionability, the agreement must have been unconscionable at the time of execution and, in addition, the party must not have been provided "fair and reasonable disclosure," not waived the right to disclosure, and did not have (or could not have had) adequate knowledge of the other's property.

   Thus, UPAA requires proof of both substantive fairness (termed "unconscionability") and procedural fairness (disclosure and voluntary execution).

H. **ALI *Principles*:** The ALI *Principles* require that premarital agreements must meet standards of substantive fairness as well as procedural fairness. A rebuttable presumption arises that the agreement satisfies the procedural fairness informed consent requirement if (1) the agreement was executed at least 30 days prior to the marriage; (2) both parties had, or were advised to obtain, counsel and had the opportunity to do so; and (3) if one of the parties did not have counsel, the agreement contained understandable information about the parties' rights and the adverse nature of their interests. ALI *Principles* §7.04(e)(a)(b) and (c).

Quiz Yourself on
PREMARITAL AGREEMENTS

6. Jane and Paul enter into a premarital agreement under which each waives any future right to the property of the other. Appended to the agreement is a general list of assets (e.g., "All shares of X Company," "All existing accounts at Bank of Blackacre in Husband's name") without valuations. At the divorce, Jane alleges that the agreement is invalid because it fails to provide full and fair disclosure of Paul's assets. Will her argument prevail? _____

7. Edmund and Charissa execute a premarital agreement that is motivated by a clause in Edmund's divorce agreement from his first wife that restricted his visitation with his son from the prior marriage. Edmund and Charissa's premarital agreement provides that, in the event of divorce, any children shall spend equal residential time with both parents. When Charissa challenges the agreement, will she prevail? _____

8. At the time that Wendy and John are contemplating marriage, bankruptcy proceedings are pending against Wendy and her former husband. Several weeks before the wedding, John asks Wendy to execute a premarital agreement because of his concern that creditors in the bankruptcy proceeding will seek to attach his assets once he and Wendy marry. They execute a premarital agreement specifying that each party retains sole title to any property acquired prior to and during the marriage and that any debts incurred prior to and during the marriage would remain the debt of the party who incurred the debt. Additionally, the parties waive rights to alimony and property. When Wendy later files for divorce from John, she alleges that the premarital agreement is invalid because she was not represented by counsel. Will her argument be successful? _____

9. The day before their wedding, Mark tells his fiancée Fran that they are going to get a marriage license but drives her instead to his lawyer's office where he insists that she sign a premarital agreement as a condition of the marriage. Mark's attorney tells her that she has a right to obtain counsel. She has the opportunity to review the document but looks at it only briefly before she signs. Upon divorce, she claims that the premarital agreement is invalid because of fraud and duress. Will her argument be successful? _____

Answers

6. No. Although courts require full and fair disclosure in premarital agreements, they do not require detailed disclosure. The general list of assets would probably fulfill the disclosure requirement. It is sufficient if the prospective wife knows that the prospective husband is worth considerable money and that she is relinquishing certain rights.

7. Yes. The parties may not enter into an enforceable premarital agreement that concerns child custody, stemming from the state's interest in child welfare.

8. No, probably not. Legal representation is not a prerequisite to the validity of a premarital agreement. Wendy never sought independent legal advice even though she had ample time to do so. She was not coerced into signing the agreement. Furthermore, when she executed the agreement, she had knowledge of the importance of independent legal advice because she had been a party to prior legal proceedings (bankruptcy and a prior divorce). In some states, however, the waiver of her right to alimony might be invalid if the state prohibits waivers of spousal support or requires that such waivers must be made after consultation with independent counsel.

9. No. Mark's pressure tactics, although deplorable, will not serve to negate the knowing and voluntary nature of the execution of the agreement because Fran had the opportunity to review the document and also to retain counsel but she chose to do neither. However, if the jurisdiction follows the ALI *Principles*, the agreement should have been signed at least 30 days before the marriage to raise a rebuttable presumption that the agreement satisfies the informed consent requirement.

III. RESTRICTIONS ON ENTRY INTO MARRIAGE

A. **Constitutional limitations on regulation of the right to marry:** All states have restrictions on who may marry. Beginning in 1967, the Supreme Court invalidated several state restrictions on marriage.

The Supreme Court established that the right to marry is a *fundamental right*. As a result, state restrictions on the right to marry are subject to *strict scrutiny* (the highest level of protection for the individual's freedom to marry).

■ *Three* different tests exist for scrutinizing the constitutionality of state statutes, regulations, practices, or policies: Under the lowest level of scrutiny (the *rational basis test*), the restriction merely must be "reasonably related to a legitimate state objective."

■ The intermediate level of scrutiny requires that the restriction must be "*substantially related to an important governmental objective.*"

■ In contrast, the *strict scrutiny test* mandates that the restriction be "necessary to a compelling state interest" in order to survive constitutional challenge.

Note: The Supreme Court treats the right to marry as part of substantive due process ("liberty") and also as part of the "fundamental rights" branch of equal protection. That is, classifications that infringe upon fundamental rights trigger strict scrutiny in the same manner as do suspect classifications. A violation of equal protection occurs when the state or federal government treats similar groups of persons differently. Under traditional equal protection analysis, classifications based on gender or illegitimacy trigger intermediate scrutiny. Strict scrutiny applies to suspect classifications based on race, alienage, and national origin.

Example: A U.S. citizen and an undocumented alien from Mexico live together in Pennsylvania for two years, during which time they have a son. They request an application for a marriage license from the county registrar. Although the undocumented alien presents his birth certificate, Mexican passport, and documents from an immigration proceeding, he is denied the application, according to local policy, because he lacks either a "green card" or a foreign passport with a visa. The couple file a civil rights suit under 42 U.S.C. §1983, alleging that the registrar violated their rights to equal protection and due process. A federal district court rules that the policy, requiring an alien seeking to marry a U.S. citizen to produce certain forms of identification, violates the parties' fundamental right to marry because, based on strict scrutiny review, the policy significantly interferes with the right to marry by placing a direct legal obstacle in their path. *Buck v. Stankovic*, 485 F. Supp. 2d 576 (M.D. Pa. 2007).

1. **Race:** The U.S. Supreme Court has held that *racial restrictions* on marriage are unconstitutional.

   Example: Mildred Jeter, an African-American woman, marries Richard Loving, a white man, in 1958 in the District of Columbia. The Lovings are forced to leave their home state of Virginia in order to marry because Virginia is one of 16 states that prohibits interracial marriage (by means of an "anti-miscegenation" statute). After their marriage, the Lovings return to Virginia. Subsequently, they are convicted of violating the statutory ban by their out-of-state marriage and given a suspended sentence of 25 years provided that they leave Virginia. They appeal their convictions, arguing that the statutory ban violates the Equal Protection Clause and the Due Process Clause. The U.S. Supreme Court holds that the state statute restricting the right to marry on the basis of racial classifications violates both the Equal Protection Clause and the Due Process Clause. *Loving v. Virginia*, 388 U.S. 1 (1967).

   Note: Rule of lex loci. Under the rule of "lex loci," a marriage valid where performed is valid everywhere. Thus, the Lovings' marriage (performed in the District of Columbia) should have been valid in Virginia. This rule is subject to the exception that a jurisdiction need not recognize the marriage if contrary to public policy. On this basis, Virginia argues that it did not have to recognize the Lovings' marriage. The Supreme Court, in effect, holds that such a racially motivated public policy is unconstitutional.

2. **Poverty:** The Supreme Court also has invalidated a restriction on the right to marry based on *poverty*.

   Example: A Wisconsin statute provides that certain state residents (i.e., noncustodial parents with court-ordered support obligations) may not marry without a court order. To obtain the court's permission, the applicant (Redhail) has to prove that his children are not public charges and are unlikely to be in the future and that he is current in his support obligation. Redhail requests the Milwaukee county clerk to issue him a marriage license. The clerk refuses because Redhail fathered a nonmarital child two years earlier (when he was a high school student) and has outstanding child support payments. His child has been a public charge since its birth. Redhail argues that the statute violates his right to marry and challenges the constitutionality of the statute on both equal protection and due process grounds.

   The Court reaffirms that the right to marry is a fundamental right protected by the Fourteenth Amendment Due Process Clause. The Court states this holding more explicitly than it did in *Loving*. It also holds that the restriction violates Equal Protection. Applying the strict scrutiny test, the Court concedes that the asserted state interests (i.e., counseling the individual regarding support obligations and protecting children's welfare) are sufficiently important. However, the Court finds that the state's chosen means are not closely tailored to achieve those interests because the statute does not compel counseling nor does it guarantee that money would be delivered to the applicant's children. The Court reasons that less drastic means are available to compel compliance with support obligations without infringing on the right to marry. *Zablocki v. Redhail*, 434 U.S. 374 (1978).

   a. **Some reasonable regulations will be upheld:** The *Zablocki* Court reaffirms the fundamental character of the right to marry. However, the Court states that *not all* state restrictions on the right to marry should receive heightened scrutiny.

      "By reaffirming the fundamental character of the right to marry, we do not mean to suggest that every state regulation which relates in any way to the incidents of or prerequisites for marriage must be subjected to rigorous scrutiny. To the contrary, *reasonable regulations that do not significantly interfere with decisions to enter into the marital relationship may legitimately be imposed." Zablocki, 434 U.S. at 386.*

The Court elaborates that only those classifications that *directly* and *substantially* interfere with the right to marry will be reviewed under heightened scrutiny. *Id.*

    b. **Direct and substantial requirements:** The *Zablocki* Court provides a clue to the meaning of "direct" and "substantially" by distinguishing *Zablocki* from *Califano v. Jobst*, 434 U.S. 47 (1977), in which the Court upheld the constitutionality of a Social Security provision that penalized marriage by the loss of benefits. According to *Zablocki*, a legal obstacle constitutes the element of "directness," in contrast to a statutory penalty that results in the individual's loss of public benefits because of the marriage (*Jobst*). Further, the ban in *Zablocki* was total (satisfying the element of "substantiality") because only the state can confer the legal status of marriage, whereas the loss in *Jobst* was merely $20 per month.

  3. **Special context: Prisons:** The Supreme Court has upheld the right to marry in such special contexts as *prisons*. Further, any governmental policy that refuses to permit prisoners to marry must be reasonably related to legitimate penological goals.

Example: A Missouri Division of Corrections regulation permits a prison inmate to marry only with the superintendent's permission and, then, only when compelling reasons exist. Although "compelling" is not defined in the regulation, prison officials interpret it to permit marriages only in cases of pregnancy or the birth of nonmarital children. Inmates who desire permission to marry challenge the rule as a violation of their constitutional right to marry. Prison officials, although conceding that the right to marry is fundamental, argue that the right does not apply in the prison context. They assert that the state's interests in prison security (i.e., prevention of "love triangles") and rehabilitation (i.e., marriage would detract from prisoners' development of necessary skills of self-reliance) support the prohibition. The Supreme Court holds that the constitutional right to marry does apply in this context and also that the prison regulation is unconstitutional because it fails to satisfy even the rational basis test, i.e., it is not reasonably related to the stated goals. *Turner v. Safley*, 482 U.S. 78 (1987).

Turner is significant for its affirmation that the right to marry applies even in those special contexts (e.g., prisons) in which the parties' rights traditionally have been limited.

Note: In *Turner*, the Supreme Court affirms its prior holding in *Butler v. Wilson*, 415 U.S. 953 (1974), that a prohibition on marriage for *life* inmates is constitutional as punishment for crime.

Quiz Yourself on CONSTITUTIONAL LIMITATIONS ON REGULATION OF THE RIGHT TO MARRY

10.   Nancy, a probation officer for the state Department of Corrections, falls in love with Mitch, one of her clients who is serving a sentence for a property offense. They plan to marry. When Nancy's supervisor learns of her romantic relationship, he informs her that she must either give up Mitch or her job, pursuant to a departmental regulation that forbids probation officers from becoming

involved socially with their clients in or out of jail. When Nancy refuses to stop seeing Mitch, she is terminated. She brings an action alleging that the departmental regulation forbidding employees from becoming socially involved with clients violates her due process right to marry. Will her argument be successful? _____

11. Patricia is convicted of harboring her fugitive husband Charlie and being an accessory after the fact. Charlie is wanted for $177,000 in unpaid child support to his former wife Victoria. Knowing that Charlie is wanted for a violation of federal criminal law, Patricia helps Charlie flee to Mexico, provides him funds, and refuses to divulge his whereabouts. She appeals her conviction, alleging that the harboring and accessory statutes impermissibly infringe upon her right to marry. Will Patricia's argument be successful? _____

12. A prison policy refuses to allow a prisoner to go to the probate court to apply for a marriage license to fulfill the state requirement of a personal appearance. The prisoner and his fiancée sue state officials alleging that the prison's policy (i.e., the prison's refusal to facilitate his ability to appear at the probate court, as required by law) violates their fundamental right to marry. Will their argument be successful? _____

Answers

10. No. The departmental regulation did not violate Nancy's due process right because it did not forbid Nancy from marrying in general or from marrying Mitch specifically. It merely made it more costly for her to marry Mitch—the cost being the loss of her job. The regulation burdened her right to marry but did not impermissibly preclude her from marrying.

11. No. The fact that a statute *affects* the marriage relationship does not mean that the statute *infringes* on the right to marry. *Loving* involved normal spousal conduct, whereas the harboring and accessory statutes punish conduct that demonstrates an intent to frustrate law enforcement. Also, there is a significant difference between the importance of the government interests involved. The purpose of the statute in *Loving* was to prevent interracial marriage, whereas the harboring and accessory statutes advance the orderly operation of essential government functions of apprehending criminals.

12. Yes. The prison's policy (refusing to allow the prisoner to go to the probate court to apply for a marriage license) completely frustrates the couple's right to marry and, therefore, violates the parties' due process rights. Prison officials must prove that the policy is reasonably related to legitimate penological objectives (such as safety concerns). The prison would have a difficult time making such a showing because it would be possible to permit the inmate to travel to the probate court (e.g., accompanied by an escort) without endangering the safety of other inmates or that of the community.

B. **Substantive restrictions: Capacity:** All states have substantive restrictions on who may marry. These refer to regulations regarding capacity to marry and state of mind. *Capacity* traditionally required that the parties (1) be of opposite sexes, (2) be married to only one spouse at a time, (3) not be related, and (4) be above the statutorily defined age. State of mind restrictions (discussed *infra*) require that the parties marry (1) voluntarily, (2) without fraud, and (3) without duress.

1. Same sex

  a. Traditional rule: Under the traditional rule, jurisdictions refused to recognize same-sex marriage. Most jurisdictions had explicit heterosexual statutory definitions of marriage as "the union of a man and a woman" that precluded same-sex marriage.

  b. Rationale for traditional rule: States offered various rationales for their prohibitions on same-sex marriage, including:

  ■ marriage is for the propagation of the species;

  ■ marriage protects the health and welfare of children;

  ■ children need two parents of the opposite sex for children's well-being; and

  ■ the state has an interest in fostering and facilitating traditional notions of marriage and the family.

  c. Early challenges based on the federal constitution: Beginning in the 1970s, plaintiffs raised a variety of unsuccessful constitutional challenges to state marriage bans on both federal and state grounds.

   i. Nature of constitutional arguments: Plaintiffs argued that state restrictions violated their federal constitutional rights to marry under the Due Process Clause, Equal Protection Clause, First Amendment right of association, First Amendment right to free exercise of religion, and the Ninth Amendment.

   ii. Obstacle based on constitutional right of privacy: *Bowers v. Hardwick* and *Lawrence v. Texas* (discussed *infra*): A significant obstacle to plaintiffs' success was *Bowers v. Hardwick*, 478 U.S. 186 (1986), upholding the constitutionality of a Georgia statute applied to consensual same-sex sodomy. However, in *Lawrence v. Texas*, 539 U.S. 558 (2003), the U.S. Supreme Court overturned *Bowers*. (*Lawrence* is discussed *infra*.)

  d. Early challenges based on state constitutions: Beginning in the 1990s, gay and lesbian plaintiffs renewed arguments that their right to marry was protected by certain state constitutional guarantees (state equal rights amendments and state constitutional protections of the rights to privacy and equal protection). *Baehr v. Lewin*, 852 P.2d 44 (Haw. 1993), marked the beginning of the change. *Baehr* held that the Hawaii ban established a sex-based classification that was subject to strict scrutiny in an equal protection challenge under the state constitution. However, the Hawaii legislature subsequently refused to recognize same-sex marriage and instead enacted legislation authorizing a form of domestic partnership (called "reciprocal beneficiaries").

  e. State and federal responses to *Baehr*: The question arose (after *Baehr* raised the possibility of state recognition of same-sex marriage) whether one state must recognize a same-sex marriage that is validly contracted in another state (such as Hawaii). Two doctrines would appear to dictate an affirmative answer: the Full Faith and Credit Clause of the Constitution, Art. IV, §1 (i.e., the requirement that a state shall give full faith and credit to "the public acts, records and judicial proceedings" of other states) and the rule of "lex loci" (i.e., a marriage valid where performed is valid everywhere).

  After *Baehr*, Congress acted swiftly to stymie efforts to legalize same-sex marriage by enacting the federal Defense of Marriage Act (DOMA). Section 2 of DOMA (discussed *infra*) permitted states to exercise discretion not to recognize same-sex marriages. In addition, the public policy exception to the rule of lex loci (i.e., a marriage contracted in one state is valid in any other state unless recognition of that marriage would be contrary to public policy) precluded same-sex marriage in some states.

f. Federal response: The Defense of Marriage Act: Congress responded to the possibility that states might recognize same-sex marriage by enacting the Defense of Marriage Act, 28 U.S.C. §1738(c), in 1996. The Act contained two provisions:

- it created a federal heterosexual definition of the term "marriage" as a union between a man and a woman and the term "spouse" (for purposes of federal law regarding federal benefits, such as immigration, Social Security survivors benefits, tax benefits, etc.) (Section 3), and

- it left recognition of same-sex marriage to state discretion under the Full Faith and Credit Clause (Section 2).

Gay rights advocates soon mounted challenges to the federal DOMA.

g. *Lawrence v. Texas*: The U.S. Supreme Court decision in *Lawrence v. Texas,* 539 U.S. 558 (2003), paved the way for recognition of same-sex marriage. In *Lawrence*, John Lawrence and Tyron Garner are convicted of engaging in same- sex sexual conduct in violation of a Texas sodomy statute (criminalizing "deviate sexual intercourse" with an individual of the same sex). They appeal, raising state and federal due process claims. The U.S. Supreme Court, overruling its decision in *Bowers v. Hardwick*, holds that the state sodomy statute violates defendants' substantive due process rights. The Court chooses a broad due process rationale, protecting the *liberty to engage in intimate personal relationships*, rather than more narrow equal protection grounds. The Court reasons that moral disapproval cannot justify criminal sanctions for private consensual sexual conduct. "Our obligation is to define the liberty of all, not to mandate our own moral code." *Lawrence*, at 571.

In his dissent, Justice Scalia predicts that *Lawrence* calls into question state laws against "bigamy, same-sex marriage, adult incest, prostitution, masturbation, adultery, fornication, bestiality, and obscenity." *Id.* at 590 (Scalia, J., dissenting). Subsequent developments confirm that prediction regarding same-sex marriage laws. (The influence of *Lawrence* on other state laws is discussed *infra*.)

h. *Goodridge v. Department of Public Health*: Massachusetts was the first state to permit same-sex marriage based on the state constitution. *Goodridge v. Department of Public Health*, 798 N.E.2d 941 (Mass. 2003).

i. Domestic partnership legislation: Before legalization of same-sex marriage, some states enacted a *range* of *limited* legal protections for unmarried same-sex couples in the form of domestic partnership laws or civil union laws. A few states continue to allow these marriage alternatives. After the Supreme Court recognized marriage equality, some states automatically converted civil unions into marriage.

j. Challenges to federal DOMA — *Windsor and Obergefell*: Same-sex spouses successfully challenged DOMA in *United States v. Windsor*, 570 U.S. 744 (2013), and *Obergefell v. Hodges*, 576 U.S. 644 (2015).

***United States v. Windsor*, 570 U.S. 744 (2013):**

Example: After 40 years together, New York residents, Edith "Edie" Windsor and Thea Spyer, marry in Canada. At that time, New York recognized same-sex marriages performed in other jurisdictions. However, because *federal* law did not recognize their marriage due to DOMA (recall that Section 3's definition of "marriage" and "spouse" precluded federal benefits), Windsor paid $363,000 in federal estate taxes upon Spyer's death. If federal law had recognized their marriage, Windsor would have paid no estate tax. As the representative of Spyer's estate, Windsor seeks a refund of the federal estate taxes and a declaration that DOMA's Section 3 violates the Fifth Amendment's Equal Protection Clause.

The Supreme Court concludes that DOMA's definition of marriage is unconstitutional as a deprivation of due process and equal protection protected by the Fifth Amendment. ("DOMA seeks to injure the very class New York seeks to protect. By doing so it violates basic due process and equal protection principles applicable to the Federal Government.") In a majority opinion authored by Justice Kennedy, the Court notes that the regulation of domestic relations is subject to the exclusive regulation of the states. However, the federal DOMA rejects that view. According to the Court, DOMA's application to federal law has the purpose and effect of depriving same-sex spouses of the benefits that stem from the federal recognition of their state-sanctioned marriages.

In addition, DOMA demeans same-sex couples and treat them unfairly. Whereas the state's decision to give same-sex partners the right to marry confers upon them dignity and status, DOMA permits the federal government to respond to this class differently and to impose federal disabilities. DOMA thus creates two different marriage regimes within the same state. The resulting injury and indignity constitute not only a deprivation of liberty but also a violation of equal protection protected by the Fifth Amendment.

Obergefell v. Hodges, 576 U.S. 644 (2015):

Example: Jim Obergefell and John Arthur, natives of Ohio, resolve to marry before Arthur succumbs to amyotrophic lateral sclerosis (ALS). Because Ohio did not permit same-sex marriage at that time, they decide to marry in Maryland, a state that permitted same-sex marriage. Arthur dies three months after their marriage. Obergefell sues to have Ohio law recognize him as a "surviving spouse" on his partner's death certificate. Plaintiffs (Obergefell sued on behalf of other same-sex couples) raise two questions: (1) do same-sex couples have a constitutional right to marry under the Fourteenth Amendment, and (2) must individual states recognize same-sex marriages that are licensed in other states? Justice Kennedy delivers the majority opinion answering the above questions in the affirmative. He bases the holdings on both the Due Process Clause and Equal Protection Clause, finding marriage to be a fundamental right inherent in the liberty protected by the Due Process Clause which the Equal Protection Clause guarantees for same-sex couples. The Due Process Clause protects the liberty to make "choices central to individual dignity and autonomy, including intimate choices that define personal identity and beliefs." Four principles and traditions support the conclusion that the right to marry applies to same-sex couples: (1) individual autonomy and dignity; (2) the importance of a two-person union to the individuals involved, with its benefits of companionship and understanding; (3) the safeguards that marriage provides to children and families; and (4) the centrality of marriage as a "keystone of our social order." Recognizing the material and dignitary harms imposed by state bans, Kennedy explains that the exclusion from the institution of marriage imposes "stigma and injury of the kind prohibited by our basic charter," because this exclusion serves not only to deny the "constellation of benefits" linked to marriage but also treats gays and lesbians as unequal and demeans them. Justice Kennedy rejects the originalist view that the Due Process Clause safeguards only rights that were protected at the time of ratification of the Constitution. Gays and lesbians seek only to have the fundamental right of marriage extended to them, not to claim a new right to "same-sex marriage"—just as *Loving* did not claim a new "right to interracial marriage." Justice Kennedy repeatedly extols the virtues of marriage, explaining that same-sex partners who seek to marry are manifesting their respect, rather than disrespect, for the institution of marriage. Finally, the majority declines to take a cautious approach by waiting for legislative change in light of the "urgent" concerns of the petitioners. The dissenters (Chief Justice Roberts, joined by Justices Scalia and Thomas) protest that the ruling violates separation of powers because the issue should be decided by the legislature through the democratic process. Precedents cited by the majority (such as *Lawrence*) pertain to privacy rights, which are "not at issue" here. Marriage laws banning same-sex marriage do not violate equal protection because distinctions between same-sex and opposite-sex marriage are rationally related to the state's legitimate interest in preserving the traditional institution of marriage. The right of opponents of same-sex marriage to exercise their religion may be adversely impacted by the ruling. Finally, the dissent makes the argument that legalization of same-sex marriage will lead to plural marriage.

Note: Commentators criticize that the majority opinion neglects to address the appropriate level of scrutiny under the Equal Protection Clause for discrimination based on sexual orientation. Further, they fear that Justice Kennedy's glorification of marriage may have harmful implications for nonmarital families and, similarly, that his language about the importance of marriage for children's well-being may have harmful implications for children raised by unmarried parents. Finally, critics contend that the majority opinion leaves open the issue of the accommodation of claims of religious liberty by those who oppose providing services to same-sex couples.

k. **Accommodation of religious liberty:** Recent cases in the context of same-sex marriage raise issues of the conflict between claims of accommodation of religious liberty and anti-discrimination principles.

Example: Based on his religious beliefs, baker Jack Phillips declines the request of Charlie Craig and David Mullins to create a cake for their wedding reception. Phillips contends that decorating cakes is an art form through which he can honor God and that it would displease God for him to create cakes for same-sex marriages. Craig and Mullins file an action claiming discrimination based on sexual orientation under the Colorado Anti-Discrimination Act (CADA) which bans discrimination based on (*inter alia*) sexual orientation in public places of business.

Phillips raises two First Amendment defenses: (1) the act of requiring him to create a cake for a same-sex wedding, pursuant to CADA, would violate his First Amendment right to free speech by compelling him to exercise his artistic talents to express a message with which he disagrees, and (2) requiring him to create cakes for same-sex weddings would violate his right to the free exercise of religion.

In a 7-2 opinion, the Supreme Court decides the case based on the ground of free exercise. The Court's point of departure is that the state (through the Colorado Civil Rights Commission) must apply the Colorado anti-discrimination law in a neutral manner regarding religion. The Court holds that the Commission violated the baker's free exercise rights by failing to consider his claim of religious liberty in a neutral and respectful fashion.

According to the Court, the Commission's consideration of the baker's arguments was tainted by hostility toward religion in two ways. First, several commissioners' comments that disparaged Phillips' beliefs cast doubt on the fairness of the agency's consideration of his claims. Second, Phillips' claims were treated differently compared to the claims of other bakers in previous cases. The Commission allowed these other bakers to refuse to serve customers whose anti-gay views the bakers deemed offensive, while sanctioning

Phillips whose religious beliefs were disparaged by Commission members.Dissenting Justice Ginsburg, joined by Justice Sotomayor, disagrees that the commissioners' comments and disparate treatment of other bakers justify the ruling in favor of the baker. Justice Kagan contends that Phillips denied services to the gay couple precisely because of their sexual orientation. Justice Gorsuch, in a concurring opinion (joined by Justice Alito), emphasized that the government must favor claims of religious freedom when claims of conscience conflict with public accommodations law. *Masterpiece Cakeshop v. Colorado Civil Rights Comm'n*, 138 S. Ct. 1719 (2018).

Note: Commentators criticize that *Masterpiece Cakeshop* fails to resolve fully the issues raised by the conflict between claims of free exercise and the equality principles of anti-discrimination law. Further, the Supreme Court did not decide the central substantive issues of whether forcing businesses to provide services for gays and lesbians, or other marginalized groups, violates the owners' rights to free exercise of religion or free speech. Instead, the Court invalidated Colorado's ruling on the narrow ground that the state Civil Rights Commission had exhibited hostility toward the baker's religious views. These issues are likely to re-emerge at the Supreme Court. The appointment of Justice Amy Coney Barrett in 2020 signifies that the Court will likely give greater deference to claims of religious liberty.

l. **Popular opinion: Public opinion about same-sex marriage has changed dramatically.** A decade before *Obergefell*, 60 percent of Americans opposed marriage equality. More recently, that same percentage of Americans support same-sex marriage. Pew Research Ctr., Attitudes on Same-Sex Marriage, https://www.pewforum.org/fact-sheet/changing-attitudes-on-gay-marriage/

m. **International developments:** Currently, almost 30 countries allow same-sex couples to marry. (The Netherlands was the first country to allow same-sex marriage in 2001, and Costa Rica is the most recent country to allow same-sex marriage in 2020.)

n. **Transgender people's right to marry:** Traditionally, cases questioned the validity of the marriage of a transgender person (i.e., a person who experiences a discrepancy between physical anatomy and psychological identity). Some courts determined the validity of such marriages by reference to *anatomy,* whereas other courts held that sexual identity is determined by *birth and chromosomes.*

Example: After his father dies intestate, a son petitions for letters of administration, naming himself as sole heir, and claiming that the marriage between his father and a postoperative male-to-female transgender person was void. The Kansas Supreme Court holds that a postoperative male-to-female transgender person is not a "woman" within the meaning of the statutes recognizing marriage, and that the marriage was void as against public policy (thereby following the chromosome approach). *In re Estate of Gardiner*, 42 P.3d 120 (Kan. 2002).

Obergefell offered hope to the transgender community by its extension of protection under the Fourteenth Amendment to "intimate choices that define personal identity and beliefs." Although gay rights advocates hoped *Obergefell* would have positive implications for transgender people's rights generally, the Trump Administration subsequently rolled back protections from discrimination against transgender people in education, employment, health care, immigration law, and the military.

In a recent landmark decision, the Supreme Court ruled that Title VII's prohibition against employment discrimination "based on sex" applies to sexual orientation and gender identity (*Bostock v. Clayton County, Ga.*, 140 S. Ct. 1731 (U.S. 2020)).

Quiz Yourself on
SUBSTANTIVE RESTRICTIONS: SAME-SEX MARRIAGE

13. Jane and Jill, who have been in a committed relationship for eight years in Whiteacre, decide to get married. After their marriage, Jane submits a request to her employer requesting spousal health benefits for her new "spouse." Is Jane's employer required to grant such benefits?_____

14. A woman "Jo" is married to Tom in the jurisdiction of Blackacre. Jo is a transgender person who has not yet undergone male-to-female sex reassignment surgery. Jo is arrested for a traffic violation. During a routine motor vehicle check, the police determine that "Jo" is really biologically male (a man named "Joe"). The police request that the state invalidate "Jo" and Tom's marriage. "Jo" and Tom argue that their marriage is valid. Will the couple's argument be successful? _____

15. John and Jerry are married in the jurisdiction of Whiteacre. John is a resident of Whiteacre; Jerry is a national of Ireland. After their marriage, Jerry asserts that, as John's "spouse," Jerry is entitled to preferential status for immigration purposes. Will Jerry's argument be successful? _

Answers

13. Yes. The Supreme Court's decision in *Obergefell* signified that same-sex couples are entitled to the same "constellation of benefits" that married couples enjoy. Therefore, Jane's employer must grant spousal health benefits to Jane's new spouse.

14. Yes. Traditionally, the couple's marriage would have been invalid under either theory that was applied to validate marriages of transgender persons because "Jo" is male by virtue of both chromosomes and current anatomy. However, after *Obergefell,* a person's gender is no longer a bar to marriage.

15. Yes. The Supreme Court's decision in *Obergefell* signified that same-sex couples are entitled to the same "constellation of benefits" that married couples enjoy. Therefore, foreign nationals who are same-sex spouses may be granted permanent legal residency in the United States on the same basis as opposite-sex spouses.

---

2. **Substantive Restrictions: Bigamy:** All states refuse to permit marriages that are bigamous (i.e., having two spouses at the same time) or polygamous (i.e., having *more* than two spouses at the same time).

   a. **Civil restrictions and criminal sanctions:** Civil restrictions specify that a person may not marry more than one spouse at a time. States also make bigamy and polygamy criminal offenses.

   Example: Nathan and Vicki Collier marry in South Carolina in 2000. Nathan later becomes involved in a committed relationship with Christine, who he also wants to marry. Both women consent to be married to Nathan simultaneously. When Nathan and Christine apply for a marriage license in Montana, the county clerk denies their application, explaining that granting the license would violate Montana's criminal prohibition on entrance into multiple marriages. Nathan, Vicki, and Christine bring suit in federal district court challenging the state's criminal as well as civil marriage laws.

The federal district court finds that plaintiffs lack standing in their criminal challenge because they have never been threatened with prosecution. The state's position is that the Colliers have not violated bigamy laws simply by living together. However, the court finds that they have standing in their civil challenge based on the denial of Nathan and Christine's application for a marriage license. Nonetheless, the court rules that the plaintiffs' claim is barred by *Reynolds v. United States* (upholding the constitutionality of a state polygamy ban). "Although *Reynolds* is almost 140 years old, it is not antiquated and is still valid, binding authority." The Colliers attempt to draw support for their claim from Chief Justice Roberts' dissent in *Obergefell*, in which he said that the majority's reasoning would support the claim of a fundamental right to plural marriage. In response, the federal district court concludes that Roberts' dissent is not binding precedent and did not overrule *Reynolds*. *Collier v. Fox*, 2018 WL 1247411 (D. Mont. 2018).

b. Background: Plural marriage is still practiced by some fundamentalist Mormon sects in accordance with the dictates of the Church of Jesus Christ of Latter-Day Saints' founder, Joseph Smith. In a famous incident, Arizona law enforcement officials raided the polygamous community of Short Creek in 1953. The raid resulted in criminal convictions of husbands, and the removal of children from their homes and their placement in foster care. This costly venture failed to eradicate polygamy. A similar raid by law enforcement and Child Protective Services in 2008 at the Yearning for Zion Ranch, in Eldorado, Texas, also resulted in the removal of many children from their homes. The Texas Supreme Court subsequently concluded that the culture of polygamy did not warrant the grant of emergency custody of all the children to the state social welfare department. *In re Texas Dept. of Family and Protective Services*, 255 S.W.3d 613 (Tex. 2008).

c. Criminal requirements: Modern courts require intent, i.e., that the defendant enter a second marriage with the knowledge that the first marriage is still valid. Some jurisdictions, however, punish a defendant despite the latter's bona fide (but erroneous) belief that the first marriage has ended.

d. Effect on validity of successive marriage: If a party to a marriage is still validly married to a prior living spouse, then the subsequent marriage is void. This rule is not applied in all cases; for example, it is subject to a presumption (discussed *infra*) in limited circumstances.

e. Defenses: Parties have asserted two defenses to criminal liability for bigamy/polygamy, one defense based on constitutional grounds and the other defense based on state grounds.

    i. Freedom of religion: Sometimes, a defendant claims that plural marriage is required by the defendant's religious beliefs and that the defendant's choice is thereby protected by the First Amendment. Courts have held that religious beliefs are not a valid defense to the crime of bigamy.

    Example: George Reynolds appeals from his conviction for bigamy. He argues that his fundamentalist Mormon church requires its members to practice polygamy. Rejecting his argument, the U.S. Supreme Court holds that the defendant's practice of plural marriage is a *religious practice* rather than a religious belief. Although the First Amendment dictates that government cannot interfere with religious beliefs, religious practices do not merit the same constitutional protection. *Reynolds v. United States*, 98 U.S. 145 (1878).

ii. **Enoch Arden statutes:** Some statutes, following English law, provide defenses to bigamy for spouses who remarry in good faith based on the defendant's belief that the previous spouse is deceased. These so-called "Enoch Arden" statutes, although not validating the subsequent marriage, permit a spouse to remarry without criminal liability after a specified time. The statutes are named after a protagonist in a Tennyson poem who was shipwrecked and returned after a long absence to find that his wife, who believed him dead, had remarried.

f. **Conflict of laws:** Bigamous marriages may present conflict-of-laws issues. Recognition of a bigamous marriage (for example, a bigamous marriage that is permitted in another country) by an American jurisdiction may depend on the purpose of the litigation. That is, a jurisdiction may recognize the marriage only for the purposes of legitimacy of children or inheritance.

Example: A native of India dies intestate (without a will) in California. When his estate is probated, two women residents of India each allege that she is entitled to share his estate as his widow according to Indian law that permits plural marriage. The court holds that the wives should share equally because public policy is not violated when neither wife contests the other's claim. Further, the two women are the only interested parties, and the purpose is inheritance. *In re Dalip Singh Bir's Estate*, 188 P.2d 499 (Cal. Ct. App. 1948).

g. **Presumptions and the burden of proof:** Problems of proof have given rise to a presumption that sometimes operates in doubtful cases. Under this presumption, the most recent marriage is valid. The party asserting the invalidity of the second marriage has the burden of rebutting the presumption by conclusive evidence.

This presumption prevails over a different presumption that a valid marriage exists until proof of its end by death or divorce. Courts are likely to apply the presumption of validity to the most recent marriage if the latest marriage is longstanding, has produced children, and the challenge involves a claim against an employer or governmental entity for benefits purposes.

Example: Hattie and Gertrude Gordon both claim to be the widow of Samuel Gordon. Both seek widows' benefits under the Railroad Retirement Act. Each has proof of marriage. Hattie's marriage to Samuel preceded Gertrude's. Gertrude and Samuel are living together at Samuel's death. During the latter 13-year marriage, they had one child. The court holds that the second wife, Gertrude, prevails based on the presumption of validity of the most recent marriage. *Gordon v. Railroad Retirement Bd.*, 696 F.2d 131 (D.C. Cir. 1983).

Example: Jerry Lee Sumners divorces Patricia O'Neil. Their Nebraska decree orders the parties to refrain from remarrying for six months. Three months later in Iowa, Jerry marries Sharon who is then pregnant with his child. When Sharon subsequently petitions for dissolution, Jerry challenges the court's jurisdiction. He argues that his marriage to Sharon, occurring before the termination of his prior marriage to Patricia, was bigamous and void. Based on the presumption of validity of the most recent marriage (a presumption that the court determines Jerry failed to rebut), the court holds that Jerry's marriage to Sharon is valid and should have been dissolved by the lower court. *In re Marriage of Sumners*, 645 S.W.2d 205 (Mo. Ct. App. 1983).

h. **Child bigamy laws:** Among the state interests underlying polygamy prohibitions is the interest in preventing the child sexual exploitation that is often associated with polygamous practices. To address this problem, the Utah legislature increased the penalty for bigamy involving teenage brides and imposed sanctions on parents for their involvement in such marriages. *See* Utah Code Ann. §76-7-101.5 (providing that marriage or cohabitation with a *minor*, while the actor is validly married to another, constitutes a second-degree felony punishable by up to 15 years); Utah Code Ann. §30-1-9.1 (providing that a parent who knowingly allows a minor to enter a marriage that is prohibited is guilty of a third-degree felony). The Utah legislature considered, but rejected, a provision that would have prosecuted church leaders who arrange marriages by inducing minors to enter a polygamous relationship.

i. **Modern developments: Challenges to state and federal bigamy laws:** In *Lawrence v. Texas*, Justice Scalia suggested, in his dissent, that *Lawrence* would call into question state laws against same-sex marriage and bigamy (as well as "adult incest, prostitution, masturbation, adultery, fornication, bestiality, and obscenity") (539 U.S. at 590). Post-*Lawrence*, plaintiffs raised challenges to state and federal bigamy laws on this basis.

    Example: Rodney Holm, a fundamentalist Mormon police officer, is legally married to Suzie Stubbs. Subsequently, he participates in a religious marriage ceremony with two other women, one of whom is 16-year-old Ruth Stubbs (who is Suzie's sister). Holm is convicted of bigamy and sexual contact with a minor. He challenges the constitutionality of the bigamy statute and alleges that his conduct is protected as a fundamental liberty interest based on *Lawrence v. Texas*. The Utah Supreme Court upholds the bigamy ban, concluding it does not violate defendant's right to freedom of association, it is not unconstitutionally vague as applied, and also that the prohibition against sexual contact with a minor does not violate equal protection by distinguishing between married and unmarried persons. The court distinguishes *Lawrence* by explaining that (1) the present case implicates the institution of marriage (rather than mere private consensual conduct) because the state has an interest in preventing the formation of marital forms it deems harmful, and (2) the present case involves a minor, and sexual conduct involving minors is outside the scope of *Lawrence*. *State v. Holm*, 137 P.3d 726 (Utah 2006), *cert. denied*, 549 U.S. 1252 (2007).

    But cf. Brown v. Buhman, 947 F. Supp. 2d 1170 (D. Utah 2013), *cert. denied*, 137 S. Ct. 828 (2017), in which a federal court invalidated a provision of Utah's bigamy statute (based on *Lawrence v. Texas*) that criminalized *cohabitation* in a marriage-like relationship when the person was already married to another. This decision was vacated when the county attorney announced that it would not prosecute, rendering the case moot.

    Note: In *Obergefell v. Hodges*, Justice Roberts suggested, in his dissent, that the majority's reasoning, in support of the fundamental right to same-sex marriage, would apply with equal force to the claim of a fundamental right to plural marriage. In the wake of *Obergefell*, plaintiffs have raised this argument.

    Example: In *Collier v. Fox*, discussed *supra*, plaintiffs challenged Montana's civil marriage laws prohibiting plural marriage based, in part, on Justice Robert's dissent in *Obergefell*. However, the Utah Supreme Court rejected plaintiffs' argument, reasoning that Justice Robert's dissent is not binding precedent and cannot overrule binding precedent.

j. Modern liberalization: In response to the Browns' lawsuit (above), the Utah legislature enacted legislation clarifying the requirement that a party must "cohabit" with the additional spouse(s) "and" (rather than "or") purport to marry the other spouse(s). Utah Code Ann. § 76-7-101. The legislature subsequently eliminated the cohabitation requirement and, instead, imposed criminal liability for bigamy if: (a) the individual purports to marry another individual; and (b) knows or reasonably should know that one or both of the individuals described (above) is/are legally married to another individual. Also, in response to the Browns' lawsuit, the Utah legislature increased the penalty from five to fifteen years if bigamy is accompanied by the crimes of domestic abuse, child abuse, sexual abuse, human trafficking or human smuggling, inducing marriage or bigamy under false pretenses, or fraud. *Id.*

In May 2020, the Utah legislature enacted a law that *decreases* liability for bigamy/ polygamy from a third-degree felony (with a penalty of up to five years in prison) to an infraction (subject to a $750 fine or community service). In contrast, cases of polygamous arrangements stemming from threat or coercion, or those that occur under fraudulent pretenses, remain a third-degree felony pursuant to Utah Code Ann. §76-7-101.

3. Substantive Restrictions: Incest: All states regulate the degrees of kinship within which persons may marry. Marriages between persons who are related within prohibited degrees of kinship are void.

a. Civil restrictions: States have *civil* restrictions requiring that prospective spouses may not be granted marriage licenses if the parties are related to each other within certain prohibited degrees of kinship.

i. Consanguinity: All states restrict marriages by *consanguinity* (i.e., blood relationships, such as those between parent and child, brother and sister, uncle and niece, aunt and nephew). Some states also prohibit first-cousin marriages.

Example: A man marries his niece in Italy. Because the parties obtain a dispensation, the marriage is legal there. The newlyweds return to Connecticut, where they reside until the husband's death. The widow petitions the probate court for a widow's allowance pursuant to state law, claiming that she is his lawful spouse. The court holds that although the marriage was valid in Italy, a marriage between an uncle and niece contravenes public policy in Connecticut. Therefore, the woman is not the decedent's legal spouse and is not entitled to a widow's allowance. *Catalano v. Catalano*, 170 A.2d 726 (Conn. 1961).

Occasionally, a question of statutory interpretation arises, for example, as to whether consanguinity restrictions prohibit marriage among half-blood relatives.

Example: An uncle and niece by the half blood (the wife's mother is the husband's half-sister) marry in Connecticut. Based on the advice of counsel that their marriage is incestuous and void, the parties seek an annulment in Connecticut. Four years later, they remarry in California where such marriages are not proscribed. Thereafter, in Connecticut, they seek to set aside the annulment. The court holds that the marriage is void. Based on strict statutory interpretation (the common meaning of "uncle" and "niece"), the court holds that marital restrictions based on consanguinity extend to relationships of the half blood as well as whole blood. *Singh v. Singh*, 569 A.2d 1112 (Conn. 1990).

    ii. Affinity: Some states also restrict marriages between parties related by *affinity* (i.e., relationships established by law, such as marriage with in-laws, step relatives, or relatives by adoption).

        Example: Martin and Tammy Israel, who are brother and sister by adoption, desire to marry. (Martin's father married Tammy's mother when Martin was 18 and Tammy was 13.) The parties are denied a license because of Colorado's express statutory prohibition on marriages between brother and sister whether "by the half or the whole blood or by adoption." The parties argue that the statute is unconstitutional as a violation of equal protection. The court holds that the provision is unconstitutional, having no rational basis (i.e., it fails to further any state interest in family harmony). *Israel v. Allen*, 577 P.2d 762 (Colo. 1978). (But cf. UMDA §207 prohibiting marriage between a brother and sister of the whole blood or who are related by adoption.)

        Example: Mr. and Mrs. X adopt a daughter who is referred to as M. The adoptive parents divorce when M is 22 years old, although the parents separated several years prior to that time. Shortly after the divorce, M gives birth to a son whose father is M's adoptive father. M and her adoptive father now desire to marry. M seeks to vacate her adoption by her adoptive father (Mr. X) so that she can marry him. Under New Jersey law, an adoption may be vacated upon a showing of "truly exceptional circumstances" when it is in the best interest of the child and adoptive parents. The court determines that these facts constitute truly exceptional circumstances in order to eradicate the legal impediment to M's marriage to her adoptive father and to legitimize the infant. *In re Adoption of M*, 722 A.2d 615 (N.J. Super. Ct. Ch. Div. 1998).

  b. Criminal sanctions: In addition to civil restrictions, states also have *criminal* provisions punishing incest.

    i. Definition: Incest is defined, for purposes of the criminal law, as marriage *or* sexual intercourse between persons who are related within the prohibited degrees of kinship.

    ii. Rationale: Common rationale for legal regulation of incest (both criminal and civil aspects) include the following:

      ■ genetic (inbreeding results in transmission of harmful genetic traits);

      ■ religious (based on biblical proscriptions);

      ■ sociobiological (the need to encourage the formation of new families);

      ■ sexual (the necessity to eliminate intrafamilial sexual competition); and

      ■ psychological (prevention of exploitation of vulnerable family members).

        Some of these rationales have been called into question in terms of some prohibited relationships. For example, the genetic concern is absent in step and adoptive relationships.

  c. Modern development: Post-*Lawrence* challenges and state incest laws: Some courts have explored whether state incest prohibitions violate the constitutional right to privacy in the wake of *Lawrence v. Texas*.

    Example: Allen Muth marries his younger sister Patricia. The couple has three children. After the couple abandons their disabled child, Wisconsin officials terminate their parental rights based on their incestuous parenthood and then charge them with criminal liability for incest. In the husband's petition for a writ of habeas corpus, he argues that the state incest statute is unconstitutional because it criminalizes a sexual relationship between consenting adults in violation of *Lawrence v. Texas*. The U.S. Court of Appeals refuses to read *Lawrence* so broadly as to create a fundamental right to engage in all forms of private sexual intimacy, reasoning that *Lawrence* had a limited focus on same-sex sodomy and also that *Lawrence* failed to apply strict scrutiny review. *Muth v. Frank*, 412 F.3d 808 (7th Cir. 2005), *cert. denied*, 546 U.S. 988 (2005).

4. Substantive Restrictions: Age

a. Generally: All states have a minimum age for marriage, generally age 18. However, most states provide for exceptions for some youth (e.g., younger teens and/or pregnant teens) to marry with parental and/or judicial consent. *See, e.g.,* N.C. Gen. Stat. Ann. §51-2.1 (pregnant minor may marry at age 14 with judicial consent). In states with parental consent requirements, the permission of one parent is generally sufficient.

b. Historical rule: At common law, a valid marriage could be contracted by a boy at age 14 and a girl at age 12. Today, statutory age provisions are gender neutral.

c. Rationale: The rationale for marital age restrictions is that maturity is necessary to promote marriage stability.

d. Effect of noncompliance: At common law, nonage was a civil disability that rendered *void* any marriage involving a minor under age seven. Marriages involving older, but still under-age, parties were *voidable* at the request of the under-age minor until the youth reached the age of capacity.

Today, defects of age or lack of consent render a marriage *voidable* upon the initiative of the under-age party. If the party fails to disaffirm, the marriage is validated when that party reaches the age of consent.

Some states permit annulment actions to be brought by the parent of the minor. Absent statutory authority, however, a parent cannot initiate annulment proceedings on the grounds of age or lack of consent.

e. Constitutionality of parental consent requirements: Courts have upheld the constitutionality of parental consent requirements against attacks based on the children's right to due process.

Example: Raoul Roe, 18 years old, desires to marry 15-year-old Maria Moe, who is the mother of his child. According to New York law, males between 16 and 18 years old and females between 14 and 18 must obtain parental consent. Maria's mother, a widow, refuses consent, allegedly because she desires to continue to receive Maria's welfare benefits. Moe and Roe institute a class action on behalf of minors who wish to marry but cannot because they lack parental consent. They charge that the provision violates their liberty under the Due Process Clause, denies them an individualized showing of maturity, and denies them the only means to legitimize their child. The court upholds the constitutionality of the parental consent requirement. According to the court, although prior cases recognized the constitutional right of privacy, the state's interest in child protection dictates use of a rational basis standard. The court finds that the statute is rationally related to the state's interests in protecting minors from immature decision making and unstable marriages as well as supporting the parent's right to act in the child's best interests. Moreover, the court reasons that the statute does not effectuate a total deprivation of plaintiffs' rights, but only a delay. *Moe v. Dinkins*, 533 F. Supp. 623 (S.D.N.Y. 1981), *aff'd*, 669 F.2d 67 (2d Cir. 1982), *cert. denied*, 459 U.S. 827 (1982).

Note: Plaintiffs did not challenge the differential age requirements for men and women. Such differences, however, appear to violate equal protection. *See, e.g., Stanton v. Stanton*, 421 U.S. 7 (1975) (holding unconstitutional a statute establishing different gender-based age requirements for parental support purposes).

Courts also have upheld state age-based marriage laws based on the challenge that the statutes violate a *parent's* due process to raise a child as the parent sees fit.

Example: A father and mother have joint custody of their daughter following their divorce. The mother and daughter relocate to New Mexico, where the 15-year-old daughter expresses her wish to marry her 48-year-old piano teacher. Because New Mexico law does not permit under-age marriages, the couple goes to Las Vegas where they obtain judicial authorization (with the mother's consent). The father, who was not notified of the judicial proceeding, petitions to vacate the order authorizing the marriage and to annul the marriage. The Nevada Supreme Court holds that a statute allowing judicial authorization of a marriage of an under-age person does not violate the substantive or procedural due process rights of a nonconsenting parent and that the father lacked standing to annul the marriage. The court reasons that a parent's constitutional right to raise his child as he sees fit is not absolute and must be weighed against the child's fundamental right to marry. *Kirkpatrick v. Eighth Judicial District Court*, 64 P.3d 1056 (Nev. 2003).

f. **Law reform: State laws:** The past few years have witnessed a trend towards increasing restrictions on teen marriages. The trend began in 2005 in response to a Nebraska case involving the marriage of a 15-year-old girl to a felon (below). Since 2016, more than a dozen states enacted reforms. Some states raised their minimum age to marry. A few states restricted marriage to persons age 18 or older.

Example: A 15-year-old girl enters a common-law marriage with a felon. The Department of Human Services files a petition challenging the validity of the marriage of the girl who is subject to a dependency and neglect proceeding. (The marriage had been entered into without parental consent.) The court of appeals holds that, because the common-law age of consent applies to common-law marriages, the 15-year-old female was competent to consent to the marriage. *In re Marriage of J.M.H. and Rouse*, 143 P.3d 1116 (Colo. Ct. App. 2006).

Note: The outcry following this case led the Colorado legislature to raise the minimum age for common-law marriage to 18, or 16 with parental and judicial approval.

g. **Federal and international reforms:** Many countries allow child marriages. The reasons are economic and the desire to control female sexuality. To address this issue, the Violence Against Women Reauthorization Act (VAWA) of 2013 requires the Secretary of State to develop and implement a strategy to prevent child marriage. This strategy focuses on empowering girls. It reflects an awareness of "the unique needs, vulnerabilities, and potential of girls younger than 18 years of age in developing countries." 122 U.S.C.A §7104(j). In 2018, 116 countries sponsored a United Nations resolution to end child marriage and forced marriage.

h. **Empirical data:** Empirical data reveals that teen brides tend to come from backgrounds characterized by poverty and they tend to remain in poverty. Further, the overwhelming majority of teen marriages end in divorce. See Tahirih Justice Center, Child Marriage in the United States (Dec. 12, 2018), https://www.tahirih.org/wp-content/uploads/2016/11/FINAL-12.12.18-Tahirih-Child-Marriage-Backgrounder_publisher-version-3.pdf

Quiz Yourself on
SUBSTANTIVE RESTRICTIONS: INCEST, BIGAMY, AGE

16. Sandra marries Tom. Tom had been previously married to Nancy. Unbeknownst to Sandra, Tom's divorce was not final when they married. Therefore, Sandra's marriage to Tom is not valid. Can Sandra be prosecuted for bigamy? _____

17. John, a Utah police officer, is terminated by his employer after his employer learns that he practices plural marriage. John seeks declaratory and injunctive relief to determine that Utah's laws prohibiting plural marriage are invalid and to enjoin their enforcement. He alleges that his discharge violates his constitutional rights. Will he be successful? _____

18. Todd and Heidi, who are first cousins, decide to marry in the jurisdiction of Blackacre. After ten years of marriage, Todd is killed in an automobile accident. Heidi petitions the probate court for a widow's allowance pursuant to state law, claiming that she is Todd's "lawful spouse." Will she be successful? _____

19. Alison is 14 years old and a freshman in high school. She and her 21-year-old boyfriend Bobby wish to marry. However, Alison and Bobby know that Alison's parents will never consent because they believe that Alison is too young to marry. Alison decides to obtain judicial consent to marry, in hopes that she will not have to obtain her parents' consent. Is her strategy likely to be successful? _____

Answers

16. No. Bigamy consists of the crime of entering into marriage when one of the parties is married to a previous spouse who is then still living. Modern courts generally require intent to commit bigamy, i.e., that the defendant enter a second marriage with the knowledge that the first marriage is still valid. Sandra did not have the requisite intent.

17. Probably not. Plaintiff's constitutional arguments are not likely to be successful. Plaintiff's First Amendment argument would not prevail based on *Reynolds v. United States*. According to *Reynolds*, although the First Amendment dictates that government cannot interfere with religious beliefs, religious practices (such as bigamy/polygamy) do not merit the same constitutional protection. Also, Plaintiff's argument that the discharge violates his constitutional right to privacy will probably fail because bigamy is distinguishable from the monogamous relationship protected by *Lawrence v. Texas*. The state could argue that it is justified, by a compelling interest, rooted in history and tradition, in upholding the discharge to protect monogamy. However, John would not incur felony

liability for bigamy/polygamy under Utah law because the legislature recently *decreased* liability for bigamy/polygamy from a third-degree felony (with a penalty of up to five years in prison) to an infraction (subject to a $750 fine or community service).

18. Perhaps. It depends on the law of Blackacre, specifically whether first-cousin marriage constitutes incest. Marriage with a first cousin constitutes incest in some, but not all, states. If Blackacre law holds that first-cousin marriages constitute incest, then the probate court is likely to hold that the marriage was void ab initio and refuse to recognize Heidi's right to claim a widow's allowance.

19. Probably not. Generally, minors must secure parental consent to marry, according to state law. However, for very young minors (such as Alison), several states require *both* judicial consent and parental consent. If Alison resides in such a jurisdiction, judicial consent would not be sufficient. Alison would need either to secure parental consent or wait until she obtains her majority. Further, Alison may face another obstacle if she lives in a jurisdiction that follows the modern trend restricting or abolishing teen marriages.

C. **Substantive restrictions: State of mind:** A majority of states provide that fraud and duress are grounds to annul a marriage. The existence of fraud or duress vitiates consent and makes the marriage voidable at the request of the injured party. Today, annulment is less important than in the past because no-fault divorce makes dissolution more easily obtainable.

   1. **Fraud**

      a. **Requirements:** Courts have adopted different tests to annul a marriage based on fraud.

         i. **Strict test:** Under the strictest test to annul a marriage, the fraud must go to the "essentials" of the marriage. Case law interprets "essentials" as referring to sexual intercourse or procreation.

            Example: When Judith files for divorce from her husband James, James counterclaims by seeking an annulment on the ground of fraud. He alleges that Judith misrepresented that her prior husband was dead. James, a practicing Roman Catholic, claims that he would not have married Judith had he known of the misrepresentation. The court holds that the defendant is entitled to an annulment because the plaintiff's fraud goes to the essentials of the marital relationship (i.e., the defendant's knowledge makes it impossible for him to perform his marital duties and obligations). *Wolfe v. Wolfe*, 389 N.E.2d 1143 (Ill. 1979).

            Example: Plaintiff marries Defendant based on his representation that he is a practicing Orthodox Jew. The marriage is consummated. When Plaintiff discovers that Defendant fraudulently misrepresented his religious beliefs, she seeks an annulment. The court holds that Defendant's fraud goes to the essentials of the marriage because Plaintiff could not perform her duties as wife and mother, following her religion, without believing that her husband shared her religious beliefs. *Bilowit v. Dolitsky*, 304 A.2d 774 (N.J. Super. Ct. Ch. Div. 1973).

         ii. **Materiality and "but for" tests:** Some jurisdictions adopt a "materiality" test (similar to the materiality standard for ordinary contracts), whereas others adopt a "but for" test requiring that the plaintiff would not have married the defendant had the plaintiff known of the misrepresentation. However, misrepresentations of health, wealth, and status are not legally sufficient grounds for annulment.

Example: Husband appeals from a judgment denying his petition for an annulment, claiming that he would not have married Wife *but for* her representations related to their son's paternity (that he sired the child). The appellate court finds sufficient evidence supporting the trial court's determination that Husband would have married Wife regardless of her representation. Husband admits that, during their two-year courtship, he fell in love with Wife. Further, both parties admit that Husband had questions about the son's paternity prior to the marriage, but he married Wife anyway. Husband's testimony therefore fails to establish that he relied upon the Wife's representation of paternity in deciding whether to marry Wife, only that it played a part in his decision to begin a relationship with her. *Blair v. Blair,* 147 S.W.3d 882 (Mo. Ct. App. 2004).

b. **Standard of proof:** Fraud generally must be proven by clear and convincing evidence.

c. **Significance of consummation:** Some jurisdictions require the highest standard of fraud (that the fraud go to the "essentials") if the marriage has been consummated. The judicial reluctance to annul such marriages stems from the historical concern that invalidation in these cases would work a hardship on the woman (i.e., because she is no longer a virgin and thereby is "tainted goods").

d. **Effect:** The existence of fraud renders a marriage voidable (rather than void) at the request of the injured party.

e. **Immigration fraud:** Marriage to a U.S. citizen exempts an alien from the quota restrictions of the Immigration and Nationality Act (INA), 8 U.S.C. §1151(a), (b). Some immigrants may contract marriage fraudulently with a U.S. citizen in an effort to obtain preferential entry status. To curb such fraud, Congress enacted the Marriage Fraud Amendments Act, 8 U.S.C. §§1154(h), 1255(e), in 1986, granting permanent resident status (following conditional status) if an applicant has remained married for two years. This rule imposed a hardship on some women who were forced to remain in abusive relationships in order to obtain permanent resident status. As a result, Congress amended the Violence Against Women Act (VAWA) to permit self-petitions by battered spouses and to establish a special visa for battered spouses. Illegal Immigration Reform and Immigration Responsibility Act of 1996 §204(a)(1), 8 U.S.C. §1154(A)(iii)(1); 8 U.S.C. §1254(a)(3).

Note: To improve oversight of the mail-order bride industry Congress, through the VAWA Reauthorization Act of 2013, authorized the Attorney General to designate a specific office to bring criminal or civil charges against International Marriage Brokers (IMBs) that violate the International Marriage Broker Regulation Act (IMBRA) (S. 47, 113th Cong. Title VIII, Sec. 808(a)(2)(A)). IMBRA requires recordkeeping by IMBs showing their compliance with background checks and age requirements for foreign brides and provides penalties for clients who lie or fail to disclose a violent or criminal history.

2. **Duress:** Marriages are voidable and may be annulled if a party enters the marriage because of duress. Traditionally, courts required that physical force or the threat of such force (the "shotgun marriage") were sufficient to overcome the plaintiff's will (a subjective test) as opposed to a reasonable person's will (an objective test)). Threats of criminal prosecution would not suffice. Subsequently, courts held that mental distress suffices if it makes a party unable to act as a free agent in entering the marriage.

Note: Forced marriages exist at home and abroad. Few legal resources prevent parents from forcing daughters into marriage or punish these parents: only ten states have laws on forced marriage. Forced child marriage is correlated with high maternal and infant mortality rates as well as violence against women.

Some countries have enacted law reforms addressed to forced marriage. For example, Germany imposes a five-year sentence on a person who forces a woman into marriage. In the United Kingdom, the Forced Marriage Act of 2008 authorizes restraining orders preventing forced unions.

3. **Effect of Voidable Marriage for Spousal Benefits:** Persons who enter marriages that are voidable as a violation of state of mind restrictions may be unable to collect spousal state benefits based on such marriages.

Example: When Robert Watkins, Jr. (Decedent) died at the age of 82, he was survived by his third wife of less than two years, Emeline. After his death, his daughter maintains that Emeline's marriage to Decedent was procured by fraud, duress, and undue influence. The daughter petitions the probate court to bar the widow from receiving any share of Decedent's estate. The court holds that evidence supports a finding that Decedent's widow procured her marriage by undue influence, and thus precludes her from obtaining an elective share of Decedent's estate. *Matter of Watkins*, 209 A.3d 135 (Md. Ct. Spec. App. 2019).

Quiz Yourself on SUBSTANTIVE RESTRICTIONS: STATE OF MIND

20. Jim meets Paula through an Internet chat room. They discuss many things — their backgrounds, religions, finances, etc. At the time, Jim has more financial resources than Paula. Paula misrepresents her wealth to appear more wealthy than she is. A few months later, they marry. After several months, they break up. Jim contends that the marriage was procured by Paula's fraud regarding her financial situation. He alleges that she wanted to marry him in order to access his finances and solve her financial difficulties. Will his argument be successful? _____

21. When Anne and Donald marry, he draws up a document that explains that the marriage is taking place against Donald's wishes and only because of Anne's threats against him (that she will blacken his name at his place of employment) and her threats against herself (that she will commit suicide). The document adds that Anne is marrying him because she is desirous of reestablishing herself in the good graces of her relatives and also because she cannot bear to continue to live with her sister. When Anne and Donald separate after a 10-year marriage, Donald argues that the marriage is invalid on grounds of duress. Will his argument be successful? _____

22. Barbara, a Polish national, is living in Washington State with David when she meets Anthony. She informs Anthony that she is looking for a husband so that she can remain in the United States. He asks her to marry him based on his affection for her, and she agrees. After a brief marriage, Barbara petitions for divorce. Anthony files a counter petition alleging the invalidity of the marriage based on fraud. He alleges that Barbara continued her intimate relationship with David after her marriage to him. Anthony contends that Barbara lied to him about the nature of her relationship with David, in order that Anthony would marry her to enable her to get permanent residency status. Will Anthony's argument be successful? _____

Answers

20. No. Jim's argument regarding Paula's alleged fraud about her financial situation is not sufficient to entitle him to an annulment based on fraud. False representations as to wealth (similar to those regarding health, character, etc.) are not legally sufficient grounds for annulment.

21. No. Donald's allegations of duress are not legally sufficient to invalidate the marriage. Here, the duress was mental (rather than physical). To succeed, Donald would have had to prove that Anne's duress (threats and persuasion) rendered him unable to act as a free agent in entering the marriage. These allegations of duress do not approach that standard. Donald could have refused to marry Anne.

22. Probably not. A finding of fraud vitiates consent to marry. Many courts hold that fraud (for annulment purposes) must go to the "essentials" of the marriage (generally pertaining to sexual intercourse or childbearing). Barbara's deception to Anthony consisted of a false representation of her affection for him. Courts have held that such misrepresentations do not go to the essentials of the marriage. Barbara's second alleged misrepresentation concerned her desire to obtain status for immigration purposes. Courts generally hold that concealment of the fact that one party married the other for the sole purpose of obtaining status for immigration purposes is sufficient misrepresentation to go to the essence in an action for annulment. However, Anthony's assertion that he would not have married Barbara had he known that she was marrying him to obtain permanent residency status is contradicted by the record (i.e., she disclosed her motive). Hence, he cannot prove that she misrepresented the truth or that he relied on such "misrepresentation."

D. Procedural restrictions: All states regulate marriage procedure. Such regulation is intended to promote the stability of marriage and facilitate the collection of vital statistics.

   1. Licensure: States require that the parties procure a marriage license, often by applying to a county clerk. The clerk may refuse to issue the license if the information provided by the parties reveals that they are ineligible to marry. Some states provide that a portion of marriage license fees shall support domestic violence programs.

   2. Physical examination and blood tests: In the 1930s, rising rates of syphilis caused a public health crisis and prompted many states to require that before county clerks could issue a marriage license, the parties had to file a health certificate, signed by a physician, stating the applicants had undergone a physical examination (including blood tests) and were free from communicable venereal disease Only one state (Montana) still requires blood tests prior to obtaining a marriage license. Other states have eliminated the requirement that couples take tests for certain diseases before they marry.

   Some states have substituted the requirement for blood tests with a provision for the distribution of a brochure that furnishes applicants with information about the statutory requirements for licenses, including information about testing for, and treatment of, genetic and sexually transmissible diseases (e.g., Cal. Fam. Code §358).

   3. Solemnization: All states require solemnization of marriage by an authorized person before witnesses (subject to some exceptions, discussed *infra*). No specific form of ceremony is required. Different states have different regulations about who can perform wedding ceremonies. States generally permit members of recognized religious denominations, judicial officers, and county clerks to officiate at weddings. Some states allow others to perform a wedding if they submit an application and pay a fee.

4. **Waiting period:** Many states impose a waiting period (ranging from one to five days) between the time of the parties' application for the license and the issuance thereof in order to deter hasty marriages. *See, e.g.,* UMDA §204 (requiring a three-day waiting period).

5. **Recordation:** The person solemnizing the marriage must sign the marriage certificate and submit it to the county clerk. The clerk then registers the marriage so that it becomes part of the public record.

6. **Failure to comply with the procedural formalities:** Failure to comply with these procedural formalities will not invalidate a marriage. This rule operates unless the jurisdiction has a statute *expressly* making a marriage invalid without a license.

   Example: Plaintiff and Defendant are married by a priest in a Roman Catholic ceremony, although they fail to obtain a marriage license. They live together for 25 years and raise 4 children. When Wife petitions for divorce, Husband alleges that the marriage is void because of their noncompliance with the statutory licensure requirement. The court holds that in the absence of a statute invalidating an unlicensed marriage, a ceremonial marriage contracted without a marriage license is not void on public policy grounds (reasoning that no useful purpose is served by nullifying a longstanding marriage). *Carabetta v. Carabetta*, 438 A.2d 109 (Conn. 1980).

   Example: Jack Harris and Derrel DePasse live together for several years. DePasse becomes terminally ill and is hospitalized. The day before she dies, the hospital chaplain performs a marriage ceremony for the couple. Although aware that a marriage license was required, the parties do not obtain a license because of her imminent death. After her death, Jack claims an interest in her estate as her surviving spouse. Her executor challenges his petition on the ground that the marriage was not valid because the parties failed to obtain a marriage license. The court finds that, based on the statutes governing marriage, the issuance of a marriage license is a mandatory requirement for a valid marriage in California. Therefore, the court denies Harris's petition to qualify as a surviving spouse. *Estate of DePasse*, 118 Cal. Rptr. 2d 143 (Ct. App. 2002).

7. **Abolition of marriage licenses:** The Alabama legislature enacted a law (Ala. Code § 30-1-9.1) in 2019 abolishing marriage licenses and replacing them with signed affidavits. This measure was enacted in the wake of *Obergefell* because some state probate judges responded to marriage equality by refusing to issue marriage licenses. This state law transforms the duty of probate judges from the issuance of marriage licenses to mere recordation of affidavits.

E. **Procedural variations:** Parties sometimes marry by resort to procedures that differ from the traditional marriage ceremony. Such procedures include proxy marriages and confidential marriages.

   1. **Proxy marriages:** Some jurisdictions recognize proxy marriages in which a substitute or "proxy" stands in for an absent bride or groom (subject to the bride or groom's authorization). Parties may resort to such marriages in times of war or other international conflict. If the proxy marriage is valid where performed, other jurisdictions will recognize it. UMDA §206(b) permits recognition of such marriages if the proxy acts with written authorization.

Example: Mary-Louise Tshiani requests a divorce from her husband Noel. Noel claims that their marriage was not valid. Both parties are natives of the Democratic Republic of Congo where they married. However, Noel was in another part of Africa during the wedding and asked his cousin to stand in for him while he participated by telephone. The couple then moved to Maryland and held themselves out as husband and wife. The court of appeals determined that the marriage was valid under Congolese law, that marriages by proxy are not prohibited by Maryland law, and concluded that such a marriage is not repugnant to Maryland's public policy. *Tshiani v. Tshiani*, 81 A.3d 414 (Md. Ct. App. 2013).

2. **Confidential marriages:** Some states provide for recognition of certain types of marriages that fail to meet all the statutory formalities. For example, California recognizes "confidential marriages" for partners who are not minors and who have been living together. Cal. Fam. Code §500. A confidential marriage license is issued by the clerk. Although the marriage must be recorded, the records are not open to public inspection except upon a showing of "good cause." Cal. Fam. Code §511. The purpose of recognition of these marriages is to encourage legalization of the relationship without subjecting the couple to potentially embarrassing publicity.

F. **Curative procedural doctrines:** Some doctrines protect the parties to a marriage who fail to observe the requisite *procedural formalities* (i.e., common-law marriage), or the party who is unaware of an *impediment* to the marriage (i.e., putative spouse doctrine).

1. **Common-law marriage**

   a. **Generally:** Common-law marriage requires no ceremony. Rather, the parties presently *agree* to enter a legal marital relationship, *cohabit*, and *hold themselves out* as husband and wife in the community. Such a relationship constitutes a valid marriage and can only be terminated by death or dissolution.

      Approximately eight states recognize common-law marriage (i.e., Colorado, Iowa, Kansas, Montana, New Hampshire, South Carolina, Texas, and Utah). Cases generally arise at dissolution or death when the survivor attempts to claim inheritance or health insurance benefits, workers' compensation, or Social Security survivor benefits.

   b. **Elements**

      i. **Present agreement:** No specific words are required. However, words or conduct must indicate a present agreement. Words of futurity are insufficient. Also, the present agreement must take place when neither party is under a legal impediment (such as from a prior marriage). Many states require a new present agreement after removal of any legal impediment.

         Example: Elizabeth and Harold marry and have a daughter. Several years later, Harold leaves Elizabeth and moves in with Mildred. He remains with Mildred until his death 20 years later. Six years before his death, he finally divorces Elizabeth. When he shows Mildred the decree, he says, "Now, we're legally married." She replies, "It's about time!" After his death, Mildred argues that she is entitled to an intestate share of his estate as his legal spouse. The court holds that Mildred was Harold's common-law wife from the date Harold was divorced from his first wife. The parties' words, upon their seeing the decree, constituted a present agreement to marry. *Estate of Garges*, 378 A.2d 307 (Pa. 1977).

ii. **Cohabitation:** The couple must cohabit in a jurisdiction that recognizes common-law marriages. Statute and case law fail to require a specific duration for cohabitation. In fact, the couple's duration in the common-law jurisdiction may be brief, although some courts require that visits be longer than a day or two.

iii. **Holding out:** The couple must have the reputation in the community of being married. This "holding out" requirement establishes evidence of the couple's reputation as married and prevents fraud. It can be accomplished by using "Mr. and Mrs.," wearing wedding rings, etc.

Example: Sandra begins dating Dave, a California baseball player. The couple spends time in California, New Jersey, and Texas. (Of these states, only Texas recognizes common-law marriage.) After Sandra becomes pregnant, Dave tells her he wants to have a private ceremony. She makes a reservation at a hotel and they stay in the "honeymoon suite." Subsequently, she informs her mother that they are married. They rent a condo with the name "Winfield" on the mailbox. Sandra continues to use her surname. She signs the baby's birth certificate with her surname. She does not wear a wedding ring. She files income tax returns and health insurance forms as single. Sandra files for divorce, claiming that she is Dave's common-law wife. The court holds that she failed to establish the requisite element of "holding out" based on her conduct. *Winfield v. Renfro*, 821 S.W.2d 640 (Tex. Ct. App. 1991).

c. **Conflict of laws:** Common-law marriages present problems when the couple resides at various times in multiple jurisdictions, i.e., both a jurisdiction that does not recognize common-law marriage as well as one that does.

i. **Initial residence in a common-law jurisdiction:** If the parties meet the requirements for a common-law marriage and first reside in a jurisdiction that recognizes such marriages, but later move to a jurisdiction that does not, the latter jurisdiction almost always recognizes the marriage.

ii. **Initial residence in a non-common-law jurisdiction:** If the parties meet the requirements for a common-law marriage but first reside in a jurisdiction that does not recognize such marriages, but later move to a jurisdiction that does, the latter jurisdiction usually recognizes the marriage.

If the parties meet the requirements for a common-law marriage and reside in a jurisdiction that does not recognize such marriage, but later *visit* a jurisdiction that does, and then return to the former jurisdiction (that does not recognize such marriages), many courts in the home state will hold that a valid common-law marriage took place in the jurisdiction that the couple visited.

Note: In general, courts appear to be more sympathetic to a finding of a common-law marriage in cases of lengthy relationships and in claims against defendants who are governmental entities.

d. **Criticism:** A criticism of the common-law marriage doctrine is that it imposes governmental regulation on parties who have chosen this intimate relationship specifically because they desire to eschew governmental regulation.

e. **Common-law marriage and same-sex couples:** Following *Obergefell*, several states conferred common-law-marriage status *retroactively* on same-sex couples as a means of providing them rights and benefits because they were previously barred from ceremonial marriages by state laws that were subsequently declared unconstitutional.

Example: Sabrina Maurer and Kimberly Underwood, longstanding same-sex partners, celebrate a commitment ceremony in Pennsylvania in 2001. They remained in Pennsylvania until Underwood's death in 2013. Although they wanted to marry, they were unable to because Underwood's death occurred six months before Pennsylvania legalized same-sex marriage. As a result, Maurer was obligated to pay inheritance taxes on Underwood's estate that would have been unnecessary had the couple been legally married. Maurer filed suit for a declaratory judgment, claiming she and Underwood had a common-law marriage dating from their commitment ceremony in 2001. Pennsylvania had abolished common-law marriages in 2004, except for those occurring prior to January 1, 2005. The Pennsylvania Court of Common Pleas ruled that the couple had a valid common-law marriage beginning in 2001 and continuing under Underwood's death in 2013, and therefore, they are entitled to all rights and privileges of spouses. *In re Estate of Kimberly M. Underwood*, 2015 WL 5052382 (Pa. Ct. Com. Pl. 2015).

2. **Putative spouse doctrine:** Another curative doctrine to protect the interests of a marital party is the putative spouse doctrine.

   a. **Definition:** The putative spouse doctrine protects a spouse who has a good-faith belief in the validity of the marriage.

   Example: When Robert meets Nancy, he tells her that he is separated from his former wife Christina. In September 2003, Robert and Nancy obtain a marriage license. The document fails to mention his previous marriage despite the fact that both parties sign under penalty of perjury. Robert and Nancy marry on September 27, 2003. His divorce from Christina becomes final on December 31, 2003. Nancy takes the document with the "Notice of Entry of Judgment" of his divorce (containing a warning that neither party should remarry prior to the "effective date of the termination of marital status") and mails it to Robert's ironworkers union with her request to be added to his medical insurance. When Robert dies in a construction accident, Nancy files an action for wrongful death, claiming that she is Robert's putative spouse. His employer contends that she lacks standing because she did not have the requisite "good faith belief" that her marriage was valid (because of her possession of the divorce decree with the cautionary note). The California Supreme Court, reversing summary judgment for the employer, clarifies that a putative spouse's status depends on subjective good faith (a genuine and honest belief in the validity of the marriage) and does not require that the belief be objectively reasonable. *Ceja v. Rudolph & Sletten, Inc.*, 302 P.3d 211 (Cal. 2013).

   b. **Purpose:** The doctrine is often relied upon in claims to confer benefits upon an "innocent" spouse at death (e.g., for inheritance purposes, state or federal death benefits, to establish standing to sue for wrongful death) or dissolution (e.g., to establish rights to marital property or spousal support).

   c. **Common-law marriage distinguished:** In a common-law marriage, the parties are aware that they have not taken part in a marriage ceremony. In contrast, under the putative spouse doctrine, the parties have undergone a marriage ceremony and at least one party has a good-faith belief that a valid marriage has occurred.

   d. **Conflicting claims:** Occasionally, both a putative spouse and lawful spouse may assert claims to a benefit stemming from the marriage.

   Example: Juan marries Mildred in 1929. They have three children and live together until his death in 1969. Josephine meets Juan in 1942. He informs her that he is divorced. She marries him in 1945 and has four children with him. He lives a double life, maintaining homes with *both* women until 1969. Upon his death in an auto accident, both wives claim an intestate share of his estate as his legal spouse. The court holds that, although Josephine's marriage was void because Juan was still married to Mildred, Josephine acquired the status of putative spouse based on her good-faith belief that she was validly married. As such, she is entitled to share equally in his estate with Mildred, his lawful spouse. *Estate of Vargas*, 111 Cal. Rptr. 779 (Ct. App. 1974).

Quiz Yourself on
PROCEDURAL VARIATIONS AND CURATIVE PROCEDURAL DOCTRINES

23. Daniel and Laverne are married while he is hospitalized with an inoperable malignant brain tumor. The clerk issues a marriage license, but Daniel never signs the application or appears before the clerk. At the ceremony, Daniel is unable to respond. A third party acknowledges the marriage vows for Daniel. When Daniel dies four days later, Laverne files a petition for letters of administration alleging her status as the decedent's wife. She contends that she married Daniel by proxy. Daniel's children from a prior marriage argue that the marriage was invalid. Will their argument be successful?

_____

24. Anna and Dickie apply for, and are issued, a marriage license. They participate in a marriage ceremony, at which the minister signs their marriage license. However, the parties never file the license. They live together for a month after the ceremony. Anna contends that they married because of Dickie's concern about his family members' belief that he would go to hell because of his sinful relationship. She claims Dickie proposed a fake ceremony and represented that the marriage would not be valid. After the ceremony, Anna burns the license, allegedly with Dickie's knowledge and consent. When Dickie files for divorce, Anna denies the existence of the marriage based on a failure to comply with the requisite formalities. Will her argument be successful? _____

25. Julian Orr separates from his wife Bernice and finally divorces her many years later (in 2009). He lives with Louisa in California and Nevada during his separation from Bernice. Although Julian and Louisa never celebrate a marriage ceremony, Louisa uses the name "Mrs. Orr." They hold themselves out as husband and wife. In 2010, Julian and Louisa visit Texas several times, the longest trip being two weeks, to visit Louisa's relatives. He is living with Louisa at the time of his death in Nevada in 2012. Although neither California nor Nevada recognizes common-law marriages, Texas does. At Julian's death, Louisa claims Social Security survivor benefits as his legal spouse. Will she be successful? _____

26. After several months of dating, Gary asks Lillie to marry him. She declines, saying she is not yet ready to marry. Several times over the next ten years of dating, Lillie asks Gary to marry her, but he does not do so. Instead, he promises to marry her at some future time. Gary stays at Lillie's house several nights each week. Each maintains a separate residence and separate bank accounts. They sometimes take vacations together. Gary never represents that he and Lillie are married. When they break up, Lillie alleges that they had a common-law marriage. Will her argument be successful?

_____

Answers

23. Probably. Even if this state legislature authorizes marriage by proxy, such deathbed ceremonies evoke suspicion about consent and fraud (whether the alleged surviving spouse took advantage of the decedent's last illness). For example, Daniel never signed the application for the marriage license or personally appeared before the clerk. He was unable to respond at the ceremony. Moreover, there was no evidence of a written proxy authorizing any representative to obtain the license or to acknowledge the marriage vows.

24. No. Failure to comply with the procedural formalities (i.e., filing the license) will not invalidate the marriage. Courts generally interpret compliance with the procedural formalities as a directory, ministerial act rather than as a mandatory requirement (absent a state statute that expressly provides that the issuance of a marriage license is a mandatory requirement for a valid marriage).

25. Yes. Louisa is entitled to benefits as the decedent's common-law spouse. Julian and Louisa cohabited and held themselves out as husband and wife. A valid common-law marriage came into existence after 2009 (when Julian divorces Bernice) based on the couple's visits to Texas (a state that recognizes common-law marriages).

26. No. Lillie failed to establish that a common-law marriage existed. She and Gary never agreed to live together as husband and wife. (Lillie rejected Gary's sole proposal.) They did not cohabit because each maintained a separate residence throughout the relationship. Gary never represented that they were married. Even if Gary intended to marry Lillie at some future point, an agreement to marry in the future is insufficient to establish the requisite agreement to establish a common-law marriage.

IV. ANNULMENT

An annulment declares a marriage *void ab initio*, i.e., the marriage never occurred. This contrasts with a divorce, which declares that a marriage that was once valid has come to an end (as of the date of the dissolution decree).

A. Reasons to seek: Annulments, historically, enjoyed great popularity prior to no-fault when divorce was difficult to obtain. Today, parties may resort to annulment, rather than divorce, for religious reasons. Or, parties may seek an annulment for jurisdictional reasons to avoid longer residency requirements for divorce or to reinstate a benefit that was lost upon marriage.

B. Void/voidable distinction: A marriage may be characterized as void or voidable. Several features differentiate a void from a voidable marriage.

    1. Void: A void marriage is invalid from inception. No legal action is required to declare its invalidity. It may be challenged by the parties themselves or by third parties, and may be collaterally attacked (in actions other than annulment) even after the death of one of the parties. A void marriage offends a strong state policy.

    2. Voidable: A voidable marriage is valid from inception and requires that one of the parties take judicial action to establish its invalidity. If neither party acts to disaffirm the marriage, the marriage remains valid. A voidable marriage may be attacked only by the parties (although some statutes permit parents of a minor to attack a marriage). A voidable marriage cannot be collaterally attacked (i.e., in actions other than annulment). Such a marriage offends public policy less than does a void marriage.

3. **Grounds:** Bigamy and incest provide grounds for a void marriage. Fraud, duress, and nonage provide grounds for a voidable marriage.

   Example: Elizabeth seeks to annul the marriage of her deceased father, comedian Richard Pryor, with Jennifer. Pryor remarried Jennifer while she was caring for him during his last illness. (He had previously been married to Jennifer briefly 20 years earlier.) After Pryor's death, his daughter discovers the later marriage and petitions to annul it on the ground of fraud, alleging that her father's name was forged on the marriage license. Finding that she lacks standing, the court reasons that Pryor's (second) marriage was voidable and not subject to collateral attack. Thus, only Pryor could have commenced an annulment proceeding. *Pryor v. Pryor*, 99 Cal. Rptr. 3d 853 (Ct. App. 2009).

4. **Relation back doctrine:** Under this doctrine, a marriage that has been annulled is considered as void from inception. The doctrine is useful in some circumstances (such as the reinstatement of an employment benefit that was lost because of the marital relationship). Judicial discretion is involved in the application of the doctrine.

5. **Effect of annulment on other's rights**

   a. **Spousal rights:** Traditionally, courts awarded alimony upon divorce, not upon annulment. Some statutes now permit spousal support awards following an annulment.

      A question sometimes arises whether annulment of a second marriage results in reinstatement of spousal support from a prior marriage. Most courts do not reinstate spousal support based on a policy of protecting the first spouse's expectations.

   b. **Children's rights:** At common law, annulment resulted in bastardizing any children born during the relationship (as a result of the strict application of the relation back doctrine). Statutes have abrogated this harsh result. *See* UMDA §207(c) providing that children who are born to a void marriage are legitimate.

Quiz Yourself on ANNULMENT

27. At the time of the marriage between Leslie and Mitchell, Leslie is working as an attorney for the state Department of Corrections. Prior to and during their marriage, Mitchell conceals from Leslie the fact that he had been convicted of a second-degree felony (theft of property) in another state. Leslie's employer discovers Mitchell's criminal record and informs her that because of her marriage to a convicted felon, her employer has determined that there is a conflict of interest and her employment would terminate. Leslie and Mitchell separate, and she requests an annulment on grounds of fraud. Is Leslie entitled to the annulment? If so, will the annulment enable her to continue her employment?

_____

28. Martha begins work as a housekeeper for widower Otto and his children. Some time later, Martha accepts Otto's proposal of marriage; however, they never take part in a marriage ceremony. They

cohabit and attend social events together. On various occasions, she registers as single (for a hospitalization), as does he (executing a mortgage), and they file tax returns as single persons. After Otto's death, Martha claims a dower interest as Otto's common-law widow. Otto's children contend that Martha is not entitled to a dower interest because there was no common-law marriage between their father and Martha. Will their argument succeed? _____

Answers

27. Yes on both counts. Courts grant annulments where one spouse has concealed from the other a criminal background because it goes to the essentials of the marriage. Mitchell's misrepresentations violated the essential purpose of the marriage (sexual intercourse and procreation). (Leslie wanted a husband and prospective father to her children of whom she could be proud.) The annulment will be held to "relate back" to the date of the marriage, and thereby, eliminate Leslie's conflict of interest.

28. Yes. Although Martha and Otto had a present agreement to marry and cohabited, Martha and Otto failed to establish the required "holding out" as married. Thus, Martha is not the decedent's common-law wife.

V. CONFLICT OF LAWS: WHICH LAW GOVERNS MARRIAGE VALIDITY?

A. **Generally:** Sometimes a court must make a determination regarding which state's law shall govern the validity of a marriage. This involves an issue regarding the conflict of laws (or choice-of-law problem).

B. **Traditional rule: Law of place of celebration:** Under the traditional rule, marriage validity is determined by the law of the state where the marriage was celebrated. Recall that under the rule of *lex loci*, a marriage valid where celebrated is valid everywhere unless recognition of the marriage would be violative of public policy. Both the Restatement (First) of Conflict of Laws and UMDA take this approach.

Example: Wife and Husband are first cousins who marry in their native Iran. When Wife later files for divorce in Louisiana, the trial court dismisses her petition based on its refusal to extend comity to a first-cousin marriage. Reversing, the appellate court rules that, because the marriage was valid in Iran where it was contracted, the marriage should be recognized as valid in Louisiana, absent a violation of strong public policy. Finding no such public policy because first-cousin marriages are not prohibited by Louisiana incest law, the court holds that the marriage was valid and reverses the dismissal of Wife's divorce petition. *Ghassemi v. Ghassemi,* 103 So. 3d 401 (La. Ct. App. 2012).

C. **Restatement (Second) of Conflicts approach:** The Restatement (Second) of Conflict of Laws §283(1) has modified the general rule, holding that, in the absence of a statutory directive as to choice of law, the validity of marriage is determined by the state that has the "most significant relationship to the spouses and the marriage." Relevant factors in the application of this rule include: the policy of the forum state and the protection of the parties' expectations. Thus, the state's interest depends on the purpose to be achieved by the rule and the relation of the state to the marriage and the parties.

D. Definitions of "domicile" and Restatement (Third) of Conflicts approach: The traditional meaning of "domicile" encompasses the twin elements of physical presence plus intent to remain. Restatement (First), Conflict of Laws § 15; Restatement (Second), Conflict of Laws §§ 15(3), 18 cmt. b.

The current Restatement (Third) of Conflict of Laws uses the term "domicile" to identify the "place where the person's life is centered for resolving choice-of-law issues" and emphasizes proof of intent by objective evidence (i.e., evidence of place of employment, voting, etc.). Restatement (Third), Conflict of Laws § 2.01(2) (Tent. Draft No. 1, 2020).

E. Uniform Marriage Evasion Act: The Uniform Marriage Evasion Act (1912) also addressed the issue of what state law applies to marriage validity. The Act declared void all marriages entered into by parties who married in another state for the purpose of evading their home state restrictions on marriage. Although the Act was not widely adopted and has been withdrawn, some states have similar statutes.

F. Divorce. The issue of which state law shall apply to determinations of marriage validity also arises at the time of divorce. For discussion of this issue, see Chapter 5 *infra*.

Exam Tips on
PREPARING TO MARRY

Premarital Controversies

☛ **Identifying the controversy:** First determine the type of premarital controversy: *breach of promise to marry* or a *gift in contemplation of marriage*.

☛ **Breach of promise to marry:** Initially address the issue whether the jurisdiction still recognizes breach of promise to marry. Only a few jurisdictions still do. However, in any case, be sure to continue to discuss the elements, defenses, and damages.

    ☞ Be sure to check whether there has been an ***actual promise*** by A to marry B. Under this cause of action, A can recover damages from B if B breaches a promise to marry. (Note that the issue of who broke the engagement may become important subsequently in actions for recovery of gifts in contemplation of marriage.)

    ☞ **Defenses:** Check whether A may exert any defenses (such as B's fraudulent misrepresentation(s), the fact that either A or B was married at the time of the engagement, and mutuality of the decision to end the engagement).

    ☞ **Damages:** Determine A's damages. Note that some jurisdictions limit damages to economic loss.

    ☞ Be sure to mention the existence of heartbalm legislation and the rationale therefor, the abolition movement, and the modern trend. Look out for exam questions that involve both types of premarital controversies (breach of promise to marry and gifts in contemplation of marriage).

In such cross-over questions, be sure to determine who was "at fault" (if anyone) in breaking the engagement because it becomes relevant in recovery or retention of an engagement ring.

☛ **Gifts in contemplation of marriage:** The usual gift that is given in contemplation of marriage is an engagement ring. Here, the important issue is the existence of fault. Be sure to determine if either party is at fault in breaking the engagement. Discuss the role of fault and the modern trend.

    ☞ Remember the two views about fault. At common law, fault (breaking the engagement) barred recovery or retention of the engagement ring. The fault-based rule is the majority approach. However, under the modern rule, fault is irrelevant, meaning that the donor can recover the ring regardless of who broke the engagement or if the termination of the engagement was mutual.

    ☞ Determine whether the suit involves recovery of only an engagement ring or other objects as well. If the latter, ascertain whether a given object was actually given in contemplation of (conditional on) the marriage. Many objects that are typically given during intimate relationships are deemed to be irrevocable gifts (i.e., they are completed transfers that are not recoverable).

    ☞ Consider the interaction of abolition of actions for breach of promise on actions for recovery of gifts given in contemplation of marriage. Many courts that have abolished the former action still permit the latter action.

☛ **Premarital contracts:** Verify whether this was an agreement between prospective spouses made in contemplation of the marriage. Determine what rights are being limited or relinquished (property rights during the marriage or after death, spousal support, etc.).

    ☞ **Different views:** Be sure to point out the traditional view (invalidating them) and modern view (upholding them) regarding the validity of premarital contracts.

    ☞ **Limitations:** Check for possible invalid limitations on child support or child custody.

    ☞ **Formalities:** Mention the requirement of a writing and that consideration is not normally required.

☛ **Validity requirements:** Check to see if *substantive* and *procedural* fairness requirements have been satisfied.

    ☞ For substantive requirements, recall that there are two *views about fairness*. Some courts require that the agreement be fair under the circumstances, whereas other courts will enforce unfair agreements (if entered into voluntarily and with full disclosure). For procedural fairness, courts require that the parties entered the agreement voluntarily, and with full and fair disclosure. Recall that full disclosure does not require detailed disclosure.

    ☞ Another aspect of procedural fairness is the presence of *independent counsel*. Determine whether the party against whom enforcement is sought (usually the woman) was represented. If not, was she informed of her right to counsel and given the opportunity to consult? Recall that courts do not require her to be represented.

    ☞ **Special rules for spousal support waivers:** Remember that some courts have restrictive rules for premarital agreements that include waivers of spousal support. Some states prohibit such waivers. Other states provide that these waivers are not enforceable without safeguards, such as requiring representation or denying enforcement if support provisions leave a spouse destitute.

☞ Two final points: Recall that the UPAA requires a *higher standard* for unfairness (unconscionability). Also, be sure to check the *time* of the fairness determination: whether the appropriate assessment of fairness is at the time of execution of the contract or the time of enforcement (dependent on the relevant statute or case law). If fairness is determined at the time of enforcement, then ascertain whether any event has occurred (e.g., spouse's illness) that would make the agreement unfair even though it was fair at the time of execution.

Restrictions on Entry into Marriage: Constitutional, Substantive, Procedural

Constitutional Limitations on Regulation of the Right to Marry: Race, Poverty

☛ In discussing constitutional rights, identify the constitutional *status* of the right (i.e., is it a fundamental right), the constitutional *source* of the right, and the appropriate level of *scrutiny*. Determine whether the restriction is a limitation on the right to marry and the nature of that limitation (for example, does it *preclude marriage* or merely make marriage more *costly*?). Remember that infringements on the right to marry can violate substantive due process as well as the fundamental rights branch of equal protection.

☛ *Identify the correct level of scrutiny*. Recall that different tests exist for scrutinizing the constitutionality of state statutes, regulations, practices, or policies. Begin with the presumption that the lowest level of scrutiny (rational basis) applies but determine if a more rigorous level of scrutiny (intermediate or strict scrutiny) should apply. Remember that suspect classifications and infringements of fundamental rights (such as racial classifications and infringements on the right to marry) trigger strict scrutiny. Classifications by sex or illegitimacy trigger intermediate scrutiny.

   ☞ In applying the correct level of scrutiny, remember that each test has a *means* (fit) and an *end* (goal or objective) component. That is, for the rational basis test, is the restriction "reasonably related" (is the "means" reasonable) to a "legitimate state objective" (is the "end" legitimate)? For intermediate level of scrutiny, is the restriction "substantially related" (the "means") to "an important governmental objective" (is the "end" sufficiently important)? Finally, for strict scrutiny, is the restriction "necessary" (the "means") to a "compelling state interest" (the "end" must be so important that it is "compelling") to survive constitutional challenge?

   ☞ Remember that *Zablocki* states that *not all* state restrictions on marriage violate the fundamental right to marry and that "*reasonable regulations that do not significantly interfere with decisions to enter into the marital relationship may legitimately be imposed.*" Therefore, you need to determine if the restriction "significantly interferes" (i.e., whether it *directly* and *substantially* interferes) with the right to marry.

   ☞ Be aware: exam questions sometimes raise cross-over constitutional issues related to the right to privacy (contraception, abortion) as well as the right to enter the marital relationship.

Substantive Limitations

☛ Identify and discuss any substantive restrictions on marriage. Remember that substantive restrictions on marriage refer both to *capacity to marry* and *state of mind*. Capacity refers to age, having one spouse at one time, and not being related. Sometimes questions may involve one or more issues of capacity. Fraud and duress are state of mind restrictions.

   ☞ Be sure to note that substantive restrictions involve both *civil* restrictions (preclusions of the right to marry) as well as *criminal* sanctions (bigamy, incest). Remember that *Lawrence v. Texas* invalidated state sodomy laws. If the discussion involves discrimination against same-sex spouses, be sure to mention constitutional issues (due process, equal protection), and the application of *Lawrence* and *Obergefell*. If a question involves the denial of services to a same-sex couple and a claim of accommodation of religious liberty, be sure to mention *Masterpiece Cakeshop*'s requirement that the state must apply anti-discrimination law in a neutral manner regarding religion.

☞ For issues of bigamy and incest, be sure to mention the potential impact of *Lawrence*. By recognizing a constitutionally protected right to engage in consensual intimate sexual relationships in the home, *Lawrence* foreshadows liberalization of restrictions on bigamy and incest. Also discuss Chief Justice Roberts' dissent in *Obergefell*, in which he said that the majority's reasoning would support the claim of a fundamental right to plural marriage.

☛ *State of mind restrictions* involve fraud and duress. For fraud, discuss the different standards (i.e., essentials, materiality, but for). For duress, ascertain whether the coercion is physical or mental. If mental, apply both subjective and objective standards.

Procedural Limitations

☛ Procedural restrictions refer to the procedural formalities associated with marriage (licensure, solemnization, blood tests, filing the license, etc.). If you find an issue regarding substantive or procedural restrictions, be sure to discuss the effect of failure to comply with these restrictions on marriage validity. Mention the void-voidable distinction and the consequences thereof, as well as potential criminal liability (bigamy, incest).

☞ **Annulment:** If a question raises annulment, be sure to identify the appropriate grounds therefor. Discuss why the plaintiff might be seeking an annulment rather than a divorce (e.g., jurisdictional, avoidance of financial implications of divorce). Discuss the traditional versus modern rule for spousal support and children's rights following annulments. Determine if the relation back doctrine applies and discuss the consequences of applying the doctrine.

Procedural Variations and Curative Procedural Devices

☛ If there are issues of marriage validity, explore the presence of procedural **variations** (i.e., *proxy marriages, confidential marriages*). Determine if any *curative devices* (i.e., *common-law marriage* or the *putative spouse doctrine*) apply to protect a party. Identify and discuss the requirements for application of each doctrine. If you establish the existence of a common-law marriage, check the chronology carefully to ensure that no *impediment* exists (such as a prior marriage) that would prevent formation of the common-law marriage. Make sure that the parties "hold themselves out" as husband and wife. Identify the aspects of *holding out* (use of joint names on documents, referring to each other as spouses, etc.). Remember that no special amount of time is necessary to establish a common-law marriage.

Conflict of Laws

☛ For questions involving marriage validity, always be on the lookout for conflict-of-laws issues. Analyze the applicability of the rule of *lex loci* and the *Full Faith and Credit Clause of the Constitution*. Remember that the Full Faith and Credit Clause applies to public acts, records, and judicial proceedings of *sister states*.

☞ For choice-of-law issues, be sure to discuss the applicable law in all relevant jurisdictions. Do not assume that discussion of the law in one jurisdiction will obviate the need to discuss the applicable law in other jurisdictions.

☞ For issues of marriage validity, be sure to discuss the changing definitions of "domicile" under the various Restatements of Conflict of Laws.

CHAPTER 3

BEING MARRIED

ChapterScope

This chapter addresses the legal regulation of marital roles and responsibilities. It explores the rights and duties of the parties at common law, under various statutory regimes, and based on constitutional doctrine. Here are key principles covered in this chapter:

- **Marriage — Contract or status:** Marriage is both a *contract* (an agreement between two parties) and a *civil status* (regulated by the state).

- **Support rights and obligations during marriage:** At common law, a husband had a duty to support his wife, and the wife had a correlative duty to render services. Modern statutes make the duty of support gender neutral. A limitation on the spousal duty of support is the *family privacy doctrine* (courts are reluctant to interfere in an ongoing marriage).

- **Regulation of roles and responsibilities:**

  - **Names:** Today, a *married woman* may retain her birth name. Parental disputes regarding *children's surnames* are resolved by resorting to the best-interests-of-the-child standard.

  - **Domicile:** At common law, a married woman lacked the capacity to establish her domicile. Today, both spouses may acquire a domicile of choice.

  - **Employment:** *Antinepotism rules* prevent one spouse from being employed by the other spouse's employer. Federal and state challenges to such policies have been raised.

  - **Parenting:** Formerly, *mandatory maternity leave policies* required female employees to leave employment when they became pregnant. Congress responded with the *Pregnancy Discrimination Act* and the *Family and Medical Leave Act*. Employers' failure to make *pregnancy accommodations* for pregnant workers with medical needs, when accommodating non-pregnant workers, violates the PDA. *Breastfeeding discrimination* violates the PDA, FMLA, and many state laws.

- **Criminal law and tort:** In both criminal law and tort law, courts and legislatures have abolished special treatment for marital parties.

  - **Testimonial privilege:** At common law, two testimonial privileges existed: the *adverse spousal testimonial privilege* and the *confidential communications privilege*. The Supreme Court vested the adverse spousal testimonial privilege in the witness-spouse, allowing that spouse to testify against the other spouse in criminal proceedings.

  - **Marital rape:** Modern jurisdictions are abolishing or limiting the *common-law marital rape exemption* under which a husband could not be guilty of raping his wife.

  - **Alienation of affections:** Most jurisdictions have *abolished* tort actions for alienation of affections (tort actions against a third party for interfering in the marital relationship).

  - **Interspousal immunity doctrine:** Jurisdictions have *abolished* the common-law doctrine of interspousal immunity that barred tort actions between husbands and wives.

I. INTRODUCTION

The law regulates marital roles and responsibilities. The women's movement and the ensuing transformation of gender roles have altered traditional marital roles and responsibilities.

A. **Historical background: Ecclesiastic versus civil jurisdiction:** In England, ecclesiastic courts maintained exclusive jurisdiction over marriage from the Norman Conquest until the mid-nineteenth century. In contrast, in the American colonies, marriage was a civil matter. Today, civil courts continue to have jurisdiction over marriage, but vestiges of canon law and practice remain (e.g., marriage procedure, grounds for annulment and divorce, etc.).

B. **Contract versus status**

1. **Marriage is a contract:** Marriage is an agreement between two people. The American colonists, rejecting the religious character of marriage, regarded marriage as a civil contract. Similar to other contracts, marriage involves parties who are legally capable of consent, rests on consideration consisting of the exchange of mutual promises, and imposes rights and obligations. It differs from other contracts because the state is also a party (imposing obligations), and because it cannot be modified as easily as other contracts.

2. **Marriage is a status:** Marriage is also a civil status. The classic view of the dual nature of marriage as a status and contract was declared in *Maynard v. Hill*, 125 U.S. 190 (1888) (upholding the constitutionality of a state's assertion of broad power over regulation of marital status):

   [Marriage] is something more than a mere contract. The consent of the parties is of course essential to its existence, but when the contract to marry is executed by the marriage, a relation between the parties is created which they cannot change. . . . The relation once formed, the law steps in and holds the parties to various obligations and liabilities. . . .

   Id. at 210-211.

II. REGULATION OF ROLES AND RESPONSIBILITIES

A. **Background: Married women's common-law disabilities:** Under the common-law doctrine of *coverture*, the husband and wife became one person upon marriage — and, as Blackstone stated, the husband was *that* one. This was sometimes called the doctrine of "marital unity" or "merger." This suspension of the wife's legal identity subjected married women to significant common-law disabilities.

Absent her husband's consent, a wife was unable to:

- sue or be sued;

- enter into contracts;

- alienate real property;

- make a will; or

- retain or control her own earnings and property.

The husband was liable for the wife's premarital and marital debts and torts. Special rules of procedure required joinder of the husband in claims against the wife. The Married Women's Property Acts (enacted during the mid- and late nineteenth century) largely eliminated these common-law disabilities.

REGULATION OF ROLES AND RESPONSIBILITIES

B. Support rights and obligations during marriage

1. **Scope of spousal duty of support:** At common law, the husband had a duty to support his wife. The wife had a correlative duty to render services to her husband. Modern statutes make the duty of support gender neutral.

2. **Limitation on spousal duty of support—family privacy doctrine:** The spousal duty of support was limited by the doctrine of family privacy in cases of intact marriages. Under this common-law *doctrine of nonintervention*, courts are reluctant to interfere in an *ongoing* marriage to settle disputes between the spouses. Rationales include: (1) a desire to preserve marital harmony, (2) a judicial reluctance to adjudicate trivial matters, (3) adherence to the view that the husband, as head of the family, should determine family expenditures, and (4) the existence of the wife's common-law disability to sue her husband.

   Example: During a 33-year marriage, Wife cooks, cleans, and performs household chores. Despite his substantial assets, Husband refuses to provide wife with clothes, furniture, household necessities (e.g., indoor bathroom, kitchen sink, or working furnace), or entertainment. Wife brings an action against Husband to recover support. The court denies Wife recovery. Because the parties are not separated, the court will not intervene to order spousal support. For public policy reasons, a married couple's disputes are not a matter for judicial resolution. *McGuire v. McGuire*, 59 N.W.2d 336 (Neb. 1953).

3. **Common-law necessaries doctrine:** A husband had a common-law duty to provide *necessaries* (i.e., necessary goods and services) to his wife and children. (The necessaries doctrine was designed to protect married women who surrendered their property to their husbands.) At common law, courts permitted indirect enforcement of the husband's duty of support. That is, notwithstanding the doctrine of nonintervention, courts allowed third parties (i.e., creditors) to sue the husband to enforce his duty to provide a wife or children with necessaries.

   a. **What constitutes a necessary:** Necessaries generally include food, clothing, shelter, and medical care. (Courts sometimes include other items.)

   b. **Constitutional challenges:** Support obligations that are payable only by the husband have been held unconstitutional.

   Example: Hospital sues Husband for services rendered to Wife, based on Virginia's statutory codification of the common-law duty of the husband to provide necessaries. Husband defends by challenging the statute as unconstitutional. The court holds that the statute, which imposes financial obligations only on the husband, constitutes gender-based discrimination under the state constitution as well as the Equal Protection Clause. *Schilling v. Bedford Cty. Mem. Hosp.*, 303 S.E.2d 905 (Va. 1983).

   c. **Modern view:** States take a variety of approaches, by case law or statute, to the necessaries doctrine in order to avoid equal protection problems. These approaches include:

   ■ abolition of the doctrine;

   ■ expansion of liability to both spouses;

   ■ imposing primary liability on the serviced spouse (i.e., make the creditor seek payment first from that spouse, and, if unable to collect, then from the other spouse).

   The emerging trend is the gender-neutral imposition of primary liability on the serviced spouse but if that spouse is unable to pay, then on the other spouse (the last alternative above).

Example: Hospital sues Wife (and Husband's estate) for services rendered to Husband during his last illness. Plaintiff contends that the common-law rule requiring Husband to pay for Wife's necessaries should extend to Wife, based on modern notions of women's increased independence, marriage as a partnership, and equal treatment. The court holds that both spouses are liable for the necessary expenses incurred by either. However, in the absence of spousal agreement to undertake the debt, creditors should first attach the assets of the spouse incurring the debt; only if those assets are insufficient should the creditor be permitted to reach the other spouse's assets. *Jersey Shore Med. Ctr. v. Estate of Baum*, 417 A.2d 1003 (N.J. 1980).

4. **Child's necessaries:** Modern statutes and case law make gender neutral the parent's common-law duty to furnish necessaries to a child.

5. **Modern statutory support obligations:** State legislation (supplementing and sometimes codifying the common-law necessaries doctrine) also imposes support obligations. Many *Family Expense Acts* (originally enacted to protect creditors) now require both spouses to provide support for the expenses of the family.

6. **Criticisms of family privacy doctrine:** Criticisms of the family privacy doctrine include the following:

   ■ The doctrine does not preserve marital harmony. Because support obligations may be adjudicated only upon separation or dissolution, the doctrine encourages the parties to terminate their relationship.

   ■ Matters of spousal disagreements are not trivial. The doctrine leaves a more vulnerable spouse without remedy.

   ■ Common-law rationales for the doctrine (husband as decision maker, wife's legal disability to sue) are outdated.

   ■ The doctrine inappropriately gives preference to third-party rights over those of an injured spouse (by permitting third-party suits but not interspousal suits).

   ■ Further, the doctrine introduces needless circularity to judicial resolution of intrafamilial disputes (by enabling only creditors to sue).

C. **Names:** A person may change his or her name in two ways: (1) the common-law method (without legal proceedings) by adopting another name and using it consistently and without fraudulent intent; or (2) a statutorily designated procedure.

   1. **Married woman's surname change:** At common law, a married woman assumed her husband's surname based on custom, not operation of law. Today, a married woman may retain her birth name so long as she has proven consistent and non-fraudulent use of that name. (Fraudulent use, for example, would involve an attempt to mislead creditors.)

   Example: Mary Emily Stuart marries Samuel Austell. Before the marriage, they orally agree that she shall retain her birth name. She registers to vote using that name but indicates that she is now married. Defendant-voter registrar notifies her that her voter registration will be canceled unless she assumes her husband's name. Defendant cancels her voter registration when Plaintiff fails to re-register. She challenges Defendant's action. The court holds that Plaintiff is entitled to continue to retain her birth name, following her marriage, if she shows that she consistently and non-fraudulently used that name. *Stuart v. Bd. of Supervisors of Elections*, 295 A.2d 223 (Md. Ct. App. 1972).

Note: Spouses are limited by state law in their choice of surnames following marriage. Only some state statutes explicitly provide for hyphenated surnames. Fewer states allow blended surnames (i.e., a combination of parts of both current surnames to create an entirely new surname).

2. **Married woman's resumption of maiden name**

   a. **During marriage:** Many states allow a married woman who has adopted her husband's surname either to resume her maiden surname or to adopt another surname that is different from her husband's, absent fraudulent intent.

      Example: Judith marries Daniel Natale, a school administrator. Husband does not wish to list his home phone. Attorney-wife desires to do so. She requests a judicial name change to Judith Natale Montague (*not* her surname prior to marriage). The trial court denies the petition based on possible detriment to third parties. Wife appeals. The court holds that Plaintiff may change her name since no evidence was presented of harm to third parties (i.e., Husband consented, possible harm to future offspring is too speculative, and no harm to state was shown). *Matter of Natale*, 527 S.W.2d 402 (Mo. Ct. App. 1975).

   b. **Upon divorce:** Statutes frequently authorize a married woman to resume her maiden name upon dissolution. Formerly, absent a statute, some trial courts expressly refused such resumption, voicing concerns about the need for a husband's consent or fear of possible harmful consequences for the children. However, appellate decisions rejected such reasoning. *See, e.g., Miller v. Miller*, 670 S.W.2d 591 (Mo. Ct. App. 1984).

3. **Men's right to change their names upon marriage:** A few state statutes expressly provide for a man to assume his spouse's surname, or allow the couple to combine some of the letters of each name, creating a new blended surname for both. *See, e.g.,* Cal. Fam. Code §306.5.

4. **Same-sex partners' name change:** Many states now permit same-sex partners to change their surnames or to choose a hyphenated name combining both surnames. *See, e.g.,* Mass. Gen. Laws c.46, §1D (applicable to any marital partner). However, even after marriage equality, many states failed to update their laws by deletion of sex-specific statutory language about marital name change.

5. **Transgender person's name change:** Traditionally, completion of gender affirming surgery (formerly known as sex reassignment surgery) was necessary before states would alter identification documents for transgender people. *See, e.g.,* Ala. Code §22-9A-19(d). Today, some states issue new birth certificates reflecting name and gender changes merely upon proof of "clinically appropriate treatment" (i.e., adherence to transitioning guidelines). *See, e.g.,* Cal. Health & Safety Code §103425. However, a few states (Ohio, Tennessee) still refuse to allow correction of gender on birth certificates even after transgender people's transition. Litigation is pending to remedy this issue.

6. **Name change for victims of domestic violence:** Victims of domestic violence who seek to change their names to escape their abusers face difficulties with open public records and publication requirements. Some states address this problem by providing that records of a name change may be sealed and any publication waived where there is a threat to safety. *See, e.g.,* N.M. Stat. Ann. §40-8-2.

7. **Choice of children's names**

   a. **Generally:** At common law, custom dictated that a child born in wedlock adopted the father's surname. Out-of-wedlock children (now termed **nonmarital children**) adopted the mother's name. Many modern statutes provide that parents may choose the father's surname, the mother's surname, or a hyphenated surname combining the two.

b. **Standard to resolve disputes:** Courts resolve parental disputes about children's surnames according to the *"best interests of the child"* standard. Relevant factors include:

- the child's preference;

- the effect of a name change on child-parent relationships; and

- parental motives.

Example: After Mother and Father divorce, Mother files a surname change application for their infant daughter (to reflect Mother's surname). Mother wants the surname change not to cause estrangement from the father but to promote ease in her daycare pick-ups and access to medical care. She alleges that Father manifested little interest in the child and threatened to kill the child when he learned of her surname change request — which he denies. He contends that he was thwarted in his attempts to visit the child and concedes that the surname change would not alter his feelings about his daughter. The trial court denies Mother's petition, reasoning (1) the child is too young to choose; (2) the name change would weaken the father-child bond; (3) the father has shown an interest in the child's welfare by paying child support; and (4) the father desires to preserve the parent-child bond. The D.C. Court of Appeals holds that the trial court erred in applying the best-interests-of-the-child standard based on gender-based assumptions and stereotypes (that a child should bear the father's surname and that the parent-child relationship would be weakened by the child's bearing another surname). The court adds that these distinctions fail to account for family diversity and raise significant constitutional issues. The relevant factors on remand should include gender neutral and child-centered factors. *Melbourne v. Neal*, 147 A.3d 1151 (D.C. Ct. App. 2016).

Example: The father of a nonmarital child, a successful businessman in a small Texas town, objects to the mother's petition to change the daughter's surname to his surname. He argues that the name change would embarrass members of his marital family by exposing his affair. The appellate court rejects the father's arguments, ruling that the best-interests test focuses on the welfare of the child and not the "self-seeking interests" of the noncustodial parent. *Scoggins v. Trevino*, 200 S.W.3d 832, 840 (Tex. App. 2006).

c. **Same-sex spouses' right to be listed as parents on birth certificates:** Following *Obergefell*, opponents of marriage equality resisted the ruling in many ways. Some states denied parentage rights to same-sex spouses by refusing to list both parents on a child's birth certificate.

Example: Two married same-sex couples live in Arkansas, although both couples were married elsewhere. Each couple has children conceived through anonymous sperm donation. In both instances, the Arkansas Department of Health refuses, in adherence to state statute, to issue birth certificates listing both spouses as "parents." The state statute requires that a child's birth certificate list the non-biological father if he is married to the biological mother, thereby precluding same-sex spouses from being listed as parents. The parents argue that the state law violates *Obergefell*. Based on the rational basis test, the state supreme court disagrees, reasoning that the law is predicated on the biological parent-child relationship and not the parents' marital status (i.e., birth certificates are intended merely to collect information about biological parents and biology justifies treating married same-sex couples differently).

Disagreeing sharply, the U.S. Supreme Court holds that the Arkansas rule denies same-sex couples *Obergefell*'s entitlement to "the same terms and conditions as opposite-sex couples." The Supreme Court explains that birth certificates are substantially more than mere markers of biological relationships; they are important records of legal parentage. The Court thereby interprets *Obergefell* broadly and reaffirms *Obergefell*'s requirement of equal treatment to all the benefits and responsibilities of marriage. *Pavan v. Smith*, 137 S. Ct. 2075 (2017).

8. **Constitutional protection for parental choice of child's name:** Some cases raise constitutional challenges to statutes restricting parental choice in the selection of children's surnames.

   Example: Debra Henne, wife of Robert Henne, bears a child fathered by Gary Brinton. She wishes to name the child "Alica Renee Brinton." Another plaintiff, Linda Spidell, who is an unmarried woman, wishes to give her daughter the same surname ("McKenzie") as that of her two other children. (Spidell chose that surname solely because she liked it.) A Nebraska statute restricts the choice of children's surnames (in cases of marriages) to: (1) the husband's surname; (2) the mother's surname; (3) the mother's birth name; or (4) a fused surname. Unmarried women may choose (a) the father's or mother's surname, or (b) a fused surname. Plaintiffs argue that the statute violates their constitutional right of privacy. The court holds that parents have no constitutional right of privacy to confer a surname with which the child has no legally recognized connection. The statute is rationally related to legitimate state interests in promoting the welfare of children, recordkeeping, and ensuring that names are not appropriated for improper purposes. *Henne v. Wright*, 904 F.2d 1208 (8th Cir. 1990), *cert. denied*, 498 U.S. 1032 (1991).

9. **International perspective:** Several countries regulate children's surnames strictly. For instance, parents in some countries must secure governmental approval for their choice of a child's name.

D. Married woman's domicile

1. **Definition:** Domicile, a legal concept defining a person's legal relationship to the state, is important in determining jurisdiction for such family matters as the validity of a marriage, the award of divorce and custody, the establishment of legitimacy, and adoption.

2. **Common-law rule:** At common law, a married woman lacked the capacity to establish, change, or retain the domicile of her choice. Instead, the law assigned to her the legal domicile of her husband.

3. **Reform:** The traditional rule began to change when the ***Restatement (Second) of Conflict of Laws*** permitted a "special circumstances" exception to the assignment of the husband's domicile and permitted a separate domicile for a wife who was living apart from her husband. *Restatement (Second) of Conflict of Laws* §21(1) (1971).

   Subsequent case law and statutory revisions further liberalized the common-law rule. See *Restatement (Second) of Conflict of Laws* §21 (Supp. 1988) (permitting unmarried and married women, as well as men, to acquire a domicile of choice).

E. Employment

1. **Common-law disability:** At common law, married women's civil disabilities prevented them from being employed in some professions.

   Example: Myra Bradwell, a married woman, seeks admission to the Illinois bar. The Illinois Supreme Court denies her request based on a married woman's common-law disability to enter into contracts. The United States Supreme Court affirms and extends the prohibition to single women as well. A concurring opinion (by Justice Bradley) rests on the ***doctrine of separate spheres*** (women belong in the private sphere of the family, whereas men belong in the public sphere). *Bradwell v. Illinois*, 83 U.S. (16 Wall.) 130 (1873).

2. **Antinepotism (or no-spousal employment) policies:** Antinepotism rules, which were formulated historically to prevent public officials from hiring unqualified relatives, prevent one spouse from being employed by the other spouse's employer.

   These rules often affect married women more than men. This result occurs because women are more likely to be the "last hired" because they enter the labor market later than men (e.g., due to childbearing or the custom of women marrying older men).

   a. **Rationale for policies:** Common rationales in support of antinepotism policies include arguments that employment of spouses in the workplace leads to:

   - increasing incidence of quarrels at work;

   - favoritism;

   - scheduling conflicts (e.g., vacations, holidays); and

   - dual absenteeism.

   b. **Grounds of attack:** Plaintiffs raise both federal and state challenges to antinepotism policies.

   i. **Constitutional challenges:** Antinepotism policies have been challenged as a violation of the ***fundamental right to marry*** under *Loving v. Virginia*, 388 U.S. 1 (1967), and *Zablocki v. Redhail*, 434 U.S. 374 (1978).

      Example: Employees of an electric power company, Jennifer and Keith, get married. When they are terminated because of an antinepotism rule, they allege that the terminations violate their constitutional rights. The court concludes that the employer's policy does not merit strict scrutiny review because it does not place a "direct and substantial" burden on the right of marriage. Based on rational basis review, the court finds that the policy advances a legitimate governmental interest (regarding fostering loyalty and discipline). The court also finds that a fact question existed on the retaliatory discharge claim (thereby precluding summary judgment) regarding whether the termination was a consequence of the employee's speech (his unwillingness to "fully agree" with the employer's rule) protected by the First Amendment and whether the termination therefore was an attempt to chill his First Amendment rights. *Vaughn v. Lawrenceburg Power System*, 269 F.3d 703 (6th Cir. 2001).

   ii. **Title VII:** Title VII of the Civil Rights Act of 1964, 42 U.S.C. §2000e-2(a)(1), may provide another vehicle to attack antinepotism policies. (Title VII prohibits discrimination based on race, color, religion, sex, or national origin.) Because Title VII does not prohibit discrimination based on marital status, most antinepotism challenges under Title VII raise "disparate impact" claims: Although the policies are facially neutral (specifying that "no spouses" may be employed), the policies adversely affect a particular class of employees (women).

      Example: Employers defend disparate impact actions by alleging that antinepotism policies are justified by ***business necessity***. The court invalidated the no-spousal policy under Title VII, reasoning that alleged business necessity did not justify the discriminatory policy. *EEOC v. Rath Packing Co.*, 787 F.2d 318 (8th Cir. 1986).

    iii. State civil rights statutes: Plaintiffs often challenge antinepotism policies based on state civil rights statutes that prohibit discrimination on the basis of marital status. Courts are split as to whether such statutes apply to no-spousal employment policies. Some courts have invalidated such policies based on state civil rights laws. However, other courts narrowly interpret the statutes to bar only discrimination based on marital *status* (i.e., whether a person is single, married, divorced) and not to bar discrimination based on the fact of marriage to a *particular individual* (i.e., another employee).

    iv. Public policy: In states without civil rights statutes, plaintiffs have challenged antinepotism policies based on public policy arguments (but generally without success).

c. Anti-fraternization rules: Some employers have anti-fraternization rules for their employees. Some rules ban all employees from dating co-workers or limit the prohibition to supervisor-subordinate relationships. Other rules ban relationships between employees in the same department, require disclosure of dating relationships to Human Resources, or allow fraternization absent the occurrence of harm in the workplace.

Some employers require that employees execute "love contracts" in which co-workers who are involved in dating relationships affirm that their dating relationship is consensual, acknowledge they have received notice of the employer's policy, and agree to adhere to professional workplace conduct during the relationship and afterwards.

F. Health care

1. Common-law duty to provide medical care: At common law, a spouse had a duty to provide medical attention to the other spouse. This requirement was based on the duty to provide necessaries.

Breach of this spousal duty of care may result in criminal liability, especially if the injured or vulnerable spouse is unable to summon aid.

Example: Husband and Wife spend the day in town drinking. That evening outside the house, in snow that is two to three feet deep, Wife passes out. Husband allows Wife to lie outside unconscious all night, knowing that she is not warmly dressed, even though she was within easy distance of the house and even though he had a hired man who lived with them who could help carry her inside. When they brought Wife into the house the next morning, Husband made no effort to secure medical care for her (she was barely conscious). Court affirms his conviction for manslaughter. The court adds that Husband's drunkenness does not excuse him from the discharge of his duty to his spouse. *Territory v. Manton*, 19 P. 387 (Mont. 1888).

However, case law holds that a spouse does not incur liability for failure to provide medical care *if* the omission is in good faith and at the request of a competent spouse.

Example: Wife requires daily medication to control epilepsy and diabetes. Husband and Wife are "born-again" Christians. After a religious meeting, Wife believes that she is healed and resolves to discontinue medication. When she suffers ensuing seizures, Husband fails to summon aid. He is indicted for criminally negligent homicide. The court holds that because Wife, a competent adult, made a rational decision and exercised her free will to refuse medical assistance, Husband is not criminally liable. *People v. Robbins*, 443 N.Y.S.2d 1016 (App. Div. 1981).

2. **Spousal right to terminate life support:** All states permit a person to express his or her wishes as to medical treatment in case of terminal illness or injury, and to appoint a proxy decisionmaker in the event the person cannot communicate for himself or herself. Depending on the state, these documents are known as "living wills," "medical directives," "health care proxies," or "advance health care directives." Many statutes confer priority upon spouses to serve as designated decision makers if the patient has not designated a preference.

3. **Property rights in spousal remains:** At common law there were no property rights in a dead body. Therefore, the decedent could not make a disposition of his or her body by a will. The prevailing American and English view now confers upon the next of kin (including a spouse) a "quasi-property" right in the disposition of the decedent's body for burial and other dispositive purposes.

Quiz Yourself on
REGULATION OF ROLES AND RESPONSIBILITIES

29. Husband is admitted to the hospital for treatment for the final stages of colon cancer. Wife gives her authorization for Husband's medical treatment, although only Husband promises to pay for all medical services to be rendered to him. Upon Husband's death, the hospital sues Wife for Husband's medical care. The hospital argues that the state's codification of the common-law duty of a husband to provide necessaries is unconstitutional and that liability should extend to the wife based on the modern view of marriage as a partnership. Is Wife liable? _____

30. Stuart Morgan calls 911 and reports that his wife Beth is unconscious. The operator tells Stuart how to start CPR (cardiopulmonary resuscitation). When paramedics and police arrive promptly, they find Beth unconscious on the floor. Stuart maintains that he has done CPR for 20 minutes, but the police notice that Stuart's hair is dripping wet and that the bathtub and shower walls are wet. Beth, who was without oxygen for more than five minutes, is placed on life support but subsequently dies. Bruising on her arms indicates drug use and that Stuart injected her with cocaine. Stuart is charged with, and convicted of, manslaughter. He appeals. Will the conviction be upheld? _____

31. When Debbie and William Jones divorce, they are awarded joint legal custody of their four children. A few months later, one of the children dies. In the midst of a dispute about child support obligations, Debbie files a petition alleging (among other claims) that she should be reimbursed by William for one-half of the medical expenses and burial expenses she had incurred with respect to the deceased child. Will Debbie prevail? _____

32. Mary Smith marries John Jones. After their marriage, they orally agree that Mary shall adopt the hyphenated surname "Mary Smith-Jones." Mary begins to use that surname on all formal and informal documents. However, after the couple marries, John's relatives refuse to recognize Mary as "Mary Smith-Jones," and persist in calling her "Mary Jones." The relatives inform Mary that her common-law name change is invalid. Are they correct? _____

33. J.P. is a transgender man who has been in the process of transitioning from female-to-male for two years. J.P. files a petition to change the name and gender on their birth certificate. The court refuses to accept J.P.'s medical documentation and denies the petition, reasoning that J.P. must have completed gender affirming surgery. On appeal, will J.P. prevail? _____

34. Rhonda and Ronald marry. Rhonda becomes pregnant. Marital difficulties lead to a divorce during which Rhonda is given primary residential custody of James (their unborn child). During the divorce, Rhonda changes her surname to "Acosta," the name of the man she plans to marry soon. Rhonda is pregnant during the divorce proceedings. When James is born, prior to entry of the divorce decree, Rhonda gives him the surname Acosta. During the divorce proceedings, Ronald challenges the refusal of the trial court to change James's surname to Ronald's and argues that custom dictates the father's choice of surname. Will Ronald succeed? _____

35. Lillian and Jack live in a rent-subsidized apartment in New York. They purchase a condo in Florida and divide their time equally between New York and Florida each year. While they are absent from New York, their apartment remains furnished and is not sublet. Jack has a Florida driver's license and has moved his assets there. Lillian, although she has no driver's license because she does not drive, does maintain personal and financial ties to New York. They file federal income tax returns listing Florida as their residence and claim a Florida homestead exemption. They have bank accounts in both states and vote in New York. Their New York landlord seeks to evict them, contending that they have forfeited their rent-subsidized apartment by acquiring a new domicile in Florida. Jack and Lillian respond that Jack's primary residence is in Florida, but Lillian's domicile remains in New York. Will the couple's argument be successful? _____

36. After Sue Smith, who is secretary to the police chief, marries a police officer, Sue is transferred to a clerk typist position in another city department. Her boss claims that he transferred her because he was afraid that her marriage would interfere with her ability to maintain the confidentiality required by his office. What constitutional arguments would you make on Sue's behalf to challenge the transfer? What counterarguments would you expect? _____

37. After Husband is pronounced dead, the hospital asks Wife to make an anatomical gift of his remains. Hospital documents Wife's refusal, based on Husband's previously expressed wishes, in the hospital records. Pursuant to established state procedures, the coroner (who fails to inquire as to the existence of objections and follows standard policy by not inspecting medical records) removes Husband's corneas. Wife institutes a suit for deprivation of property (i.e., her property interest in her husband's corneas) under color of state law, alleging a violation of due process. Will she prevail?

_____

38. Grace and John's three-year relationship is characterized by severe physical abuse. Even after Grace leaves John, he continues to contact her despite her restraining order. Grace believes her life to be in danger. As a result, she seeks to move, change her name, and get a fresh start. To obtain a name change in her jurisdiction, Grace must publish notice of her name change application in a newspaper of general circulation in the county in which she resides. Grace believes the publication of her name change will provide John with her address and new name and thereby jeopardize her safety. As a result, she files a motion to waive the requirement of publication. Will Grace succeed?

_____

_____

Answers

29. Probably. Wife may be held liable for Husband's necessary medical expenses. At common law, the husband had a duty to pay for the wife's necessaries, including medical care. Because of successful constitutional challenges to this doctrine (based on the equal protection doctrine), states now adopt a variety of approaches, either by case law or statute, to avoid this form of gender-based discrimination. Some states have abolished the doctrine; others expand liability to both spouses. The emerging trend is to impose primary liability on the serviced spouse (i.e., to make the creditor seek payment first from the serviced spouse's estate, and, if unable to collect, then from the other spouse). Depending on the approach that this jurisdiction follows, Wife may incur liability. If the jurisdiction follows the emerging trend, the hospital may recover from Wife if the hospital unsuccessfully sought payment from Husband's estate.

30.   Yes. The husband's violation of the duty to provide medical care to his wife and the duty to summon aid for someone he helped place in danger amounted to recklessness. His actions (including his delay in summoning assistance) provided a sufficient basis on which to rest a manslaughter conviction.

31.   Yes. The necessaries doctrine requires that both parents (even divorced parents) are jointly and severally liable for the medical and funeral expenses of their minor children. Although some states have statutes so providing, other states have determined that such a duty exists at common law. On this basis, Debbie has a good argument that William should have to reimburse her for one-half of the deceased child's medical and burial expenses.

32.   No. A person may change his or her name at common law without legal proceedings by adopting another name and using it consistently and absent fraudulent intent. A common-law name change is valid despite the failure or refusal of others to recognize and rely on the new name. The validity of the name change does not require that it be recognized or accepted by anyone other than the person who assumes the new name.

33.   Perhaps, depending on the jurisdiction. Traditionally, completion of gender affirming surgery was necessary before states would alter identification documents. Today, although a few states refuse to allow correction of gender on birth certificates, some states will issue new birth certificates with name and gender changes merely upon proof of adherence to transitioning guidelines.

34.   No. Courts generally resolve parental disputes about children's surnames according to the best-interests-of-the-child standard. In this case, a court would weigh Rhonda's versus Ronald's reasons for the name change. Rhonda would argue that James should take the name "Acosta" because James will be physically present in her home and will bear the same surname as his mother and new stepfather. On the other hand, Ronald would argue that James should have Ronald's surname because Ronald has an interest in the preservation of his parental relationship, which could be weakened if James does not bear his surname. A court might find that the best interests of James dictate that he should be permitted to take the new surname "Acosta." Ronald's concerns might be addressed by having him strengthen the father-child bond in other ways during the exercise of his visitation rights.

35.   Yes. A wife now has the same capacity to acquire a domicile of choice as her husband. A wife's domicile no longer is deemed to be the domicile of the husband. Each spouse may have a separate domicile. Jack may choose Florida as his domicile, and Lillian may choose New York.

36.   Sue would argue that the governmental action burdens her constitutional right to marry. Therefore, she would argue that the policy is subject to strict scrutiny and cannot be shown to be narrowly tailored to serve a compelling government interest. The police chief would counter that the policy did not deny her right to marry and that the transfer was necessary to serve a compelling government interest in the effective functioning of the police department (by preserving confidentiality in such matters as discipline and access to private information).

37.   Yes. Wife has a legitimate claim of entitlement in Husband's remains.

38. Perhaps, depending on the jurisdiction. Grace may be entitled to waive publication if she resides in a state providing that records of a name change may be sealed and any publication waived where there is a threat to safety.

III. PARENTING

The entrance into the workplace of more women with children, as well as the increasing number of women of childbearing age, prompted calls for greater protection of women against employment discrimination. Employment discrimination based on pregnancy is prohibited by law. Pregnancy discrimination affects women of all races and ethnicities, although women of color and immigrants are at particular risk because they are more likely to hold physically demanding and low-wage jobs that present specific challenges for pregnant workers.

A. **Mandatory maternity leave policies:** Many employers' mandatory maternity leave policies formerly required employees to leave their employment when they became pregnant. Plaintiffs challenged these rules on constitutional grounds.

   Example: School board requires pregnant teachers to take maternity leave without pay beginning five months before birth and requires them to wait until their child is three months old before returning to work. Another school district's policy requires their pregnant teachers to give six months' notice and to leave work four months prior to birth. Plaintiffs challenge the policies as violations of due process and equal protection. The U.S. Supreme Court holds that these regulations violate plaintiffs' due process rights by the conclusive presumption that pregnant employees are unable to work. The rationale of administrative convenience fails to justify the constitutional defect. *Cleveland Bd. of Educ. v. LaFleur*, 414 U.S. 632 (1974).

B. **No maternity leave policies:** Some employers provided for disability leave but not pregnancy leave. Plaintiffs unsuccessfully challenged these policies on equal protection grounds and under Title VII. *See Geduldig v. Aiello*, 417 U.S. 484 (1974) (finding that California's state disability plan did not violate equal protection since the exclusion was rationally related to legitimate objective of cost containment); *General Electric v. Gilbert*, 429 U.S. 125 (1976) (finding that private employer's disability insurance plan did not violate Title VII). Dissatisfaction with the Supreme Court's holdings that pregnancy discrimination did not constitute sex discrimination led to enactment of the Pregnancy Discrimination Act.

C. **Pregnancy Discrimination Act**

   1. **Generally:** Congress enacted the Pregnancy Discrimination Act (PDA), 42 U.S.C. §2000e(k), in 1978. The PDA is an amendment to Title VII of the Civil Rights Act of 1964 that prohibits discrimination in employment. The PDA has two prongs:

      ■ it amends the definitional section of Title VII to provide that employment discrimination on the "basis of pregnancy, childbirth and related medical conditions" is sex discrimination for purposes of the Act (thus overruling prior Supreme Court cases); and

      ■ it provides that women affected by pregnancy, childbirth, or related medical conditions shall be treated the same for employment purposes as other persons who are disabled from work.

      Employers with fewer than 15 employees are exempt from the Act.

Note: The PDA does not mandate pregnancy leave. Rather, it is an anti-discrimination rule that requires employers to treat pregnancy *the same as other temporary disabilities* of employees in terms of leave and other employment benefits.

2. **PDA's preemption of state statutes:** Following enactment of the PDA, a question arose as to the effect of the PDA on those state statutes that affirmatively provided for employment-related pregnancy benefits.

   Example: California statute requires employers to provide four months maternity leave and to provide a qualified right to reinstatement (unless business necessity renders employee's former job not available). Bank policy permits employees to take unpaid leaves for pregnancy but does not mandate employee's reinstatement. When receptionist Lillian Garland desires to return to work after her maternity leave, the bank tells her that her job has been filled and that no similar positions are available. She charges the bank with a violation of state statute. Employer defends on the ground that the state statute is invalid because it is preempted by Title VII. The U.S. Supreme Court holds that the California statute is not invalid as preempted by Title VII because it is not inconsistent with the purposes of Title VII. Congress intended PDA to be a "floor" below which maternity benefits could not drop and not a "ceiling" (i.e., a state can provide more expansive benefits if it wishes). *California Federal Savings & Loan Assn. ("Cal. Fed.") v. Guerra*, 479 U.S. 272 (1987).

3. **Discrimination after the PDA:** Despite the PDA, employees continue to report acts of discrimination in the workplace. Such acts sometimes take the form of "family responsibilities discrimination," that is, adverse employment decisions based on caretaking duties (discussed *infra*).

4. **Criticisms of the PDA:** The PDA treats pregnancy as a "disability," rather than as a normal stage of a woman's life. In addition, by mandating employers must provide the *same* benefits for pregnancy as for persons with other disabilities, the PDA permits employers to have *no* policy for pregnancy if they have no policy for disability generally. The PDA has also been criticized for covering only discrimination arising from pregnancy and not addressing other issues necessary to secure equality for women in the workplace, such as adequate child care.

D. **Pregnancy accommodations:** Pregnant employees may need workplace accommodations that enable them to continue working while pregnant. Employees have challenged workplace policies that refuse to accommodate pregnant employees with medical needs despite accommodating workers with other disabilities.

   Example: A pregnant UPS delivery driver requests workplace accommodations after her physician restricts her from lifting more than 20 pounds. UPS denies her request because their policy requires employees to be able to lift 70 pounds. However, UPS provided accommodations to other non-pregnant employees. UPS places Young on leave without pay, and, as a result, she loses her medical benefits. Young files suit, alleging that her employer engaged in pregnancy discrimination in violation of the Pregnancy Discrimination Act (PDA) by refusing to accommodate her pregnancy-related lifting restriction. The Supreme Court holds that failure to accommodate pregnant workers with medical needs, when an employer similarly accommodates non-pregnant employees, violates the PDA when the employer's policies impose a "significant burden" on pregnant workers and the employer has not raised a "sufficiently strong" justification. *Young v. United Parcel Service (UPS)*, 575 U.S. 206 (2015).

E. **Breastfeeding discrimination:** Some employers have workplace policies that impose restrictions on breastfeeding mothers. As a result, many new mothers face the choice between breastfeeding and keeping their jobs. Low-income workers and employees in male-dominated workplaces have the least supportive work environments. Some state and federal protections exist (discussed below).

   1. **Constitutional protection:** An early case, decided before the PDA and the FMLA, held that breastfeeding is protected by the Constitution.

      Example: Janice Dike, a kindergarten teacher, breastfed her infant at work until her employer directs her to stop because of a school board directive against bringing employees' children to work. The school board denies her request to nurse the baby off school grounds. As a result, Dike is compelled to take an unpaid leave of absence. She files suit against the schoolboard, alleging a violation of her constitutional rights. The Fifth Circuit Court of Appeals rules that breastfeeding is entitled to constitutional protection based on the right of privacy and that the trial court erred in dismissing her complaint without trial to determine whether the school board's interests were strong enough to justify the regulations and whether the regulations were sufficiently narrowly drawn. *Dike v. School Board*, 650 F.2d 783 (5th Cir. 1981).

   2. **Protection under the PDA and FMLA:** Breastfeeding discrimination violates the PDA as well as the FMLA. Employers must treat requests for breastfeeding accommodations the same as they treat requests for accommodations from non-pregnant workers.

      Example: Stephanie Hicks is working as a narcotics investigator when she becomes pregnant. She takes the full 12 weeks of FMLA leave, despite her supervisor's urging her to take only 6 weeks leave. On her return, she experiences a toxic workplace: she is written up for minor infractions; is subject to derogatory remarks from her supervisor and colleagues; demoted to patrol duty (resulting in a pay decrease, weekend work, and the loss of her service vehicle); and required to wear a ballistic vest that impedes her ability to breastfeed. After her supervisor denies her request for accommodations to a desk job, she files suit alleging pregnancy discrimination, constructive discharge, FMLA interference, and FMLA retaliation.

      The jury determines that Hicks suffered discrimination in violation of the PDA as well as FMLA interference and FMLA retaliation. The Eleventh Circuit Court of Appeals upholds the jury verdict for pregnancy discrimination, finding that the defamatory language plus temporal proximity of 8 days from her return until her reassignment support her claim of intentional discrimination under the PDA. The court reasons that lactation is a "related medical condition" to pregnancy and therefore is covered under the PDA. The court also holds the defendants liable for constructive discharge under Title VII, finding that the proposed accommodations for breastfeeding (not wearing a vest or wearing one too large) were so inadequate that any reasonable person would have resigned. Finally, the court agrees that Hicks suffered FMLA retaliation when she was reassigned and demoted only 8 days after her return from FMLA leave. *Hicks v. City of Tuscaloosa, Alabama*, 870 F.3d 1253 (11th Cir. 2017).

   3. **Federal protection:** An Affordable Care Act (ACA) provision (Break Time for Nursing Mothers) requires employers to provide employees with reasonable break time to express breast milk for one year after birth in a private place (not a bathroom). Smaller employers (those with fewer than 50 employees) are exempt if the requirements impose undue hardship. 29 U.S.C. §207(r)(1)-(4).

Congress is presently considering the Fairness for Breastfeeding Mothers Act, S. 528, H.R. 866, 116th Cong. (2019-2020), requiring federal buildings to provide a lactation room, other than a bathroom, that is hygienic and available to breastfeeding mothers. The legislation passed the House of Representatives but awaits passage in the Senate.

4. **State protection:** State protections for breastfeeding include exemptions of breastfeeding from public nudity and other criminal statutes, protection of breastfeeding mothers in any public or private location, protection of breastfeeding in civil rights remedies, encouragement or mandating employer accommodation of breastfeeding, and exemptions of breastfeeding women from jury duty.

F. Parental and family leave policies

1. **Generally:** In the 1970s, many persons began advocating for a federal leave policy, claiming that the United States was one of few industrialized countries without such a policy. Some commentators urged that the proposed policy should adopt an "equal treatment" approach (i.e., gender-neutral parental leaves), rather than a "special treatment" approach (i.e., gender-based maternity leaves). At the same time, fathers began demanding that courts recognize fathers' roles in child rearing.

2. **Judicial challenges:** Parents initiated judicial challenges on constitutional grounds to gender-based leave policies.

   Example: Husband and Wife are university teachers. When Wife becomes pregnant, couple agrees that Wife will continue working and Husband will care for Child. Husband requests but is denied a "parental" leave of absence. Such leaves are routinely granted to women. He charges that the denial is a violation of equal protection. The court holds that Husband may have a colorable claim and may proceed to trial (court denies employer's motion for summary judgment). (The case never went to trial because the Board of Education amended its policy to include fathers.) *Danielson v. Bd. of Higher Educ.*, 358 F. Supp. 22 (S.D.N.Y. 1972).

3. **Legislative reform: The Family and Medical Leave Act**

   a. **Generally:** Congress enacted the Family and Medical Leave Act (FMLA), 29 U.S.C. §§2601 et seq., in 1993 to provide job-protected leave to eligible employees for designated reasons. The Act requires that:

   - employers of 50 or more;

   - must provide eligible employees (those who are employed for at least one year);

   - with unpaid leave for up to three months;

   - because of birth, adoption, foster care placement, or to care for a family member with a "serious health condition," or to address the employee's "serious health condition."

   Courts have interpreted the term "serious health condition."

   Example: Caldwell, a single mother, sues her employer, alleging that the latter terminated her employment in violation of the Family and Medical Leave Act after she took time off work in order to care for her three-year-old son who suffered from a serious ear infection. Caldwell's son required constant care for more than three days and he required two postoperative doctor visits. The trial court grants the employer's motion for summary judgment, holding that Caldwell's son did not suffer a "serious health condition" under the FMLA. The appellate court reverses, holding that Caldwell presented sufficient evidence to raise a question of fact as to whether her son's ear infection incapacitated him for more than three days and whether he received subsequent treatment for his condition. *Caldwell v. Holland of Texas, Inc.*, 208 F.3d 671 (8th Cir. 2000).

   b. Criticisms: The FMLA has been criticized for the following reasons, among others:

   ■ FMLA provides only unpaid leave (i.e., many women cannot afford to take unpaid leave);

   ■ FMLA contains a traditional definition of a parent as biological or adoptive and, when enacted, failed to provide adequately for nontraditional family members such as same-sex co-parents;

   ■ FMLA allows employers to contact health care providers to verify information about leaves, thereby raising privacy concerns for employees.

   c. FMLA and same-sex partners: The Department of Labor (DOL) later revised the FMLA definition of "spouse" to include same-sex married parents. Unmarried same-sex parents are covered by a different rule providing for entitlement to the FMLA leave for a person who will "co-parent a same-sex partner's biological child." U.S. Dept. of Labor, Wage & Hour Div., Fact Sheet #28B (July 2015).

G. Work-family conflict and accommodating family needs in the workplace: Employees face issues engendered by the work-family conflict (i.e., workplace problems experienced by employees who struggle to accommodate family needs).

Family responsibilities discrimination (FRD): FRD is a form of discrimination against workers based on their caregiving responsibilities for children, elderly parents, or ill spouses and partners. FRD includes not only pregnancy discrimination and the "maternal wall" that blocks women's advancement when they become mothers, but also discrimination against men who seek to take on a larger family caregiving role for young children, elderly parents, or ill spouses than traditional gender stereotypes of men envision. Examples of FRD include assigning a mother to less important "mommy track" work based on the assumption that she will be less committed to work or retaliating against a male employee who takes time off to care for his elderly parent or ill wife. *See* Joan C. Williams, *Reshaping the Work-Family Debate: Why Men and Class Matter* (2008).

H. State paid leave legislation: A few states (e.g., California, New Jersey, and Washington) offer *paid* family leave programs financed through the use of unemployment insurance programs, temporary disability insurance, or tax incentives.

I. International perspectives: Until the FMLA, the United States was one of two industrialized countries (with South Africa) without national family leave. However, even after the FMLA, other countries provide more generous parental leave policies.

Quiz Yourself on
PARENTING

39. Speedy-Clean, the employer of a small dry cleaning establishment (with 15 employees), has no medical leave policy for pregnancy or other disabilities. Speedy-Clean defends the lack of a policy by arguing that the business is not sufficiently profitable to enable them to provide such a policy. Pauline, a pregnant employee, challenges the employer's lack of a maternity leave policy under the Pregnancy Discrimination Act. Will she prevail? _____

40. Same basic facts as above. Pauline also challenges the employer's lack of a maternity leave policy under the Family and Medical Leave Act. Will she prevail? _____

41. Candice returns to her job in a children's toy manufacturer after her first baby. She decides to breastfeed her baby. Her health insurance covers a state-of-the-art breast pump, and she plans to pump milk during the workday. Upon her return to work, she asks her supervisor where she can pump milk. Her supervisor seems irritated and says that he guesses she would have to go into the bathroom stall or the lunchroom. He gruffly explains that there is no extra space for breast pumping in a factory employing 200 workers. Candice threatens to file a complaint under the Patient Protection and Affordable Care Act (PPACA). Will she be successful? _____

Answers

39. No. Pauline will not be successful on her PDA claim. The PDA requires that employers treat pregnant employees the same as other disabled employees. Because Speedy-Clean has no policy for pregnancy, and has no policy for other disabilities, the employer is treating all employees alike and, therefore, will not be liable.

40. No. Pauline will not be successful on her FMLA claim. The FMLA only requires employers of 50 or more employees to provide unpaid leave. Therefore, the FMLA would not apply to Speedy-Clean, an employer with only 15 employees.

41. Yes. Under the PPACA, all employers must provide a private, non-restroom space for breastfeeding employees to pump for a year after the baby is born. Small employers may obtain a hardship exemption, but Candice's factory employs 200 workers. Her supervisor was clearly wrong in suggesting the bathroom; moreover, a lunchroom for 200 workers could hardly be considered a private space. The factory must find a way to provide Candice with a place to pump that complies with the law.

IV. CRIMINAL LAW AND TORT LAW

In both criminal and tort law, courts and legislatures have abolished many of the special evidentiary privileges for spouses that were mandated by the common law.

A. Crimes involving spouses

1. Testimonial privileges

a. **Common-law rules:** At common law, special evidentiary rules applied to spouses, including the adverse spousal testimonial privilege and the confidential marital communications privilege.

   i. **Rule of spousal disqualification:** At common law, the spouse of a party was not considered a competent witness. A common-law rule of disqualification prevented a spouse from testifying for or against the other spouse in criminal or civil proceedings. The rule was based on the legal fiction of marital unity, the possibility of bias, and the judicial desire to foster harmony and to promote the sanctity of marriage. The rule of spousal disqualification evolved from a rule of absolute disqualification to a rule of privilege.

   ii. **Privacy of marital communications:** The common law recognized the confidential marital communications privilege. Private communications between husband and wife were privileged absolutely. Either spouse could invoke this privilege.

   Today, different rules apply in the federal courts to these two types of marital privileges.

b. **Modern approach to testimonial privileges:**

   i. **Competence:** The majority of jurisdictions now regard a spouse as a competent witness to testify for or against the other in *civil* proceedings. Most states permit the defendant's spouse to testify *for* the defendant in *criminal* cases as well. Jurisdictions are divided, however, concerning *adverse* spousal testimony in *criminal* cases.

   ii. **Adverse spousal testimony—state approaches:** The case of *Trammel v. United States*, 445 U.S. 40 (1980) (discussed *infra*), adopted the rule regarding adverse spousal testimony that is applicable in criminal proceedings in the federal courts.

   Prior to *Trammel*, states adopted one of four approaches:

   ■ some adhered to the common-law rule of disqualification;

   ■ some vested the privilege against adverse spousal testimony in the defendant, or in the husband and wife jointly;

   ■ some states vested the privilege in the witness-spouse; and

   ■ some states abolished the privilege.

   iii. **Confidential communications privilege—modern development:** One state recently abolished the *confidential communications* privilege on policy grounds.

   Example: David Gutierrez killed his first wife's uncle who had raped her several times when she was a teenager. He discloses his commission of the murder to his wife, shows her the body, and threatens to kill her if she ever tells anyone. They divorce and Gutierrez remarries. He also tells his second wife about the murder. More than 13 years after the homicide, a grand jury indicts Gutierrez for the murder. By the time of his trial, Gutierrez is estranged from his second wife. At trial, he invokes the spousal communications privilege to preclude both women from testifying about his role in the killing.

   The state supreme court concludes that the admission of the women's testimony was harmless error (thereby affirming the defendant's first-degree murder conviction). The court reasons that the first wife's testimony was not privileged because she testified as to what she saw (the corpse). Defendant's statements to the second wife were not privileged because defendant was unable to prove that he made the statements during the marriage. (Communications must be made during the marriage to be privileged.) Turning to the issue of the continued vitality of the rule, the court criticizes assumptions underlying the privilege: married people are unaware of it and do not rely on it in deciding to disclose information to their spouses. In addition, the privilege is outdated, perpetuates gender imbalances (i.e., benefiting men more than women), and shields marital violence. The court abrogates the privilege prospectively. The dissent argues that the privilege plays an important role in protecting marital privacy. *State v. Gutierrez*, 2019 WL 4167270 (N.M. 2019).

c. **State exceptions:** In some states, the spousal evidentiary privileges are inapplicable in cases on interpersonal crimes. Several states extend the exception to include cases of child abuse by a spouse. Another common exception is the case of fraudulent (sham) marriages.

d. **Federal approach:** In *Trammel*, the U.S. Supreme Court vested in the witness-spouse the adverse spousal testimonial privilege, allowing a witness-spouse to testify about spousal communications in the presence of third parties. (*Trammel* leaves intact the confidential marital communications privilege.)

Example: Husband and Wife (and two other men) are arrested for importing heroin. Husband is indicted. The indictment also names Wife as an unindicted co-conspirator. Wife agrees to testify against Husband under a grant of immunity and a promise of lenient treatment. Husband asserts the defense of marital privilege to prevent Wife from testifying against him. The district court and court of appeals rule that Wife can testify as to communications made in the presence of third parties, but not as to confidential marital communications. The U.S. Supreme Court affirms, holding that the adverse spousal testimonial privilege (protecting communications made in the presence of third parties) vests in the witness-spouse. That is, if she chooses to give adverse testimony, she may do so. The Court reasons that this modification of the rule furthers the interest in marital harmony without unduly impeding legitimate law enforcement objectives. *Trammel v. United States*, 445 U.S. 40 (1980).

e. **Exceptions to *Trammel*:** Several exceptions exist to the *Trammel* rule.

- if the spouses have jointly participated in the crime;

- if the spouses are permanently separated at the time of the communication; and

- if the underlying offense was committed against a spouse or a child of either spouse (a "familial offense").

Note: *Trammel* is applicable in federal courts. States are free to adopt whatever rule they choose.

2. **Wiretapping:** Federal law (Title III of the Omnibus Crime Control Act, 18 U.S.C. §§2510-2520) provides civil and criminal liability for wiretapping. Many states enacted wiretapping statutes that are similar to the federal statute. According to the majority rule, federal courts may impose liability on spouses for *interspousal* wiretapping under Title III. *See Glazner v. Glazner*, 347 F.3d 1212 (11th Cir. 2003).

Example: Barry and Paula divorce after 40 years of marriage following her discovery of Barry's affairs. When Barry's lawyer asks for proof of Barry's infidelity, her lawyer produces email communications from Barry to several women that were allegedly forwarded to Paula's account. Barry sues Paula and her lawyer, alleging that they violated the federal Wiretap Act through the interception and disclosure of his emails. The court finds that Barry stated a valid claim against his ex-wife. However, the court refuses to find the lawyer liable, reasoning that the lawyer did not "disclose" anything because Barry already knew the contents of the intercepted emails and, further, he invited their disclosure by requesting them in discovery. Finally, Barry did not prove the lawyer's "use" of the emails for the purpose of embarrassing him. The concurring judge (Judge Richard Posner) raises the policy question of whether courts should allow interspousal suits ("so lacking in any social benefit") that permit a spouse to invoke the Wiretap Act to hide evidence of adultery. *Epstein v. Epstein,* 843 F.3d 1147 (7th Cir. 2016), *cert. denied,* 137 S. Ct. 2168 (2017).

3. **Marital rape**

   a. **Common-law rule:** A common-law rule provided for a marital exemption from rape. Under this rule, a married man could not be guilty of raping his wife. The rule is based on the wife's implied consent to intercourse, the idea of the wife as property, the fiction of marital unity, and the doctrine of family privacy (i.e., the judicial reluctance to disturb marital harmony).

   b. **State approaches:** Currently, all states have abolished or limited the exemption either by statute or case law. States that limit the exemption take one of the following approaches:

   - some states preclude the husband's resort to the exemption if the parties are living apart;

   - other states preclude resort to the exemption if one party has initiated legal proceedings; and

   - still other states require that the parties are living apart *and* one party has initiated legal proceedings.

   Several states now make their rape statutes gender neutral. Note, however, that the marital rape exemption is not obsolete.

   c. **Modern trend:** Some states still provide preferential treatment to spousal rapists by making marital rape a lesser, separate offense to rape and/or providing some form of exemption for spouses who sexually assault their partners when the latter are drugged or otherwise incapacitated. Law reform efforts are ongoing to repeal these laws.

   Example: Husband, while separated from Wife because of his intimate partner violence, calls Wife to request to visit Son. Wife agrees to his visit and agrees to return to his motel with the child provided that a friend will be present. At the motel, the friend leaves. Husband forcibly rapes and sodomizes Wife in front of their two-year-old son. Husband, although unable to resort to the marital rape exemption because of the legal separation order, attempts to defend by contending that the exemption violates equal protection.

   Reasoning that no rational basis exists for distinguishing between marital rape and nonmarital rape, the court rules that the marital rape exemption violates equal protection. The court rejects the following rationales for the law: prosecutions will lead to fabricated complaints by vindictive wives, disrupt marital privacy, and impede reconciliation; and marital rape is not as serious as other rapes. Disagreeing that the exemption protects against governmental intrusion in marital privacy, the court reasons that only consensual acts are protected by the privacy doctrine. Although finding that the exemption is unconstitutional, the court does not reverse Husband's conviction. *People v. Liberta*, 474 N.E.2d 567 (N.Y. 1984).

4. **Crimes against spousal property:** At common law, a spouse could not be liable for a criminal act involving the other spouse's property based on the fiction of marital unity (husband and wife constitute a single legal entity). Modern case law rejects this common-law rule.

B.   Tort actions against third parties

1. **Generally:** At common law, the husband had a right to sue a third party in tort for interference with the marital relationship. Each spouse had a legally cognizable interest in *consortium*, i.e., the services, companionship, and affection of the other spouse, as well as the sexual relationship.

   A third party's tortious interference with the husband-wife relationship might precipitate a legal action for:

   ■ alienation of affections, and/or

   ■ criminal conversation.

2. **Modern trend:** Courts and legislatures in the 1930s began abolishing actions for alienation of affections and criminal conversation via anti-heartbalm legislation (sometimes, confusingly, referred to as "heartbalm statutes")—the same legislation that eliminated actions for breach of promise to marry.

3. **Reasons for abolition:** Reasons for abolition include: (1) the modern view that marital dissolution is never solely attributable to a third party's intervention, (2) the excessive awards, (3) the difficulty of assessing damages, (4) the inappropriateness of awarding monetary damages as compensation for dissolution, (5) the lack of deterrent effect, and (6) a reluctance to equate spousal affection with a property right.

4. **Problems posed by abolition:** The abolition of such actions creates problems for plaintiffs who seek to impose civil liability on psychologists and religious officials who engage in sexual misconduct while in the course of marital counseling. Often, such suits must proceed on other grounds (negligence, infliction of emotional distress, etc.).

5. **Specific tort claims**

   a. **Alienation of affections**

      i. **Generally:** At common law, a spouse could bring an action against a third party for alienation of affections for causing damage to the marriage, often resulting in divorce.

      ii. **Elements:** To prevail, a plaintiff must show:

         ■ plaintiff's valid marriage;

         ■ defendant's wrongful conduct with plaintiff's spouse;

         ■ an ensuing loss of consortium; and

         ■ a causal connection between defendant's conduct and plaintiff's loss.

         In assessing damages, a court may consider the quality and duration of the relationship. Further, punitive damages may be awarded if a defendant's conduct is malicious, and the defendant has the ability to pay.

Example: A husband (Ryan Ammarell), who lives with his wife in Alabama, has an affair with Megan France in North Carolina where he owns a business. The affair eventually comes to light when France calls the wife and describes the sexual relationship, in an effort to persuade the wife to leave her husband. Mrs. Ammarell asserts common-law causes of action for alienation of affection and criminal conversation.

The case reveals the elements of these causes of action as well as the status of the tort in the post-*Lawrence* era. The court rejects defendant's defense based on *Lawrence*. The court reasons that the right to private intimate conduct protected in *Lawrence* does not protect France's intimate conduct because the state has a legitimate interest in protecting the institution of marriage and *Lawrence* does not apply where private intimate conduct causes injury to a third party. The court also rejects defendant's First Amendment defense, reasoning that the wife's alienation of affection claim does not infringe on defendant's rights to freedom of speech or association because alienation of affection targets France's actions and not her expression. *Ammarell v. France*, 2018 WL 2843441 (W.D. N.C. 2018).

iii. **Defenses:** Consent of the plaintiff's spouse is not a defense.

Example: Donna Jones and Todd Swanson, former high school sweethearts, meet again after both have married other persons and have families. They have an affair. Donna admits the affair to her husband, Richard, and tells him that she wants a divorce. Richard files suit against Todd for alienation of affections. Richard prevails. Todd appeals, contending that there was insufficient evidence to support the claim, no causal connection existed between the affair and the divorce, and the damages were excessive. The court finds that there was sufficient evidence and a sufficient causal link because Donna still had affection for Richard. The court takes no notice of Todd's claim that Donna was a willing participant, reasoning that the consent of the plaintiff's spouse is irrelevant. Finally, the court rejects Todd's argument that he did not intend to harm Richard, reasoning that intent to harm is not an element of the tort. The court affirms the judgment in favor of Richard but reduces the damages. *Jones v. Swanson*, 341 F.3d 723 (8th Cir. 2003).

iv. **Modern trend:** The modern trend is to abolish the cause of action. Most states have abolished the tort either by statute or case law. Only about six states currently recognize alienation of affections (i.e., Hawaii, North Carolina, Mississippi, New Mexico, South Dakota, and Utah).

v. **Jurisdictional issues:** In states that continue to recognize the action, jurisdictional issues may arise when the alleged acts of sexual misconduct occur *outside* the forum state.

Example: Mary Beth sues her husband's paramour, Tracy, for interfering with Mary Beth's marital relationship with husband, Skip. Defendant moves to dismiss for lack of jurisdiction, alleging that she had insufficient contacts with the forum because she never had sexual relations with the husband *in North Carolina* or did anything to avail herself of the laws and privileges *of North Carolina*. Her contacts with the husband allegedly consisted of numerous telephone conversations and email messages while she resided in Georgia and he resided in North Carolina (although the husband disputes her claim that they never had sex while in North Carolina). The appellate court rules that the exercise of personal jurisdiction over Defendant, based on the aforementioned contacts, does not violate her due process rights, because there was a direct link between Defendant's contacts with the state and the plaintiff's injuries. *Fox v. Gibson*, 626 S.E.2d 841 (N.C. Ct. App. 2006).

b. Criminal conversation

i.   **Generally:** This action was available only to the husband at common law. The rationale was to prevent the husband from having to support illegitimate children. Damages were for the plaintiff's humiliation, loss of reputation, and loss of consortium.

ii. **Elements:** To prevail, a plaintiff had to show:

- proof of a valid marriage; and

- defendant's sexual intercourse with the plaintiff's spouse.

   The law presumed a resultant loss of affection.

   Example: Patricia and Frank are married and have two children. Patricia meets a supervisor in her real estate office. Suspecting that Patricia is having an affair with the supervisor, Frank hires detectives who substantiate Patricia's presence in the supervisor's apartment on two occasions. Frank sues the supervisor for criminal conversation. The supervisor appeals the jury's award of punitive damages ($28,000 actual damages and $270,000 punitive damages). The court finds the defendant liable for criminal conversation (based on the circumstantial evidence), but concludes that the punitive damage award is unsupported by the evidence (i.e., defendant's conduct was not malicious and he did not have sufficient assets to pay such an award). *Albertini v. Veal*, 357 S.E.2d 716 (S.C. Ct. App. 1987).

iii. **Defenses:** Criminal conversation was considered a strict liability offense because the defendant could not defend by showing that the plaintiff's wife consented, nor that the spouses were living apart.

iv. **Alienation of affections distinguished:** Whereas criminal conversation requires evidence of sexual intercourse between the defendant and the plaintiff's spouse, a claim for alienation of affection may be brought without proof of such conduct.

c.   **Policy issue:** Critics contend that the amatory torts are out-of-sync with the sexual attitudes of modern society and question whether the harm caused by adultery is actually alleviated by money damages.

C. Interspousal tort actions

1. Interspousal immunity doctrine

a.   **Historical background:** The common-law doctrine of interspousal immunity, based on the legal fiction of marital unity, barred tort actions between husbands and wives. Thus, a wife could not sue her husband (or vice versa) at common law for either negligence or an intentional tort (assault, etc.).

b.   **Rationale:** Traditional rationales for the interspousal immunity doctrine are that the bar:

- promotes marital harmony;

- prevents involvement of the judiciary in trivial matters;

- prevents the spouses from collusion to defraud insurance companies; and

- prevents double recovery (because the plaintiff-spouse would share any recovery with the wrongdoer).

c. **Reform:** The Married Women's Property Acts in the mid- to late nineteenth century liberalized the rule to permit a wife to sue a husband for torts concerning her property. Gradually, case law and statutory law permitted recovery for negligent torts and, subsequently, for intentional torts. A majority of courts have either abolished or limited the doctrine.

d. **Family exclusion clauses:** Insurance companies have responded to the abolition of the interspousal immunity doctrine by the insertion into policies (i.e., automobile, homeowners') of "family exclusion clauses" that exclude co-resident family members from coverage. Courts are split on whether such clauses violate public policy.

2. **Sexual torts:** Interspousal tort liability also exists for negligent transmission of venereal disease. Whereas some courts formerly barred recovery based on the interspousal tort immunity doctrine, many states now impose liability.

a. **Duty to disclose:** The Restatement of Torts postulates that a spouse has a duty to disclose physical conditions that make cohabitation dangerous. Restatement (Second) of Torts §554 (1977).

b. **Liability for constructive knowledge:** A majority of courts holds that liability for negligent transmission of venereal disease extends to situations in which the defendant has *constructive*, not merely actual, knowledge that he or she is infected.

Example: Wife sues Husband for infecting her with HIV (human immunodeficiency virus), claiming intentional and negligent infliction of emotional distress, fraud, and negligence. An issue arose as to whether spouses have a duty to disclose to each other their HIV-related status. The California Supreme Court holds that, in the balance of the husband's state constitutional right to privacy against the wife's right to discover relevant facts, the husband's medical records and sexual history (extending to six months prior to his negative HIV test) are discoverable. Further, the court holds that liability for negligent transmission of HIV extends to situations when a person had reason to know of the infection (constructive knowledge). *John B. v. Superior Court*, 137 P.3d 153 (Cal. 2006).

c. **Disclosure by third parties:** Courts are reluctant to extend liability to third parties to require them to disclose a family member's exposure to the innocent spouse or sexual partner.

Example: A woman files suit against her fiancé's parents, alleging fraudulent and negligent misrepresentation, for their informing her that their son's medical condition was metal poisoning and Lyme disease when he actually was HIV positive and had been diagnosed with AIDS (Acquired Immunodeficiency Syndrome). The appellate court holds that the parents' failure to disclose is not actionable for negligent misrepresentation because state law prohibits disclosure of HIV testing or status. The court also holds that Plaintiff's reliance was not justifiable because she should have directed her concerns about her own health to medical professionals. The state supreme court affirms. *Doe v. Dilling*, 888 N.E.2d 24 (Ill. 2008).

3. **Intentional infliction of emotional distress:** Several courts recognize the interspousal tort of intentional infliction of emotional distress (IIED) to enable a spouse to recover damages for

acts of extreme cruelty by the other. Such tort claims are generally brought after the termination of the marriage.

Example: Wife brings a post-divorce action against Husband for intentional infliction of emotional distress, alleging that he physically and mentally abused her during and after their marriage. Husband claims Wife failed to allege sufficient facts giving rise to an action for IIEE and further that the statute of limitations has run on the alleged misconduct. The Illinois Supreme Court finds the allegations showed a type of domestic violence extreme enough to be actionable and that Wife sufficiently alleged that she suffered severe emotional distress. Further, the court finds that the "continuing tort rule" applies (explained *infra*). *Feltmeier v. Feltmeier*, 798 N.E.2d 75 (Ill. 2003).

a. **Statute of limitations:** Statutes of limitations may prevent recovery for damages for the tortious acts that occurred early in the marriage because victims sometimes wait years after the occurrence of physical abuse before they file suit. Some courts (such as *Feltmeier*, *supra*) resolve this problem by adoption of the "continuing tort theory"—ruling that domestic violence constitutes a continuing injury (rather than a series of discrete incidents) such that the limitations period does not begin to run until the date of the last injury or the date the tortious acts cease. Therefore, the statute of limitations does not bar the action (or preclude admission of specific abusive acts that occurred early in the relationship) because the course of continuing domestic violence is regarded as a "single act" rather than a series of isolated incidents.

b. **Claim preclusion:** Courts are split regarding whether a battered spouse's claim is barred in a separate post-divorce tort action because of the res judicata effect of the divorce decree.

c. **Joinder:** States also differ in their approach to joinder, i.e., whether the tort claim for IIED must be joined to the spouse's suit for dissolution. A majority of jurisdictions adopt a permissive approach, i.e., permitting but not mandating joinder. *See Chen v. Fisher*, 843 N.E.2d 723, 726 (N.Y. 2005).

4. **Intimate partner violence**

a. **Traditional rule:** At common law, a husband had the privilege of "moderate chastisement" to punish his wife. A wife was barred by the interspousal immunity doctrine from suing her husband for intentional torts (e.g., assault, battery).

b. **Modern state approaches:** The women's movement focused public attention on intimate partner violence and contributed to the formation of legal policy. Currently, all states address domestic violence by statute and case law. Legal policy takes several forms, including (among others):

  ■ civil and criminal remedies against the abuser;

  ■ rules liberalizing the admission of battered woman's syndrome evidence;

  ■ remedies against law enforcement personnel; and

  ■ remedies for children's exposure to domestic violence.

c. **Role of age:** Age plays a role in the law's response to intimate partner violence.

  i. **Teen Dating Violence:** Teenagers as well as the elderly experience intimate partner violence.

Example: A mother files for a protection order on behalf of her 13-year-old daughter against her respondent-boyfriend. Respondent has been in an on-and-off dating relationship with the daughter during which the respondent committed acts of forcible touching and sexual assault. He contends the family court lacks jurisdiction to issue the restraining order because the statute requires that respondent be a "member of the same family or household" as the victim. However, the legislature amended the definition to include "persons who are not related by consanguinity or affinity and who are or have been in an intimate relationship regardless of whether such persons have lived together at any time." The appellate court upholds the family court determination that the couple's intermittent dating relationship qualifies as an intimate relationship within the scope of the statute. *Samantha I. ex rel. Emily K. v. Luis J.*, 997 N.Y.S.2d 510 (2014).

Note: Currently half the states have laws that address teen dating violence by encouraging or requiring schools to teach teen-dating-violence-prevention education.

   ii. **Elder abuse:** All states have laws addressing elder abuse. The most common perpetrators are adult children or spouses. Elder abuse consists of physical abuse, abandonment, psychological abuse, financial abuse, and neglect. Federal law (the Elder Justice Act, enacted as part of the Affordable Care Act (ACA)), serves to "prevent, detect, treat, understand, intervene in and, where appropriate, prosecute elder abuse, neglect and exploitation."

d. **Other influential factors:** Gender, sexual orientation, disability, race and ethnicity, and immigration status all play a role in the law's response to intimate partner violence.

   i. **Gender:** Women are significantly more likely than men to be victims of intimate partner violence, including physical, sexual, psychological, or stalking. Women are also likely to suffer more severe injuries and to be killed by an intimate partner.

   ii. **Sexual orientation:** Intimate partner violence among same-sex couples occurs with the same or greater frequency as among opposite-sex couples. LGBT victims are reluctant to seek help because they fear consequences such as loss of child custody, homophobia, or discrimination. Congress expanded federal protection for LGBT victims in the Violence Against Women Act (VAWA) Reauthorization Act of 2013 by including "sexual orientation" and "gender identity" in the definition of "underserved populations," thereby expanding eligibility for services.

   iii. **Disability:** Women with disabilities face a higher risk of IPV. They also suffer abuse by multiple partners, more severe abuse, more types of abuse, and abuse for longer durations. VAWA 2000 provided for additional funding for services for victims with disabilities.

   iv. **Race and ethnicity:** Domestic violence affects all race and ethnic groups, although Native American women and African-American women are at particularly high risk. Native American women experience IPV largely at the hands of non-Native men. African-American women often hesitate to report abuse because of their fear that disclosure will subject their partners to a racist or violent response from the police.

   v. **Immigration status:** Immigrant women suffer high rates of domestic violence. They face language barriers, social isolation, and the lack of financial resources. Moreover, abusers frequently use their partners' immigration status as a tool to force victims to remain in the relationship.

Congressional concern about abusive marriages involving immigrants led to the creation in VAWA of a "battered spouse waiver" and a "self-petitioning" option to allow abused foreign wives to submit a special petition to immigration authorities for legalization of their residency status without the assistance of their citizen-spouse.

VAWA 2000 created a U-Visa program to enable a victim of crime who cooperates with law enforcement to petition for a temporary visa, provided she suffered "substantial physical or mental abuse" as the result of a designated crime.

Victims of domestic violence face difficulties in applying for asylum. In 2018, U.S. Attorney General Jeffrey Sessions issued a legal decision concluding that domestic violence victims are ineligible for asylum because they do not fit into a "particular social group" for the reason that they are defined by their "vulnerability to private criminal activity." *Matter of A-B-*, 27 I&N Dec. 316 (A.G. 2018).

   e. **High lethality crimes:** Risk factors have been identified that help predict cases in which intimate partner violence is most likely to result in severe physical violence or homicide. High lethality factors include non-fatal strangulation (choking), stalking, forced sex, and threats to kill.

The Danger Assessment Instrument is an important tool that measures a victim's risk of homicide or severe physical violence. Many states require or encourage the police, prosecutors, court personnel, and service providers to use this tool.

Example: Anthony Elonis begins posting violent threatening statements and imagery on his social networking website (Facebook) under the guise of "rap lyrics." He posts a photograph of himself holding a toy knife to a co-worker's neck, captioned "I wish." He also threatens his ex-wife by posting violent material threatening to kill her. After his ex-wife secures a restraining order, Elonis questions (again in a Facebook post) whether the order is "thick enough to stop a bullet." He adds that he has "enough explosives to take care of the State Police and the Sheriff's Department"; threatens to "slit [the] throat" of the FBI agent who visited his home to question him, and threatens to commit a school shooting in a kindergarten class. He is charged with five violations of federal law (the Interstate Communications Act) for transmitting communications in interstate commerce "containing [a] threat . . . to injure the person of another." 18 U.S.C. §875(c). In addition to his threats against his ex-wife, he is charged with threatening a co-worker, law enforcement, an FBI agent, and a kindergarten class.

Elonis contends that his postings are intended to be "therapeutic," and that he did not intend to harm anyone. The Third Circuit Court of Appeals affirms his convictions, holding that section 875(c) requires only that the defendant communicate words that a reasonable person would understand as a threat. The Supreme Court reverses. Although the Court fails to set forth the correct legal standard, the Court holds that the determination of the correct mental state requires more than negligence for a communication to be viewed as a threat. The Supreme Court remands the case to the Third Circuit Court of Appeals to re-try Elonis under the correct legal standard. *Elonis v. United States*, 575 U.S. 723 (2015).

On remand, the Third Circuit Court of Appeals upholds the convictions. *United States v. Elonis*, 841 F.3d 589 (3d Cir. 2016).

   f. **Battered woman's syndrome**

      i. **Admissibility of evidence of battered woman's syndrome:** Courts initially were reluctant to admit evidence of the battered woman's syndrome. The trend is to permit admission of such evidence.

ii. Definition of battered woman's syndrome: The battered woman's syndrome is a theory of behavior, based on the work of psychologist Lenore Walker, that explains the cycle of violence (i.e., abuse occurs within a gradual escalation of tension during a relationship) and the concept of "learned helplessness" (i.e., women stay in an abusive relationship because they become so depressed by the abuse that they lose the motivation to respond).

iii. Rationale for admission of evidence: Expert testimony on the battered woman's syndrome can support a battered woman's claim of self-defense in cases of homicide (i.e., when a battered woman kills her abuser). To rely on the doctrine of self-defense, a defendant must prove that she reasonably feared that she was in imminent danger of serious bodily harm. Evidence of the battered woman's syndrome addresses the reasonableness of the perceptions of imminence and the danger that a woman faces.

iv. Requirements for admissibility of evidence: To admit evidence of the battered woman's syndrome, courts generally require that the evidence be *relevant* to the woman's claim of self-defense and that the evidence meets the *scientific acceptance test*.

Example: Husband, when drunk, frequently assaults wife during seven-year marriage. In the midst of one argument, Wife stabs Husband to death with a pair of scissors. At trial, she claims self-defense stemming from her fear that he was going to kill her. To establish the requisite state of mind for self-defense, Wife calls an expert witness to testify about the battered woman's syndrome. The trial court rules the evidence inadmissible. The appellate court reverses Wife's conviction. The court states that the admissibility of evidence of the battered woman's syndrome depends on (1) whether the evidence is relevant to the defendant's claim of self-defense, and (2) whether the standards for admission of expert testimony (general acceptability in the scientific community) are met. The court concludes that the testimony was relevant to support Wife's testimony that she honestly believed she was in imminent danger of death. However, the court remands for a new trial on the issue of the acceptability of the syndrome evidence in the scientific community. *State v. Kelly*, 478 A.2d 364 (N.J. 1984).

Federal courts (and many state courts) traditionally evaluated the admissibility of novel scientific evidence based on the *Frye* standard (*Frye v. United States*, 293 F. 1013 (D.C. Cir. 1923)), permitting admission of evidence if it has become generally accepted by scientists in the relevant field of study. That standard was replaced by the standard in *Daubert v. Merrell Dow Pharmaceuticals*, 509 U.S. 579 (1993), that adopted Federal Rule of Evidence 702 (holding that evidence may be admitted if it is helpful to the trier of fact and if the methodology is scientifically valid).

Note: Whereas *Daubert* technically applies to the federal courts, many state courts also follow it.

g. Remedies against the batterer: All states have criminal and civil statutes addressing intimate partner violence.

i. Criminal: A batterer may incur criminal liability for assault and/or battery. Historically, police departments were reluctant to treat wife-beating as seriously as other assaults. Legal policy addresses this reluctance by means of case law (i.e., federal civil rights actions against municipalities and police departments, discussed *infra*) as well as statutory law (i.e., statutes that eliminate police discretion by requiring mandatory arrests of batterers).

ii. **Civil:** All states also have legislation providing for civil protective orders (temporary and permanent). Restraining orders restrain a batterer from entering a dwelling or from committing further acts of abuse. Orders of protection also permit awards of temporary child custody, child support, and spousal support.

h. **Remedies against law enforcement for failure to protect battered women**

i. **Federal civil rights action under §1983:** Courts have recognized federal civil rights claims against law enforcement and/or municipalities for the failure to protect battered women. Claims are based on 42 U.S.C. §1983, which imposes liability on governmental officials for deprivation of the victim's constitutional rights (e.g., generally due process and/or equal protection) under color of law (i.e., the official was serving in his/her governmental capacity).

Generally, no right to police protection exists for private acts of violence. However, a cause of action may arise under the "special relationship" requirement or the "state-created danger doctrine."

ii. **Special relationship requirement:** For a limited time, courts applied the "special relationship doctrine" to enable battered women to recover in suits against law enforcement agencies. Under the general rule, a cause of action will not arise for failure to provide a specific individual with police protection (because the police owe a duty to the public at large) unless a "special relationship" exists between the governmental agency and the individual.

To establish a special relationship, the governmental agency must:

- assume an affirmative duty to act on behalf of the injured party;

- have knowledge of the consequences of inaction;

- have direct contact with the injured party; and

- incur the injured party's justifiable reliance on the municipality's affirmative undertaking.

iii. **Limitation on doctrine: *DeShaney v. Winnebago*:** The Supreme Court subsequently limited the "special relationship" exception in a child abuse case that had significant implications for battered women. In *DeShaney v. Winnebago*, 489 U.S. 189 (1989), the Court holds that no special relationship exists between a child protective service agency and an abused child even though the agency was investigating the family and was aware of the continuing abuse. Absent a special relationship, the state has no constitutional duty to protect its citizens against deprivation of life, liberty, or property committed by private individuals. The Court reasons that a special relationship might arise, however, if the agency placed the child in custody or in a worse position than she/he would have occupied in the absence of state intervention.

Courts apply *DeShaney* in the context of spousal abuse to foreclose claims by battered women on *substantive* due process grounds.

iv. **State-created danger doctrine:** The state-created danger doctrine is another exception to *DeShaney*. State actors may be liable under §1983 to protect an individual against private violence if the state officials *created* or *enhanced* the danger of the violence. Case law liberalized the doctrine for some abused spouses.

Example: Michele Okin is physically abused by her boyfriend. Over a 15-month period, police repeatedly respond to her calls for assistance, but they fail to interview or arrest the abuser. At times, they respond to her allegations with sarcasm. Okin brings a §1983 action against the police department and individual officers, alleging that they violated her rights to due process and equal protection by failing to respond to her complaints. The Second Circuit Court of Appeals holds that a genuine issue of material fact existed as to whether police officers implicitly but affirmatively encouraged the abuse, precluding summary judgment with respect to the state-created danger theory. The holding liberalizes the requirement that police must explicitly enhance the danger by permitting an affirmative act to qualify if it merely communicates an implicit sanction of the violence. The court also allows the officials' repeated inaction to suffice to condone the violence. *Okin v. Village of Cornwall-on-Hudson Police Dept.*, 577 F.3d 415 (2d Cir. 2009).

v. **No procedural due process protection:** The Supreme Court later addressed a question left unanswered by *Deshaney*, i.e., whether the state violates *procedural* due process rights by failing to provide police protection in *Town of Castle Rock v. Gonzales*, 545 U.S. 748 (2005). The Supreme Court thereby held that a constitutional claim for failure to protect does not lie under the theory of procedural due process for failure to enforce a restraining order.

Example: Jessica Gonzales alleges that city officials in Castle Rock, Colorado, violated her due process rights and those of her children (pursuant to 42 U.S.C. §1983) by police officers' failure to enforce her restraining order against her former husband, specifically by their failure to respond to her repeated reports over a day's period that her ex-husband had abducted the couple's three daughters. In the early morning hours after the abduction, the father arrived at, and fired on, the police station. In the ensuing gun battle, the police killed the father and later discovered the bodies of the three children in the back of his truck (and concluded that he murdered the children earlier). The U.S. Supreme Court holds that the Due Process Clause does not entitle the mother to recognition of a property interest in the enforcement of her restraining order. The Court reasons that, although the restraining order statute provided that police "shall" use every reasonable means to enforce the restraining order, the language did not make the enforcement of restraining orders mandatory but rather discretionary, essentially because arrest was not always possible or practical; the statute provided for an alternative to immediate enforcement (initiation of an arrest warrant and the right to initiate contempt proceedings), and did not expressly give a protected person a right to demand an arrest. *Town of Castle Rock v. Gonzales*, 545 U.S. 748 (2005).

Epilogue: Jessica Gonzales later successfully alleged that the actions of the police and the decision of the Supreme Court violated her human rights. The Inter-American Commission on Human Rights concluded that the American Declaration of the Rights and Duties of Man (the source of legal obligation for the Commission's member states) imposes an affirmative duty to protect citizens from private acts of domestic violence.

i. **Difficulties for prosecutors:** Problems arise for prosecutors because corroboration of abuse may be difficult (as the violence takes place in private), and victims may not be able to testify (e.g., due to fear, unwillingness, or death). The admissibility of hearsay evidence was restricted by the U.S. Supreme Court in *Crawford v. Washington*, 541 U.S. 36 (2004), a holding with implications for prosecutions of domestic violence.

Example: During investigation of a stabbing, the suspect's wife makes a recorded statement that contradicts her husband's claim of self-defense. At trial, the state seeks to admit her prior out-of-court recorded statement because her testimony was barred at trial by the husband's assertion of the marital privilege. The U.S. Supreme Court reverses the husband's conviction, holding that the use of the wife's statement violated the Confrontation Clause because the Sixth Amendment requires witness unavailability *and* a prior opportunity for cross-examination when prosecutors seek admission of out-of-court testimonial statements.

   i. Implications of *Crawford*: *Crawford* severely limits the opportunity for admission of victims' and witnesses' out-of-court statements if these persons are "unavailable" for trial (e.g., afraid to testify), and if their out-of-court statements are deemed "testimonial" (i.e., made for the purpose of prosecution).

   ii. Meaning of testimonial hearsay: The Supreme Court clarified the meaning of "testimonial hearsay" in two post-*Crawford* domestic violence cases. In *Davis v. Washington*, 547 U.S. 813 (2006), the Court held that statements to 911 operators are not testimonial and therefore admissible because they are elicited to resolve an *ongoing emergency*. However, in the consolidated case of *Hammon v. Indiana,* the Court held that admission of a victim's statement to a responding police officer violates the right to confrontation (absent the opportunity for cross-examination) because the officer was investigating a possible crime.

   iii. Exception to *Crawford*: An exception has developed to the *Crawford* rule that bars the use of "testimonial" statements, as a violation of the Confrontation Clause, in some cases of witness unavailability. The "forfeiture by wrongdoing" exception (based on the public policy of deterring wrongdoing threatening the legal process) holds that a person who obtains the absence of a witness by wrongdoing (for the purpose of preventing the witness from testifying) forfeits the constitutional right to confrontation. In the case of battered spouses, a wrongdoer might make a witness "unavailable" at trial by any number of means, ranging from killing the witness (in an intimate partner homicide) to using coercion to prevent the witness from testifying. *See Giles v. California*, 554 U.S. 353 (2008).

j. Mandatory arrest: Over half of the states require mandatory arrest for misdemeanor domestic-violence offenses. The benefits and detriments of mandatory arrest are contested. Advocates argue that mandatory arrest protects victims effectively by providing immediate relief. Opponents suggest that mandatory arrest may unnecessarily escalate the confrontation, sometimes results in mutual arrests, and often fails to comport with the victim's wishes (to stop the abuse but not to have the abuser arrested).

k. No-drop policies: No-drop policies also dispense with discretion, requiring the state to prosecute batterers even if the victim does not wish to pursue the matter. No-drop policies also present controversial policy issues of ensuring the victim's protection versus diminishing the victim's autonomy.

l. Federal legislative reforms: The federal approach to intimate partner violence consists of the following:

   ■ funding for shelters;

   ■ remedies pursuant to the Violence Against Women Act (VAWA); and

   ■ regulation of firearm possession by perpetrators of domestic violence.

i. Shelters: Federal legislation began providing funding for battered women's shelters in 1984 with the passage of the Family Violence Prevention and Services Act (FVPSA) (Title III of P.L. 98-457). Shelters provide a victim and her children with housing as well as other social services.

ii. Violence Against Women Act: In 1994, Congress enacted the Violence Against Women Act (VAWA), 42 U.S.C. §§14014 et seq. VAWA has several purposes, including: (1) the authorization of grants for purposes of funding battered women's shelters, implementing mandatory arrest policies, and providing education about domestic violence generally; (2) the imposition of federal criminal liability upon an individual who crosses a state line with intent to injure or harass a current or former spouse or intimate partner or to violate a protection order; (3) the provision of full faith and credit for protection orders; and (4) the provision of a federal cause of action for victims of crimes of violence motivated by gender.

Note: In *United States v. Morrison*, 529 U.S. 598 (2000), the Supreme Court held that Congress exceeded its power under the Commerce Clause in authorizing a private cause of action under VAWA for gender-motivated crimes. The Court reasoned that gender-motivated crimes are not analogous to economic activity so as to evoke regulation of interstate commerce. However, some states have similar provisions.

Congress reauthorized VAWA several times, most recently in 2013 with the expansion of protections for LGBT victims of intimate partner violence, prohibition on discrimination based on sexual orientation or gender identity in all VAWA-funded programs, expansion of protections for Native American victims, and an increase in funding for teen dating violence prevention and victim service programs. The VAWA Reauthorization Act of 2020 is pending in Congress.

iii. Firearm restrictions: Federal legislation prohibits firearm possession by any person convicted of a misdemeanor crime of domestic violence (MCDV) or subject to a protective order. Federal firearm regulation of domestic violence misdemeanants was challenged after the U.S. Supreme Court struck down a statutory ban on handguns as a violation of the Second Amendment right to keep firearms for private use in the home. *District of Columbia v. Heller*, 554 U.S. 570 (2008).

Nonetheless, following *Heller*, several courts upheld the constitutionality of federal restrictions on handgun ownership for persons subject to domestic violence restraining orders or those convicted of misdemeanor crimes of domestic violence. *See, e.g., U.S. v. Skoien*, 614 F.3d 638 (7th Cir. 2010). Subsequently, the U.S. Supreme Court expanded the reach of the federal ban on firearm possession by convicted domestic violence misdemeanants by holding that *violent* physical force is *not* a necessary predicate for a state MCDV conviction that would subject the offender to the federal firearm ban. Rather, according to the Supreme Court, the common-law meaning of force (namely, an offensive touching) applies—thereby subjecting a broader category of perpetrators of domestic violence to the federal firearm ban. *U.S. v. Castleman*, 572 U.S. 157 (2014).

m. Children's exposure to intimate partner violence: State laws are increasingly recognizing that children suffer harm resulting from witnessing domestic violence. The law takes three approaches to children's exposure to domestic violence:

■ tort liability for intentional infliction of emotional distress (IIED);

- criminal liability for child endangerment; and

- liability for child maltreatment as a form of child abuse or neglect.

Example: Sharwline Nicholson brings a class action under 42 U.S.C. §1983 against the New York City Administration for Children's Services (ACS), alleging that ACS removed children from mothers who were victims of domestic violence without due process. Plaintiffs allege that this policy constitutes an unlawful interference with parents' constitutionally protected liberty interest in the custody and care of their children. The district court grants a preliminary injunction. The Second Circuit Court of Appeals affirms the finding that ACS's practice of removing children from their home based on parents' failure to prevent their children from witnessing domestic violence amounted to a "policy" of ACS and that in some circumstances these removals raise questions of federal constitutional law. However, the Second Circuit certifies questions to the New York Court of Appeals regarding the scope of the statutes under which the city had acted, particularly the question of whether New York law authorized such a policy and whether the definition of "child neglect" included a parent's exposure of his or her child to domestic violence.

The Court of Appeals determines that in order for a child to be removed from the home due to neglect, there must be proof of actual physical, emotional, or mental impairment to the child, a causal connection between the basis for the neglect petition and the circumstances that produce the child's impairment or imminent danger of impairment, and proof that the parent failed to exercise a minimum degree of care. Evidence that a caretaker allowed a child merely to witness domestic violence is insufficient, without more, to satisfy the statutory definition of "neglect," and also witnessing IPV alone does not give rise to a presumption of such injury. *Nicholson v. Scoppetta*, 820 N.E.2d 840 (2004).

Quiz Yourself on
CRIMINAL LAW AND TORT LAW

42. Donna separates from Cedric. Before their divorce becomes final, Cedric visits their young daughter at Donna's residence. He comes across documents there that indicate that Donna filed the false loan applications for which she is eventually convicted. At the request of the FBI, Cedric agrees to tape a conversation with Donna at which she makes incriminating statements. When the taped conversation is admitted into evidence, Donna objects based on the marital communications privilege. Will her argument be successful? _____

43. Husband is charged with drug offenses. The prosecution wishes to introduce testimony of the Wife regarding statements of the Husband concerning his drug use that were made in the presence of third parties and also statements that were made in private. Wife and Husband are separated but they are in marriage counseling. Wife asserts the privilege against adverse spousal testimony and confidential marital communications. Will she prevail? _____

44. Amy and Tim have a tumultuous relationship. One night, the neighbors call police after hearing a woman scream and loud, pounding noises. When the police arrive, Amy is outside on the porch, visibly beaten, and sobbing. One responding officer begins asking her questions, while the other officer finds Tim pacing inside. Amy explains that Tim started yelling at her when she telephoned a

male coworker. Then she adds that Tim beat her in the face, threw her against the wall, and attempted to strangle her. The police arrest Tim. A few days later, Amy leaves town to visit some relatives in Mexico. At Tim's trial, the prosecutor wants to put the responding police officer on the stand to testify as to what Amy said on the night of the incident. Will the prosecution's strategy succeed?

_____

45. After Katherine and Bill have a child, she tells him that he should quitclaim a half interest in his home to her to protect their child if Bill should die. Trusting Katherine because she is an attorney, Bill quitclaims his interest, only to discover later that she lied about the law. Katherine also opens numerous credit cards by forging Bill's name and makes false allegations that cause him to be investigated for embezzlement. Bill and Katherine divorce. Bill sues Katherine for fraud, breach of fiduciary duty, defamation, and malicious abuse of process. Katherine argues that interspousal immunity bars these claims. Will she prevail? _____

46. Wife and Husband have been married for 20 years and have three children. They have grown apart and sleep in separate bedrooms. When Wife decides to attend art classes at a nearby college, she leases an apartment there to allow her more time to study. She considers this a "trial" separation. She establishes a relationship with Winston, a wealthy insurance salesman, telling him that she is divorced. When Husband discovers the Wife's intimate relationship, he sues Winston for alienation of affections. Is Husband likely to be successful? _____

Answers

42. No. The marital communications privilege applies to communications made between spouses. However, these spouses, although still technically married, were living separate lives with no reasonable expectation of reconciliation, so the court might reason that there was no marital harmony to promote. Further, at least one state has abolished the confidential marital communications privilege on policy grounds.

43. Probably. Because the privilege against adverse spousal testimony vests in the witness spouse (Wife), and the privilege as to confidential marital communications vests in either spouse, Wife will likely prevail as to both assertions to prevent admission of her testimony. Further, although this couple is separated, there is still the possibility of reconciliation so the court might reason that there is marital harmony to protect.

44. No. *Crawford* severely limits the opportunity for admission of victims' out-of-court statements if these persons are "unavailable" for trial, and if their out-of-court statements are deemed "testimonial" (i.e., made for the purpose of prosecution). Amy, who is in Mexico, is unavailable to testify. Although the prosecution will argue that her statements were non-testimonial, as the police were responding to an "ongoing emergency," the court is not likely to agree. Amy was outside on the porch when officers arrived, clearly shaken and scared, but the attack had stopped. Tim was not on the run; he was easily apprehended. The primary purpose of Amy's statements to the police officer was to provide evidence to be used against Tim, not to stop an ongoing crime or emergency. Hence, the responding police officer's testimony regarding Amy's statements will be inadmissible.

45. No. Katherine's claim will be rejected because most jurisdictions have abolished the interspousal immunity doctrine. In addition, the court probably will not be concerned about the policy of preservation of marital harmony because the couple is now divorced.

46. No. To recover for alienation of affections, Husband must prove a valid marriage, defendant's wrongful conduct, an ensuing loss of consortium, and a causal connection between defendant's conduct and plaintiff's loss. Although Husband can prove the validity of the marriage, he will have difficulty establishing the other elements. Winston had no intention to alienate Wife's affections because he believed she was divorced. Husband's loss of consortium, as well as the loss of Wife's affections, predated Winston's relationship with Wife and were not attributable to Winston's actions. Further, most courts have abolished this cause of action because it is based on outdated views of marriage and divorce.

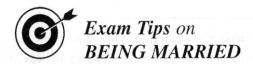

Exam Tips *on* BEING MARRIED

Regulation of Roles and Responsibilities

☞ **Identifying the marital role or responsibility at issue:** First, determine the nature of the controversy: support, names, employment, health care, or parenting. Does the issue involve civil or criminal law?

☞ **Duty of support:** Determine if the question involves support rights and obligations *during* marriage. If so, you will need to discuss the *family privacy doctrine*, i.e., the common-law doctrine of nonintervention in an ongoing marriage.

　　☞ Check if the disputed item involves *necessaries*. Define necessaries. If necessaries are at issue, you will need to discuss the common-law necessaries doctrine. Determine *who* is initiating the suit—a spouse or third party (such as a creditor)—and on whose behalf (spouse, child).

　　☞ Be on the lookout for any *constitutional issues* (gender-based obligations that might violate equal protection doctrine). Be sure to discuss modern responses to equal protection problems (i.e., expansion of liability, or the imposition of primary liability on the serviced spouse and secondarily, from the other spouse).

☞ **Names:** Identify the naming dispute. Does it involve a *married woman's name* or a dispute over a *child's surname*? Clarify *who* is initiating suit (i.e., a married woman, a governmental entity, the other parent of a child). Determine whether the suit involves *retention* or *resumption* of a surname or the *adoption of a new surname*. Discuss the two *methods* of name change (common-law and statutory). If the question involves a divorced woman, discuss the special statutes that authorize divorced women to restore their former surnames.

　　☞ If the dispute concerns a child's surname, discuss the *prevailing standard* to resolve the dispute (the best interests of the child). Take into account all relevant factors in determining which surname would be in the child's best interests. **Tip**: Be sure to look for any *constitutional challenges* to naming restrictions, such as the right of the state to restrict parental choice in children's surname selection. Discuss the judicial views on whether parents have a *fundamental right* of privacy to confer a surname on a child and discuss *equal protection* issues in cases favoring one parent's right to name a child.

☞ **Domicile:** Be sure to look for any "lurking" issues regarding the domicile of the parties. If the question involves the domicile of a married woman, explain the *common-law* rule, the *Restatement*

(Second) of Conflict of Laws view, the *Restatement (Third) of Conflict of Laws* view, and the *modern view* that permits either a husband or wife to acquire a domicile of choice.

☛ **Employment:** Look for issues of a *married woman's common-law disability* and *antinepotism policies*. If you spot an issue regarding an antinepotism policy, be sure to explain the nature of the policy (does it prevent one spouse from being employed by the other spouse's employer, or is it broader and prevents employment of any "relative"?). Identify the *business rationale* for such policies. Be sure to determine if the common business rationale is applicable to the facts at hand.

☞ If an antinepotism policy is being challenged, discuss all possible grounds of attack: *federal* (constitutional and Title VII) and *state*. In terms of federal constitutional issues, be sure to discuss the *fundamental right to marry*. For *Title VII*, be sure to explain that Title VII does not prohibit discrimination based on marital status; therefore, plaintiffs must raise claims under "disparate impact" analysis. In the latter cases, discuss the usual employers' defense of business necessity. For state issues, be sure to discuss *state civil rights statutes* prohibiting discrimination on the basis of marital status. Mention the *split of opinion* as to whether such statutes apply to no-spousal employment policies: Some states apply such statutes but other states narrowly interpret the statutes to bar only discrimination based on the status of being single, married, or divorced (and not to bar discrimination based on marriage to a particular individual).

☛ **Health care:** Determine if there is an issue regarding the *duty to provide medical care to a spouse* or if the issue concerns the *termination of life support* (by a spouse or other family member). If the former, discuss the spouse's *common-law duty* to provide medical care to the other. Determine if the injured spouse requested the other spouse not to provide care (because in such cases, the latter does not incur liability for the failure to provide care). If the issue is the termination of life support, discuss the applicability of state *advance directives*.

☛ **Parenting:** The primary issues here concern *parental and family leave policies* (including pregnancy accommodations and breastfeeding discrimination) and the *work-family conflict*.

☞ Be sure to check for the applicability of federal legislation (Pregnancy Discrimination Act, the Family and Medical Leave Act, Title VII). Recall that the PDA does not provide affirmative protection for pregnant women, but only guarantees equal treatment between pregnant women and other disabled workers. Recall, too, that the FMLA has its limitations, such as unpaid leave and its application to employers of 50 or more employees.

☛ **Criminal and tort law:** Identify whether the question concerns issues of criminal and/or tort law. For crimes involving spouses, look for issues of *testimonial privileges*, *wiretapping*, *marital rape*, and *property offenses*.

☞ If the question involves testimonial privileges, be sure to mention that *two* possible privileges exist (confidential marital communications and spousal communications made in the presence of third parties).

☞ Identify which privilege is at issue because different rules apply. Discuss the impact of the U.S. Supreme Court's *Trammel decision* on the privilege regarding spousal communications in the presence of third parties (leaving intact the confidential marital communications privilege). Remember that *Trammel* applies to criminal proceedings in federal courts (although the case has influenced state court proceedings).

☞ If the question involves wiretapping, be sure to point out the *source of wiretapping liability* (Title III of the Omnibus Crime Control Act) that provides for civil and criminal liability. Note the *modern trend* in federal courts to impose liability for spousal wiretapping.

☞ If the question involves a ***victim's prior out-of-court statement***, be sure to discuss the Sixth Amendment guarantee of confrontation, the *Crawford* case, rules about the primary purpose of the police response to violence (to address an "ongoing emergency" or to collect evidence for a prosecution), the implications for the admissibility of the victim's statement (i.e., testimonial hearsay), and the forfeiture-by-wrongdoing doctrine (holding that one who obtains the absence of a witness by wrongdoing, in order to prevent the witness from testifying, forfeits his or her constitutional right to confrontation).

☞ Determine whether the question involves marital rape. Explain the ***marital rape exemption*** (exempting husbands from the crime of rape of their wives). Discuss the ***transition*** from the common-law rule to the modern trend (to abolish or limit the exemption). Point out that the marital rape exemption is not defunct.

☛ **Tort issues:** Identify all possible tort issues. Are there tort actions against ***third parties*** or ***interspousal*** actions? If the claims are against third parties, are there legal actions for ***alienation of affections***, ***criminal conversation***, and/or ***loss of consortium***? Be sure to discuss the ***elements*** of each claim and determine if they apply to the facts. Explore whether the defendant has defenses. Be sure to point out the difference between criminal conversation and alienation of affections (the former requires that the defendant have sexual intercourse with the plaintiff's spouse). For loss of consortium, determine the time of the injury. Be sure that it occurred during the marriage (i.e., there may be problems with recovery if the injuries occurred pre- or post-marriage).

☞ If the action is an interspousal tort claim, determine whether the interspousal immunity doctrine applies. Be sure to explain the doctrine (as barring tort actions between husbands and wives) and its rationale.

☛ **Domestic violence:** Determine if the claims involve ***civil*** and/or ***criminal*** actions. Explain the ***common-law privilege*** of moderate chastisement and point out the ***family privacy*** doctrine that led to a policy of judicial nonintervention in an ongoing marriage.

☞ If there is an issue of a battered wife who killed her husband, be sure to discuss the admissibility of evidence of ***battered woman's syndrome***. Define the syndrome and discuss the rationale for the admission of such evidence. Discuss the requirements for admissibility. Mention the ***different standards*** for admissibility of novel scientific evidence (***Frye, Daubert***).

☛ Determine whether the plaintiff is seeking remedies against the ***batterer*** or against a ***governmental entity*** (i.e., for failure to protect battered women). If the latter, examine whether the victim can make a claim of the special relationship requirement (that the police owe victim a duty because a special relationship exists such as caused by their knowledge of a protection order) or the state-created danger doctrine (that the state has an affirmative duty to act if the state creates or enhances the danger to the individual from private violence).

☞ Be sure to mention the limitation on the special relationship doctrine of ***DeShaney v. Winnebago*** and the liberalization of the state-created danger rule by *Okin v. Village of Cornwall-on-Hudson Police Dept.*

Examine the question for the existence of possible *federal* issues regarding VAWA or firearms restrictions. If the issue involves VAWA, determine whether the claim involves the VAWA provision regarding the private cause of action for victims of gender-motivated crimes that the Supreme Court declared unconstitutional in ***Morrison***. If the question raises ***firearms restrictions*** on abusers, be sure to discuss the constitutionality of the restriction under *Heller* as well as the ban on firearm possession by persons who are convicted of domestic violence misdemeanors (*Skoien, Castleman*).

CHAPTER 4

NONTRADITIONAL FAMILIES

ChapterScope ———————————————————————————————

This chapter addresses the legal regulation of nontraditional family forms, as well as the changing legal meaning of the term "family." Here are a few of the key principles covered in this chapter:

- **Traditional definition of the family:** The traditional definition of the family was limited to relationships based on a *ceremonially initiated marriage, consanguinity,* and/ or *adoption*.

- **Modern definition:** With the decline of the traditional nuclear family, many people now reside in *nontraditional* family forms, such as *cohabitation, same-sex relationships, multi-parent families*, and *extended families*.

- **Same-sex marriage:** Same-sex marriage is valid in all jurisdictions. In addition, a few states have domestic partnerships or civil unions that confer a range of legal protections on same-sex unmarried partners and, sometimes, opposite-sex unmarried partners.

- **Extended families:** The Supreme Court has held that the constitutional right to *family privacy* applies to extended families (i.e., those based on blood relationships that extend beyond the traditional nuclear family) and enables them to live together.

- **Communal families:** The Supreme Court has held that communal families (of unrelated persons) have *no fundamental constitutional right to association or privacy*.

- **Unmarried couples:** The traditional legal response to unmarried couples (opposite-sex and same-sex) was *punitive*, based on the state's desire to uphold moral standards. Today, the Supreme Court has held that the constitutional *right to privacy* protects the individual against state interference in private sexual conduct between consenting adults (*Lawrence v. Texas*).

- **Unmarried cohabitants:** According to the majority rule, unmarried cohabitants *may enter into express agreements*. In addition, some courts recognize both express and implied agreements between these partners.

- In *tort law*, however, *courts are divided* about permitting cohabitants the same legal rights as traditional family members.

- In many states, cohabitants still face discrimination in some legal contexts, such as housing and inheritance.

- The U.S. Supreme Court recently ruled that employment discrimination based on sexual orientation and gender identity violates Title VII of the Civil Rights Act of 1964.

I. INTRODUCTION

    A. Background: The traditional nuclear family, consisting of a husband and wife and their co-resident children, is on the decline. Currently, only one in five families fits the traditional model. The decline is attributable, in part, to the rising incidence of divorce, a change in sexual mores (i.e., the decreasing stigma of sexual relations outside marriage), and widespread disillusionment with the institutions of marriage and the family.

B. Types of nontraditional families: Many people now reside in nontraditional families. Such families include quasi-marital relationships (such as opposite-sex and same-sex cohabitants), multi-parent families, communal arrangements, and extended families. The growth of nontraditional families stems, in part, from the fact that fewer Americans are getting married. Over the past four decades, the annual number of marriages has decreased by more than 50 percent.

C. Legal recognition: The law confers legal recognition on some nontraditional families for some purposes. This chapter explores the extent to which the legal system treats members of nontraditional families similarly to, or differently from, members of traditional family units. The chapter, thereby, sheds light on just what is meant, in legal policy, by the term "family."

II. FUNCTIONAL DEFINITION OF FAMILIES

A. Formal versus functional: The *formal* definition characterizes a "family" according to blood ties or legal ceremony (such as marriage or adoption). In contrast, the *functional* approach defines a family by virtue of its functions.

Example: Plaintiffs (households of unrelated individuals) challenge a provision of the federal Food Stamp Act. Jacinta Moreno, a 56-year-old diabetic, resides and shares expenses with Ermina Sanchez and the latter's three children. Sanchez, who is on public assistance, also helps care for Moreno. Sheilah Hejny, a married woman with three children, took in a 20-year-old girl with emotional problems in order to care for her. Victoria Keppler, whose daughter attends a school for the deaf, shares her apartment with another woman on public assistance in order to be able to afford to live near her daughter's school. At issue is the constitutionality of Food Stamp Act §3(e), providing food stamp benefits, that defines an eligible "household" as a group of *related individuals*, living as one economic unit sharing cooking facilities, and purchasing food in common. Plaintiffs allege they have been or will be excluded even though they satisfy eligibility requirements. They seek declaratory and injunctive relief, arguing that the "unrelated person" provision violates their rights to equal protection and due process. Based on rational basis review, the Supreme Court holds the legislation unconstitutional. Although finding that minimization of fraud is a legitimate interest, the Court concludes that the restriction to related persons is not rationally related to this objective. The Court scoffs at the government's contentions that households of unrelated persons are more likely to fraudulently report income and make detection of abuse more difficult. The majority explains why a morality-based rationale cannot justify the restriction.

Concurring, Justice Douglas would require higher scrutiny because the provision burdens association. He analogizes the act of welcoming persons into the home (because of poverty or to "bring[] happiness to the household") to such other "peripheral First Amendment rights" as sending a child to religious school and the marital right of privacy. He points out that this provision penalizes "the poorest of the poor" who band together against adversity. Dissenting, Justice Rehnquist argues that Congress might reasonably conclude that the restriction ensures the existence of a household for some purpose other than to collect food stamps. *U.S. Dept. of Agriculture v. Moreno*, 413 U.S. 528 (1973).

Note: Commentators have long criticized *Moreno* for its unwillingness to address the degree to which the Constitution protects the rights of persons to choose with whom to share a home.

B. Legal protection: Formal families created through biology and legal ceremonies are granted automatic protections under the law, such as protection against housing discrimination and recognition of custody rights of the parents. Unmarried partners (whether same-sex partners or opposite-sex partners) lack these automatic legal protections. The extent of their protection often depends on the legal context (contract, tort, inheritance, etc.).

III. EXTENDED FAMILIES

A. Nature of the constitutional protection for the extended family: To a limited extent, the Constitution protects the freedom of family members to choose to live together as an *extended family*. An extended family consists of those members who are related to each other more remotely than the parent-child dyad (e.g., grandparents, aunts, and uncles).

Example: Mrs. Moore (Plaintiff) lives with her son (Dale Sr.) and two grandsons (Dale Jr. and John Moore Jr.). The grandsons are cousins rather than brothers (one grandson is Dale Sr.'s child, the other grandson is Plaintiff's son John's child). A city housing ordinance limits occupancy of a dwelling to members of a "single family." As defined, the term fails to include Plaintiff's extended family. Specifically, the ordinance permits a head of household to live with one dependent child and that child's dependent children (i.e., it would have permitted Mrs. Moore to live with Dale Sr. plus Dale Sr.'s child but not with her other son's child). The city informs Plaintiff that she is violating the ordinance. When she refuses to comply, she is charged with a criminal offense. She argues that the ordinance violates her right to due process. The U.S. Supreme Court concurs, reasoning that the ordinance fails to serve the stated governmental interests (i.e., prevention of overcrowding, minimizing traffic and parking congestion, and avoiding an undue financial burden on the school system). Reasoning that the tradition of the extended family is rooted in history, the Court concludes that the extended family is equally deserving of constitutional protection as the traditional family. *Moore v. East Cleveland*, 431 U.S. 494 (1977).

Criticism: Some commentators argue that the plurality in *Moore* erased race from the analysis by failing to consider the straightforward purpose of the ordinance: to exclude from a middle-class, predominantly black community (that saw itself as socially and economically upwardly mobile) other black families characteristic of a lower-class lifestyle. The Court thereby refused to honor the community's desire to preserve its middle-class identity.

B. Scope of the constitutional protection for the extended family: Although the Constitution provides some protection to the extended family from state interference, it does not require a state to provide *governmental benefits* to assist members of extended families to maintain a residence together. *See, e.g., Lipscomb v. Simmons*, 962 F.2d 1374, 1378 (9th Cir. 1992) (upholding constitutionality of state-funded foster care benefits to nonrelatives but not relatives).

IV. COMMUNAL FAMILY

A. Federal protection (or lack thereof) for the communal family: In contrast to the legal recognition accorded to the extended family for zoning purposes, the Supreme Court refuses to provide similar protection to the communal family. Courts have consistently applied rational basis review to uphold zoning provisions that limit the number of unrelated individuals residing in single-family dwellings.

Example: Six unrelated students at Stony Brook rent a house together in the village of Belle Terre on Long Island. A village ordinance restricts land use to "single family" dwellings and defines single family as "persons related by blood, adoption or marriage, living and cooking together as a single housekeeping unit," and prohibits more than two unrelated persons to reside together. A communal resident challenges the constitutionality of the zoning ordinance as an interference on the right to travel and the freedom of association. The U.S. Supreme Court upholds the constitutionality of the statute, maintaining that it does not interfere with the right to travel or with any fundamental right. The Court reasons that the statute bears a rational relationship to the permissible state objectives of limiting congestion and noise as well as promoting family values. *Village of Belle Terre v. Boraas*, 416 U.S. 1 (1974).

B. State protection for the communal family

1. **Generally:** Communal families have received more favorable treatment in zoning challenges based on state, rather than federal, constitutional law.

   Example: A group of 12 adults rent a ten-bedroom, six-bath house on a one-acre lot in Santa Barbara owned by Ms. Adamson (who also resides in the house). The occupants include a business woman, graduate biochemistry student, real estate broker, lawyer, and others. The city brings an action to enforce a municipal zoning ordinance that restricts the number of unrelated individuals (i.e., unrelated by blood, marriage, or adoption) who may live in single-family zones to "a group . . . not to exceed five persons . . . living together as a single housekeeping unit." The court grants the city a preliminary injunction and restraining order. Three residents of the house appeal, arguing that they regard their group as "a family" and that they consist of "a single housekeeping unit" because they share expenses, rotate chores, and eat evening meals together. The California Supreme Court holds that unrelated persons have a constitutional right (based on the state constitution's right of privacy) to live with others who are not related by blood, marriage, or adoption. The court finds that the city failed to demonstrate that a compelling state interest justifies its restriction on communal living (i.e., reasoning that the assumption that groups of unrelated persons cause an immoral environment for families with children is not legitimate). *City of Santa Barbara v. Adamson*, 610 P.2d 436 (Cal. 1980).

2. **Requirement: Familial-like:** In order to merit legal recognition in some jurisdictions, communal families must evidence certain familial-like criteria. However, courts differ as to the importance they attach to the various criteria that qualify a group as a "single family." This approach leads to inconsistent legal treatment.

   Example: Ten unrelated state college students rent a house together in the Borough of Glassboro. The town's zoning ordinance limits the occupancy of residences to families, defined as: "one or more persons occupying a dwelling unit as a single non-profit housekeeping unit, who are living together as a stable and permanent living unit, being a traditional family unit or the functional equivalency thereof." When the town seeks an injunction against the students' use and occupancy of the house, the students challenge the ordinance. The New Jersey Supreme Court declines to consider the constitutional issues, but affirms the factual finding that the students' occupancy constitutes a single housekeeping unit because they eat together, share household chores, pay expenses from a common fund, and plan to remain together for three years (thereby satisfying the requirement of a "stable and permanent living unit"). The court adds that the purpose of noise regulation and regulation of socially disruptive behavior can be achieved by other means than land use restrictions. *Borough of Glassboro v. Vallorosi*, 568 A.2d 888 (N.J. 1990).

Example: A nonprofit corporation negotiates the purchase of a house in Brewer, Maine, to serve as a group home for the mentally disabled and a few employees. The city's zoning ordinance restricts single-family residential uses to "a collective body of persons doing their own cooking and living together . . . as a separate housekeeping unit . . . based upon birth, marriage or other domestic bond as distinguished from a group occupying a boarding house, lodging house, club, fraternity or hotel." The nonprofit corporation appeals the denial of an occupancy permit based on the group's failure to qualify as a single-family use, contending that the purpose of the group home is to create a family environment for the residents. The court holds that the denial of the occupancy permit was appropriate because the group home lacks certain familial-like qualities. Specifically, the facility employs rotating staff, thereby lacking any permanent residential authority figure analogous to a parent or parents. The average stay of residents is short, thereby failing to demonstrate cohesiveness and permanence. Finally, the staff, rather than residents, is responsible for meal preparation and the operation of the household. As a result, the court reasons that the facility is more like a club, boarding house, or fraternity rather than a traditional family. *Penobscot Area Housing Dev. Corp. v. City of Brewer*, 434 A.2d 14 (Me. 1981).

V. UNMARRIED COHABITANTS (OPPOSITE-SEX AND SAME-SEX COUPLES)

State courts also regulate the relationships between cohabitants, between cohabitants and third parties, and between cohabitants and the state. The legal treatment accorded these family members often depends on the purpose for which, or the context in which, their families are being regulated. In short, the law confers recognition on some nontraditional families but not others, and on these families for some purposes but not others.

A. Criminal sanctions for sexual conduct: Traditional response: Traditionally, the law regarded with disfavor unmarried couples who were living together. The traditional legal response was the imposition of criminal sanctions for such "misconduct" in the form of penalties for fornication and cohabitation.

B. Zoning: Zoning ordinances and the First Amendment: Some state courts extend the Supreme Court's refusal to recognize communal families by the denial of constitutional protection to unmarried couples for zoning purposes. *See, e.g., City of Ladue v. Horn*, 720 S.W.2d 745 (Mo. Ct. App. 1986). However, *Lawrence v. Texas* casts doubt on that holding.

C. Housing: States have made much progress in terms of remedying housing discrimination against unmarried couples (opposite-sex and same-sex couples).

   1. Occupancy rights to a rent-controlled apartment: In a landmark decision, New York recognized the rights of gay partners to be free from housing discrimination. In reaching its holding, the New York court of appeals adopted a broad functional definition of family.

   Example: Miguel Braschi resides with his gay partner, Leslie Blanchard, in a rent-controlled New York City apartment for 11 years. Following Blanchard's death, the building owner notifies Braschi that because Blanchard was the tenant of record, Braschi must vacate the apartment. New York City Rent and Eviction Regulations provide protection from eviction to either the "surviving spouse of the deceased tenant or some other member of the deceased tenant's family." Braschi seeks to enjoin the owner from evicting him. Although the term "family" is not defined by the code, Braschi maintains that he qualifies as a member of Blanchard's family within the meaning of the regulations. The court declares that the term "family," as used in the rent-control laws, should not be limited to marital or adoptive relationships. Legal protection against sudden eviction should "find its foundation in the reality of family life." Courts should determine entitlement based on an examination of the parties' relationship, including (but not limited to):

- the exclusivity and longevity of that relationship;
- the level of emotional and financial commitment;
- the manner in which the parties conduct their lives and hold themselves out; and
- the reliance the parties place on each other for daily family services.

The court finds that Braschi demonstrated a likelihood of success on the merits because of the parties' lengthy relationship, their recognition by family and friends as spouses, and their emotional and financial commitment to each other. *Braschi v. Stahl Assocs.*, 543 N.E.2d 49 (N.Y. Ct. App. 1989).

Note: LGBT advocates speculate that the recent U.S. Supreme Court case of *Bostock v. Clayton County* (discussed *infra*) might lead to abrogation of housing discrimination against LGBT people under federal and state statutes.

2. **Occupancy rights under the Fair Housing Act (FHA):** Landlords sometimes refuse to rent to an individual on the basis of sex, sexual orientation, or familial status. Under the FHA, the term "familial status" signfies protection against discrimination for families involving one or more individuals (who have not attained the age of 18 years) who are domiciled with (1) a parent or another person having legal custody of such individual or individuals; or who are domiciled with (2) the designee of such parent or other person having such custody, with the written permission of such parent or other person. 42 U.S.C. §3602(k).

Example: Deepika Avanti refuses to rent her townhouse to the Smith family, consisting of a married couple (Tonya Smith and her spouse, Rachel Smith, who is a transgender woman) and their two children. Avanti informs Tonya of the housing denial in an email, saying that the Smiths are not welcome because of neighbors' concerns about their children and "noise" and because Avanti does not want the notoriety that would stem from renting to them because of the Smiths' "unique relationship." The Smiths file suit in federal district court, claiming that the defendant violated two provisions of the federal Fair Housing Act as well as the Colorado Anti-Discrimination Act (refusal to rent based on "sex" as well as "family status," and making statements indicating such discrimination). The court expands protection against housing discrimination to those who do not conform to sex stereotypes (but not to same-sex couples facing discrimination based solely on sexual orientation or gender identity). *Smith* is a landmark case for its interpretation of Title VII as encompassing gender identity or expression, as well as sexual orientation, provided that the housing provider employed sex stereotyping in the adverse housing decision. *Smith v. Avanti*, 249 F. Supp. 3d 1194 (D. Colo. 2017).

Note: In 2020, the United States Supreme Court determined that employers who fire employees based on their sexual orientation or gender identity violate Title VII of the Civil Rights Act of 1964. *See Bostock v. Clayton Cty., Georgia*, 140 S. Ct. 1731 (U.S. 2020). Commentators speculate that the holding regarding employment discrimination might be extended eventually to ban housing discrimination based on sexual orientation and gender identity because Title

VII employment cases often provide guidance in decisions involving housing discrimination under the FHA.

3. **Occupancy rights under state nondiscrimination statutes in the face of a landlord's First Amendment claims:** Landlords sometimes refuse to rent to unmarried couples, alleging that such rentals would violate landlords' *religious* beliefs. Many courts refuse to recognize an exemption for landlords from state nondiscrimination statutes on this basis.

Example: A landlord refuses to rent an apartment to an unmarried couple on the basis that she would be committing a sin by renting to persons who would be engaging in nonmarital sex. The state fair housing agency rules that the landlord is discriminating against prospective tenants on the basis of marital status, in violation of state housing law. The landlord appeals. The state supreme court affirms the state agency's decision that the landlord's refusal to rent to the unmarried couple violated the state fair housing law and also rules that the federal Religious Freedom Restoration Act does not exempt the landlord from the application of the state anti-discrimination statute. *Smith v. Fair Employment & Hous. Comm'n.*, 913 P.2d 909 (Cal. 1996). *But cf. North Dakota Fair Housing Council v. Peterson*, 625 N.W.2d 551 (N.D. 2001).

D. **Tort law:** States are divided about recognition of the legal rights of cohabitants in the tort context. Some jurisdictions permit cohabitants to recover in tort for injuries to each other by third parties, whereas other jurisdictions refuse to do so. In the latter jurisdictions, an unmarried partner does not have a claim either for loss of consortium or for negligent infliction of emotional distress (NIED) arising from an injury by a third party to the other partner.

Example: Catrina Graves has been living with Brett Ennis for seven years. The couple is engaged to marry. One day, Brett is riding his motorcycle while Graves is following behind in a car. Defendant Frank Estabrook fails to yield at a stop sign, colliding with Brett's motorcycle. Catrina views the accident and runs to Brett's aid. She stays by his side while he is being treated. Brett dies the next day. Catrina sues Defendant for negligent infliction of emotional distress. The New Hampshire Supreme Court recognizes her claim because plaintiff was a bystander who witnessed the accident and also because she was engaged in a stable, enduring, substantial, and mutually supportive relationship with the cohabitant-victim. *Graves v. Estabrook*, 818 A.2d 1255 (N.H. 2003).

Example: Unmarried cohabitants, Richard Elden and Linda Eberling, are injured in a car accident caused by Robert Sheldon's negligence. Elden sustains serious injuries; Eberling dies. Elden sues Sheldon for his own injuries, for NIED caused by witnessing Eberling's injuries, and for loss of consortium. The court analyzes the NIED claim under the *Dillon v. Legg* factors, especially whether the plaintiff was sufficiently closely related to the victim. Under this test, the court rejects Elden's NIED claim, finding that the state has a strong interest in the marriage relationship, such claims would unduly burden the courts with a difficult examination of each relationship, and such claims would magnify the number of persons to whom the defendant owes a duty of care. The court similarly rejects plaintiff's loss of consortium claim, finding that the claim has never applied to unmarried couples. *Elden v. Sheldon*, 758 P.2d 582 (Cal. 1988).

Unmarried partners generally are precluded from suing for wrongful death. *See, e.g., Clark Sand Co., Inc. v. Kelly*, 60 So.3d 149 (Miss. 2011). Validly married same-sex spouses, of course, have the same right to sue for wrongful death as other spouses.

Note: The California legislature overruled *Elden v. Sheldon* to allow *registered* domestic partners to recover damages for negligent infliction of emotional distress to the same extent as spouses

(Cal. Civ. Code §1714.01). California domestic partnerships apply to same-sex couples since 2003 and opposite-sex couples since January 1, 2020.

E. **Support and property rights of unmarried partners:** The law regulates and protects marital parties' rights (e.g., support and property rights) upon dissolution. Historically, this legal protection has not been available to members of unmarried couples.

   1. **Traditional rule: Refusal to enforce agreements:** Under the traditional rule, courts refuse to enforce agreements between members of unmarried couples (formerly termed *meretricious relationships*). Courts hold such agreements are invalid as contrary to public policy (similar to contracts for prostitution). The rationale for the policy was the deterrence of immorality ("living in sin").

   Changing sexual mores (i.e., deceasing stigma of sexual relations outside of marriage) and increasing attention to the rights of women (who appear to be unfairly treated by the traditional rule) have contributed to reform. Currently, jurisdictions adopt one of three approaches to recognition of the rights of unmarried partners:

   - some continue to adhere to the traditional rule and refuse to recognize such claims based on public policy grounds (the minority view);

   - others recognize claims if based on an express agreement;

   - still others recognize claims if based on express *or* implied agreements.

   2. **Minority view: Traditional rule:** Some courts refuse to recognize the rights of nonmarital parties to enter contracts with each other about property rights.

   Example: Victoria lives with Robert for 15 years. When Victoria becomes pregnant, Robert tells her that no formal ceremony is necessary for them to be husband and wife. They notify their relatives that they are married and hold themselves out as spouses. Victoria later alleges that in reliance on Robert's promise to share his property with her, she contributed to his education and assisted him in his career. When Robert ends the relationship, Victoria files suit, requesting an equal share of all property. The Illinois Supreme Court holds that contracts between unmarried cohabitants are unenforceable as contrary to public policy. The court reasons that the negative impact of the recognition of such contracts on society and the institution of marriage outweighs the rights of the parties. *Hewitt v. Hewitt*, 394 N.E.2d 1204 (Ill. 1979). *See also Williams v. Ormsby*, 966 N.E.2d 255 (Ohio 2012) (pointing out that palimony claims are not recognized by state statute or case law).

   Note: *Hewitt* was subsequently reaffirmed in *Blumenthal v. Brewer* (discussed *infra*).

   3. **Majority view: Modern judicial approaches**

      a. **Express agreements**

         i. **Statement of the rule:** Unmarried partners may enter into express contracts with each other regarding the ownership of property acquired during their relationship. Under this rule, the contractual rights of nonmarital parties are similar to those of spouses.

         ii. **Limitation: Illicit consideration:** A court will not enforce a contract between nonmarital partners, however, if illicit sexual relations form part of the consideration for the agreement.

         Example: Plaintiff and Defendant live together for over 20 years. They have two children. They file joint tax returns. When the relationship ends, the woman seeks $250,000 in damages. She alleges, first, the existence of a contract based on her provision of domestic duties and business services at Defendant's request, her expectation of payment, and Defendant's acceptance of her services knowing she expected compensation. Second, she claims that she and Defendant entered into a partnership agreement whereby she agreed to perform domestic and business services and, in return, Defendant agreed to support and maintain her. Affirming the order granting Defendant's motion to dismiss, the New York Court of Appeals holds that Plaintiff failed to show an express contract (reasoning that she performed voluntarily) and finds that an implied contract cannot be implied from this "partnership agreement." Clarifying the law, the court holds that express contracts of unmarried couples are enforceable provided that they are not based on unlawful consideration. However, implied contracts for personal services are not enforceable because such services often are rendered gratuitously in intimate relationships. The court points to policy reasons for its reluctance to recognize implied contracts (fear of fraud inherent in claims for contractual damages) as well as the difficulty of proof. *Morone v. Morone*, 413 N.E.2d 1154 (N.Y. 1980).

   iii. Limitation: Cohabitation requirement: Another limitation is that the parties must have actually cohabited, although courts differ as to whether part-time cohabitation suffices.

   Example: Attorney Johnnie Cochran begins a relationship with Patricia in 1966, at a time when he is still married to his first wife. The couple has a son, buys a house together, and places title in both their names as joint tenants. Johnnie also owns another home. They never live together full-time, but Johnnie stays with Patricia and their son two to four nights per week, keeps clothes there, and eats meals there. Johnnie divorces his wife, but never marries Patricia. Nevertheless, he holds himself out as Patricia's husband during some of their 25-year relationship. When Patricia and Johnnie separate, she claims that Johnnie promised to support her for the rest of her life. He contends that because they never cohabited, any alleged agreement would not be subject to *Marvin* (discussed *infra*). The appellate court holds that a triable issue of fact exists as to whether the couple "cohabited" precluding summary judgment, based on their part-time cohabitation over the 17-year period, holding themselves out as husband and wife, and joint ownership of a home where they spent "family time." The court explains that the cohabitation requirement may be satisfied in appropriate cases by living arrangements that are less than full time. *Cochran v. Cochran*, 106 Cal. Rptr. 2d 899 (Ct. App. 2001).

b. Express and implied agreements

   i. Rule: Some courts recognize ***both*** express and implied agreements between nonmarital cohabitants. Recognition of implied agreements becomes important because nonmarital parties often fail to have express agreements about their support and/or property rights.

   Implied contracts may be either implied-in-fact or implied-in-law. In an implied-in-fact agreement, the court infers contractual intent from the parties' conduct. On the other hand, a court imposes implied-in-law remedies to prevent unjust enrichment (i.e., the parties' intent is irrelevant).

   ii. *Marvin* case: The landmark case of *Marvin v. Marvin*, 557 P.2d 106 (Cal. 1976) [hereafter *Marvin I*], recognized the rights of nonmarital partners to make express and implied agreements.

   Marvin v. Marvin: Michelle Triola Marvin lives with actor Lee Marvin from 1964 until Lee ends the relationship in 1970. (Lee is legally married to another woman for part of that time.) Michelle and Lee never marry, although Michelle changes her surname legally to Marvin. Upon dissolution of the relationship, Plaintiff claims that she and Defendant entered into an oral agreement whereby they agreed to share all earnings and property and to hold themselves out as husband and wife. She further alleges that she agreed to give up her lucrative singing career, and to render services to Defendant as companion, housekeeper, and cook in return for his promise to provide financial support for the rest of her life.

Plaintiff asks the court to determine her support rights and rights to the property held in Defendant's name (approximately $1 million in real and personal property, including motion picture rights earned during the relationship), and to impose a constructive trust on half of the accumulated property (i.e., treating her as if she were a legal spouse in a community property jurisdiction).

Defendant raises four arguments:

- the court should not enforce contracts between nonmarital partners because such agreements are contrary to public policy as immoral;

- the alleged contract also violates public policy because it impairs the community property rights of his first wife (from whom he was not yet divorced);

- enforcement of any agreement is barred by the Statute of Frauds requiring contracts for marriage settlements to be in writing; and

- enforcement is barred because the legislature has abolished actions for breach of promise to marry.

The California Supreme Court holds that express agreements between nonmarital partners are enforceable except to the extent that such contracts rest on unlawful consideration. The court, in reversing the trial court, reasons that adult cohabitants are as competent as other persons to contract regarding their property rights. The court notes that changing social mores dictate imposition of a standard that is not based on an abandoned moral code.

Addressing Defendant's arguments (above), the California Supreme Court responds:

- agreements between nonmarital partners fail only to the extent that they rest on illicit sexual services (any severable portion will be enforced);

- the actor's first wife's rights are not impaired because her rights were fixed by her divorce action (in which she had the opportunity to assert her rights);

- the contract at issue is not a contract for a marriage settlement; and

- agreements to pool earnings and to provide support are not barred by abolition of actions for breach of promise to marry.

In the absence of an express agreement, the court holds that implied contracts (both implied-in-fact and implied-in-law) between cohabitants are enforceable to protect the fulfillment of the parties' reasonable expectations. Courts may inquire into the conduct of the parties to fashion relief through a constructive trust, resulting trust, or quantum meruit.

c. Additional equitable remedies

i. **Dictum of *Marvin I*:** *Marvin I* also states, by way of dictum (see fn. 25 of the opinion), that courts may utilize their broad equitable powers to grant relief to nonmarital partners in order to protect the expectations of the parties. *Marvin*, 557 P.2d at 122.

ii. ***Marvin II*:** Taking up the California Supreme Court's invitation (in *Marvin I*) to rely on broad equitable powers to fashion a remedy, the trial court, on remand, awards Michelle Marvin $104,000 as equitable relief. The monetary award was for the Plaintiff's economic rehabilitation until she could become self-supporting. The court fixed the award at the highest salary she had ever earned ($1,000/week). *Marvin v. Marvin*, 5 Fam. L. Rep. 3077 (1979) [hereafter *Marvin II*].

iii. ***Marvin III*:** In *Marvin III*, a California Court of Appeals reverses the trial court's award of $104,000, on remand, to Michelle Marvin. The appellate court reasons that such an award is not based on traditional notions of equity. The appellate court determines, instead, that Defendant was not unjustly enriched nor did he commit any wrongful act. As a result, the award has no basis in law or equity. "A court of equity admittedly has broad powers, but it may not create totally new substantive rights under the guise of doing equity." *Marvin III*, 176 Cal. Rptr. 555, 558 (Ct. App. 1981).

Note: *Marvin II* misinterpreted the California Supreme Court's call for the courts to use their broad equitable powers to fashion remedies. Here, it is questionable whether Defendant committed any legally cognizable wrong or whether Defendant received a legally cognizable benefit because Plaintiff also received benefits that must be offset.

d. **Application of *Marvin* to same-sex couples:** Some jurisdictions apply *Marvin* to same-sex couples and recognize the cohabitation contracts of former same-sex partners However, a few jurisdictions refuse to do so.

Example: Elizabeth Swain and Mona Cates cohabit from 2000 to 2006. In 2003, they move to Seattle where Cates buys a home and the two cohabit. Swain testifies that she gave Cates money in order to contribute to the down payment. Additionally, the couple make various improvements towards the home, which later sold for $300,000. The couple then move to Mississippi where Cates buys another home. Swain contributes financially to that home as well. Upon dissolution, Swain brings suit against Cates to recover for her monetary contributions toward the purchase and improvement of the joint residences. The court determines relief may be granted to Swain based on the theory of unjust enrichment, which applies to situations where there is no legal contract and the person sought to be charged is in possession of money or property, which in good conscience and justice they should deliver to another. Here, Cates remained in the Mississippi home after the dissolution of the relationship, and therefore, Cates was unjustly enriched by Swain's contributions to the home. *Cates v. Swain*, 215 So. 3d 492 (Miss. 2013).

Example: Dr. Jane Blumenthal and her intimate partner Judge Eileen Brewer live together for more than 25 years and raise three children together. At dissolution, Blumenthal sues for partition of the jointly owned family home. Brewer counters with a claim for reimbursement for her investment in Blumenthal's lucrative medical practice and for a share of the "marital" assets, accumulated during the time when Brewer was devoting considerable time to raising the couple's children. The state supreme court reaffirms *Hewitt v. Hewitt*'s public policy stance precluding recovery. The court reasons that such a rule does not violate state or federal guarantees of due process and equal protection in order to disfavor recognition of mutually enforceable property rights to "knowingly unmarried cohabitants" and to "uphold the institution of marriage." The court adds that the rule also prevents cohabitants from evading the statutory prohibition on common law marriage. *Blumenthal v. Brewer*, 69 N.E.3d 834 (Ill. 2016).

4. **Meretricious relationships in Washington state:** Washington state was in the forefront of the movement to extend property rights to unmarried cohabitants upon dissolution. *See Connell v. Francisco,* 898 P.2d 831 (Wash. 1995) (adopting an equitable doctrine that confers property rights at dissolution for partners who have a "meretricious relationship," that is, a "stable, marital-like-relationship where both parties cohabit with knowledge that a lawful marriage between them does not exist").

5. **ALI** *Principles*: The ALI *Principles* adopt a **status-based,** rather than a **contractual,** approach to the dissolution of cohabitants' relationships (opposite-sex and same-sex). That is, if cohabitants satisfy the ALI requirements, they will be accorded the same treatment as spouses upon dissolution in terms of property division and "spousal" support (termed "compensatory payments").

   According to the ALI provisions, parties who live together with their common child for a statutorily designated period (suggested: two years), are deemed domestic partners. Childless cohabitants are presumed to be domestic partners merely if they share a common household for a statutorily designated period (suggested: three years). Childless cohabitants who reside together for less than the statutorily designated period may still qualify (based on a rebuttable presumption) if one partner shows that they shared a common household and lived together for "a significant period of time."

F. **Employment:** Unmarried opposite-sex, as well as same-sex, couples encounter discrimination from employers.

1. **Withdrawal of offer of employment or discharge:** In one celebrated case, a lesbian lost an offer of employment when her employer learned of her planned marriage to another woman.

   Example: Defendant-state Attorney General Bowers withdraws his offer of employment after he learns that Plaintiff Shahar plans to marry another woman. Plaintiff alleges violations of her rights to freedom of association, freedom of religion, equal protection, and due process. The Eleventh Circuit Court of Appeals vacates its earlier ruling that Plaintiff's right of association was protected, grants a rehearing en banc, and holds that Shahar's rights were not violated. The court first assumes that Plaintiff's right of intimate association encompasses the right to marry another woman (an assumption on which the court has "considerable doubt"). The court then determines that strict scrutiny is inappropriate and evaluates the Attorney General's decision by resort to the *Pickering* [*Pickering v. Bd. of Ed.*, 391 U.S. 563 (1968)] balancing test (that is applicable to scrutinize a government employer's decision to limit an employee's exercise of her right to free speech). The court considers the Attorney General's claims that Shahar's employment would impugn the credibility of his office, interfere with the ability to handle controversial matters such as enforcing the law against homosexual sodomy, and endanger working relationships within the department. The court concludes that the Attorney General's interests outweigh Shahar's associational rights. 224 F.3d 1097 (11th Cir. 1997), *cert. denied,* 522 U.S. 1049 (1998).

2. **Note:** At the time of Shahar's suit, Title VII did not apply to employment discrimination based on sexual orientation. Therefore, Shahar brought suit on constitutional grounds. Recently, the U.S. Supreme Court determined that Title VII's prohibition against employment discrimination applies to discrimination based on sexual orientation or gender identity.

   Example: Gerald Bostock, a gay man, began working for Clayton County, Georgia, in 2003 as a child welfare services coordinator. In 2013, Bostock began playing on a gay recreational softball league. Soon after, influential members in the community became aware of Bostock's sexual orientation. Bostock was fired for conduct "unbecoming of its employees." He filed suit under Title VII, alleging he was discriminated against on the basis of his sexual orientation. (The case was consolidated with the case of an employee who was fired because of being transgender.) The Supreme Court held that an employer violates Title VII when it intentionally fires an employee based on sex. The Court reasoned that it is impossible to discriminate against an employee for being homosexual or transgender without discriminating against that individual "based on sex." For example, an employer who fires a male employee because he is attracted to men, discriminates against him for traits and actions it tolerates in his female colleague. Sex plays a "necessary" and "undisguisable" role in the firing decision. *Bostock v. Clayton County,* 140 S. Ct. 1731 (U.S. 2020).

2. **Proposed federal legislation:** Unsuccessful federal efforts to ban employment discrimination based on sexual orientation date from 1974. In 2019, the U.S. House of Representations passed the Equality Act (H.R. 5, 116th Cong. (2019-2020)), which would have banned discrimination on the basis of sexual orientation or gender identity in employment, housing, credit, education, public accommodations, federal funding, and jury service. However, the bill has little likely of passage in the Republican-controlled Senate.

3. **State laws:** On the state level, 21 states and the District of Columbia currently have laws prohibiting employment discrimination based on sexual orientation and gender identity.

4. **Military discharge:** Gay and lesbian members of the armed forces traditionally faced discharge if they revealed their sexual orientation. The military policy of "Don't Ask, Don't Tell" (DADT), Pub. L. No. 103-160, 10 U.S.C. §654, prohibited any person who was not heterosexual from disclosing his or her sexual orientation, or from speaking about any gay and lesbian relationship, while serving in the armed forces. Congress repealed the policy in 2010. However, advocates suggest that although lesbian, gay, and bisexual service members are able to openly serve in the military, the military culture has been slow to change.

   Service members historically could also be discharged for being transgender. In 2016, transgender troops began serving openly in the military after the Obama Administration lifted the ban for those service members already enlisted. The military set July 1, 2017, as the date when transgender people would be allowed to enlist. Before that date, however, the Trump Administration banned transgender people from either serving or enlisting in the military.

G. **Inheritance law:** Courts traditionally *refuse* to permit a member of an unmarried couple (opposite-sex or same-sex) to inherit an *intestate share* of the deceased partner's estate. That is, courts refuse to treat unmarried cohabitants as legal spouses. (Intestacy refers to the state of dying without a will.) However, in a few modern jurisdictions, statutes modify this result. That is, states with domestic partnerships or civil unions generally confer intestacy rights on *registered* partners.

H. **Parentage rights of unmarried fathers**

1. **Constitutional rights:** The U.S. Supreme Court recognizes the constitutional rights of unmarried fathers in some circumstances.

   Example: Joan and Peter Stanley live together intermittently for 18 years although they never marry. They have three children whom Peter supports. Upon Joan's death, the state removes the children from Peter's custody (via a dependency proceeding) pursuant to a state statute providing that unmarried fathers are not "fit" parents and their children become wards of the state upon the death of the mother. Peter challenges the statute on due process and equal protection grounds. The Supreme Court determines that he was denied procedural due process because he was entitled to a hearing regarding his parental fitness before removal of the children from his custody. The state interest in administrative convenience (i.e., by the application of presumptions) is outweighed by the father's interest in raising his children. *Stanley* is both a procedural due process case (guaranteeing a hearing to a parent for the purpose of proving a lack of fitness before terminating parental rights) and also a substantive due process case that limits the circumstances under which the state may remove children from parents. That is, the state must prove (not presume) lack of fitness prior to removing children from parents' custody. *Stanley v. Illinois*, 405 U.S. 645 (1972).

Note: Subsequent Supreme Court cases (*Quilloin v. Walcott*, *Caban v. Mohammed*, and *Lehr v. Robertson*) (discussed in Chapter 10 *infra*) establish that if the biological father manifests a substantial relationship with the child (i.e., "indicia of parenthood"), his parent-child relationship will be accorded constitutional protection (thereby conferring rights on him in the adoption process).

The U.S. Supreme Court held that, when an unmarried biological father's rights *conflict* with the rights of a married father, the *married father will prevail* if the child was born into an intact family (even in the face of contrary biological evidence of paternity).

Example: Carole, while married to Gerald, has an affair with her neighbor, Michael. When Carole gives birth to Victoria, Gerald is listed as the father of Victoria on her birth certificate. Blood tests indicate a 98.07 percent likelihood that Michael is Victoria's father. After Carole and Gerald separate, Carole and Victoria visit Michael in St. Thomas, where his business is located. They remain there for three months and subsequently live with him in Los Angeles for eight months. In St. Thomas, Michael holds out Victoria as his child. After Carole reconciles with Gerald, she rebuffs Michael's attempts to visit Victoria. Michael files an action to establish his paternity and visitation rights. Victoria files a cross-motion seeking to maintain her filial relationship with both Michael and Gerald. Under California law, a child born to a married woman is conclusively presumed to be the child of the marriage. Michael contends that the presumption violates his due process rights. The Supreme Court addresses the following issues: (1) whether this presumption infringes upon the due process rights of unmarried biological fathers, and (2) whether the presumption infringes upon the constitutional rights of children to maintain relationships with their biological fathers.The plurality (Justice Scalia) concludes that the presumption does not infringe Michael's due process rights because biological fathers, such as Michael, do not possess a constitutionally protected liberty interest in maintaining a relationship with their children. The Court reasons that no historical, social, or legal tradition protects a non-biological parent-child relationship when the child is born during the mother's marriage. To the contrary, policy supports the state's interest in legitimacy and preservation of family integrity. The Court dismisses Victoria's claims on the same grounds. *Michael H. v. Gerald D.*, 491 U.S. 110 (1989).

2. **Rebuttable presumptions of paternity:** Most states (including California, the setting of *Michael H.*) now have *rebuttable* presumptions of paternity. California amended its conclusive presumption of legitimacy to allow a putative father to move for blood tests within two years of birth if the putative father received the child into his home and openly held out the child as his child. Cal. Fam. Code §7541(b).

3. **Dual fatherhood:** Courts in at least a dozen states now hold that children can have more than two parents (such as the mother's husband as well as the biological father) in some

circumstances, thereby altering the result in *Michael H.* Further, under UPA (2017) §613 (Alternative B), a state might allow a child to have more than two parents if the court makes a finding that the failure to recognize more than two parents would be detrimental to the child.

4. **Voluntary paternity establishment:** Another way in which unmarried fathers can establish parentage rights to their nonmarital children is through voluntary acknowledgements of paternity. Federal law (PRWORA) currently requires all states to recognize Voluntary Acknowledgments of Paternity forms that are available at hospitals. *See* 42 U.S.C. §666(a)(5)(C) (providing that a valid acknowledgment of paternity should be treated as equivalent to a judicial determination of paternity).

5. **Extending paternity laws to unmarried former same-sex partners**

   a. **Traditional approach:** Paternity establishment has long been necessary to confer rights and obligations on nonmarital children and their parents. Traditionally, the law was not concerned with "maternity establishment" and its ensuing rights and obligations because the woman who gives birth to a child is easily identifiable. However, the traditional approach caused problems for same-sex second parents in their attempt to establish parentage rights to the children of their former partners in cases when the children were not biologically related to the second parent.

   b. **Modern approach:** With the development of reproductive technology and the advent of marriage equality, courts are faced with the issue of determining what role paternity laws should play in the establishment of parental rights of lesbian and gay partners. Courts are increasingly recognizing the rights of the second parent through a variety of approaches, including equitable approaches (de facto parentage, psychological parent, etc.) and extension of the Uniform Parentage Act.

      The trend is to extend the original UPA's presumed-parent provisions in a gender-neutral manner to same-sex partners. UPA §4(a)(4)(1973) provided: "A man is presumed to be the natural father of a child" if the man "receives the child [as a minor] into his home and openly holds out the child as his natural child."

      Example: Chatterjee and King are lesbian partners who adopt a child from Russia. King formally adopts the child but Chatterjee, although providing support and co-parenting, never does. When the couple breaks up, King prevents contact between Chatterjee and the child. Chatterjee files a petition to establish parentage and visitation, alleging that she is a presumed natural parent under the state UPA. The state supreme court concludes that the Act's parentage provision should not be limited to men. The court reasons, first, that the Act contemplated establishment of parentage by conduct rather than biology and that a woman can fulfill this requirement as easily as a man. Second, the court points to intent, noting that commentary to the original UPA explains that paternity provisions should not be limited to males. Third, public policy supports a liberal interpretation of the Act by ensuring that children have financial support and parental relationships. Finally, a restrictive interpretation would evoke equal protection issues. Therefore, the court allows Chatterjee the opportunity to establish parentage. Her failure to adopt the child does not alter the decision because parents are often allowed to establish paternity without taking official steps to formalize the relationship. Further, she does not have to establish King's unfitness before seeking custody herself. *Chatterjee v. King*, 280 P.3d 283 (N.M. 2012).

Note: A few states address the rights of *unmarried same-sex parents* by allowing them to execute gender-neutral forms (Voluntary Agreements of Parentage (VAP)). *See supra.*

c. **Contrast with same-sex *spouses'* parental rights:** States cannot deny same-sex *spouses* the same benefits afforded to opposite-sex spouses (according to the Supreme Court in *Obergefell* and *Pavan*). In addition, the marital paternity presumption violates the constitutional rights of non-biologically-related same-sex spouses to due process and equal protection.

Example: Kimberly and Suzan McLaughlin marry in California and decide to have a child via artificial insemination. During Kimberly's pregnancy, they move to Arizona. There, they execute two legal documents: (1) wills declaring Suzan to be an equal parent and (2) a parenting agreement stating that in the event of a separation, Suzan would maintain shared custody, have regular visitation, and be responsible for child support. Kimberly gives birth to a boy ("E"), and Suzan stays home to care for him. Two years later, Kimberly moves out, taking the boy with her, and cuts off contact with Suzan. Suzan files a petition to recognize her parental rights. The Arizona Supreme Court holds that *Obergefell* requires that Arizona's statutory paternity presumption be applied in a gender-neutral manner and declares Suzan as presumptive parent under the statute. The court reasons that Arizona's statute is a benefit attendant to marriage and, therefore, it applies equally to same-sex spouses. *McLaughlin v. Jones*, 401 P.3d 492 (Ariz. Sup. Ct. 2017).

d. **Uniform Parentage Act (2017):** The modern trend applies the original UPA's presumed-parent provisions to same-sex partners. UPA (2017) addresses this issue through express statutory provisions, such as the replacement of gender-based terminology in the "holding provision" of the original UPA (§4(a)(4)) ("A man is presumed to be the natural father of a child if . . .") with gender neutral language ("An *individual* is presumed to be a parent of a child if . . ."). UPA §204(a)(2).

Note: Although equitable parenthood doctrines provide certain parental rights relating to custody and visitation, the UPA's "holding out" provisions establish *full legal parentage* for individuals who have acted like parents despite their lack of genetic connection to the child.

I. **Citizenship by descent:** Rules governing citizenship by descent ("derivative citizenship") for foreign-born children of a U.S. citizen-parent traditionally depended on the citizen-parent's marital status and gender. Formerly, unmarried children of a U.S.-citizen-mother were treated differently, for citizenship purposes, from unmarried children of a U.S. citizen-father. The U.S. Supreme Court changed that result in 2017.

Example: Luis Ramón Morales-Santana, born in 1962 in the Dominican Republic, is the adult son of an unmarried U.S.-citizen father and a non-citizen mother. Morales-Santana moved to the U.S. when he was 13 years old. After the federal government sought to deport him (as an adult) for violating New York criminal law, Morales-Santana claimed U.S. citizenship ("citizenship by descent") based on his father's citizenship status. At the time, the derivative citizenship law of the federal Immigration and Nationality Act (INA) contained gender-based distinctions that treated foreign-born children of unwed U.S.-citizen *mothers* more favorably than foreign-born children of unwed U.S.-citizen *fathers*. If the citizen-parent was the child's father, the child could obtain citizenship if the male parent had lived in the U.S. for *five years* prior to the child's birth and after the male parent had attained the age of 14. However, if the citizen-parent was the child's mother, the child could obtain citizenship if the female parent had lived in the United States for *one year* prior to the child's birth. Immigration officials denied Morales-Santana's claim to citizenship because at the time of Morales-Santana's birth, his father had not satisfied the requirement of five-year's physical presence after the age 14.

Morales-Santana claimed, on his deceased father's behalf, that his unmarried father was a victim of gender-based discrimination. Justice Ginsburg, writing for the six-person majority, determines that the derivative citizenship law violated equal protection under the Fifth Amendment because it was based on "stunningly anachronistic" sexual stereotypes about gender roles. However, the Court concludes that the appropriate remedy is to apply the five-year requirement to children born of *both* unwed parents, i.e., unmarried U.S.-citizen- mothers as well as U.S.-citizen-fathers. The Court sends a signal that laws allocating gender-based rights and responsibilities between parents in the nonmarital family are vulnerable to challenge and must serve important governmental interests. *Sessions v. Morales-Santana,* 137 S. Ct. 1678 (2017).

J. **Domestic violence:** All states have civil and criminal legislation addressing domestic violence, including protections for married, as well as unmarried, intimate partners.

   1. **Federal law:** The Violence Against Women Act (VAWA), enacted by Congress in 1994, applies to intimate partners whether married or unmarried. Congress expanded the VAWA Reauthorization Act of 2013 to prohibit any VAWA-funded program from discriminating against domestic violence survivors on the basis of sex, sexual orientation, or gender identity.

   2. **Protection orders:** All states have civil and criminal legislation addressing domestic violence, including provisions for protective orders. Until recently, many state laws on protection orders were silent on their application to same-sex partners, and a few state laws explicitly precluded these partners from obtaining restraining orders because of "opposite-sex" language. Some states have declared these gender-based laws to be unconstitutional.

       Example: Jane Doe seeks a protection order against her former same-sex partner (with whom she cohabited for five years). Doe alleges that she felt threatened when her ex-partner followed her from her home to her workplace. She calls law enforcement who arrive and file an incident report for the charges of "simple assault" and "assault-intimidation." The Family Court denies Doe's petition, citing the definition of "household member" in state law (as a "male and female who are cohabiting or formerly have cohabited"). Doe then petitions for a declaratory judgment, arguing that the statutory definition of "household member" violates the Fourteenth Amendment because it leaves unmarried same-sex victims without the remedy afforded to their opposite-sex counterparts. The state supreme court holds that the statutory definition of "household member" is unconstitutional as applied to Doe. *Doe v. State*, 808 S.E.2d 807 (S.C. 2017).

   3. **Obstacles for LGBT partners:** Congress expanded federal protections for LGBT victims in the VAWA Reauthorization Act of 2013. These victims continuously face obstacles in accessing services, such as shelter services, by providers who lacked cultural competency or an understanding of diversity. As a result, VAWA 2013 lists both "sexual orientation" and "gender identity" in the revised definition of "underserved populations" in order to expand eligibility of LGBT victims for various grant programs. (42 U.S.C.A. §13925(a)(39)). VAWA 2013 also prohibits discrimination on the basis of sexual orientation or gender identity in all VAWA-funded programs. 42 U.S.C.A. §13925(b)(13)(A).

Note: The pending VAWA Reauthorization Act of 2020, H.R. 1585, 116th Cong. (2019-2020) proposes an expansion of those protections.

K. Parentage: Recent decades have witnessed a transformation in family structure due to the rising rate of nonmarital births as well as unmarried cohabitation. Traditionally, nontraditional families experienced limitations on support and inheritance rights.

1. **Support rights of nonmarital children:** Traditionally, the law regarded nonmarital children as *ilius nullius* and bastards ("illegitimate"). That status affected the child's right to support and inheritance. Nonmarital children had no right to support from their father and no right to inherit from him intestate. Today, statutes require *both* parents to support the child regardless of the parents' marital status.

   Example: Cherlyn Clark files a complaint for support on behalf of her minor daughter. Clark named Gene Jeter to be the father. A blood test finds that Jeter is 99.3 percent likely to be the father. However, Jeter moves to dismiss on the ground the action is barred by the state's six-year statute of limitations for paternity actions involving nonmarital children. (Clark waited ten years.) In contrast, a legitimate child may seek support from a father at any time. Plaintiff challenges the statute as a violation of the Equal Protection and Due Process Clauses.

   Applying an intermediate level of scrutiny, the Court declares the Pennsylvania statute unconstitutional on equal protection grounds. The Court concludes that the six-year statutory period does not provide a mother with a reasonable opportunity to assert a claim on behalf of her nonmarital child. Furthermore, the six-year statute is not substantially related to the state's interest in avoiding litigation of stale or fraudulent claims. According to the Court, the fact that Pennsylvania permits paternity to be litigated in other contexts more than six years post-birth (for example, intestate claims) casts doubt on the state's asserted interest here. *Clark v. Jeter*, 486 U.S. 456 (1988).

   Note: Under federal law, all state programs currently must permit paternity establishment at any time before a child turns 18 years old.

2. **Uniform Parentage Act (UPA):** The original UPA was promulgated in 1973 to address the prevailing unequal treatment of nonmarital children and also to respond to the need to provide guidance to the states in response to U.S. Supreme Court decisions on the rights of nonmarital children. The Uniform Law Commission (ULC) promulgated a new UPA in 2000 and revised it again in 2002. The most recent version (UPA 2017) makes the Act gender-neutral and applies to same-sex couples. All revised versions reaffirm the equal treatment of children regardless of the parents' marital status.

Quiz Yourself on
NONTRADITIONAL FAMILIES

47. Roger lives with his gay partner, Paul, for several years until Paul's death. After Paul's death, Roger files an action against Paul's estate. Roger argues first that he should be treated as a "surviving spouse" in terms of the distribution of Paul's estate, and second, that he has a claim on an express oral agreement in which Roger was to provide services as "lover, companion, homemaker, traveling companion, housekeeper and cook" in exchange for Paul's promise to share their jointly accumulated property. Will Roger's arguments be successful? _____

48. Jonathan and Michael live together in a rent-controlled apartment in Blackacre for ten years until Michael dies of AIDS. Jonathan has been taking care of Michael for the last two years of Michael's illness. Both men's families are aware of their relationship. Because Michael was the named tenant on the lease, the landlord begins procedures to evict Jonathan in order to offer the apartment at a higher rent. Jonathan argues that he is a "family member" for the purpose of protection from eviction. The rent-control statute prohibits eviction following death of a "family member." However, the provision includes a restrictive definition that limits family members to husband, wife, son, daughter, step-relationships, nephew, niece, uncle, aunt, grandparents, grandchildren, and in-law relationships. When Jonathan challenges the eviction, will he be successful? _____

49. Lucy lives with Allen for approximately one year. They pool their earnings and expenses. They plan to marry but postpone the wedding date. In expectation of their marriage, they jointly purchase a home, taking title in both names. Again, they set the wedding date. Eight days before the wedding, Allen dies at the scene of an automobile accident, allegedly caused by defendant's negligence. Lucy, who witnessed the accident, sues the defendant to recover for negligent infliction of emotional distress. Will Lucy prevail? _____

50. Same facts as above. Lucy now files suit for wrongful death under a statute that permits "heirs" to bring the action. The statute defines "heirs" as those entitled to succeed to decedent's property based on the laws of intestacy. Will Lucy be successful? _____

51. Mr. and Mrs. Sears are employees of "Abbott House," a private nonprofit agency licensed by the state to care for neglected children. The Searses, their two children, and ten foster children (seven of whom are siblings) lease a home in an area of the city of White Plains. The parents and their children, natural and foster, live together as a family, and cook and eat all meals together. The city restricts land use to "single-family" dwellings, defining family as: "one or more persons limited to the spouse, parents, grandparents, grandchildren, sons, daughters, brothers, or sisters of the owner or the tenant or of the owner's spouse or tenant's spouse living together as a single housekeeping unit with kitchen facilities." The city seeks to enforce its zoning ordinance and to enjoin the Searses' use of their home in this way. When the Sears family challenges the city's actions, will they be successful? _____

52. Melissa and Michelle lived together in a committed relationship for three years. During this time, Michelle often has angry outbursts involving verbal abuse, threats, property destruction, and physical abuse. By the end of the third year, Melissa moves in with her mother. However, after the breakup, Melissa finds threatening notes directed at her on her mom's front porch, her car windshield, and her workplace. Melissa believes Michelle has left these notes. A few weeks after the breakup, Michelle begs Melissa to take her back. Melissa refuses, and Michelle physically assaulted Melissa. Melissa seeks a protection order, which is denied by a judge because the definition of "household member" in the protection order statute does not apply to same-sex partners. Melissa appeals, claiming this is a violation of the Equal Protection Clause. Will she be successful? _____

53. Jody and John begin a four-month long dating relationship in the small town of Whiteacre. A month after the relationship ends, Jody discovers that she is pregnant. She decides to keep the baby. Seven years after the baby's birth, she files a complaint for child support. A blood test determines that John is 99.8 percent likely to be the father. However, John moves to dismiss the complaint on the ground that under the laws of Whiteacre, Jody's claim is barred due to the state's six-year statute of limitations for paternity actions. Will John be successful? _____

54. Anne, while married to Dave, has an affair with Tom. Nine months later, Anne gives birth to a son. All parties live in the jurisdiction of Blackacre. On the birth certificate, she lists Dave as the father. But she tells Tom her belief that he is the biological father. A blood test later confirms Tom's

paternity. Unaware of Anne's duplicity, Dave holds the child out to be his. As the child gets older, Anne allows Tom to visit the child occasionally. When Anne later decides to cut off Tom's contact with the child, he files an action to establish paternity and the right to visitation. In response, Dave files a motion for summary judgment, contending that there are no triable issues of fact because he was married to Anne when the child was born. Will Dave be successful? _____

Answers

47. Probably not. Courts traditionally refuse to permit a member of an unmarried couple (either opposite-sex or same-sex) to inherit an intestate share of the deceased partner's estate. However, Roger might be successful if he resides in one of the few jurisdictions in which state law modifies this result by recognition of domestic partnerships or civil unions. In terms of Roger's contract claim, under the traditional rule, courts refuse to recognize the rights of nonmarital partners to contract with each other about property rights. However, because of changing sexual mores and the increasing acceptance of cohabitation, most courts now permit opposite-sex unmarried partners to enter into agreements about their property. Roger would argue that gay and lesbian partners have the same rights as opposite-sex unmarried partners (under *Marvin* and *Lawrence v. Texas*) to enter into express contracts with each other about the ownership of property acquired during their relationship. Even if the court recognizes this argument, however, Roger would face another hurdle. Courts apply a limitation to the rule that recognizes express agreements between partners: A court will not enforce such a contract if the consideration for the agreement encompasses the provision of sexual services. This limitation stems from the fact that contracts for an illegal act are void. Because the provision of sexual services was inseparably part of the consideration for Roger and Paul's agreement (Roger was to provide services as "lover"), Roger's claim will be denied.

48. Perhaps. Jonathan should argue that he is protected despite the restrictive definition of family under the Blackacre rent-control provision. He should argue that a functional definition applies because the purpose of the restrictive provision is analogous to the broad rent-control ordinance at issue in *Braschi*—to protect family members from hardship and dislocation following death. Further, the two men's relationship meets the *Braschi* standard: manifesting a long duration, a high level of emotional commitment, care of each other's needs, and an openness about their relationship.

49. Perhaps. Lucy will try to show that, as Allen's fiancée, she was sufficiently closely related to enable her to recover under the *Dillon v. Legg* factors (i.e., she was at the scene of the accident, she suffered severe emotional distress from observing the accident, and she bore the requisite close relationship to the victim). However, states are divided about whether cohabitants can recover in tort for injuries to each other by third parties.

50. No. Because the action is purely statutory, Lucy will not qualify as a lawful spouse in order to bring an action for wrongful death purposes.

51. Probably. The group home manifests permanency and constitutes a single housekeeping unit within the meaning of the ordinance. The group home promotes family values and therefore is analogous to a traditional family unit. Further, case law would support recognition of the group home's claim because the home is more analogous to the extended family of *Moore* (the grandmother's purpose to care for her grandchildren) than to the transient college student commune of *Belle Terre*.

52. Yes. All states authorize protection orders to safeguard victims from intimate partner violence. However, until recently, some statutes were silent on the application to same-sex partners, and other statutes precluded these partners from obtaining restraining orders because of explicit "opposite-sex" language. Today, virtually all states extend eligibility for protection orders to same-sex partners. Further, differential treatment of same-sex partners for purposes of protection orders would violate equal protection.

53. No. John will not succeed in dismissing the support claim on the basis that the statute of limitations bars the claim. The Supreme Court held that a six-year statute of limitations violates the Equal Protection Clause because the statute treats nonmarital children differently from children of married parents because a legitimate child may seek support from a father at any time (*Clark v. Jeter*). Further, federal law currently requires states to permit paternity establishment at any time before a child turns 18 years old.

54. Perhaps. It depends on Blackacre law. The U.S. Supreme Court has affirmed constitutional protection for a putative father's parental rights if he has established a substantial relationship with his child by his commitment to the responsibilities of parenthood. Tom has not established the requisite relationship because he never lived with the boy or provided support (he only visited him occasionally). Tom also faces another obstacle—Anne and Dave were married at the time of the boy's birth. The Supreme Court upheld a conclusive statutory presumption that a man living with the mother at the time of a child's birth is the legal father despite the existence of biological evidence that another man fathered the child (*Michael H. v. Gerald D.*). If the state follows this conclusive presumption, the court could determine that Dave, who was married to Anne at the time of the birth, is the child's legal father. If Blackacre follows the modern trend, however, Tom might prevail because most states now have a rebuttable presumption of paternity. Further, about a dozen states now permit dual fatherhood.

Exam Tips on NONTRADITIONAL FAMILIES

The central theoretical question here is the extent to which the legal system treats members of non-traditional families similarly to, or differently from, members of the traditional family. This question necessarily implicates the legal definition of the family.

Extended Families

☛ The central issue is the nature of the constitutional protection for the extended family.

    ☞ First, examine and explain the ***nature*** of the particular regulation of the extended family that is at issue. For example, does the regulation prevent the family from residing together (as in *Moore*)?

    ☞ Another threshold issue involves the determination of ***whether the particular household qualifies*** as an extended family. That is, in order to qualify, the group or household must contain members who are related to each other in some familial relationship. If the members are all unrelated persons, then the group is not an extended family but rather a communal family (see discussion below).

    ☞ Be sure to make clear that the extent of constitutional protection for extended families depends on the nature of the governmental infringement. That is, the Constitution provides protection for family members to choose to ***live together*** as an extended family but ***does not require a state to provide benefits*** to assist that family to remain together.

Communal Families

☞ Here two issues arise. The first question is the ***constitutional*** protection (or lack thereof) for the communal family. The second question concerns the extent of protection for communal families under ***state law***. The usual context in which these questions arise is ***zoning***.

☞ Explain that the Supreme Court has ***refused*** to extend constitutional protection to communal families from state regulation for zoning purposes. Point out that such treatment ***differs*** from that accorded to the extended family. Contrast the Supreme Court's treatment of communal families with state treatment of such families. That is, clarify that communal families have received ***more favorable*** treatment in zoning challenges based on state, rather than federal, constitutional law.

☞ In discussing a regulation of communal families under ***state law***, be sure to highlight the requirement that, in order for such families to merit legal recognition in some jurisdictions, they must evidence ***familial-like criteria***. Be sure to ***analyze which aspects*** of "group living" qualify (e.g., financial dependence, emotional dependence, eating together, sharing chores, pooling resources, etc.).

    ☞ Be sure to discuss the possible ramifications for recognition of communal families based on *Lawrence v. Texas* (recognizing the individual's right to enter into sexual relationships between consenting adults in the home).

Unmarried Couples

The two important points to remember here are (1) the law confers recognition on ***some***, but not other, nontraditional families; and (2) the law confers recognition on such nontraditional families for some ***purposes*** but not others. Be sure to identify whether the couple is married or merely cohabiting because same-sex partners who are validly married must be treated the same as legal spouses.

☞ First, identify the context of the regulation: sexual conduct, zoning, housing, tort law, contract law, employment, inheritance law. If the issue concerns sexual conduct, explain the traditional legal response (criminal sanctions for nonmarital sexual conduct) versus the modern legal response (based on *Lawrence v. Texas*, recognizing protection of the individual's privacy right to enter into consensual sexual relationships in the home).

☞ ***Zoning*** cases necessarily implicate constitutional issues, such as the First Amendment (freedom of association) and Fourteenth Amendment right to familial privacy, as well as state issues of the police power to regulate definitions of the family. Point out that some state courts have extended the U.S. Supreme Court's refusal to recognize communal families by denying constitutional protection to unmarried couples for zoning purposes. Point out too that *Lawrence* raises doubts as to the constitutionality of such decisions.

☞ Issues of ***housing discrimination*** evoke claims under state civil rights statutes. Here, an important issue is the need to balance constitutional rights (i.e., to balance the landlord's First Amendment right to refuse to rent to unmarried couples on religious grounds versus the couple's right to live where they choose free of discrimination).

    ☞ Explain that landlords' claims have met with varying success under state nondiscrimination statutes because of states' narrow versus broad interpretations of the statutory term "marital status."

    ☞ Explain the recent Supreme Court decision (*Bostock v. Clayton County*) holding that Title VII's prohibition against employment discrimination applies to discrimination based on sexual orientation or gender identity. Suggest its potential application to issues of housing discrimination.

☛ An exam question may raise **issues of tort law**. The most likely tort claims are for loss of consortium and/or negligent infliction of emotional distress arising from an injury to a cohabitant. Remember the threshold issue that bystander liability requires the plaintiff-cohabitant to have been a bystander, i.e., have witnessed the accident to the injured partner.

☞ Mention the split of opinion on recovery. Some jurisdictions permit cohabitants to recover in tort for injuries to each other, whereas other jurisdictions reject such claims.

☞ Point out that the existence of laws on registered domestic partnerships or civil unions may allow recovery. Mention that only a few jurisdictions have these laws and that they differ in terms of legal benefits.

☛ **Contract claims** (regarding support and property rights) may also arise when the unmarried couple terminates their relationship. Usually such claims occur following dissolution of the relationship, but occasionally such claims follow termination of the relationship by death. In dissolution cases, the claim will be "inter se" — one member of the couple suing the other for breach of contract. In cases of death of a partner, the plaintiff generally institutes a contract claim against the deceased partner's estate. Both scenarios require analysis under traditional contract principles. Clarify the nature of the offer, acceptance, and consideration.

☞ Discuss the traditional rule (refusal to enforce agreements) and its rationale (morality, public policy).

☞ Discuss the modern view, based on *Marvin v. Marvin*, that permits express and implied agreements between partners so long as the consideration for the agreement does not include the provision of sexual services.

☞ Discuss the minority view (*Hewitt v. Hewitt, Blumenthal v. Brewer*) holding that public policy precludes recognition of the rights of cohabitants (opposite-sex or same-sex).

☛ Be sure to conclude by discussing the impact of domestic partnership/civil union laws that equate the rights of same-sex partners to married couples in some states as well as the ALI *Principles* that pertain to dissolution of such relationships.

☛ **Employment** issues generally concern (1) employment decision making (i.e., refusals to hire a cohabitant, withdrawal of an offer of employment, or discharge of an employee), or (2) the denial of employment-related health benefits.

☞ In the first case, point out that Title VII does not protect against discrimination based on marital status. Plaintiffs, alternatively, may raise constitutional issues, such as violations of the right to freedom of association, due process, and equal protection.

☞ In terms of the denial of employment-related health benefits, an issue is whether such decisions constitute permissible marital status discrimination. Point out that many municipalities and private employers currently provide such benefits to domestic partners.

☛ Be sure to explain the recent Supreme Court decision (*Bostock v. Clayton County*), holding that Title VII's prohibition against employment discrimination applies to discrimination based on sexual orientation or gender identity.

☛ Finally, ***inheritance issues*** may arise when one of the partners of an unmarried couple dies. The issue typically is whether the surviving partner qualifies as a "spouse" under the statutory scheme for intestate distribution. The death of a partner without a will triggers application of state statutes that limit inheritance rights to designated family members ("spouses," "children," etc.). Be sure to contrast the traditional versus modern response. That is, courts traditionally refuse to permit a member of an unmarried couple (opposite-sex or same-sex) to inherit an intestate share of the deceased partner's estate. However, a few modern jurisdictions modify this result by domestic partnership or civil union laws. In the context of death, be on the lookout for cross-over questions that address issues of contract (i.e., *Marvin*-type claims), intestacy (spousal definition), and tort (i.e., loss of consortium, negligent infliction of emotional distress).

CHAPTER 5

DIVORCE

ChapterScope

This chapter explores the traditional fault-based system of divorce and the system of no-fault dissolution that replaced it. Here are a few of the key principles covered in this chapter:

- Historically, courts granted divorces based on *marital fault*.

- Traditional fault-based *grounds* include:

  - adultery;

  - cruelty; and

  - desertion.

- Traditional fault-based *defenses* include:

  - recrimination;

  - condonation;

  - connivance; and

  - collusion.

- *No-fault divorce* is available in every state, although "no fault" does not mean the same thing in all states.

- A *reform movement* attempted to re-introduce fault in the dissolution process. *Covenant marriages* reflect that movement.

- *Denial of access* to the courts by imposing filing fees and court costs violates indigents' right to due process.

- *Divorce discrimination* may constitute *marital status discrimination* pursuant to some states civil rights laws.

- Jurisdictions regulate *sexual relations* between attorneys and clients.

- *Subject matter jurisdiction* is necessary for the plaintiff to secure a divorce.

- A state has jurisdiction to dissolve a marriage based on plaintiff's *domicile* in the forum state.

- *Personal jurisdiction* over the defendant is not necessary to dissolve a marriage if the plaintiff is domiciled in the forum state but *notice* to the defendant that complies with due process is required.

- *The Full Faith and Credit Clause* of the Constitution requires that a state recognize the decrees of a sister state, provided that the sister state had jurisdiction.

- The *domestic relations exception* to federal jurisdiction signifies that federal courts can refuse to hear cases involving divorce, alimony, or child custody.

I. BACKGROUND

American divorce law was more liberal than English ecclesiastic practice. England did not permit judicially granted "absolute divorce" until the Matrimonial Causes Act in 1857. English law distinguished between "absolute divorce" (akin to our modern idea of divorce in which the parties can remarry) and "divorce a mensa et thoro" (i.e., from "bed and board"). The latter is analogous to our concept of a judicial separation—that is, it did not permit the spouses to remarry. Until 1857, the only recourse for English spouses was to seek either an annulment or the rare legislative divorce.

In contrast, by the nineteenth century in America, almost all northern colonies permitted judicial divorce. In the southern colonies during the same period, many legislatures dissolved marriages. Gradually, however, judicial divorce replaced legislative divorce.

Despite increasing demand, divorce was not easily obtainable until the early 1970s. Until that time, states required that a plaintiff establish fault-based grounds for divorce. Grounds varied considerably in the different states. Furthermore, divorce was awarded only to the innocent party. The innocent party received support, property, and custody. The "guilty" spouse was punished by having to pay (support and/or property) and by the denial of a custody award.

Today, all states have enacted some form of no-fault dissolution (i.e., divorce without proof of fault). Some jurisdictions are pure no-fault, whereas others have engrafted no-fault grounds onto their former fault-based system. It is important to note that "no fault" does not mean the same thing in all jurisdictions. For example, some states make divorce more difficult if only one spouse desires the divorce. Further, some states define "no fault" to mean that the parties must have "irreconcilable differences"; other states define "no fault" to signify a marital breakdown that results in the parties physically living apart for a statutorily defined period of time. The various meanings of "no fault" are explored below.

II. FAULT-BASED GROUNDS

All jurisdictions now have some variation of no-fault divorce. However, fault-based grounds still exist in some jurisdictions. The most common fault-based grounds for divorce in the fault era were cruelty and adultery.

A. Cruelty: Cruelty provided a traditional ground for divorce and remains a fault-based ground in some states. Statutes sometimes include the terms of "cruel and inhuman treatment" or "indignities to the person." Cruelty was the most common ground for divorce prior to no-fault (i.e., more frequently pleaded than adultery).

1. **Elements:** To prove cruelty a plaintiff must show:

   ■ a course of conduct that is so severe as to

   ■ create an adverse effect on plaintiff's physical or mental well-being.

   A single act of cruelty does not suffice to satisfy the "course of conduct" requirement unless the act is particularly severe.

2. **Physical versus mental cruelty:** Early American courts required actual or threatened physical violence. Courts gradually permitted mental cruelty to suffice.

   Example: Wife files for divorce, alleging that Husband's demands that she relocate to an Islamic community constitute cruel and inhuman treatment. Wife claims that the community's restrictions and rules (e.g., the requirement that women obtain permission from their husbands before leaving the confines of the community) are oppressive. Although Husband did not physically harm Wife, the court holds that the Husband's conduct constitutes mental cruelty. *Muhammad v. Muhammad*, 622 So.2d 1239 (Miss. 1993).

Note: Some courts required that the mental cruelty be sufficiently severe as to pose a danger to plaintiff's well-being. The requirement of adverse effect was thought necessary to overcome the judicial concern regarding fraudulent claims.

B. Adultery

1. **Elements:** To prove adultery a plaintiff must show:

   ■ opportunity to commit the offense; and

   ■ disposition to commit it.

   Although courts generally require corroboration for fault-based grounds, they permit circumstantial evidence to prove adultery because the sexual conduct occurs in private.

   Example: Judy and Orville are married for 17 years. Judy works as a secretary, bookkeeper, and office manager for Orville's construction company. Judy becomes suspicious that Orville is having an affair with his new receptionist, Sheila, because the pair spends considerable time together and are absent from work at the same time. In addition, Orville gave Sheila $2,500. Judy fires Sheila, but Orville rehires her and fires his wife. Judy sues for divorce based on adultery. The court finds that there is sufficient testimony that Orville and Sheila had opportunities to conduct their affair and, despite Orville's denials, the facts are sufficient to establish his infatuation. *Lister v. Lister*, 981 So.2d 340 (Miss. Ct. App. 2008).

   Jurisdictions traditionally required that acts of sexual intercourse were necessary to establish adultery, although the requirement has been liberalized to permit a lesser showing (noncoital acts).

2. **Criminal versus civil overlap**

   a. **Definition:** Adultery is a *crime* as well as a *civil* ground for divorce. At common law, the crime could be committed only with a married woman. For divorce purposes, the definition is broadened to include sexual misconduct with any person other than the defendant's legal spouse.

   b. **Double standard:** Historically, a double standard existed regarding proof of adultery for divorce purposes. For a wife, a single sexual act might satisfy the requirements, whereas a *course* of adulterous conduct was required for a husband.

C. Desertion

1. **Elements:** Desertion, or abandonment, serves as another traditional ground for divorce. It requires:

   ■ a voluntary separation;

   ■ with intent not to resume cohabitation;

   ■ that is without consent or justification.

2. **Constructive desertion:** Constructive desertion serves both as an alternative ground for divorce and as a defense. It constitutes conduct that either causes a spouse to leave or justifies the spouse's departure.

Example: Wife files for divorce, claiming constructive desertion. She identifies the following marital problems as justifying her departure: (1) Husband's sexual difficulties, (2) his excessive work habits, (3) his failure to assist in rearing their four children, and (4) a general lack of intimacy within the marriage. The court denies Wife's petition, finding that Husband's periodic impotence and long working hours did not justify Wife's departure. Instead, the court holds that, because Wife's response to the marital problems was to terminate marital cohabitation and file for divorce, she committed desertion (and thereby forfeited her right to spousal support). *Reid v. Reid*, 375 S.E.2d 533 (Va. Ct. App. 1989).

D. **Other grounds:** Other fault-based grounds for divorce include:

- habitual drunkenness or drug addiction;

- incurable impotence;

- failure to support;

- criminal conviction and/or imprisonment; and

- insanity.

III. FAULT-BASED DEFENSES

Fault-based defenses to divorce include recrimination, connivance, condonation, and collusion. These defenses are not relevant if the divorce is sought on no-fault grounds.

A. **Recrimination:**

1. **Rule:** Recrimination is the doctrine that bars divorce in cases in which both spouses are at fault (i.e., both spouses have grounds for divorce).

   Example: Wife seeks a divorce for cruel and inhuman treatment and presents evidence showing a pattern of Husband's systematic, continuous abuse that resulted in her hospitalization for anxiety-related disorders. Husband contends that Wife was guilty of adultery and that the defense of recrimination prohibits the granting to her of a divorce. The court rejects Husband's defense of recrimination, reasoning that Wife's adultery occurred only after the parties' separation (although some jurisdictions do consider adultery that occurs post-separation). *Parker v. Parker*, 519 So.2d 1232 (Miss. 1988).

2. **Policy rationale:** Policy rationale includes the clean hands doctrine, the idea that divorce should be permitted only for an innocent spouse, preservation of marriage, and the need to provide economic protection to women by denying divorce in order to force husbands to continue to support wives.

3. **Criticism:** Critics charge that the doctrine denies divorces for marriages that genuinely deserve to end.

4. **Limitations:** The harshness of the doctrine led some courts to develop the **doctrine of comparative rectitude** by which a court could determine the degrees of fault and award the divorce to the party who was least at fault.

   Example: Danielle and Christopher separate after he discovers that she is having an affair. She petitions for a divorce on both fault and no-fault grounds. He cross-petitions on the same dual grounds. Eleven months after the wife files for divorce, the husband has an affair (with the wife of the husband with whom his wife had had an affair). The petitioner-wife alleges the defense of recrimination (i.e., husband's adultery). The trial court grants the wife's motion and enters a final decree of no-fault divorce. The husband appeals, arguing that his adultery cannot be used as the basis for the defense of recrimination because it did not cause the breakdown of the marriage given that his adulterous conduct occurred 11 months after his wife filed for divorce. The wife counters that he was not an "innocent party," as the statute required. The state supreme court agrees with the wife. The court explains that, although the statute requires an "innocent party," the timing of the husband's adultery is irrelevant because he was still married when he had his affair. The court also finds that causation is not an element of the defense of recrimination. *Ire Matter of Ross*, 146 A.3d 1232 (N.H. 2016).

B. Connivance: Connivance is participation in, or consent to, the defendant's wrongful conduct. The doctrine was usually limited to suits for adultery.

Example: Suspecting that Wife is fond of their chauffeur, Husband intentionally gives the chauffeur ample opportunity, both during the daytime and at night, to be with Wife. Husband also hires detectives to spy on Wife and inform him of her activities. Husband seeks a divorce on ground of adultery. The court denies the divorce because Husband actively facilitated Wife's commission of adultery and made no effort to warn her or to fire his employee. *Sargent v. Sargent*, 114 A. 428 (N.J. Chancery Div. 1920).

C. Condonation: Condonation means that a spouse who has once condoned marital misconduct, such as adultery, is barred from using that misconduct as a grounds for divorce. Condonation exists if the wronged spouse resumes sexual relations with the wrongdoer following knowledge of the wrongdoer's misconduct. Some courts require both forgiveness and the resumption of sexual intercourse after the misconduct; others hold that either element suffices. The policy rationale is to encourage reconciliation. One criticism of the condonation doctrine is its harsh application to the forgiving spouse.

Example: Joesie confesses an affair to her husband Michael but not its lengthy duration (she admits only that she had "a brief fling"). Joesie and Michael file for no-fault divorce, but they put the divorce complaint on hold for two years during Michael's military commitment. When Michael wants to finalize the divorce, Joesie withdraws her consent to a no-fault divorce. Both file for fault-based divorce on the ground of adultery (the details of Michael's alleged adultery are unspecified). The trial judge awards a no-fault divorce, finding that neither party is entitled to a fault-based divorce: Joesie failed to establish adultery on his part, and Michael proved adultery (based on her confession) but condoned her adulterous conduct. Michael appeals. The Mississippi Supreme Court grants Michael's petition for a fault-based divorce (based on his wife's adultery), finding that Michael condoned only the "fling" but not the entirety of her affair because she never disclosed it. *Gerty v. Gerty*, 265 So. 3d 121 (Miss. 2018).

Some states limit the defense of condonation to dissolutions based on adultery.

Example: Wife petitions for divorce based on abandonment as well as cruel and inhuman treatment, claiming that Husband left the marital home and engaged in adultery (with the adultery serving as the "cruel and inhuman treatment" under New York law). Husband responds by asserting, first, that his departure was justified because Wife admitted her long-term extramarital affair and, second, that his adultery could not constitute cruel and inhuman treatment because it followed on the heels of Wife's revelations. Wife then asserts the defense of condonation, claiming that Husband forgave her infidelity and that the parties attempted to reconcile. The court rules that her defense of condonation fails because that defense is applicable only to a cause of action for adultery (pursuant to New York law) and not to the ground of cruel and inhuman treatment (as pleaded here), and also because condonation requires proof of a resumption of marital relations that Wife failed to establish. Instead, the court finds that Husband has proven grounds for divorce because of Wife's extramarital conduct. *P.K. v. R.K.*, 820 N.Y.S.2d 844 (Sup. Ct. 2006).

D. Collusion

1. **Rule:** Collusion occurs when the spouses agree (or fabricate evidence) that one partner commits a marital offense to provide grounds for divorce.

   Example: Husband seeks, and is granted, a divorce on the ground of adultery. Wife defaults. Wife seeks to set aside the default and defend, alleging that she never committed adultery and only agreed to give plaintiff a divorce because he promised that if she did so, she could have custody of their child. The court grants Wife's motion to set aside the default for the policy reason that courts desire to prevent collusion. *Rankin v. Rankin*, 124 A.2d 639 (Pa. Super. Ct. 1956).

2. **Connivance distinguished:** Connivance includes *consent* by one spouse to the other spouse's marital misconduct, whereas collusion includes a spousal *agreement* to commit a marital wrong.

E. Insanity: Insanity was both a traditional ***ground*** for divorce as well as a ***defense***.

Quiz Yourself on
FAULT-BASED GROUNDS AND DEFENSES

55. Husband files for divorce in a fault-based jurisdiction, alleging that Wife is guilty of cruel and inhuman treatment. Husband alleges that Wife posted YouTube videos to discuss the couple's marital troubles and to humiliate Husband. Husband claims that, in response, he left the marital home, sought medical treatment from his doctor for stress, and obtained psychological counseling. Will Husband be successful? _____

56. Husband and Wife are married for 20 years. Several years ago, Wife has an extramarital affair of which Husband was aware. After the Husband's discovery of Wife's affair, the couple continues to live together and have sexual relations. Wife petitions for divorce on the ground of Husband's cruelty in a fault-based jurisdiction. She maintains that he frequently is drunk, vomits throughout the house, provokes arguments, threatens violence, and makes excessive sexual demands. Husband defends by alleging Wife's adultery. Will Wife prevail? _____

57. Husband is aware that Wife has had several extramarital affairs during the marriage (as has he). He arranges for a private detective either to engage in an intimate relationship with Wife or to hire persons to do so. Detective employs numerous persons, at least one of whom does engage in sexual conduct with Wife. Husband petitions for divorce on the ground of Wife's adultery in a fault-based jurisdiction. Will Husband's suit for divorce be successful? _____

Answers

55. Yes. Wife engaged in a course of conduct that was severe by posting multiple YouTube videos designed to publicly humiliate Husband. Wife's actions prompted Husband to seek medical and psychological treatment, thereby satisfying the "adverse effect" requirement.

56. Yes. The divorce was properly granted on the ground of Husband's cruelty. Under the recrimination doctrine (where both parties are at fault), Wife's adulterous conduct would prevent her from obtaining the divorce she sought. However, here Husband condoned her adultery by continuing to live with Wife and have sexual relations with her, after he had knowledge of her sexual indiscretion.

57. No. Wife has a claim of connivance that constitutes a defense to Husband's claim of adultery. Husband intentionally provided opportunities for Wife's adultery.

IV. NO-FAULT DIVORCE

- A. **Early no-fault grounds:** Early no-fault grounds were "living separate and apart" and "incompatibility."

  - 1. **Living separate and apart:**

    - a. **Elements:** Some state laws predated the no-fault revolution by providing for divorce based on the parties' separation for a statutorily designated period of time. This divorce ground eliminated proof of fault. Today, most states continue to provide for no-fault divorce based on the ground of physical separation. Some states require that marital breakdown be shown by a separation for a statutorily designated period. Other states engraft this ground upon fault-based grounds. That is, these states require that if marital breakdown cannot be proven by physical separation for the statutorily designated period (between six months and two years), the parties may resort to fault-based grounds.

    - b. **Meaning of separate and apart:** The term "living separate and apart" may refer to both the physical separation and the intention to dissolve the marriage. Courts differ as to the relevance of, and interpretation of, these two requirements.

    - c. **Physical separation:** Some courts hold that the spouses have lived "separate and apart" even though they live in the same house (e.g., in separate bedrooms). Other courts require that the spouses maintain separate residences (despite the financial burden this requirement imposes).

  - 2. **Incompatibility:** Incompatibility was one of the earliest no-fault grounds. The standard was not as widely adopted as the marital breakdown standard of either California or UMDA (discussed *infra*).

- B. **Modern no-fault legislation:** All states now have some form of no-fault divorce. The no-fault revolution was initiated by *California* legislation in 1968. The Uniform Law Commission later promulgated another approach with the *Uniform Marriage and Divorce Act* (UMDA).

  The policy underlying no fault is the recognition that divorce is not caused by a party's "fault" (i.e., an act or acts of misconduct). Rather, divorce is caused by a gradual breakdown in the marital relationship. As a result, neither party should be punished in the dissolution process.

1. **Variations in no-fault regimes**

    a. **Definitions of no fault:** States define no fault differently. Some states equate no fault with "irreconcilable differences" between the parties. Other states define "no fault" to signify a marital breakdown that results in the parties physically living apart for a statutorily defined period of time.

    b. **Pure no-fault v. mixed jurisdictions:** Some states are pure no-fault jurisdictions, i.e., eliminating proof of fault. Other states merely add a no-fault ground (such as "incompatibility," "living separate and apart," or "marital breakdown") to their fault-based grounds.

    c. **Unilateral or mutual consent:** Some states permit a no-fault divorce only if both parties consent. If these states, if mutual consent is lacking, then divorce is available only on fault grounds. In contrast, most states permit a no-fault divorce if only one spouse desires it.

2. **California approach:** California legislation permits divorce on the ground of "irreconcilable differences which have caused the irremediable breakdown of the marriage." Cal. Fam. Code §2310(a).

    Irreconcilable differences are defined as: "those grounds which are determined by the court to be substantial reasons for not continuing the marriage and which make it appear that the marriage should be dissolved." Cal. Fam. Code §2311.

3. **UMDA approach:** UMDA permits divorce if the marriage is "irretrievably broken." "Irretrievable breakdown" may be established by either: a six-month separation, or a showing of "serious marital discord adversely affecting the attitude of one or both of the parties to the marriage." UMDA §302(a)(2).

4. **Problems accompanying the trend to no-fault:** A number of problems accompanied the shift from fault-based grounds to no fault:

    ■ some confusion existed as to the continued viability of fault-based defenses;

    ■ a few states wrestled with whether a no-fault divorce could be granted in cases of nonconsensual divorces (where only one party desired the divorce).

    A minority of states currently limit the availability of nonconsensual divorces to fault-based actions. The majority, in contrast, will grant a no-fault divorce even if only one spouse contends that the marriage is ended.

5. **New York reform:** New York was the last state to adopt pure no-fault in 2010. Prior to 1967, the only ground for divorce in New York was adultery. Subsequently, divorce was permitted on several fault-based grounds (i.e., cruelty, abandonment, incarceration, adultery), as well as the no-fault ground of "living separate and apart" for one year based upon either a judicial separation decree or a separation agreement between the parties. If the spouses could not reach an agreement on any marital settlement term (custody, support, property), they were required to resort to fault grounds.

6. **Re-emergence of fault reform movement:** Despite the widespread adoption of no fault, some states still consider fault to be relevant in the division of marital property and the determination of spousal support.

    Note: UMDA precludes consideration of marital misconduct as a factor in property division (UMDA §307) or spousal support (UMDA §308).

7. **Covenant marriage:** A reform movement in the 1990s culminated in the adoption of "covenant marriage" laws in a few states (Louisiana in 1997, Arizona in 1998, and Arkansas in 2001) that make it more difficult for couples to obtain no-fault divorces. Generally, covenant marriage laws permit divorce only after a two-year separation or proof of fault (e.g., adultery, commission of a felony or domestic violence, or abandonment).

Quiz Yourself on *NO-FAULT DIVORCE*

58. Mary and Larry, a married couple, cease having sexual relations after Mary suffers a stroke rendering her completely paralyzed. Eight years later, because of marital discord, Larry moves out of the house and into a travel van adjacent to the house. He continues to help Mary with household chores. This arrangement continues for several years. When Larry files suit for divorce based on the grounds of living separate and apart for at least two years without cohabitation, will he prevail? _____

59. Gail and Richard have been married for 20 years when Richard moves out of the house and begins engaging in affairs with several women. Three months later, Gail retains legal counsel and files for dissolution. If Gail resides in a jurisdiction that permits divorce on the ground of "irreconcilable differences," will she prevail? _____

60. Same basic facts as above. If Gail resides in a jurisdiction that follows the UMDA approach, will she prevail? _____

61. After 22 years of marriage, Barbara petitions for divorce and also sues Henry for intentional and negligent infliction of emotional distress. She alleges that Henry was verbally abusive by criticizing and belittling her, being explosive and rageful (i.e., having frequent temper tantrums although he never physically assaulted her), and tightly controlling all finances (i.e., refusing to let her write checks, giving her only $20 at a time for groceries, and insisting on buying all her clothes). Will Barbara be successful on her claim of emotional distress? _____

Answers

58. Perhaps. The term "living separate and apart" may require both physical separation and the intention to dissolve the marriage. Some courts require that the spouses maintain separate residences and hold themselves out to the public as not living together. Depending on the jurisdiction, Larry's living in the travel van adjacent to the house may or may not qualify as living separate and apart. Similarly, the fact that the couple continued to hold themselves out as married may militate against a finding that they lived separate and apart. Finally, there was no cessation of marital duties because Larry continued to help with household chores—an additional factor that might militate against a finding that the couple lived separate and apart.

59. Yes. Irreconcilable differences (based on the model California no-fault legislation) are those differences that have caused the irremediable breakdown of the marriage. Gail could successfully argue that Richard's conduct caused the marriage to break down and that such a situation was irremediable.

60. Yes. UMDA permits divorce if the marriage is "irretrievably broken." This divorce ground may be established *either* by a six-month separation or by a showing of "serious marital discord adversely affecting the attitude of one or both of the parties to the marriage." Although Richard and Gail have only been apart for three months (not the requisite six months), Gail could prove that Richard's extramarital affairs were adversely affecting her attitude toward continuation of the marriage.

61. Perhaps. For claims of infliction of emotional distress, courts generally require that a defendant's conduct be extreme and outrageous. Barbara will prevail if a jury finds that Henry's conduct (verbal abuse, rage, and controlling all finances) was sufficiently outrageous. The policy question is whether the allowance of interspousal claims for emotional distress in divorce actions reintroduces fault into the divorce process.

V. ACCESS TO DIVORCE

A. Religious limitations: The Get

1. **Judicial redress for husband's denial of divorce:** Under Orthodox Jewish law, a wife whose husband civilly divorces her without granting her a religious divorce (a "Get") is unable to remarry. If she does remarry, the subsequent marriage is adulterous: any ensuing children are considered illegitimate and are unable to marry another Jew. Some husbands use the threat of denying their wives a "Get" to exact financial concessions from them.

    Women have challenged judicial refusal to enforce a "Get" based on tort and contract principles. Some defendants have raised constitutional defenses, contending that judicial enforcement of the "Get" violates the First Amendment's Free Exercise Clause (the husband's right to practice or not practice his religion), as well as the Establishment Clause (prohibiting governmental entanglement in religion).

2. **Legislative reform:** The New York legislature enacted a "Get" statute in 1983, providing that no final judgment of divorce may be granted unless the petitioner has taken all steps within his or her power to remove all barriers to remarriage. N.Y. Dom. Rel. Law §253. In addition, a New York equitable distribution statute permits a judge to consider any "barriers to remarriage" in determinations regarding property distribution and spousal support. N.Y. Dom. Rel. Law §236B(5)(h). A bill (A.B. 392) is pending in the New York legislature to require *both parties* (rather than only the petitioner as formerly) to remove all religious barriers to remarriage within 90 days of filing as well as to impose sanctions on recalcitrant spouses of $2,500 per week until all barriers are removed.

B. Financial limitations: Filing fees:
The state cannot require an indigent to pay filing fees and court costs prior to filing for divorce.

Example: Connecticut law requires that litigants pay court fees and costs for service of process in order to bring an action for divorce. Welfare recipients challenge the statute as a violation of their due process rights. The state asserts an interest in prevention of frivolous litigation and the need to use fees and costs to allocate scarce resources, and the striking of a reasonable balance between a defendant's right to notice and the plaintiff's right of access. The U.S. Supreme Court holds that the statutory cost requirement violates due process because the cost forecloses an indigent's right to be heard (when the bona fides of indigence and desire for divorce are undisputed). The Court bases its holding on the position of marriage in society's hierarchy of values as well as the state monopolization of the means for divorce (divorce courts are the only forum available).

None of the state's asserted interests are sufficient to override the plaintiff's right to access: No connection exists between assets and seriousness in bringing suit; alternatives exist to fees and cost requirements to deter frivolous litigation (penalties); and alternatives exist to costly personal service of process (mailing). *Boddie v. Connecticut*, 401 U.S. 371 (1971).

Note that some states currently impose fees on divorce filings for the purpose of funding domestic violence centers and/or services.

C. **Right to counsel:** Jurisdictions are divided on whether an indigent person has a right to counsel in divorce proceedings based on state constitutional or statutory law.

Example: Brenda is the primary caretaker of the couple's three children during a ten-year marriage. At the divorce proceeding, the husband (Michael) is represented by counsel, whereas Brenda proceeds pro se. After the trial court awards custody to Michael but visitation to Brenda, Brenda moves for a new trial. When her request for court-appointed counsel is denied, she argues that an indigent parent has a due process right to counsel in dissolution proceedings based on the state constitution. The Washington Supreme Court disagrees, holding that a parent's due process right of access to the courts, as guaranteed by the state constitution, does not include a right to publicly funded counsel in a dissolution action (and distinguishes the case from parental termination proceedings in which counsel is provided because the state seeks to sever the parent-child relationship permanently). *King v. King*, 174 P.3d 659 (Wash. 2007).

Example: Christine is awarded a divorce from her husband David and all the marital property. David, who is serving a life sentence in state prison, moves for relief from the default judgment and for appointment of court-appointed counsel due to his indigent status. A state statute imposes a mandatory duty on the courts to appoint counsel for civil litigants who meet the statute's requirements. The state supreme court determines that the statute requires appointment of counsel for indigents in civil actions, including divorce, and that such counsel must be compensated. *Sholes v. Sholes*, 760 N.E.2d 156 (Ind. 2001).

D. **Summary dissolution:** A few jurisdictions provide for summary dissolutions of marriage. For example, California permits dissolutions without hearings in cases of short marriages (less than five years), for couples with no minor children and no real property, who have agreed to the disposition of marital property, and who waive claims for support. Cal. Fam. Code §2400.

E. **Pro se divorce:** Pro se divorces permit an individual to act as his or her own lawyer, thereby decreasing the costs of divorce. A considerable number of family law cases, including dissolutions, involve individuals who represent themselves.

F. **Comparative perspective:** The Philippines and Vatican City are the last two countries that ban divorce.

VI. DISCRIMINATION ON THE BASIS OF DIVORCE

Courts have held that discrimination on the basis of divorce violates the Constitution as well as state civil rights statutes.

A. **Constitutional protection:** One court has ruled that divorce discrimination violates the constitutional right to privacy.

Example: Linda Littlejohn, an untenured elementary school teacher, receives positive evaluations. Untenured teachers normally are rehired for the following year. Littlejohn and her husband divorce. Despite the principal's recommendation that Linda be rehired, the superintendent decides not to do so, telling the principal that the refusal is based on Linda's divorce. Linda institutes an action in federal district court, contending that the superintendent's action was a violation of her constitutional right to privacy. The school district moves for, and is granted, a directed verdict. The appellate court holds that the district court's grant of a directed verdict for the school district was improper. A denial of employment based on an employee's impending divorce is constitutionally impermissible as a violation of plaintiff's fundamental right to privacy regarding her marital status. *Littlejohn v. Rose*, 768 F.2d 765 (6th Cir. 1985), *cert. denied*, 475 U.S. 1045 (1986).

B. **State civil rights protection:** Some courts hold that divorce discrimination constitutes "marital status" discrimination under state civil rights laws.

Example: Robert Smith is a paramedic/EMT employed by a medical transport company, Millville Rescue Squad (MRS). His wife Mary is also employed at MRS. In 2005, Robert has an affair with an MRS volunteer. Their mutual supervisor suggests to Robert "that he could not promise that the affair would not affect plaintiff's job" and that his continued employment depended on "how it shakes down." After the marriage ends, the supervisor tells Robert that he predicts "an ugly divorce," that he might have to take the issue to the Board of Directors and gives Robert eight months to "make things right." The Board fires Robert, citing reasons of poor performance and restructuring. Robert later refutes those reasons by asserting that he had an excellent employment record, was never subjected to formal discipline, was promoted twice, and received annual raises.

Robert sues for wrongful discrimination based on sex and marital status in violation of state anti-discrimination law. The state employment discrimination statute protects against employment discrimination based on "race, sex, marital status, national origin, and age." The term "marital status" is not defined. The New Jersey Supreme Court adopts a broad interpretation of "marital status," concluding that the term includes persons who are single or married as well as those who are "in transition from one [marital] state to another." The court reasons that such a holding is in accord with the "purpose and goals" of the statute (i.e., the goal of eradicating discrimination in the workplace) and would prevent an employer from resorting to stereotypes in its assessment of an employee that bear no relation to the employee's actual performance. The court remands, saying that the evidence presented a jury question regarding whether the employee was terminated because of his marital status. *Smith v. Millville Rescue Squad*, 139 A.3d 1 (N.J. 2016).

Note: No federal law expressly prohibits discrimination based on marital status.

VII. ROLE OF COUNSEL

Several ethical issues arise in the representation of family law clients.

A. **Joint representation**

1. **Different approaches:** Divorcing parties occasionally seek joint representation to decrease the costs associated with divorce. Some states regard *dual* or *joint representation* (i.e., an attorney represents both spouses) in a divorce action as unethical because it presents an inherent conflict of interest.

   Other states, following the ABA Model Rules of Professional Conduct (promulgated in 1983), permit the practice only if the attorney informs the clients about the risks of dual representation and obtains each client's written consent thereto (Model Rules of Professional Conduct, Rule 1.7). If potential or actual conflicts of interest do arise (e.g., regarding support, property, or custody), the attorney must withdraw or face disciplinary charges.

2. **Dispelling the aura of dual representation:** An attorney may not give advice to an unrepresented opposing party. Further, the attorney owes a duty to an unrepresented opposing party not to give the impression that the attorney is representing both parties. ABA Model Rule 4.3 requires a lawyer to refrain from implying that she or he is disinterested and also to correct an unrepresented client's misunderstanding to that effect. An attorney who takes advantage of an opposing client's lack of representation may be disciplined, and any resulting agreement may be set aside on the ground of fraud.

Example: Wife employs Lawyer who contacts and makes an appointment with unrepresented Husband. Lawyer then informs Husband that he and Wife must divide their property and that Husband has to pay Wife spousal support. When Husband inquires whether he needs independent representation, Lawyer replies that Husband should let Lawyer represent both parties for cost reasons. Husband (who has minimal education, has just started a business, and earns considerably less than Wife) agrees to unfavorable provisions regarding property (i.e., waiving his community property rights) and spousal support. Lawyer refuses to explain to Husband the terms of the agreement, or to give him time to read them, and secures his stipulation as to a default without Husband's knowledge or understanding. Husband subsequently retains separate counsel and seeks to have the agreement set aside. The trial court cancels the marital settlement agreement, holding that the agreement was procured by extrinsic fraud. Attorney's fraud consisted of omissions and deceptive representations that prevented Husband from acquiring knowledge of his rights. *Adkins v. Adkins*, 186 Cal. Rptr. 818 (Ct. App. 1982).

3. **Confidentiality issues:** One of the dangers of joint representation is that an attorney who previously represented one or both spouses may use knowledge that was acquired in the earlier representation adversely to one of the former clients. The ABA Model Rules of Professional Conduct (Rule 1.6) address this problem by requiring that a lawyer not reveal confidential information or use such information to the disadvantage of a client or to the advantage of a third person.

Example: Husband and Wife meet with Lawyer to discuss their marital problems. Lawyer believes he is "counseling" them in hopes of reconciliation. Husband and Wife decide to divorce and both retain separate counsel (not Lawyer). Subsequently, Husband meets with Lawyer, discusses the case with him and asks him to represent him. Lawyer defers a decision on representing Husband. A few days later, Lawyer agrees to represent Wife. He later withdraws when Husband protests. Husband files a complaint with the bar association against Lawyer. The court holds that Lawyer violated rules of professional conduct and should be reprimanded. Lawyer obtained confidential information when he "counseled" both spouses. Thereafter, he could no longer represent either. It was also improper for Lawyer to agree to represent Wife after Lawyer discussed marital problems with Husband. *In re Braun*, 227 A.2d 506 (N.J. Super. Ct. 1967).

B. **Representation of clients in different suits involving related matters:** Representation of clients involved in different lawsuits that deal with "substantially related" matters may give rise to prohibited conflicts of interest.

Example: Lawyer represents Husband and Wife in their acquisition of a business. Lawyer then represents Husband in the couple's divorce. The conflict of interest arose because the business was an asset of the marital estate, and Counsel would have had to argue on behalf of Husband that he was entitled to a greater share of the business. When Wife later complains, Lawyer fails to show that Wife consented to such a conflict, and it is shown that Lawyer used personal information to the detriment of his former client (Wife). The Florida Bar determines that Lawyer violated several rules of attorney conduct and recommends that his license be suspended. *Florida Bar v. Dunagan*, 731 So.2d 1237 (Fla. 1999).

Courts often must determine whether two legal matters are sufficiently "substantially related" to result in disqualification or sanctions of an attorney.

Example: Counsel represents Wife in a personal injury action. Counsel then represents Husband in the couple's divorce action. The court holds that the attorney was properly disqualified from subsequently representing Husband in the divorce because the two matters (personal injury action and the divorce) were "substantially related" given the fact that the attorney had obtained confidential information from Wife in the personal injury action concerning her health, her employment history, and her response to contested litigation that could be used to her detriment in the dissolution action regarding issues of custody, support, and property. *Hurley v. Hurley*, 923 A.2d 908 (Me. 2007).

Example: Counsel represents a man in a bankruptcy proceeding. Counsel then represents the man's former lover in her defense against a paternity action brought by the bankruptcy client. The court holds that Counsel violated the disciplinary rule prohibiting representation that would conflict with the representation of a former client because Counsel obtained confidences from the first client (in the bankruptcy proceeding) regarding his finances that created a conflict of interest in the attorney's subsequent representation of the second client in the paternity action that would cause injury to the first client regarding custody and support. *In re Conduct of Balocca*, 151 P.3d 154 (Or. 2007).

C. Sexual relations with clients

1. **Different approaches:** An increasing number of states regulate attorney-client sexual relationships. These states adopt a variety of approaches.

   - Some states prohibit any sexual relationship between attorneys and clients (this per se prohibition is the strictest approach);

   - Some states ban attorney-client sexual relations but exempt those sexual relationships that predate the representation;

   - Some states prohibit only those attorney-client sexual relationships that adversely affect the practice of law.

   At least one state's ban (New York) on attorney-client sexual relationships applies specifically to domestic relations attorneys during the course of representation (22 NYCRR §1200.0; Rule 1.8(j)). Finally, some states permit the imposition of tort liability and/or sanctions (criminal sanctions or sanctions for violations of state business and professions code).

   Example: Lawyer has sex with client on several occasions over a five-month period while representing her in a dissolution proceeding. The court finds that Lawyer violated Iowa Code of Professional Responsibility for Lawyers DR 5-101(A) (an absolute prohibition on a lawyer's engaging in sexual relations with a client) and DR 1-102(A)(1) and (6) (providing that a lawyer shall not violate a disciplinary rule or engage in any other conduct that adversely reflects on the fitness to practice law). The court imposes a three-month suspension because Lawyer was previously admonished for making sexual advances toward another client only eight months before. *Iowa Supreme Court Attorney Disciplinary Bd. v. Morrison*, 727 N.W.2d 115 (Iowa 2007).

Some critics object to these restrictions, arguing that they interfere with the rights to freedom of expression and association.

2. **Background:** California was the first state, in 1991, to adopt restrictions on sexual relations with clients (such as in cases involving coercion).

3. **Special case of coercion:** Courts take a particularly dim view of attorneys' sexual misconduct with clients when the sexual relationship is coerced.

4. **ABA Rule:** ABA Model Rules of Professional Conduct Rule 1.8(j) ("Sexual Relations with Clients") prohibits sexual relations between attorney and client absent a preexisting consensual sexual relationship.

5. **States without specific bans may still find ethical violations:** Even without a specific state prohibition on attorney-client sexual relations, a state may nonetheless determine that the attorney's sexual conduct constitutes a violation of *general* conflict-of-interest rules (such as ABA Model Rules of Professional Conduct Rule 1.7: "Conflict of Interest: Current Clients").

   Example: Lawyer engages in a sexual relationship with a client while he is representing her in a dissolution proceeding. He ends the sexual relationship a few weeks later. The client enters psychological treatment as a result of the affair. In a disciplinary hearing, the state supreme court rules that Lawyer's sexual conduct warrants a 30-day suspension, reasoning that the sexual relationship constituted a prohibited conflict of interest even though the relationship was consensual, the client retained Lawyer to represent her in a subsequent action, and there was no evidence of incompetent representation. *In re Tsoutsouris*, 748 N.E.2d 856 (Ind. 2001).

D. **Fees:** Unlike in civil actions where the litigants pay their own attorneys' fees, a court may order one spouse in a divorce proceeding to pay the other's fees. Note that contingent fees in divorce actions are unethical based on the rationale that an attorney may discourage reconciliation if his or her fee depends on the granting of a divorce.

Quiz Yourself on ## *ROLE OF COUNSEL*

62. Husband calls Lawyer, who has previously represented Husband in business dealings, and asks Lawyer to represent Wife and Husband in their divorce. Lawyer agrees and draws up a complaint and property settlement. Lawyer gives documents to Husband who has Wife execute them. Wife later charges Lawyer with malpractice when she discovers that she surrendered her right to an interest in certain community property—the existence of which Husband did not disclose to Lawyer. Will Lawyer incur liability for dual representation? _____

63. Atticus Attorney is retained to represent Cleo Client in a family law matter. During Atticus's representation of Cleo, Atticus's wife files for divorce on several grounds, including adultery. During Atticus's representation of Cleo, and while his own divorce action is pending, Atticus is observed leaving Cleo's residence at 3:00 A.M. on a night that Cleo had custody of her minor child. In a disciplinary proceeding, may Atticus be suspended from the practice of law? _____

Answers

62. Yes. Many states regard dual representation in a divorce action as unethical because it presents an inherent conflict of interest. In this dual representation situation, Lawyer breached his duty of care to Wife. Lawyer should have obtained verification of Husband's financial statement or, at least, informed Wife of the limited representation that she was receiving and pointed out that she might need independent advice.

63. Probably yes. Depending on the jurisdiction, a court might find that suspension is an appropriate disciplinary sanction for an attorney who engages in sexual behavior with a client after the attorney separates from his wife and while representing his client. Here, Atticus failed to inform the client of the possible negative implications of their sexual relationship on the issue of child custody.

VIII. DIVORCE JURISDICTION

A. Terminology

1. **Jurisdiction in the divorce context:** Jurisdiction refers to *subject matter jurisdiction* that is necessary for the plaintiff to secure a divorce (i.e., durational residency and/or domiciliary requirements) and *personal jurisdiction* over the defendant. (Jurisdictional rules pertaining to personal jurisdiction over the defendant in the divorce context differ from personal jurisdiction rules in other civil contexts, as explained below.)

2. **Definition of domicile:** Domicile includes the twin elements of: physical presence plus intent to remain permanently. Generally, domicile is distinguishable from "residence" because a person may have more than one residence (e.g., a college student) but only one legal domicile. However, some states' "durational residency" requirements for divorce are construed so as to be indistinguishable from "domicile."

3. **Ex parte versus bilateral divorce:** In an *ex parte (or unilateral) divorce*, the court has personal jurisdiction over only one spouse. In a **bilateral divorce**, the court has personal jurisdiction over both spouses. A bilateral divorce, because it is premised on jurisdiction over both parties, cannot be collaterally attacked.

4. **Divisible divorce:** Under this doctrine, a court in an ex parte divorce has jurisdiction *only over the marital status* of the parties. That is, the court can render a divorce decree. *However, the court may not determine the support and property rights of the absent spouse.* This result follows because the court does not have personal jurisdiction over the "stay-at-home" spouse.

B. Subject matter jurisdiction

1. **Traditional rule: Domiciliary jurisdiction:** A state has jurisdiction to dissolve a marriage based on the petitioner's **domicile** in the forum state. Thus, a state's domiciliary requirements, sometimes termed "durational residency requirements" (generally applicable to the divorce petitioner), confer subject matter jurisdiction over the marriage upon a given court. Further, jurisdiction for divorce purposes is "in rem," i.e., over the marital status.

2. **Importance of domiciliary requirement:** The domiciliary requirement assumed considerable importance during the fault era for a spouse who might want to evade strict fault-based grounds

in the marital forum. The importance of the domiciliary requirement diminished with the advent of no fault. It still has relevance, however, for those spouses who relocate to another state at some point during the marital breakup (e.g., for employment or other personal reasons) and who desire to obtain a divorce in the new forum.

3. **Restatement view: Divorce without domicile:** Presence alone, normally, is insufficient to confer jurisdiction for divorce purposes. The Restatement (Second) of Conflict of Laws relaxes the traditional domiciliary requirement. According to the Restatement, a state can dissolve a marriage:

   - if both spouses are domiciled in the state (§70); or

   - if one of the spouses is domiciled in the state (§71); or

   - if neither spouse is domiciled in the state provided that either spouse has "such a relationship to the state as would make it reasonable for the state to dissolve that marriage" (§72).

   The relaxation of the traditional rule would enable a member of the military or that person's spouse, for example, to obtain a divorce in the jurisdiction where the member of the armed services is stationed. See also UMDA §302(a)(1) (authorizing divorce for a member of the armed services based on that person's "military presence" in the state).

4. **Durational residency requirements:** Some states impose durational residency requirements instead of a domiciliary requirement, or in addition to that requirement. Durational residency requirements require a petitioner to be a state resident for a period varying from a minimum of six weeks to one year.

   Durational residency requirements may pose a barrier to a divorce petitioner who has recently moved to a state. The U.S. Supreme Court has held that these state requirements are constitutional.

   Example: Wife separates from Husband in New York and then moves with her three children to Iowa. One month later, she petitions an Iowa court for divorce. Husband, who was served with notice during a visit to Iowa to see the children, contests jurisdiction. The Iowa court dismisses Wife's petition on jurisdictional grounds because Husband is not a resident of Iowa, and Wife failed to satisfy the statutory requirement of one-year residency preceding her filing of the petition. Wife appeals, contending that Iowa's one-year residency requirement violates her constitutional right to travel. The U.S. Supreme Court upholds Iowa's residency requirement, reasoning that it minimizes the susceptibility of a state's decrees to collateral attack and avoids one state's interference in matters in which another state has an important interest. Further, Iowa's residency requirement does not foreclose a plaintiff's access to the courts but merely delays it. *Sosna v. Iowa*, 419 U.S. 393 (1975).

5. **Full Faith and Credit Clause:** The Full Faith and Credit Clause of the Constitution (Article IV, §1) requires that a state give full faith and credit to the decrees of sister states provided that the sister state had jurisdiction.

   This requirement was interpreted and applied to the divorce context by the U.S. Supreme Court (*Williams I* and *Williams II*, explained below).

   a. **The *Williams* cases:** The doctrine announced by the U.S. Supreme Court in the case of *Williams v. North Carolina* determines whether, and in what circumstances, a divorce decree granted by one state will be recognized by another state under the Full Faith and Credit Clause.

b. ***Williams I*: Whether to give full faith and credit:** *Williams I* holds that a court in State A must give full faith and credit to the divorce decree of a sister state (State B) when one of the parties is domiciled in that sister state (State B). That is, a state must recognize, under the Full Faith and Credit Clause, a divorce granted to a spouse who is domiciled in a sister state even though the stay-at-home spouse does not appear and is not served with process in the sister state.

Example: A shopkeeper in a small town in North Carolina elopes with his clerk's wife. The couple goes to Nevada to seek a divorce. After residing there for six weeks, they file for, and are granted, divorces from their respective spouses. They marry and return to their home town in North Carolina. They are tried and convicted of bigamous cohabitation and appeal. The convictions are overturned based on the U.S. Supreme Court's interpretation and application of the Full Faith and Credit Clause. The U.S. Supreme Court holds that a court in North Carolina must give full faith and credit to the divorce decree of Nevada when one of the spouses is domiciled in Nevada. Because the divorce decree states that the husband of one couple and the wife of the other couple were domiciled in Nevada, North Carolina must give full faith and credit to the decree. *Williams v. North Carolina*, 317 U.S. 287 (1942).

c. ***Williams II*: When to give full faith and credit:** *Williams II* examines the circumstances in which a jurisdictional determination of domicile for divorce may be challenged. In this case, the bona fides of the spouses' domicile in *Williams I* was at issue. Refining the rule of *Williams I*, the Supreme Court holds that one state's determination of a petitioner's domicile is not binding on another state. That is, the decree-granting state's finding of domicile may be reexamined by another state to determine the bona fides of a petitioner's domicile.

Example: North Carolina retries the shopkeeper and his second wife for bigamous cohabitation. The state asserts that the Nevada decree need not be recognized under Full Faith and Credit because the parties lacked a bona fide domicile in Nevada. The jury instructions charge that the statement in the Nevada decree that the petitioners were domiciled in Nevada is prima facie evidence of domicile. If, however, the jury finds that the petitioners went to Nevada for the sole purpose of obtaining a divorce, then the petitioners never established domicile there and Nevada's assertion of jurisdiction was invalid. The convictions are upheld this time. Although a state has the power to grant a divorce entitled to Full Faith and Credit (*Williams I*), the bona fides of the party's domicile in the decree-granting state may be re-examined. North Carolina may make its own determination of the bona fides of the parties' domicile in Nevada. *Williams v. North Carolina*, 325 U.S. 226 (1945) (*Williams II*).

d. ***Williams'* limitation to the ex parte situation:** The *Williams* rules (permitting judicial reexamination of the findings of jurisdiction by a sister state) operate if the divorce decree was entered in ex parte proceedings. However, the appearance of both parties in a bilateral divorce confers jurisdiction on the court and prevents reexamination of findings of jurisdictional fact.

Example: Margaret and Edward marry and live together in Massachusetts. Following marital strife, Wife takes their two children to Florida, allegedly for a visit. Wife files for divorce in Florida on the ground of cruelty. Husband retains Florida counsel, and enters a general appearance to deny the allegations. The Florida court grants the divorce. Wife remarries.

After two months in Florida, the newly married couple returns to Massachusetts. Former Husband files an action alleging that the Florida decree is invalid and Wife's subsequent marriage is void. The Supreme Court holds that the decree is valid and comports with due process. The Court reasons that, unlike in *Williams*, the finding of jurisdiction was made in a proceeding in which Husband appeared and participated. Full Faith and Credit requires recognition of a decree rendered by a court that has jurisdiction over both parties. *Sherrer v. Sherrer*, 334 U.S. 343 (1948).

Note: A special appearance by a defendant (i.e., defendant's participation in the proceedings for the limited purpose of contesting jurisdiction) will prevent application of the *Sherrer* rule.

C. **Personal jurisdiction over the defendant:** Personal jurisdiction over the defendant is not required to terminate a marriage if the plaintiff is domiciled in the forum state. This special jurisdictional rule, which varies from the usual rule in civil actions requiring personal jurisdiction over the defendant, dates back to *Pennoyer v. Neff*, 95 U.S. 714 (1878). Nonetheless, notice to the defendant in divorce cases that complies with due process is required to inform the defendant of the pendency of the action.

Furthermore, if personal jurisdiction over the defendant is not obtained, then the court may adjudicate only the issue of marital status (i.e., the termination of the marriage) but not the economic issues (i.e., spousal support, property division). This result follows because depriving the defendant of property rights (i.e., regarding support or property division) without due process would violate the Constitution.

Example: Wife, a citizen of Japan, challenges an Iowa court's jurisdiction to dissolve her marriage on the ground that petitioner-Husband failed to comply with Iowa's residency requirements and contends that Japan was the more convenient forum. The appellate court finds that (1) the trial court could exercise jurisdiction in the action brought by Husband, a permanent resident alien, without violating the wife's due process right, even though Wife was absent from Iowa, had never been there, and was constructively rather than personally served; (2) Husband established that his domicile was in Iowa for purposes of divorce jurisdiction (he had lived in Iowa for 13 months and had established residence in good faith); and (3) the refusal to dismiss the dissolution proceeding on *forum non conveniens* grounds was not an abuse of discretion because Husband would have been denied protection of Iowa's no-fault divorce law if the proceeding was held in Japan, Wife enjoyed vigorous representation in Iowa, and Iowa's rules on alimony and property division were beneficial to Wife. *In re Marriage of Kimura*, 471 N.W.2d 869 (Iowa 1991).

1. **Proper notice:** Proper notice, to comport with due process, must meet the standards established by the Supreme Court. That is, notice must be "reasonably calculated under all the circumstances, to apprise interested parties of the pendency of the action and afford them an opportunity [to be heard]." *Mullane v. Central Hanover Bank & Trust Co.*, 339 U.S. 306, 314 (1950). A divorce that does not meet proper notice requirements may be challenged for lack of jurisdiction.

   If the divorce petitioner knows of the defendant's whereabouts, then notice should be either by personal service or mail. However, if the defendant's whereabouts are unknown, notice may be satisfied by constructive service, such as notice by publication or posting.

   Example: Javin files a petition in Coffee County, Tennessee, to divorce his wife Mary. The petition states that Mary is a nonresident who resides in Miami Beach, Florida. He gives Mary notice by publication in a Tennessee county newspaper. After he is awarded a divorce based on

Mary's default, he remarries. Shortly thereafter, he dies. Mary files an action to set aside the divorce decree for lack of jurisdiction. The court holds that notice by publication fails to satisfy Wife's due process rights. Wife should have received *Mullane* notice ("notice reasonably calculated under all the circumstances, to apprise interested parties of the pendency of the action and afford them an opportunity [to be heard]." Javin knew or could have ascertained Mary's mailing address. *Baggett v. Baggett*, 541 S.W.2d 407 (Tenn. 1976).

2. **Long-arm statutes:** Although personal jurisdiction over a defendant is not essential for the sole purpose of ending a marriage, the assertion of personal jurisdiction is necessary to resolve the financial incidents of the divorce and also to ensure that a decree is entitled to full faith and credit. Long-arm statutes facilitate the assertion of personal jurisdiction over nonresident defendants.

   According to the traditional rule, personal jurisdiction must accord with the requirements of state long-arm statutes and the Constitution's Due Process Clause. Prior to the 1970s, many states permitted the assertion of jurisdiction over nonresidents in domestic relations cases by expansive readings of their long-arm statutes (e.g., by construing the divorce defendant's actions to be "the conduct of business" or "a tortious act," etc.).

   Beginning in the 1970s, many states substantially increased the scope of jurisdiction over nonresidents in domestic relations cases by revising their long-arm statutes to include specific provisions for the assertion of jurisdiction in claims for spousal support and child support. The U.S. Supreme Court curtailed somewhat this state court expansion of personal jurisdiction over nonresident defendants in *Kulko v. Superior Court*, 436 U.S. 84 (1978), by delineating the scope of due process limitations. Subsequently, in *Burnham v. Superior Court*, 495 U.S. 604 (1990), the Court further clarified the requisites of due process in the divorce context.

   Example: Sharon and Ezra Kulko, who live in New York, marry during a three-day stopover in California en route to Ezra's tour of duty in Korea. They live in New York until their separation when Sharon moves to California. Pursuant to a written agreement (that Sharon flies to New York to sign), the children remain in New York but spend school vacations in California. Sharon obtains a Haitian divorce that incorporates the terms of the spouses' agreement. Their daughter comes to live with her mother in California. Then, the son decides that he wants to join her. She sends him a plane ticket, unbeknownst to Ezra. After the son arrives, Sharon commences an action in California, seeking to establish the Haitian decree as a California judgment, to modify the judgment to give her full custody, and to increase Ezra's support obligation. Ezra appears specially to quash service of the summons. The U.S. Supreme Court agrees with Ezra and holds that California's assertion of personal jurisdiction violated his right to due process because he lacks minimum contacts with the forum. His marriage there did not confer jurisdiction, none of his actions were "purposeful acts" by which he benefited from California's laws (such as agreeing to his daughter's move), he did not cause an injury to anyone in California and could not have foreseen that his actions would subject him to jurisdiction in California. Basic considerations of fairness point to New York as being the proper forum. (Ezra remained in the state of the marital domicile; therefore, Sharon should bear the expense of litigating in another state.) *Kulko, supra*.

   Note: *Kulko* establishes the rule that personal jurisdiction over the respondent that comports with due process/minimum contacts is required for orders determining financial rights and obligations in the divorce context.

3. **Transitory presence:** A state may acquire jurisdiction for divorce purposes over a nonresident defendant who is physically present in the state. Thus, *transitory presence* suffices to satisfy due process requirements even when a defendant has no substantial connection to the forum. This accords with the rule that is applicable to civil actions generally: Personal jurisdiction over the defendant is satisfied by service of process while in the forum state.

Example: Dennis marries Francie Burnham. They live in New Jersey for ten years. When they agree to separate, Francie moves to California with their children. Before she leaves, they both agree to file for a no-fault divorce. Subsequently, Dennis files in New Jersey for divorce on grounds of desertion, refusing to adhere to their prior agreement. She files suit for divorce in California. When Dennis comes to California on a business trip and to visit his children, he is served there with a copy of his wife's divorce petition. He makes a special appearance moving to quash service of process for lack of jurisdiction because he did not have minimum contacts with California. The U.S. Supreme Court holds that the assertion of jurisdiction for divorce purposes over nonresident defendants who are physically present in the state does not violate due process. *Burnham v. Superior Court*, 495 U.S. 604 (1990).

D. **Foreign decrees**

1. **Comity doctrine: Recognition of divorce decrees rendered by a foreign country:** During the fault era, many Americans sought divorces in other countries (e.g., Mexico, Haiti, or the Dominican Republic) that had more liberal divorce grounds or residency requirements. The *comity doctrine* concerns the extent to which a state recognizes the decrees of foreign countries.

   The prevailing view, expressed by the Restatement (Second) of Conflict of Laws §98, provides that an American jurisdiction may recognize a judgment of a foreign nation provided that the judgment was rendered after a fair hearing by a court that has personal jurisdiction over one or both of the parties.

   Example: Husband and Wife, who are Connecticut domiciliaries, fly to Mexico to obtain a divorce on the ground of incompatibility (not recognized by Connecticut). Their support and property agreement is made a part of that decree. The agreement provides that Husband will pay their children's medical and college expenses. Several years later, Wife alleges that daughter must attend private school, based on doctor's orders, and that, therefore, the "medical" expense should be payable by Husband. She seeks to have the Mexican decree made a decree of the Connecticut court and then enforced. Husband contends that Connecticut cannot enforce the Mexican decree. The court determines that the Mexican divorce decree should be recognized by Connecticut because the Mexican court had jurisdiction over both parties and because recognition would not violate Connecticut's public policy (which subsequently adopted no-fault divorce). *Yoder v. Yoder*, 330 A.2d 825 (Conn. 1974).

   a. **Judicial discretion:** A court is not *required* to give the same deference to a divorce decree of a foreign country as to a decree from a sister state (the recognition of the latter is mandated by the Full Faith and Credit Clause). Courts may refuse to apply the comity doctrine to recognize foreign divorces if such recognition would violate public policy.

      Example: After a 17-year marriage, Wife files for divorce in New Hampshire on the basis of irreconcilable differences. Husband moves to dismiss, asserting that the trial court lacks jurisdiction in light of the fact that he had secured a Lebanese divorce, based on Islamic law, by declaring that he divorced Wife three times in her presence and by going to Lebanon to consult an attorney and sign divorce papers. The New Hampshire family court refuses to recognize the Lebanese ex parte divorce. The court reasons that Wife would be forced to bear the burdensome cost of traveling to Lebanon to seek relief from the divorce decree and also that recognition of an ex parte divorce obtained in a foreign nation where neither party is domiciled would frustrate New Hampshire laws regulating divorce. *In re Ramadan*, 891 A.2d 1186 (N.H. 2006).

   b. **Rationale:** The rationale supporting recognition of foreign decrees includes the achievement of finality. Opposing rationale stem from due process concerns.

2. **Full faith and credit distinguished:** Comity is a discretionary doctrine that governs the recognition of decrees rendered by the courts of a foreign country. On the other hand, the Full Faith and Credit Clause of the Constitution mandates judicial recognition of the decrees of sister states (i.e., of the "public acts, records and judicial proceedings" of other states).

   The Full Faith and Credit Clause of the Constitution does not apply to divorces that are granted by foreign nations.

3. **Estoppel:** Many courts in the fault-based era refused to recognize foreign divorces. (The comity doctrine applied only in a minority of states.) Nonetheless, such divorces might be protected by means of the estoppel doctrine. That is, a spouse who obtains a foreign divorce may be estopped from denying its validity subsequently.

   Example: Dr. King and Mrs. Clagett decide to divorce their respective spouses and marry each other. They both obtain Mexican divorces. They marry but the marriage does not work out. Wife seeks a separation and spousal support. Dr. King counters, seeking an annulment on the ground that neither he nor Wife were eligible to marry each other because their divorces from their prior spouses were invalid. The court holds that the Mexican court was without jurisdiction to grant his divorce because the divorcing spouses were domiciliaries of Maryland. However, the husband is barred by estoppel from asserting the invalidity of the Mexican divorce because he sought that divorce. *Clagett v. King*, 308 A.2d 245 (D.C. Ct. App. 1973).

E. **Domestic relations exception to federal jurisdiction: *Ankenbrandt v. Richards*:** The domestic relations exception to federal court jurisdiction provides that federal courts can refuse jurisdiction in those cases in which a party is seeking divorce, alimony, or custody decrees because such matters are more suitable for state courts. The U.S. Supreme Court narrowed the domestic relations exception to federal jurisdiction in *Ankenbrandt v. Richards*, 504 U.S. 689 (1992). Thus, *Ankenbrandt* permits federal courts to adjudicate a broader variety of disputes involving the divorcing parties.

   Example: Carol Ankenbrandt, a Missouri citizen, files suit against her former husband and his female companion, seeking monetary damages for the defendants' sexual and physical abuse of her daughters. Plaintiff alleges diversity jurisdiction. The district court dismisses based on the domestic relations exception to diversity jurisdiction and the abstention doctrine. The abstention doctrine, as announced in *Younger v. Harris*, 401 U.S. 37 (1971), states that federal courts may decline to exercise their jurisdiction in extraordinary circumstances because of federalism concerns (e.g., a reluctance to intervene if the state proceeding involves important state interests). The Fifth Circuit Court of Appeals affirms. Reversing, the U.S. Supreme Court holds that federal subject matter jurisdiction was proper. The Court maintains that the domestic relations exception is still valid only insofar as it divests federal courts of the power to issue divorce, alimony, and child custody decrees. Because plaintiff is not seeking such a decree, federal subject matter jurisdiction exists. The Court adds that application of the abstention doctrine was in error because no state proceeding was pending, nor did Defendant assert that the federal courts should not interfere because important state interests were at stake. *Ankenbrandt v. Richards*, 504 U.S. 689 (1992).

Several courts have held that intraspousal claims for intentional infliction of emotional distress do not fall within the domestic relations exception.

Example: Woman brings action, based on diversity of citizenship, against her lover following the breakup of their 23-year relationship, alleging that he promised to divorce his wife and marry her, and asserting claims for promissory estoppel and intentional infliction of emotional distress. After his death, his personal representative argues that the case should be dismissed based on the domestic relations exception to diversity jurisdiction. The court of appeals disagrees, stating that this case grew out of the dissolution of an intimate relationship; and the woman's claims do not sound in the specific areas of divorce, alimony, and child custody. *Norton v. McOsker*, 407 F.3d 501 (1st Cir. 2005).

IX. ALTERNATIVES TO DIVORCE: ANNULMENTS AND SEPARATIONS

A. **Divorce, annulment, and separation distinguished:** A divorce terminates a valid marriage. An annulment is a judicial declaration that a marriage never took place. A legal separation is a judicial declaration that the parties are separated.

English ecclesiastic practice distinguished between an *absolute divorce* and *divorce a mensa et thoro* (from bed and board). An absolute divorce permitted the parties to remarry. However, a *divorce a mensa et thoro* decreed that the parties could live separate and apart and might include orders as to temporary support and custody but did not permit the parties to remarry.

B. **Reasons to seek:** In the fault era, when spouses had difficulty obtaining a divorce in the absence of fault-based grounds, the parties might seek an annulment or legal separation as an alternative. Today, a spouse might seek an annulment for religious reasons (because some religions hold that a divorce bars a party from remarriage), or to reinstate a benefit that was lost upon marriage. Alternatively, a spouse might seek an annulment or legal separation in order to avoid a particular state's lengthy durational residency requirement for divorce.

For further distinctions between divorce and annulments, see Chapter 2.

X. ALTERNATIVE DISPUTE RESOLUTION PROCESSES

The movement toward alternative dispute resolution was spurred by criticisms of fault-based divorce (especially the acrimony and hostility accompanying judicial divorce). The most common alternatives are arbitration, conciliation, and mediation.

A. **Arbitration, conciliation, and mediation distinguished:** Arbitration provisions are present in some separation agreements. Such provisions require the parties to submit future disputes (for example, support, property, or custody issues) to an arbitrator prior to initiating court action. Arbitration is an adjudicatory process, an alternative to traditional judicial resolution, by which a neutral third party (an "arbitrator") makes a determination that is binding upon the parties.

Conciliation is marriage counseling with an eye toward reconciliation (thereby avoiding divorce). In the fault era, some states established court-connected conciliation services.

Divorce mediation is a process by which the parties themselves, with the help of a mediator, resolve their disputes. Unlike in arbitration, the parties do not cede their authority to a neutral third party to resolve their dispute. In mediation, the parties make their own agreements with the mediator serving as a facilitator.

Of the three above alternatives, arbitration is most similar to judicial resolution because arbitration is still considered "adversarial." During arbitration, each of the disputing parties attempts to convince a third party who acts as decision maker. However, arbitration involves less time, expense, and effort than a full-scale trial.

B. **Enforceability of arbitration provisions:** Several states enforce agreements to arbitrate disputes in the divorce context. A few of these states maintain that arbitration of, specifically, custody and visitation disputes violates public policy.

Example: Susan and Roger divorce after 17 years of marriage and four children. Prior to their divorce, they execute a marital settlement agreement regarding spousal support, child support, and custody. The agreement requires binding arbitration for any financial disputes between the parties. When Susan claims that Roger is in arrears on support payments and has defaulted on a promissory note regarding property, Roger cross-claims to compel arbitration. After the arbitrator makes an award, Roger argues that arbitration clauses involving domestic disputes should not be permitted as a violation of public policy and also that this award was erroneous. The court disagrees, holding that public policy supports the enforcement of arbitration provisions (by providing an effective alternative to judicial resolution, by reducing court congestion and hostilities, and by providing an opportunity for private resolution of sensitive matters). *Faherty v. Faherty*, 477 A.2d 1257 (N.J. 1984).

C. **Mandatory mediation:** A few states have mandatory mediation for some divorcing parties. For example, California requires mediation, prior to judicial action, for couples who have disputes about custody or visitation. Cal. Fam. Code §3173.

For additional material on custody mediation, see Chapter 7.

D. **Collaborative law procedure:** The term "collaborative law" was coined in the late 1980s by a Minnesota divorce lawyer to signify an agreement by the parties and their attorneys to the use of cooperative techniques without resort to judicial intervention. (If the parties and lawyers are unable to resolve their differences through cooperative techniques, the lawyers must withdraw and cannot serve as counsel.) The collaborative law movement arrived in California in 1993 and spread from there to at least 20 states. In 2001, Texas became the first state, by statute, to recognize collaborative law in divorce proceedings.

Note: Collaborative law's requirement that the divorcing parties' lawyers must withdraw if settlement negotiations fail may pose a violation of state rules of professional conduct. *See, e.g.,* Colorado Bar Association, Ethics Opinion 115, Ethical Considerations in the Collaborative and Cooperative Law Contexts (Feb. 24, 2007) (suggesting that such a provision violates state professional conduct rules that bar a lawyer from representing a client if the representation is "materially limited by the lawyer's responsibilities to . . . a third person," because it creates an insurmountable conflict of interest impairing the lawyer's independent judgment about the need for litigation). However, the ABA finds that virtually all other state ethics opinions conclude that collaborative law is consistent with professional conduct rules. ABA Standing Comm. On Ethics and Professional Responsibility, Formal Op. 07-447, 8/9/07.

Quiz Yourself on
DIVORCE JURISDICTION

64. Wife obtains a degree of separation in Illinois where Husband and Wife reside. Husband, a college teacher, writes to a Nevada attorney inquiring about obtaining a divorce there. He learns that Nevada has a six-week residency requirement. Husband discusses marriage with his new girlfriend. Husband moves to Nevada, telling his employer that he will return to teach in the Fall but retaining saving and checking accounts in Illinois. He obtains an ex parte Nevada divorce. Wife claims that the Nevada decree is not entitled to full faith and credit in Illinois. Will she prevail? _____

65. Husband and Wife reside in Iowa. Following a period of marital strife, Wife leaves Husband to live with her parents in Missouri. Husband files a petition for divorce in Iowa based on the ground of desertion. He neglects to forward to Wife a notice of the filing of the petition or to serve Wife with a copy of the summons and complaint. He dies shortly after obtaining the divorce. Wife enters a claim for Social Security benefits as his legal wife. Will she prevail? _____

66. Husband and Wife live as a married couple in New York. Wife then moves to Vermont solely to take advantage of its no-fault divorce law. For two years, Wife continues to work in New York, but obtains a Vermont driver's license, votes in Vermont, pays Vermont taxes, and leases property in Vermont. She then files for divorce in Vermont. Does the Vermont court have subject matter jurisdiction over the divorce? _____

Answers

64. Yes. Husband's divorce decree, obtained ex parte, is not entitled to full faith and credit because Husband failed to establish a bona fide domicile in Nevada. Based on the Supreme Court decisions of *Williams I* and *Williams II*, Illinois is entitled to determine for itself the jurisdictional facts upon which the Nevada decree was based. Illinois should determine that the husband was not domiciled in Nevada because he did not intend to abandon his Illinois domicile (as evidenced by his retaining his job and bank accounts in Illinois).

65. Yes. Because proper service of process is required for jurisdiction over a defendant, the decree of divorce is invalid. Wife was denied her due process rights because Husband knew her mailing address and should have provided Wife with *Mullane* notice. Therefore, Wife is entitled to Social Security benefits as Husband's legal spouse.

66. Yes. Although Wife's stated intent in moving to Vermont was to take advantage of its more favorable divorce laws, her actions (i.e., obtaining a driver's license, voting, paying taxes, and leasing property in Vermont) demonstrate an intent to remain there indefinitely. She thereby satisfied the domicile requirement for subject matter jurisdiction. In addition, because Wife lived in Vermont for at least two years, she met any durational residency requirement imposed by the state.

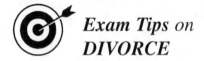

Exam Tips *on*
DIVORCE

☛ Begin the discussion of divorce-related issues by referring to your answer on **marriage validity**. That is, only if a valid marriage exists do you need to worry about dissolving it. However, do not assume that the invalidity of the marriage obviates the need to discuss divorce. Take care of this problem by saying something like, "Assuming that a valid marriage exists, then the plaintiff must terminate that relationship by divorce." (For annulment, see discussion below.)

☛ Even though all jurisdictions have adopted some form of no-fault dissolution, it is still necessary to determine whether a plaintiff may/must resort to a **fault-based ground** or grounds (adultery, cruelty, desertion, etc.). (This is important because some jurisdictions still retain fault-based grounds.)

 ☞ Also determine if the defendant may raise any **fault-based defenses** (condonation, collusion, recrimination, connivance). Identify the requisite elements of these grounds and defenses. Remember that **more than one ground or defense** may exist.

☛ Next, explore the applicability of no fault. Determine the **meaning of no fault** in the relevant jurisdiction (i.e., "irreconcilable differences," or "living separate and apart"). Do not assume either that a given jurisdiction follows no fault or that the adoption of no-fault dissolution means that fault-based grounds are irrelevant.

 ☞ In discussing no fault, determine if **both spouses consent** to a no-fault divorce (see jurisdiction discussion below). In either case (if they both consent or one does not), discuss what difference this might make regarding the application of state statute and/or judicial willingness to grant the divorce.

 ☞ Mention the reemergence of fault (the **reform movement**). Determine if the **covenant marriage** doctrine is relevant, and if so, explain and apply that doctrine.

☛ Examine the question to see if there are any issues involving **alternatives** to divorce (i.e., annulment or separation). Determine if reasons exist (jurisdictional, religious, etc.) for plaintiff to seek separation or annulment rather than divorce.

 ☞ For annulment, explore possible **grounds** (i.e., fraud, duress) and the application of the "**relation back**" doctrine.

 ☞ The **void-voidable** distinction may be relevant here as well.

☛ Be on the lookout for possible **jurisdictional** issues. Determine if there are issues regarding subject matter jurisdiction (i.e., domicile/durational residency requirements), personal jurisdiction over the defendant, or notice to the defendant.

 ☞ Determine if this is a **unilateral** (ex parte) or **bilateral** divorce. That is, is only one party before the court or are both spouses present?

 ☞ If the question involves an ex parte divorce, remember that the court in this case is able to grant only the divorce. That is, a court cannot adjudicate the financial aspects of an ex parte divorce because the court lacks jurisdiction over the absent spouse.

☞ For issues of ***subject matter jurisdiction***, determine if the plaintiff has established a bona fide domicile. Be sure to check whether personal jurisdiction issues involve cross-over questions with constitutional law. Common issues are due process, and full faith and credit.

☞ To establish ***personal jurisdiction*** over the defendant for purposes of support or property, recall that the assertion of jurisdiction must comport with the requirements of the Due Process Clause. For constitutional issues, analyze whether the defendant has sufficient contacts with the forum.

☞ Also, make sure that ***notice to the defendant*** complies with the *Mullane* doctrine.

☞ If you find a full faith and credit issue, be sure to discuss the *Williams* cases.

☞ If a plaintiff seeks a divorce in a foreign country, explore the ***comity doctrine***. Remember that full faith and credit does not apply to divorce decrees issued by a foreign country.

☛ Before leaving issues of divorce, determine if there are any minor issues involving ***access*** to divorce (e.g., poverty or religious divorce), ***discrimination*** on the basis of divorce (again, a cross-over topic with constitutional law), or ***the role of counsel***. Issues concerning divorce attorneys might involve cross-over issues with ***professional responsibility*** (e.g., dual representation, conflicts of interest, or sexual relations with clients).

☛ Always be on the lookout as well for the application of ***the domestic relations exception to federal jurisdiction***. Normally, federal courts refuse to adjudicate family law matters, such as divorce, alimony, and custody, because such matters are more suitable for resolution by state courts. Any time a plaintiff initiates a lawsuit in federal court, be sure to discuss the domestic relations exception to federal jurisdiction (***define it and discuss its applicability***) and analyze the potential ***impact of Ankenbrandt v. Richards*** (narrowing the domestic relations exception to federal jurisdiction, thereby permitting federal courts to adjudicate a broader variety of disputes) for the particular fact pattern.

CHAPTER **6**

FINANCIAL CONSEQUENCES OF DISSOLUTION

ChapterScope ━━━

This chapter addresses the financial consequences of dissolution. Specifically, it focuses on the legal rules that courts apply in their allocation of the financial obligations surrounding dissolution (i.e., awards of property, spousal support, and child support). Here are a few of the key principles covered in this chapter:

- Upon divorce, the court divides the spouses' property and may also award spousal support and child support, absent an agreement between the spouses.

- Two marital property regimes exist:

  - *common law*; and

  - *community property*.

- Different *rationales* characterize the division of marital *property* and the award of *spousal support*.

  - The traditional rationale underlying both property divisions and awards of spousal support was *fault*.

  - The *partnership/contribution* approach has replaced the traditional rationale for *property* division.

  - Modern rationales of *self-sufficiency* and *loss compensation* are replacing the traditional rationale for spousal support.

- *Statutory guidelines* have replaced *discretion* as the method of determining child support.

- Courts generally apply a standard of *substantial and material change of circumstances* in order to grant modifications of spousal support or child support.

- Traditionally, changes in *either spouse's circumstances* may warrant reduction or termination of the spousal support obligation. Remarriage and cohabitation are common circumstances.

- An *alimony reform movement*, leading to the Massachusetts Alimony Reform Act, led to many states' efforts to limit the duration of alimony.

- To make or modify an award of child support or spousal support, a court must have *personal jurisdiction* over the obligor.

- Absent *merger* or *incorporation* into a judicial decree, a separation agreement is only a contract.

━━━

I. STANDARDS FOR THE INITIAL AWARD OF PROPERTY, SPOUSAL SUPPORT, AND CHILD SUPPORT

At divorce, unless the spouses reach their own agreement, the court will divide the property acquired by one or both spouses and may also award spousal support (formerly called "alimony"). In addition, if the couple has minor children, a court will award child support.

A. Division of property

1. Marital property regimes defined: Two marital property regimes exist in the United States: common law and community property. Most states follow the common-law approach.

a. Common law: At common law, all property belonged to the spouse who acquired it. This included any property derived from that property (rents, profits, etc.). Upon divorce, a court awarded property to the spouse who had title. This was called the "title system." Thus, a homemaker, for example, had no right to share in the property acquired by her income-earning husband.

b. Community property: Community property is the marital property regime in nine predominantly southern and western states (Arizona, California, Idaho, Louisiana, Nevada, New Mexico, Texas, Washington, and Wisconsin). This system derives largely from Spanish and French influences (except for Wisconsin, which follows a community property system because of its adoption of the Uniform Marital Property Act). The guiding principle of such property regimes is that marriage is a partnership.

Note: Statutory variations do exist in community property states. For example, some community property states require an equal division of the community property. However, other community property states adopt equitable distribution (discussed *infra*). Further, even the meaning of equitable distribution varies in community property jurisdictions, especially regarding the treatment of separate property (discussed *infra*).

2. Equitable distribution generally: A majority of jurisdictions now adhere to a system of equitable distribution. Equitable distribution has replaced the title system of property ownership. The objective of the equitable distribution system is to order a fair distribution, under all the circumstances, of the spouses' property.

The women's movement, in large part, contributed to the adoption of equitable distribution. Feminists argued that the common-law system failed to reflect and recompense women's non-financial contributions to marriage.

a. Meaning of equitable distribution: The equitable distribution regime requires courts to take into account a number of statutory factors in determining the most equitable allocation of property between the spouses. Many states adopted equitable distribution based on the Uniform Marital and Divorce Act (UMDA) as originally formulated in 1970.

Currently, UMDA §307(a) provides four factors that courts may consider in arriving at a "just" division of marital property:

1. the contribution of each spouse to that property (including homemaking services);

2. the value of the property set apart to each spouse;

3. the duration of the marriage; and

4. the economic circumstances of each spouse at the time of dissolution, including the desirability of awarding the family home to the primary custodian of the children.

According to UMDA §307(b) (Alternative B), marital property includes property acquired by the parties *subsequent* to the marriage but does *not* include property (1) acquired by gift or inheritance, (2) exchanged for separate property, or (3) subject to a valid agreement of the parties. This alternative addressed property distribution for community property states.

A later version of UMDA §307 (Alternative A) proposed an alternative model for common law states that gives courts authority to divide equitably the "hotchpot" of assets owned by either spouse, whenever or however acquired. This alternative is based on the principle that *all* the property of the spouses (separate property and marital property) should be regarded as assets of the married couple and available for distribution. Upon divorce, most equitable distribution states follow UMDA and divide only marital property, although some equitable distribution states divide both separate and marital property.

In general, "equitable" (as in "equitable distribution") does not mean the same as "equal." However, in a few jurisdictions, a presumption exists that the most equitable division is an *equal* division, although in these jurisdictions courts are free to deviate from that presumption if it would lead to a more equitable result.

b. **Treatment of separate property:** Separate property merits different treatment under the various property regimes. For example, in some community property jurisdictions (e.g., California), courts divide only the jointly acquired marital property (excluding separate property from the division of assets). In other community property jurisdictions (e.g., Washington and Wisconsin), statutes give courts authority to include separate property in the equitable distribution of assets. Similarly, some non–community property jurisdictions that follow equitable distribution also subject to division both separate and jointly acquired property. The rationale for the inclusion of both separate and jointly acquired property is that courts in equitable distribution jurisdictions are allowed considerable latitude in arriving at a fair division.

Gifts and inheritances to one spouse, according to both the majority approach and UMDA, are considered nonmarital property (separate property) and therefore are awarded to the party who received them.

Example: Jane and David marry in 1973 and have three children. In 1992, Jane files for divorce. They cannot agree on an equitable division of their property. The trial court excludes from consideration certain gifts (worth approximately $40,000) made to Jane during the marriage by her family. David argues that these gifts should not be treated as Jane's separate property and that, on this basis, the ensuing property division (of $70,000 to Jane and $15,000 to David) was not equitable. Reversing, the state supreme court determines that under equitable distribution, a trial court must consider all relevant factors. The court concludes that the trial court erred by treating gifts to Jane as separate property rather than as marital property. (This view represents the minority approach.) *Gaulrapp v. Gaulrapp*, 510 N.W.2d 620 (N.D. 1994).

3. **Traditional rationales:** Several different rationales traditionally characterized the distribution of property.

   a. **Fault:** The most longstanding principle of property distribution is fault. That is, a court divides the property so as to punish the spouse who caused the marital breakup. Only innocent spouses traditionally received property (and spousal support) upon divorce.

   b. **Need:** According to the need rationale, a court divides property based on a spouse's need for support. Thus, a nonworking, dependent wife is in "need" of property and spousal support. A determination based on need ignores the duration of the marriage.

   c. **Status:** Based on the status principle, a court divides property based on the status that the parties enjoyed during the marriage. A determination based on status also rejects the duration of the marriage as a factor.

4. Modern rationale: A modern rationale characterizes the distribution of property.

   a. Contribution: The partnership model: A contribution rationale takes into account the contributions of both spouses. The partnership model of marriage is based on this contribution rationale. Under this view, the court divides property based on the view that marriage is an economic partnership. Spousal earnings, as well as assets acquired with those earnings, belong to the partnership and are subject to division upon divorce.

      i. Valuation of homemaker services: A problem that arises in the partnership model is how to calculate the noneconomic contribution of a spouse who is a homemaker and who contributes services rather than property. The traditional devaluation of housework leads to a low estimate of the value of the stay-at-home spouse's contribution.

      Judicial and legislative reforms have addressed this problem by providing that homemaker services may be taken into account.

      Example: Linda and Billy separate after 24 years of marriage, during which Linda was a homemaker and Billy was a cable repairman. Linda files for divorce based on Billy's adultery. The trial court judge grants Linda the divorce and awards her alimony (both monthly and a lump-sum payment to replace Billy's gifts to his mistress), as well as a one-half interest in Billy's pension and stocks and the marital homestead debt-free. Billy appeals, contending that the assets (home, pension, and stocks) are titled in his name and constitute his separate property. The court disagrees and abrogates the title theory in favor of equitable distribution, reasoning that the traditional title theory fails to recognize the homemaker's noneconomic contribution to the marriage. *Ferguson v. Ferguson,* 639 So. 2d 921 (Miss. 1994) (en banc).

      ii. Community property and the contribution approach: The community property regime, based on the idea of marriage as a partnership, reflects the contribution rationale. The partnership concept applies not only at dissolution but during the marriage. That is, a community property regime gives rise to present vested interests in both spouses in all property acquired during the marriage (other than that acquired by gift or inheritance). Management of the community property also is shared.

      iii. ALI innovative approach to contribution: The American Law Institute (ALI) has formulated *Principles of the Law of Family Dissolution* that reconceptualize some of the financial consequences of dissolution. The objective of the *Principles* is to obtain uniformity among the states and to permit greater predictability of outcomes. One provision (§4.18) recharacterizes separate property as marital property for the dissolution of *long-term marriages* (unless the trial court makes written findings that preservation of the separate character of the property is necessary to avoid substantial injustice). This provision is based on the fulfillment of the reasonable expectations of the parties in long-term marriages.

   b. Limited role for fault as a modern rationale: Despite the widespread adoption of no-fault, marital fault still plays a limited role in some states' equitable distribution schemes. This occurs, for example, if the fault includes adultery, cruelty, or the waste of marital assets.

   Example: Mary has an extramarital affair and her husband John engages in long-standing verbally abusive behavior. A Virginia statute prevents awards of spousal support in cases of adultery, unless the denial of support would be a manifest injustice based on both parties' relative degrees of fault and a disparity in their economic circumstances. The appellate court determines that this exception applies because John's 20-year history of profane behavior outweighs Mary's adultery, and also because of the parties' economic disparities in light of John's high-paying job. *Congdon v. Congdon*, 578 S.E.2d 833 (Va. Ct. App. 2003).

c. **Reform movement: Re-emergence of fault:** Some commentators, as well as legislators, urge that fault should play a more salient role in the determination of the parties' financial rights and responsibilities upon divorce (see discussion in Chapter 5).

Quiz Yourself on
DIVISION OF PROPERTY: RATIONALES

67. Howard and Lillian are married in a common-law fault-based jurisdiction. Both spouses work during the marriage. They have four children, the youngest of whom is not the biological child of Howard, but rather is the product of Lillian's extramarital affair. Lillian's affair lasted for much of the marriage. Howard petitions for divorce and requests equitable division of the property with the bulk of the property going to him based on Lillian's adultery. Will he succeed? _____

68. Laura and Bob have been married for 24 years. They have two teenage children. They live in the jurisdiction of Blackacre. During the marriage, Laura was a traditional homemaker. Bob worked for a local telephone company. All their jointly acquired property is held in Bob's name. The couple divorces, following a mutually agreed upon separation. When the court awards all the marital property to Bob, Laura appeals. Will she be successful? _____

69. Same basic facts as above, except Bob and Laura live in a community property jurisdiction. All the couple's jointly acquired property is held in Bob's name. At the couple's dissolution, the court awards all the community property to Bob. Laura appeals. Will she be successful?_____

70. Janet and Peter have been married for ten years. At the beginning of their marriage, Janet received a legacy of $100,000 upon the death of her mother. She purchased stock with the money and titled the stock in her name. When the couple divorces in a jurisdiction that has adopted the Uniform Marriage and Divorce Act, will the court divide the stock between Janet and Paul? _____

Answers

67. Perhaps, depending on the jurisdiction. At common law, upon divorce, only spouses who were innocent of marital fault were eligible to receive property or spousal support. Lillian was guilty of marital fault because she committed adultery. Therefore, Lillian's fault may bar (or reduce) her share of the division of the property or spousal support. However, today, many fault-based jurisdictions require "egregious fault" in order to grant an unequal property division. Adultery usually does not meet this standard.

68. Probably. Under common-law jurisdictions that followed the title theory, each spouse was considered the owner of all property that was titled in his or her name. Formerly, based on this theory, a court would have been correct in awarding all the marital property to Bob because all property was titled in his name. Today, however, the title theory has been replaced by equitable distribution. Under this

theory, the court divides the couple's property, upon divorce, based on a determination of fairness (often in reliance on statutory factors).

69. Yes. In a community property jurisdiction, each spouse owns a present undivided equal interest in the community ("marital") property. Even though the couple's jointly acquired property is titled in Bob's name, Laura still retains the right to her half of the jointly acquired property based on the fact that the spouses were domiciled in a community property state during the period of acquisition of their property.

70. No. UMDA follows a system of equitable distribution. According to UMDA §307(b)(Alternative B), marital property includes property acquired by the parties *subsequent* to the marriage but does *not* include property acquired by gift or inheritance (which is considered each spouse's separate property), or property that is exchanged for separate property. Because Janet purchased the stock with funds that were acquired by virtue of an inheritance from her mother, the stock will be considered Janet's property and not subject to division. Note that separate property merits different treatment under various property regimes. For example, in some community property states, courts exclude separate property (such as inheritances) from the division of assets, whereas other community property jurisdictions permit courts to include separate property in the equitable distribution of assets. Similarly, some non–community property jurisdictions that follow equitable distribution also subject both separate and jointly acquired property to division. The majority of jurisdictions exclude gifts and inheritances from the equitable distribution of assets.

---

5. **Property Distribution: Process:** There are three basic steps in dividing property in a dissolution action:

  ■ *Characterization*: First, the court must determine whether the property is marital or separate property (or, in a community property state, "community property," "separate property," or "quasi-community property").

  ■ *Valuation*: Next, the court must assign a value to the property either by means of the parties' agreement or an appraisal.

  ■ *Division*: After the property has been characterized and valued, the court turns to dividing the property.

Property that a spouse acquires after a judgment of legal separation or while "living separate and apart" is generally considered separate property (rather than marital property). "Living separate and apart" generally requires that the parties have come to a parting of the ways with no present intent to resume their marriage (i.e., their conduct must manifest a complete and final break in the marital relationship). States differ on whether the separated spouses must reside in separate residences to be "living separate and apart."

6. **What is property?**

  a. **Professional licenses and degrees:** During some marriages, one spouse (often the wife) contributes earnings and services while the other spouse attains a professional license or degree. The supporting spouse does so in the hope that both partners will benefit subsequently from an enhanced standard of living. If the marriage dissolves before that time, the partnership model of marriage dictates that the supporting spouse's contributions be compensated in some manner.

Increasingly, courts are asked to determine whether the license or degree is an asset subject to distribution upon dissolution. This *characterization* involves a question of statutory interpretation (e.g., is the license or degree "property" within the meaning of an equitable distribution statute).

i. **Characterization: Majority approach:** Virtually all states *refuse* to treat professional degrees, licenses, and enhanced earning capacity as marital property. However, many courts find alternative theories for compensating the supporting spouse in an effort to reach a fair result.

    Example: Stephanie and Jason separate after a two-year marriage. Stephanie worked full-time during the marriage to put Jason through chiropractic school. At their divorce, the trial court considers Stephanie's contributions to Jason's education, training, career potential, and license. The court then awards her a greater share of the marital property ($30,000 compared to his share of $5,000) despite the short duration of the marriage — as well as $18,000 to be paid in 24 monthly installments as spousal support. The appellate court affirms both awards, reasoning that professional licenses do not constitute property subject to division as a marital asset and the contributing spouse must receive some form of compensation for her contributions in the expectation that the marital unit will prosper in the future. Jason relied on Stephanie for support during his chiropractic training and his anticipated income was expected to increase substantially when he received his license. The appellate court also reasons that the trial court had authority to award maintenance to Stephanie despite the fact that her petition requested that neither party be awarded maintenance. *In re Marriage of Thornley*, 838 N.E.2d 981 (2005).

    Some states take licenses and degrees into account in awards of *spousal support*.

    Example: Jackie and Lane are married for 16 years. Wife works during his undergraduate years as well as during his dental school education. Upon graduation, he joins his father's dental practice and begins to earn $100,000/year. Wife leaves her employment after their second child to care for the children. Husband later acquires his father's dental practice and begins making $355,000/year. Wife works in husband's business part-time. They live an upper-class lifestyle. At the divorce, the trial court denies compensatory spousal support to Wife, reasoning that her contribution during the marriage was typical and expected "for a spouse at the age and place in their lives." Wife appeals. State supreme court holds that wife made "significant" contributions to husband's career that were sufficient in amount, duration, and nature to weigh in favor of an award of compensatory spousal support. *In re Marriage of Harris*, 244 P.3d 801 (Or. 2010).

    Other states provide for *reimbursement* of expenses to the supporting spouse. *See, e.g.,* Cal. Fam. Code §2641(b)(1) (providing for reimbursement of the community for contributions to the education or training of a party that substantially increases the earning capacity of that party).

ii. **Characterization: Minority approach:** The minority approach characterizes a professional license or advanced degree as a marital asset subject to property division. *See, e.g.,* O'Brien v. O'Brien, 489 N.E.2d 712 (N.Y. 1985) (but see New York law reform *infra*).

iii. **Criticism of minority characterization of licenses and degrees as property:** Most courts have difficulty characterizing professional licenses or degrees as property for the following reasons:

- A degree or license lacks the traditional attributes of property (i.e., it cannot be bought or sold, has no exchange value, is personal to the holder, terminates on the death of the holder, and is not inheritable);

- Future earning capacity is too difficult and speculative to value;

- A degree or license is a product of only one spouse's intelligence and skills; and

- Valuation as property would result in indentured servitude forcing one spouse to work to pay the other.

iv. **Modern development: New York law reform:** The New York legislature enacted a law in 2016 providing that a spouse's enhanced earning capacity in the form of a professional license or advanced degree is no longer considered marital property subject to equitable distribution upon divorce. The new law provides, instead, that the degree or license may be *one factor* in the determination of post-divorce *maintenance and equitable distribution* (N.Y. Dom. Rel. Law §236(B)(6)(d)(7) ("in arriving at an equitable division of marital property, the court shall consider the direct or indirect contributions to the development during the marriage of the enhanced earning capacity of the other spouse")).

In short, the non-title owning spouse is entitled to a share of the wealth (in the property division) that the professional license or degree produced but does not hold equity in the license or degree itself. In the spousal support determination, the court may again consider a recipient-spouse's contribution to the licensed spouse's enhanced earnings (N.Y. Dom. Rel. Law §236B(5)(d)(7)).

v. **ALI approach:** The ALI *Principles* adopt the majority rule and refuse to treat earning capacity as divisible property. Instead, the *Principles* provide for "compensatory payments" to reimburse the supporting spouse for the financial contributions made to the other spouse's education or training. ALI *Principles* §§4.07, 5.12. The education must have been completed in less than a specified number of years (set out in a rule of statewide application) before the filing of the dissolution petition. *Id.* at §5.12.

b. **Goodwill:** Another intangible asset of a marriage is the ***goodwill*** of a spouse's business or professional practice (e.g., law, medicine, accounting). Goodwill is the ***reputation of the business*** that signifies the probability of future earnings.

The majority of states take the position that personal goodwill is not marital property because it is tied to the skills of a particular person. However, enterprise goodwill is marital property because it is a business asset by virtue of its arrangements with suppliers and customers.

c. **Other enhanced earning capacity:** Courts also must determine whether other enhanced earning capacity (e.g., a spouse's celebrity status) is an asset subject to distribution upon dissolution.

Example: Upon dissolution of a 17-year marriage, the husband of opera singer Frederica von Stade Elkus argues that her celebrity status constitutes marital property subject to equitable distribution. At the time of the marriage, von Stade was beginning her career (earning $2,250 annually). During the marriage, she became highly successful (earning $600,000 annually). Her husband served as her voice coach and photographer. He claims that he sacrificed his own career to help her and raise their two children. The trial court determines that her celebrity status is not marital property because the husband benefited financially during the marriage and would be compensated adequately by division of their substantial assets. He appeals. Reversing and remanding, the court holds that celebrity status is marital property subject to equitable distribution to the extent that the appreciation in her career is attributable to the husband's efforts and contributions. *Elkus v. Elkus*, 572 N.Y.S.2d 901 (App. Div. 1991).

d. Pensions and retirement benefits: Pension benefits may constitute a significant part of the marital property for many couples. Two central issues arise:

- whether pension benefits (vested and nonvested) should be *characterized* as marital property; and

- what is the appropriate method of *valuing* pensions.

   i. Definition: *Vested* pension rights are not subject to forfeiture if the employment terminates (voluntarily or involuntarily) prior to retirement. *Nonvested* pensions are subject to such forfeiture.

   ii. Characterization as marital property: Majority and minority views: Under the majority rule, vested *and* nonvested pensions are marital property subject to equitable distribution. Under the minority rule, vested (but *not* nonvested) pensions are marital property subject to equitable distribution.

   Example: Wife files for divorce after a 20-year marriage. Husband was employed as a firefighter for almost the entire duration of the marriage. He is entitled to a pension after 25 years of service. (His pension, therefore, is nonvested.) Husband appeals the trial court decision awarding Wife one-half of his nonvested pension benefits as marital property. Affirming, the state supreme court holds that Husband's nonvested pension benefits are sufficiently concrete, reasonable, and justifiable as to constitute a presently existing property interest for equitable distribution purposes. The court reasons that any uncertainty regarding vesting is more appropriately handled in the valuation and distribution stages, rather than in the classification stage. *Bender v. Bender*, 785 A.2d 197 (Conn. 2001).

   iii. Valuation: Jurisdictions choose among different methods of pension valuation, including:

   - calculating the employee's contributions to the plan, plus interest, and awarding the nonemployed spouse an appropriate share (most useful for pension plans funded by employer contributions rather than those in which only the employee contributes a portion);

   - calculating the present value of the prospective benefits when they vest, discounted to present day (based on several speculative possibilities); or

   - determining the spousal shares by a formula but retaining jurisdiction until payments actually are received (the reserved jurisdiction approach).

   iv. Federal pension benefits and federalism principles: The distribution of *federal* pension benefits may involve a conflict between federal law versus state equitable distribution or community property law. The issue is whether state courts dividing marital property interfere with certain rights guaranteed under federal law. That is, does federal legislation preempt, under the Supremacy Clause of the Constitution, state statutes that regulate the division of property acquired during the marriage?

(a) **Railroad employees' retirement benefits:** Federal legislation provides for retirement benefits for certain federal employees, such as railroad employees. In *Hisquierdo v. Hisquierdo*, 439 U.S. 572 (1979), the U.S. Supreme Court held that federal law preempted state marital property regimes in ruling that federal railroad employees' retirement benefits under the Railroad Retirement Act (RRA) are not community property subject to distribution upon divorce. Congress subsequently changed this result by amending the RRA to extend benefits to those divorced spouses who have been married to the railroad employee for at least ten years. 45 U.S.C. §231a(c)(4)(i-iii).

(b) **Military retirement benefits:** The U.S. Supreme Court again confronted, in the context of military retirement benefits, the issue of federal preemption of state law in terms of state court distribution of federal benefits upon dissolution. In *McCarty v. McCarty*, 453 U.S. 210 (1981), the U.S. Supreme Court ruled that military retirement benefits were the separate property of the retiree, thereby refusing again to permit state court interference in federal retirement benefit law.

Considerable dissatisfaction with this result led to enactment of the Uniformed Services Former Spouses Protection Act (USFSPA), 10 U.S.C. §1408, that overruled *McCarty*. USFSPA permits state courts to apply state law in determining the divisibility of military retirement benefits upon divorce. Payments can be made to former spouses who have been married to a service member for at least ten years of service.

Note: USFSPA permits, but does not require, state courts to divide the federal pension.

v. **Federal pension benefits regulation: ERISA, REA, and QDROs:** The comprehensive federal pension law, ERISA (the Employee Retirement Income Security Act of 1974), 29 U.S.C §§1000 et seq., originally limited the rights of a nonemployee spouse (e.g., the wife of a covered employee) to share in the employee's pension upon divorce. ERISA's "anti-alienation rule" states that pension plan benefits may not be assigned or alienated.

The purpose of the rule was to ensure that the participant does not consume retirement savings prior to retirement. ERISA made no special exceptions for domestic relations claims against an employee's pension plan. In the wake of ERISA, federal and state courts split on whether the anti-alienation rule barred distribution of pension benefits to a nonemployee spouse pursuant to a divorce.

Congress enacted the Retirement Equity Act of 1984 (REA), Pub. L. No. 98-397, 98 Stat. 1426 (codified in scattered sections of 26 and 29 U.S.C.), to remedy this problem experienced primarily by ex-wives. REA permits a court to divide pension benefits as a marital asset. REA mandates that the ERISA anti-alienation rule must yield to certain state domestic relations decrees, i.e., those "qualified domestic relations orders" (QDROs).

A QDRO facilitates the enforcement of awards of spousal support and child support by authorizing retirement plan administrators to make payments directly to a former spouse, thereby enabling that spouse not to be dependent on the plan beneficiary to pay the amount awarded by the divorce decree. QDROs apply to both spousal and child support.

e. Bankruptcy discharge

i. Generally: Sometimes, events occur during or after dissolution that affect a spouse's ability to pay a property award or spousal support. One such event is bankruptcy. To further the protective policy behind the federal Bankruptcy Code, 11 U.S.C. §541, a debtor may claim exemption for certain property (e.g., home, car, etc.). The Code also permits a debtor-spouse to be discharged from certain divorce-related obligations.

ii. Rule: Nondischargeability from support obligations: The traditional rule was that the obligations attributable to a *property* division upon divorce were dischargeable in bankruptcy. However, *spousal support and child support obligations were not*. This rule was called "the support-property distinction."

Because of this difference in treatment, it was important to determine whether an obligation could be classified as support or a property division. Such characterization was difficult because judicial decrees and parties' settlement agreements tend to blur the distinction between support and property. Therefore, the particular label in the decree or agreement is not determinative. One method to overcome this problem was reliance on the "intent" and "function" of the financial obligation: The court looked behind the label of "property" or "alimony" to find the (court's or spouses') intention in creating the underlying financial obligation and the function of that obligation (i.e., to divide property or furnish support). The trend among courts was to construe "support" broadly to result in nondischargeability.

Bankruptcy reform (discussed *infra*) eliminated the different treatment of support and property for Chapter 7 bankruptcies (involving liquidation of debts) but not for Chapter 13 bankruptcies (involving reorganization of debts).

iii. Stay of proceedings: Federal bankruptcy law provides that the filing of a bankruptcy petition will halt state proceedings (except for the establishment or modification of spousal support orders). Bankruptcy Code, 11 U.S.C. §362(b)(2).

iv. Bankruptcy Reform Act (BRA) of 1994: The Bankruptcy Reform Act, 11 U.S.C. §523(a)(15), modified the traditional rule that property obligations are dischargeable. It provided that debtor-spouses could no longer discharge property obligations but provided for affirmative hardship defenses permitting the debtor-spouse to discharge property obligations if he/she could show (a) the need for these resources for support and that of dependents, or (b) the benefit of the discharge would outweigh the creditor-spouse's detriment.

v. Bankruptcy Abuse Prevention and Consumer Protection Act of 2005: The Bankruptcy Abuse Prevention and Consumer Protection Act of 2005 (BAPCPA), 11 U.S.C., §523(a)(15), further modified the traditional rule that property obligations were dischargeable. More debts are now *nondischargeable* under Chapter 7. Property obligations stemming from dissolution judgments or separation agreements are no longer dischargeable in Chapter 7 bankruptcies. However, the support-property distinction continues to control dischargeability for purposes of Chapter 13 bankruptcies. See 11 U.S.C. §1328(a)(2) (excepting §523(a)(5) obligations from discharge but not §523(a)(15) obligations). (Chapter 7 provides for straight bankruptcy liquidation, whereas Chapter 13 involves a repayment plan, usually partial, of debts.) Note that the determination of whether an obligation is nondischargeable is governed by federal, rather than state, law.

Example: In Shane and Sondra's divorce decree, Shane is ordered to make payments on a repossessed car. Shane then files for Chapter 7 bankruptcy and is discharged from his debts. The creditor demands payment from Sondra for the car loan. She files a motion for contempt to enforce Shane's obligation. He contends that he was discharged from the debt. The appellate court construes the car debt as a nondischargeable "debt to a former spouse under a divorce decree" pursuant to BAPCPA. The court reasons that the couple's divorce decree actually had two obligations: an obligation to pay the creditor on the marital debt and a separate obligation *to Sondra* to pay the car loan (apparently the decree lacked a "hold harmless" clause). Therefore, the appellate court determines that the trial court could properly enforce Shane's obligation *to Sondra* under the decree even if Shane's obligation *to the bank* on the repossessed car had been discharged. *Howard v. Howard*, 336 S.W.3d 433 (Ky. 2011).

Note: Better practice would dictate the inclusion of an "indemnification and hold harmless clause" in a divorce decree or marital settlement agreement to avoid this problem.

Quiz Yourself on WHAT IS PROPERTY?

71.   Harry and Wilma are both teachers. When Harry chooses to pursue a medical degree, Wilma continues to teach and contributes all her earnings to their joint support. Harry completes his education and begins employment as a radiologist. A year later, he announces to Wilma that he wants a divorce. At trial, Wilma's expert testifies that the present value of Harry's medical license is $1,000,000 and that the value of Wilma's contribution to Harry's medical education was $200,000. Wilma contends that Harry's medical degree and license are marital property subject to distribution. The jurisdiction follows equitable distribution. Will Wilma prevail? _____

72.   Jennie and Doug are married. A few months later, Doug is hired by the Whiteacre City Fire Department. He immediately begins making contributions from his wages to the state firemen's retirement fund. Jennie and Doug divorce after a 20-year marriage. At that time, Doug has completed 19 years of employment with the city fire department. Under his employer's policy, Doug cannot draw a pension from the retirement fund until he has completed 20 years of service. In the divorce proceedings, the trial court finds that the value of the couple's marital property interest in the firemen's retirement fund consists of Doug's cash contributions to the fund until the date of the divorce (i.e., the cash surrender value of Doug's pension contributions) and awards Jennie half that amount. Jennie appeals, arguing that she has a property right in Doug's nonvested pension benefits. Will she prevail? _____

73.   Wife and Husband divorce in a common-law jurisdiction after a 30-year marriage. At the time of the divorce, Husband is eligible to receive military retirement benefits based on his service in the marines. Husband argues that his military retirement benefits are exempted from distribution by the divorce court because military retirement benefits are subject to federal law. (At the time, federal law provides that military retirement benefits are the serviceman's separate property.) Wife contends that state courts have the ability to value and distribute military pension rights. Will she prevail?
_____

74.   Karen and Chad meet at New York University and marry in New York in 2016. Throughout their marriage, Karen works as an accountant, while Chad attends law school. He graduates, is admitted to the Bar, and works at a top firm New York law firm making six figures annually. After five years of marriage, Karen files for divorce. She argues that Chad's professional degree and license should be considered as marital property subject to equitable distribution upon divorce. Will Karen prevail?

Answers

71.   Probably not. The court must determine whether Harry's license or degree is "property" within the meaning of the state's equitable distribution statute. If the couple's jurisdiction follows the majority approach, the court will refuse to treat Harry's medical degree and license as marital property. However, even in a jurisdiction that follows the majority approach, Wilma may not be totally out of luck. She may have a claim, depending on case law or statute, that would reimburse her for her contributions and services during the time Harry was in medical school. If Wilma and Harry live in a jurisdiction that follows the ALI *Principles,* Wilma similarly will be unsuccessful in her effort to have Harry's medical license or degree characterized as divisible marital property. The ALI *Principles* adopts the majority rule and refuses to treat earning capacity as divisible property. Instead, the *Principles* provides for "compensatory payments" to reimburse the supporting spouse for the financial contributions made to the other spouse's education or training, provided that the education was completed in less than a specified number of years (set out in a rule of statewide application) before the filing of the dissolution petition. Because Harry completed his training shortly before he sought a divorce, Wilma would probably be successful in her effort to seek "compensatory payments" for reimbursement under the ALI approach.

72.   Yes. The traditional rule was that nonvested pension rights were not property but were a mere expectancy and thus not an asset subject to division upon dissolution of a marriage. However, a majority of courts currently hold that the marital community has a property interest subject to division at divorce in the employee spouse's nonvested retirement benefits. Thus, Jennie has a property right in Doug's nonvested pension benefits in the firemen's retirement fund.

73.   Yes. The United States Supreme Court held (in *McCarty v. McCarty*) that military retirement benefits are exempted from distribution by state divorce courts on the basis of federal statute. However, subsequently, Congress overruled *McCarty* with the enactment of the Uniformed Services Former Spouses' Protection Act. As a result, a state court has the ability to distribute military pension rights. Wife will be able to claim a share of Husband's military pension benefits.

74.   No. According to current New York law, a spouse's enhanced earning capacity in the form of a professional license or advanced degree is no longer considered marital property subject to equitable distribution upon divorce. However, the court may consider Karen's "direct or indirect contributions" to Chad's enhanced earning capacity (his law degree and license to practice law) as *one factor* in the determination of both spousal support and equitable distribution of their property.

B. Spousal support

1. **Definition:** Spousal support (formerly "alimony") is an award of future payments to one spouse payable from the future earnings of the other spouse. It is also sometimes called "maintenance." The movement toward gender-neutral roles and the desire to remove the stigma from divorce led to a change in nomenclature.

2. **Background:** Our modern law of spousal support derives from English ecclesiastical law and practice. For generations, England permitted only legal separation, not divorce. Neither party was free to remarry. Because societal constraints and marital property law dictated that wives were economically dependent on their husbands, a separated wife needed a means of support. As a result, courts awarded wives alimony (so long as the wife was not "at fault"). Alimony, thus, represented a continuation of the husband's marital duty of support.

   The purpose of spousal support has changed today, influenced by the women's movement and the acceptability of no-fault divorce. In addition, spousal support is no longer a gender-based award.

   Example: After a 36-year marriage, a lawyer-husband and homemaker-wife divorce. An Alabama statute provides that only husbands, not wives, must pay alimony upon divorce. Husband challenges the constitutionality of the statute as a violation of equal protection. The U.S. Supreme Court holds that the gender-based statute is unconstitutional. The Court reasons that the dual objectives offered by the state (to provide help to needy spouses, using sex as a proxy for need, and to compensate women for past discrimination during marriage) do not justify the statute. Because courts routinely conduct individualized hearings upon divorce, courts have no reason to use sex as a proxy for need. Further, courts may address the compensatory rationale without burdening only husbands. *Orr v. Orr*, 440 U.S. 268 (1979).

3. **Rationale for spousal support**

   a. **Traditional theories**

      i. **Need:** At common law, the husband had a duty to support his wife. Because women were economically dependent on men, women "needed" support in the event of a marital breakdown.

         Courts based awards on the plaintiff's *need* plus the defendant's *ability to pay*. The measure of need was the couple's standard of living during the marriage.

         Although most awards of spousal support formerly were granted to needy wives, in appropriate cases spousal support was awarded to needy husbands.

      ii. **Fault:** In a fault-based regime, only the innocent spouse is awarded spousal support. The guilty spouse is "punished" for his/her marital transgressions by denial of awards of spousal support (and property).

          Theories of need and fault have been undermined by the spread of no-fault divorce and the transformation of gender roles brought about by the women's movement.

   b. **Modern rationales**

      i. **Self-sufficiency:** Many commentators urge that, because the original purposes of alimony awards (fault/need) are no longer relevant, spousal support should be abolished or else awarded infrequently and for short periods of time.

UMDA was influential in the adoption of self-sufficiency as a rationale for awards of spousal support. For example, UMDA provides for awards of spousal support only for those spouses who do not have sufficient property to provide for their reasonable needs, are unable to support themselves through employment, or have custody of very young children. UMDA §308(a). UMDA aims to provide for a divorced spouse by way of a property settlement rather than spousal support. (The effectiveness of this approach depends, of course, on the existence of property to distribute.)

Example: Brenda and James live a lavish lifestyle based on gifts from her family's business. Several years later, Brenda files for divorce, alleging adultery and extreme cruelty. James receives an award of alimony because of his economic dependence on Brenda. When Brenda appeals, contending that his fault should preclude alimony, James argues that fault should play no part in alimony determinations. Brenda argues that the court should consider fault under the "catch-all" statutory category that considers any relevant factor in an equitable distribution. The state supreme court adopts a third view that considers fault in limited circumstances (the ALI view). The court holds that "in cases in which marital fault has negatively affected the economic status of the parties it may be considered in the calculation of alimony." The court adds that fault may also be considered in cases of egregious fault, such as cases of attempted murder of a spouse or infecting a spouse with an STD. Because James's marital misconduct had no economic impact, the court remands for a reconsideration of spousal support that is not based on fault. *Mani v. Mani*, 869 A.2d 904 (N.J. 2005).

    ii. **ALI's loss compensation:** The ALI *Principles* propose an innovative rationale of "loss compensation" for spousal support. A spouse would make "compensatory spousal payments" to the other spouse to compensate for certain losses that the second spouse experienced during the marriage. Examples of compensable losses include loss attributable to child care responsibilities and the loss of a standard of living. Thus, for example, a homemaker wife would be entitled to compensation upon dissolution for the reduced standard of living she experienced based on her residual loss of earning capacity stemming from the fact that she was the primary caretaker during the marriage and lost employment opportunities thereby. ALI *Principles* §5.05.

c. Alimony reform

    i. **Background: Massachusetts alimony reform movement:** An influential alimony reform movement began in Massachusetts when a businessman (Stephen Hitner), who was in the midst of a long, contentious divorce, formed a law reform organization consisting primarily of divorced husbands and their second wives. The organization was created due to members' discontent about purportedly unjust long-term alimony awards.

    ii. **Massachusetts Alimony Reform Act (2011):** The alimony reform movement led to the Massachusetts Alimony Reform Act that was signed into law in 2011. Reformers had several goals, including making alimony awards more predictable, promoting self-sufficiency for the recipient-spouse, linking the duration of alimony to the length of the marriage, terminating awards of permanent alimony, freeing payers from obligations after retirement, and terminating alimony upon the recipient's cohabitation.

    iii. Criticisms: Critics argue that the alimony reform movement ignores the income inequality wrought by divorce for women in lengthy marriages who gave up careers to be stay-at-home mothers and who face poor employment prospects following divorce.

    iv. Influence of Massachusetts reform: The Massachusetts law reform movement had far-reaching consequences. For example, the New Jersey legislature later amended its alimony statute (after *Mani, supra*) to reflect many features of the Massachusetts statute.

4. Spousal support and property division distinguished: Despite the tendency in case and statutory law to blur the distinctions between awards of property and spousal support, important differences exist.

    a. Modifiability: Unlike awards of property, spousal support traditionally was *modifiable* upon proof of a subsequent substantial change of circumstances. Property distributions are final.

    b. Terminability: Traditionally, spousal support, unlike payments for purposes of property settlements, was *terminable upon remarriage* of the recipient-spouse or the *death of either* spouse.

    c. Enforcement by contempt power: Spousal support obligations, unlike awards of property, are enforceable by means of the contempt power.

    d. Discharge in bankruptcy: Traditionally, property awards (but not awards of spousal support) were dischargeable obligations if the payor-spouse declared bankruptcy. Reforms have eroded the "support-property" distinction in some situations.

    e. Tax consequences: Finally, different tax consequences (discussed *infra*) flow from the two awards. For discussion of the Tax Cuts and Jobs Act of 2017 (TCJA), see *infra*.

5. Types of alimony

    a. Temporary: By statute, either spouse may obtain temporary spousal support (termed "alimony pendente lite") during the pendency of the divorce proceedings.

    b. Permanent: Permanent alimony was more commonly awarded during the fault-based era to homemaker spouses in long-term marriages who were free from fault. Permanent alimony is rarely awarded today.

    c. Modern view: Two modern forms of alimony are *rehabilitative alimony* and *reimbursement alimony*.

        i. Rehabilitative alimony: In accordance with the modern trend to limit awards of spousal support, many courts award "rehabilitative alimony" in lieu of permanent spousal support. This type of support lasts for only a limited period, as determined by the time necessary for the dependent spouse to obtain training or employment and to become self-supporting.

        ii. Reimbursement alimony: "Reimbursement alimony" refers to spousal support that is awarded in cases in which one spouse has supported the other through a professional program during the marriage. It recompenses the supporting spouse for her contributions (monetary and nonmonetary) to the education and training of the other. Reimbursement alimony represents a compromise by courts and legislatures between adherence to a rule denying relief and the practical difficulties of characterization/valuation of a professional degree or license as property. See also the discussion ("What is Property?"), *supra*, on licenses and degrees.

Quiz Yourself on
SPOUSAL SUPPORT

75. Husband and Wife divorce after 38 years of marriage. She agrees to waive spousal support. Husband receives the bulk of the marital property. At the time of the divorce, Husband also receives income from a deferred profit-sharing account worth $250,000. Wife suffers from physical disabilities that prevent her from working. She subsequently challenges her waiver of spousal support as unconscionable. Will she prevail? _____

76. Margaret and Jonathan divorce after a ten-year marriage. Jonathan agrees to pay Margaret $2,500 per month as spousal support for a four-year period. Two years after the divorce, Jonathan is seriously injured in an automobile accident and is unable to return to work while he undergoes extensive physical therapy. He requests a modification of his spousal support to $500 per month—a sum that he can more easily pay from his disability insurance. Will his request be granted? _____

Answers

75. Yes. The traditional standard for spousal support is need and ability to pay. Here, Husband has the ability to pay, and Wife has substantial basic needs that she cannot meet on her own. Further, under the modern view, as illustrated by UMDA, spousal support may be awarded to spouses who do not have sufficient property to provide for their needs, who are unable to support themselves through employment, or who have custody of very young children. Because Wife does not have sufficient property or employment to provide for her own needs, her challenge will succeed.

76. Yes. To succeed in his request for modification, Jonathan must show a substantial and material change in circumstances. Given that the automobile accident seriously affected his health and his ability to work, Jonathan's request for a decrease in his spousal support payments should be granted.

C. Child support

1. **Liability of both parents:** At common law, the father was liable for the support of all children born during a marriage. The modern trend is to consider *both* parents responsible for the support of their children.

2. **Standards**

   a. **Discretion: Traditionally**, vague statutory standards permitted courts to use considerable discretion in the award of child support. Criticisms arose regarding arbitrariness, the inadequacy of awards, and the lack of uniformity.

   b. **Guidelines:** A trend developed in the late 1970s and 1980s to limit judicial discretion by the adoption of more specific standards. The current statutory approach adopts mathematical formulae called "guidelines."

   i. UMDA: UMDA began the trend by its provision that a court may order either or both parent(s) to pay child support, without regard to marital fault, after considering all relevant factors, including:

- the financial resources of the child, the custodial parent, and the noncustodial parent;

- the family's pre-divorce standard of living; and

- the "physical and emotional condition of the child and his educational needs."

UMDA §309.

   ii. Federal law: The Child Support Enforcement Amendments of 1984, 42 U.S.C. §651, facilitated the movement to guidelines by requiring states to have guidelines in place or else risk losing a percentage of federal welfare funds. The Family Support Act of 1988 (FSA), 42 U.S.C. §667(a)-(b), extended the application of the guideline requirement to all cases (not merely to families on welfare), providing that the guidelines should serve as a rebuttable presumption and requiring states to regularly update their guidelines.

3. Models of determining support: Because federal law does not recommend any particular set of guidelines, states implemented guidelines based on one of three models:

- the income shares model;

- the percentage of income model; or

- the Melson formula.

a. Income shares model: The income-shares model is the most popular model. It requires that both parents make a monetary contribution to child support. This model is based on a belief that a child should receive the same proportion of parental income as if the parents lived together. First, a court computes the support obligation based on the combined income of the parents in the former intact household. This obligation then is pro-rated in proportion to each parent's income. Finally, the model permits consideration of work-related child care and extraordinary medical expenses.

b. Percentage of income: The percentage of income model, the second most popular model, is the simplest. It allocates child support based on a percentage of the obligor's income and the number of children. For example, in some states, an obligor must pay 17 percent for one child, 25 percent for two children, 29 percent for three, 31 percent for four, and 34 percent for five or more. The obligor pays the same amount regardless of the custodial parent's income. In jurisdictions that adhere to this model, provision may be made for the obligor's support, child care expenses, or extraordinary medical expenses. However, adjustments may be made for shared physical custody and additional dependents.

c. Melson formula: The Melson formula, despite its praise by commentators and courts, has been adopted by only a small number of jurisdictions (including Delaware, where it arose). It involves more complex calculations than the other models. Its fundamental assumption is that the child's needs must be met first before a parent may retain any income beyond that necessary for the parent's basic support needs. That is,

- parents may keep sufficient income to meet their basic needs but not more than what is required for their own self-support; and

- children are entitled to share in any additional income so that they can benefit from the absent parent's higher standard of living.

Under this model, statutory factors for determining the amount of support include: the health, financial circumstances, and earning capacity of the parties; the parties' subsistence requirements; and the standard of living to which the parties were accustomed prior to the divorce.

4. **Deviation from guidelines:** A court may order a deviation from the statutory guidelines in appropriate cases, but the court should explain the reasoning for the deviation.

    Example: When Raymond and Jessica divorce, the court orders joint legal and physical custody of their children. Using the statutory child support formula, the court determines Raymond's support obligation to be approximately $900 a month based on his share of the couple's income. However, the court applies a parenting-time deviation, thereby reducing the award to $500 per month but also requires him to pay two-thirds of the children's expenses for their extracurricular activities. Raymond files a petition for review, which does not challenge the decision to deviate from the presumptive child support obligation but argues instead that the trial court erred by failing to explain how it calculated the deviation. He is concerned that he is paying twice for the cost of extracurricular activities because (he argues) those costs are included in the presumptive amount of child support. The state supreme court agrees, explaining that when the court determines that a deviation should apply, "the order must explain the reasons for the deviation [and state how] the presumptive amount of child support would be . . . inappropriate and how the best interest of the children . . . will be served by the deviation." Because the trial court did not make the requisite findings, the court reverses and remands. *Turner v. Turner,* 684 S.E.2d 596 (Ga. 2009).

5. **Liability of stepparents**

    a. **Stepparent liability during marriage to child's parent:** At common law, a stepparent had no legal duty to support a stepchild.

    Some modern statutes, as well as case law, change the common-law rule and impose liability on stepparents. Some of these laws limit liability to co-resident stepchildren or to the duration of the marriage that gave rise to the step-relationship. Courts have upheld the constitutionality of stepparent liability statutes.

    b. **Stepparent liability upon divorce from child's parent:** At common law, because a stepparent had no legal duty to support a stepchild, courts had no authority to award child support for that stepchild upon termination of the stepparent's marriage to the child's biological parent.

    In contrast, some modern courts hold that stepparent liability may continue after the dissolution of the marital relationship that gave rise to the step-relationship. A few states impose post-divorce stepparent liability by means of a variety of doctrines (e.g., the "in loco parentis" doctrine or equitable estoppel).

6. **Post-majority support:** Traditionally, a parent's duty to support a child ceased upon the child reaching the age of majority. Although the age of majority used to be 21, most states lowered the age to 18. This change gave rise to the issue whether a noncustodial parent is liable for post-majority child support, especially for college expenses.

Example: At Kristi and Robert's divorce, the court awards Kristi custody. Robert is ordered to pay child support. At that time, Robert is earning $30,000. Over the next decade, his income increases to $250,000 annually. When the eldest child enrolls in college, Robert promises to cover the child's educational expenses, but he fails to do so. The state supreme court reconsiders prior case law that held that ordering a noncustodial parent to pay college expenses violated equal protection. Here, the state supreme court finds there is a rational basis to treat divorced parents differently than non-divorced parents because the state has a legitimate interest in ensuring that children of divorced families are not deprived of educational opportunities solely because their families are no longer intact. The court holds that an award of post-majority educational support does not violate equal protection *under limited circumstances* (e.g., if the parents would *otherwise* have paid for their children's education but for the divorce). Applying this rule to these facts, the court orders the father to pay the educational support for the reason that he promised to do so, he had the means to pay, and he would have likely done so had the family remained intact. *McLeod v. Starnes*, 723 S.E.2d 198 (S.C. 2012).

a. **Different state approaches:** States adopt different approaches to this issue:

- The majority of states fail to authorize post-majority educational support.

- A few states, by statute or case law, permit support through college through a variety of legal doctrines (e.g., construing "children" and "educational expenses" broadly to extend dependency). *But cf. Ex parte Christopher*, 2013 WL 5506613 (Ala. 2013) (holding that plain meaning of term "child" means minor and thereby refusing to award post-majority support).

b. **Constitutional attacks on statutes:** Some courts have upheld the constitutionality of statutes requiring divorced parents to provide post-majority educational support. *See, e.g., McLeod v. Starnes, supra.* Other courts hold that such statutes violate equal protection. *See, e.g., Curtis v. Kline*, 666 A.2d 265 (Pa. 1995).

c. **Separation agreements:** Courts have more latitude to permit post-majority support if the parties have provided for that eventuality in a separation agreement.

d. **ALI Principles:** The ALI *Principles* (§3.16) suggest that post-majority educational support be dependent on a judicial inquiry into parental resources and the likelihood of such support had the parents remained together.

7. **Support rights of nonmarital children**

a. **Traditional rule:** Traditionally, nonmarital children had a right to support and inheritance only from their mother.

b. **Modern rule:** According to the modern view, both parents have the duty to support children regardless of the legitimacy of the children. Further, modern law expands the inheritance rights of nonmarital children (explained *infra*).

c. **Statutes of limitations:** Traditionally, states had short statutes of limitations within which a parent had to bring a paternity action in order to seek support for a nonmarital child. The U.S. Supreme Court invalidated short statutes of limitations as a denial of equal protection.

d. **Federal legislation:** Congress lengthened the period for paternity establishment by enacting the Child Support Enforcement Amendments of 1984, 42 U.S.C. §666(a)(5)(A)(ii), which extended the statutory period until 18 years post-birth.

The Family Support Act (FSA) of 1988, 42 U.S.C. §1305, further strengthens the procedures for paternity establishment. The FSA

- requires states to permit paternity establishment for children whose actions previously were dismissed based on short state statutes of limitations;

- requires states to enact procedures to order all parties to submit to blood tests to determine paternity (subject to a good cause exception); and

- makes available to state agencies the Parent Locator Service to facilitate enforcement of child support obligations.

e. **Uniform Acts:**

i. **Paternity:** The Uniform Parentage Act (UPA) §4 facilitated paternity establishment by providing for legal parenthood by fathers who receive a child into their homes and publicly acknowledge the child or acknowledge the child in writing to a court or administrative agency. As amended in 2002, UPA §5 revised the UPA §4(4) presumption that arose by conduct ("holding out"). Because the original act failed to specify a time frame for the "holding out," uncertainty existed regarding whether the presumption could arise if the receipt of the child into the man's home occurred for a quite limited time or took place long after the child's birth. The 2002 amendments made the "holding out" presumption subject to an express durational requirement that the man reside with the child for the first two years of the child's life.

Note: UPA 2017 (the latest version of the UPA) makes the law gender-neutral in order to clarify its application to same-sex couples. It also reaffirms the equal treatment of children regardless of their parents' marital status.

ii. **Inheritance:** Uniform Probate Code §2-117 declares that a parent-child relationship exists between a child and the biological parents regardless of the parents' marital status. This provision enables a nonmarital child to inherit, for example, from a biological father by application of intestate succession law (subject to proof of paternity).

f. **Discrimination against nonmarital children:** Beginning in the 1960s, the U.S. Supreme Court held that some forms of discrimination (specifically, certain statutory benefits schemes) against nonmarital children were unconstitutional. *See, e.g., Weber v. Aetna Casualty and Surety Co.*, 406 U.S. 164 (1972) (state workers' compensation law); *Levy v. Louisiana*, 391 U.S. 68 (1968) (wrongful death).

However, the Court was less willing to invalidate some restrictions on nonmarital children's inheritance rights. *Compare Lalli v. Lalli*, 439 U.S. 259 (1978) (upholding a statute that requires judicial establishment of paternity in order for a nonmarital child to inherit from his father), with *Trimble v. Gordon*, 430 U.S. 762 (1977) (holding that a statute permitting nonmarital children to inherit from their fathers only if their fathers marry their mothers post-birth or acknowledge the child violates equal protection).

g. **Voluntary paternity establishment:** Welfare reform legislation strengthens procedures for voluntary paternity establishment. Legislation establishes that voluntary acknowledgments of paternity (subject to a 60-day rescission period) are legal findings and requires states to improve their paternity establishment procedures. Personal Responsibility and Work Opportunity Reconciliation Act of 1996 (PRWORA), 42 U.S.C. §666.

8. **Support rights of children of same-sex couples:** Some courts have held that children of same-sex couples have a right to child support from *both* same-sex parents.

Example: Jennifer and Sandra marry in New Mexico. During the marriage, Sandra gives birth to a child using sperm from a male friend who volunteered to help the couple get pregnant. During the pregnancy, Jennifer attends Sandra's doctor visits and is present at the birth. Both women take family leave. One year later, Jennifer moves out. Sandra files for divorce and child support. Jennifer argues that she is precluded from paying child support because she is not biologically related to the child and the Texas Family Code defines "parents" in terms of a mother and a father. Sandra argues that the Texas Family Code must be read in accord with the U.S. Supreme Court's recognition of same-sex marriage in *Obergefell*. The Texas court determines that the child "born of the marriage" is the child of both Sandra and Jennifer and that they will be treated as any other married couple, thereby obligating Jennifer to pay child support. *Treto v. Treto*, 2020 WL 373063 (Tex. App. 2020).

II.   MODIFICATION OF SPOUSAL AND CHILD SUPPORT AWARDS

A. Standard

1. **General rule:** The standard for modification of spousal and child support is a *substantial and material change of circumstances since the entry of the decree*. Courts have broad discretion in how they define that term. For purposes of spousal support awards, certain circumstances (such as the cohabitation of the recipient-spouse) may lead to modification or termination of support either by statute or agreement between the parties.

2. **UMDA restrictive rule for modification of spousal support:** UMDA, which adopts a restrictive standard for spousal support generally, also provides for a restrictive standard for *modification of spousal support*. Under UMDA, spousal support may be modified only if a change in circumstances has occurred that is "so substantial and continuing as to make the terms unconscionable" (§316).

3. **Restrictive rule for retroactive modification of child support.** Most jurisdictions refuse to allow *retroactive* modification of *child support* obligations (i.e., alterations of payments that are past due).

B. Relevant factors:
Sometimes, circumstances occur that may affect the support obligation. Changes in *either* former spouse's circumstances may warrant reduction or termination of spousal support. Circumstances that may affect a family member's needs and/or a spouse's ability to pay include:

- a voluntary change in the payor's occupation;
- the payor's remarriage and resulting increased family responsibilities;
- the payor's increased resources;
- the payor's deteriorating health; and
- the payee's remarriage or cohabitation.

1. **Payor's changed circumstances:** An involuntary change in circumstances results from events beyond a person's control, such as the loss of employment or illness, and may justify a reduction

in the support obligation. On the other hand, a *voluntary* change in circumstances generally does not justify a reduction in the support obligation.

a. **Change of occupation:** When a parent changes employment, his or her child support obligation may be reduced only if (1) the change was in good faith (not attributable to an attempt to avoid paying support); and (2) the action will not deprive the child of reasonable financial support. The existence of good faith is a factual determination. If a parent is voluntarily unemployed or underemployed, the child support obligation will be calculated based on imputed *earning capacity*.

    Example: Husband and Wife are both attorneys. Following their divorce, Father petitions to reduce his child support obligation, alleging that his income decreased while he trained for a new career in teaching. The trial court denied his request, finding that Husband was voluntarily underemployed and that he still possessed the same earning capacity. The trial court reasons that, although Husband is free to change careers, his child should not be expected to finance his choice. The Alaska Supreme Court affirms, explaining that even if the career change was undertaken in good faith, Husband's statements that he was a failure at law were undermined by his failure to keep regular office hours and his efforts to reduce his workload. *Olmstead v. Ziegler*, 42 P.3d 1102 (Alaska 2002).

b. **Payor's remarriage and subsequent family obligations:** A court will consider the payor's remarriage if it places increasing demands on his financial resources.

    Example: Mother and Father marry and have two children. They divorce ten years later. According to their separation agreement, the parties agreed Father would pay Mother $3,000 dollars monthly in child support. A few years later, Father requests to modify support based on a change in circumstances (his remarriage and two additional children). The trial court reduces Father's child support to $2,400 per month, concluding that Father proved a substantial change in circumstance. Further, a court may consider a deviation from the child support guidelines if it determines that a parent is responsible for supporting others. *Trombley v. Trombley*, 2018 WL 2187894 (Ohio Ct. App. 2018).

c. **Payor's increased resources:** A significant improvement in the payor's resources may constitute a substantial and material change of circumstances justifying an increase in spousal support. On the other hand, a few courts have held that the recipient-spouse should not receive a windfall merely if the payor subsequently experiences success for the reason that the appropriate yardstick for support is the standard of living during the marriage.

d. **Payor's deteriorating health:** The payor's health problems sometimes may result in a reduction in payment of spousal support and/or child support.

2. **Recipient's changed circumstances**

a. **Remarriage:** Some jurisdictions follow a rule of automatic termination upon a recipient's remarriage. The reason for terminating maintenance at remarriage is because the former husband's duty of support has been replaced by that of the new husband.

b. **Cohabitation:** A few states permit modification or termination of spousal support presumptively when the recipient-spouse cohabits with a new intimate partner. *See, e.g.,* Cal. Fam. Code §4323 (rebuttable presumption of decreased need for spousal support exists if recipient is cohabiting with a nonmarital partner). The policy rationale is that cohabitation generally results in a decreased need for support.

Some states reduce or terminate alimony automatically regardless of a diminution in the recipient's need whereas other states require such proof. A relevant factor in some states is the length of time the couple shares a residence. Durational requirements range from three months (Massachusetts) to one year (North Dakota, Virginia).

When the issue of cohabitation arises for purposes of alimony modification, the former spouses often argue about whether the divorced spouse's new intimate relationship rises to the requisite degree of "cohabitation." The payor-spouse generally introduces evidence that the alimony recipient attempts to refute.

Example: Husband and Wife end their 13-year marriage. According to the marital settlement agreement, alimony ($5,500 monthly) would terminate in the event of the wife's remarriage or cohabitation "in a relationship tantamount to marriage." Upon discovery of his ex-wife's longstanding relationship with her significant other (J.K.), the ex-husband moves to terminate alimony. The appellate court rules that he failed to prove that his ex-wife's cohabitation established the requisite change in circumstances. According to the court, the test is whether the relationship has reduced the financial needs of the former spouse. The ex-husband was able to prove only that his ex-wife and her new partner had a social relationship (i.e., J.K. spent considerable time at her house and attended social/family events with her) but not a dependent financial relationship (i.e., no shared living expenses, no intertwined finances or proof of an enforceable promise of support). *Mennen v. Mennen*, 2019 WL 1468745 (N.J. Super. Ct. App. Div. 2019).

III. JURISDICTION AND ENFORCEMENT OF CHILD SUPPORT AWARDS

Child support enforcement is difficult when the parties reside in different states. Traditionally, a custodial parent had a limited ability to enforce interstate child support obligations for several reasons:

1. the original state lacked personal jurisdiction over the noncustodial parent in the latter's new state;

2. the noncustodial parent's new state could not help because no nexus existed between that state and the custodial parent; and

3. limits were imposed by federalism.

The limits imposed by federalism were that support orders, as continuing obligations, were not enforceable under the Full Faith and Credit Clause, U.S. Const. art. IV, §1, which applies only to final and nonmodifiable child support orders. *Sistare v. Sistare*, 218 U.S. 1 (1920).

To establish or enforce a support order, a custodial parent had to travel to the noncustodial parent's new state and initiate new proceedings there — a costly and burdensome procedure. This problem, to some extent, has been remedied.

A. **Jurisdiction generally:** To make (or modify) an award of child support or spousal support, a court must have *personal jurisdiction* over the obligor. Although a court may award an ex parte divorce without jurisdiction over one spouse, a court may not resolve the financial incidents of the divorce without personal jurisdiction over both spouses. This is the ***doctrine of divisible divorce*** (affirmed by the U.S. Supreme Court in *Vanderbilt v. Vanderbilt*, 354 U.S. 416 (1957)).

The trend is to expand the traditional methods of acquiring personal jurisdiction over nonresidents for support purposes. The reform results from efforts to address the increasing number of parents with unpaid child support obligations. State and federal reforms and Uniform Acts are indicative of this trend.

B.   State long-arm statutes

1. **Types of long-arm statutes:** According to the traditional rule, personal jurisdiction must accord with the requirements of state long-arm statutes and the Constitution's Due Process Clause.

    Prior to the 1970s, states occasionally permitted the assertion of jurisdiction over nonresidents in domestic relations cases by liberal interpretations of their long-arm statutes (construing the obligor's actions to be "a tortious act," or "the infliction of harm," etc.). Other states (e.g., California) provided similarly broad parameters by permitting the assertion of jurisdiction so long as it met the "constitutional requirements of due process."

    In recent years, many states substantially increased the scope of jurisdiction over nonresidents in domestic relations cases by revising their long-arm statutes to include specific provisions for the assertion of jurisdiction in claims for family obligations (both spousal support and child support). In addition, the U.S. Supreme Court clarified the scope of due process limitations in *Kulko v. Superior Court, infra*, and, subsequently, in *Burnham v. Superior Court, infra*. (See the discussion of these cases in Chapter 5.)

2. **Constitutional limits of long-arm statutes:** The assertion of personal jurisdiction by means of long-arm statutes must comport with the requisites of due process. The U.S. Supreme Court in *Kulko v. Superior Court*, 436 U.S. 84 (1978), identified those requirements in the child support context.

    Example: Ezra marries Sharon during a three-day stopover in California en route to a tour of duty. Both parties are domiciled in New York. They live there with their two children until their separation. Sharon moves to San Francisco. They execute a separation agreement in New York providing that the children will continue to live in New York with their father but spend vacations in California with their mother. Ezra agrees to pay $3,000 annually in child support. Sharon obtains a Haitian divorce that incorporates the terms of the agreement. She returns to California and remarries. Soon, the children decide (first the daughter, then later the son) that they want to live with Sharon. Ezra sends the daughter to California. Sharon, unbeknownst to Ezra, sends the son a ticket. After the son's arrival, Sharon files an action in California to establish the Haitian divorce decree as a California judgment and to modify it to award her custody and increased child support. Ezra appears specially, arguing that the court lacks jurisdiction over him. The California Supreme Court holds that Ezra's "purposeful act" in sending the daughter to live in California warranted the exercise of personal jurisdiction over him. Reversing, the U.S. Supreme Court holds that California's assertion of personal jurisdiction over the defendant violates due process. By Defendant's sending his daughter to California, he did not "purposefully avail" himself of the benefits of California law or do anything whereby he might have expected to litigate an action in California. Considerations of fairness (i.e., the stay-at-home spouse should not bear the burden of litigating in a new forum) and the fact that the controversy arose in New York militate against California's assertion of jurisdiction. *Kulko v. Superior Court*, 436 U.S. 34 (1978).

C. Interstate enforcement: URESA, RURESA, and UIFSA

1. General procedure: The Uniform Law Commission formulated the Uniform Reciprocal Enforcement of Support Act (URESA), in 1950, and its revised version, RURESA, in 1968, to facilitate establishment and interstate enforcement of child support orders.

2. Continuing problems led to UIFSA: In response to continuing problems of multiple conflicting support orders, the Uniform Interstate Family Support Act (UIFSA) superseded URESA and RURESA in 1992. UIFSA aims to eliminate cases in which more than one child support order applies to a child (or children) and also to encourage states to apply restraint in the modification of existing child support orders, especially if modification is sought in a state other than the rendering state. UIFSA contains new procedures for *establishing, enforcing, and modifying* support orders.

Welfare reform legislation in 1996 spurred the enactment of UIFSA by requiring states to enact UIFSA in order to qualify for the receipt of federal welfare funds. Personal Responsibility and Work Opportunity Reconciliation Act (PRWORA), 42 U.S.C. §666(f).

3. UIFSA

    a. Scope: UIFSA provides for the establishment, modification, and enforcement of temporary and permanent support orders, and also provides for enforcement by civil and criminal contempt. UIFSA §305(b).

    b. Reforms: UIFSA permits the enforcement of support orders in another state without registration, and does not require reciprocity (i.e., that the other state also adopt the legislation) to establish or enforce a support order.

    To eliminate multiple orders, UIFSA provides that only one support order can be in effect at any one time—i.e., the "One-Order-One-Time" rule. That is, the court entering the original support order maintains continuing, exclusive jurisdiction until that state ceases to be the residence of the child or the parties, or a party files consent to another state's jurisdiction. If no state has continuing, exclusive jurisdiction, an order made by the child's home state has priority. UIFSA §205.

    Also, UIFSA provides for one-state proceedings, as an alternative to the former two-state proceedings. That is, UIFSA §201 provides an expansive long-arm statute that permits the assertion of personal jurisdiction over the obligor by the originating state.

    UIFSA has also made other changes in the traditional two-state proceedings. Under former law, the initiating state determined whether the obligor owes a duty of support. Under UIFSA, the initiating tribunal forwards support documents to the responding tribunal that determines jurisdiction.

    UIFSA addresses the modification of support orders as well. Formerly, the original state and the responding state could modify a support order. Under UIFSA, however, only the state with continuing, exclusive jurisdiction can modify a registered order unless the parties file a written consent to assertion of jurisdiction or the original state is no longer the residence of the child or the parties. UIFSA §205(a).

D. Federal legislation: Full Faith and Credit for Child Support Orders Act: On the federal level, attempts have been made to encourage widespread adoption of UIFSA. In 1994, Congress enacted the Full Faith and Credit for Child Support Orders Act (FFCCSOA), 28 U.S.C. §1738(B), that

requires states to enforce the child support orders of other states. The Act is aimed at eliminating the problem of the multiplicity of support orders under URESA and ensuring that only one child support order at a time will be in effect.

1. **UIFSA serves as model:** FFCCSOA incorporates many UIFSA concepts. Specifically, FFCCSOA

   ■ requires that a state enforce the child support order made by a court of another state, provided that the court in the originating state had subject matter jurisdiction and personal jurisdiction over the parties;

   ■ limits modification of child support orders in a manner similar to UIFSA;

   ■ requires that the forum state's law applies in proceedings to establish, enforce, or modify support orders, unless the court is merely interpreting the support order (in which case the law of the originating state applies); and

   ■ provides that the longer of two different statutes of limitations will apply in enforcement actions. 28 U.S.C. §1738B(e) and 28 U.S.C. §1738B(g)(3).

2. **Federal preemption:** Courts are split as to whether the Full Faith and Credit for Child Support Orders Act preempts UIFSA. However, most courts (like *LeTellier v. LeTellier*, *infra*) agree that the statutes can be harmonized (i.e., that the FFCCSOA does *not* preempt UIFSA).

   Example: Teresa and Steven divorce. The District of Columbia awards Teresa custody and orders Steven to pay child support. Teresa later moves with their son to Tennessee. Steven moves to Virginia. Subsequently, Teresa files a petition in Tennessee, seeking to register the D.C. support order and to modify it. The Tennessee court grants the father's motion to dismiss, agreeing that the Tennessee court lacks subject matter jurisdiction to modify the award, and orders the case transferred to Virginia, where Father resides. Mother appeals. The Tennessee Supreme Court agrees, holding that the Tennessee court lacked subject matter jurisdiction, and also that the jurisdictional provisions of the Federal Full Faith and Credit for Child Support Orders Act (FFCCSOA) do not preempt the jurisdictional provisions of UIFSA. According to the court's reasoning, Mother, as a Tennessee resident, cannot meet the UIFSA requirement governing modification of the child support order of another state (she is not a "petitioner who is a nonresident of this state seek[ing] modification") and, thus, UIFSA's provision does not confer subject matter jurisdiction upon the Tennessee court to hear her petition to modify the District of Columbia's child support order. *LeTellier v. LeTellier*, 40 S.W.3d 490 (Tenn. 2001).

E. **Enforcement remedies:** Several state and federal remedies address the problem of enforcement of child support obligations.

   1. **Traditional state remedies:** State remedies include money judgments, criminal nonsupport proceedings, and the contempt power.

      a. **Money judgments:** Most jurisdictions provide for enforcement of child support obligations by money judgments. These include: the imposition of liens, sequestration, attachment of property, and wage garnishment. Resort to these remedies normally requires that the custodial parent obtain personal jurisdiction over the noncustodial parent or over his/her property. Further, such remedies are available only in cases of arrearages (not to collect future payments).

b. **Criminal nonsupport proceedings:** The custodial parent may also institute a criminal proceeding for nonsupport based on state statute. All states have statutes that result in the imposition of criminal sanctions on noncustodial parents who fail to support or abandon their children.

c. **Contempt:** The most common state remedy for nonpayment of child support is contempt. Under its broad equitable power, a court may hold in contempt a noncustodial parent who refuses to pay child support. This results in incarcerating the parent until he or she pays or agrees to pay. To be found in contempt, a court must determine that the obligor first had the ability to pay.

   i. **Civil v. criminal nature of contempt:** Contempt may be either civil or criminal in nature, although sometimes it is difficult to determine which it is. The distinction becomes important because a criminal defendant is entitled to due process protections.

   Additional distinctions between criminal and civil contempt include:

   ■ in civil contempt, punishment is *remedial* (imprisonment only until defendant performs a required act) and for the benefit of the *petitioner*;

   ■ in criminal contempt, the sanction is *punitive* (imprisonment for a definite period without the possibility of purging) and to vindicate a *court*;

   ■ in civil contempt, any fine is payable to the petitioner;

   ■ in criminal contempt, any fine is payable to the court.

   ii. **Role of counsel in contempt proceedings.** The U.S. Supreme Court holds that the Due Process Clause does not *automatically* require the provision of counsel in civil contempt proceedings for an indigent who is subject to a child support order. However, due process may require counsel in some circumstances.

   Example: Michael Turner fails to pay court-ordered child support. He is found in contempt and sentenced to 12 months incarceration. He challenges his incarceration, claiming a right to counsel. Given the civil nature of the proceeding (his ability to purge the sentence by payment of the arrearage), the Court determines that the Fourteenth Amendment's Due Process Clause applies (rather than the Sixth Amendment), thereby triggering consideration of the *Mathews v. Eldridge* test (424 U.S. 319 (1976)), requiring consideration of: (1) the nature of the private interest affected, (2) the comparative risk of an erroneous deprivation of that interest with and without additional or substitute procedural safeguards, and (3) the nature and magnitude of any countervailing interest in not providing additional or substitute procedural requirements.

   Although the private interest (loss of liberty) argues strongly for a right to counsel here, the Court nonetheless decides that counsel is not required because (1) the proof of indigence to demonstrate the need for counsel is the same issue as that on the merits (inability to pay); (2) in some cases (as here), the opposing party lacks representation, thereby causing an unfair asymmetry; and (3) there are alternative procedural mechanisms to determine his ability to pay (e.g., financial forms or judicial findings). Because Turner lacked any of these protections, lacked counsel, and lacked any determination of his inability to pay, his due process rights were violated. *Turner v. Rogers,* 564 U.S. 431(2011).

      iii. ***Turner* Guidelines:** Federal reforms prompted by *Turner* (called "*Turner* Guidelines"), effective in 2017, make several changes in child support enforcement. Federal rules strengthen due process requirements by providing guidance on the factors for consideration when determining which cases should be referred for civil contempt, including a determination of the noncustodial parent's ability to pay. The new provisions also prohibit state child support programs from treating incarceration as voluntary unemployment, thereby leading to the possibility of modifying child support orders during periods of incarceration.

2. **Modern state remedies: License suspension:** Some statutes provide for the suspension of professional, occupational, business, driver's, or recreational licenses of obligors with child support arrearages. Other states provide for the *denial of a new license or denial of a renewal* of certain licenses for obligors with outstanding child support obligations. Courts have upheld the constitutionality of such statutes.

3. **Federal remedies:** Important federal legislation provides tools for the enforcement of child support orders.

    a. **Federal crime:** In 1992, Congress enacted the Child Support Recovery Act (CSRA), 18 U.S.C §228(a), making it a federal crime to willfully fail to pay a "past due support obligation" for a child who resides in another state. The Act defines a "past due support obligation" as an amount determined by a state court that remains unpaid for longer than one year or exceeds $5,000. The Act provides for incarceration and restitution for the unpaid support. Congress amended and strengthened the CSRA in 1998 with the Deadbeat Parents Punishment Act (codified at 18 U.S.C §228(a)). The amendment provides that a debt of longer than two years or over $10,000 is punishable by fine or imprisonment of up to 24 months or both. Courts have upheld the constitutionality of the statute.

    b. **Garnishment or income withholding:** Wage garnishment, the most effective weapon in the federal arsenal, permits an employer to pay an employee's child support obligation directly to the other spouse on behalf of a child. The federal Child Support and Establishment of Paternity Act of 1974, 42 U.S.C. §659, permits the garnishment (or income withholding) of federal wages to facilitate payment of child support to welfare recipients.

    Early legislation was so effective that Congress expanded the program by the Child Support Enforcement Amendments of 1984 (CSEA) to require that *all support orders* include a conditional order for wage withholding to begin when payments are one month *in arrears*.

    The Family Support Act of 1988 (FSA) goes even further by mandating automatic wage withholding in *all cases, regardless of whether support payments were one month in arrears as formerly*. States must institute wage withholding absent a judicial finding of good cause or a written parental agreement providing otherwise.

    Federal welfare reform legislation facilitates collection procedures by providing for a governmental agency to collect funds for obligees and also by requiring reports of newly hired employees to a state agency that forwards this information to the federal government. Personal Responsibility and Work Opportunity Reconciliation Act of 1996 (PRWORA), §§312, 653(a).

    c. **Tax refund intercept:** CSEA also provides for the interception of federal (and state) tax refunds of all obligors to meet an obligor's unpaid child support obligations.

    d. Passport denial: Federal welfare legislation authorizes the denial, revocation, or nonrenewal of a passport for reason of the nonpayment of support obligations.

    e. Other mechanisms: CSEA also mandates that states adopt other collection procedures for enforcing child support orders, including: expedited enforcement (administrative processes for establishing and enforcing support obligations), liens against real and personal property, posting a bond or giving security for overdue support, and disclosure of overdue support to consumer reporting agencies.

Quiz Yourself on CHILD SUPPORT

77. Richard pays $512 each month to his ex-wife for support of their minor child. At the time of their divorce, Richard is an assistant professor of English. Shortly after the divorce, Richard voluntarily resigns his position to attend law school. He petitions the court for a modification in child support based on his reduction in income. Will he succeed? _____

78. Mark divorces Sylvia after a five-year marriage in order to marry Glenice. At the time of the divorce, Mark and Sylvia have one daughter, age three. Glenice is a young widow who has been working part-time as a receptionist to take care of her three young children because her husband died from cancer. At the time of the divorce, Mark agreed to pay Sylvia $750 per month as child support. One year later, Mark requests a modification of his support obligation to $500 per month for the reason of his remarriage and additional financial responsibilities to Glenice and her children. This jurisdiction follows the modern (rather than common-law) approach regarding the imposition of stepparent liability. Will Mark prevail? _____

79. Jeffrey and Shanon have two nonmarital children. After the parents separate, a court enters an order establishing Jeffrey's paternity and orders him to pay $723 per month for child support. Jeffrey never makes a voluntary payment but has his income withheld for some of the amount he owes. Eventually, he owes more than $52,000 in unpaid support. He tells Shanon that he won't pay because, "They're your girls." He is indicted for willful failure to pay child support. He argues that because he is unable to pay the entire amount of child support, his failure is not "willful." Will he prevail? _____

80. Charles and Yetta, both accountants, divorce when their daughter Helen is 15 years old. The court orders Charles to pay $800 a month as child support. Three years later, Yetta seeks an increase in child support to pay for costs associated with Helen's college education. Helen is an excellent student and has just been accepted at a private college. Charles contends that an order of child support would unlawfully require him to support Helen past her majority. Will he prevail? _____

81. Chip and Joanna are married for 15 years and have three children. When they divorce, the court awards Joanna sole custody of the children and orders Chip to pay $5,000 per month in spousal support. Two years later, Joanna and the children begin living with Joel, who is Joanna's significant other. When Chip learns of the new living arrangement, he seeks to terminate Joanna's spousal support. Chip introduces evidence that, although Joanna and Joel are not married, they have been living together for two years, attend social and family events together, and share a checking account. Will Chip prevail? _____

Answers

77. Perhaps. According to the general rule, a voluntary change of occupation that results in the payor's reduced earnings generally does not justify a decreased award of support. Here, Richard gave up a steady salary as a professor to become a law student. However, if Richard chooses to attend law school to seek an improved financial situation and the change was made in good faith (not simply to reduce his support payments), and his occupational change will not deprive his child of reasonable financial support, then a court may grant his request for a reduction.

78. Probably yes. Remarriage is a relevant consideration in the modification of support obligations if the remarriage places increasing demands on a payor's financial resources. Mark's remarriage to a woman with three children has resulted in substantial new financial obligations. Further, although at common law, a stepparent had no legal duty to support a stepchild, many modern statutes and some case law impose liability on stepparents for co-resident stepchildren. Thus, because Glenice's three children reside with Mark and Glenice, Mark may have a statutory duty to support his stepchildren. Mark's request for a modification should be granted.

79. No. A parent may be criminally convicted for willful failure to pay child support if he has the ability to pay and refuses to do so. Courts reason that a parent should seek modification if he or she is unable to pay, rather than wait to challenge the child support determination until being incarcerated for nonpayment. Here, a court could reason that Jeffrey has the ability to pay because his income was withheld to pay support in the past, and his words to Shanon clearly indicate an intentional refusal to pay. Therefore, his conviction will be upheld.

80. Perhaps. Traditionally, child support payments could not extend past a child's majority except in extraordinary circumstances (i.e., disability). However, an increasing number of states, by statute or case law, permit child support through college through a variety of legal or equitable doctrines. Depending on the law in this jurisdiction, it is possible that Yetta may be successful in her claim for Helen's post-majority support for college expenses. Several courts look to the following factors: the child's aptitude, the parents' financial resources, the parents' college background, and the family's expectations had the marriage remained intact. Because of Helen's excellent record and her parents' financial abilities and college backgrounds, it is possible that Charles will have to contribute to Helen's college expenses. However, some courts have ruled that a post-divorce order for a parent to contribute to college expenses violates the Equal Protection Clause.

81. Perhaps, depending on state law. Some states reduce or terminate alimony *automatically* regardless of a diminution in the recipient's need, whereas other states require such proof. In the former states, a court may well reduce or terminate Joanna's alimony given that she and the children have been living with Joel for two years. A relevant factor in some states is the length of time the couple shares a residence. The court might determine that Joanna's two-year cohabitation is sufficient to decrease or terminate her spousal support, especially because she and her new significant other have commingled their finances (sharing a checking account). However, in other states, Chip may have to prove that Joanna was *financially dependent* on Joel in order for the court to reduce or terminate her spousal support.

IV. SEPARATION AGREEMENTS

Separation agreements (sometimes called "marital settlement agreements") are contracts entered into by divorcing spouses that concern the division of property, the support rights of a spouse and children, and sometimes child custody as well.

A. Premarital agreements distinguished: Separation agreements are distinguishable from premarital agreements. A separation agreement is entered into by the parties *during* the divorce process. A premarital agreement is entered into *before* the marriage.

B. Validity: The validity of a separation agreement is determined by contract law. Such agreements may be set aside for fraud, duress, or overreaching.

C. Policy: Formerly, courts regarded separation agreements with suspicion because such agreements were thought to encourage divorce. Courts now favor separation agreements because they reduce the expense, delay, and animosity associated with litigation.

D. Modification: The modifiability of a separation agreement depends on whether it is characterized as "contractual" or "decretal." Courts cannot rewrite the terms of a contract. However, courts can modify some provisions of a judicial decree (e.g., support provisions but not property divisions) in light of changed circumstances.

Example: Husband and Wife's separation agreement contains a provision that Husband must provide Wife with health and dental insurance until her remarriage, but no alimony. The court incorporates the agreement in the divorce decree. Six years later, based on his unemployment and deteriorating health, Husband seeks to terminate his obligation to provide insurance. The trial and appellate courts deny his request, finding that he cannot modify the provision because the insurance coverage was not a form of spousal support. He appeals. The state supreme court reverses, finding that the "maintenance of health insurance has the hallmark of spousal support: it provides the receiving spouse a benefit which is normally incident to the marital relationship." Further, the court finds that Husband presented sufficient evidence of a substantial change in circumstances that entitled him to modification. *Miles v. Miles*, 711 S.E.2d 880 (S.C. 2011).

E. Enforcement of settlement agreement: Merger: A settlement agreement may be enforceable by means of the contempt power if the agreement has been **incorporated** and **merged** in the divorce decree.

Once an agreement is incorporated into the divorce decree, its provisions become part of the decree and may be enforced by court order, including contempt. On the other hand, if the agreement is incorporated, but is *not merged* into the decree, it remains a separate enforceable agreement and is *not* enforceable by contempt.

Example: Joseph and Ida execute a separation agreement providing that Joseph would pay Ida $2,425 a month for spousal support, which may be terminated if Ida remarries or either party dies. The separation agreement also contains a nonmodification agreement, providing that "[t]he terms of this Agreement shall not be subject to modification or change, regardless of the relative circumstances of the parties. . . ." The court finds that the agreement is not unconscionable and incorporates it into the divorce decree. Several years later, Joseph seeks termination of the spousal support, claiming that Ida tried to have him killed. The court refuses because of the nonmodification clause, which (according to the court) was not unconscionable and did not offend public policy, despite the acts of Ida. *Richardson v. Richardson*, 218 S.W.3d 426 (Mo. 2007).

V. TAX CONSIDERATIONS

Tax issues often arise in connection with a dissolution.

A. Traditional approach: Spousal support

1. **Taxable to the recipient:** The Internal Revenue Service (IRS) treats spousal support (called "alimony" under the Internal Revenue Code), as income, similar to salary. Traditionally, alimony was *taxable* to the recipient (i.e., included in his or her gross income).

2. **Deductible by the payor:** Traditionally, the IRS permitted a deduction to the payor-spouse for the alimony that the payor-spouse paid to the recipient-spouse. That is, alimony was *deductible* by the payor-spouse.

   According to this traditional view, in order to qualify as deductible by the payor-spouse, alimony payments must have manifested the following characteristics:

   - be in cash (not property or services);

   - be received by or on behalf of the other spouse according to a divorce decree or written separation agreement; and

   - terminate upon the recipient's death.

     In addition, to qualify, the parties could not live together or file a joint tax return after the payments began.

B. Modern approach: Spousal support

The federal Tax Cuts and Jobs Act (TCJA), Pub. L. No. 115-97, enacted by Congress in 2017, made several notable reforms regarding payment of alimony.

   i. Alimony: TCJA eliminates the tax deduction for payor-spouses for alimony payments and no longer requires the recipient-spouse to report alimony as income.

   ii. Timing: After the TCJA, the timing of a finalized divorce or separation agreement is vital. The TCJA provision is effective for divorce or separation agreements executed after December 31, 2018. The TCJA also applies to any divorce or separation instrument that was executed on or before December 31, 2018, and was *modified* after that date, if the modification expressly provides that the amendments made by this section apply to such modification.

C. Transfers of property to spouse incident to divorce:
Property transfers between spouses do not result in the recognition of income during the marriage or so long as the transfers are "incident to divorce" (if the transfer occurs within one year after the date of divorce or is "related to the cessation of the marriage"). The property transferred is treated as a gift to the recipient, so any gain or loss inherent in the property is not recognized at the time of the transfer. Further, the recipient takes the donor's basis in the property. This means that the recipient will have the tax burden (or benefit) of any gain (or loss) inherent in the property at the time of transfer.

Before TCJA, payor-spouses might have been motivated to disguise property transfers as deductible alimony in order to receive the more favorable tax treatment accorded to alimony. After TCJA, because there is no longer an alimony deduction for the payor-spouse, the incentive to disguise property transfers as alimony disappears.

D. Child support:
Alimony does not include child support payments. Child support payments are *nontaxable* to the recipient-spouse and *nondeductible* by the payor-spouse. This rule remains unchanged.

Quiz Yourself on
SEPARATION AGREEMENTS

82. Upon their divorce, Husband and Wife enter into a property settlement agreement. The agreement provides that "in consideration of the payment to Wife of $10,000 per year for four years for spousal support, and the conveyance of $20,000 to Wife in personal property, Wife agrees to and does release all rights of inheritance in Husband's estate." The agreement is referred to in the divorce decree and is approved by the court but is not actually made part of the decree. Husband conveys to Wife the $20,000 in personal property in the form of stocks and bonds; however, he fails to make any payments for spousal support. Wife attempts to enforce the agreement by contempt proceedings. Will she prevail? _____

Answer

82. No. A settlement agreement between the spouses may be enforced by contempt if the agreement has been incorporated and merged in the divorce decree. If the agreement is not merged into the decree, it remains a separate enforceable agreement and is enforceable in a separate contract action but not enforceable by contempt. Because Husband and Wife's agreement was referred to in the decree and approved by the court, but not merged into the decree, the marital separation agreement is not enforceable by contempt. Wife will have to sue for breach of contract.

Exam Tips on
FINANCIAL CONSEQUENCES OF DISSOLUTION

General Issues Regarding Support and Property

☛ Before analyzing support and property issues, be sure to identify various ***threshold issues***.

   ☞ For example, note who is petitioning for divorce in the designated forum. Identify whether one spouse is petitioning or both. Remember that if the facts involve a ***unilateral divorce*** (by one spouse only), the respondent might be able to assert that the court lacks jurisdiction over him or her. (A court lacking jurisdiction over the respondent can only terminate the marriage and cannot adjudicate the financial incidents of the divorce.)

   ☞ Be sure to note also whether the divorce is being sought on ***fault-based grounds or no fault***. If the divorce is sought by a party (or parties) on fault-based grounds, then fault may bar awards of spousal support and property in some jurisdictions.

Property

☛ For property questions, clarify the ***type of marital property regime*** in the given jurisdiction. If the question states no specific regime, then answer the question as if each of the regimes (common law, community property) would apply. Be sure to explain the rationales of each type of marital property regime (e.g., community property is based on the partnership model, etc.).

☞ Mention the shift from the *traditional* rationale for *property* division to the *contribution* approach.

☞ Explain that most states now adhere to *equitable distribution*. Clarify the meaning of the term "equitable distribution." If the issue involves separate property, be sure to mention the *lack of uniformity of treatment of separate property* under the scheme of equitable jurisdiction. (That is, some equitable distribution jurisdictions treat gifts and inheritances as separate property, whereas others treat those items as marital property.)

☛ Be on the lookout for *frequently tested property issues*. Such issues include: professional licenses and degrees, goodwill, pensions, and bankruptcy. Always specify relevant majority and minority approaches. For example, if the issue involves a professional license or degree, explain the majority rule that most states refuse to treat professional licenses and degrees as marital property. Clarify the reasons underlying that rule. Explain, too, that some jurisdictions find ways to mitigate the harshness of this rule. Be sure to mention the ALI *Principles'* approach here (and wherever relevant).

☛ For questions involving pensions, explore whether the problem involves *vested and/or nonvested pension rights*. Explain the difference between vested and nonvested pension rights. In the determination of whether an employee-spouse's rights have vested, be sure to take note of the numbers of years' service that are necessary for the vesting of pension rights.

☞ Discuss the majority versus minority approach to nonvested pension rights. Remember to clarify that under the majority rule, vested *and* nonvested pension benefits are marital property subject to equitable distribution.

☞ Finally, determine if there are any issues regarding *federal-state preemption*. Such issues are likely to arise if the pension rights involve federal benefits (military retirement pay, etc.). Discuss the about face in treatment of preemption issues. That is, the U.S. Supreme Court first ruled that certain federal retirement schemes were exempt from application of state marital property rules; however, subsequently Congress overruled that policy by the enactment of federal legislation.

☛ For questions involving *bankruptcy*, explain the protective policy behind the federal bankruptcy legislation.

☞ Discuss the *"support-property distinction"* — the traditional rule that obligations attributable to a property division upon divorce were dischargeable in bankruptcy but that support obligations (child support, spousal support) were not dischargeable. Because of this rule, it is necessary to determine whether a particular obligation could be classified as support or property. Recall that the determination is not always crystal clear. In such a case, discuss the implications of a finding that a particular obligation could be classified as either support or property.

☞ Be sure to point out the impact of BAPCPA that made property obligations stemming from dissolution judgments or separation agreements no longer dischargeable in Chapter 7 bankruptcies (although the support-property distinction continues to control dischargeability for purposes of Chapter 13 bankruptcies).

Support

☛ When analyzing issues of support, be sure to distinguish if the question is asking about spousal support and/or child support. Different rationale, rules, and policies will apply.

☞ Mention that the traditional rationales underlying awards of alimony were *fault* and *need*. However, the modern rationales of *self-sufficiency* and *loss compensation* (ALI) replace the traditional rationales.

☞ Remember that support statutes with *gender-based* provisions are unconstitutional (*Orr v. Orr*).

☞ Remember, too, that different forms of spousal support are available (*rehabilitative alimony* and *reimbursement alimony*). Be sure to explain the meaning of each term and determine whether each form would (or should) be available.

☛ Many questions involve issues of both spousal support and property. In such cases, be sure to remember the *distinctions* between the awards. For example, spousal support is *modifiable*; property awards are not. Spousal support is *terminable* upon remarriage; property awards are not. Spousal support awards are enforceable by the *contempt* power; property awards are not.

☛ For questions involving spousal support and child support, clarify whether the question involves an *initial award* or *modification*. Always look for cross-over issues between spousal support and property, such as those raised by licenses and degrees.

☞ When addressing modification of spousal support, be alert for *common fact patterns involving changed circumstances* (especially remarriage, cohabitation, deteriorating health).

☞ Remember that a determination of changed circumstances requires that the change be *substantial* and *material* since the entry of the divorce decree.

Child Support

☛ For child support issues, determine if the jurisdiction is relying on the traditional *discretionary* standard or *guidelines*.

☞ If the approach is unspecified, discuss both. If the jurisdiction has adopted guidelines, determine which *model* it follows (i.e., income shares model, percentage of income model, or Melson formula) and apply that model to the facts. If no model is specified, discuss all three approaches.

☛ Be alert for *frequently tested issues*, such as post-majority support, stepparent liability, and support of nonmarital children.

☞ For questions involving *post-majority support*, be sure to mention that states have different approaches to this issue. Be on the lookout for possible issues regarding the constitutionality of a post-majority support statute.

☞ For issues of *stepparent liability*, mention the traditional view (of no duty) and the modern view that imposes liability in some cases.

☞ If the question involves *support of nonmarital children*, be sure to look for constitutional issues of discrimination against nonmarital children (e.g., denial of equal protection), and issues involving statutes of limitations. In the latter case, be sure to mention the influence of federal legislation (Child Support Enforcement Amendments) that extends the statutory period until age 18. Be alert to possible issues regarding the standard of proof, indigents' rights in paternity establishment cases, and voluntary paternity establishment.

☛ When addressing *modification of child support* (just like modification of spousal support), be alert for *common fact patterns involving changed circumstances* (i.e., remarriage, cohabitation, deteriorating health, increased resources, occupational changes).

     ☞ Remember that a determination of changed circumstances requires that the change (since the prior custody order) be both *substantial* and *material*. Discuss the rule and apply it to the given fact pattern.

☛ Finally, be alert for issues involving *jurisdiction* and *enforcement* of child support awards.

     ☞ To make or modify an award of child support (or spousal support), a court must have *personal jurisdiction* over the obligor.

     ☞ Determine if the obligor is a *nonresident* (a frequent fact pattern). If so, note the trend to expand traditional methods of acquiring personal jurisdiction over nonresidents for support purposes. For questions involving personal jurisdiction over a nonresident obligor, remember to discuss both *state law* (i.e., the different types of *long-arm statutes*) and *constitutional due process*. In discussing the constitutional limits of long-arm statutes, be sure to discuss and apply the U.S. Supreme Court's decision in *Kulko v. Superior Court*.

☛ Common fact patterns involving *interstate enforcement* issues arise whenever the noncustodial parent leaves the state and refuses to pay support, whenever the custodial parent relocates to another state but wants to enforce a preexisting order, or whenever petitioner seeks modification in a forum that is different from the original forum.

     ☞ If the question involves the possibility (or actuality) of multiple support orders from different jurisdictions, be sure to discuss and apply the Uniform Interstate Family Support Act (UIFSA). Remember that UIFSA applies to initial awards as well as modifications of support orders.

     ☞ If a petitioner is seeking a modification of support in another state (other than the original forum), be sure to discuss and apply UIFSA's concept of *continuing, exclusive jurisdiction* (i.e., the court entering the original support order maintains continuing, exclusive jurisdiction until that state ceases to be the residence of the child or any party, or a party files consent to another state's jurisdiction).

     ☞ For enforcement, discuss both *state and federal* remedies.

CHAPTER 7

CHILD CUSTODY

ChapterScope

This chapter examines child custody in the divorce context. Here are a few of the key principles covered in this chapter:

■ Historically, courts applied ***presumptions*** to aid the determination of custody disputes.

- ■ The ***"tender years presumption"*** favored an award of custody to the mother of young children. Courts have held that this presumption violates the Equal Protection Clause.

- ■ The ***"primary caretaker presumption"*** favors an award of custody to the parent providing primary care. While no state continues to follow this presumption, many states consider it as a factor in custody decision making.

■ The modern prevailing standard in custody decision making is ***"the best interests of the child."***

■ Certain ***constitutional issues*** may arise in the determination of the best interests of the child.

- ■ ***Race*** cannot be the determinative factor in custody decisions.

- ■ The constitutional right to ***freedom of religion*** also restricts consideration of the role of religion in custody decision making.

- ■ Courts may also consider other factors regarding ***fitness*** in custody determinations.

- ■ Most states now consider ***domestic violence*** as a factor in custody decision making. Some states adopt a ***rebuttable presumption*** against custody awards to an abusive parent.

■ Almost all states now permit some form of ***joint custody***. Joint ***legal*** custody grants legal custody to both parents, i.e., responsibility for making major childrearing decisions (education, religion, medical). Joint ***physical*** custody grants responsibility for day-to-day caretaking to both parents.

■ Traditionally, the noncustodial parent received ***visitation rights*** to the child. Courts have discretion to define the scope, time, place, and circumstances of visitation. Courts deny visitation rights reluctantly.

■ Custody and visitation are ***not dependent*** variables: failure to support a child may *not* result in infringement of the parent's visitation rights.

■ A ***rebuttable presumption*** favors the biological parent in a custody dispute pitting a ***parent versus a nonparent***. However, the modern trend favors recognition of the parentage rights of former same-sex partners who are not biologically related to the child (i.e., no longer treating them as nonparents).

■ All states have ***visitation*** statutes permitting ***third parties*** (such as grandparents) to petition for visitation in certain circumstances.

■ Many states consider a ***child's preference*** in making custody decisions.

■ ***Representation for a child*** in a custody dispute is ***discretionary***.

■ Custody *modification* generally requires proof of a *material or substantial change in circumstances*.

■ The *Uniform Child Custody Jurisdiction and Enforcement Act* (UCCJEA) governs jurisdiction and enforcement of child custody decision making. It harmonizes differences between the original Uniform Child Custody Jurisdiction Act and the Parental Kidnapping Prevention Act.

■ The *Uniform Child Abduction Prevention Act* (UCAPA) enables the court to order measures to prevent child abductions.

■ Some jurisdictions mandate *mediation* in cases involving custody or visitation disputes. Mediation is a dispute resolution process by which the divorcing spouses, with the aid of a neutral third person, consider issues in hope of reaching a consensual agreement without resort to judicial intervention.

■ Some states have **collaborative law**, a process by which divorcing spouses *and their attorneys* agree to use cooperative dispute resolution techniques without resort to judicial intervention.

I. INTRODUCTION

This chapter concerns child custody disputes in the context of divorce. In the vast majority of divorces, parents reach private agreements about custodial arrangements. However, contested cases can be particularly acrimonious.

A. Definition of custody: Custody refers to the right to the care and control of a child, including the ability to make decisions regarding the child's residence, discipline, education, training, medical care, etc.

Traditionally, upon divorce, the court awarded custody to one parent (often the mother) granting that parent broad rights to the care and control of the child. Simultaneously, the court awarded *visitation* rights (sometimes called "parenting time") to the other parent (usually the father) that encompassed more limited decision making while the child was temporarily residing with the noncustodial parent. (The concept of joint custody is explained *infra*.)

B. Functions of custody law: Custody law has two functions: private dispute settlement and child protection.

C. Historical background: Prior to the nineteenth century, a rule of paternal preference prevailed: the father was entitled to custody. Beginning in the mid- to late nineteenth century, feminists advocated for the right to custody. Custody law began to reflect a maternal preference for mothers of young children. This maternal preference was abrogated in the 1980s because of its constitutional shortcomings.

Fault also played a role, historically, in custody decision making. Upon divorce, custody was awarded to the innocent spouse (i.e., the spouse who was not guilty of a fault-based ground for divorce).

The original version of the Uniform Marriage and Divorce Act (UMDA) rejected fault-based notions in custody determinations. However, UMDA §402 currently provides: "The court shall not consider conduct of a proposed custodian that does not affect his relationship to the child."

II. STANDARDS FOR SELECTING THE CUSTODIAL PARENT

A. **Presumptions:** Some states invoke presumptions to adjudicate child custody disputes.

   1. **Tender years doctrine (the maternal preference)**

     a. **Definition:** Historically, the tender years presumption provided that the biological mother of a young child is entitled to custody unless the mother is found to be unfit.

     b. **Effect:** Courts treated the tender years presumption as:

- a rule requiring maternal custody if all other factors are equal,

- a rule placing the burden of persuasion on the father to show that paternal custody is in the best interest of the child, or

- a rule affecting the burden of proof that required the father to prove maternal unfitness.

     c. **Constitutionality:** Beginning in the 1980s, courts invalidated the tender years presumption as a violation of equal protection. *See, e.g., Devine v. Devine*, 398 So.2d 686 (Ala. 1981).

     d. **Modern view:** Today courts assume that both parents are capable of caring for a child. However, courts still may consider the age of a child as a relevant factor in custody decision making.

   2. **Primary caretaker**

     a. **Definition:** The primary caretaker presumption briefly replaced the maternal preference in a few states. The primary caretaker presumption is a gender neutral custodial presumption that favors an award of custody to the parent who has assumed the status of the primary caretaker.

     b. **Relevant factors:** Several factors are relevant to the determination of primary caretaker status:

- preparing and planning meals;

- bathing, grooming, and dressing the children;

- purchasing, cleaning, and caring for the clothes;

- obtaining medical care for the child;

- arranging for children's social interactions with peers;

- arranging alternative care;

- putting the children to bed at night and tending to children who awaken during the night;

- managing discipline;

- supervising the child's religious, cultural, or social education; and

- teaching elementary skills.

Garska v. McCoy, 278 S.E.2d 357, 363 (1981).

     c. **Modern view:** The primary caretaker presumption was not widely adopted. Many states currently consider primary caretaker status as a relevant *factor* in custody decision making, although they no longer treat it as a presumption.

    d. ALI "approximation" approach: The American Law Institute's *Principles* provide for rules regarding the "allocation of custodial and decisionmaking responsibility" for children. Parties seeking custody must submit a "parenting plan" (a written agreement that specifies caretaking and decision-making authority and the manner for resolution of future disputes). If the parents agree, the court should enforce that agreement unless it was not voluntary or would be harmful to the child. ALI *Principles* §2.06(1)(a), (b).

    If the parents cannot agree, the court should award custody based on an *approximation standard* that allocates custody based on the amount of responsibility assumed by each parent prior to the separation. ALI *Principles* §2.08(1). The objective is to replicate the division of custodial responsibility that was followed when the family was intact.

  3. Other presumptions: Several other custody presumptions exist, including: custody of a nonmarital child vests in the mother, the separation of siblings is not in their best interest, custody awards to a biological parent are favored over awards to nonparents, and custody should not be awarded to a parent who has perpetrated domestic violence.

B. Best interests of the child: Most jurisdictions follow the "best interests of the child" standard when resolving custody disputes. Despite its widespread adoption, commentators criticize this standard as highly discretionary and imprecise. Several factors are relevant when applying this standard.

  1. Constitutional factors

    a. Race: The U.S. Supreme Court determined that race may not serve as the decisive factor in custody decision making.

    Example: When Linda and Anthony divorce, Linda is awarded custody of their three-year-old daughter. Subsequently, a court divests Linda of custody because she is living with, and later marries, an African American. The trial court finds that due to the social stigma accompanying an interracial marriage, the child's best interests will be served by awarding the father custody. The U.S. Supreme Court holds that an award of custody based on race violates the Equal Protection Clause. Race, although it may be a factor in custody decision making, may not be the determinative factor. The effects of racial prejudice cannot justify a racial classification that divests custody from a biological mother who has not been found to be unfit. *Palmore v. Sidoti*, 466 U.S. 429 (1984).

    Note: The ALI *Principles* prohibit courts from considering the race or ethnicity of the child, parent, or other member of the household in determining custody. ALI *Principles* §2.12(1)(a).

    b. Religion

      i. General rule: The First Amendment serves as a limitation on judicial consideration of religion as a factor in awarding custody. Under the Free Exercise Clause, a court may not interfere with a parent's right to practice religion. Under the Establishment Clause, a court may not favor one parent's religion or religious observance over another parent's religion or nonobservance.

      Example: Mother and Father marry in India. They move to the U.S. and have a daughter. When they separate, Mother is granted custody of the child with liberal visitation granted to Father. During the marriage, the parents practiced the Hindu faith. They now disagree about performance of a religious ceremony ("Chudakarana") on their daughter. The ceremony involves shaving the child's head, placing a mark on her head, and conferring blessings. The court refuses Father's request to order the ceremony, reasoning that granting Father's right to free exercise and his right to control the upbringing of the child would repudiate the Mother's equivalent rights. Further, neither parent provided evidence of a compelling state interest to justify the interference with the other parent's free exercise of religion because it was unclear whether performance of the ceremony would promote the child's welfare. The court decides to postpone the ceremony until the child can make her own decision. *Sagar v. Sagar*, 781 N.E.2d 54 (Mass. App. Ct. 2003).

ii. **Limitation:** A court may consider the *effect* of a parent's religion on the child.

Example: Three years after the spouses divorce, conflict develops about the religious upbringing of their young daughter. Husband is Roman Catholic. Wife recently joined the Pentecostal Church, which has several lifestyle restrictions (concerning clothes, make-up, jewelry, sports, dance) that affect daughter. The daughter was baptized a Catholic. Both parents seek sole custody. The trial court awards Husband sole custody. The appellate court holds that Wife's refusal to place child's needs above her religious convictions justified the custody modification in favor of father because the parents' conflict contributed to the child's confusion, guilt, and fear. However, the court added that any prohibition on Wife's taking the child to her church was unwarranted. *Holder v. Holder*, 872 N.E.2d 1239 (Ohio Ct. App. 2007).

iii. **ALI *Principles*:** The ALI *Principles* prohibit a court from considering the religious practices of either a parent or child in custody decision making except in the following situations: (1) if the religious practices present "severe and almost certain harm" to the child (and then a court may limit the religious practices only to the minimum degree necessary to protect the child) or (2) if necessary to protect the child's ability to practice a religion "that has been a significant part of the child's life." ALI *Principles* §2.12(1)(c).

2. **Fitness factors:** Courts consider numerous factors relevant to the determination of a parent's fitness. Some of these include sexual conduct, wealth, domestic violence, and disability.

   a. **Sexual conduct**

      i. **Generally:** Traditionally, a parent's acts of adultery and/or cohabitation resulted in a denial of custody. However, according to the modern view, a parent's sexual conduct is only relevant if it has an ***adverse effect*** on the child. *See* UMDA §402 ("The court shall not consider conduct of a proposed custodian that does not affect his relationship to the child").

      Example: Mother and Father divorce when their son (M.J.) is two years old. The court awards joint custody but names Mother as primary physical custodian. Father appeals, arguing that Mother's adultery should have resulted in an award of primary physical custody to him. Affirming, the appellate court concludes that the trial court could have been influenced by Mother's testimony that, although she had been in an intimate relationship since separating from Father, her relationship did not have a detrimental impact on her parenting skills or on the child's best interest. *In re M.J.*, 2010 WL 3042438 (Tex. App. 2010).

      ii. **Same-sex sexual conduct:** Courts traditionally adopted one of three basic approaches to the role of same-sex sexual conduct in custody decision making:

■ same-sex sexual conduct is evidence of parental fitness per se;

■ same-sex sexual conduct leads to a presumption of adverse impact that can be rebutted by the parent's showing of absence of harm; or

■ custody will be denied only if the parent's sexual orientation has or will have an adverse impact on the child.

This third view, the **nexus test**, represents the modern approach (and the view of the ALI *Principles* discussed *infra*).

Example: Beth and Tim divorce on the ground of irreconcilable differences. During the divorce proceedings, Tim testifies that his only concern with leaving their son Zach in Beth's permanent custody was the "homosexual environment" in which Zach would be raised. Tim felt that Beth was qualified in every other way to raise the child. When the trial court awards Tim custody, Beth appeals. The appellate court holds that the trial judge abused his discretion by placing too much weight on Beth's "moral fitness," the judge never found the mother unfit, no evidence was presented regarding any detrimental effects on the child as a result of living with the mother, and the judge ignored the voluminous evidence supporting Beth as the preferred custodial parent. *Hollon v. Hollon*, 784 So. 2d 943 (Miss. 2001).

iii. *Lawrence v. Texas*: *Lawrence v. Texas* may apply to custody decisions that restrict LGBT parents' custody rights based on parents' sexual conduct. In *Lawrence v. Texas*, the U.S. Supreme Court held that state sodomy laws banning same-sex, but not opposite-sex, sodomy violate the individual's constitutionally protected liberty and that moral disapproval is not a legitimate interest to justify such differential treatment.

After *Lawrence,* as well as *Obergefell v. Hodges*, many commentators believe that sexual orientation can no longer be used to restrict child custody rights. Commentators argue that *Lawrence* and *Obergefell* limit the extent to which courts can rely on moral disapproval as a basis for limiting LGBT parents' custodial rights, reasoning that it is impermissible to deny or restrict child custody because a parent is engaging in constitutionally protected conduct.

On the other hand, in the decade following *Lawrence*, critics point out that no LGBT parent has successfully invoked *Lawrence* to keep custody of a child or to challenge restrictions on the exercise of visitation rights. *See, e.g.,* Nancy Polikoff, *Custody Rights of Lesbian and Gay Parents Redux: The Irrelevance of Constitutional Principles,* 60 UCLA L. Rev. Disc. 226, 229 (2013).

Some courts hold that a child's best interest is a sufficiently compelling state interest to overcome *Lawrence*'s application to the custody context.

Example: A father seeks to modify primary custody in the child's mother based on her intimate lesbian relationship. The trial court awards the father custody and the mother appeals, arguing that prior Alabama case law was no longer good law after *Lawrence v. Texas*. The appellate court disagrees, holding that *Lawrence* does not overrule state precedent. The appellate court distinguishes *Lawrence* by explaining that *Lawrence* involved a challenge to a criminal statute, and that neither prior state law nor the present case requires the court to "address the lawfulness of a statute or the morality of homosexuality." The court affirms the custody award to the father, reasoning that the evidence warranted the change of custody because (among other factors) the mother was engaged in a same-sex affair and had moved out of city where the child had lived her entire life to be with her partner. *L.A.M. v. B.M.*, 906 So. 2d 942 (Ala. Civ. App. 2004).

    iv. ALI *Principles*: The ALI *Principles* prohibit a court from considering either the extramarital sexual conduct or the sexual orientation of a parent except upon a showing that such conduct causes harm to the child. ALI *Principles* §2.12(1)(d).

b. Wealth: The relative wealth of the parties is not determinative unless one parent is unable to provide adequately for the child.

c. Domestic violence: Virtually all jurisdictions consider the role of domestic violence in child custody disputes.

    i. Approaches: Jurisdictions adopt a variety of approaches:

- The majority of states consider domestic violence as a *factor* in the application of the best interests standard. One state specifies that the safety of the child and the abused party is the *most important factor* in the best interests test. *See, e.g.,* Colo. Rev. Stat. §14-10-124.

- The modern trend applies a *rebuttable presumption against an award of custody* to a parent who has committed domestic violence. Jurisdictions differ in terms of the evidence necessary to establish the presumption (e.g., a severe incident or a pattern of abuse, or a criminal conviction).

- Many states now provide protection for victims of domestic abuse in *custody mediation*.

    ii. Mutual acts of domestic violence: Abusers may contend that the domestic violence was "mutual," i.e., that the victim provoked the abuse. In response, courts must determine whether one or both spouses perpetrated domestic violence.

Example: Roland and Jenese marry after she became pregnant with their son. One year later, after experiencing several instances of physical abuse by Roland, Jenese files a complaint seeking dissolution of the marriage. The court grants Jenese a divorce on the grounds of adultery, extreme cruelty, and irreconcilable differences. Upon finding Roland had committed domestic violence, the court awards physical custody of their son to Jenese and provides Roland "closely supervised" visitation. Roland appeals, claiming, inter alia, that the trial court erred when it found that he had committed domestic violence and Jenese had not. The North Dakota Supreme Court affirms, holding that although Jenese may have struck, hit, or scratched Roland during their relationship, her actions were largely in self-defense and were far less serious in nature and degree than Roland's domestic violence. *Peters-Riemers v. Riemers*, 644 N.W.2d 197 (N.D. 2002).

According to the ALI *Principles*, acts of self-defense do not constitute abuse. Rather, if one spouse's act is more extreme or dangerous, "it may be appropriate for the court to impose limits on the primary aggressor but not on the primary victim." ALI *Principles* §2.11(c) cmt.

Critics charge that mutual protective orders are based on misconceptions (the victim must have provoked the abuse), constitute gender bias, serve to blame the victim, fail to give guidance to law enforcement on how to enforce the order, and jeopardize the victim's custody rights because most states favor the nonabusive parent in custody decision making.

   iii. Effect of "friendly parent" provisions: Statutes sometimes contain *friendly parent provisions* that require courts, in determining the best interest of the child, to consider which parent is more likely to maintain the child's relationship with the other parent. Because these provisions disadvantage abused spouses, some states abrogate the doctrine in cases of domestic violence. *See, e.g.,* Minn. Stat. §518.17(13).

   d. Disability: UMDA §402(5) and many state statutes require consideration of the parents' mental and physical health when applying the best interests standard.

   When the parent is disabled, courts generally focus on the *effect* of the disability on the child.

   Example: A husband and wife separate, executing an agreement granting custody of their sons to the father. The father moves to California and begins living with a woman who becomes the sons' stepmother. A few years later, the father becomes a quadriplegic as a result of an accident. During his year-long hospitalization and recuperation, the children visit him several times a week. Five years after the separation, the mother files an action for divorce and modification of custody. The mother has not seen the sons since the separation. The trial court grants a modification of the couple's prior custodial agreement and awards custody to the mother. The court reasons that the father's disability prevents him from establishing a normal relationship with his sons. Reversing, the California Supreme Court holds that a physical handicap affecting the ability to participate in physical activities with children is not a changed circumstance of sufficient relevance and materiality to necessitate a custody change. The court notes that the essence of a child-parent relationship lies in emotional and intellectual guidance. *In re Marriage of Carney*, 598 P.2d 36 (Cal. 1979).

C. Joint custody (also called "shared custody"): An increasing number of jurisdictions now permit joint custody. California initiated the movement in 1979. *See* Cal. Fam. Code §3080.

   1. Terminology: Custody involves the concepts of legal custody and physical custody. Legal custody confers responsibility for major decision making such as upbringing, health, welfare, and education. Physical custody confers responsibility for day-to-day decisions regarding physical care. Joint custody allows both parents to share legal responsibility for major childrearing decisions regarding upbringing, health, welfare, and education.

   Note: The joint custody label in decrees and separation agreements may be confusing. For example, an award of "joint legal custody" does not signify that parents have "joint physical custody." Moreover, "the label of joint physical custody often does not reflect the social reality." Eleanor E. Maccoby & Robert H. Mnookin, *Dividing the Child: Social and Legal Dilemmas of Custody* 159 (1992). That is, joint physical custody may involve maternal residence, paternal residence, or dual residence.

   Note: The ALI uses the term "custodial responsibility" to refer to the concept of physical custody and the term "decisionmaking responsibility" to refer to the concept of legal custody.

   2. Rationale: Joint custody is based on the rationale that children benefit from continued and frequent contact with both parents and that both parents play an important role in childrearing.

   3. Modern trend: Courts initially were reluctant to order joint custody, fearing the difficulties incumbent upon divorcing parents and the effects upon the children. However, most states currently provide for joint custody.

4. **Different state approaches:** States adopt one of the following approaches:

- Joint custody is a *presumption*. Some states following this approach require parental agreement.

- Joint custody is a *preference*.

- Joint custody is *one factor* in the best interests determination.

  The third approach is the most common.

5. **"Joint" custody does not mean equal time:** A popular misconception is that joint custody (or joint physical custody) means equal time with each parent.

6. **Parental agreement:** Parental agreement and parental cooperation are not prerequisites to an award of joint custody. Some jurisdictions grant joint custody even if both parents do not agree. However, severe parental conflict may militate against an award of joint custody.

7. **Joint custody reform:** Almost two dozen state legislatures recently considered stricter measures to make joint custody a legal presumption. The movement stems from lobbying by fathers' rights advocates who highlight the concerns of divorced fathers who feel alienated from their children and burdened by child support obligations.

8. **Criticisms of the joint custody reform movement:** Critics, including women's rights groups and some legal associations, contend that stricter joint custody laws endanger battered women, unwisely abrogate judicial discretion, are unnecessary because most divorcing parents prefer shared custody, and lead to the elimination of child support.

D. **Pet custody disputes:** Pet custody cases sometimes arise. The traditional analysis treats the pet as personal property and focuses on whether the pet is separate property and/or a gift. In contrast, a custody analysis focuses on the issue of the pet's "best interests" in terms of nurturing, emotional needs, and happiness.

Example: Shannon and Trisha are same-sex spouses. Before their marriage, Shannon buys a dachshund puppy that the couple names "Joey." When the couple separates two years later, Trisha takes Joey with her without Shannon's consent. Shannon files for divorce and moves for an order for Trisha to return the dog and for the court to award Shannon "sole custody" of Joey. Shannon argues that Joey is her property because she bought him with her separate property. She alleges that she was Joey's primary caretaker and that it would be in Joey's "best interests" to be returned to her. Trisha counters that Joey was a gift from Shannon as consolation for Trisha's having to give away her cat at Shannon's insistence. Trisha adds that she shared care and financial responsibility for Joey, she is closest to Joey because his bed was "next to her side of the marital bed," and he has been living with her since the break-up. The court explains that, according to the traditional property analysis (for replevin), Joey would be awarded to the party with the superior possessory right (probably Shannon as her separate property unless Trisha can prove Shannon gave him to her as a gift). However, the court holds that property-based arguments are only one factor in the analysis and notes that many courts currently consider at least some factors traditionally associated with a child-custody analysis. The court grants Shannon's motion for a hearing to determine who shall have final possession of the dog and advises the application of the standard of "best for all concerned." *Travis v. Murray,* 977 N.Y.S.2d 621 (N.Y. Sup. Ct. 2013).

E. **Parenting plans and parenting coordinators:** Many states provide for *parenting plans* — written agreements by which parents specify caretaking and decision-making responsibility authority for their children (and often the manner in which future disputes are to be resolved). The ALI

Principles reflect this trend by requiring a party seeking custody to submit a parenting plan. ALI *Principles* §2.06(1)(a), (b).

The majority of states currently authorize appointment of *parenting coordinators* to help divorcing parents resolve disputes. Parenting coordinators tend to be mental health professionals or family law practitioners who are trained to work as neutral parties helping parents resolve issues in high conflict divorces.

Quiz Yourself on
STANDARDS FOR SELECTING THE CUSTODIAL PARENT

83.   Pauline and Peter's constant bickering leads them to begin discussing divorce. While their discussions are ongoing, Pauline begins a sexual relationship with Sarah, a female co-worker. When Pauline and Peter ultimately decide to seek a divorce, they cannot agree as to custodial arrangements of their two children (ages one and three). Pauline has been doing most of the childcare since the children were born. At a subsequent hearing, Peter asks the court to grant him sole custody. He argues that Pauline's sexual conduct with Sarah renders Pauline an unfit custodian. Pauline asks the court to award sole custody to her based on the tender years presumption. Will Pauline's argument be successful? _____

84.   Same basic facts as above. Now, Pauline asks the court to award sole custody to her based on the primary caretaker presumption. Will her argument be successful? _____

85.   Same basic facts as above. Will Peter prevail in his argument that Pauline is an unfit custodian because of her sexual conduct with Sarah? _____

86.   Meg, a yoga instructor, and Ryan, a financial analyst, divorce. They have a four-year-old daughter Susan. At the time of the divorce, Meg needs hospitalization for an operation. Ryan agrees to care for Susan until Meg recuperates. In the divorce proceeding, Ryan petitions for custody based on Meg's disability. Ryan also argues that he should be awarded custody because he has superior financial resources (i.e., he can provide Susan with her own room, and send her to private schools). Will Ryan's arguments be successful? _____

87.   Monica and Adiel have a nonmarital son (J.D.). Monica is a Jehovah's Witness, and Adiel is a Muslim. Monica, who has been the primary caretaker of J.D., has raised J.D. as a Jehovah's Witness. When J.D. is four, Monica files an action for paternity establishment and determination of custody. At trial, Adiel argues that Monica should not receive custody because her religion is harmful to J.D. In particular, Adiel argues that Monica proselytizes door-to-door on weekends, has caused J.D. anxiety socially due to her religious beliefs, and teaches J.D. that non–Jehovah's Witnesses will be annihilated, thereby harming J.D. and alienating Adiel. Will Adiel prevail? _____

88.   Diana, who is Caucasian, marries Livingston, a native of Nigeria and a naturalized U.S. citizen. Six years later when the couple divorces, the court awards custody of their son to Diana and orders Livingston to pay child support. Livingston appeals, arguing that the son's biracial heritage warrants placement with him. He claims that Diana's recent relocation from a Midwestern city with a relatively large African-American population to a smaller town which has no African-American children would

be detrimental to his son because the boy would be denied daily contact with any racially diverse individuals. Will Livingston's argument be successful? _____

Answers

83. No. Regarding Pauline's request for sole custody, courts no longer apply the tender years presumption (or maternal preference doctrine). That doctrine permitted awards of custody to the mother when the children were "of tender years" (i.e., preschool age). Several courts have declared the doctrine unconstitutional as a violation of the Equal Protection Clause.

84. No. Pauline will not prevail on the basis of the primary caretaker presumption. That presumption would dictate that a court award custody to the parent who was the child's primary caretaker, i.e., the parent who performed such tasks as meal preparation, grooming, discipline, bathing, and putting the child to bed, etc. Even though Pauline might be able to prove that she was the children's primary caretaker, such a showing would be unlikely to result in the application of a presumption in her favor because no jurisdiction currently accords the doctrine presumptive status. Rather, the court would most likely follow the majority of jurisdictions that consider primary caretaker status as one among many factors in the determination of the best interests of the child.

85. Probably not. States are split as to the role of a parent's same-sex sexual conduct in custody determinations. States adhere to different standards: the parent's same-sex sexual conduct is evidence of unfitness per se, presumptively has an adverse impact, or is relevant only if there is proof of adverse impact (majority rule). Where there is no evidence of adverse effect, Pauline's sexual relationship with Sarah should not result in a custody denial in most jurisdictions. Moreover, *Lawrence v. Texas* and *Obergefell v. Hodges* raise doubts about the constitutionality of custody restrictions for LGBT parents.

86. No. The court should accord no weight to Meg's disability. Although many courts and UMDA permit consideration of the parties' mental and physical health, courts generally focus on the effect of a disability on the child. That is, unless a parent's physical disability has harmful effects on a child, it should not be a decisive factor in custody decision making. Ryan has presented no evidence here that Meg's physical condition has resulted in any harm to Susan. In terms of Ryan's argument regarding his superior financial resources, the court should not give any weight to the relative wealth of the parties unless a party's lack of resources inhibits his/her ability to care for the child adequately. Therefore, the court should not take into account Ryan's superior financial resources as a financial analyst compared to Meg's resources as a yoga instructor unless Meg is unable to provide adequately for Susan.

87. No. Monica has had primary responsibility for the child's religious upbringing for the first four years of his life. As a custodial parent, she has the right to determine the child's religion and also to practice her own religion under the First Amendment. In addition, Adiel has failed to show significant actual harm to J.D. resulting from Monica's religious beliefs or religious practices. Therefore, a court will reject his argument and determine custody on nonreligious grounds.

88. No. Livingston is basing his request for custody of his son solely on the argument that he would be a better parent to raise his biracial child, given the fact that his former wife is Caucasian and would raise the child in a Caucasian community. According to the U.S. Supreme Court's decision in *Palmore*, race cannot be the dominant or controlling factor in a custody decision. That decision would preclude an award of child custody to a fit parent (such as Diana) based on the sole ground of race. Therefore, Livingston's argument will not be successful.

III. STANDARDS FOR SELECTING THE NONCUSTODIAL PARENT: VISITATION

A. Denial of visitation

1. **General rule:** Courts are reluctant to impose a total denial of visitation because the parent-child relationship is constitutionally protected. However, some extreme situations (e.g., severe physical or sexual abuse, substance abuse) may bring about such an outcome.

2. **Visitation and support: Independent variables:** The right to visitation and the duty of support are not interdependent. That is, a parent may not condition visitation upon the other parent's payment of child support. Conversely, if one parent withholds support, the other parent may not deny visitation as retaliation. Some courts make an exception, however, and deny or restrict visitation based on a parent's willful and intentional failure to pay child support that is detrimental to the child.

   Example: A court grants visitation rights to a father and orders him to pay child support. After he is unable to make his support payments and his request for reduction is repeatedly denied, the court finds him in civil contempt and orders him to serve a six-month sentence to be purged upon payment of arrearages (i.e., $40,908.86 past support). The court suspends the father's visitation before his release from jail because he fails to pay the support. He appeals the suspension of his visitation rights. The appellate court holds that the facts do not warrant the suspension of visitation. Child custody and visitation decisions should be guided by the best interests of the child and are not intended to be punitive. The denial of visitation is warranted only when the noncustodial parent is financially able to pay support but refuses to do so. *Turner v. Turner*, 919 S.W.2d 346 (Tenn. Ct. App. 1995).

B. Conditions on visitation: Courts sometimes place conditions on a parent's visitation rights. Factors that commonly lead to such conditions include domestic violence, sexual abuse, religious practices or beliefs, and a parent's sexual conduct. Courts also determine the time, place, and circumstances of visitation.

1. **Domestic violence:** Courts occasionally order supervised visitation in cases of domestic violence. Supervised visitation may be conducted by a visitation service or a private individual. Restrictions may encompass extensive or minimal supervision. Visitation may be held either at, or away from, a program center.

2. **Sexual abuse:** In cases of sexual abuse, courts may place conditions on visitation or even terminate visitation.

   Example: Mother's ex-husband admits sexual abuse of his 11-year-old stepdaughter that occurred six years earlier. The court orders unsupervised visits with the parties' four-year-old daughter. After a visit, the child complains that her father has inappropriately touched her. A subsequent medical examination determines that abuse is a possibility. The court allows unsupervised visits to continue and even orders overnight visitations. The mother requests review of the court's order granting overnight visitation. Reversing, the appellate court holds that when a parent is justified in believing sexual abuse has occurred, the parent is not required to submit the child for visitation without stringent safeguards. The trial judge should have provided a specific place for the supervised visitation that would have protected the child and should have required supervisors that were satisfactory to both parties. *Hanke v. Hanke*, 615 A.2d 1205 (Md. Ct. Spec. App. 1992).

3. **Religious practices or beliefs:** A parent's exercise of religion sometimes leads to disputes about visitation. However, First Amendment concerns limit a court's power to settle religious disputes. In imposing restrictions on religion, courts sometimes look to the effect of the exposure to the religious practices or beliefs on the children.

   Example: Mother is a Catholic, and Father is a member of the Latter Day Saints (LDS). Their children have been raised for ten years in the Catholic faith. Upon Mother and Father's divorce, as part of its determination of custody, the court orders that the children continue to practice their Catholic faith, although the court permits them to attend LDS church with Father if the children wish to do so. A few months later, Mother petitions to modify custody to obtain sole legal custody, arguing, among other things, that Father is violating the order on the children's religion by "forcing" them to attend the LDS church. The trial court awards Mother sole legal custody and orders that the children be raised only as Catholics and prohibits Father from taking them to LDS church. The appellate court affirms, finding the trial court justified in imposing the limitation on Father's visitation where the children needed consistency in their religious upbringing. *Franco v. Franco*, 2008 WL 4814415 (Ariz. Ct. App. 2008).

4. **Sexual conduct:** A parent's sexual behavior may also lead to conditions on visitation.

   a. **Traditional response:** Formerly, courts were especially likely to impose restrictions on visitation when the noncustodial parent was involved in a nonmarital intimate relationship.

      Example: The trial court orders that the father not have a female companion stay overnight when the children visit. The father appeals, arguing the order violates his right to privacy. The mother argues that the moral welfare of her children might be endangered by the presence of an overnight female friend in the father's home. Affirming, the court holds that the mother has an interest in the moral welfare of her children. The court reasons that, although no evidence exists of improper conduct between the father and his companion, there is the possibility of harm to the children's moral welfare. *DeVita v. DeVita*, 366 A.2d 1350 (Super. Ct. N.J. App. Div. 1976).

   b. **Modern view:** Most courts no longer impose restrictions on visitation in the context of opposite-sex relationships. Although some courts impose such restrictions when a noncustodial parent is gay or lesbian, the constitutionality of these restrictions is doubtful after *Lawrence v. Texas* and *Obergefell v. Hodges*.

      Example: Mother and Father have two daughters. Upon their divorce, the court awards shared legal and physical custody. Three years later, Mother seeks primary physical custody and restrictions on Father's visitation. She argues that Father recently began to cohabit with another man and that Father was unwilling to seek professional help to deal with explaining his sexual orientation to the children. The magistrate judge agrees, awarding Mother sole legal and physical custody of the children and prohibiting Father from having overnight visitation in the presence of his partner. The state supreme court affirms, pointing out that under *Lawrence*, a court cannot deprive a parent of custody rights based solely on his sexual orientation, absent a showing of harm to the children. However, the court finds that the restriction on overnight visitation in the presence of Father's partner was appropriate given the hostile relationship between the partner and ex-wife (the partner had tried to make trouble for her at work and with the police). *McGriff v. McGriff*, 99 P.3d 111 (Idaho 2004).

5. Substance abuse: A parent's substance abuse might lead to conditions on, or denial of, visitation.

Example: Wife files for divorce. The trial court awards sole custody of a ten-year-old child to the mother and denies Husband visitation. Husband appeals. The state supreme court affirms the trial court order, holding that the denial of visitation was not an abuse of discretion because of Husband's chronic use of illegal drugs, inter alia, and not because of his status as an adoptive, rather than a biological, parent. *Taylor v. Taylor*, 646 S.E.2d 238 (Ga. 2007).

C. Interference with visitation rights: Noncustodial parents may institute proceedings to enforce their visitation rights. Possible remedies for custodial interference include civil contempt, a change of custody, tort damages, or makeup parenting time.

1. Civil contempt: If a parent refuses to comply with visitation orders, a court may find that parent in contempt.

2. Change of custody: The custodial parent has a duty to foster a child's relationship with the noncustodial parent. Interference with that relationship sometimes will be remedied by a change in custody.

Example: Mother is the children's primary caregiver during and after the marriage. After the divorce, Father petitions for modification of custody. He seeks primary physical custody after Mother (who lives in Louisiana) refuses to relocate to Utah as required in the original custody order, refuses to help pay travel costs so that Father can visit the children, hangs up on Father when the children attempt to talk to him on the phone, makes the children feel guilty about visiting Father, and repeatedly calls the children during their visitation with Father. The court awards Father primary physical custody, finding that Mother's interference with Father's visitation rights constitutes a material change in circumstances and that the children's best interests are served by modifying custody. *Hanson v. Hanson*, 223 P.3d 456 (Utah Ct. App. 2009).

3. Tort actions: A parent may seek tort damages for the other parent's interference with visitation rights. However, some courts refuse to recognize the tort of custodial interference based on public policy concerns.

Example: Father and Mother have two children. Mother obtains sole legal and physical custody, moves to New Jersey, changes her telephone number, and blocks all of Father's attempts to contact the children. After Father locates the children, he sues for IIED, arguing that Mother has engaged in extreme and outrageous conduct that poisoned his relationship with the children. The court dismisses his cause of action as contrary to public policy, finding that such a lawsuit is harmful to the children where neither parent, in bringing or defending the suit, is considering the children's best interests. *Segal v. Lynch*, 993 A.2d 1229 (N.J. Super. Ct. App. Div. 2010).

Note: Custodial interference is also a crime in some jurisdictions. *See, e.g.*, Wash. Rev. Code §9A.40.060.

Quiz Yourself on STANDARDS FOR SELECTING THE NONCUSTODIAL PARENT: VISITATION

89. Diane and Gary are the divorced parents of 13-year-old Sandra. Prior to the divorce, Gary was charged with sexually molesting Sandra. The charges were dropped when Gary agreed to undergo psychological counseling. During the divorce proceedings, Diane requests that the court deny Gary visitation rights because of the sexual abuse. Will she prevail? _____

90. Joan and William are the divorced parents of three-year-old Don. For the past year, William has failed to pay court-ordered child support to Joan. Joan brings an action to hold William in contempt. A court finds William in contempt of court, orders him to pay his child support arrearages, and conditions William's visitation rights on the payment of his past child support. William appeals. Will he prevail? _____

Answers

89. Probably not. Courts are reluctant to impose a complete denial of visitation because the parent-child relationship is constitutionally protected. As a result, the trial court will probably restrict Gary's visitation rights by requiring supervised visitation (specifying the time and place for visitation) in order to protect Sandra.

90. Yes. The appellate court should reverse the trial court decision. According to the general rule, visitation and support are independent variables. That is, visitation should not be conditioned or denied based on payment of support. Thus, although the trial court can hold William in contempt and order him to pay his past-due child support obligations, it should not condition or terminate William's visitation rights based on the fulfillment of his child support obligations.

IV. STANDARDS: PARENT VERSUS NONPARENT DISPUTES

    A. Biological parent presumption: A presumption favors biological parents in custody disputes involving nonparents. That is, courts apply a rebuttable presumption that custody should be awarded to a biological parent absent evidence of parental unfitness, voluntary relinquishment, or other extraordinary circumstances. However, psychological parents (sometimes called "de facto" parents) may overcome this presumption.

    Example: When his wife and infant daughter are killed in a car accident, the father asks the wife's parents to care for his son temporarily. A year later, the father remarries and wants the return of his son. When the grandparents refuse, the father sues for custody. The court holds that the child's best interests will be served by remaining with the grandparents (thereby refusing to apply the biological parent presumption). The court bases its decision on the grandparents' financial and education background and living situation. Whereas the grandparents are college graduates, have a comfortable home, and are respected in their community, the father never finished college, lives in Berkeley, California, is financially insecure, and aspires to be a freelance writer/photographer. The court also relies on the testimony of a child psychologist to the effect that the child regards the grandparents as parental figures and that removal from their home would be detrimental to the child. *Painter v. Bannister*, 140 N.W.2d 152 (Iowa 1966).

B. Custody and visitation rights of third parties: Custody disputes sometimes involve third parties, such as grandparents, stepparents, or former same-sex partners.

1. Grandparents

   a. Common-law rule: At common law, grandparents had no right to visitation with grandchildren in the face of parental objection or in the face of death, divorce, or termination of parental rights of the custodial parent(s).

   b. Grandparent visitation statutes as a challenge to family autonomy: The U.S. Supreme Court has held that grandparent visitation constitutes a challenge to family autonomy when a fit custodial parent opposes visitation.

   Example: Tommie Granville and Brad Troxel live together for several years and have two nonmarital daughters. When the parents separate, Brad lives with his parents and regularly brings his daughters there for weekends. Brad commits suicide. Several months later, Tommie (who has remarried) informs the grandparents that she wishes to limit their visits to one visit per month. The grandparents petition for visitation rights, requesting two weekends of overnight visitation per month and two weeks of visitation each summer.

   The Washington statute provides that "any person" may petition the court for visitation "at any time" and that the court may order visitation rights whenever visitation serves the best interests of the child. The U.S. Supreme Court holds that the statute, as applied, violates the mother's due process rights because it contravenes the traditional presumption that a fit parent will act in his/her child's best interests and accords no special weight to a fit mother's determination of those best interests. *Troxel v. Granville*, 530 U.S. 57 (2000).

   In the wake of *Troxel*, many states revised their visitation statutes to limit the persons who could seek visitation and to give deference to a fit parent's wishes. In addition, some states required that grandparents must demonstrate a significant prior relationship with the child in order to obtain visitation rights.

   c. Standard: States differ on the standard to apply in grandparent visitation disputes. A majority of states apply the best interests test. However, some jurisdictions adopt the more stringent harm standard (requiring that a lack of visitation would result in harm or potential harm before a grandparent may be awarded visitation rights).

   Example: Maternal grandparents seek visitation rights with their grandchildren after the death of the children's mother from breast cancer and the father's remarriage. The father appeals the order granting the grandparents' petition. The appellate court concludes that the visitation order was reasonable and furthered the children's best interest. The court also holds that due process does not require a showing of harm prior to an award of grandparent visitation, but rather courts must consider a broad array of factors in determining whether visitation with grandparents is in the child's best interests. *Dodd v. Burleson*, 967 So.2d 715 (Ala. Civ. App. 2007).

   Example: A grandmother brings an action against the child's father, seeking visitation rights. The appellate court holds that the grandmother's allegations that the father abused the child's mother were sufficient to rebut the presumption of the father's fitness and made the requisite showing that visitation could be necessary to protect the child from significant harm. The court reasons that, although the grandmother was estranged from the child's mother, the grandmother submitted sufficient proof in the form of affidavits from her daughter's employment supervisors that described the mother's abuse by the father as occurring on many occasions prior to the mother's disappearance, allegedly at the hands of the father. *Sher v. Desmond*, 874 N.E.2d 408 (Mass. App. Ct. 2007).

2. **Stepparents:** Case and statutory law sometimes grant visitation rights to former stepparents, especially if they have had a long-term relationship with the child.

Example: Katherine gives birth to a daughter, K.A. Shortly thereafter, Katherine marries Robert, and they have twins. K.A. has lived with Katherine and Robert for her entire life, and has had minimal contact with her biological father. Robert has never adopted K.A. When Katherine and Robert divorce, Robert receives visitation rights with K.A. Katherine appeals. The state supreme court finds that because Robert is the only father K.A. has known and he has cared for her like his biological children, he has established "extraordinary circumstances" justifying a third-party award of visitation rights over the objection of the mother. *Edwards v. Edwards*, 777 N.W.2d 606 (N.D. 2010).

3. **Lesbian co-parents:** Courts are increasingly receptive to recognition of the custody rights of former same-sex partners.

   a. **Traditional view:** Traditionally, courts were not receptive to recognition of lesbian co-parenting rights after dissolution of a lesbian relationship.

   b. **Modern View:** The modern trend (influenced by *Lawrence* and *Obergefell*) increasingly recognizes the parental rights of the "second parent" (i.e., the non-biological parent) in gay and lesbian families. (Adoption by "second parents" is discussed in Chapter 10.)

   Example: Alicia Bethany and Emily Jones are same-sex partners for eight years, during which time Bethany had a child, E.B. After the couple splits up, they agree to continue co-parenting three-year-old E.B. However, after Bethany begins a new intimate relationship, she denies visitation to Jones. When Jones petitions for a custodial determination, Bethany argues that Jones lacks standing. The court disagrees based on the "in loco parentis" doctrine, finding that Jones served as a parent to E.B. because Jones was a stay-at-home mom, E.B. called her "Mommy," Jones' parents were considered E.B.'s grandparents, and the two partners intended to co-parent the child. The court also determines that visitation is in E.B.'s best interest. The court rejects Bethany's argument that this decision would open the floodgates for anyone (grandparents, babysitters, boyfriends) to seek visitation, distinguishing such third parties from those persons who serve as a parent based on the parties' intent. *Bethany v. Jones*, 378 S.W.3d 731 (Ark. 2011).

   c. **Uniform Parentage Act (2017):** UPA (2017) addresses the issue of second-parent custody rights through an *express* statutory provision that abrogates the gender-based terminology in the "holding provision" of the original UPA. According to the original UPA, "A *man* is presumed to the natural father of a child if . . ." UPA §4(a)(4). That section provides recognition of parentage based on a father's social relationship to his child (i.e., his conduct in receiving the child into his home and openly holding out the child as his own). The new UPA makes this language gender neutral. According to the new UPA, "An *individual* is presumed to be a parent of a child if . . ." UPA §204(a)(2).

Further, UPA (2017) provides enhanced protection for de facto parents. The new UPA permits the establishment of parentage by those who claim to be a *de facto parent* provided that the person proves (by clear and convincing evidence) residence for a significant period with the child as a regular member of the child's household, consistent caretaking, taking on the responsibilities of a full and permanent parent without compensation, treating the child as a biological child and presenting the relationship as a parent-child relationship, having established a bonded and dependent parent-child relationship with at least one legal parent's approval, and demonstrating that the continuation of the relationship with the child is in the child's best interests. UPA §609.

4. **Uniform Nonparent Custody and Visitation Act (UNCVA) (2018):** The Uniform Law Commission (ULC) gave final approval in 2018 to the UNCVA, a statutory framework for resolving conflicts about third-party access to children. The Act recognizes the role of nonparents with whom children have a close relationship, especially if the nonparent was engaged in co-parenting, or (for those nonparents who never resided with the children) have had regular contact with them. The ULC's recognition of the role of nonparents was accentuated by the role of grandparents who cared for their grandchildren during the opioid epidemic.

5. **ALI *Principles*:** The ALI *Principles* recognize both parenthood by estoppel (§2.03(1)(b)), and de facto parenthood (§2.03(1)(c)). Under the latter, a person must have performed an equal or greater share of caretaking as the other parent, lived with the child for at least two years, and acted as a parent for nonfinancial reasons and with the agreement of a legal parent. A parent by estoppel is a person who: (1) is liable for support; (2) has a good faith belief that he is the biological father; (3) enters into a co-parenting agreement prior to the birth; and (4) lives with the child for at least two years, while holding out the child as a parent pursuant to an agreement with the legal parent, when the court finds that recognition as a parent is in the child's best interests.

Quiz Yourself on
STANDARDS: PARENT VERSUS NONPARENT DISPUTES

91. Linda and Dustine, two women, have three children by artificial insemination during their relationship. When they break up, Dustine (the biological mother) relocates with the children. Linda sues for visitation rights and arguing that she was the children's primary caretaker, supported them, and held them out as her own. She argues that Dustine agreed to the co-parenting arrangement and that shared parenting is in the children's best interests. Will she prevail? _____

92. After Amber and Joe (the father of three-year-old Hunter) separate, Amber begins dating and eventually marries. Joe agrees to terminate his parental rights to enable Amber's new husband to adopt Hunter. Prior to this time, Hunter had a substantial relationship with Joe's parents. The grandparents babysat him several days a week. After her remarriage, Amber finds alternative childcare and refuses further visits with the grandparents. The grandparents petition for visitation. At the hearing, Amber contends that she wants to end visitation because she does not want Hunter to learn that Joe voluntarily gave up his parental rights until Hunter is old enough to process that information. Also, she wants to focus on her new family, and their integration into her new husband's extended family. At the hearing, the grandparents show that they spent substantial time with Hunter. Two of their friends testify

that Hunter cried and didn't want to leave the grandparents' home, and the another friend testified that Hunter was excited and called out to the grandmother upon arriving at their house. Will the grandparents prevail? _____

Answer

91. Probably yes. Although courts traditionally denied parenting rights to a lesbian co-parent who was not the biological parent of the children, courts increasingly use various theories (e.g., equitable estoppel, "de facto parenthood") to justify awards of custody and/or visitation rights over the objection of the biological parent. Here, because Dustine has allowed Linda to co-parent the children, and because Linda actively assumed a parenting role in the children's lives, a court can apply either equitable estoppel or de facto parenthood doctrines to recognize Linda's rights. Further, if the jurisdiction has adopted UPA (2017), then Linda can derive support for her parentage claims by resort to the UPA's express statutory affirmation of parentage rights of former same-sex partners as well as the UPA provision for the establishment of parentage by those who claim to be de facto parents (i.e., unrelated persons who have functioned as a parent).

92. Probably no. Although it is obvious that Hunter spent substantial time with his grandparents, their evidence is probably not sufficient under the strictest test to show that he will be harmed if he no longer sees them. Hunter is still young, and his mother presents compelling reasons for wanting to end their relationship, some of which suggest that Hunter may actually suffer harm if he does continue the relationship. Finally, under *Troxel*, there is a presumption that favors the wishes of a fit custodial parent, and there is no evidence that Amber is an unfit parent.

V. ROLE OF SPECIAL PARTICIPANTS

    A. Child's preference: Most states, either by statute or case law, require consideration of a child's wishes when making custody determinations.

        1. Different statutory approaches: Statutes fall into one of four types:

            ■ those which require consideration of the child's wishes (modeled after UMDA §402(2));

            ■ those which require a consideration of the child's preference after a preliminary finding that the child has sufficient mental capacity;

            ■ those which give controlling weight to the preference of a child of a certain age; or

            ■ those which leave the consideration of a child's preference completely to the court's discretion.

        2. Procedures to obtain child's preference: States also take different procedural approaches to determine a child's preference. States may:

            ■ have the child testify in open court;

            ■ have other witnesses testify concerning the child's preference;

- have the judge interview the child regarding the parental preference in chambers, either with or without opposing counsel present; and/or

- require that a record be made of in-chamber interviews.

B. Counsel for the child: In most states, appointment of a child's legal representative is discretionary. Controversy exists about the appropriate role of counsel (either as the child's attorney or a best interests attorney).

Example: The judge appoints counsel for the children in a divorce case. At the end of the trial, the court awards custody to the mother. The father appeals, arguing that due process requires that the judge have clarified the role of the child's counsel in order for the parents to properly present their evidence. The appellate court holds that, while such a procedure would have been preferable, the omission was harmless error. The court also criticizes the lack of clarity regarding the possible roles of the child's counsel generally (i.e., decision maker, guardian ad litem, and investigator). *Leary v. Leary*, 627 A.2d 30 (Md. Ct. Spec. App. 1993).

The Uniform Representation of Children in Abuse, Neglect and Custody Proceedings Act addresses representation of children in custody-related proceedings (defined to include custody and abuse/neglect, but not delinquency). The Act specifies the attorney's role and responsibilities, and provides that, at the time of the initial hearing, the court may appoint *either* a child's attorney or a best interests attorney.

C. Expert testimony: Experts frequently testify in custody determinations. They may conduct evaluations, make recommendations, furnish a second opinion, rebut testimony, or act as mediators in custody disputes. Although a judge may base a custody decision on expert opinion, the judge is the ultimate authority.

Example: The trial court awards the mother sole custody, subject to visitation by the father. The mother petitions to terminate the father's overnight visitation and to require supervised visitation when she learns that the father is sleeping in the same bed as the child. The father cross-petitions for sole custody. At the hearing, a clinical psychologist who interviewed the mother, father, and child testifies that the child's best interests require the transfer of custody to the father. Another psychologist, a social worker, and the child's legal guardian also recommend a change in custody, reasoning that the mother was overly punitive and tried to exclude the father from the child's life. The mother's expert, who only interviewed the mother, testifies that custody should remain with the mother. The appellate court determines that the trial court erred in rejecting most of the expert testimony that favored the father. *In re Rebecca B.*, 611 N.Y.S.2d (App. Div. 1994).

VI. MODIFICATION

A. Standard for modification: Courts have continuing power to modify custody orders. The parent seeking the modification has the burden of proof. The standard for modification is higher than for an initial custody determination.

    1. Rationale for higher standard: The rationale for the higher modification standard, which favors finality of judgments, is to avoid the disruptive effect of changes in children's lives post-divorce.

    2. Traditional standard: Courts generally apply one of several standards. The most commonly accepted standard requires the petitioner to show that a *material or substantial change of* *circumstances* has occurred, after the original decree. Courts differ as to what constitutes a "substantial" change of circumstances. Some courts require very little.

Example: Mother is granted custody of six-year-old son. Father requests, and is granted, modification based on the fact that the boy, who is now 12, wants to live with his father in order to engage in hunting, fishing, and hiking. Mother appeals. Affirming, the court holds that a substantial increase in the age of the child, standing alone, constitutes a sufficient change of circumstances to warrant modification. *McMillen v. McMillen*, 602 A.2d 845 (Pa. 1992).

3. **Strictest standard:** Some states follow UMDA and require endangerment. UMDA §409(b) requires serious endangerment (of the child's physical, mental, moral, or emotional health) for nonconsensual changes. Absent serious endangerment, UMDA §409(a) provides for a two-year waiting period following the initial decree.

4. **Most liberal standard:** A few states require only that modification be in the best interests of the child regardless of any change in circumstances.

5. **Modification of joint custody:** Some jurisdictions ease the traditional modification rule (from substantial change in circumstances to best interests) when sole custody is modified to joint custody. Similarly, some courts do not require the stricter standard if the requested modification is merely a rearrangement of parenting time in a joint physical custody schedule.

Example: Mother and Father are awarded joint legal and physical custody of their three-year-old daughter. Father has physical custody each weekend when Mother works. Mother subsequently seeks to modify Father's parenting time when her work schedule changes and because the child attends school full time. After finding a change of circumstances, the trial court decreases father's parenting time, awarding him physical custody three out of four weekends per month. Father appeals, contending that the court applied the wrong modification standard. The Missouri Supreme Court affirms based on the best-interests-of-the-child standard, explaining that the substantial-change-in-circumstances test is not appropriate for a modification of parenting time in a joint custody award. The court explains the rationale for lowering the standard by saying that the higher standard developed in a different era when gender-based custody preferences and fault-based divorce prevailed. *Russell v. Russell*, 210 S.W.3d 191 (Mo. 2007).

B. Relocation controversies

1. **Generally:** Relocation controversies often arise in the post-decree period when the custodial parent decides to move due to remarriage, employment, educational opportunities, or the promise of support from relatives.

Disputes most often arise in the following contexts:

- a decree or statute requires the custodial parent to seek permission to leave the jurisdiction;
- absent a statute, the noncustodial parent petitions to enjoin the move; or
- faced with an impending move by the custodial parent, a noncustodial parent requests a custody modification.

2. **Standards to resolve disputes:** Courts employ different standards in relocation cases. Some adopt a custodial-parent presumption favoring the custodial parent's right to relocate. Most courts, however, adopt the best interest standard, taking into account all relevant facts (e.g.,

reasons for the move, future quality of life in the new location, alternative visitation schedule for the noncustodial parent).

Example: At Mother and Father's divorce, Mother is appointed primary residential parent of Connor. Father has two weekends and two weekday evenings of visitation per month. When Mother is laid off, her employer asks her to relocate to another state where Mother's relatives live. Mother petitions to relocate, but Father opposes her motion. A special advocate determines, and the trial court agrees, that relocation would result in significantly reducing Father's presence in Connor's life. Mother appeals, alleging a violation of her constitutional right to travel. The state supreme court finds that recent statutory amendments replaced the custodial parent presumption with the best interests standard in which both parents share the burden of demonstrating the child's best interests. The court then rules that the trial court abused its discretion by failing to consider factors favoring the mother (i.e., the advantages of relocation, extended family support, the mother's improved financial situation) and, therefore, unconstitutionally infringed on her right to travel. *Ciesluk v. Ciesluk*, 113 P.3d 135 (Colo. 2005).

3. **ALI *Principles* standard:** The ALI *Principles* provide that the custodial parent should be permitted to relocate so long as the relocation is "in good faith for a legitimate purpose," to a location that is reasonable in light of that purpose. ALI *Principles* §2.20(4)(a). Relocation justifies a change of custody (i.e., constitutes a substantial change in circumstances) only when it "significantly impairs" either parent's ability to exercise responsibilities under a parenting plan. *Id.* at §2.17(1).

4. **Parental motives:** Many courts consider good faith on the part of the custodial parent as a threshold requirement in relocation disputes. Thus, courts may deny relocation requests if the relocation is sought for the sole purpose of restricting the noncustodial parent's visitation rights. Recall the ALI *Principles*' approach (*supra*) that requires that the move be in good faith.

5. **Infringement on the constitutional right to travel:** Feminists criticize relocation restrictions for their disproportionate impact on women (who generally have custody) and the ensuing interference with women's constitutional right to travel. Some courts hold that conditioning a parent's primary custody on remaining in the noncustodial parent's location violates the former's right to travel. *See, e.g., Watt v. Watt*, 971 P.2d 608 (Wyo. 1999). *But cf. Mason v. Coleman*, 850 N.E.2d 513 (Mass. 2006) (holding that the child's best interests trump the parent's constitutional right to travel).

6. **Domestic violence:** Relocation restrictions may present significant risks for victims of domestic violence because they serve as obstacles to the victim's efforts to flee from the abuser.

Quiz Yourself on
ROLE OF THIRD PARTIES AND MODIFICATION

93. Mary and Frank have been married for six years and are the parents of five-year-old Timmy. They separate because of Frank's temper and alcoholism. The trial court awards custody to Mary and provides that Frank would have no visitation rights until a psychiatrist (who had been chosen by the parties) recommends when visitation should commence and on what terms, guidelines, and locations. The psychiatrist refuses to continue treatment until the father pays the balance of his fees, thereby effectively denying the father visitation. When Frank challenges the court order as an abuse of discretion, will he prevail? _____

94. Miriam and Toby divorce. The court awards custody of two-year-old Dolly to Miriam. A few months after the divorce, Miriam is in a minor automobile accident. Toby agrees to care for Dolly until Miriam recovers. However, when Miriam recovers, Toby refuses to return Dolly. Toby petitions for a modification of custody. Based on the best interests test, the court modifies custody and awards custody to Toby. Miriam appeals. Will she be successful? _____

95. Jean and David divorce after a marriage that was marked by severe domestic violence. During the marriage, Jean had been seriously injured many times, often in front of their daughter Andrea, who is 15 at the time of the divorce. The violence was well documented in police reports and orders of protection. When Jean files for custody, Andrea expresses a preference to live with her father. She also denies that any violence takes place in their home. David is very involved in Andrea's school work and activities. He buys her things (e.g., a TV, clothes, a horse, a trip to Europe), and calls her his "princess." In contrast, Andrea claims that her mom is not really involved in her schooling or her activities and she does not like her mom or being around her. How should the court rule?

_____

Answers

93. Yes. The appellate court should invalidate the delegation of authority about visitation (by Frank to Timmy) to the psychiatrist. Jurisdiction over custody and visitation is vested in the court's discretion; no authority exists for the delegation of such jurisdiction to someone outside the court.

94. Probably. Miriam should be successful in seeking a reversal of the custody award for several reasons. First, the trial court may have used the wrong standard for modification. The prevailing standard requires a substantial change of circumstances since the original decree. Only some jurisdictions follow the best interests standard or the strictest standard of serious endangerment. Second, nothing has occurred that would constitute a material or substantial change of circumstances. Miriam's injuries from a minor auto accident probably will not qualify. Certainly, no endangerment to Dolly has occurred. In the interests of maintaining the child's stability, the court should permit Dolly to remain in Miriam's custody.

95. Courts accord greater weight to older children's custodial preferences. Therefore, a court might give considerable weight to Andrea's custodial preference because she is 15 years old. However, the judge should be concerned that Andrea's custodial preference might be coerced by her father, she might become a victim of his abuse in the future, or she might have psychological problems because she appears to be in denial about the existence of violence in her parent's marriage.

VII. JURISDICTION AND ENFORCEMENT

A. Jurisdiction

1. **Traditional rule:** According to the traditional rule, a court could assert jurisdiction to adjudicate custody if the child was domiciled in the state. However, courts increasingly rejected the domicile rule, and permitted assertions of jurisdiction if another state had a substantial interest in the child's welfare. This interest might be based on the child's domicile, residence, or temporary presence; or the domicile or residence of one or both parents.

This broad standard frequently led to concurrent assertions of jurisdiction. Two statutes were promulgated to redress problems of custody jurisdiction: the Uniform Child Custody Jurisdiction Act (UCCJA) and the Parental Kidnapping Prevention Act (PKPA).

The UCCJA was drafted in 1968 to reduce jurisdictional competition and confusion, as well as to deter parents from forum shopping to re-litigate custody. The Parental Kidnapping Prevention Act (PKPA), adopted in 1980, was also applicable to jurisdiction and enforcement of child custody. Congress felt that the PKPA was necessary because, at the time of its enactment, it was not clear that all states would enact the UCCJA. Moreover, Congress wanted to encourage uniformity because state courts were interpreting the UCCJA in different ways. The PKPA aimed to ensure that state custody decrees would receive recognition and enforcement in other states through *full faith and credit*. Both statutes were superseded by the Uniform Child Custody Jurisdiction and Enforcement Act (UCCJEA).

2. **The UCCJEA:** The Uniform Child Custody Jurisdiction and Enforcement Act (UCCJEA), adopted in 1997, intended to harmonize some of the differences between the UCCJA and the PKPA. The primary differences among the UCCJEA, the UCCJA, and the PKPA are:

   ■ The UCCJEA follows the PKPA in giving priority to home state jurisdiction (i.e., the state in which the child had lived for at least six consecutive months at the time of the commencement of the proceeding) unlike the UCCJA, which did not prioritize among the different bases of jurisdiction;

   ■ The UCCJEA eliminates the "best interests" language (that it is in the best interest of the child that a court of the state assume jurisdiction because the child and parents have a significant connection with the state and there is substantial evidence there concerning the child's care);

   ■ The UCCJEA severely restricts the use of emergency jurisdiction to the issuance of temporary orders;

   ■ The UCCJEA provides strict requirements for modification (restricting the exercise of modification jurisdiction to exclusive continuing jurisdiction, like the PKPA but not the UCCJA);

   ■ The UCCJEA clarifies the meaning of "child custody determination" to encompass all custody and visitation decrees (temporary, permanent, initial, and modification); and

   ■ The UCCJEA expands the definition of "child custody proceedings" to include those related to divorce, separation, abuse and neglect, dependency, guardianship, paternity, termination of parental rights, and protection from domestic violence.

   Virtually all states have enacted the UCCJEA.

3. **Jurisdiction over Native American children: The Indian Child Welfare Act:** The Indian Child Welfare Act (ICWA) of 1978, 25 U.S.C. §§1901-1963, provides that the Indian tribe has exclusive jurisdiction as against any state concerning a child welfare proceeding involving a Native American child. The Act applies to foster care placements, adoption, termination of parental rights, and guardianship. (See the discussion of the Indian Child Welfare Act, Chapter 9.)

B. **Enforcement of custody orders:** Civil and criminal remedies to enforce custody determinations include the following: contempt proceedings, writ of habeas corpus, tort recovery, and criminal prosecutions for child abduction.

1. **Contempt:** A parent will be found in contempt of court if that parent could have complied with the custody order, yet willfully failed to do so. Contempt may either be civil (resulting in a fine or a temporary jail sentence until the parent complies with the custody order), or criminal (resulting in a conviction with a fixed sentence).

2. **Habeas corpus:** A writ of habeas corpus was originally used by prisoners claiming illegal arrest or unlawful detention but has also been utilized in custody cases to compel the production of a child who is being wrongfully held or retained. The petitioner must prove both the validity of the custody order and the person who is entitled to custody under that order.

3. **Tort recovery:** Tort recovery is another possible avenue for a custodial parent who has been deprived of a child's custody. Possible tort claims include: intentional infliction of emotional distress and custodial interference.

   Courts are divided about permitting recovery for custodial interference in claims brought by custodial parents. *Compare Silicott v. Oglesby*, 721 S.W.2d 290 (Tex. 1986) (recognizing the tort of custodial interference), with *Larson v. Dunn*, 460 N.W.2d 39 (Minn. 1990) (refusing to recognize the tort of custodial interference, but permitting claims for intentional infliction of emotional distress). Some courts express the fear that such litigation is not in the child's best interests because it subjects the child to increased parental hostility.

4. **Criminal sanctions:** Parents who wrongfully remove or retain children may also incur criminal liability for violation of state statutes on child abduction.

VIII. CHILD ABDUCTION

Many child abductions are perpetrated by family members. Formerly, most child abductions were carried out by noncustodial fathers. Currently, most child abductions are carried out by custodial mothers who are fleeing domestic violence. The traditional approach imposed criminal liability on the perpetrator. The modern approach is to provide for judicially ordered abduction prevention mechanisms.

A. **Uniform law:** The Uniform Child Abduction Prevention Act (UCAPA), approved in 2006, enables a party (i.e., parent, prosecutor, or the court) to bring an action seeking "abduction prevention measures" after establishing the existence of a credible risk of abduction. Such measures include the imposition of travel restrictions.

B. **Federal law:** The International Parental Kidnapping Crime Act (IPKCA), 18 U.S.C. §1204, enacted in 1993, makes it a federal crime for a parent to wrongfully remove or retain a child outside the United States. The felony is punishable by a fine, imprisonment (for up to three years), or both. Courts have rejected constitutional challenges to the IPKCA.

C. **International Treaty on International Child Abduction:** The Hague Convention on the Civil Aspects of International Child Abduction is a widely adopted international treaty that proposes guidelines on international child abduction. It has been implemented in the United States via the International Child Abduction Remedies Act (ICARA), 42 U.S.C. §§11601-11611. The Hague Convention was based on the rationale that the likely abductor was a noncustodial father. Today, however, most international abductions are carried out by custodial mothers, many of whom are fleeing domestic violence.

Article 13 of the Convention specifies three affirmative defenses to defeat the child's return: (1) if the taking parent establishes that the child's caretaker was not exercising custody rights at the time of removal or retention or consented to removal or retention; (2) if the taking parent establishes a grave risk that the return would entail physical or psychological harm to the child; and (3) if the court in the the taking parent's forum finds that the child, who has attained an appropriate age and maturity (based on the court's discretion), objects to the return. Recent efforts to make domestic violence an explicit exception to automatic return have been unsuccessful.

The U.S. Supreme Court has held that a child's habitual residence under the Hague Convention depends on the totality of the circumstances specific to the case, not on categorical requirements such as an actual agreement between the parents. *Monasky v. Taglieri*, 140 S. Ct. 719 (2020).

IX. PROCESS TO RESOLVE DISPUTES

Most divorcing parents reach private agreements regarding custody. In cases of parental disagreement, several dispute resolution processes exist: the adversary process, custody mediation, and collaborative law.

A. **Adversary process:** In the adversary process, a court asserts authority over child custody and is the ultimate decision maker. Commentators criticize the adversary process for its hostility, accentuation of differences, high rates of re-litigation, and long-term negative psychological effects for the participants.

B. **Mediation:** is a process by which the parties, with the aid of a neutral third party, identify disputed issues, develop and consider options and alternatives, and reach a consensual agreement. Unlike the adversary process in which a judge makes the ultimate decision, mediation respects the parties' autonomy in decision making.

Mediation has several advantages: it is less expensive and less hostile than the adversarial process, gives the parties an active role in decision making, results in increased satisfaction by the parties with the dissolution process, is less likely to result in re-litigation, and yields better long-term consequences for parents and children. The disadvantages include domination by the stronger partner in negotiations, reinforcement of gender role stereotypes (i.e., mother as caretaker), and the risk of subjecting abused women to revictimization by their abusers.

1. **Voluntary vs. mandatory:** Many statutes provide for custody mediation, although a few states mandate it (e.g., Cal. Fam. Code §1830).

2. **Waiver:** Many states permit mediation to be waived for good cause, or if a party will suffer severe emotional distress. Some states use these waiver provisions to exclude domestic violence cases from mediation. Other states provide for separate mediation sessions in cases of domestic violence or allow the abused spouse to bring a support person to the mediation.

3. **Qualifications of a mediator:** Mediation may be provided either by publicly funded court services or by mediators in private practice. Mediators frequently are lawyers or mental health professionals. Statutes generally specify the requisite qualifications for court-connected mediators. However, the lack of regulation for *private* mediators has been a longstanding problem.

In 1984, the ABA adopted "Standards of Practice for Lawyer Mediators in Family Disputes." Under the Standards, a lawyer mediator has six duties:

1. to define and describe the process and cost before the parties reach an agreement to mediate;

2. not to voluntarily disclose the information obtained through the mediation process without the prior consent of both participants;

3. to be impartial;

4. to assure that the participants make decisions based upon sufficient information and knowledge;

5. to suspend or terminate mediation whenever continuation of the process would harm one or more of the participants; and

6. to advise each of the participants to obtain legal review prior to reaching any agreement.

4. **Domestic violence:** Mediation poses special dangers for abused spouses, especially the risk that the mediation sessions will subject the victim to revictimization. Several schools of thought exist about the wisdom of mediation in domestic violence cases. Some believe that mediation should never be used in cases of domestic violence. Others contend that mediation should be used with adequate safeguards. Still others believe that the choice of mediation should be left to the victim.

5. **Ethics**

   a. **Conflicts of interest and dual representation:** Ethical questions may arise for lawyer mediators. Early concerns focused on whether a lawyer mediator violates the prohibition on representing conflicting or potentially conflicting interests, or the prohibition against dual representation of husband and wife.

      State bar ethics committees have ruled that a lawyer mediator can mediate a dispute for the husband and wife so long as the mediator (1) informs the parties that the mediator represents neither of them, (2) will refrain from representing either if the mediation proves unsuccessful, and (3) advises the parties to seek independent legal counsel.

   b. **Confidentiality:** Confidentiality is a central part of the mediation process. A controversial issue concerns whether the mediator can make a recommendation to the court if the parties' attempts at mediation prove unsuccessful. In addition to presenting a breach of confidentiality, the practice also raises due process concerns if the mediator is not subject to cross-examination.

      Example: A father in a custody dispute moves for a "protective order" that would permit him to cross-examine the mediator (following the mediator's in-court recommendation) if the parties are unable to reach an agreement on custody. California's mandatory mediation statute requires that all mediation proceedings be private, confidential, and privileged. Once a mediator makes a recommendation and is subject to cross-examination, the mediator may have to divulge confidential communications. To address this problem, local court rules require that a mediator not state his/her reasons for a recommendation and therefore denies the parties the right to cross-examination. The court holds that the policy of denying cross-examination is unconstitutional. If local practice permits the mediator to make a recommendation, the court concludes that due process requires that the mediator be subject to cross-examination. *McLaughlin v. Superior Court*, 189 Cal. Rptr. 479 (Ct. App. 1983).

C. **Collaborative law:** Collaborative law is an innovative form of alternative dispute resolution whereby the parties and their attorneys sign a binding agreement in which they agree to use cooperative techniques without resort to judicial intervention except for court approval of the agreement. If the parties are unable to reach an agreement through collaborative law procedures, their attorneys must withdraw from representation. Texas became the first state, in 2001, to provide, by statute, for resolution of certain family law matters by collaborative law procedures (Tex. Fam. Code Ann. §153.0072).

The Colorado Bar Association's Ethics Committee (Ethics Opinion No. 115 (Feb. 24, 2007)) declared that collaborative law is per se unethical based on the provision in the attorney-client agreement that if settlement negotiations fail, the lawyers must withdraw. The concern is that this restriction creates a conflict of interest impairing the lawyer's independent judgment about the need for litigation. However, the ABA and most state bar associations find that collaborative law is consistent with professional ethics.

Quiz Yourself on
JURISDICTION AND ENFORCEMENT

96. Patricia and Kirk's Texas divorce decree incorporates the couple's agreement that Patricia shall have primary custody of the couple's two daughters. Shortly thereafter, Patricia decides that she would like to move to Arizona. She asks Kirk, and he agrees, to take the children for a few months until Patricia finds employment and is able to establish a home for them in Arizona. Kirk then moves with the children to Minnesota with his new fiancée, to be near her extended family. Before Patricia is able to move to Arizona, Kirk files a custody modification motion in Minnesota two months after his arrival there. Does the Minnesota court have jurisdiction to modify the Texas custody decree? _____

97. Casey and Mason divorce after three years of marriage. Casey, a high school graduate, is a stay-at-home mom for two young children. Mason is a cardiologist who often works as an expert witness in medical malpractice cases. Mason maintains strict control of the couple's finances. He rarely informs Casey about financial considerations but simply places an allowance in an account for her every month. Mason often remains late at work, citing the long commute, and meets with a female colleague on the weekends. Most disturbing to Casey is the fact that Mason berates and belittles her when he is angry, threatens to leave her and take the children, and tells her that she will never see the children again because, if they divorce, he is familiar with court procedures. Eventually, Mason files for divorce. He asks Casey to participate in mediation. Casey comes to your family law practice for advice. Is Casey a good candidate for mediation? _____

Answer

96. No. To determine which state (Minnesota or Texas) has jurisdiction for modification purposes, it is necessary to examine the requirements of the UCCJEA. Under the UCCJEA (which superseded the UCCJA and PKPA), a state that has made a prior custody determination has "continuing exclusive jurisdiction" for purposes of modification if the initial court continues to have jurisdiction and the former state is the residence of the child or any contestant. In this case, Texas would be the proper forum under the UCCJEA because Texas rendered the decree and Patricia continues to reside there.

97. Probably not. Many commentators agree that, in relationships that include abuse or intimidation, mediation is often not a good idea. It seems that Casey may be suffering from emotional and financial

abuse because of Mason's pattern of intimidation. As a result, many would agree that mediation is not appropriate for Casey.

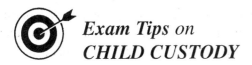

Exam Tips on
CHILD CUSTODY

☞ *Custody*: For questions involving child custody, be precise about the facts. Identify important facts, such as the age, race, religion, etc., of all children because these facts may be highly relevant subsequently. Clarify whether the request for custody is for sole or joint custody. **Define relevant terms** (sole custody, primary custody, joint custody, etc.). Always specify the **different possible standards**, even if one standard seems to fit the facts best.

☞ Be on the alert for **cross-cut issues**. For example, examine facts about the marriage. Was the couple validly married? Or does the question deal with unwed father's rights? If the couple was divorced, were fault-based grounds present? If so, be prepared to discuss the relevance or irrelevance of fault in awards of custody.

☞ Make sure, also, that you take note of whether the question deals with an **initial** award or a **modification**. If the petitioner requests a modification, specify that **different standards** apply for modification than for initial awards. Look for **common areas of disputes for modifications** (religious disputes, relocation, etc). Always explore possible **constitutional** issues (e.g., First Amendment issues in religious disputes, right to travel issues in relocation disputes).

☞ If the question involves an initial grant of custody, then explore the application of the **relevant standards** for selection of the **custodial parent**: presumptions (i.e., tender years presumption, primary caretaker), the best interests of the child, and joint custody. For **joint custody**, identify whether it operates as a **presumption**, **preference,** or **option**. Note problems with the application of presumptions: the tender years presumption raises **constitutional problems** (equal protection) and the primary caretaker presumption has been abandoned by the two jurisdictions that adopted it originally but still remains a factor in custody decision making in many jurisdictions.

☞ Point out that the **best interests** of the child is the **prevailing standard** for determination of custody disputes. When discussing **factors** relevant to the best interests, always be on the lookout for **constitutional cross-over** issues (especially those involving race, religion, or gender). Remember that in questions involving race-based discrimination, *Palmore* specified that **race** cannot be the **determining** factor in custody decision making. For examples of **gender-based** discrimination, be sure to specify the different possible **levels of scrutiny** (under the Constitution, the test is whether the classification is substantially related to an important governmental objective, but some states apply a strict scrutiny standard).

☞ After discussing issues involving the custodial parent, turn to issues involving the **noncustodial parent**. Such issues generally involve **visitation** disputes. Determine if the question involves a **denial** of, or **conditions** on, visitation. Restrictions on visitation may be a fertile area for a constitutional cross-over question (e.g., First Amendment). Termination of visitation rights (or of custody rights of the custodial parent) may involve cross-over issues with adoption. Determine if the noncustodial parent is experiencing problems with visitation (e.g., **interference** with visitation rights). If so, explore possible ***enforcement*** remedies (e.g., contempt, change of custody, tort or criminal liability for custodial interference).

☛ Identify and analyze any possible issues regarding ***third-party rights***. Frequently tested issues concern stepparents, grandparents, and same-sex partners. Discuss the biological parent presumption that would apply to favor the biological parent over a third party. If grandparent visitation is involved, discuss the application of *Troxel*. If same-sex partners are involved, be sure to discuss whether the partners are legal spouses or unmarried partners. If the same-sex partners are not legal spouses, then discuss the traditional restrictive view and the more liberal modern trend (equitable estoppel, de facto parentage, UPA (2017)) that recognizes the parenting rights of the same-sex partner who is not biologically related to the child. Also, explore whether any other third-party issues exist (e.g., the child's right to representation, experts' role).

☛ Always look for issues of ***enforcement*** and ***jurisdiction***. Remember to explore and discuss both civil and criminal remedies for enforcement of custody orders (e.g., contempt proceedings, habeas corpus, tort recovery, and criminal prosecutions for child abduction). Jurisdiction is a frequently tested issue. Recall that the UCCJEA may be applicable in cases of jurisdictional disputes involving initial assertions of jurisdiction or requests for modification.

☛ Finally, before finishing your analysis of custody, analyze whether any possible issues of ***alternative dispute resolution process*** (such as custody mediation or collaborative law) are present. For example, if the couple sought custody mediation, determine if ***ethical*** issues exist (i.e., conflicts of interests, dual representation, confidentiality) or ***constitutional*** problems (i.e., due process).

CHAPTER 8

PROCREATION

ChapterScope

This chapter addresses the legal regulation of reproductive freedom and reproductive control. It examines reproductive rights in the contexts of contraception, abortion, and assisted reproduction. Here are a few of the key principles covered in this chapter:

- The right of *access to contraception* does *not* depend upon *marital status*. Both unmarried and married persons have a constitutional right to determine whether or not to bear a child.

- The Constitution protects a woman's *right to choose* to have an *abortion*. The U.S. Supreme Court extended the right of privacy to encompass the right to an abortion in *Roe v. Wade*. Since *Roe v. Wade*, the Supreme Court has limited the scope of that right.

- A state law that imposes an *undue burden* (i.e., has the purpose or effect of placing a substantial obstacle) on the right to abortion is unconstitutional.

- A state may *not* require *spousal consent or notification* prior to an abortion.

- A state *may* require *parental consent and/or notification* prior to a minor's abortion, provided that the state offers an alternative of a *judicial bypass*.

- After *Roe v. Wade*, state legislatures enacted numerous *restrictions on abortion*, including (among others) restrictions on abortion funding, Targeted Regulation of Abortion Providers (TRAP), bans on late-stage abortions, and fetal protection legislation.

- *Fetal protection legislation* includes laws protecting the fetus, such as fetal homicide laws, personhood laws, gestational limits, fetal heartbeat laws, and fetal remains laws.

- After *Roe v. Wade*, states enacted laws that allow health care professionals to *refuse to provide* reproductive health services. Almost every state has **religious refusal laws** (also called conscience clauses) regarding abortion.

- The traditional legal response toward surrogacy is to regard *surrogacy contracts as void.* However, an increasing number of states *permit surrogacy subject to state regulation*.

- Several jurisdictions permit a *pre-birth determination* of the *legal status* of the intended parents of a child born via surrogacy.

I. CONTRACEPTION

The foundation of a woman's reproductive rights rests on the constitutionally protected right to privacy. The recognition of this right stems from two U.S. Supreme Court cases, decided in the mid-1960s and early 1970s, dealing with access to contraceptives. In both cases, the Court invalidates state restrictions on contraception. In the first case, the Court enunciates the constitutional right to privacy and, in the second, extends the scope of that right from married people to the individual.

A. **Access to contraception generally:** The right of access to contraception does not depend upon marital status. Both unmarried and married persons have a constitutional right to determine whether or not to bear a child. The Supreme Court enunciates this right for married persons in *Griswold v. Connecticut*, 381 U.S. 479 (1965), and subsequently for unmarried persons in *Eisenstadt v. Baird*, 405 U.S. 438 (1972) (both discussed *infra*).

B. **Historical background:** Harsh restrictions on contraception date from the 1870s. In 1873, a vice crusader and ex-dry goods salesman, Anthony Comstock, spearheaded passage of federal legislation (known as the "Comstock law") that banned the circulation and importation through the mail of obscene materials (defined to include contraceptives and abortifacients). Many states enacted similar legislation. As a result, physicians were unable to prescribe birth control devices and disseminate information about contraception. Courts upheld the constitutionality of such state legislation as a valid exercise of the police power until the Supreme Court invalidated the Connecticut law in 1965.

C. **Married persons' rights to contraception:** Married persons have the right to determine matters concerning birth control without interference from the state. This guarantee has its foundation in the constitutional right to privacy.

   1. **Case and holding:** A Connecticut statute prohibits any person from using "any drug, medicinal article or instrument for the purpose of preventing conception," or from aiding and abetting another to use contraceptive devices. The statute epitomizes the most stringent of state Comstock laws by prohibiting the "use," rather than merely the distribution, of contraceptives, and by not providing an exclusion for women whose lives would be endangered by a pregnancy. Estelle Griswold (the Executive Director of the Planned Parenthood League of Connecticut, which provides information about contraception as well as contraceptives to *married* persons) and the League's medical director are charged with violating the "aiding and abetting" provision of the statute. They argue that the statute violates their married patients' right to privacy under the Fourteenth Amendment. The Supreme Court holds that the restriction is an unconstitutional interference with the right of marital privacy. The case establishes that the right to privacy, although not explicitly mentioned in the Constitution, nonetheless has a constitutional basis.

   2. ***Griswold* concurrence:** Justice Goldberg, in a concurring opinion joined by Chief Justice Warren and Justice Brennan, locates the constitutional right to privacy in the Ninth Amendment. He points out that the Ninth Amendment was intended to grant to the people those essential rights that are not specifically enumerated in the Bill of Rights.

   3. ***Griswold* dissent:** Justices Black and Stewart, in their dissent, argue that the Court is usurping the power of state legislatures by enabling the judicial invalidation of any "legislative act which the judges find irrational, unreasonable, or offensive" under the relevant constitutional provisions. *Griswold*, 381 U.S. at 511.

   4. **Rationale:** The Court invalidates the statute based on the recognition of a constitutional right to privacy. The Court reasons that the statutory prohibition on the *use* of contraceptives (rather than their manufacture or sale) infringes on marital privacy because enforcement would necessitate police searches of the bedroom.

   5. **Source of the constitutional right to privacy:** Justice Douglas, author of the majority opinion, reasons that the right of privacy is found in the "penumbras" (*Griswold*, 381 U.S. at 483) "formed by emanations from those guarantees [in the Bill of Rights] that help give them life and substance." Douglas states that these guarantees create "zones of privacy." Among the specific guarantees, he cites: the First Amendment's right of association, the Third Amendment's prohibition against quartering soldiers without the owner's consent during time

of peace, the Fourth Amendment's protection against unreasonable search and seizure, the Fifth Amendment's privilege against self-incrimination, and the Ninth Amendment's identification of unenumerated rights.

Other justices, although concurring that there is a constitutional right to privacy, locate the source of that right in the Ninth Amendment (see "*Griswold* concurrence" *supra*). Neither view of the source of the privacy right is accepted today. Constitutional doctrine since *Griswold* (discussed *infra*) identifies the source of the right to privacy in the Fourteenth Amendment's Due Process Clause ("liberty").

6. **The importance of marriage to *Griswold*'s holding:** Protection of the rights of *married* persons was central to the holding of *Griswold*. The case is clear that the right of privacy inheres in the marital relationship. Both the majority and concurring opinions emphasize the importance of marriage. Justice Douglas speaks of "notions of privacy surrounding the marriage relationship" and the "sacred precincts of *marital* bedrooms" (*Griswold*, 381 U.S. at 485) (emphasis added). Justice Goldberg's concurrence speaks of "the right of marital privacy" (*id.* at 486), "the marital relationship and the marital home" (*id.* at 494), "the intimacy of husband and wife" (*id.* at 498), and "the institution of marriage" (*id.* at 499). Justice Douglas concludes the opinion by stating:

   > Marriage is a coming together for better or for worse, hopefully enduring, and intimate to the degree of being sacred. It is an association that promotes a way of life, not causes: a harmony in living, not political faiths; a bilateral loyalty, not commercial or social projects. Yet it is an association for as noble a purpose as any involved in our prior decisions. *Id.* at 486.

7. **Curtailment of police powers:** The U.S. Supreme Court decides *Griswold* during the civil rights movement. Justice Douglas's opinion reflects an abhorrence of police excesses, particularly regarding governmental invasions into private homes and private matters. Douglas reasons that in order to enforce the prohibition on the use of contraceptives, the police would have to enter and search the home: "Would we allow the police to search the sacred precincts of marital bedrooms for telltale signs of the use of contraceptives? The very idea is repulsive to the notions of privacy surrounding the marriage relationship." *Id.* at 485.

8. **Fundamental right:** *Griswold* points out that the right to privacy is "fundamental." Constitutional doctrine accords fundamental rights strict scrutiny review (i.e., restrictions on those rights must be *necessary* to a *compelling* state interest).

9. ***Griswold* and the constitutionalization of family law:** Prior to *Griswold*, the U.S. Supreme Court decided few family law cases. Family law was regarded as a matter of state law. However, *Griswold* heralded the beginning of the "constitutionalization of family law," i.e., the development, application, and extension of constitutional doctrine to family matters.

10. **Subsequent extension of the right to privacy:** The constitutional right to privacy, first recognized in *Griswold* in regard to contraceptives, was extended subsequently to protect the rights of the unmarried to contraception, a woman's rights to abortion (both discussed *infra*), and the right to engage in adult consensual sexual conduct (in *Lawrence v. Texas*, discussed in Chapter 2).

D. Unmarried persons' rights to contraception

1. **Generally:** Unmarried persons have the same constitutional right as married persons to make intimate decisions regarding childbearing. This right was announced by the U.S. Supreme Court in *Eisenstadt v. Baird* (discussed *infra*).

2. **Background to *Eisenstadt*:** Prior to *Griswold*, some married persons were able to evade statutory bans on the sale and use of contraceptives by seeking the services of private physicians. Such alternatives were not available to the unmarried. Doubt arose after *Griswold* as to how far the Supreme Court might extend *Griswold*'s reasoning with regard to unmarried persons. This doubt stemmed from the Court's emphasis in *Griswold* on a right to *marital* privacy.

3. ***Eisenstadt v. Baird***

   a. **Case and holding:** A Massachusetts statute provides a maximum five-year term for anyone (other than a licensed physician or pharmacist) who "gives away . . . any drug, medicine, instrument or article whatever for the prevention of conception." Mass. Gen. Laws Ann., c. 272. Married persons are permitted to obtain contraceptives, for the purpose of pregnancy prevention, from physicians or pharmacists; single persons are unable to obtain contraceptives from anyone. William Baird, a moral crusader and ex-director of a pharmaceutical company, decides to challenge the Massachusetts ban. In the course of a lecture on contraception that he delivers to Boston University students, he hands a female student a package of vaginal foam. Baird is arrested, charged, and convicted of violating the statute. He challenges the constitutionality of the statute. The U.S. Supreme Court holds that unmarried persons have a constitutional right of access to contraceptives. *Eisenstadt v. Baird*, 405 U.S. 438 (1972).

   b. **Rationale: Equal protection:** Extending the reasoning of *Griswold*, the Court finds that the statute violates the Equal Protection Clause by providing dissimilar treatment for those persons (married/unmarried) who are similarly situated. The Court states: "[W]hatever the rights of the individual to access to contraceptives may be, the rights must be the same for the unmarried and the married alike." *Id.* at 453.

   c. **Rejection of proffered state interests:** The Court rejects both of the proffered state interests (i.e., the deterrence of premarital sex and the promotion of health). The Court reasons that "[i]t would be plainly unreasonable to assume that Massachusetts has prescribed pregnancy and the birth of an unwanted child as punishment for fornication." *Id.* at 448. The Court rejects the health measure rationale by pointing out that federal and state laws already regulate the distribution of harmful drugs.

   d. **Privacy: Not a marital, but an individual, right:** The Court states that the right of privacy belongs to the individual and not to the marital relationship or to married partners.

   > It is true that in *Griswold* the right of privacy in question inhered in the marital relationship. Yet the marital couple is not an independent entity with a mind and heart of its own, but an association of two individuals each with a separate intellectual and emotional makeup. If the right of privacy means anything, it is the right of the individual, married or single, to be free from unwarranted governmental intrusion into matters so fundamentally affecting a person as the decision whether to bear or beget a child. *Id.* at 452.

   e. **Criticism of equal protection approach:** Commentators criticize the doctrinal basis of *Eisenstadt*. They argue that the case should have rested not on equal protection grounds, but rather on substantive due process. That is, the Court should have extended the substantive right to privacy that the Court delineated earlier in *Griswold*.

   f. **Significance of *Eisenstadt* for same-sex sexual conduct**

      i. **Unanswered question:** An open question after *Eisenstadt* concerned the parameters of the right to privacy, especially in regard to the protection of the sexual conduct.

Specifically, did *Eisenstadt* protect, narrowly, procreational freedom (i.e., access to contraceptives) or, more broadly, sexual conduct between consenting adults? The question assumed special importance for gays and lesbians who faced stringent criminal penalties in many jurisdictions for their sexual activity.

ii. *Bowers v. Hardwick*: The Court's decision in *Bowers v. Hardwick*, 478 U.S. 186 (1986), first addressed the question left unresolved by *Eisenstadt* concerning same-sex sexual acts. *Bowers* upheld the constitutionality of a Georgia statute criminalizing sodomy that was applied to an adult male committing sexual acts with another adult male in the bedroom of the former's home.

Example: Michael Hardwick is charged with violating a Georgia statute criminalizing sodomy (defined as "any sexual act involving the sex organs of one person and the mouth or anus of another"). He challenges the constitutionality of the statute. The district court grants the state's motion to dismiss for failure to state a claim. The federal court of appeals reverses, finding that the statute violates the defendant's fundamental rights because same-sex sexual activity between consenting adults is protected by the Due Process Clause. The U.S. Supreme Court reverses and upholds the constitutionality of the statute, maintaining that the Constitution does not confer a fundamental right upon homosexuals to engage in sodomy. The Court bases its holding on the irrelevance of prior privacy cases (dealing with family, marriage, and procreation), the existence of ancient Judeo-Christian proscriptions against homosexual sodomy, and the fact that criminal penalties for sodomy are widespread in other states. The Court also distinguishes *Stanley v. Georgia*, 394 U.S. 557 (1969), which protected possession of pornography in the home (such possession would not have been protected outside the home) by reasoning that illegal conduct is not immunized because it occurs in the home. *Bowers v. Hardwick, supra.*

iii. **Criticism of *Bowers*: Failure to extend the right to privacy:** The *Bowers* dissent (Justice Blackmun, joined by Justices Brennan, Marshall, and Stevens) disagrees that the Georgia statute fails to implicate the constitutionally protected right to privacy. In addition, Justice Blackmun argues that the prohibition involves the privacy interest regarding both intimate decision making and the conduct of private activities in the home.

iv. *Lawrence v. Texas*: The U.S. Supreme Court overturns *Bowers* in *Lawrence v. Texas*, 539 U.S. 558 (2003). *Lawrence* holds unconstitutional a state (Texas) sodomy statute criminalizing same-sex sexual conduct. The U.S. Supreme Court rules that the state statute violates the defendants' substantive due process rights. The Court chooses a broad due process rationale, protecting the individual's *liberty to engage in intimate personal relationships*, rather than more narrow equal protection grounds. The Court reasons that moral disapproval cannot justify criminal sanctions for private consensual sexual conduct. (*Lawrence* is discussed further in Chapter 2.)

E. **Minors' rights to contraception:** The U.S. Supreme Court has held that minors have a constitutionally protected right of privacy to obtain contraceptives. Some state laws permit *all* minors to consent to contraceptive services. However, other states explicitly limit the class of minors who can consent to contraceptive services (e.g., married minors, minors who are parents, minors who are or have been pregnant, mature minors).

1. **Access:** The Supreme Court wrestled with minors' reproductive rights in *Carey v. Population Servs. Int'l*, 431 U.S. 678 (1977).

a. **Case and holding:** *Carey* invalidates a New York statute restricting the distribution of contraceptives to minors under age 16. The Court thereby extends the constitutional right of privacy to minors' contraceptive choices.

   Example: A New York statute makes it a crime (1) for any person to *sell or distribute a contraceptive to a minor* under 16 years of age, (2) for anyone *except a pharmacist* to distribute contraceptives to *persons over 16*, and (3) for anyone, including pharmacists, to *advertise or display* contraceptives. The district court holds unconstitutional the prohibition regarding the distribution of nonprescription contraceptives to minors. The state appeals, arguing that the regulation is constitutionally permissible as a deterrent to sexual promiscuity. The U.S. Supreme Court holds that the right of privacy protects the right of access to contraceptives for minors as well as for adults. *Carey v. Population Servs. Int'l, supra.*

b. **Rationale: Rejection of proffered state interests:** The *Carey* Court finds no rational basis to uphold the statute. The Court rejects the proffered state interests (deterrence of teenage sexual activity and unwanted pregnancies). The Court doubts whether limiting access to contraception will discourage early sexual behavior.

c. **Relevance of minors' abortion rights:** The Court bases its protection of minors' right to contraceptives on prior constitutional doctrine regarding abortion. The Court reasons that because the state may not prohibit a minor from terminating her pregnancy (*Planned Parenthood v. Danforth*, 428 U.S. 521 (1976)), the state cannot deny the distribution of contraceptives to minors.

d. **Miscellaneous provisions:** The Court also invalidates the requirement that only licensed pharmacists can sell nonmedical contraceptives to adults, finding no compelling state interest (health, morality) to justify it. The Court reasons that the requirement imposes a significant burden on the individual's right to use contraceptives (i.e., limiting accessibility, reducing the opportunity for privacy, and lessening the possibility of price competition). In addition, the Court invalidates the prohibition on contraceptive advertising and displays.

e. **Significance of *Carey* for minors' rights generally:** Although the Court in *Carey* extended the right of privacy to minors' contraceptive decision making, the Court also made clear that the scope of permissible state regulation is broader with respect to minors than adults.

2. **Parental notification for minors' access to contraceptives:** Neither state nor federal law requires parental *notification* for minors' use of contraceptives. Further, federally-funded providers of family planning services (including contraceptives) under Title X are not required to notify parents or guardians when the providers prescribe contraceptives to minors. *See Planned Parenthood Federation of America v. Heckler*, 712 F.2d 650 (D.C. Cir. 1983) (invalidating "squeal" rule that required parental notification).

3. **Minors' access to emergency contraception:** The Food and Drug Administration (FDA) approved the use of emergency contraceptives for all women, including minors, without a prescription and without proof of age.

   Example: Women's health organizations challenge the FDA's denial of their petition to expand access to emergency contraceptive ("the abortion pill") to women of all ages (including minors). A federal district court judge finds that FDA's denial was politically motivated and orders the FDA to approve non-prescription access for teenagers 17 and older. He remands for the FDA to reconsider access for younger adolescents. *Tummino v. Torti*, 603 F. Supp. 2d

519 (E.D.N.Y. 2009). During the ensuing three-year reconsideration period by the FDA, the Administration approves a different version of the abortion pill but with similar restrictions for minors. Plaintiffs again institute suit to expand access. The same federal judge finds that the FDA's restriction is not entitled to deference because it was based on an order by Health and Human Services Secretary Kathleen Sebelius that was "politically motivated, scientifically unjustified, and contrary to agency precedent." The court orders the FDA to make emergency contraceptives available without a prescription to women of all ages. *Tummino v. Hamburg*, 936 F. Supp. 2d 162 (E.D.N.Y. 2013).

F. **Misrepresentation of contraceptive use:** A woman's misrepresentation about her contraceptive use does not provide a man with a defense to her claim for *child support.*

Example: Peter and Kellie have an intimate sexual relationship. Kellie stops taking birth control pills without informing Peter. After she has a baby, Peter sues her for fraud and breach of contract. He argues that he will suffer substantial economic injury by virtue of having to pay 18 years of child support. Rejecting Peter's claims, the appellate court characterizes his suit as an attempt to circumvent his child support obligation. The court holds that public policy requires the imposition of financial liability on *both* parents. Finally, the court notes that if Peter did not desire children, he should have used contraceptives himself. *Wallis v. Smith*, 22 P.3d 682 (N.M. Ct. App. 2001).

G. **Right of refusal of health care providers and pharmacists:** Some state laws allow health care providers and pharmacists to refuse to prescribe or dispense contraceptives (including emergency contraceptives) based on their moral or religious beliefs. These provisions are called "conscience protection laws."

In contrast, other states *require* health care providers and pharmacists to fulfill all prescriptions even if such an act would violate their moral or religious beliefs.

Example: A pharmacist refuses to fill or transfer a patient's prescription for an oral contraceptive. He appeals the state pharmacy licensing board's reprimand. The appellate court holds that the pharmacist engaged in unprofessional conduct by failing to perform in a minimally competent manner, and concludes that his decision resulted in the patient's missing her medication and her suffering emotional harm from worrying about an unplanned pregnancy. According to the court, state licensing statutes are enacted not for the benefit of the individuals licensed, but rather for the benefit and protection of the public. *Noesen v. State Dept. of Regulation & Licensing, Pharmacy Examining Bd.*, 751 N.W.2d 385 (Wis. Ct. App. 2008).

H. **Health insurance coverage of contraceptives:** The Patient Protection and Affordable Care Act (PPACA, also called "Obamacare") requires employers of more than 50 employees to offer health care plans that cover free contraceptive services and FDA-approved contraceptives without out-of-pocket costs to patients (known as the "contraceptive mandate"). Federal regulations offered exemptions from the ACA's mandate to religious employers (such as churches) and accommodations to nonprofit employers with religious objections. A *for-profit* closely-held family corporation challenges the constitutionality of these regulations.

Example: A corporation owned by devout fundamentalist Christians claims an exemption from the ACA's contraceptive mandate based on the business owners' religious objections to covering four specific contraceptive methods that the owners deem "life-terminating." They argue that their constitutional right to religious freedom protects their decision not to cover contraceptives that violate their religious beliefs. They contend that the contraceptive mandate substantially burdened their religious beliefs in violation of the federal Religious Freedom Restoration Act (RFRA).

A closely divided Supreme Court sides with the challengers. The majority reasons that the contraceptive mandate, as applied to for-profit closely held corporations (private corporations with relatively few owners), substantially burdens the exercise of religion for purposes of RFRA; and that less restrictive means were available to meet the governmental interest in public health and gender equality. The majority bases its ruling on the assumption that the female employees in question would have coverage for all approved, essential medical care without cost from some other source, and disclaims any implications for religion-based objections to other types of health care or employee benefits (such as those triggered by same-sex marriage). *Burwell v. Hobby Lobby Stores, Inc.*, 573 U.S. 682 (2014).

I. **Contraceptive coverage: Recent developments:** In 2018, the Trump Administration issued an *expanded conscience rule* significantly broadening the pool of employers and health care providers who can refuse to cover or perform services by allowing employers (both nonprofit and for-profit) to exclude some or all contraceptive methods and services from their health plans if employers have religious objections *and* moral objections. Several federal courts blocked enforcement of these regulations on various procedural and substantive grounds.

Example: The Commonwealth of Pennsylvania, joined by the State of New Jersey brought an action for declaratory and injunctive relief against the President and the Departments of Health and Human Services (HHS), Treasury, and Labor, asserting substantive and procedural challenges under the Administrative Procedure Act to the agencies' issuance of final rules exempting employers, with religious or moral objections, from mandate to provide no-cost contraceptive coverage under the Affordable Care Act. The Little Sisters of the Poor, a religious nonprofit organization of Catholic nuns that operated homes to care for the elderly poor intervened, arguing that compliance with the contraceptive mandate violated their religious belief that avoidance of reproduction through medical means is immoral.

The Supreme Court ruled against the two states, holding that the Trump Administration had legal authority to allow private employers with moral or religious objections to opt out of the contraceptive mandate to providing no-cost contraceptive coverage. According to Justice Clarence Thomas, writing for the 7-2 majority, "We hold today that the departments had the statutory authority to craft that [religious] exemption, as well as the contemporaneously issued moral exemption." He added, "We further hold that the rules promulgating these exemptions are free from procedural defects." *Little Sisters of the Poor v. Pa.* and *Trump v. Pa.*, 140 S. Ct. 2367 (U.S. 2020).

II. ABORTION

A. **Generally:** The U.S. Supreme Court extended the right of privacy to encompass the right to an abortion in *Roe v. Wade*, 410 U.S. 113 (1973). Since then, however, the Court significantly limited the scope of that right.

B. **Historical background:** Early American proscriptions against abortion date from the 1820s. The anti-abortion movement escalated in the second half of the nineteenth century. Approximately 40 states enacted restrictive abortion regulations from 1860 to 1880. Physicians (especially the American Medical Association) spearheaded legislative reform in an effort to end the lucrative abortion practices of nonmedical practitioners. The anti-abortion movement also benefited from the nineteenth century "social purity" campaign supporting the Comstock laws' restriction of access to contraceptives.

Reform began in the 1960s when a number of states adopted the American Law Institute (ALI)'s Model Penal Code abortion provisions liberalizing abortion for pregnancies resulting from rape or incest, those involving a deformed fetus, and those whose continuation would impair the mother's mental or physical health (i.e., "therapeutic abortions"). The backlash against *Roe v. Wade* ushered in a new era of abortion restrictions.

C. **A woman's right to an abortion:** The U.S. Supreme Court held in *Roe v. Wade* that a woman has a constitutionally protected right to an abortion. The constitutional source for this protection is the right to privacy.

   1. *Roe v. Wade*

      a. **Case and holding:** Jane Roe, an unmarried pregnant woman who desires an abortion, seeks a declaratory judgment that the Texas criminal abortion statute is unconstitutional. The Texas statute makes abortion illegal except for the purpose of saving the life of the mother. Jane Roe is unable to obtain a legal abortion in Texas because her life is not threatened by the continuation of the pregnancy; nor can she afford to travel to another jurisdiction where abortion is legal. The U.S. Supreme Court invalidates the Texas statute based on the woman's constitutionally protected right to privacy. *Roe v. Wade, supra.*

      b. **Source of the constitutional right to privacy:** The Court finds the right to abortion situated in the Fourteenth Amendment's concept of personal liberty.

      Note: Many feminist commentators prefer an equal protection rationale, rather than a privacy-based approach on the theory that reproductive freedom is a feature of gender equality.

      c. **Abortion as a fundamental right requiring strict scrutiny:** *Roe* holds that the right to an abortion is *fundamental*. The Court, therefore, applies strict scrutiny to the statute. This test requires that the state have a *compelling* interest in restricting abortion and the statute must be *narrowly tailored* to effectuate that interest.

      d. **The governmental interests in abortion regulation:** The state offers three possible government interests for restricting abortion: (1) to discourage illicit sexual conduct, (2) to protect the mother from the hazardous nature of the abortion procedure, and (3) to protect the state's interest in potential life.

      The Court dismisses the first governmental interest ("it appears that no court or commentator has taken the argument seriously"). *Id.* at 148. However, the Court accepts the remaining interests (protection of the mother's health and potential life) as compelling. The Court determines that these competing interests must be balanced against the woman's right. Specifically, the woman's right to an abortion is not absolute and must be weighed against the important state interests in regulation.

      e. **The role of the physician:** Justice Blackmun's opinion in *Roe* confers the right to make decisions regarding abortion to the *woman in consultation with her physician*. Blackmun's high regard for the medical profession (he was counsel to the Mayo Clinic) led to his emphasis on the physician's role as well as the appropriation of the trimester framework (the medical approach to pregnancy). Subsequent abortion decisions do not retain this emphasis.

      f. **Trimester framework:** Justice Blackmun, writing for the majority, reaches an accommodation of these competing interests by a trimester framework.

i. **First trimester:** In the first trimester, the woman has an unqualified right to an abortion that may not be infringed upon by the state. This results from the fact that the stated governmental interests are not sufficiently compelling to justify regulation at this point. Abortion is not a health risk this early in pregnancy; nor does the state have an interest in potential life at this stage, according to the Court. Thus, prior to the end of the first trimester, the Court states that the abortion decision must be left to the woman in conjunction with "the medical judgment of the pregnant woman's attending physician." *Id.* at 163-164.

ii. **Second trimester until viability:** After the first trimester and until the point of viability, the state may regulate abortion in the interest of maternal health. The state may not place an outright ban on abortions in this period, but it may regulate the abortion procedure for the purpose of protecting the mother's health and safety. For example, the state may regulate the qualifications and licensure of medical personnel who perform abortions, and the conditions and licensure of the facilities in which the procedure is performed. Viability is defined as the point at which a fetus is capable of survival outside the womb.

iii. **Third trimester:** After viability (loosely defined, at the time of *Roe*, as the beginning of the third trimester), the state's interest in protecting potential life justifies the state in regulating, and even proscribing, abortion except when necessary for the preservation of the life or health of the mother.

g. **Criticisms of *Roe*:** *Roe* engendered considerable criticism. Critics questioned the Court's enunciation of the right of privacy and the trimester scheme, neither of which is explicit in the Constitution. Criticisms also focused on the Court's emphasis on the importance of viability (as the benchmark in defining the state's interest in prenatal life), in part, because the definition of viability changes as technological advances occur.

Further, some feminists (the most prominent of whom are Catharine MacKinnon and Justice Ruth Bader Ginsburg) argued that the right to abortion should be based on equal protection doctrine (rather than the amorphous right to privacy) because abortion restrictions affect only women.

2. **Constitutional challenges to procedural requirements:** Immediately after *Roe v. Wade*, states began adopting a flurry of restrictions on abortion. Restrictions on *procedures* made abortion more difficult to obtain. The federal courts began addressing the constitutionality of these restrictions.

   a. **Hospitalization requirements**

   i. ***Doe v. Bolton:*** *Doe v. Bolton*, 410 U.S. 179 (1973), addresses the constitutionality of Georgia's ALI-inspired abortion legislation. The Court invalidates the requirements that (1) the abortion must be performed in an accredited hospital; (2) the woman must secure advance approval by a hospital committee; and (3) the abortion must be justified by at least three physicians. The Court reasons that (1) the requirement of accreditation is not legitimately related to the state's objective in protecting the mother's health; (2) the requirement of a committee's advance approval substantially limits women's rights to medical care as prescribed by her physician as well as the physician's right to make medical decisions; and (3) the three-physician requirement is unable to withstand constitutional challenges regarding the patient's needs and the physician's right to practice.

ii. ***Akron v. Akron Center for Reproductive Health***: Three abortion clinics and a physician challenge the constitutionality of an Akron city ordinance that requires: (a) the performance of all second-trimester abortions in a hospital; (b) physicians to notify patients of fetal development, physical and emotional complications resulting from an abortion, and the availability of adoption; and (c) a 24-hour waiting period (among other provisions). Reaffirming *Roe v. Wade*, the Court holds the above provisions unconstitutional.

The Court concludes that (1) the hospital requirement does not reasonably further the state's interest in maternal health because it imposes a heavy burden on women's access to a relatively inexpensive and safe medical procedure, (2) the informed consent requirement goes beyond permissible limits in protecting health by attempting to influence the woman's choice of abortion versus childbirth and also intrudes on the physician's discretion, and (3) the waiting period does not further any legitimate state interest because it fails to guarantee the abortion will be performed more safely or to address the concern that the woman's decision be informed. *Akron v. Akron Ctr. for Reproductive Health*, 462 U.S. 416 (1983).

Note: The case is noteworthy for the dissent's criticisms of *Roe* and its foreshadowing of *Planned Parenthood of Southeastern Pennsylvania v. Casey* (*infra*). Justice O'Connor, in her dissent (joined by Justices White and Rehnquist), sharply criticizes *Roe*'s trimester framework, stating that it is "clearly on a collision course with itself." *Id.* at 458. Also, O'Connor disagrees with the importance of viability as a benchmark, stating that the state's compelling interests in maternal health and potential life "are present throughout pregnancy." *Id.* at 459. She advocates a preference for limiting strict scrutiny review to "unduly burdensome" abortion restrictions. *Id.* at 461.

b. **Consent:** Informed consent in health care requires that patients understand the risks, benefits, and alternatives involved in a medical treatment or procedure prior to giving authorization to a non-emergency medical procedure. Medical treatment without first having obtained the patient's consent is considered a form of battery.

Many states have abortion-specific informed consent laws, i.e., specific provisions that are required solely for abortion patients.

i. **"Right to Know" Laws:** Almost two dozen states require that health care providers impart certain verbal and/or written information to women seeking an abortion. Some of these laws (sometimes termed "Right To Know" laws) require a woman seeking an abortion to be given factual information concerning the alternatives to abortion (e.g., adoption), the availability of public and private financial assistance to encourage childbearing, and certain medical facts (e.g., the possibility that the procedure inflicts fetal pain; and the speculative links between breast cancer, suicide, and abortion). The information is designed to make the women hesitant about undergoing the abortion.

Courts have upheld the constitutionality of "Right to Know" provisions.

Example: A South Dakota statute requires doctors to tell women that abortion increases the risk of suicide as well as "terminates the life of a whole, separate, unique living human being." An abortion provider brings an action to enjoin the informed consent law on the ground that it violates physicians' First Amendment right to be free from compelled speech. The Eighth Circuit Court of Appeals disagrees, finding that the statements are permissible. Upon rehearing en banc to address only the suicide advisory, the Court of Appeals determines (after reviewing social science and medical evidence) that the advisory is not a misrepresentation but rather a statement that women need to hear in order for them to give informed consent. *Planned Parenthood Minn., N. Dakota, S. Dakota v. Rounds*, 686 F.3d 889 (8th Cir. 2012).

    ii. Informed consent plus waiting period requirement: The U.S. Supreme Court upheld an abortion-specific informed consent requirement in ***Planned Parenthood of Southeastern Pennsylvania v. Casey***. In *Casey*, the Supreme Court retreated from *Roe*'s guarantee of abortion freedom, gave less constitutional protection to the abortion right, and announced a new standard for scrutiny of abortion restrictions.

Example: The Supreme Court examines the constitutionality of a Pennsylvania statute that provides for:

- an informed consent requirement (informing the woman of the nature and health risks of the procedure, alternatives to abortion, fetal age) and a 24-hour waiting period;

- notification of a married woman's husband prior to an abortion;

- a one-parent consent requirement with judicial bypass for pregnant minors;

- a medical emergency exception; and

- reporting requirements for abortion facilities.

The Court upholds all the Pennsylvania restrictions except the spousal notification requirement. Although reaffirming *Roe v. Wade*, the Court rejects *Roe*'s trimester scheme. Further, rather than continuing to speak of abortion as a fundamental right, the court demotes it to a *liberty interest*. ("The controlling word in the case before us is 'liberty.'") *Id.*

Restrictions on abortion no longer are subject to strict scrutiny — only those restrictions that impose an *undue burden*. *Casey* enunciated a new *undue burden standard* in place of *Roe*'s strict scrutiny for constitutional review of abortion regulations. Only those regulations that impose an undue burden on the woman's abortion decision will be subject to strict scrutiny.

The Court defines undue burden as "the conclusion that a state regulation has the purpose or effect of placing a substantial obstacle in the path of the woman." *Id.* at 877. The Court concludes that neither the informed consent requirement nor the 24-hour waiting period creates undue burdens.

Casey recognizes the importance of viability, stating that the state may not impose an undue burden on the woman's decision before viability. However, this stance is weakened (perhaps, even contradicted) by the Court's recognition "that there is a substantial state interest in potential life *throughout* pregnancy" (emphasis added). *Id.* at 876. *Casey*'s seeming condonation of state restrictions on abortion "throughout pregnancy" undermines *Roe*'s heightened protection of the right to an abortion during the first trimester.

   c. TRAP laws: Many states have so-called "targeted regulation of abortion providers" or "TRAP" laws that impose requirements on abortion providers that are more stringent than the regulations applied to other medical practitioners. For example, some TRAP laws mandate waiting periods, ultrasounds, and abortion-specific informed consent procedures.

Other TRAP laws require that abortion facilities be licensed as more costly ambulatory surgical care centers and require providers to have admitting privileges at local hospitals.

Example: Texas abortion providers seek an injunction to prevent enforcement of two provisions of a Texas TRAP law: (1) an admitting-privileges requirement that requires physicians performing abortions to have admitting privileges at a hospital within 30 miles of the facility, and (2) an ambulatory surgical care center requirement that requires abortion clinics to meet minimum standards for ambulatory surgical centers. Health care providers argue that admitting privileges at local hospitals are often unattainable for abortion providers as well as unnecessary because abortion is such a safe procedure. (Admitting privileges are unobtainable because providers cannot generate sufficient patients, given the safety of abortion, that hospitals require as a condition of granting such privileges.) They also argue that surgical care center building requirements are prohibitively expensive and, similarly, unnecessary as a health issue because abortion is such a safe procedure. The state argues that the requirements are necessary to promote women's health.

The Supreme Court invalidates both provisions as medically unnecessary and a substantial burden on women's access to abortion. Justice Breyer's majority opinion clarifies the undue burden by explaining that whether an abortion restriction is constitutional depends in part on whether the burdens it imposes on women in fact outweigh the benefits. After conducting a fact-based inquiry to evaluate the burdens and benefits, the Court reasons that abortion-related complications are rare and most often occur long after the patient had left the facility. As a result, neither admitting privileges nor surgical-center standards would advance the state's purported interest in maternal health. The Court recognizes the substantial obstacles imposed by the two requirements, i.e., the closure of more than 75% of the clinics in Texas, thereby severely limiting access to abortion and forcing women to travel long distances. In view of the "virtual absence of any health benefit," the two provisions, taken together, constitute an undue burden. *Whole Woman's Health v. Hellerstedt*, 136 S. Ct. 2292 (2016).

Example: A Louisiana law requires abortion providers to have admitting privileges at a hospital within 30 miles of the abortion facility. The law is virtually identical to the Texas law invalidated by the Supreme Court in *Whole Woman's Health, supra*. Abortion providers argue that the law unconstitutionally imposes an undue burden on the right to obtain an abortion. The U.S. Supreme Court invalidates the law. A plurality opinion by Justice Breyer (joined by Justice Roberts who files a separate concurring opinion) holds that the law imposes the same undue burden on access as the Texas law invalidated in *Whole Woman's Health*. The plurality finds that enforcement of the admitting-privileges requirement would leave Louisiana with just one clinic with one provider to serve 10,000 women annually, resulting in longer waiting times and longer driving distances—burdens that would fall disproportionately on poor women. Plaintiffs also raise the issue of third-party standing (whether health care providers can assert the claims of pregnant patients). The Court rules that the state waived its standing challenge when it sought to obtain an expedited decision from the district court on the merits of plaintiffs' claim. *June Medical Servs. v. Russo*, 140 S. Ct. 2103 (U.S. 2020).

Concurrence: The significance of the opinion rests on Justice Roberts' concurring opinion in which he disagrees with the benefit-burden test adopted in *Whole Woman's*

Health (requiring courts to consider the burdens that a law imposes together with the benefits conferred). He criticizes that courts cannot assign weight and compare the "imponderable values" in the abortion context. He points out that *Planned Parenthood v. Casey* did not require such balancing—focusing instead on whether the restriction imposes a substantial obstacle on women's access. Roberts advocates a return to *Casey*'s framework (an approach, parenthetically, that would allow more restrictions on access). According to Roberts, so long as the state has a legitimate purpose in enacting the abortion restriction and the restriction is reasonably related to that goal, "the only question for a court is whether the law has the 'effect of placing a substantial obstacle in the path of a woman seeking an abortion of a nonviable fetus.'" *Id.* at 2138.

    d. Proposed federal legislation: A bill introduced in Congress, the Women's Health Protection Act (WHPA), S.1645/H.R.2975, 116th Cong. (2019-2020) would protect the right to access to abortion care by creating a safeguard against state bans and medically unnecessary restrictions that are inapplicable to other medical procedures. WHPA establishes a *statutory right* for health care providers to provide, and for their patients to receive, abortion free from medically unnecessary restrictions.

D. The abortion funding cases: Although the Supreme Court held in *Roe* that a woman has a constitutionally protected right to an abortion, the Court also held that the government is under no obligation to provide funds for abortion. This raises the question of how meaningful is a guaranteed right to an abortion without provision of the means to secure that right? A series of abortion funding cases restrict access to abortion by permitting limitations on abortion funding, thereby making it difficult or impossible for indigents to secure an abortion.

    1. Background: The abortion funding cases arise in the context of challenges to federal funding of medical care. A federal statute, Title XIX of the Social Security Act, establishes a joint federal-state Medicaid program to assist indigents with medical costs. Prior to 1976, a significant percentage of legal abortions were funded by the Medicaid program.

    State attempts to limit Medicaid funds for abortion led to constitutional challenges. In *Beal v. Doe*, 432 U.S. 438 (1977), the U.S. Supreme Court determines that Title XIX does not require states to fund nontherapeutic (i.e., elective) abortions as a condition of participation in the Medicaid program. In *Maher v. Roe*, 432 U.S. 464 (1977), the Court upholds the funding of only medically necessary abortions, determining that the exclusion of elective abortions from Medicaid does not violate the Equal Protection Clause.

    2. Restrictions on funding medically necessary abortions: *Harris v. McRae:* In another attempt to limit Medicaid funding for abortion, Congress enacted the *Hyde Amendment* in 1977 to prohibit expenditure of Medicaid funds unless the mother's *life* is endangered or she is a victim of *reported rape or incest*. The Hyde Amendment guarantees that Medicaid cannot cover abortion even when a patient's *health* is at risk and her doctor recommends the abortion. The effect of the Hyde Amendment is to prevent low-income pregnant women (especially minority women) who seek abortion from access to safe, legal medical care.

    Example: A Medicaid recipient in the first trimester of pregnancy, together with a provider of abortion services, challenged the constitutionality of the Hyde Amendment on due process and equal protection grounds. The Supreme Court held that the Hyde Amendment violates neither due process nor equal protection. Rejecting the argument that the Amendment impinges on the liberty interest recognized in *Roe v. Wade*, the Court reasoned that a woman's freedom of choice does not mandate a constitutional entitlement to the financial resources to effectuate that choice. Because the government does not create the obstacle to the woman's abortion (i.e., indigence), the government is not required to remove the obstacle.

In terms of equal protection analysis, the Court pointed out that the Hyde Amendment does not implicate a suspect classification (poverty). Based on rational basis review, the Court finds that the Hyde Amendment is rationally related to the legitimate government objective of protecting potential life. *Harris v. McRae*, 448 U.S. 297 (1980).

Note: Congress has renewed the Hyde Amendment since *Harris* with its limitation of Medicaid coverage only to those pregnancies caused by rape or incest or to life-saving abortions. The Hyde Amendment, although banning the use of federal Medicaid to cover almost all abortions, does not limit a state's ability to use its *own* funds to cover abortion. Fifteen states extend state funding for abortion coverage to low-income Medicaid patients (although some of these states still make it difficult to access abortion).

3. **Prohibition on use of public hospitals and public employees:** In *Webster v. Reproductive Health Services*, 492 U.S. 490 (1989), the U.S. Supreme Court upholds a prohibition on the use of public hospitals and employees in the performance of elective abortions (not necessary to save the mother's life), relying on the abortion funding cases rationale. The Court reasons that the state's refusal to allow public employees to perform abortions leaves women in no worse position, i.e., women can still have abortions at private facilities performed by private physicians.

4. **Funding restrictions on abortions for military personnel:** Federal law prohibits the use of federal funding for abortions for military servicewomen and female military dependents except to save the life of the mother or if the pregnancy is the result of rape or incest. 10 U.S.C. §1903(a) & (b). This means that these women must travel off base to seek abortion in the civilian community (if abortion is possible there).

5. **Enhanced right to abortion funding under state constitutions:** Indigent plaintiffs have been more successful in securing funding for abortion under some state constitutions. *See, e.g., Committee to Defend Reproductive Rights v. Myers*, 625 P.2d 779 (Cal. 1981) (holding that the right of privacy explicitly guaranteed by the California constitution mandates public funding of abortions for indigents).

E. **Clinic access and FACE laws:** Abortion access is also a problem for pregnant women who are confronted with anti-abortion activists' tactics at clinics. In response to the murder of abortion providers and the harassment of patients at abortion clinics, Congress enacted the Freedom of Access to Clinic Entrances (FACE) Act, 18 U.S.C. §248, in 1996. FACE provides criminal and civil penalties for the use of "force, threat of force, or physical obstruction" aimed at injuring, intimidating, or interfering with any patients or providers of reproductive health services.

Several states enacted clinic access laws, modeled on the federal legislation, making it a ***state crime*** to obstruct access to clinics. States adopt two approaches to protect abortion providers. Some states have enacted laws similar to the federal Act that *prohibit specific activities* such as obstruction of access to clinics. Other states attempt to create *buffer zones* around clinics that prohibit protestors from coming too close to abortion patients without the latter's consent.

Courts are split on the constitutionality of buffer zones. The U.S. Supreme Court upheld a state law requiring an 8-foot buffer zone around patients within 100 feet of the clinic entrance but invalidated another state law that placed a 35-foot buffer zone around clinic entrances.

Example: A Colorado law makes it unlawful to "knowingly approach" within 8 feet of another individual to pass a pamphlet, show a sign, or engage in protest, education, or counseling without consent if the individual is within 100 feet of a health care facility's entrance. The U.S. Supreme Court upholds the statute against a First Amendment challenge, finding that it is a content-neutral, narrowly tailored, valid "time, place, and manner" restriction that served significant governmental interests. The case established the constitutional standard for these types of ordinances (expressive activity, even in public forums, is subject to reasonable time, place, or manner restrictions provided that they are content neutral, are narrowly tailored to serve a significant governmental interest, and leave open ample alternative channels for communication of the information). *Hill v. Colorado*, 530 U.S. 703 (2000).

Example: A Massachusetts law makes it a crime to stand within 35 feet of an abortion clinic entrance or obstruct access to an abortion clinic. Anti-abortion protestors claim that the 35-foot buffer zone hampers their "counseling efforts." They seek to enjoin the Act's enforcement on the ground that it violates the First and Fourteenth Amendments, both on its face and as applied. The U.S. Supreme Court reasons that, because the Act is neither content- nor viewpoint-based, it need not be analyzed under strict scrutiny. Recognizing that the government's ability to restrict speech in the public forum is limited, the Court holds that the statute is not narrowly tailored because it burdens substantially more speech than is necessary to further the government's legitimate interests in protecting patient access to health care and thus violates free speech guarantees. *McCullen v. Coakley,* 573 U.S. 464 (U.S. 2014).

F. **Partial-birth abortion bans:** Both state and federal laws ban partial-birth abortions. A "partial-birth" abortion involves abortion of later-stage pregnancies (those pregnancies in or past the fifth month) by terminating the life of the fetus after extraction of the fetal head intact from the mother's body. Late termination of pregnancy is more controversial than abortion in general.

1. **State legislation on partial-birth abortions:** Many state legislatures enacted partial-birth abortion bans in the 1990s and early 2000s.

2. *Stenberg v. Carhart:* Before enactment of the federal partial-birth abortion ban of 2003 (discussed *infra*), the U.S. Supreme Court *upheld* a Nebraska ban on partial-birth abortions.

   Example: A physician who performed abortions brought suit on behalf of himself and his patients challenging the constitutionality of the Nebraska statute banning partial-birth abortions unless that procedure is necessary to save the mother's life. "Partial-birth abortion" was defined as: "delivering into the vagina a living unborn child, or a substantial portion thereof, for the purpose of performing a procedure that . . . does kill the unborn child." The U.S. Supreme Court held that the statute was unconstitutional because it lacked a "health exception" that would have allowed physicians to perform the banned method to protect the mother's health and because the statute imposed an undue burden on a woman's abortion right by restricting the most common and safest dilation and evacuation (D & E) procedure as well as the dilation and extraction (D & X) procedure. *Stenberg v. Carhart*, 530 U.S. 914 (2000).

3. **Federal legislation on partial-birth abortions:** *Gonzales v. Carhart:* In 2003, Congress enacted the Partial-Birth Abortion Ban Act (PBABA), 18 U.S.C. §1531, that prohibited a certain type of intact dilation and evacuation (D & E) abortion procedure in which the physician partially delivers, and then kills a living fetus, unless necessary to preserve the life of the mother. The U.S. Supreme Court upheld the federal ban in *Gonzales v. Carhart*, 550 U.S. 124 (2007).

Example: Abortion providers and advocacy organizations challenge the constitutionality of the federal Partial-Birth Abortion Ban Act. The Supreme Court holds that the prohibition on intact dilation and evacuation procedure is not void for vagueness on its face, reasoning that the statutory requirement that a living fetus be delivered to one of two anatomical landmarks establishes sufficient guidelines to govern law enforcement, and the scienter requirement ("knowingly performs") limits prosecutorial discretion. The Court also concludes that the ban does not sweep too broadly to include an alternative late abortion D & E procedure in which the fetus is removed from the uterus in pieces, and thus does not impose an undue burden on second-trimester abortions based on overbreadth.

The Court finds that the stated congressional purposes of protecting innocent human life from an inhumane procedure and protecting the medical community's ethics and reputation are furthered by the enactment of the ban. Justice Kennedy claims that the ban is also supported by the state's interest in ensuring that the woman's choice is well informed. He suggests that doctors may tend to withhold information from women about the grisly nature of the procedure. The ban thereby prevents women who discover the details of the procedure after the abortion, he contends, from "struggl[ing] with grief more anguished and sorrow more profound" (*id.* at 159) than those other women who generally "come to regret their choice" of abortion (*id.*).

Gonzales marked the first time that the Supreme Court allowed a ban on a *method* of abortion. The case also held, for the first time, that regulations on abortion procedures do not have to include a health exception. In so ruling, the Court permitted considerable judicial deference to the legislature, based on its reasoning that such deference is appropriate in the face of medical uncertainty regarding the necessity of the procedure to preserve women's health given the availability of safe alternative procedures.

Dissent: Justice Ginsburg criticizes the absence of a health exception for the mother. She is also critical of the majority's decision to blur the line between pre-viability and post-viability abortions. In her opinion, the Act does not further any governmental interest. Further, she scoffs at Justice Kennedy's suggestion that the ban protects women from subsequent regret about their abortion decision, pointing out that "[e]liminating or reducing women's reproductive choices is manifestly not a means of protecting them" (*id.* at 184 n.9).Critics charged that the case ushered in a new era of abortion restrictions, the Court gave too much deference to congressional fact-finding that was rejected by the appellate courts, and led to the emergence of a new paternalistic governmental interest in regulating abortion (i.e., protecting women from psychological harms associated with the abortion decision).

4. **Modern restrictions on late stage abortions:** Several states currently ban or severely restrict the most common method of late stage abortion in the interest of protecting potential life. These restrictions (that are distinguishable from state partial birth abortion bans) include: (1) physicians may legally perform a D&E abortion only if they first cause "fetal demise" or, alternatively, confirm that a fetus's life is terminated in utero before completing the D&E; and (2) patients receive extensive counseling prior to receiving a D&E abortion—thereby requiring at least three trips to a clinic.

G. **Medication abortions:** In 2000, the FDA approved medication for termination of early pregnancies. The medication is known as RU-486, or "mifepristone," or more commonly, the "abortion pill." Medication abortions are approved for patients who are up to ten weeks pregnant. They account for approximately 40% of abortion procedures.

Medication abortion is subject to FDA requirements that require that medication must be dispensed only by certified prescribers and only in clinics, medical offices, or hospitals. Currently, more than a dozen states have bans or restrictions on the use of medication abortions. Many of these state laws require the *physical presence* of the prescribing health care provider when medication abortion is dispensed, effectively banning the use of telemedicine for this form of abortion. The COVID-19 pandemic highlighted the importance of access to medication abortions.

Courts have split on the validity of restrictions on medication abortions. The U.S. Supreme Court has yet to rule on their constitutionality.

Example: State law permits administering the abortion pill only by protocols using an obsolete regimen that has been rejected by doctors, medical experts, and leading professional organizations. A coalition of reproductive rights organizations brings a challenge to the constitutionality of the state statute. The state supreme court holds that the statutory requirement that physicians adhere to an outdated protocol, rather than the current version, places a substantial obstacle in the path of patients who desire an abortion by making abortion more difficult to obtain and thereby, imposes an undue burden. *Cline v. Oklahoma Coalition for Reproductive Justice*, 292 P.3d 27 (Okla. 2012), *cert granted, writ dismissed as improvidently granted*, 571 U.S. 985 (U.S. 2013).

Example: State law prohibits administering the abortion pill except according to protocols originally approved by the FDA. Health care providers challenge the constitutionality of the statute. The Sixth Circuit Court of Appeals upholds the law, reasoning that it is not unconstitutionally vague because it provides physicians with a reasonable opportunity to know what is prohibited, and the limitation does not create a substantial obstacle for the large fraction of women in deciding whether to have an abortion. *Planned Parenthood Southwest Ohio Region v. Dewine*, 696 F.3d 490 (6th Cir. 2012). *Accord Planned Parenthood of Greater Texas Surgical Health Servs. v. Abbott*, 734 F.2d 406 (5th Cir. 2013) (finding that state restriction on medication abortions does not place an undue burden on women's right to have an abortion).

Note: In July 2020, a federal judge in Maryland granted a preliminary injunction enjoining the Food and Drug Administration (FDA), during the COVID-19 pandemic from enforcing the "In-Person" rules requiring that pregnant women must physically visit a medical facility in order to receive oral medication to induce an abortion or manage a miscarriage. *Am. Coll. of Obstetricians & Gynecologists v. U.S. Food & Drug Admin.*, 2020 WL 3960625 (D. Md. 2020).

H. State sanctions for abortion participants: Some states have enacted laws punishing abortion providers. Other states have laws punishing pregnant women who seek an abortion.

   1. Providers: At the time of *Roe*, the law punished only the abortion provider. However, some recent state laws similarly impose criminal sanctions on doctors who perform abortions.

   2. Pregnant women: The longstanding view exempted women from criminal liability for having an abortion. Nonetheless, seven states currently have laws criminalizing self-induced abortions. The idea of punishing women received renewed attention in 2016 when former President Donald Trump ignited a bipartisan firestorm for his suggestion of prosecuting women for having an abortion.

I. Husband's rights in the abortion context: A husband has *no* constitutional right to influence his spouse's abortion decision making.

   1. Spousal consent: A state may not require a spouse's *prior written consent* to an abortion.

   Example: A Missouri statute requires the prior written consent of the spouse of a woman seeking an abortion during the first 12 weeks of pregnancy unless the abortion is medically necessary to preserve the woman's life. A number of physicians and surgeons challenge this and other provisions of the Missouri statute. The state defends the provision as necessary for the protection of family values in encouraging joint decision making. The U.S. Supreme Court invalidates the provision, holding that the state may not constitutionally delegate to a spouse that power which the state, itself, is prohibited from exercising during the first trimester by *Roe v. Wade. Planned Parenthood v. Danforth*, 428 U.S. 52 (1976).

2. **Spousal notification:** A state may not require spousal *notification* prior to an abortion.

   Example: Plaintiffs challenge the constitutionality of a Pennsylvania statute requiring that a married woman cannot receive an abortion without providing her physician with a signed statement certifying that she has notified her husband of her abortion plans. Under the statute, notification is not required if: (1) the husband is not the father, (2) the husband cannot be located, (3) the pregnancy is the result of reported spousal rape, or (4) the woman believes notification will cause her bodily injury. The Supreme Court finds that the spousal notification requirement places a significant obstacle (i.e., an "undue burden") in the path of women's exercise of their right to an abortion. The Court relies on *Danforth* (discussed *supra*), the woman's liberty interest in her body, and empirical evidence suggesting that this provision would prevent many battered wives from securing an abortion. *Planned Parenthood of Southeastern Pennsylvania v. Casey,* 505 U.S. 833 (1992).

J. Minor's right to an abortion: A minor's right to an abortion is more limited than an adult's right. Many states mandate parental consent and/or notification when minors seek an abortion. In states with parental involvement laws, minors who do not wish to seek parental consent or notification may petition for a judicial bypass. Thus, pregnant teens do not have to obtain parental consent or notification to obtain an abortion, but, if they do not, they must undergo a judicial bypass proceeding.

1. **Parental consent**

   a. *Bellotti v. Baird:* A Massachusetts statute regulates a minor's right to an abortion by providing (1) an unmarried minor must obtain the consent of both parents, and (2) if one or both parents refuse, the minor may obtain judicial consent upon a showing of good cause. Abortion rights activists and an unmarried minor challenge the constitutionality of the statute as unduly burdening the right to seek an abortion. The U.S. Supreme Court invalidates and enjoins the statute. Although the Court supports parental involvement, it holds that the statute fails constitutional muster because it permits judicial authorization to be withheld from a mature minor (as determined by a court) and because it imposes a blanket parental consent requirement without providing an alternative procedure. The Court reasons that limitations on the freedom of minors are justified by: (1) children's vulnerability, (2) children's inability to make mature, informed decisions, and (3) the importance of the parental role in childrearing. If a state requires one or both parents' consent, the state must provide an *alternative authorization procedure* whereby the minor may show that she is either mature enough to make the decision herself, or, if she cannot make such a showing of maturity, that an abortion, nonetheless, would be in her best interests. *Bellotti v. Baird*, 443 U.S. 622 (1979).

   b. **Parental consent statutes under state constitutions:** Plaintiffs are more successful in securing abortion rights under state constitutions because some state constitutions protect a broader right to privacy than the federal right.

   Example: A California statute prohibits unemancipated minors from obtaining abortions without either the consent of a parent or judicial authorization. Health care providers challenge the constitutionality of the statute. The state supreme court counters the state attorney general's reliance on U.S. Supreme Court decisions by pointing to the explicit *state* constitutional guarantee of a right of privacy and prior case law (*Committee to Defend Reproductive Rights v. Myers*, discussed *supra*) affording the right to indigents to have public funding for abortion. Although conceding that the asserted state interests (protection of the physical, emotional, and psychological health of minors and promotion of the parent-child relationship) are compelling, the court finds that the statute does not further these interests (i.e., it harms minors' health and is detrimental to the parent-child relationship). Examining the statute under strict scrutiny as required under the state constitutional right of privacy, the court concludes that the statute violates a minor's right to privacy. *Am. Academy of Pediatrics v. Lungren*, 66 Cal. Rptr. 2d 210 (Cal. 1997).

2. **Parental notification:** State laws also restrict minors' abortion rights by means of parental notification requirements. The U.S. Supreme Court has upheld such restrictions. *See, e.g., Planned Parenthood of Southeastern Pennsylvania v. Casey*, 505 U.S. 833 (1992) (upholding statute requiring parental notification of one parent plus informed consent requirement with judicial bypass); *Hodgson v. Minnesota*, 497 U.S. 417 (1990) (holding that judicial bypass procedure makes two-parent notification requirement constitutional).

3. **Judicial bypass:** A judicial bypass is an order from a judge that allows a minor to get an abortion without the notification or consent of her parents. The Supreme Court (*Bellotti, supra*) requires that parental involvement laws must include exceptions (called judicial bypass procedures) which require minors to receive court approval to access abortion care when they do not have their parents' knowledge or consent.

   According to the U.S. Supreme Court in *Bellotti, supra*, a pregnant minor must prove at the bypass proceeding that (1) she is mature enough and well enough informed to make the abortion decision independently of her parents' wishes; or (2) even if she is not able to make this decision independently, an abortion would be in her best interests. Once the minor makes either showing, the bypass petition must be granted.

   For many pregnant teenagers, judicial bypass is not a viable alternative. In states that mandate parental involvement, many pregnant minors do not know that judicial bypass is available or the manner to obtain it; and they lack access to transportation to travel to court. Further, forcing teens to reveal the details of their private lives to strangers causes them extraordinary fear, anxiety, and shame.

4. **Undocumented minors' right to abortion:** Unaccompanied undocumented adolescent girls, as well as undocumented adult women, face high rates of sexual assault in their trek across the border. Once in the United States, these women and adolescents in immigration detention face virtually insurmountable barriers in accessing reproductive health care. Under the Obama Administration, governmental policies allowed them access to abortion. Under the Trump Administration, however, immigration officials exercised a unilateral veto over immigrant minors' decision to choose an abortion. Undocumented minors brought a class action lawsuit to challenge the policy.

   Example: Pregnant unaccompanied immigrant minors in the custody of the Office of Refugee Resettlement (ORR) bring a class action suit, challenging the governmental policy that precludes them from obtaining an abortion even after securing judicial approval in a bypass proceeding. After the district court grants a preliminary injunction in favor of the minors, the government appeals. The D.C. Circuit Court of Appeals affirmed the issuance of the preliminary injunction, holding that the ORR policy was not a mere refusal to facilitate or subsidize abortion but rather constituted an undue burden on the minors' right to choose to terminate their pregnancies. The possibility of a minor's voluntary departure from United States or appointment of a sponsor did not remove such undue burden. *J.D. v. Azar*, 925 F.3d 1291 (D.C. Cir. 2019).

Note: In September 2020, the Trump Administration reversed its policy. The new policy provides that the Office of Refugee Resettlement must allow teenagers in its custody to obtain abortions.

III. FETAL PROTECTION LEGISLATION

Federal and state legislatures have enacted laws that protect the fetus. These laws establish the crime of fetal homicide, restrict abortion based on the personhood of the fetus and its gestational age, restrict abortion based on the detection of a fetal heartbeat, and regulate the disposition of fetal remains.

A. **Federal fetal homicide laws:** Federal law criminalizes the killing of a fetus during the commission of a *federal* crime.

    1. **Federal legislation:** Congress enacted the Unborn Victims of Violence Act (UVVA), 18 U.S.C.A. §1841, in 2004. The Act is dubbed "Laci and Conner's Law" in memory of a California woman who was murdered by her husband when she was eight months pregnant. The Act creates a criminal offense for the killing or injuring of an unborn child (at any period of gestation) during the commission of a federal crime involving a pregnant woman (thus recognizing two victims of the crime). For the first time, the federal government confers legal rights on a fetus — a result that critics claim may have implications narrowing a woman's right to an abortion. Note: the UVVA applies only to conduct that is charged as a *federal* crime.

    2. **State laws:** Most states have fetal homicide laws imposing state criminal liability for harm committed to the fetus as well as the pregnant woman. The laws vary in terms of the degree of protection and the stage of pregnancy at which criminal liability attaches.

B. **Personhood laws and gestational limits:** Some state policymakers have attempted to provoke a challenge to Roe v. Wade by banning abortion before viability. More than a dozen state legislatures have introduced bans on abortion by bills protecting "fetal personhood." Federal and state courts have consistently blocked enforcement of laws that ban abortion before 13 weeks. However, more than a third of states have successfully implemented 20-week abortion bans that are based on the unfounded assertion that a fetus can feel pain at 20 weeks postfertilization. According to the American College of Obstetricians and Gynecologists (ACOG), evidence indicates that a fetus cannot perceive pain until the third trimester at the earliest, well past viability.

C. **Fetal heartbeat laws:** Several states have enacted so-called "fetal heartbeat" laws. These laws ban abortion as early as six weeks into pregnancy. The laws prohibit abortion once a fetal heartbeat can be detected. Critics point out that these laws, which prohibit abortion before many women know they are pregnant, amount to a near-total ban on the procedure.

D. **Fetal remains laws:** Some state laws regulate the disposal of fetal remains by mandating burial or cremation of fetal tissue. Critics argue that these requirements increase costs for patients, burden providers, and shut down clinics.

Example: Plaintiffs challenged two provisions of a 2016 Indiana law (HB 1337). The first provision mandated that health care facilities, such as hospitals and abortion clinics, either bury or cremate fetal remains from abortions and miscarriages instead of disposing of fetal tissue along with other surgical tissue. The second provision of the law prohibits abortions on the basis of the sex, race, or disability of the fetus. The Supreme Court reversed a federal appellate court ruling blocking the provision of the Indiana law requiring fetal remains to be buried or cremated, thereby allowing Indiana's fetal burial law to stand. The Court declined to hear the challenge on the second provision. *Box v. Planned Parenthood of Indiana and Kentucky*, 139 S. Ct. 1780 (2019).

Quiz Yourself on *ABORTION*

98.   The Blackacre legislature enacts a statute imposing a new restriction on abortion, i.e., a requirement that all second-trimester abortions be performed in a hospital. Physicians who fail to comply with the requirement will be subject to criminal liability. Service providers and physicians bring an action challenging the constitutionality of the abortion restriction. Will Plaintiffs prevail?

 _____

99.   The Greenacre legislature enacts a law regulating the practice of abortion. The new law has two provisions. The first provision sets forth requirements for the design and construction of abortion clinics, such as requirements for specific size/types of rooms or hallways, and regulations about necessary medical equipment. The second provision requires that health care providers who counsel patients seeking abortions must notify the women, if they are more than 20 weeks pregnant, that the fetus will feel pain during the abortion procedure. Reproductive rights providers challenge the constitutionality of these provisions. Will they prevail? _____

100. Husband and Wife have been married for five years. They have been trying unsuccessfully to conceive. However, serious marital problems develop and the couple seeks a divorce. Both parties are surprised to learn, during the pendency of the dissolution proceedings, that Wife is a few weeks pregnant. After much soul-searching, Wife decides to have an abortion. She believes that the marriage is dead and that she can better pursue her ambition of becoming a physician if she is unencumbered by a child. When she informs Husband of her decision, he files an action for an injunction seeking to prohibit Wife from terminating her pregnancy. Will he be successful?

 _____

101. Mary Moe, who is 14 years old and in the first trimester of pregnancy, petitions the Superior Court to authorize her abortion. She prefers not to inform her parents that she and her 15-year-old boyfriend have been sexually active. Mary tells the judge that her decision to have an abortion is based on the following considerations: She believes that she is too young to raise a child, she wants to avoid disrupting her education, and her doctor tells her that the medical risks of pregnancy and childbirth for a young teenager far exceed the risks of a first-trimester abortion. The judge determines that Mary is not sufficiently mature to give informed consent to the procedure. He adds that he cannot determine whether an abortion would be in Mary's best interests unless Mary consults at least one of her parents. He therefore denies her petition. Mary appeals. Will she be successful?

 _____

Answers

98. Probably yes. Based on *Roe v. Wade*, Plaintiffs would argue that a woman's right to terminate her pregnancy is encompassed by the right to privacy guaranteed by the federal Constitution. Here, the state would respond that the purpose of the requirement is the protection of maternal health, arguably a compelling state interest. However, the regulation probably would be invalidated as it is not sufficiently narrowly tailored to achieve that objective because second-trimester abortions can be performed safely outside a hospital setting (i.e., in outpatient facilities). Moreover, Plaintiffs could argue that the hospitalization requirement constitutes an "undue burden" under *Casey* in light of the fact that the hospitalization requirement significantly increases the cost of an abortion (thereby creating a "substantial obstacle" in the woman's decision) and also precludes poor women from obtaining an abortion.

99. Possibly not. A court might uphold the regulation of the design of abortion clinics to protect the health of women who are undergoing a serious medical procedure. Recall that *Roe v. Wade* permitted state regulation to serve the goal of maternal health. A court also might uphold the patient advisory about fetal pain, determining that health care providers are simply providing patients with information to assist their informed judgment about whether to undergo an abortion. Because such information does not prevent a woman from having an abortion or significantly increase the cost of the procedure, a court might conclude that it does not create an undue burden on the constitutional right to an abortion under *Casey*. A court might reach this conclusion even in the face of medical uncertainty about the ability of a fetus to feel pain. (Recall that the U.S. Supreme Court wrestled with a similar situation in *Gonzales v. Carhart* involving medical uncertainty about the need for partial birth abortions).

100. No. The injunction should not be granted because it would violate Wife's constitutional rights as set forth in *Roe v. Wade* and *Planned Parenthood v. Danforth*. *Roe* guarantees that a woman has a constitutionally protected right to an abortion. *Danforth*, by invalidating a statutory provision requiring the prior written consent of a husband to his wife's abortion, holds that the state may not delegate to a husband that power that the state is prohibited from exercising during the first trimester by *Roe v. Wade*. This latter ruling has been reaffirmed by the U.S. Supreme Court in *Planned Parenthood v. Casey*, invalidating a spousal notification requirement.

101. Yes. The appellate court should overturn the denial of Mary's petition for judicial authorization of her abortion. The trial court committed judicial error in conditioning its consent on Mary's consultation with at least one parent. The U.S. Supreme Court has provided for a judicial authorization procedure as an *alternative* to parental consult. Based on *Bellotti v. Baird*, after a judge determines that a minor is not sufficiently mature to make the abortion decision, the judge has to determine whether the abortion would be in the minor's best interests. Here, Mary has demonstrated her thoughtful consideration of several factors involved in the abortion decision. The trial judge should have determined that Mary was sufficiently mature enough to make the abortion decision or, in the alternative, ruled that an abortion would be in her best interests.

IV. ASSISTED REPRODUCTIVE TECHNOLOGY

Scientific advances have made possible various forms of assisted reproductive technologies, including collaborative reproduction involving third parties, such as surrogate motherhood. The use of these reproductive methods raises many legal issues.

A. Early technique to address infertility: Artificial insemination

1. **Definition:** Artificial insemination is a reproductive technique to combat problems of, primarily, male infertility. In cases when a man is sterile, has a low sperm count, or carries a genetically transmissible disease, the man's wife or female partner may be inseminated with the sperm of an anonymous third-party semen donor. Semen is washed, concentrated, placed in a catheter, and deposited into the uterus.

2. **Legitimacy of children conceived thereby:** Many statutes legitimize the resulting offspring of artificial insemination as the product of the marriage. Often, statutes require the woman's husband's written consent as a prerequisite. The original version of the Uniform Parentage Act §5a (approved in 1973) provides that the husband of a woman who is artificially inseminated is treated, legally, as if he were the biological father (provided that he consents and the procedure is carried out under the supervision of a licensed physician).

3. **Role of husband's consent in child support obligation:** A husband's consent to the artificial insemination of his wife gives rise to his obligation for financial support for any ensuing child.

4. **Sperm donor's rights regarding anonymity:** Sperm donors have received legal protection.

    i. **Traditional view:** Traditionally, sperm donors were assured anonymity. The original UPA (§5) explicitly provided for sealed records concerning donor insemination.

    ii. **Evolving view:** The recent UPA (2017) addresses the right of children born through assisted reproductive technology (ART) to access their medical and identifying information regarding gamete providers. Article 9 requires infertility treatment centers to ask donors if they want to have their identifying information disclosed when the resulting child attains age 18. The 2017 UPA also requires disclosure of the *non-identifying medical history* of gamete donors (not merely the medical history of sperm donors).

    iii. **Influence of the Internet:** The Internet diminishes the importance of law reforms guaranteeing sperm donors' rights. The popularity of DNA tracking services makes anonymity difficult. Donor-conceived children have been highly successful in tracking down their biological parents and half-siblings.

B. Modern technique to address infertility: In vitro fertilization

1. **Definition:** In vitro fertilization (IVF) is a process in which the ovaries are stimulated to produce numerous eggs that are later extracted via suction under general anesthesia. The eggs are placed in a Petri dish with sperm where fertilization occurs and the embryos can be incubated for three to five days. Some of the resultant embryos are then placed into a catheter and deposited into the uterus, and the remaining embryos may be frozen for subsequent use.

2. **Status of posthumously conceived children:** IVF is sometimes used to accomplish posthumous conception (i.e., children who are conceived after a parent's death with sperm that was stored before the parent's death). This procedure is sometimes used after a person, who would like to be a father, is diagnosed with a life-threatening illness.

i. **Donor's explicit written consent:** State law generally requires that a donor's explicit written consent must be obtained prior to death for his sperm to be harvested and used posthumously based on the rationale of the individual's right to autonomy.

ii. **Posthumously conceived children's right to inherit:** State law differs on the inheritance rights of posthumous conceived children. Several states place a time limit on the child's birth following posthumous conception for inheritance purposes from a deceased parent.

iii. **Social Security survivors' benefits:** The Social Security Act relies on state law to determine parentage and inheritance rights. The U.S. Supreme Court held that the right of posthumously conceived children to Social Security survivors' benefits depends on state intestacy law. Some state laws (like that of Florida in the example below) preclude inheritance by posthumously conceived children via intestate succession whereas other state laws permit it.

Example: Robert dies from cancer three years after his marriage to Karen. Karen becomes pregnant with sperm that Robert had frozen before he underwent chemotherapy. She files for Social Security survivors' benefits for her posthumously conceived twins. The Social Security Administration denies her application for benefits. The Supreme Court concludes that the twins are not eligible for benefits based on its interpretation of the meaning of "children" in the Social Security Act, the Act's reference to state law of domicile on matters of family status, and Florida state intestacy law (where Robert was domiciled at the time of his death). The Court interprets the federal statute to entitle biological children to Social Security survivors' benefits solely if they qualify for inheritance from the decedent under state intestacy law. *Astrue v. Capato*, 566 U.S. 541 (2012).

iv. **Uniform law:** According to the Uniform Parentage Act (UPA §708 (2017)), for an individual to be considered a parent of a child conceived by assisted reproduction, the embryo must be either (a) in utero not later than 36 months after the individual's death or (b) the child must be born not later than 45 months after the individual's death.

3. **Sperm donors' rights regarding child support:** Most state laws provide that a sperm donor has no parental rights or financial obligations vis-à-vis a child born from a sperm donation. These statutes are modeled on the original UPA (§5(b)). A prerequisite is that a licensed physician must perform the insemination. The rationale of these laws is to encourage sperm donation to infertile couples while protecting the sperm donor from subsequent parental responsibility.

However, in cases of *known* sperm donors, courts are divided about the recognition of the sperm donor's legal rights. Some courts *refuse to recognize* agreements in which a sperm donor agrees to relinquish his parental rights in return for the mother's agreement not to seek child support (reasoning that public policy precludes parents from bargaining away the child's entitlement to support). Other courts *uphold such agreements* based on a variety of rationales.

Example: Former intimate partners agree that the man will furnish sperm in an arrangement that reflects all the hallmarks of an anonymous sperm donation (i.e., the sample will be provided in a clinical setting and lacking any rights/obligations on the part of the sperm donor). Nonetheless, after the birth, the mother seeks child support. The trial court finds that the parties' oral agreement, in which the sperm donor relinquished his right to visitation in return for the mother's agreement not to seek child support, was unenforceable as against public policy, and orders the sperm donor to pay child support. The state supreme court reverses, holding that the agreement was enforceable based on the parties' intention, the fact that the artificial insemination took place in a clinical setting, the negotiation of the agreement outside a traditional romantic relationship, and the parties' behavior that conformed to the agreement for five years following the birth. *Ferguson v. McKiernan*, 940 A.2d 1236 (Pa. 2007).

4. **Parentage rights of same-sex partners:** Same-sex partners sometimes engage in disputes post-dissolution about the parental rights of the "second parent" (i.e., the non-biologically related parent) regarding children conceived by assisted reproductive technology.

   a. **Traditional view: Biological parent presumption:** Based on traditional doctrine, the second parent faced an insurmountable obstacle because the *biological parent presumption* trumped the custody rights of a non-biological/non-adoptive parent.

      Example: Hawkins and Grese are unmarried same-sex partners in a ten-year relationship. Grese becomes pregnant via artificial insemination and gives birth to B.G. The parties never marry and Hawkins never adopts B.G. The child is raised by both women until their relationship ends seven years later. The women informally share custody for an additional two years. Eventually, Grese terminates B.G.'s contact with Hawkins. The trial court awards the biological mother full custody of the child. Hawkins appeals, claiming that the trial court violated her Fourteenth Amendment liberty and equality rights by declining to recognize her status as a parent and perform a best interest determination. The appellate court affirms, reasoning that Hawkins failed to demonstrate special facts and circumstances sufficient to rebut the biological parent presumption. *Hawkins v. Grese*, 809 S.E.2d 441 (Va. Ct. App. 2018).

   b. **Evolving view:** The evolving view treats the second parent as a legal parent based on the belief that the traditional third-party framework is inappropriate when both same-sex partners act as parents and the child has a strong attachment to both.

      Example: Dr. Lisa Colon (gynecologist/obstetrician) and Victoria Adjmi (businesswoman) live together as intimate partners for 18 years. When they decide to start a family, both women are involved in the selection of the donor, the pregnancy, and birth. Colon gives birth to a baby girl ("Charlie"). Shortly afterwards, Colon signs a notarized document conferring sole custody rights to Adjmi in the event of her death; executes a will bequeathing her property jointly to Charlie and Adjmi; and executes a power of attorney giving Admi authority on all matters relating to Charlie's care. They sign a domestic partnership agreement (in Louisiana) providing that each would have joint custody and visitation rights in the event of a breakup. Adjmi never adopts the child. Seven years after Charlie's birth, they break up when Colon becomes romantically involved with another woman and limits Adjmi's role in Charlie's life. Adjmi asserts a constitutional right to custody of the child. The appellate court affirms the trial court finding that the child's best interests would be served by joint custody. The court reasons that the third-party statute is not well tailored to the situation of same-sex parents because of the inapplicability of the "substantial harm" standard with its presumption of unfitness of one or both parents; the fact that the second parent lived with the child and parented the child from birth; and the third party is more likely to be a co-parent from the child's perspective. *In re C.A.C.*, 231 So. 3d 58 (La. Ct. App. 2017).

C. **Disposition of frozen embryos at divorce:** Couples sometimes fight about the fate of their excess frozen embryos after the end of their relationship. Courts apply different approaches in these disputes.

Example: Mandy and Drake Rooks use IVF to conceive three children. Their agreement with the fertility clinic fails to specify the allocation of any remaining pre-embryos upon divorce. The agreement merely provided that "the disposition of our embryos will be part of the divorce/ dissolution decree paperwork." At the time of the divorce, Ms. Rooks wants to preserve the six remaining pre-embryos for future implantation, but Mr. Rooks wants them discarded. The trial court awards him the pre-embryos. The appellate court affirms. Mrs. Rooks appeals.

The state supreme court first surveys different state approaches: the intent-based approach contained in the parties' agreement; balancing the parties' interests; and the requirement of the parties' mutual contemporaneous consent. The court then determines that, because the parties' written agreement does not resolve the dispute in the event of divorce, the disposition of the embryos must be resolved by balancing the parties' interests. Reasoning that the lower courts considered "inappropriate factors" in balancing these parties' interests, the court reverses and remands the case with directions to balance these interests under a new suggested framework. Proposed factors include the intended use of the party seeking to preserve the disputed pre-embryos, the demonstrated physical ability (or inability) of that party to have biological children through other means, the parties' original reasons for pursuing IVF, the hardship for the person seeking to avoid becoming a genetic parent (including emotional, financial, or logistical considerations), and either spouse's bad faith or attempt to use pre-embryos as unfair leverage in divorce proceedings. *In re Marriage of Rooks*, 429 P.3d 579 (Colo. 2018).

D. Surrogacy

1. **Definition:** Surrogacy is a contractual arrangement whereby a woman agrees to be artificially inseminated with the sperm of a man whose partner is unable to conceive or bear a child, and then to surrender the ensuing child to the commissioning parents. Surrogacy is also used by gay couples who wish to have children. Early surrogacy arrangements involved surrogate mothers as egg donors. Scientific advances have led to increasing use of gestational surrogacy in which the carrying mother bears the child but contributes no genetic material.

2. **Traditional view:** According to the traditional view, surrogacy contracts are void because they violate public policy. Opponents contend that surrogacy agreements violate babyselling statutes, prohibitions on pre-birth consent to adoption, and determinations of custody based on the best- interests standard. In addition, opponents argue that surrogacy exploits women and commodifies children (i.e., devalues them by treating them as objects).

3. **Modern view:** States adopt a variety of approaches to surrogacy. Only about half the states have surrogacy statutes. Some states ban the practice. *See, e.g.,* N.Y. Dom. Rel. Law §§121-123. Other states permit surrogacy but subject it to regulation. *See, e.g.,* Fla. Stat. Ann. §63.213 (allowing "preplanned adoption agreement" by a "volunteer mother," with a right of rescission for her biological child).

   Example: A woman (D.B.) and her husband enter into a gestational surrogacy contract with J.F. (the intended and biological father). D.B. agrees to be inseminated with donor eggs and with semen from J.F. The agreement provides that, in return for $20,000 plus expenses, D.B. will terminate her parental rights upon the birth of any child(ren). A custody dispute follows the birth of triplets. J.F. sues D.B. for breach of contract. The trial court grants summary judgment for D.B. and her husband, concluding that the surrogacy contract violates public policy. The Pennsylvania Supreme Court disagrees, holding that no articulated state public policy bans surrogacy contracts. *J.F. v. D.B.*, 879 N.E.2d 740 (Ohio 2007).

4. **Theories to resolve disputes:** States have adopted several different theories to resolve surrogacy disputes.

   a. **Intent-based parentage:** Some courts follow the "intent-based parentage" approach in which the parties' intentions at the time of formation of their contract presumptively determine legal parenthood.

   Example: Husband and Wife enter into an agreement with another woman for her to carry their child. Wife donates an egg that is fertilized by Husband's sperm. The zygote is implanted in a surrogate mother (a co-worker of Wife) who agrees to relinquish her parental rights for $10,000. After the birth, the surrogate sues to assert her parental rights. The California Supreme Court holds that where artificial insemination results in a child not genetically related to the birth mother, the birth mother is not the child's mother. The court adopts an *intent-based theory of parenthood*: where a genetic mother and a birth mother both exist, the woman who intends to bring the child into being is the natural mother. The court rejects the birth mother's claim to a liberty interest in the right to care and companionship of her child, reasoning that that right can only be asserted to the detriment of the genetic mother's right. *Johnson v. Calvert*, 19 Cal. Rptr. 2d 494 (Cal. 1993).

   b. **Uniform Parentage Act: Revised:** Several states rely on applications of the Uniform Parentage Act to evaluate surrogacy agreements. UPA (2002), amending earlier versions of the Act, permitted surrogacy agreements (termed "gestational agreements") provided that the agreement was "validated" by procedures tantamount to a preconception adoption (including a home study and judicial approval) prior to making the intended parents the child's legal parents. A gestational agreement without validation was not enforceable. *See* UPA §§802, 803, 809 (2002). States were slow to adopt these UPA surrogacy provisions.

   Other features of the revised UPA include:

- payment is permitted to the carrying mother;

- the intended parents may be married or unmarried;

- the intended parents must both be parties to the gestational agreement;

- the agreement may not limit the right of the gestational mother to make decisions about her health or that of the fetus; and

- a party to a non-validated gestational agreement, who later refuses to adopt the resulting child, may be liable for support.

   For a court to validate a gestational agreement, the "intended parents" in a gestational surrogacy arrangement must prove their infertility and undergo a home study to confirm their fitness. UPA §§801(b), 803(b). The parties can terminate a validated gestational agreement only before the pregnancy begins or, alternatively, they can terminate it judicially for good cause.

   c. **Uniform Parentage Age (2017):** In 2017, the ULC amended the UPA and updated the surrogacy provisions in several ways. First, the new UPA removes gender-based language and recognizes intended parents without regard to sex or sexual orientation (thereby facilitating surrogacy by same-sex couples). Second, the new UPA liberalizes state enforcement of surrogacy contracts. Previously, many states treated surrogacy like adoption by requiring the intended parents to appear in court, requiring a home study, and allowing the birth mother the opportunity to withdraw consent after the child is born. However, UPA (2017) removes courts from parentage determinations, treating the intended parents as the legal parents provided that they follow designated procedures. UPA treats only traditional (genetic) surrogacy like an adoption by requiring prior judicial approval and providing for post-birth change of mind. Finally, UPA (2017) provides new eligibility requirements for gestational carriers and intended parents. *See* UPA §802 (2017).

d. **Common law approaches:** Some courts emphasize conduct (such as de facto parenthood or equitable estoppel) in determinations of parentage in surrogacy situations.

5. **Obstacles to parentage determinations:** Some obstacles stand in the path of the commissioning parents when they seek parentage determinations.

a. **Presumption of legitimacy:** The parties to a surrogacy agreement must overcome the presumption of legitimacy if the surrogate is married because the surrogate's husband is presumed to be the biological father of any children who are born during the marriage. The typical surrogacy contract, therefore, requires that the surrogate's husband be a party to the agreement and relinquish any parental rights he may have.

b. **Adoption consent statutes:** Another obstacle is the prohibition in adoption consent statutes of pre-birth consent. All states have laws that prohibit a mother from granting irrevocable consent to adoption before the child's birth. The purpose of such laws is to ensure that consent is knowing, voluntary, and without duress.

6. *Baby M.:* The most famous surrogacy case, *In re Baby M.*, holds that surrogacy contracts are unenforceable.

Example: Mr. and Mrs. Stern desire a child. Mr. Stern's parents are Holocaust survivors, so he has a keen desire to continue his lineage. Mrs. Stern, who has multiple sclerosis, fears that a pregnancy will worsen her condition. The couple enters into a surrogacy contract, with the help of a surrogacy organization, with Mary Beth Whitehead. For $10,000, Whitehead agrees to bear the child and terminate her parental rights. After the child's birth, Mrs. Whitehead refuses to relinquish the child. Mr. Stern seeks specific enforcement. The trial court holds that the surrogacy agreement is valid. The court terminates Mrs. Whitehead's parental rights and awards sole custody to Mr. Stern. On appeal, the New Jersey Supreme Court reverses.

The New Jersey Supreme Court holds that (1) the surrogate contract conflicted with laws prohibiting babyselling in adoption, laws requiring proof of parental unfitness or abandonment before termination of parental rights or adoption is granted, and laws making surrender of custody and consent to adoption revocable in private placement adoptions; (2) the surrogate contract conflicted with state public policy; and (3) the constitutional right of procreation did not entitle the biological father and his wife to custody of child. Nonetheless, the court concludes that the best-interests-of-child standard justified awarding custody to the father and his wife, and awards visitation rights to Whitehead. *In re Baby M*, 537 A.2d 1227 (N.J. 1988).

Note: The New Jersey legislature enacted a new law (New Jersey Gestational Carrier Act) in 2018 making gestational surrogacy contracts enforceable. According to the new law, intended parents can exercise their parental rights by obtaining a pre-birth parentage order.

7. **Methods of fixing parental status:** Some states provide for determinations of parentage status *prior* to the child's birth.

a. **Pre-birth stipulations and judgments:** Some courts permit a pre-birth determination of the legal status of the intended parents of a child born pursuant to a surrogacy agreement, especially if the surrogate mother is in agreement. However, other courts refuse to permit such pre-birth determination of the child's legal status.

Example: Marla and Steven Culliton, a married couple, enter into an agreement with Melissa Carroll for her to bear their child using the Cullitons' genetic material. Melissa becomes pregnant with twins. A few months later, the Cullitons seek a declaration of paternity and maternity, as well as a pre-birth order designating them as the twins' father and mother on their birth certificates. They were joined in the complaint with the gestational carrier. The family court dismissed their claim. On appeal, the Supreme Judicial Court held that the family court had authority to consider the merits of the relief sought. *Culliton v. Beth Israel Deaconess Medical Center*, 756 N.E.2d 1133 (Mass. 2001).

Example: Husband and Wife apply for a pre-birth declaration of parentage for the biological child of the husband and an anonymous ovum donor that was carried to term by a gestational carrier. The New Jersey Supreme Court denied the couple's request. The court thereby rejected the couple's constitutional arguments that (1) the wife had a fundamental right under the state constitution to create a legal parental relationship to the child at birth and (2) the state Parentage Act's recognition of parental status for an infertile husband, but not an infertile wife, violated the wife's equal protection principles under the state constitution. *In re T.J.S.*, 54 A.3d 263 (N.J. 2012).

b. **Birth certificates:** Some states permit the issuance of birth certificates in the names of the commissioning parents prior to birth for children who are born via surrogacy arrangements.

Example: A married couple contracts with a gestational carrier to bear their child using the couple's genetic material. However, when the child is born, the birth certificate lists the gestational carrier and her husband as the child's parents. The intended parents (joined by the gestational carrier and her husband) seek a declaration of parentage. The trial court enters an order declaring the father's paternity but concludes that it lacked statutory authority to declare maternity. On appeal, the state supreme court reverses, finding that the trial court had the statutory authority to declare maternity in favor of the genetic mother. After receiving the judgment of parentage, the parents were permitted to submit it to state officials with a request that the child's birth certificate be corrected. *Nolan v. LaBree*, 52 A.3d 923 (Me. 2012).

c. **Registration:** Other states permit the intended parents to establish parentage by registering the surrogacy agreement prior to the birth. *See, e.g.,* 750 Ill. Comp. Stat. 47/1-47/75.

8. **Divorce during surrogacy process:** The commissioning parents are responsible for the care and support of a child born via surrogacy even if the intended parents separate and divorce during the process.

Example: When Husband and Wife divorce, Wife petitions to establish herself as mother of their child (biologically unrelated to either) who was born by surrogacy. The appellate court holds that the intended parents are treated in law as the child's biological parents, and the husband is obligated to support the child because of his acquiescence to the child's conception by the gestational surrogacy arrangement. *In re Marriage of Buzzanca*, 72 Cal. Rptr. 2d 280 (Ct. App. 1998).

9. **International law:** England has long recognized private surrogacy agreements (permitting payment for expenses but not services), although it bans commercial surrogacy. Surrogacy Arrangements Act, 1985 (C. 49 Eng.). The legislation recognizes the pregnant woman as the mother but authorizes a court order treating the "applicants" as a child's parents. Applicants must be a married couple or cohabiting partners. The child must be conceived with the gametes of one of the applicants. Human Fertilisation and Embryology Act of 2008, ch. 22, §§33, 54 (U.K.).

In 1996, Israel adopted the Surrogate Motherhood Agreements Act, S.H. 1577, which permits compensation and commercial surrogacy, and provides for government approval of all surrogacy arrangements. Surrogacy in India has become a multi-million dollar industry since the practice was legalized in 2002.

E. Three or More Parents

1. **Traditional view:** Traditionally, the law recognized only two parents for a child — one parent of each gender.

2. **Modern approach:** Today, assisted reproductive technology makes possible multiple parenthood that separates biological parents from intended parents. For example, as many as five people are involved if the birth is commissioned by two intended parents who use donor games (donor eggs and sperm) and the child is born by an unrelated gestational carrier.

3. **State law reform:** Approximately a dozen states have laws that allow children to have more than two parents, although states take different approaches. Some state courts recognize third-parent adoptions. Other courts allow a third parent to have standing in custody and/or visitation disputes.

   Example: Two male spouses (David and Raymond) agree with a female friend (Samantha) to conceive and raise a child. Both men contribute sperm, although David is later determined to be the biological father. All parties select the midwife, attend medical appointments, are present for the birth, and select the child's name ("Matthew"). The three share childrearing responsibilities. After friction develops regarding the extent of the men's access, the men seek legal custody and shared parenting time. They request that Raymond (the non-biological parent) be granted standing to seek custody and visitation and ask the court to declare him the third legal parent. Samantha cross-petitions, seeking sole custody, but allowing the men reasonable visitation. She concedes that Raymond should have standing, but she opposes a declaration that he is a legal parent.

   The court grants Raymond standing but refuses to declare him a legal parent. The court bases its standing decision on the existence of the parties' tri-parenting agreement and legislative intent underlying the state custody statute applicable to nontraditional families. The court reasons that the marital presumption of legitimacy (which would bar Samantha's claim) is not relevant because it can be rebutted by the parties' tri-parenting agreement. Nonetheless, the court refuses to declare Raymond a legal parent, explaining that such a declaration lacks precedent and the issue is not properly before the court because no petition was filed for paternity. The court defers the issue of parentage for future consideration, such as if there were a need to make a child support award. *Raymond T. v. Samantha G.*, 74 N.Y.S.3d 730 (N.Y. Fam. Ct. 2018).

4. **Landmark California legislation:** California was the first state to pioneer landmark legislation in 2013 (dubbed the "third parent law") that allows children to have more than two legal parents. *See* Cal. Fam. Code §§3040(d), 7612(c). The bill was intended to address the situation

in which same-sex couples have a child with an opposite-sex biological parent as well as a response to a California case (below).

Example: Melissa breaks up with her female partner, Irene, and begins a relationship with a male partner Jesus. She becomes pregnant during their brief relationship. However, Melissa and Irene reconcile and later legally marry. Both women's names are placed on daughter Emily's birth certificate. About a year later, Melissa resumes contact with Jesus, and he begins to pay child support. At Jesus' request, Melissa takes the child to visit his family. When Irene is hospitalized and Melissa is in jail (for assaulting Irene), the state social services department takes Emily into custody. The Department of Social Services refuses to return Emily to Irene's care because she is unemployed and homeless. Jesus asks the court for custody as Emily's "parent."

The appellate court grants legal status to only two of these three parents. Despite Irene's lack of a parent-child relationship, the court finds that she is a presumed mother under the UPA because she and Melissa were married at the time of the child's birth. Additionally, the court finds that Jesus is the quasi-presumed father. Even though he never welcomed the child into his home, he paid some financial support and fostered a relationship between the child and his family. The appellate court remands for the lower court to resolve the competing parental presumptions: to determine "the presumption which on the facts is founded on the weightier considerations of policy and logic controls" by clear and convincing evidence. However, the court challenges the legislature to reconsider the two-parent rule, and the legislature responds with California's three parent law. *In re M.C.*, 123 Cal. Rptr.3d 856 (Cal. App. 2011).

5. **Uniform law:** UPA §613 (Alternative B) (2017) allows a state to choose in some circumstances to allow more than two parents. A court must find that the failure to recognize more than two parents would be detrimental to the child. The UPA explains that the finding of detriment does not require a finding of unfitness in the other parent(s). Among the relevant factors in the finding of detriment, the court shall consider the harm if the child is removed from a stable placement with a person who served as a psychological parent for a substantial period.

F. **Legal Regulation of Sperm banks**

1. **Disclosure of medical information:** Donor-conceived adult children are lobbying for increased government regulation of fertility centers. In 2018, two states (Washington and Vermont) first required clinics to collect donors' medical history and to disclose that information to resulting children.

2. **Federal law:** The Food and Drug Administration rejected a petition from a donor offspring group that sought to limit the number of births per donor, mandate reporting of donor-conceived births, and require donors to provide post-conception medical updates. According to an FDA spokesperson, such oversight exceeds the FDA's mission which is limited to screening donors for communicable diseases.

3. **Model law:** The ABA adopted a model act in 2019 that regulates fertility agencies but does not go as far as many in the donor-conceived community wish. *See* ABA Model Act Governing Assisted Reproductive Technology Agencies (2019). The Act requires fertility agencies to obtain a license and sets forth affirmative duties to maintain that license (such as not giving medical or legal advice, providing clients an easy-to-read description of their services, maintaining client confidentiality, and requiring funds be held in an escrow account). The Act also specifies the repercussions for noncompliance, including fines of up to $25,000 for any violation. The Act emphasizes the importance of engaging in fair practices.

4. **State laws:** Several states have criminalized *fertility fraud* by fertility physicians who fathered children with women who did not consent to being inseminated in this manner. The misconduct consists of medical malpractice and a violation of medical ethics (i.e., a conflict of interest in the physician-client relationship). One fertility specialist (Dr. Donald Cline) was found guilty of obstruction of justice for lying to investigators about whether he inseminated patients using his own sperm. Cline used his own sperm to father at least 61 children in the 1970s and 1980s in his fertility practice.

5. **International regulation:** Some countries impose far more oversight on fertility service providers than the United States. For example, the United Kingdom created a national agency (Human Fertilisation and Embryology Authority) in 1990 to oversee fertility clinics.

Quiz Yourself on *ASSISTED REPRODUCTIVE TECHNOLOGY*

102. Sarah, an unmarried woman, decides to use a surrogate after Sarah discovers that she is unable to bear a child. She locates a gestational surrogate (Monica), a sperm donor, and an egg donor. She executes a "Surrogacy Agreement" with Monica. The agreement provides that Sarah is to be the intended mother, Monica will relinquish all rights to the child upon its birth, and all children born as a result of the Surrogacy Agreement will be the children of Sarah. Monica signs the agreement after stating that she sought independent counsel. When the child is born, it has serious medical problems. Sarah gives the child up for adoption to a third party. Monica petitions the court to establish maternity and to obtain custody rights. Will she succeed?

   _____

103. Serena and Courtney are same-sex partners in a committed relationship who live in the jurisdiction of Blackacre. Serena is a successful accountant, Courtney is an elementary school teacher. Several years later, they decide to have a child. The women determine that Courtney will go to the sperm bank and undergo IVF. They also decide that both women will serve as the parents of any ensuing children. Courtney becomes pregnant and gives birth to a baby girl, Polly. When Polly is seven, the couple separates. Serena files for visitation, and Courtney files for child support from Serena. Will Serena and Courtney, respectively, prevail? _____

104. Same facts as above. Before Polly's birth, Serena and Courtney apply to the Blackacre family court to obtain an order that requires the inclusion of both their names on the prospective child's birth certificate. Will they be successful? _____

Answers

102. Perhaps. Monica might claim the invalidity of the Surrogacy Agreement (i.e., that it violates public policy) and then try to establish maternity by showing that she gave birth to the child. In addition, pursuant to the revised Uniform Parentage Act (which some courts have held to be applicable to determinations of maternity as well as paternity), Monica can show that a court did not validate the Surrogacy Agreement, thereby making the gestational agreement unenforceable. On the other hand,

under general contract principles, Sarah can argue that the gestational agreement is a valid contract, consisting of an offer, acceptance, and consideration, and is not unconscionable or fraudulent. The Surrogacy Agreement thus constitutes a "declaration of maternity," equivalent to a declaration of paternity, and should be upheld, she would argue. If so, Sarah would have parental rights and would have the right to relinquish the child to a third party for adoption.

103.   Yes. The court should award Serena visitation and should award Courtney child support. Serena served as Polly's mother for seven years. Therefore, Serena's parentage claim would be successful based either on equitable estoppel principles (her conduct demonstrated that she acted as Polly's mother) or the UPA (she took Polly into her home and held her out as her daughter). Further, Serena could argue that the couple clearly intended to have the baby together and to co-parent her. After seven years of support, care, and building a parent/child relationship, Serena is likely to get visitation. Under *Elisa B.*, Courtney should be awarded child support from Serena. Courtney could argue that Serena acted as Polly's legal "parent" under the equitable estoppel doctrine or the UPA. Further, as *Elisa B.* explains, a child may have two parents, both of whom are women. Because Serena supported Courtney's desire to become pregnant and agreed to raise any ensuing child, Serena should be liable for child support.

104.   Probably. Some states permit the issuance of birth certificates in the names of the commissioning parents prior to the birth of children who are born via assisted reproduction. In these states, the family court has the authority to assume jurisdiction to declare the women's parentage and then order the inclusion of names on the child's birth certificate. The only question might be whether the court can declare that both women are mothers. Case law exists, however, that holds that a court has statutory authority to declare maternity in favor of a child born of assisted reproduction.

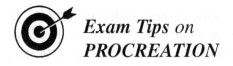

Exam Tips on
PROCREATION

☞ *Abortion* is a frequently tested family law issue. First, identify and explain the *nature* of the abortion restriction. For example, does the restriction pertain to *abortion procedures, funding, TRAP laws, clinic access,* or **medication abortions**? Clarify whether the restriction applies to abortions prior to, or after, the point of *viability* because different rules may apply given the stage of fetal development (see discussion below).

☞ Point out whether the restriction is based on *state or federal law*. Remember that sometimes both may be involved in a particular question (e.g., clinic access is regulated by federal and state law).

☞ Identify the appropriate *standard of review* to use in evaluating the constitutionality of the stated governmental restriction. *Strict scrutiny* applies to infringements of fundamental rights, and such rights may be infringed only if the restriction is necessary to achieve a compelling interest. *Fundamental rights* include: contraception, abortion (under *Roe v. Wade*, but not after *Casey*), the right to engage in adult consensual sexual conduct (as well as previously studied rights such as the right to marry and to maintain family relationships). On the other hand, if none of these fundamental rights is involved, then the appropriate level of scrutiny may be *rational basis* (unless gender discrimination is involved, which calls for an intermediate level of scrutiny) or the *undue-burden test* for abortion restrictions (see *infra*). Mention the source of the constitutional right to an abortion.

☞ Remember that the above analysis may require consideration of both means and ends. That is, be sure to identify the ***end*** (what the restriction is trying to accomplish) and then determine whether the state interest is legitimate, important, or compelling. Then, identify the chosen ***means*** of achieving that objective (how the restriction accomplishes its aim).

☛ Determine also whether the restriction imposes an ***undue burden*** on the woman's decision to have an abortion. According to *Casey*, regulations that impose an "undue burden" on the woman's abortion decision will be subject to ***strict scrutiny***. An undue burden is a ***substantial obstacle***. Because the Supreme Court gave little guidance on what constitutes a substantial obstacle, each case must be determined on its facts.

☛ Discuss whether the restriction attaches to a particular stage of fetal development. For example, does the restriction apply pre- or post-***viability***? Before viability, *Roe v. Wade* held that women had a fundamental right to an abortion. *Casey* later changed the rule so that only if a state law imposes an ***undue burden***, it will be unconstitutional. ***Post-viability***, the state may ***regulate and even proscribe*** abortion (to promote its interest in human life) except where necessary for the preservation of the mother's life or health (although *Gonzales v. Carhart* casts doubt on the continued need for a health exception). Recall that *Casey*'s seeming condonation of state restrictions on abortion "throughout pregnancy" undermines *Roe*'s heightened protection of abortion during the first trimester.

   ☞ Clarify ***whose rights*** are being restricted. Does the restriction infringe upon the ***woman's***, ***husband's***, or ***minor's rights*** regarding abortion? Remember that different rules apply to each participant in the abortion decision. *Roe v. Wade* and *Casey* protected a ***woman's*** right to an abortion. ***Danforth*** provided that the state may not require ***spousal consent*** prior to an abortion.

   ☞ Minors' rights may be curtailed more than adult women's rights (***Bellotti***) because of the minor's vulnerability, inability to make informed decisions, and the importance of the parental role. Thus, a state may require ***parental consent and/or notification*** prior to a minor's abortion, provided that the statute offers an alternative procedure. If a minor does not wish to (or cannot) obtain parental consent or notification, then determine if the statute provides for an alternative such as a judicial bypass proceeding. At that proceeding, the minor may show that she is either mature enough to make the decision herself, or, if she cannot make such a showing of maturity, that an abortion, nonetheless, would be in her best interests. Apply these tests to the minor's case.

☛ Issues involving ***contraception*** are less frequently tested. If the constitutionality of a restriction on contraception is at issue, be sure to identify whether the restriction implicates ***due process*** or ***equal protection*** rights. Apply the relevant level of scrutiny. (Review the discussion *supra* about strict scrutiny and rational basis review.)

☛ Remember that restrictions on contraception implicate fundamental rights and therefore require strict scrutiny. Identify the source of constitutional protection (e.g., the substantive due process notion of "family privacy," which is encompassed in the liberty aspect of the Fourteenth Amendment). Mention that the right of ***access to contraception*** does ***not*** depend upon ***marital status***. That is, both unmarried and married persons have a constitutional right to determine whether or not they wish to bear a child (based on *Griswold*, *Eisenstadt*).

☛ ***Surrogacy contracts*** are another commonly tested area. Determine threshold issues: ***who*** has breached the agreement (i.e., the surrogate or the couple); the ***nature of the breach*** (e.g., the surrogate refuses to relinquish the child, the couple refuses to accept the child); and the ***type of surrogacy*** (i.e., if the gestational mother is also the egg donor, she may have greater rights).

☛ A major issue is the ***validity*** of the contract. Point out the ***different approaches***: the traditional view (by case law or statute) holds that the surrogacy agreements are unenforceable. However, an increasing number of jurisdictions permit surrogacy subject to state regulation. Mention the different versions of the Uniform Parentage Act. The 2002 version authorizes gestational surrogacy agreements subject to court approval. The 2017 version dispenses with court approval for gestational surrogacy contracts (thereby recognizing the intended parents as legal parents) if the intended parents follow designated procedures. In addition, the recent version facilitates gestational surrogacy contracts by same-sex couples.

☞ In terms of validity issues, remember that many courts have held that surrogacy contracts violate public policy and babyselling statutes. Even if the court rules that the contract is invalid, however, the court must still decide the ***custody of the child***. Courts often resort to the best-interests-of-the-child standard, which involves a determination of all relevant factors.

☞ Be sure to note whether the surrogate is ***married***. Her marital status may raise parentage issues regarding who is the child's legal father. Specifically, her marital status may serve as an obstacle to the father's determination of his parentage. In such a case, it will be necessary to discuss and apply the presumption of legitimacy: The husband of a married woman is presumed to be the father of her child. To rebut this presumption (in favor of the commissioning father), discuss the theory of "intent-based parenthood" (*Johnson v. Calvert*).

☛ Finally, be sure to discuss and apply ***relevant legislation*** (including model legislation and uniform laws) on the subject of gestational surrogacy.

CHAPTER 9

THE PARENT-CHILD-STATE RELATIONSHIP IN SPECIAL CONTEXTS

ChapterScope ━━

This chapter explores the parent-child-state relationship in special contexts (tort, contract, property, education, and medical care). Here are a few of the key principles covered in this chapter:

- At common law, *parents* were *not liable* for their children's torts.

- Although *children are liable* for their own torts, they are subject to a *different standard of care* than adults.

- At common law, the contracts of a minor are *voidable*. If a party tried to enforce a contract against the minor, the minor could *disaffirm* the contract (i.e., assert a *defense of infancy*).

- A parent had a common-law right to a child's *services and earnings*.

- A child may inherit *property*, although the court may appoint a guardian to manage that property.

- The *emancipation doctrine* permits a child the right to dispose of his or her own earnings.

- The U.S. Supreme Court significantly extended the contours of the constitutional *right of family privacy* first mentioned in the context of education.

- School students do not possess the same *First Amendment rights* as adults.

- School students do not possess the same *Fourth Amendment rights* as adults. They may be subject to *random drug testing* and searches based on *reasonable suspicion* rather than probable cause.

- At common law, only a parent could *consent to medical treatment* for a child. Today, some state laws provide that minors may sometimes consent, themselves, to their medical treatment.

━━

I. TORTS

A. Children's liability: Traditional rule: Children are generally liable for their intentional and negligent torts.

   1. Standard of care: Although children are liable for their torts, they are subject to a different standard of care than for adults.

      a. Traditional rule: The traditional rule takes into account the minor's *age and experience*.

      Example: If the actor is a child, the standard of conduct to which he must conform to avoid being negligent is that of a reasonable person of like age, intelligence, and experience under like circumstances. Restatement (Second) of Torts §283A (1965).

      b. Modern rule: The modern rule continues to take into account the minor's age and experience but provides for explicit exceptions for children who are younger than five years old and those who are engaging in an adult activity.

According to the Restatement (Third) of Torts §10:

(a) A child's conduct is negligent if it does not conform to that of a reasonably careful person of the same age, intelligence, and experience, except as provided in Subsection (b) or (c).

(b) A child less than five years of age is incapable of negligence.

(c) The special rule in Subsection (a) does not apply when the child is engaging in a dangerous activity that is characteristically undertaken by adults.

2. **Contributory negligence:** Contributory negligence by the plaintiff is normally a bar to recovery despite the defendant's negligence. Jurisdictions adopt different approaches when the contributorily negligent plaintiff is a child.

   a. **Majority rule:** The majority rule (sometimes called the "Massachusetts Rule") considers the relevance of age in the standard of care for a child's contributory negligence. Thus, a child's capacity to be contributorily negligent depends on age, intelligence, and experience in comparison with other children in similar circumstances.

   b. **Minority rule:** A minority of jurisdictions adopt a rebuttable *presumption* based on age, holding that children below a certain age (e.g., age seven) cannot be held to be contributorily negligent.

   Example: Parents of a 13-year-old boy (Kodi) bring a wrongful-death suit against the school. During basketball practice, Kodi blacks out. His mother later instructs the coach that Kodi should not participate in running or strenuous activity, but that he can "walk through plays." Two days later, during practice, the coach requires the players to perform a running drill. During the drill, Kodi dies. The school district argues that Kodi's negligence (in running when he had been told not to do so) contributed to his death. The state supreme court affirms a judgment for the parents, recognizing a rebuttable presumption that children between the ages of 7 and 14 are incapable of contributory negligence. *Clay City Consolidated School Corp. v. Timberman*, 918 N.E.2d 292 (Ind. 2009).

   c. **Modern view:** The Restatement (Third) of Torts goes further, adopting an *irrebuttable* presumption holding that the extreme youth of a child (i.e., below age five) precludes a finding of contributory negligence. Restatement (Third) of Torts §10(b).

B. **Exception to rule of liability: Children's conduct of adult activities:** The modern view abrogates an age-based standard of care when a minor is performing an adult activity (driving a motor vehicle, boat, etc.). In such cases, the adult "reasonable person" standard is applicable. Restatement (Third) of Torts §10(c).

C. **Parents' liability for children's torts:** Although parents were not vicariously liable at common law for the negligent or intentional torts of their children, they may be liable in certain circumstances today by statute. *See, e.g.,* Cal. Civ. Code §1714.1 (imputing liability to parents for minors' willful misconduct that results in injury or property damage).

Other exceptions to the general rule include situations in which: (1) a parent employs his or her child, (2) a parent permits a child to use a dangerous instrumentality (negligent entrustment), or (3) a parent has knowledge of the child's similar acts or disposition and fails to warn a third party (negligent supervision).

Example: Christopher P., a 13-year-old boy, hits a neighbor child (Danielle) in the eye with his paintball gun. Christopher's parents knew that he had a paintball gun and permitted its use. Danielle's parents bring a personal injury action against Christopher's parents. The trial court holds that Christopher's parents are liable for Danielle's injuries under the doctrine of negligent entrustment. The court reasons that a parent owes a duty to protect third parties from harm that is clearly foreseeable from a child's improvident use of a dangerous instrument when the parents are aware of its use. Here the parents knew their son was using a paintball gun, which was an illegal act under N.Y. Penal Law (possessing an air gun while being under age 16), and assisted the illegal activity by enabling him to purchase ammunition. *Danielle A. v. Christopher P.*, 776 N.Y.S.2d 446 (Sup. Ct. 2004).

(The above case illustrates the imposition of parental liability based on statute, as well as the tort of negligent entrustment.)

Quiz Yourself on *TORTS*

105. Andy is the eight-year-old son of divorced parents. Andy has attention-deficit hyperactivity disorder (ADHD) (i.e., he has difficulty sitting still, listening, and paying attention). One day, while playing with a lighter, he starts a fire at his maternal grandfather's house. The garage sustains major property damage. Andy's custodial father was not present at the time of the incident. The maternal grandfather and the grandfather's insurance company file a complaint against Andy's father for negligence. Will Andy's father be liable for property damage caused by Andy? _____

106. Same basic facts as above. Andy's grandfather's insurance company now files a complaint against *Andy* for negligence. Will Andy be liable? _____

107. Jeannette and her husband Pearce are fishing from their boat on a Minnesota lake. Sam, a 12-year-old boy, is operating a boat with an outboard motor. Because of Sam's inexperience, he crosses too closely behind Jeannette and Pearce's boat. Jeannette feels a jerk on her fishing line. The reel hits the side of the boat, breaks, and a fragment flies into Jeannette's eye. She sues Sam, asserting that he was negligent. The trial judge instructs the jury to modify the traditional standard of negligence to take into account Sam's age, intelligence, and experience under the circumstances. Jeannette appeals a jury verdict for the defendant, arguing that the trial court erred in its instruction. Will she prevail? _____

Answers

105. No. At common law, parents were not liable for the torts of their child. Parental liability arises, however, if the child's injury is the foreseeable consequence of the parent's negligent act. Because it was not foreseeable that Andy would cause a fire by playing with a lighter (this was the first instance in which his acts caused a fire), the child's father did not owe a duty to the grandfather and his insurer on the claim of negligent parental supervision.

106. No. Children have limited liability for acts of negligence. The traditional rule takes into account the minor's age, intelligence, and experience. Andy, an eight-year-old child who has ADHD, cannot be held to the same standard of care as an average eight-year-old child. The insurance company will not prevail in imputing liability to Andy for negligence in starting the fire at his grandfather's house.

107. Yes. The traditional rule dictates that the minor's age and experience should be taken into account in applying the relevant standard of care. Applying this rule might well absolve Sam of liability based on his status as a novice. However, the modern view abrogates the traditional standard of care where a minor is performing an adult activity. Because Sam was engaged in an adult activity (driving a motorboat), he should be held to the adult standard of care. His activities exposed others to significant hazard.

II. CONTRACTS

A. **Common-law rule:** At common law, the contracts of a minor are *voidable*. According to the general rule, when a minor entered into a contract with another party, if the other party attempted to enforce that contract, the minor could *disaffirm* the contract. That is, the minor could assert a *defense of infancy*. The minor's disaffirmance could occur at any time during his or her minority or even within a reasonable time after he or she reached majority.

B. **Majority rule:** Most jurisdictions still follow the common-law rule permitting minors to disaffirm their contracts.

C. **Policy:** The policy behind permitting minors to disaffirm contracts is to protect minors from overreaching by adults and from their own immaturity.

D. **Modern view: Special contexts.** Some courts and legislatures change the common-law rule in limited situations (e.g., the entertainment industry).

   Example: Brooke Shields, a well-known actress, was hired as a ten-year-old model. She was required to pose nude in a bathtub for *Playboy* magazine. The photographs were intended for use in that publication. When the plaintiff reaches majority, she learns that several photos appeared in another magazine. She commences an action in contract and tort to prevent further use of the photos. A New York statute confers upon a minor's parent or guardian the right to make binding contracts for the minor. The court holds that Ms. Shields may not disaffirm the contract executed by her mother. The court reasons that, although at common law a minor could disaffirm his or her written consent or a contract executed by another on his or her behalf, the state legislature abrogated the minor's common-law right to disaffirm. The court explains that the statute is intended to bring certainty to an important industry that employs minors. The dissent argues that the state's interest in child protection should prevail over concerns for commercialism. *Shields v. Gross*, 448 N.E.2d 108 (N.Y. Ct. App. 1983).

E. **Modern view: Restitution of benefits.** The modern view (adopting the minority rule) requires minors to make restitution of any benefits that they received under their voided contracts. Restatement (Third) of Restitution & Unjust Enrichment §33 (2011).

Quiz Yourself on
CONTRACTS

108. Stephen Barry leaves royal service after serving as Prince Charles's valet for 12 years. Barry desires to publish a book about his experiences with the royal family. He accepts a lucrative book contract even though he signed a pledge of confidentiality at the time he began employment at age 17. When the royal family sues him for breach of contract, he claims that his contract with the royal family is not binding. Will he prevail? _____

Answer

108. Yes. At common law, a minor could disaffirm his contracts with another party, i.e., assert a defense of infancy, if the minor was sued. Because Stephen Barry executed his contract of royal service while he was still a minor (age 17), he should be able to disaffirm the contract.

III. PROPERTY

A. Earnings

1. **Common-law rule:** A parent had a common-law right to a child's services and earnings. Many modern statutes incorporate this common-law rule. *See, e.g.*, Cal. Fam. Code §7500.

   Example: A creditor obtains a judgment against Claude Kreigh, the father of three daughters. The sheriff seizes and sells 15 sheep in partial satisfaction of the judgment. Before the sale, the plaintiffs-daughters contend that some of the sheep constitute their property (i.e., lambs that were fed and raised by them or, perhaps, even the lambs of those lambs). The plaintiffs sue the creditor for conversion. The creditor appeals a judgment for the plaintiffs. Affirming, the court reasons that, according to the common-law rule (announced by Blackstone), only the services and earnings belong to the parent. Any other property belongs to the child. Thus, the execution of the judgment levied on the sheep did not affect the children's title to the sheep. *Kreigh v. Cogswell*, 21 P.2d 831 (Wyo. 1933).

2. **Emancipation:** *Emancipation* is the doctrine that signifies the child's release from parental control. The doctrine confers upon a child the right to dispose of his or her own earnings. At common law, emancipation occurred in cases of a minor's marriage or military service. Today, many jurisdictions have codified the doctrine. Some state statutes also permit emancipation in cases of minors who live independently from their parents with or without their consent. *See, e.g.,* Conn. Gen. Stat. §46b-150b.

B. Inheritance

1. **Traditional rule:** A child may inherit property (e.g., stocks, bonds, cash, real estate). At common law, if a child inherited property or was given property that required active management, a

court appointed a "guardian of the child's person *and estate*." Today, many states follow the same rule.

2. Guardianship and inheritance

a. **Definition:** A guardian may be of two types: "a guardian of the person" (who is charged with personal decision making) or "a guardian of the estate or property" (who is charged with asset management). In the event that a child inherits property (e.g., from a grandparent), a court may appoint one of the child's parents as the guardian of the child's estate.

b. **Problems with guardianship:** Guardianships have several shortcomings. First, a guardianship is expensive to administer because judicial supervision and approval is required for acts of the guardian. Expenses include court costs, attorneys' fees, the posting of a bond, and annual accountings. Second, the powers of a guardian (e.g., power of investment) are limited. Third, guardianship terminates at the age of majority (typically age 18), which may result in the release of considerable property to an inexperienced youth.

3. Inheritance rights of nonmarital children

a. **Traditional rule:** Traditionally, nonmarital children could inherit by intestate succession only from their mother. (Intestate succession occurs when a decedent dies without a valid will.)

b. **Modern approach:** The modern approach eliminates differences in the treatment of nonmarital versus marital children for succession purposes. Both the U.S. Supreme Court and the Uniform Parentage Act (UPA) liberalized the rights of nonmarital children in the 1970s.

Example: Gordon dies intestate at age 28 as the result of a homicide. He leaves surviving a nonmarital child, Deta Mona Trimble. Prior to Gordon's death, the child's mother, Jessie Trimble, prevailed in a paternity suit and obtained court-ordered child support. Upon Gordon's death, Trimble petitions to administer his estate and to determine the heirs. The court excludes Deta Mona from succession based on a provision of the Illinois Probate Code that provides that a nonmarital child may inherit from her mother but only from her father if two conditions are met: the parents marry (following her birth) and the father acknowledges the child as his. The mother challenges that the statute violates equal protection. The U.S. Supreme Court agrees. The Court determines that the statute has only the "most attenuated relationship" to the asserted goal of promoting legitimate family relationships. And, the statute is not reasonably related to the second goal regarding the efficient disposition of property at death (although such a purpose is legitimate). Therefore, the legislature's chosen means of overcoming the problems posed by proof of paternity do not justify the statute. *Trimble v. Gordon,* 430 U.S. 762, 767 (1977).

Example: Mario openly acknowledges his nonmarital child, Robert, as his son and provides him with a written acknowledgment of paternity by granting him permission to marry when Robert is underage. When Mario dies, Robert attempts to claim a share of Mario's estate. A New York statute requires a paternity establishment during the putative father's lifetime in order for a nonmarital child to inherit intestate from his father. The son challenges the constitutionality of the statute. The U.S. Supreme Court upholds the statute, finding that, unlike the statute in *Trimble, supra*, the New York statute survives rational basis review. The Court distinguishes *Trimble* on two grounds: (1) New York law does not have as its purpose the encouragement of legitimate family relationships and (2) the New York statute is more limited than the Illinois statute (i.e., the Illinois requirement of marriage, in addition to acknowledgment of paternity, was simply too strict). *Lalli v. Lalli,* 439 U.S. 259 (1978).

Note: The Court's underlying concern was proof of paternity. The Court was satisfied with the proof of paternity in *Trimble* (judicial declaration) but not in *Lalli* (informal written acknowledgment).

    c. Uniform Parentage Act: The Uniform Parentage Act (UPA) began the trend of expanding the rights of nonmarital children. Many states have adopted the original 1973 version of the UPA with its presumptions for identifying the father of a nonmarital child. One method was by the father's conduct. Specifically, UPA §4(a)(4) (1973) created a presumption of paternity if "while the child is under the age of minority," the parent "receives the child into his home and openly holds out the child as his natural child."

    The revised versions of the UPA (2000, 2002, and 2017) reaffirm the original policy of equal treatment of children regardless of parents' marital status. The 2017 revision affirms equal treatment for children of same-sex couples.

4. Inheritance rights of posthumously conceived children: The U.S. Supreme Court held that the right of posthumously conceived children to Social Security survivors' benefits depends on the children's eligibility to inherit property under *state intestacy law*. *See Astrue v. Capato*, 566 U.S. 541 (2012) (discussed in Chapter 8).

5. Methods of holding property for a minor: When a minor receives a gift, the minor's property typically is held in the name of a guardian (*supra*), or in a trust, or registered in the name of a custodian under the Uniform Transfers to Minors Act.

    a. Trusts: A minor may be the beneficiary of a trust in which property is held in trust for the minor by a trustee. The trustee has a fiduciary responsibility to manage, invest, and spend the proceeds for the minor consistent with the terms of the trust instrument. Although an inter vivos trust, unlike a guardianship, does not necessitate the expense and inconvenience of judicial supervision, a trust may involve attorneys' fees to create it.

    b. Uniform Transfers to Minors Act: Virtually all states have some form of the Uniform Transfers to Minors Act (UTMA). These statutory provisions permit certain property to be registered in the name of a *custodian* who has broad powers to manage the property without court supervision. Although not as flexible as a trust, gifts based on UTMA are more easily transferred and the assets more easily administered. UTMA is an extension of the Uniform Gift to Minors Act which was limited to the transfer of securities.

Quiz Yourself on
PROPERTY

109. Grandma ("Granny") Smith is delighted when her first grandson Max is born. She wants to welcome Max into the world with a substantial gift of $5,000 in shares of a mutual fund to be used for Max's college education. Granny does not want to subject Max's parents to the problems of court supervision relating to the gift, nor does she want to entail the expense of establishing an inter vivos trust with Max as the beneficiary. How would you advise Granny to proceed?

Answer

109. Granny should be advised to establish a gift for Max under the Uniform Transfers to Minors Act (UTMA). Granny's jurisdiction, similar to most states, probably has enacted a version of UTMA. This uniform statute would allow Granny to purchase the shares in the mutual fund and to have those shares registered in the name of a qualified custodian (probably Max's mother or father). The custodian then could hold that property until Max reaches age 18 or 21 (as required by state statute) or could sell the property so long as the proceeds are used for Max's benefit.

IV. EDUCATION

A. **Parents' right to control the upbringing of their children:** In a trilogy of cases, the U.S. Supreme Court announces a principle of enormous constitutional significance. Parents have a constitutionally protected right to control the upbringing of their children. These cases arose in the context of parents' right to dictate the form of their children's education.

The cases establish the constitutional underpinnings of a right to family privacy (a private realm in which the family is protected from state intervention). These cases, thereby, constitute the genesis of the right to privacy that the Supreme Court subsequently extended to contraception, abortion, etc.

Example: A schoolteacher, who teaches reading in German in the Zion Parochial School, is convicted of violating a Nebraska law that prohibits the teaching of foreign languages to children below the 8th grade. The children's parents (members of a German-speaking religious community) strongly desire that their children be educated in German. The state argues that the statute (which was enacted during World War I in response to anti-German sentiment) is intended to promote civic development. The state supreme court affirms the conviction. The U.S. Supreme Court holds that the statute is unconstitutional because it lacks a rational basis. The Court reasons that, although the object of the legislation is legitimate, the means exceed the proper limitations on the power of the state and conflict with the defendant's Fourteenth Amendment right to due process (i.e., liberty to engage in his occupation) and the parents' rights to control the education of their children. *Meyer v. Nebraska*, 262 U.S. 390 (1923).

Example: An Oregon statute requires parents of children between the ages of 8 and 16 to send their children to public schools or be subject to criminal liability. Two Oregon private schools (the Society of Sisters and the Hill Military Academy) argue that the statute interferes with their ability to engage in their chosen business and constitutes a deprivation of their property without due process. The trial court holds the statute unconstitutional as a deprivation of the schools' property rights and also an infringement on the parents' constitutionally protected "liberty" to direct the education of their children. The U.S. Supreme Court affirms. Relying on *Meyer v. Nebraska*, the Court concludes that the statute infringes on the defendants' property rights and unreasonably interferes with the liberty of parents and guardians to direct the upbringing and education of children. *Pierce v. Soc'y of Sisters*, 268 U.S. 510 (1925).

Example: Members of the Amish Mennonite Church challenge the constitutionality of Wisconsin's compulsory attendance law that requires them to send their children to school until age 16. Parents of two Amish children, ages 14 and 15, refuse to send their children to public school any longer.

The parents' decision is based on their religious beliefs that school attendance will expose their children to negative influences and threaten the survival of the Amish community, and a desire to educate the children by informal vocational training. The parents argue that the compulsory attendance law violates their First and Fourteenth Amendment rights. The parents appeal their convictions for violating the statute. The U.S. Supreme Court holds the statute unconstitutional under the First and Fourteenth Amendments. The Court reasons that the state interest in preparing citizens for a democratic way of life is not sufficient to override the Amish parents' interests in the free exercise of their religion. The Court finds that the additional two years of schooling required by the statute will not advance appreciably the state's interest. *Wisconsin v. Yoder*, 406 U.S. 205 (1972).

B. Minors' First Amendment rights

1. **Political speech:** In the civil rights era of the 1960s, the U.S. Supreme Court recognizes that students have a right to freedom of expression in the context of political speech. However, students do not possess the *same* First Amendment rights as adults. Students' exercise of the right to free speech is subject to limitation based on the possibility of disruption of school authority or invasion of the rights of others.

   Example: Three students (a 15-year-old boy, a 16-year-old boy, and a 13-year-old girl) wear arm bands to their respective schools to publicize their objection to the war in Vietnam. The various schools learn of the plan and adopt a policy that students who refuse to remove arm bands will be suspended until the students agree to return without the arm bands. The youths wear the arm bands and are suspended. They petition for an injunction restraining the school officials from disciplining them. The district court upholds the constitutionality of the action as reasonable to promote school discipline. The Court of Appeal for the Eighth Circuit affirms. The U.S. Supreme Court reverses. The Court holds that students, like teachers, possess First Amendment rights. ("It can hardly be argued that either students or teachers shed their constitutional rights to freedom of speech or expression at the schoolhouse gate.") However, the state has an interest in proscribing misconduct in the schools. In order to justify the prohibition of a particular expression of opinion, the conduct must *materially and substantially interfere with the requirements of appropriate discipline in the operation of the school or invade the rights of others.* Here, the students' wearing of arm bands neither interrupted school activities nor intruded in school affairs. *Tinker v. Des Moines Indep. Community Sch. Dist.*, 393 U.S. 503, 506 (1969).

2. **Free speech in the context of school-sponsored and school-approved activities:** Following *Tinker*, the Court circumscribes students' rights to freedom of expression in other contexts (i.e., school-sponsored newspapers, school-approved rallies for patriotic purposes).

   Example: High school journalism students desire to publish articles in the school newspaper, *Spectrum*, concerning teen pregnancy and the impact of divorce on children. In accordance with school practice, the journalism teacher submits the issue of the newspaper containing the stories to the school principal for prior approval. The principal censors the articles, believing that the content is inappropriate for younger students. The principal then deletes the pages (not just the articles) on which the articles appear. The students contend that the principal's action violates their First Amendment rights. The U.S. Supreme Court holds that school officials do not violate students' First Amendment rights when they exercise control of the content of student speech in *school-sponsored* activities, provided that the school officials' actions are reasonably related to legitimate pedagogical goals. Here, the Court reasons that the principal's decision was reasonable in light of his concerns with the protection of privacy of other students. The Court distinguishes *Tinker*, saying that this case concerns whether the school must affirmatively *promote* student speech (i.e., in school-sponsored activities), whereas *Tinker* concerns whether educators must *tolerate* student speech.

In a strongly worded dissent, Justice Brennan (joined by Justices Marshall and Blackmun) maintains that the principal violated the students' First Amendment rights. Applying *Tinker*, the dissent reasons that the student expression neither disrupted school work nor invaded the rights of others. *Hazelwood Sch. Dist. v. Kuhlmeier*, 484 U.S. 260 (1988).

Example: Joseph Frederick displays a "BONG HITS 4 JESUS" banner during a corporate-sponsored Olympic torch-passing rally occurring across the street from his high school. The student body, teachers, and administrators are dismissed from school to attend the rally. The school principal confiscates the banner. When Frederick is suspended, he alleges a violation of his First Amendment rights. The Ninth Circuit Court of Appeals reverses the district court's grant of summary judgment for the school, holding that the message was a form of protected speech and that it had not given rise to a substantial risk of disruption of the rally. The U.S. Supreme Court reverses. Because the message advocated illegal drug use and had been disseminated at school, the Court concludes that the school could stifle the message without violating the First Amendment. The Court went on to say that *Tinker*'s "substantial disruption" formula was not the only basis for regulation but that students' First Amendment rights were limited in light of the school's mission of deterring illegal drugs, and that that was a sufficient basis for finding that there had been no violation of the First Amendment. *Morse v. Frederick*, 551 U.S. 393 (2007).

3. **Minors' right to obtain sexually explicit and violent materials**: The U.S. Supreme Court has adopted a somewhat paradoxical position in upholding restrictions on the right of minors to obtain sexually explicit materials but refusing to restrict minors' right to violent materials.

   Example: The owner of a luncheonette appeals his conviction for violating a New York statute prohibiting the sale to minors under age 17 of obscene materials that the statute defines as harmful only to minors ("girlie magazines"). Affirming the conviction, the U.S. Supreme Court thereby approves a variable standard of obscenity (i.e., a more restrictive standard for minors). Specifically, the Court concludes that the statute does not invade minors' freedom of expression and that the statutory definition of obscenity on the basis of its appeal to minors under 17 is rationally related to the state's interest in promoting child welfare. *Ginsberg v. New York*, 390 U.S. 629 (1968).

   Example: Companies that create, rent, and sell video games seek a declaratory judgment that California's statutory restrictions on the sale or rental of "violent video games" to minors violate the First Amendment. The U.S. Supreme Court holds that video games qualify for First Amendment protection and that the state failed to show that the law was justified by a compelling government interest, or that the law was narrowly drawn to serve that interest. Refusing to circumscribe minors' rights to violent materials, the Court reasoned that video games were analogous to books, plays, and movies in terms of their communication of ideas. The Court thereby refused to add new categories of unprotected speech to the existing exceptions for obscenity, incitement, and fighting words. *Brown v. Entertainment Merchants Assn.*, 564 U.S. 786 (2011).

4. **Schools' ability to punish students for their expressive activity**: The U.S. Supreme Court also addresses the *procedural* rights of school students in the context of the First Amendment.

The Court holds that schools may discipline students for their expressive activity in certain situations without implicating students' First or Fourteenth Amendment rights.

Example: At a student assembly, Mathew Fraser gives a speech nominating a fellow student for student government. The speech contains no patently offensive language but does refer to the candidate using a sexual metaphor. Following the speech, the assistant principal notifies Mathew that he has violated a school disciplinary rule for disruptive conduct, suspends him for three days, and removes his name from the graduation speaker list. Mathew alleges violations of his First Amendment right to freedom of speech and his Fourteenth Amendment right to procedural due process. The district court agrees that Mathew's constitutional rights were violated; the court of appeals affirms. Reversing, the U.S. Supreme Court refuses to apply the *Tinker* standard. Reasoning that *Tinker* applies only to political speech, the Court applies a balancing test to other forms of student speech. Here, the Court reasons that the school official's interest in inculcating proper values and maintaining a proper educational environment outweighs Mathew's interest in free speech. The Court also rejects Mathew's argument that the discipline violates his right to procedural due process. Because the suspension was so brief, according to the Court, it did not give rise to due process rights. *Bethel v. Fraser*, 478 U.S. 675 (1986).

C. Minors' Fourth Amendment rights in schools

1. **Applicable standard:** The U.S. Supreme Court holds that the Fourth Amendment's prohibition against unreasonable searches and seizures ***does apply*** to searches of juveniles by public school officials. However, the standard for searches of juveniles (*reasonable suspicion*) is lower than that for adults (*probable cause*). Thus, the law permits searches of juveniles that would be unconstitutional as applied to adults.

   Example: A high school teacher finds two girls smoking in the bathroom in violation of school rules. The teacher takes the girls to Assistant Vice Principal Choplick. When Choplick asks if they were smoking, one girl admits the infraction, but the other (T.L.O.) denies it. Choplick demands to see T.L.O's purse. He finds cigarettes, rolling papers, marijuana, and documents therein that implicate T.L.O. in dealing marijuana. Choplick gives the evidence to the police. The state brings delinquency charges. T.L.O. moves to suppress the evidence, claiming that the search was unlawful and that the evidence was tainted by the unlawful search. The juvenile court denies the motion to suppress, finds her to be delinquent, and sentences her to one year of probation.

   The U.S. Supreme Court concludes that the Fourth Amendment applies to school authorities. However, the standard in this context (reasonable suspicion) differs from the standard that is applicable to adults. Neither a warrant nor probable cause is required. Rather, the legality of the search depends on "reasonableness under the circumstances." Specifically, the determination of reasonableness requires an exploration of whether the search was justified at its inception and whether it was reasonably related in scope to the circumstances justifying the search. The later inquiry requires balancing the need to search against the invasiveness of the search (in light of the age and sex of the student, and the nature of the infraction). Reasoning that a child has a decreased interest in privacy and the school has a substantial interest in maintaining discipline, the Court concludes that the search was not unreasonable under the Fourth Amendment. *New Jersey v. T.L.O.*, 469 U.S. 325 (1985).

   Note: *T.L.O.* did not resolve the issue of the constitutionality of random (suspicionless) searches of juveniles because individualized suspicion existed in *T.L.O.* The Supreme Court later addressed the constitutionality of random drug testing in both *Vernonia School District v. Acton* and *Board of Education v. Earls* (discussed *infra*).

2. **Random drug testing:** The Supreme Court subsequently reaffirms that school children's Fourth Amendment rights differ from those of adults. The Court upholds the constitutionality of random drug testing of athletes (*Vernonia*) and also of students in competitive extracurricular activities (*Earls*).

   Example: A school district adopts a new drug policy that authorizes random urinalysis testing of students who participate in school athletic programs. The district is motivated by a concern with widespread drug use by students, including student athletes, and the worry that drug use increases the risk of sports-related injuries. A seventh-grader, James, is denied participation in the football program when he and his parents refuse to sign the testing consent forms. The student and his parents file suit, seeking declaratory and injunctive relief on the grounds that the policy violates the Fourth and Fourteenth Amendments. The district court denies the claims, but the court of appeals reverses. The U.S. Supreme Court holds that the policy does not violate the student's constitutional rights. The Court reasons that school children have lesser privacy expectations with regards to medical examinations than the general population, and student athletes have even less expectation of privacy. *Vernonia Sch. Dist. v. Acton*, 515 U.S. 646 (1995).

   Example: A high school institutes a policy requiring all students who participate in competitive extracurricular activities to submit to urinalysis drug testing. Several students challenge the constitutionality of the school's suspicionless policy. The U.S. Supreme Court holds that the policy is a reasonable means of furthering the school district's important interest in preventing and deterring drug use among its schoolchildren and therefore does not violate the Fourth Amendment. *Board of Educ. v. Earls*, 536 U.S. 822 (2002).

3. **Canine sniffing:** Courts are divided on the issue of whether "dog sniffing" violates students' Fourth Amendment rights. *Compare B.C. v. Plumas Unified Sch. Dist.*, 192 F.3d 1260 (9th Cir. 1999) (holding that random suspicionless dog sniff of student infringes the reasonable expectation of privacy, and thus constitutes a search for Fourth Amendment purposes), *with Doe v. Renfrow*, 475 F. Supp. 1012 (N.D. Ind. 1979) (holding that dog sniffing is not a search within the meaning of the Fourth Amendment because of students' lessened expectations of privacy).

4. **Locker searches:** Most courts have held that student locker searches are constitutional, relying on the theory that students have no expectation of privacy in their lockers (which are school property).

5. **Strip searches:** The U.S. Supreme Court has held that a strip search of a middle school student violates the Fourth Amendment.

   Example: School officials conduct a strip search of a 13-year-old middle school student based on a tip from another student that she possessed four prescription-strength ibuprofen pills and one over-the-counter naproxen (all of which were prohibited by school rules without advance permission). No pills are found. The student's mother files suit against the school district and school officials, alleging that the strip search violated her daughter's Fourth Amendment rights. The U.S. Supreme Court holds that school officials were justified in searching the student's backpack and outer clothing but that the search of her undergarments was unreasonably intrusive. (However, because the Court found that the law regarding student strip searches was not clearly established at the time, the officials were entitled to qualified immunity.) *Safford Unified School Dist. No. 1 v. Redding*, 557 U.S. 364 (2009).

6. **Special needs doctrine:** The "special needs doctrine" provides the justification for states to circumvent the warrant and probable cause requirements of the Fourth Amendment as applied to minors in certain circumstances. Specifically, if the state asserts a "special need" for a search (such as the importance of maintaining discipline in the classroom or safety concerns), the court will balance the governmental interest (deterrence of students' drug use) against the individual's privacy interests. Based on this doctrine, federal courts upheld warrantless, suspicionless drug-testing programs as applied to athletes (*Vernonia, supra*) and minors in competitive extracurricular activities (*Earls, supra*).

Quiz Yourself on *EDUCATION*

110. A high school junior reports to the principal that the sum of $200 from cheerleading candy sales is missing from her unlocked gym locker. The principal orders all the girls in the gym class to place the contents of their pockets on the table. Then, based on the fact that two girls are fidgeting and nervous, the principal requires two eighth-grade students (Amber and Lacy) to submit their backpacks for a search in a private room by a female teacher. No money is found. The girls seek a declaration that the searches are unconstitutional. Will they prevail? _____

Answer

110. Probably not. The Fourth Amendment prohibits unreasonable searches and seizures by state officials. *T.L.O.* established that high school students have a Fourth Amendment right to be free from "unreasonable" searches in the school setting, the search must be based on reasonable grounds to suspect that the student has violated the law or school rule, and the search is permissible in scope when the school employee's actions are not excessively intrusive in light of the age and sex of the student and the nature of the infraction. Here, the girls could argue that the school officials' search of their backpacks for allegedly stealing $200 lacked a reasonable basis from its inception for the officials to believe that the particular students had committed the crime. However, random searches of students have been upheld in some cases (e.g., for athletes and participants in extracurricular competitive activities). Nonetheless, the girls could argue that these exceptions were not applicable here. In addition, the girls could argue that there was no individualized suspicion as in *T.L.O.* and also that the resulting search was highly intrusive given the age and sex of the students. However, the search was not a strip search (prohibited by *Safford*) — only a search of backpacks and it was conducted in a private room by a female teacher. Thus, a court would probably hold that Amber and Lacey's Fourth Amendment rights were not violated.

V. MEDICAL CARE

A. Requirement of parental consent: At common law, only a parent could give consent to medical treatment for a child. The child lacked capacity to consent. This rule of parental consent accorded with notions of family privacy, parental autonomy, and parental financial responsibility.

B. Minor's consent: Some state laws provide that a minor may consent to medical treatment in special circumstances (i.e., for drug treatment) or that certain minors (i.e., emancipated minors or "mature" minors) may consent to medical treatment.

   1. Specific circumstances: In many jurisdictions, statutes provide that the minor may consent to medical treatment in cases of venereal disease, alcohol or drug abuse, and pregnancy-related complications (but *not* abortion services).

   2. Emancipated minors' ability to consent: An emancipated minor (i.e., a minor who is living apart from parents and managing his or her own financial affairs, or who is married, in the armed services, or has secured a judicial declaration of emancipation) may consent to medical treatment on the same terms as an adult.

   3. Mature minors' ability to consent: Many states allow "mature minors" to obtain medical treatment without parental consent. This common-law doctrine (codified in some states) permits unemancipated minors who possess sufficient capacity to understand the "nature and consequences" of a proposed medical treatment to consent on the same basis as an adult. *See, e.g.,* Ark. Stat. Ann. §20-9-602(7).

C. Exceptions and limitations to parental consent requirements

   1. Emergency exception: Under the common-law rule (now codified in many states), physicians may provide medical treatment to a child without parental consent in the event of an *emergency* if a parent is unavailable and if delay would endanger the child.

   2. State-imposed health requirements: The state limits parental prerogatives to consent to their child's medical treatment by certain mandatory health requirements. For example, most states require children to undergo newborn testing and screening, compulsory immunizations prior to school attendance, and school screening procedures (e.g., hearing and eyesight screenings).

   3. Neglect limitation: Another limitation on the rule of parental consent occurs in terms of child neglect. Based on common law and statute, parents have the duty to provide their child with necessary medical care. If the parents refuse to provide consent to medical treatment, they may be subject to criminal and/or civil liability. Further, under the neglect jurisdiction, a juvenile court may declare the child neglected or dependent and then order the appropriate medical treatment.

    Example: Mr. and Mrs. B. decide to place their infant son Phillip, who suffers from Down syndrome, in a residential care facility. He is diagnosed with a congenital heart defect that requires surgery to avoid damage to his lungs. His biological parents refuse to consent to the surgery. The juvenile probation department files a petition in juvenile court alleging that Phillip is a neglected child and requesting that the court declare him a dependent child for the purpose of ordering the cardiac surgery. The trial court dismisses the petition and the appellate court affirms. The court of appeals notes that, although parental autonomy is not absolute and the state may interfere to safeguard the child, the trial judge found no clear and convincing evidence to support the petition. The appellate court determines that, because the experts disagreed about the likelihood of success of the surgery, the trial court's decision did not constitute error. *In re Phillip B.*, 152 Cal. Rptr. 48 (Ct. App. 1979).

Example: Phillip B. (the child in the preceding case) develops a close relationship with Mr. and Mrs. H., who are volunteers at Phillip's facility. They teach him skills, include him in their activities, and give him his own room in their house. He refers to them as his "mother" and "father" and refers to their residence as "his" house. His biological parents forbid this contact, and remain emotionally detached from him. Mr. and Mrs. H. file a petition to be appointed guardians of his person and estate (in part, so that they may order the necessary surgery). The biological parents object. The court of appeals determines that Phillip's best interests will be served by awarding guardianship to his foster parents. The court explains that, before a court may award custody to a nonparent, it must make a finding that an award of custody to a parent would be detrimental to the child and that the award to the nonparent would serve the best interests of the child. Here, the court reasons that the biological parents' retention of custody would cause Phillip severe harm. *Guardianship of Phillip B.*, 188 Cal. Rptr. 781 (Ct. App. 1983).

Note: The assertion of neglect jurisdiction fails because the court determines that the evidence about the success of the surgery is conflicting. However, the guardianship petition succeeds because the standard is the more subjective "best interests of the child" and because the presumption favoring the biological parents is overcome by the judicial finding that their continuing care is detrimental.

Quiz Yourself on
MEDICAL CARE

111.   Fifteen-year-old Kevin Sampson suffers from a disease causing a massive deformity of his face and neck. The disease is not life-threatening but results in a grotesque appearance that adversely affects Kevin's self-esteem. Kevin's physicians believe that he should have surgery to correct the condition. His mother, a Jehovah's Witness, is willing for him to have the surgery, but she refuses to consent, on religious grounds, to blood transfusions during the surgery. Can Kevin's physicians proceed without his mother's consent? _____

Answer

111.   Yes. The physicians may report the case to the county authorities to have them petition the juvenile court to declare Kevin a neglected (i.e., medically neglected) child. Juvenile court statutes typically permit a juvenile court to assert jurisdiction when a parent refuses to provide a child with necessary medical care. If the juvenile court determines that Kevin is neglected, the juvenile court would then order a guardian to consent to the operation with the necessary blood transfusions.

Exam Tips on
THE PARENT-CHILD-STATE RELATIONSHIP IN SPECIAL CONTEXTS

Identify the special context that is being tested (tort, contract, property, education, or medical care). Remember that special rules may be applicable to the particular context and that such rules have policy implications concerning the appropriateness of differential treatment of children and adults.

Torts

☛ If the issue involves *liability* for children's tortious acts, explain the different rules for parents and children. That is, at common law, parents were *not liable* for their children's torts. Children are liable for their torts—both intentional and negligent torts. However, although children are liable for their torts, they are subject to a *different subjective standard of care*. Explain the traditional rule that takes into account the minor's age and experience, and then apply that rule to the facts. Determine whether the child may have been contributorily negligent. If so, explain the minority rule establishing a rebuttable presumption that children below a certain age (e.g., age seven) cannot be held contributorily negligent and the new Restatement (Third) of Torts rule that establishes an irrebutable presumption that children below age five are incapable of contributory negligence. Next, determine whether the child was performing an adult activity (e.g., driving a car or boat) in which case the adult "reasonable person" standard would apply.

☞ Also, be sure to explore whether an exception to the traditional rule of parental nonliability is applicable. That is, is there a special statute that establishes parental liability? Was the parent employing his or her child? Did the parent permit the child to use a dangerous instrumentality such as a weapon? Did the parent have prior knowledge of the child's aggressive acts or disposition and fail to warn the victim?

Contracts

☛ Determine the nature of the contract at issue. Clarify the offer (especially the terms), acceptance, and consideration. Explore whether the minor would like to *disaffirm* (breach the contract), and explain the reason for the breach (i.e., what the minor gains by the breach). Describe the common-law doctrine that a minor's contracts are voidable (i.e., the minor can disaffirm the contract and assert a defense of infancy). Apply the rule to the facts. Mention that this common-law rule is the **majority rule**. Explain also the policy underlying the rule (to protect minors from overreaching by adults and their own immaturity). Explore whether the problem includes one of the **limited situations** (i.e., entertainment contracts) that change the common-law rule. Determine also whether the problem involves a fact pattern in which a court might determine that the minor has been unjustly enriched and has to make restitution for any benefits conferred, pursuant to the new Restatement (Third) of Restitution.

Property

☛ Explore whether the problem involves a property-based issue. If so, identify the particular issue. For example, does the problem involve the child's right to services or earnings? Does it involve inheritance? Does it involve a gift?

☛ Apply the relevant law to the circumstances. Remember that at common law, a parent had the right to a child's services and earnings and that many modern statutes incorporate this common-law rule. If the issue involves inheritance, point out that at common law (and still true today), a court appointed a guardian of the child's estate (i.e., the child's property). Explain the notion of guardianship as involving a guardian of the person and of the estate. Point out the problems with guardianship (i.e., expensive, cumbersome).

☞ For issues involving ***inheritance***, verify whether the child was born during a marriage or outside marriage. Point out the traditional rule of discrimination for nonmarital children—i.e., they could inherit from their mothers who died intestate (if the mother died without a will) but not from their fathers who died intestate. Explain that the modern rule eliminates ***differences in treatment*** of nonmarital versus marital children for succession purposes. Discuss the U.S. Supreme Court cases in *Trimble v. Gordon* and *Lalli v. Lalli*.

☞ If the issue involves a ***gift to a minor***, clarify the nature of the property that is being given and the donor. Mention the ***different methods of holding property for a minor***. Discuss whether the use of a trust or the Uniform Transfers to Minors Act might be appropriate. Be sure to define and explain the features of various options. Mention, too, the advantages and disadvantages of the use of trusts versus the Uniform Act.

☞ Be sure to identify whether the minor is ***emancipated***. If so, explain the emancipation doctrine and its effect (permitting children to acquire the right to dispose of their earnings). Point out that emancipation is a common-law as well as statutory doctrine. Identify whether common-law grounds (e.g., marriage, service in the armed forces) or particular statutory grounds are relevant.

Education

☛ The most commonly tested issues in the educational context are minors' ***First Amendment*** and ***Fourth Amendment*** rights. First, determine the nature of the restriction on minors' rights. Then determine if a state actor or agency is involved. Does the restriction involve a ***prior restraint*** on speech or a ***punishment*** of students for their ***expressive*** activities? Point out that different rules apply to these two types of restrictions.

☛ If the question involves minors' right to freedom of expression, determine the type of speech that is being restricted. For example, does the question involve ***political speech***? Political speech is entitled to the most protection under the Constitution. If political speech is involved, then discuss and apply the rules in *Tinker*. That is, does the conduct ***materially and substantially interfere*** with the requirements of appropriate discipline in the operation of the school or ***invade the rights of others***? Remember that the *Tinker* test has two prongs—the disruptive aspect and the invasion-of-rights aspect.

☞ If the restriction on student speech does not involve political speech, determine if the speech occurred in the context of a ***school-sponsored activity*** (such as a school newspaper). Point out that the Supreme Court circumscribes students' rights to freedom of expression in the context of school-sponsored activities (*Hazelwood*).

☞ If the restriction does not involve political speech, determine if the speech involves entertainment. That is, does it pertain to minors' access to sexually explicit materials? If so, explain that the U.S. Supreme Court has established a ***variable standard of obscenity*** that permits greater regulation of minors' rights to sexually explicit materials (*Ginsberg*). On the other hand, if the restriction involves minors' access to violent materials, point out that the Court refuses to apply a variable standard in this context (*Brown v. Entertainment Merchants Assn.*).

☞ If the problem involves **punishment** of students for their **expressive** activities, then remember to discuss not only students' First Amendment rights but also students' right to procedural **due process**. That is, the Supreme Court has held that schools may discipline students for their expressive activity in certain situations (*Bethel v. Fraser*). Remember that *Bethel* involved the student's **brief** suspension (three days), which the Court held did not give rise to an infringement of the due process right. Therefore, it is important to note the specific nature of the school's punishment. *Bethel* also applied a balancing test to student speech. Discuss and apply that balancing test (i.e., balancing the school official's interest, for example, in inculcating property values and maintaining a proper educational environment against the student's interest in freedom of expression).

☞ Students' **Fourth Amendment rights** are also a frequently tested issue. First, identify the nature of the search. What was the object of the search (to find drugs, cigarettes, money, firearms, etc.)? Who was conducting the search (a school official and/or police officer)? Recall that the search in *T.L.O.* was conducted only by a school official. Therefore, a higher standard than reasonable suspicion might be required if a search was conducted in concert with, or at the request of, law enforcement personnel.

☞ Identify the item being searched (i.e., the student's person, locker) because different rules apply to the student's expectation of privacy. For example, a student has a **lessened expectation of privacy in school property** (e.g., lockers).

☞ Discuss and apply the Supreme Court's holding in *New Jersey v. T.L.O.* Specifically, explain that the Supreme Court held that the Fourth Amendment applies to searches conducted by public school officials, but that a lower standard applies (**reasonable suspicion**) to searches of juveniles compared to adults (probable cause). Explain the reasonable suspicion standard — reasonableness under the circumstances.

☞ Discuss the "special needs" exception that allows the school to dispense with the warrant and probable cause requirements for the search if the school can establish a "special need," such as the need to maintain school discipline or to safeguard student safety. After the school asserts a "special needs exception," the court must balance the governmental interest against the individual's privacy interests.

☞ In evaluating the individual's privacy interests, apply the *T.L.O.* standard. Specifically, explain whether the search was justified at its inception (i.e., were there reasonable grounds at the time for suspecting that a law or school rule had been violated), and whether the scope of the search was reasonably related to that need. In terms of the latter, it will be necessary to balance the **need to search** against the **invasiveness of the search** (the invasiveness depends on the age and sex of the student, and the nature of the infraction). In discussing the factor of "invasiveness," mention *Safford v. Redding* (holding that a strip search of a student's undergarments for prescription and non-prescription" drugs was not justified by the nature of the circumstances).

Determine whether the search involved **individualized suspicion** or a **random** suspicionless search. If the latter, then discuss and apply the Supreme Court's holdings in *Vernonia* and *Earls*. Explain the school policy and its object. Explore the facts that motivated the school policy. Determine who is being searched. Remember that the reasoning of *Vernonia* applied to athletes and the reasoning of *Earls* applies to students in competitive extracurricular activities.

Analyze the students' expectation of privacy (e.g., are they similar to athletes who have a lessened expectation of privacy), the seriousness of the intrusion on students' privacy (e.g., a urine test is less intrusive than a body search), and the state interest (e.g., protection of students from drug use, promotion of civic values). Be sure to point out that *T.L.O.* left many issues unresolved (i.e., the standard if law enforcement is involved, the constitutionality of various types of searches).

Medical Care

☛ Identify the *context* for medical treatment and the *health care provider* (physician, hospital, etc.). Clarify the age and sex of the child. Determine the major issues—*parental consent, minor's consent*. Explain the common-law rule providing that only a parent could consent to medical treatment for a child because the child lacked capacity to consent. Discuss the modern view that many statutes authorize minors to consent themselves for certain types of medical treatment (drug treatment, venereal disease, substance abuse, etc.).

    ☞ Explore whether there are any *exceptions and/or limitations* to parental consent requirements. That is, is this an emergency? Is the parent unavailable? Would delay endanger the child? In such cases, the *emergency exception* would enable physicians to provide treatment to a child without parental consent. Is this a situation involving state-imposed health requirements (i.e., newborn screening)? In this case, the law limits parental prerogatives to consent because of the need to promote child welfare by compliance with health requirements.

    ☞ Other exceptions involve the emancipation doctrine and the "mature minor" rule.

    ☞ If the parents refuse their consent, remember to discuss the *neglect limitation* on parental consent requirements. That is, although parental consent is generally required, if the parents refuse to give their consent, they may be subject to *civil and/or criminal liability*. Discuss whether a state actor should resort to the neglect jurisdiction of juvenile court. That is, should a juvenile court declare the child neglected in order to authorize the necessary medical treatment? Be sure to determine if the minor is emancipated. Remember that if the minor is emancipated, he or she may consent to medical treatment on the same terms as an adult (and parental consent is not required).

CHAPTER 10

ADOPTION

ChapterScope

This chapter addresses the adoption process which creates a new parent-child relationship. Here are a few of the key principles covered in this chapter:

- Adoption was not recognized by the English common law; therefore, American adoption law is entirely *statutory*.

- The guiding standard in adoption law is the *best interests of the child*.

- Several factors, including *race, religion,* and *sexual orientation,* may be relevant in adoption.

- Despite marriage equality, *discrimination persists by faith-based adoption agencies* that refuse to provide services to same-sex partners based on claims of religious freedom.

- State statutes generally require *consent of the biological parents* before an adoption takes place.

- In the absence of voluntary consent, the state can terminate parental rights *involuntarily* in cases of *parental abuse or neglect*. Involuntary termination of parental rights must comport with procedural and substantive due process requirements.

- The Supreme Court has held that an *unmarried father* is entitled to constitutional protection of his parental rights so long as he manifests certain *indicia of parenthood*.

- A biological parent may relinquish a child to a public or privately licensed adoption *agency* for adoption, or arrange for a *private* (i.e., *independent*) adoption by which a private person/intermediary facilitates the adoption.

- States have *criminal penalties* for *baby selling*.

- An adoption agency may be liable for the tort of *wrongful adoption* (i.e., a form of misrepresentation).

- All states provide *subsidized adoption programs* to facilitate adoption of those children who are *difficult to place*.

- Courts generally uphold *open adoption* agreements if the agreements are found to be in the best interests of the child.

- Many states now permit adoptees to have *access to their adoption records*.

I. INTRODUCTION

A. **Definition:** Adoption is the legal process of creating a parent-child relationship. By adoption, an individual acquires a new parent (or parents). An adoption terminates the legal rights and responsibilities (e.g., custody, support, inheritance) of the biological parent(s) and creates new legal rights and responsibilities in the adoptive parent(s). After an adoption, the state seals the child's original birth certificate and issues a new birth certificate, thereby reflecting the adoptee's "new" legal parentage.

B.   **Best interests of the child**: The guiding standard in adoption law (as in child custody law) is the *best interests of the child*.

C.   **Historical background:** Adoption was not recognized by the English common law. This policy stemmed in large part from British emphasis on the importance of the blood line. As a result, American adoption law is entirely statutory law. Massachusetts enacted the first adoption statute in 1851.

D.   **Voluntary versus involuntary termination of parental rights:** Adoption results in the termination of the biological parents' rights. This termination may be voluntary or involuntary. On the one hand, a biological parent may *choose* to relinquish ("surrender") a child for adoption. On the other hand, a biological parent may have his or her parental rights terminated by a court because of parental misconduct (i.e., abuse, neglect, abandonment). The termination of parental rights and the adoption may take place either in the same proceeding or two separate proceedings. Involuntary termination of parental rights must comport with substantive and procedural due safeguards.

E.   **Social reality:** The adoption rate in the United States has declined in the past few years. The decline is due, in large part, to the significant decrease in the number of intercountry adoptions. At the same time, the number of infant adoptions has remained constant, and the rate of special needs adoptions has increased. Children with "special needs" include those with medical or psychological problems, disabilities, or sibling groups (and often include children of color). State and federal programs provide financial assistance to encourage adoption of children with special needs.

F.   **Influence of the Internet:** The Internet has dramatically changed the face of the adoption process. Social media currently compete with traditional adoption service providers to broaden the market for adoptable children. Social media also enable adoptees to locate birth relatives with relative ease (thereby contributing to the demise of the longstanding principle of confidentiality). The Internet has also facilitated the growth of an unregulated adoption market leading to placements that are unknown and unsupervised by social welfare agencies or the courts.

II. SELECTION STANDARDS FOR ADOPTIVE PARENTS

A.   **Generally:** The adoption process generally begins when a birth parent *voluntarily* relinquishes (or "surrenders") the child to a state-licensed or state-operated agency. The agency takes legal custody of the child and selects an adoptive family. Case law highlights the factors (disability, marital status, race, sexual orientation) that agencies and the state can consider in choosing an adoptive placement.

B.   **Relevant factors**

1.   **Preference for relatives:** Some statutes incorporate a presumption that placement with relatives is in the child's best interests, absent a showing of good cause or detriment to the child.

Example: D.L. is born to an African-American mother who is not living with D.L.'s father. The mother's three other children are being cared for by their African-American maternal grandparents. The mother relinquishes D.L. at birth for adoption. D.L. is placed in foster care with Caucasian foster parents. Following termination of the biological mother and father's rights, the foster parents and maternal grandparents all file adoption petitions. The trial court places the child with the maternal grandparents, based on a statutory preference that "the court shall give preference, in the absence of good cause to the contrary, to (a) a relative or relatives of the child, or, . . . (b) a family with the same racial or ethnic heritage as the child." The foster parents appeal, contending that the statute violates equal protection by establishing a family preference only for adoption of minority children. The state supreme court affirms. Without addressing the constitutional issues, the court reasons that adoption law has long favored child placement with family members, regardless of race or ethnic heritage. Further, according to the court, the possibility of harm caused by separation from the foster parents cannot defeat the family preference. *Matter of Welfare of D.L.*, 486 N.W.2d 375, 377 (Minn. 1992).

2. **Sexual orientation:** Gays and lesbians have long been willing to adopt or serve as foster parents for hard-to-place children (especially older children as well as children with disabilities and psychological issues). State laws vary in their recognition of the rights of gay and lesbian parents in adoptive and foster care placements.

   a. **Traditional rule:** Traditionally, some states restricted adoptions by same-sex partners. Disqualification was explicit as well as implicit. That is, some states indirectly restricted adoptions by LGBT partners by limiting adoption eligibility to opposite-sex married adults.

      Example: Gay and lesbian foster parents and guardians challenge the constitutionality of the Florida prohibition on adoption of children by same-sex partners. The Eleventh Circuit Court of Appeals holds that the foster parents and legal guardians have no due-process-protected liberty interest in family integrity, and also that the statute does not violate the Equal Protection Clause because it is rationally related to the legitimate state interest in furthering the best interests of adopted children by placing them with married parents. *Lofton v. Secretary of Dept. of Children and Family Servs.*, 358 F.3d 804 (11th Cir. 2004).

   b. **Permissive jurisdictions:** Most states today permit adoption of children by LGBT adopters and foster parents. Some state laws *explicitly* prohibit such discrimination.

      The Florida ban, discussed above, was declared unconstitutional under the state constitution in the following case.

      Example: Two boys, X.X.G. and N.R.G., are placed in the care of F.G., a gay man, when the boys were four and six months, respectively. Each child had significant medical and other needs. They thrive in F.G.'s household. F.G. petitions to adopt the children after the state terminated the biological parents' parental rights because of neglect. F.G. is precluded from adopting the children because of a state law that prohibits adoption by "homosexuals." He challenges the constitutionality of the statute under the state constitution. A Florida appellate court holds that the statute violates equal protection. The court reasons that the restriction is not rationally related to the state interest in promoting child welfare because the statute permits adoptions by single adults as well as long-term foster care by gays and lesbians. The court draws support from scientific research findings revealing that there is no difference in the parenting by gays and lesbians or the adjustment of their children. *Florida Dept. of Children & Families v. Adoption of X.X.G.*, 45 So.3d 79 (Fla. Dist. Ct. App. 2010).

   c. **Modern *implicit* restrictions:** Several states continue to restrict adoptions and/or foster care placements by gay and lesbian parents. Such discrimination persists, despite *Obergefell*, based on service providers' constitutional claims of religious freedom and free speech. Various groups are challenging the constitutionality of states' protections or restrictions of faith-based adoption agencies that refuse to provide services to LGBT parents. The cases pit state anti-discrimination laws against guarantees of free exercise of religion and free speech. Recall *Masterpiece Cakeshop* (Chapter 3) (service providers' religious-based opposition to same-sex relationships).

Example: After the city of Philadelphia learns that two of its foster care providers refuse to license same-sex couples to be foster parents, the city ceases referring children to these agencies. One agency (Catholic Social Services (CSS)) and four foster parents sue the city, asking the court to order the city to renew the agency's contract. CSS argues that its right to free exercise of religion and free speech entitles it to reject qualified same-sex couples. A federal district court denies CSS's motion for a preliminary injunction and rejects the argument that child welfare agencies have a right to discriminate. The Third Circuit Court of Appeals upholds the district court ruling. The United States Supreme Court granted certiorari. *Fulton v. City of Phila.*, 922 F.3d 140 (3d Cir. 2019), *cert. granted*, 140 S. Ct. 1104 (2020).

Example: New York law prohibits state-licensed adoption agencies from discriminating against prospective adoptive parents based on sexual orientation and gender identity (among other factors) (18 NYCRR §421.3(d)). A privately funded Christian agency, New Hope Family Services, provides adoptive homes and foster care, consistent with its religious belief in the sanctity of (opposite-sex) marriage. New York State's Office of Children and Family Services (OCFS) informs New Hope that the agency policy violates state nondiscrimination laws and requires them to change their policy or terminate operations. New Hope challenges OCFS's directive based on claims of freedom of religion, free speech, and equal protection. The federal district court denies New Hope's petition for a preliminary injunction, concluding that New Hope failed to plead any plausible constitutional claims.

The Second Circuit Court of Appeals reverses and remands the case for further consideration. The court holds that the agency stated a plausible claim for violation of its First Amendment rights. The court of appeals distinguishes *Fulton v City of Philadelphia* (limiting the free exercise of religion of an agency (CSS) that is an agent of the state) by explaining that the relationship between CSS and Philadelphia was "contractual and compensatory," whereas New Hope's adoption services are not performed pursuant to any government contract and government funding. *New Hope Fam. Servs., Inc. v. Poole*, 966 F.3d 145 (2d Cir. 2020).

d. **Proposed federal rule:** The Trump Administration proposed a rule in 2019 that would undo Obama-era protections for LGBT parents and allow foster care and adoption agencies to deny services to LGBT families on faith-based grounds. 84 Fed. Reg. 63831-01. (Nov. 19, 2019).

e. **Full faith and credit:** States wrestle with the impact of marriage equality on the recognition of same-sex couples' *out-of-state* adoption decrees. Before *Obergefell*, some states declined to recognize adoption decrees issued to same-sex couples in other states. However, after *Obergefell*, the U.S. Supreme Court determined that a state must accord full faith and credit to another state's judgment so long as the court in the original forum had jurisdiction over the relevant parties.

Example: V. L. and E. L. were in a relationship for six years. Through assisted reproductive technology, E. L. gave birth to a child and later to twins. The women raised the children jointly. V. L. filed a petition to adopt the children in Georgia. A final decree recognized both women as legal parents. The women separated while living in Alabama. When E.L. denied access to the children, V.L petitioned the Alabama court to enforce the Georgia judgment and award her custody or visitation rights. The Alabama Supreme Court rejected her claim, holding that the Full Faith and Credit Clause does not require Alabama courts to respect the Georgia judgment. The Supreme Court reversed, ruling that because the Georgia superior court had subject-matter jurisdiction to decide the adoption petition, the Alabama court had a full faith and credit obligation to enforce the Georgia judgment. *V.L. v. E.L.*, 136 S. Ct. 1017 (2016).

3. **Race**

   a. **Generally:** A longstanding practice of racial matching existed in the selection of adoptive parents that required placement of children in adoptive homes with parents of the same race as the child.

   b. **Policy debate:** Race-matching policies have been the subject of a controversial policy debate. During the civil rights era of the 1960s, transracial adoption was regarded positively. However, in 1972, the National Association of Black Social Workers adopted a resolution stating that African-American children should be placed only with African-American families in foster care or adoption. The resolution arose from the fear of cultural genocide.

   Some commentators argue that limits on transracial adoption harm children by restricting the number of possible adoptive homes. In contrast, others argue that transracial adoption results in the loss of children's and the community's racial and cultural heritage. Several authorities believe that, although same-race placements are ideal, transracial placements are preferable to long-term foster care.

   c. **Federal law:** Congress responded to the practice of racial matching in 1996 by legislating the "removal of barriers to interethnic adoption," providing that no state or other entity in a state receiving federal funds can "deny to any individual the opportunity to become an adoptive or a foster parent, on the basis of the race, color, or national origin of the individual, or of the child, involved." 42 U.S.C. §1996b (amending the earlier, less restrictive Multi-Ethnic Placement Act). Nonetheless, federal legislation continues to support matching regarding Native-American children and parents (discussed *infra*).

   d. **Indian Child Welfare Act (ICWA):** The Indian Child Welfare Act provides placement preferences for Indian children. *See* discussion *infra*.

4. **Religion:** Religion also may be a relevant factor in the selection of adoptive parents. Some states have ***religious-matching provisions*** that match the religion of the child and adoptive parent when possible. Courts have rejected constitutional challenges to these provisions.

   Example: The county Department of Social Services denies permission to a prospective adoptive couple on the ground of the couple's lack of religious affiliation. Both the state constitution and adoption statute provide that a child should be placed, when practicable and consistent with the child's best interests, in the custody of a person of the same religious background. The couple appeals the lower court's finding of constitutionality, arguing that the provision violates the First Amendment. The appellate court holds that religious-matching provisions are constitutional because they fulfill a secular legislative purpose, reflect a benevolent neutrality toward religion, and do not foster an excessive government entanglement with church interests. *Dickens v. Ernesto*, 281 N.E.2d 153 (N.Y. Ct. App. 1972), *appeal dismissed*, 407 U.S. 917 (1972).

5. **Preference for the infertile:** A few states give explicit preference to couples who are unable to have children.

6. **Indian Child Welfare Act (ICWA) of 1978:** Federal legislation dictates that Native-American origins are relevant in adoption. In 1978, Congress enacted the Indian Child Welfare Act (ICWA), 25 U.S.C. §§1901-1963, stemming from the concern in the mid-1970s that large numbers of Native-American children were being separated from tribes through adoption or foster care, thereby leading to the loss of their language and culture. The Act provides placement preferences for Indian children in adoption and child welfare matters, i.e., they shall remain in the tribal community whenever possible.

   a. **Exclusive jurisdiction and tribal preference:** Two provisions of the ICWA (§§1911 and 1915), apply to jurisdiction and the establishment of priority in adoption. Section 1911 grants tribal courts *exclusive jurisdiction* over proceedings concerning an Indian child who resides, or is domiciled, on a reservation. Section 1915(a) mandates a *preference for tribal members*. Absent good cause, adoptive placements must be made to members of the child's extended family, other members of the same tribe, or other Indian families.

   b. **Definition of "Indian child":** ICWA defines "Indian child" as any unmarried minor who is either (a) a member of an Indian tribe or (b) is eligible for membership in an Indian tribe and is the biological child of a member of an Indian tribe (25 U.S.C. §1903(4)).

   c. **"Active efforts" requirement:** ICWA provides that any party seeking to terminate parental rights to an Indian child under state law "shall satisfy the court that active efforts have been made to provide remedial services and rehabilitative programs designed to prevent the breakup of the Indian family and that these efforts have proved unsuccessful." (25 U.S.C. §1912(d)).

   d. **"Existing Indian family" (EIF) exception:** Some courts have held that the ICWA does not apply if the Indian child was being raised by a non-Indian parent with no tribal contact. This rule is called the "existing Indian family" exception.

   e. **Baby Veronica.** The Supreme Court held that the application of ICWA (giving preference to tribal members) is limited to the types of cases envisioned by Congress when it passed the Act (i.e., those cases in which government officials seek to remove Indian children from an existing Indian family). That is, ICWA does not apply to Native American biological fathers who are not custodians of an Indian child (i.e., who have never lived with the child).

   Example: A Hispanic woman who lives in Oklahoma agrees to the adoption of her infant daughter by a South Carolina couple after the baby's father disclaims (by text message) any interest in supporting or raising the child. However, when the father (who is a registered member of the Cherokee Nation) learns of the adoption, he objects. He explains that he was willing to surrender his parental rights when he thought the birth mother would be rearing the child herself. The father contests the adoption on the grounds that he was not properly notified in accordance with the ICWA. He prevails in the trial court and the South Carolina Supreme Court. The latter court disallows termination of his parental rights based on the ICWA's goal of protecting Native-American culture.

   The U.S. Supreme Court reverses, holding that the ICWA's "active efforts" requirement prior to termination of parental rights (see *supra*) does not apply where an Indian parent abandoned the Indian child prior to birth and the child had never been in that parent's legal or physical custody; and that the ICWA's tribal placement preference does not bar a non-Indian family from adopting an Indian child when no other eligible tribal candidates have sought to adopt the child. The Court remands for a determination of the child's adoption and custody under state law. *Adoptive Couple v. Baby Girl* (commonly known as the "Baby Veronica" case), 570 U.S. 637 (2013).

Epilogue: The trial court approved the adoption of Baby Girl by the adoptive couple. That decision was eventually stayed by the Oklahoma Supreme Court, but the stay was later lifted.

f. Constitutionality of ICWA: The constitutionality of ICWA was challenged in a lawsuit brought by several states (i.e., Indiana, Louisiana, Texas), foster parents, and prospective adopters.

Example: A federal district court in Texas held that ICWA violates the U.S. Constitution on the basis that it accords preferential treatment based on race (thereby invoking strict scrutiny) in violation of the Fifth Amendment's equal protection guarantee. In response to appeals by the federal government and intervening tribal nations, a three-judge panel from the Fifth Circuit reverses that decision, thereby reaffirming the constitutionality of ICWA. The Fifth Circuit Court of Appeals agrees to rehear the case *en banc*. *Brackeen v. Bernhardt*, 937 F.3d 406 (5th Cir. 2019), *reh'g en banc granted*, 942 F.3d 287 (5th Cir. 2019).

Quiz Yourself on
SELECTION STANDARDS FOR ADOPTIVE PARENTS

112. Mr. and Mrs. Allen wish to adopt a child. They file an application with the state social services agency. The application asks them for their religious affiliation. Mrs. Allen is Jewish. Mr. Allen is Catholic. Mr. Allen also has a problem with alcoholism and a history of arrests for drunk driving. The social services agency subsequently refuses to place a Catholic infant with them, explaining that "one of the reasons was your differing religions." The agency has a stated policy to match the baby's birth mother's religion and that of the adoptive parents whenever possible. Mr. and Mrs. Allen challenge the agency policy (i.e., disclosure of their religious affiliation and the denial of their application) as unconstitutional. Will they prevail? _____

Answer

112. No. Religious-matching provisions (i.e., matching the baby's religion to that of the prospective adoptive parents) have been upheld as constitutional. Further, religion may be one of several factors taken into consideration when selecting an adoptive parent. Here, the agency could argue that it took into account other factors in denying Mr. and Mrs. Allen's application for adoption. That is, the agency would claim that it would not be in the best interests of the child to be placed in a home where a parent (such as Mr. Allen) has a history of alcoholism.

III. CONSENT

A. Background: State statutes generally require *voluntary consent* of the biological parents before an adoption may take place. For married parents, consent by *both* parents is generally required.

In some cases, parental consent is unnecessary. For nonmarital children, courts sometimes dispense with the father's consent if he has not indicated sufficient "indicia of parenthood." In addition, some states authorize "putative father registries," which eliminate the need for adoption notification or consent for unmarried fathers who fail to register. Note that registration in putative father registries does not establish parentage but only invokes due process protections for the putative father (i.e., notification to the putative father and an opportunity for him to oppose the adoption).

Further, the state can terminate parental rights *involuntarily* in cases of parental abuse, neglect, or abandonment. Involuntary termination of parental rights must comport with procedural and substantive requirements (discussed *infra*).

B. Consent by the unmarried father

1. **Ramifications of *Stanley v. Illinois*:** The U.S. Supreme Court has held that a state may not deprive a biological father of custody if he has consistently cared for a child. Recall *Stanley v. Illinois* (discussed in Chapter 4 *supra*) in which the Supreme Court holds that a statute addressing an unmarried father's rights (by presuming that, on the death of the mother, the father is unfit) violates the father's procedural due process rights by denying him a preremoval hearing on the issue of fitness.

   Although *Stanley* deals with custody, the case has implications for the rights of unwed fathers in adoption cases. Prior to *Stanley*, many states allowed adoption with the mother's consent alone. In the wake of *Stanley*, many legislatures amended their statutes to confer greater rights on putative fathers. The Supreme Court has addressed the constitutionality of several such statutes in cases that have implications for unmarried fathers' rights in adoption.

2. **Indicia of parenthood:** The Supreme Court holds, in a trilogy of cases, that an unmarried father is entitled to constitutional protection of his parental rights so long as he manifests certain *indicia of parenthood*. That is, an unwed father does not have an absolute right to notice and an opportunity to be heard before his child may be adopted. Rather, his constitutional rights depend on the degree to which he reveals a ***willingness to assume parental responsibilities*** (i.e., a custodial, personal, or financial relationship). Failure to act in a ***timely*** manner may result in relinquishment of his constitutional rights.

   Example: Jessica is born out of wedlock. Her biological father, Jonathan, lives with her mother prior to her birth, and visits the mother in the hospital following her birth. However, he is not listed on the birth certificate, never provides support, does not live with the mother after the birth, and never offers to marry the mother. Shortly after Jessica's birth, her mother marries Richard. Two years later, Richard successfully petitions to adopt Jessica. Jonathan argues that the adoption is invalid because he was not given notice. A New York statute provides that a father must register with the "putative father registry" in order to receive notice of an adoption. Jonathan contends that the statute is unconstitutional as a deprivation of his liberty interest (i.e., his actual or potential relationship with his child) without due process. He argues that he has a constitutional right to notice and a hearing before being deprived of that interest. The U.S. Supreme Court holds that the rights of only *some* putative fathers merit constitutional protection that requires advance notice and a hearing. Those unwed fathers who demonstrate a full commitment to the responsibilities of parenthood are entitled to due process protection. However, "the mere existence of a biological link does not merit equivalent constitutional protection. . . ." Because Jonathan did not seek any legal recognition of his relationship with Jessica until she was two years old, he relinquished the opportunity to form such a relationship. *Lehr v. Robertson*, 463 U.S. 248, 261 (1983).

Example: Shortly after a mother gives birth to a child, she marries a man who is not the child's father. The biological father (Quilloin) never lives with the mother and/or child and never admits paternity. He makes sporadic support payments and occasionally visits the child. Nine years later, when the mother's husband petitions to adopt the child, the biological father petitions that the adoption be denied. The Georgia statute provides that a mother's consent is sufficient for the adoption of a nonmarital child unless the father legitimates the child by marriage or by court order. Quilloin challenges the constitutionality of the statute, arguing that due process prohibits terminating his parental rights without a finding of unfitness and that the distinction between unmarried and married fathers violates equal protection. The Supreme Court rejects both claims. The Court reasons that due process is not violated (i.e., no showing of unfitness is required) because Quilloin never had custody or ever sought custody. The Court also concludes that Quilloin's interests are distinguishable from those of a married father who has legal responsibility for the rearing of his children. *Quilloin v. Walcott*, 434 U.S. 246 (1978), *reh'g denied*, 435 U.S. 918 (1978).

Example: Abdiel lives with Maria for five years, during which time they have two children. When they separate, the mother moves in with another man whom she subsequently marries. Abdiel continues to see the children frequently and contributes to their support. At one point, the mother gives him physical custody when she leaves the country. When Maria and her husband petition to adopt the children, Abdiel and his new wife cross-petition to adopt them. The trial judge approves Maria's petition. Abdiel appeals, alleging that the statute, which provides that a nonmarital child can be adopted with the consent of the mother alone, violates his right to equal protection. The U.S. Supreme Court agrees, holding that the statutory distinction between unwed mothers and fathers violates the Equal Protection Clause because it does not bear a substantial relationship to the state interest in promoting adoption of nonmarital children where (as here) "the father has established a substantial relationship with the child and has admitted his paternity." *Caban v. Mohammed*, 441 U.S. 380, 392 (1979).

In the above cases, the Supreme Court recognizes the rights of only Abdiel Caban, who was most involved in his children's lives (saw them frequently, supported them, and had custody for a period). The other biological fathers (Lehr and Quilloin) never sought or had custody, paid little or no support, and did not see their children frequently. Thus, only Caban's parental relationship meets the requisite criteria of "indicia of parenthood."

3. **Consent requirement where father never has opportunity to develop a relationship:** Supreme Court decisions (i.e., the trilogy above) address cases in which the biological father has an opportunity to develop a relationship with the child. The most difficult cases occur when a father never has such an opportunity—either because he does not know of the child's birth or because the mother's actions prevent the development of his relationship with the child.

Note: The dissent in *Lehr* raises this issue (suggesting that the mother prevented the father from establishing a relationship with the child). However, the *Lehr* majority fails to address this issue.

Example: Marquette is born prematurely. He never lives with his mother. His foster parents, Jeffrey and Karen, have taken care of him since birth and paid for his medical expenses. Seeking to adopt him, they petition to terminate the parental rights of his mother, Denise, and his unknown father. Denise's parental rights are terminated, but she is unable to identify the father of the child. The Child Welfare Bureau locates the father, Bobby, and serves him notice of the pending proceeding to terminate his parental rights. For the first time, Bobby learns that he has a child. Bobby begins to make efforts to contact Marquette and expresses interest in a parent-child relationship. The trial court terminates Bobby's parental rights based on his failure to assume parental responsibilities, and reasons that his actions after learning of the child are irrelevant. Bobby appeals. The Wisconsin Supreme Court reverses, finding that Bobby's attempts to establish a parent-child relationship with the child are relevant in deciding whether to terminate his parental rights. *In re Marquette S.*, 734 N.W.2d 81 (Wis. 2007).

C. **Noncustodial parent's consent in the face of a stepparent adoption:** Rising rates of divorce and remarriage result in an increase in reconstituted or blended families. Traditionally, state adoption laws have included provisions for stepparent adoptions in which one parent's spouse adopts the child after termination of the other parent's rights.

Case law and statutory law have become more favorable to stepparent adoption. Such procedures are often used by same-sex couples. In addition, some jurisdictions now permit stepparent adoptions without the noncustodial parent's consent in limited circumstances (e.g., cases of nonsupport and failure to communicate with the child). Due process generally requires, however, that a divorced noncustodial parent first be given notice and an opportunity to be heard before termination of parental rights.

Quiz Yourself on
CONSENT

113. Following a brief intimate relationship with Bill, Stephanie gives birth to a son Michael. Stephanie and Bill never live together. Although Stephanie informs Bill of Michael's birth, Bill never offers support or visits Michael. When Michael is two years old, Bill marries Andrea. After discovering that Andrea is unable to conceive, Bill decides that he would like to obtain custody of Michael or establish visitation rights. Meanwhile, Stephanie, herself, has remarried. Her husband Larry desires to, and does, adopt Michael. When Bill learns of the adoption, he argues that it is invalid because he was not given notice and an opportunity to be heard. Larry argues that Bill's consent was not necessary because he failed to support or to visit the boy. Will Larry prevail? _____

Answer

113. Yes. The Supreme Court has held (in *Lehr*, *Caban*, and *Quilloin*) that an unwed father is entitled to constitutional protection of his parental rights so long as he manifests certain "indicia of parenthood." That is, his constitutional rights depend on the degree to which he reveals a willingness to assume a custodial, personal, or financial relationship with the child. Here, Bill has not provided support or

visited his son Michael for two years. Bill's failure to assume any parental responsibilities probably will result in relinquishment of his constitutional rights to notice and an opportunity to be heard.

IV. PLACEMENT PROCEDURE

A. **Background:** A biological parent (or parents) may relinquish a child to a public or privately licensed *adoption agency* for adoption. The agency then undertakes to investigate prospective adoptive parents. The agency's investigation often includes an evaluation called a "home study," (i.e., individualized screening of the parents and their home before the adoption may become final).

Alternatively, a biological parent (or parents) may arrange for a private (i.e., *independent*) adoption by which a private person/intermediary facilitates the adoption. In independent adoptions, the birth parents generally select the adopters themselves (with the assistance of the intermediary) and place the child directly with the adopters (pending the court's issuance of a final adoption decree). The adoptive parents often pay birth parents' expenses in independent placement.

Note that payment of the birth parents' medical and other expenses by the adoptive parents is permissible (despite prohibitions against baby selling and trafficking).

B. **Agency's role: Disclosure requirements:** An agency that discloses information to prospective adoptive parents about a child's biological parents or medical history has a duty to disclose the information *fully* so as not to mislead the adoptive parents. If the agency breaches this duty, the agency may be liable for the tort of *wrongful adoption* (i.e., a form of misrepresentation). However, most courts have not extended an agency's responsibility to include an affirmative duty to *investigate* and discover health information about a child. See also the discussion of "wrongful adoption" below.

C. **Independent placement: Intermediary's role:** Parents who wish to place their child for adoption may arrange for a private or independent adoption rather than an agency adoption. Private adoptions are often performed through an intermediary, such as an attorney or physician.

Some statutes limit or prohibit independent adoption. Attorneys who act as intermediaries must be careful not to violate conflict of interest rules.

Example: An attorney arranges an adoption for a birth mother who is pregnant with twins, unemployed, and unmarried. He represents both the birth mother and the adopting parents. He charges the adopting parents a $50,000 fee, plus $10,000 in medical expenses, in addition to a nonrefundable $1,500 retainer. Five days after the birth, the attorney files accountings in the probate court because he is required to disclose any and all disbursements of value related to the adoptions. The attorney, who paid the birth mother's living expenses and received over $60,000 from the prospective adoptive parents, represents that no disbursements had been made. The court disbars the attorney, finding that the attorney's deliberate falsification of documents to avoid disclosure of exorbitant fees and dubious payments was contrary to the professional qualities of honesty, justice, and good character. *Stark Cty. Bar Ass'n v. Hare*, 791 N.E.2d 966 (Ohio 2003).

Some rules of professional conduct will allow an attorney to represent multiple clients, but only after full disclosure and consent has been obtained.

Example: Gregory and Barbara (Couple 1) consult an attorney about adopting an infant. The parties agree that if the couple locates a baby for adoption, the attorney would assist them. Later, the couple refers an expectant mother to the attorney. The attorney contacts the couple with regard to adopting the child, and the couple indicates their interest. Shortly thereafter, the attorney recommends that the biological mother place her child with another couple (Couple 2) who also contacted him. When the first couple learns that the child was placed with the other couple, they call the attorney and request that the child be placed with them. The attorney refuses. Gregory institutes a complaint with the state bar, alleging that the attorney violated rules regarding conflicts of interest. The court determines that the attorney should be censured for violating conflict of interest rules by (1) accepting employment from Couple 2, without consent and full disclosure, after having agreed to represent Couple 1; and (2) by continuing multiple employment (of both couples) when such representation would adversely affect the interests of other clients. Censure, rather than suspension, is appropriate because the record does not unequivocally reveal that the attorney knew of the conflict (i.e., he may have been negligent in determining whether the conflict existed). *Matter of Petrie*, 742 P.2d 796 (Ariz. 1987).

Note: The Model Rules of Professional Conduct, in addressing the role of attorneys as adoption intermediaries, requires full disclosure of the implications of common representation, client consent thereto, full explanations of each decision to be made, and withdrawal from the matter upon request or dissatisfaction. Further, the attorney must reasonably believe the matter can be resolved impartially and consistent with the clients' best interests. Model Rules Prof'l Conduct R. 2.2 (2004).

D. **Criticisms of independent adoption:** The benefits of independent adoption include: (a) the process allows birth parents to select the adoptive parents; (b) prospective adoptive parents can avoid lengthy agency waiting lists; and (c) adoptive children avoid the necessity of spending a transitional period in foster care. Criticisms of independent adoption include: (a) the process is largely unregulated by the state; and (b) independent adoptions primarily help adults who are seeking a child to adopt, sometimes at the expense of child welfare.

V. SUBSIDIZED ADOPTION

A. **Background:** All states provide subsidized adoption programs to facilitate adoption of those children who are difficult to place for reasons of age, physical or mental disability, or racial or ethnic background. Specifically, states appropriate funds to social service agencies to provide assistance to adoptive parents who care for these children. The subsidy varies in duration and type (services and funds), and the needs of the child.

B. **Federal legislation:**

1. **Adoption Assistance and Child Welfare Act:** Although state subsidies first began in 1969 in New York, the federal Adoption Assistance and Child Welfare Act of 1980 (AACWA), 42 U.S.C. §§620-628, §§670-679(a), encourages the establishment and expansion of such state programs. Hoping to address "foster care drift" (i.e., lengthy stays in foster care), legislators desired to provide assistance especially to those foster parents who would like, but financially were unable, to adopt needy children in their care. The Act provides funds to states that qualify by enacting statutes that authorize subsidies for adoption of children with "special needs."

2. Adoption and Safe Families Act: The Adoption and Safe Families Act (ASFA) of 1997 strengthens the provisions of the AACWA by providing incentives to states to promote the adoption of children with special needs and those in foster care as well as requiring states to provide for health insurance for such children. 42 U.S.C. §673b (incentives); §671(a) (insurance).

Subsequent amendments decreased ASFA's earlier emphasis on family preservation in order to promote adoption by requiring states to seek termination of parental rights after children spent a designated length of time in foster care (42 U.S.C. §675(5)). Critics point out that this provision of ASFA no longer reflects best practices, causing harm to children of color.

VI. INTERNATIONAL ADOPTION

A. Background: Interest in intercountry adoption is attributable to several factors, including the domestic shortage of white infant adoptees, strict agency restrictions on adopters, and a belief that intercountry adoptions are less vulnerable to post-placement challenges. Poverty and natural disasters, as well as unrest among religious groups, also motivate U.S. citizens to adopt children from abroad.

B. Criticisms:

International adoption, the practice by which an American couple adopts a child from a foreign country, has generated considerable controversy. Advocates of the practice argue that international adoptions protect children in third-world countries from institutional care and poverty. Opponents point out the underlying colonialism reflected by the practice as well as the argument that these adoptions deprive children of their cultural heritage.

C. Decline: Intercountry adoptions have plummeted in recent years. International adoptions declined by half from their peak in 2004 until 2010, and then decreased again by half in 2015. Reasons for the decline include foreign governments' dislike of lax practices by U.S. adoption service providers (e.g., careless home studies, poor supervision, and nonexistent or fraudulent postplacement reporting) and inadequate federal and state regulation. Politics also played a role: Russia banned U.S. citizens from adopting Russian children in 2012, purportedly in retaliation for a U.S. law (Magnitsky Act) that sanctioned Russian officials and nationals for human rights abuses.

D. Applicable laws: Different laws apply to international adoption. The prospective adoptive couple must first meet the relinquishment requirements of the foreign country. Then the parents must satisfy federal immigration laws when they bring the child into the United States. Finally, the parents must meet state adoption standards when they petition to adopt the child.

E. Hague Convention: The Hague Convention on Protection of Children and Cooperation in Respect of Intercountry Adoption was adopted in 1993 to facilitate international adoptions by requiring determinations that adoption serves the child's best interests and by establishing supervisory authorities. The United States ratified and enacted implementing legislation for this Convention in 2001. 42 U.S.C. §§14901 to 14954. The legislation applies only when both countries involved are convention signatories. It was designed to protect against the risks of illegal, irregular, premature, or ill-prepared adoptions abroad.

VII. THE LEGAL CONSEQUENCES OF ADOPTION

By its termination of the rights and responsibilities of biological parents and the creation of a new legal relationship with adoptive parents, adoption sometimes results in unique civil consequences.

A. Cutoff rule: An adoption decree terminates ("cuts off") the legal relationship between the adoptee and his or her biological relatives and replaces it with ties to the adoptive family. The "cut off rule" treats the adopted child as if she or he were a biological child of the adoptive parent(s) for all purposes.

B. Marriage limitations: Occasionally, persons related by adoption may wish to marry each other. Whether they may do so depends on state statute or judicial interpretation. Some state laws prohibit persons related by adoption from marrying each other.

> **Example:** Martin and Tammy, a brother and sister related by adoption, are denied a license to marry. A statute prohibits marriage between a brother and sister "whether the relationship is by the half or the whole blood or by adoption." Martin's father married Tammy's mother when Martin was 18 and living away from home, while Tammy was 13 and living with her mother. Martin's father adopts Tammy. Martin and Tammy argue that the statutory provision violates the Equal Protection Clause. The court holds that the provision prohibiting marriage between adopted children is unconstitutional because it fails to satisfy the rational basis test. The court reasons that the traditional objections to such marriages (fear of genetic defects in offspring and moral condemnation) are absent. *Israel v. Allen*, 577 P.2d 762, 763 (Colo. 1978).

> **Note:** In *Israel v. Allen*, *supra*, petitioners did not grow up together or live together as a family. Some courts are more reluctant to permit such marriages if the individuals do so.

C. Inheritance

  1. Intestate succession: By or from the adopted child: Following a child's adoption by adoptive parents, the child traditionally loses the right to inherit from the biological parents. In particular, an adopted child loses the right to inherit by *intestate succession* (i.e., when a biological parent dies without a will). Instead, the adopted child is treated as a member of the adoptive family for purposes of inheritance. Thus, the child inherits by intestate succession only from the adoptive parents.

  A corollary is that if the adopted child predeceases a parent, the child's intestate estate passes to the adoptive parent(s) and not to the biological parent(s). This is the rule of inheritance "by or from" the adopted child.

  2. Inheritance and stepparent adoption: Some state laws now provide that an adopted child is still considered a child of a noncustodial biological parent when the child is adopted by the spouse of the custodial biological parent (i.e., following a remarriage).

  3. Stranger-to-the-adoption rule: A troublesome question for many courts, following the enactment of adoption statutes, is whether an adopted child inherits under the will of a person who is a relative of an adoptive parent (i.e., who is a literal "stranger" to the adoption). Under the "stranger-to-the-adoption rule," courts refuse to construe class gift language in a will or trust (i.e., language such as "to my nephews," or "to my sister's children") in such a way as to include adoptees—except in instruments executed by adoptive parents. Application of this rule precludes an adoptee from inheriting *through* either the biological parent's or the adoptive parent's family line when a relative of that biological or adoptive parent dies. The rationale for the "stranger-to-the-adoption rule" is a preference for relatives of the blood line.

Because of the harshness of the doctrine, many states carve out exceptions to the rule. A common exception permits an adopted child to take if the child is adopted before (but not after) the testator's death (i.e., so that the decedent is aware of the child's adoption and could have altered his or her will to preclude the child if desired). Some states apply the stranger-to-the-adoption rule to preclude inheritance by adult adoptees.

D. **Custody and visitation:** Stepparent adoption sometimes gives rise to visitation disputes when a child's grandparents desire to maintain contact with grandchildren in a post-divorce adoption situation. See the discussion of grandparent visitation in Chapter 5.

Quiz Yourself on *THE LEGAL CONSEQUENCES OF ADOPTION*

114. Miranda was born to Anne and Bob. When she was three years old, Anne and Bob put Miranda up for adoption because they are heavy drug abusers and determine that adoption is the best option for her future. Miranda is adopted by Stephanie and Todd. Five years later, Anne and Bob both pass away intestate, without leaving any close relatives, due to an airplane accident. Their estates collect $500,000 based on the airline's negligence. Miranda seeks to inherit Bob and Anne's real property. Will Miranda succeed?

Answer

114. No. Miranda will not succeed. Following a child's adoption by adoptive parents, the child traditionally loses the right to inherit intestate from the biological parents. Instead, the adopted child is treated as a member of the adoptive family (Stephanie and Todd's family) for purposes of inheritance. Miranda cannot inherit from Anne and Bob's intestate estates.

VIII. OPEN ADOPTION

A. **Definition:** Traditionally, the severance of the biological parent-child relationship also extinguishes a biological parent's visitation rights. Sometimes, however, the biological parent desires and arranges post-adoption visitation. *Open adoption* is a form of adoption that reflects a continuation of contact, following an adoption, between the biological parent and the adopted child.

B. **Modern trend:** The modern trend is to recognize open adoption.

C. **Best interests standard:** Courts, increasingly, are asked to enforce written agreements by adoptive and biological parties that authorize these arrangements. Courts generally uphold such agreements if the agreements are found to be in the best interests of the child.

Example: Debbie gives birth to Laci. Three years later, Debbie permits Mr. and Mrs. Clark (a couple with whom she is acquainted) to adopt Laci. Debbie refuses to give her consent to the adoption unless the Clarks permit her to have visitation rights. Both the Clarks and Debbie sign a post-adoption visitation agreement that grants such visitation. The Clarks abide by the agreement for over a year. Subsequently, when Debbie wants to visit Laci on Laci's birthday, the Clarks refuse and tell Debbie that she can no longer visit the child. Debbie requests specific performance of the agreement. The trial court determines that the adoption terminated Debbie's parental rights and holds the visitation agreement unenforceable. The state supreme court concludes that courts should give effect to post-adoption visitation agreements when continued visitation is in the best interests of the child and remands for such a determination. *Groves v. Clark*, 920 P.2d 981 (Mont. 1996).

Quiz Yourself on
OPEN ADOPTION

115. Samantha, a college student, has just given birth to a daughter, Gail, as the result of a casual relationship. After taking a semester off to care for the child while she works part-time, Samantha decides it would be better to place Gail for adoption. Samantha is convinced that she cannot properly care for Gail at this time because Samantha is not financially independent and also would like to finish her education. Samantha wishes, however, to maintain contact with Gail. With the help of one of her professors, Samantha locates a professional couple, Dr. and Mrs. Jones, who would like to adopt Gail. Dr. and Mrs. Jones agree to sign an agreement that permits Samantha to have visitation rights following the adoption. Following the adoption, Samantha visits Gail every few weeks. Two years later, when Gail is going through "the terrible twos," Dr. and Mrs. Jones decide that it might be better for Gail psychologically not to have further contact with Samantha. Samantha sues to enforce the agreement. Will she prevail? _____

Answer

115. Yes. A modern court is likely to uphold the agreement (for an "open adoption") if the court finds such an arrangement to be in the best interests of the child. Here, Samantha cared for Gail for several months and continued to visit Gail regularly even after the adoption. Gail and Samantha have formed psychological bonds. A court might well decide that it would be in the child's best interests to enforce the agreement.

IX. EQUITABLE ADOPTION

A. **Definition:** Equitable adoption is an equitable device whereby courts effectuate an adoption (or effectuate the consequences of an adoption) in cases in which a legal adoption never occurred.

B. **Inheritance purposes:** The doctrine is most often invoked to permit a child to *inherit from* a foster parent who agreed to, or attempted to, adopt the child but never completed the necessary legal procedure. Occasionally, courts invoke the doctrine to permit a child to *inherit through* a foster parent (i.e., from relatives of the foster parent). However, some courts require clear and convincing evidence of intent to adopt.

Example: A child claims an intestate share of his foster father's estate as an equitably adopted son. (The foster father died without issue or a surviving spouse.) The California Supreme Court holds that, although the evidence revealed a close family relationship (i.e., the child lived with his foster parents from the ages of 2 to 22), there is insufficient proof of an intent to adopt him (i.e., that the family ever made an attempt to adopt him or stated their intent to do so), as required by statute. *Estate of Ford*, 82 P.3d 747 (Cal. 2004).

C. **Theories:** Courts apply various theories to cases of equitable adoption.

1. **Contract theory:** Contract theory is often based on part performance or specific performance when a person has agreed to adopt a child but has failed to fully perform the contract. This theory has doctrinal difficulties in applying specific performance (e.g., enforcement after the death of a party and a reluctance to enforce personal service contracts).

   Example: Mr. and Mrs. Daggett desire to adopt a six-year-old girl (Plaintiff) subject to her father's consent. Plaintiff is being raised by her aunt and uncle. Plaintiff's biological father, upon being informed of the Daggetts' desire, permits the aunt and uncle to deliver Plaintiff to the Daggetts. The Daggetts change the child's name to theirs, baptize her, and raise her as their daughter although they never formally adopt her. When Mr. Daggett dies intestate, Plaintiff seeks to share in his estate as his adopted child. The court decrees an equitable adoption to the extent that Plaintiff becomes an heir of the couple. The court reasons that the remedy is appropriate because the couple took Plaintiff into their home with the understanding that they could adopt her. Although the adoption never occurred, Plaintiff's biological father fully performed his side of the agreement. *Long v. Wiley*, 391 S.W.2d 301 (Miss. 1965).

2. **Estoppel theory:** Other courts apply estoppel theory to protect the child (who has "relied" on the representation that she is adopted) from the adoptive parents' neglect in order to complete the adoption. This theory has conceptual difficulties based on the assumption of the child's detrimental reliance on the contract, especially as applied to children who are adopted young, unaware of the adoption, and lack any meaningful alternative.

3. **Equitable relief:** Other states recognize equitable adoption based on equitable considerations (the promotion of fairness and the presumed intent of the decedent). Some courts interpret decedent's intent liberally whereas other courts apply a strict approach.

   Example: Rosa North Ford died intestate. She raised several foster children, including Raymond North-Bey who she held out as her son, obtained a Social Security card for him bearing her last name, and enrolled him in school under that name. He lived his life believing he was her adopted child. After her death, he assumes he had inherited her property and moves into her house. One of the other foster children files a petition to probate her estate. North-Bey files a motion asking the court to recognize his right to inherit as an equitably adopted child. The trial court denies his claim. The D.C. Court of Appeals concedes that the intestacy statute would bar his claim. Based on the law of other jurisdictions, however, the court determines that the intestacy statute does not foreclose equitable relief. The court reverses and remands, holding that an individual can claim the status as the decedent's child as a matter of equity. *In re Estate of North Ford*, 200 A.3d 1207 (D.C. Ct. App. 2019).

Example: David Fried asserts that he was equitably adopted by his stepfather (decedent) when he was three years old after his mother married decedent who treated Fried as his son. Fried argues the equitable adoption was based on an implied agreement to adopt him. He claims that the only reason decedent did not legally adopt him was because his birth father refused consent. He produces testimony that decedent told a relative that Fried would inherit his possessions. Decedent's brother objects, arguing that decedent died intestate and without a spouse or biological children. The appellate court affirms the trial court order rejecting Fried's claim and determining that decedent's brother Paul is the sole beneficiary. The court reasons that Fried failed to provide clear and convincing evidence that decedent impliedly agreed to adopt him. *Matter of Intestate Estate of Feinstein*, 2019 WL 7187444 (N.J. Super. Ct. App. Div. 2019).

Some states require (for an equitable adoption) that the parent-child relationship began during the child's minority and a legal obstacle existed to the adoption (such as refusal of the birth parent's consent). *See, e.g.,* Cal. Prob. Code §6454.

Quiz Yourself on EQUITABLE ADOPTION

116. Mary and John have twin girls. When the twins are only a few months old, Mary is diagnosed with terminal cancer. She dies shortly thereafter. John has extreme difficulty coping with his wife's death and trying to raise the twins. Sally and Tom Lambert, an infertile couple whom John knows, inquire whether John would be willing to let them adopt the girls. John agrees. The Lamberts take the twins into their home and raise them as their own daughters, telling their friends and family that the girls are adopted. In reality, the Lamberts never complete a legal adoption. The Lamberts die intestate, victims of an automobile accident, when the twins are approaching adulthood. The twins petition the probate court to permit them to take a share of the Lamberts' intestate estates. The Lamberts' relatives argue that the twins should not share in the estate because they are not biologically related children. Will the relatives prevail? _____

Answer

116. No. Application of the doctrine of equitable adoption would permit the twins to claim their shares in their foster parents' estate. Courts invoke the doctrine as an equitable remedy in cases in which the foster parent(s) promised to adopt a child but never actually does so. Here, the Lamberts agreed with the children's father that the Lamberts would adopt the twins. Under either a theory of specific performance (the Lamberts and the father agreed to the adoption; the father performed his side of the agreement by surrendering the children), or a estoppel theory (the twins "relied" on the agreement by assuming they were the Lamberts' children). Therefore, the Lamberts' relatives should be estopped to deny the adoption), a court should equitably decree that the children share in the Lamberts' estates.

X. ADOPTEE'S RIGHT TO KNOW OF ORIGINS

A. **Traditional rule:** State adoption statutes traditionally required strict confidentiality. Thus, following an adoption, the original birth certificate and adoption records are sealed so that neither the adopted child nor a biological parent may determine the identity of the other. Historically, courts permitted disclosure only upon "good cause" (e.g., a medical necessity). This traditional rule applied to adoption agencies. However, the agencies often chose to release limited information for genetic or medical purposes.

   Example: Roger B. is an adult adoptee who has searched for his biological parents for three years. Roger petitions the court to secure access to his adoption records. He acknowledges that he has no medical or psychiatric need to know. A statute places birth and adoption records under seal and allows their release only for "good cause." Roger argues that the right to know his identity is a constitutionally protected fundamental right based on the right of privacy. The court holds that an adoptee does not have a fundamental right to examine adoption records, reasoning that no fundamental right or right of privacy is implicated. Further, the statute is rationally related to the legitimate purpose of protecting the confidentiality of the adoption process. *In re Roger B.*, 418 N.E.2d 751, *appeal dismissed*, 454 U.S. 806 (Ill. 1981).

B. **Modern view:** A growing movement allows and facilitates the exchange of information between an adopted child and the biological parents. Some states now permit biological parents to consent to the release of information pertaining to their identity or location. Other states allow those adoptees who have reached the age of majority to have access to their adoption records, to request a state or private agency to investigate the location of a birth parent, or to authorize the agency to release identifying information to family members who may make a similar inquiry.

C. **The Internet.** Social media websites currently enable adoptees to locate their birth relatives with relative ease, thereby hastening the demise of the principle of anonymity.

Quiz Yourself on *ADOPTEE'S RIGHT TO KNOW OF ORIGINS*

117. Timothy, an adoptee, seeks nonidentifying information about the medical history of his biological mother. In his petition to unseal the adoption records, he provides affidavits from his physicians stating that the medical information would be "very helpful" and "should assist" the physicians in better diagnosing and more effectively caring for Timothy and his children. Timothy has no current medical reason for his request. A state statute provides that a court may unseal adoption records for "good cause." Will Timothy succeed? _____

Answer

117. No. Although medical necessity traditionally constitutes "good cause" to unseal adoption records, here Timothy has not established a serious health condition necessary to establish a "medical necessity." A court generally will not unseal an adoption record simply because the knowledge of hereditary information might be useful. Thus, Timothy's request will not succeed.

XI. ADULT ADOPTION

A. **General rule:** Most states allow adoption of an adult by statute or case law. However, some states impose special limitations on such adoptions (i.e., co-residence, close relatives, or age restrictions).

B. **Requirements:** Adult adoption generally requires only the consent of the parties (unlike the adoption of a child which is predicated on the best-interests-of-the-child standard).

C. **Limitations:** Some jurisdictions inquire into the purpose of the adult adoption. Although adoptions may not be for fraudulent, illegal, or frivolous purposes, they may effectuate inheritance purposes.

D. **Adoption of same-sex partners:** Before the advent of marriage equality, same-sex partners sometimes sought to establish an adoptive relationship to confer legal benefits on their partners and to secure some form of societal recognition of their relationship. Historically, however, some states refused to permit adult adoption by gays and lesbians. Courts in these jurisdictions reasoned that permitting adoption in contexts other than parent-child would distort the idea of adoption and confer legitimacy on same-sex relationships.

    Example: A 57-year-old male petitions to adopt his 50-year-old male partner. The couple has lived together for 25 years and desires the adoption for social, financial, and emotional reasons. The Family Court denies the petition, reasoning that the adoption would subvert the adoption process for purposes that are more appropriately served by marriage, wills, and business contracts, and also that the couple's relationship is not that of parent and child. The court finds that the legislature could not have intended to permit a lover to adopt the other partner. Because these parties do not intend a parent-child relationship and their relationship reveals no incidents of a parent-child relationship, the statute cannot sanction an adoption that would "distort [ ] the function of adoption" and be "an unreasonable or absurd result." The court concludes that adoption is not a means of obtaining legal recognition for a nonmarital sexual relationship. *In re Robert Paul P.*, 471 N.E.2d 424, 427 (N.Y. Ct. App. 1984).

E. **Modern view:** The recognition of marriage equality eliminated the need for adult adoptions by same-sex partners. For a discussion of the role of sexual orientation in the adoption of children, see Section II.B.2, *supra*.

XII. ADOPTION FAILURE: REVOCATION AND ABROGATION

Adoptions may fail either because of the actions of a biological parent who revokes consent or because of the desires of the adoptive parent(s) to abrogate (vacate) the adoption.

A. **Revocation of consent:** Statutes confer the right on a biological parent to revoke consent to an adoption in limited circumstances (i.e., fraud, duress, and coercion).

    Historically, many jurisdictions permitted a birth parent to revoke consent at any time prior to the final decree. Stemming from a concern with certainty and finality, most jurisdictions now *limit the period* for revocation of consent.

    Example: A Colombian woman conceives a child out of wedlock. Fearing shame to herself and her family, she moves to New York to have the child. She relinquishes the four-day-old infant to an adoption agency. Ten days later, the agency places the infant with a couple for adoption. Five days later, the mother changes her mind. After learning that her wealthy parents will assist her to raise the child, she requests that the child be returned to her. When the agency refuses, she files a habeas corpus proceeding seeking return of the child. The relevant statute permits a birth mother to revoke consent unless she is proven unfit. After the court refuses to allow the prospective adoptive parents to intervene, the prospective adoptive parents argue that the court's refusal deprives them of due process. The court holds that the best interests of the child dictate that the child should be returned to her biological mother whose relinquishment decision was improvident and motivated by concern for the child. The court reasons that the mother has not been proven unfit, and is educated, financially secure, and in a position to assume the child's care. The trial court's refusal to permit the adoptive parents to intervene did not violate due process because the prospective adoptive parents do not have legal custody (i.e., the agency does). *Scarpetta v. Spence-Chapin Adoption Serv.*, 269 N.E.2d 787 (N.Y. Ct. App. 1971).

Epilogue: The prospective adoptive parents flee to Florida with the child before the New York court's decision. When the mother files a habeas corpus petition in Florida, the prospective adoptive parents argue that they are not bound by the New York decision because they were not parties to the litigation (i.e., the court did not permit them to intervene). A Florida court subsequently holds that, based on the best interests of the child, the baby should remain with the adoptive parents. The New York legislature subsequently overruled *Scarpetta* by statute (N.Y. Dom. Rel. Law §115-b(6)(d)(v)) to make it more difficult for the birth mother to revoke her consent.

B. Abrogation

1. **Definition:** Abrogation is the annulment of an adoption by the adoptive parents.

2. **Traditional view:** Courts are reluctant to permit abrogation. Concerns focus on whether abrogation serves the best interests of the child and who will support a child whose adoption has been annulled. Some states allow abrogation only if there is evidence of fraud or misrepresentation on the part of the agency or a procedural defect in the adoption.

3. **Wrongful adoption:** Some states that refuse to permit abrogation may permit *damages* in a tort suit against the agency for "wrongful adoption" (i.e., negligent or intentional misrepresentation).

   Example: Richard and Charlene adopt a baby from the Children's Home Society (CHS) and name him Jordan. They are told by the agency that the child has no medical history of substance abuse. Several months later, Charlene becomes curious about Jordan's unusual facial features and contacts a CHS caseworker to ask if Jordan's birth mother used alcohol during pregnancy. The caseworker assures Charlene that, to the best of her knowledge, his birth mother did not consume alcohol during her pregnancy, and that his unusual facial features are merely a "familial look." Later, Charlene requests information on the reason for Jordan's developmental delays, and CHS again assures her that fetal alcohol syndrome was not involved. In fact, agency records reveal that the birth mother admitted that she was an alcoholic and that she frequently got drunk during the pregnancy. Charlene and Richard file suit against CHS, alleging intentional and negligent misrepresentation and breach of contract. The court holds that the adoptive parents stated an actionable claim against the adoption agency for its intentional and negligent misrepresentation of facts regarding alcohol abuse by the child's birth mother. *Wolford v. Children's Home Soc'y of W. Va.*, 17 F. Supp. 2d 577 (S.D. W. Va. 1998).

Quiz Yourself on ABROGATION

118.   Mr. and Mrs. Xavier file an application with the ABC Adoption Agency to adopt a child. The agency informs Mr. and Mrs. Xavier that a baby is available. The agency also tells them that the child's paternal grandmother died of a genetic disease, Huntington's disease. The agency also informs Mr. and Mrs. Xavier that, because the child's father tested negative for the disease, the child is not at risk. In fact, no such test existed. The child is diagnosed with the disease four years later. The adoptive parents sue the agency for "wrongful adoption" (negligent misrepresentation). Will they prevail? _____

Answer

118.   Yes. The agency assumed the duty of informing the adoptive parents, the Xaviers, about the child's medical background (i.e., the family history of Huntington's disease and about the child's chances of developing the disease). Having done so, the agency breached their duty by informing the Xaviers that the child's biological father tested negative for the disease when no such test existed.

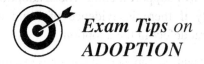 *Exam Tips on* ADOPTION

- ☛ *Commonly tested issues* in the area of adoption include: selection standards for adoptive parents; consent; placement procedures; various types of adoption (open adoption, equitable adoption, adult adoption); the adoptee's right to know of origins; and adoption failure.

- ☛ First, discuss the *legal effect of adoption* (i.e., the creation of a new parent-child relationship and termination of the legal rights and responsibilities of the biological parents). Determine whether there are any initial issues regarding the validity of the termination of the biological parents' rights (e.g., cross-over issues with the child abuse context such as whether the court had jurisdiction and whether the parents' due process rights were safeguarded). Explain the guiding *standard* in adoption law (*the best interests of the child*). Then, explore whether there are issues of *selection standards* for the adoptive parents. Look for frequently tested standards involving *religion, race,* and *sexual orientation*. Discuss the traditional rules on the relevance of each factor (i.e., religious matching, race matching, sexual orientation). Discuss possible *constitutional issues* (First and Fourteenth Amendments) if public adoption agencies are involved. Then, apply the best-interests-of-the-child test to the particular facts.

  - ☞ If the question involves the issue of *sexual orientation*, clarify whether the issue is adoption of adults or children. Discuss the *different views* (traditional and modern) that restrict or permit such adoptions.

☞ Remember that if the question involves placement of a Native-American child, federal legislation (the *Indian Child Welfare Act*) is relevant. That Act mandates a preference for tribal members, absent good cause. If the ICWA is relevant, be sure to discuss the "existing Indian family" exception and Supreme Court developments (the "Baby Veronica" case). Discuss the current constitutional challenge to ICWA.

☛ Another commonly tested issue is *consent*. Consent issues may arise concerning the *biological mother or biological father*. For example, was the mother's consent valid, or subject to *fraud or duress*? Consent issues also may concern the *biological father*. Determine if the child's parents were married or unmarried. If the question involves an *unmarried father*, determine how his rights may have been infringed. What relief is he seeking? Is he seeking notice of the adoption proceedings and an opportunity to be heard? Is his objection to the adoption timely? Has he registered in the paternity register in the requisite jurisdiction?

☞ If the unmarried father is alleging that his procedural *due process* rights have been infringed (i.e., his right to notice and an opportunity to be heard), be sure to discuss and apply U.S. Supreme Court rulings in *Stanley v. Illinois*, *Quilloin v. Walcott*, *Caban v. Mohammed*, and *Lehr v. Robertson*. Explain and apply the rule that an unmarried father is entitled to constitutional protection of his parental rights so long as he manifests certain *indicia of parenthood*. Application of the rule requires an exploration of the father's actions vis-à-vis the mother and the child: Did the father pay for the mother's medical expenses (and support) prior to, and/or after, the child's birth? Did the father attend birthing classes with the mother? Did the parents live together before and/or after the birth? Is the father named on the birth certificate? Did the father provide support for the child after the birth? Did the father communicate and/or visit with the child after the birth? If the father has not manifested the requisite indicia of parenthood, explore the reason why. For example, did the birth mother *thwart* his efforts? If so, did he act in a timely manner once he learned of the child's birth or location and manifest his willingness to assume parental responsibilities? Discuss the relevance of laws that permit termination of a father's parental rights over his objection in some circumstances.

☛ Keep in mind the issue of whether this is an *agency adoption* or an *independent adoption*. If the former, did the agency follow the *proper procedures* (regarding consent and disclosure)? If the latter, make sure that no criminal statutes for *baby selling* are implicated. Point out that some states limit or prohibit participation of independent agents in the adoption process. If the intermediary is an attorney, check whether there is a violation of any rules of professional conduct (e.g., conflicts of interest).

☛ Explore whether various forms of adoption might be relevant — open adoption, equitable adoption, and/or adult adoption. For *open adoption*, discuss the *traditional view* of confidentiality and the *modern view* that favors open adoption. Explain and apply the rule that courts generally uphold open adoption agreements if found to be in the child's best interests. Remember that the *equitable adoption* doctrine is used to permit a child to *inherit* from a foster parent. Discuss and apply the various theories (contract theory, estoppel theory, intent) that courts utilize in equitable adoption cases. For adult adoption, discuss the *general rule* (permitting adults to adopt other adults) and the various *limitations* (e.g., the requirement of a preexisting parent-child relationship beginning during the adoptee's minority).

☛ Determine whether an adoptee is seeking *access to his or her birth records*. If so, discuss the *traditional view* of confidentiality (permitting release of medical records for good cause) and the *modern trend* permitting broader access.

☞ Explore whether *adoption failure* is an issue. If so, explore which aspect of adoption failure is involved: a biological parent who revokes consent and/or an adoptive parent who seeks to vacate the adoption. In the former case, specify the traditional rule that permits revocation of consent in limited circumstances. Explore whether those circumstances (fraud, duress) exist.

☞ If abrogation is involved, determine whether the biological parent revoked his or her consent in a *timely* manner. Explain the *modern trend* that state statutes and model legislation now limit the time period within which a birth parent may revoke consent and the policy underlying that trend (to ensure stability for the child). If an agency is involved, explore whether the adoptive parents might have an action for *wrongful adoption*. Mention that some jurisdictions permit such tort claims against adoption agencies. Then, explore whether the requisite elements of the tort claim are present. For example, was there an intentional or negligent misrepresentation (or failure to disclose) on the part of the agency? What was the nature of that misrepresentation (or failure to disclose)? And finally, did the adoptive parents rely on that misrepresentation when they adopted the child?

Essay Exam Questions

QUESTION 1: Rachel and Samuel Martin have been married for eight years and reside in the jurisdiction of Blackacre. Samuel is 32 years old; Rachel is 30 years old. Both are in good health. They are the parents of four children, ranging in age from seven years to one month.

Rachel works as a teacher in a local preschool. She is able to bring her infant son with her to work, where he is cared for by her co-workers at the preschool. Rachel currently earns $50,000 a year. Throughout the marriage, Samuel, a scholar of linguistics, has been unemployed. When they married, Rachel agreed to support the family while Samuel devoted himself to the study of ancient languages and the completion of his Ph.D. The couple manages financially with Rachel's salary plus approximately $15,000 annually in gifts to Samuel from Samuel's parents. Samuel uses all of his parents' financial gifts in furtherance of his scholarly work, which includes drafting a treatise explaining biblical texts.

Serious marital difficulties have arisen. Six months ago, Rachel moved out of the marital bedroom and into quarters in the basement. She recently filed for divorce. Samuel continues to refuse, as he has throughout the marriage, to provide financially for Rachel and the children. Samuel argues that he is not purposely seeking to avoid his support duties. Rather, he points out that his life's work as a linguistics scholar prevents him from acquiring an income-producing vocation.

Before the couple's marital difficulties force Rachel to move into the basement, she approaches Attorney Aaron Atwood. She requests Atwood's advice as to how she might force Samuel to provide for her and the children—now and in the future—in the event of a divorce. Rachel wonders on what grounds she should petition for divorce. If a divorce should occur, she informs Atwood that she is thinking of leaving Blackacre to reside with her parents (who live in another jurisdiction). She would like to refuse to allow Samuel to see the children unless he provides support.

Rachel tells Attorney Atwood that she has been the sole provider for the family during the marriage. As a result, she believes that she should be entitled to all of the marital property, which includes the equity in the family residence as well as the funds in a savings account in Samuel's name (approximately $50,000) that were derived solely from gifts from Samuel's parents. She also wonders whether she has a claim for repayment of any funds derived from her employment that Samuel spent in furtherance of his Ph.D. studies during the marriage.

Further, Rachel wonders if she has any right to any of the royalties from a linguistic treatise that Samuel just published. The treatise is being hailed as a major achievement and has led to national recognition of Samuel as a linguist of extraordinary ability. Royalties on the treatise are expected to be approximately $25,000 a year.

What advice should Attorney Atwood provide to Rachel about child support and spousal support (now and in the future), possible grounds for divorce, and the division of the couple's property?

QUESTION 2: Ellen meets Trenton Smith while she is employed as a computer programmer in Trenton's business. Soon after, they move in together, and Ellen gives birth to a daughter Katie. Ellen and Trenton live together with their daughter in the jurisdiction of Greenacre for four years. Their friends and acquaintances believe that they are married, although they have never undergone a marriage ceremony. Ellen uses the name "Smith" for all purposes. The names "Mr. and Mrs. Smith" appear on their mailbox. Ellen and Trenton travel together frequently for purposes of Trenton's business, especially to the jurisdiction of Redacre, where Ellen's parents reside and where Trenton has a business supplier. On numerous occasions, they stay in Redacre hotels for business, for periods ranging from three days to three weeks. Unlike Greenacre, Redacre recognizes common-law marriages.

Ellen and Trenton's relationship begins to be stormy. They have frequent fights about money and about Trenton's indulgent childrearing practices. On one occasion while they are visiting Redacre, Ellen threatens to leave Trenton. Trenton tells her that she cannot leave, because "you are my wife in the eyes of God." She agrees to patch up the quarrel, responding, "I'm as married to you as I ever could be."

Several months after their return to Greenacre, Trenton announces that now he wants to separate. Ellen agrees to move out. She and Trenton enter into a joint custody agreement whereby they agree that Katie will remain in Ellen's physical custody but Trenton will have liberal visitation rights. Ellen and Katie subsequently move to Redacre where Ellen's parents reside and where Ellen has employment.

After Ellen and Katie have been in Redacre for eight months, Trenton files a petition in Redacre for modification to sole custody in his favor. Trenton is angry that Ellen has decided to move in with her new partner, Linda. Katie has written to Trenton that Katie does not like life in Redacre and that she particularly does not like her mother's new girlfriend. Katie is depressed because she misses her best friend from Greenacre. Although Katie is doing well in school and likes her new school, she has not yet made friends there and is sometimes teased about her mother's same-sex relationship. Ellen believes that Trenton's request for custody modification is not justified.

While the custody battle is in progress, Trenton dies intestate (i.e., without a will). Discuss Ellen's claims in the custody dispute and Ellen's claim to Trenton's estate as Trenton's alleged common-law wife.

QUESTION 3: Carl Brady is arrested and charged with armed robbery. Pending his trial, he marries Diana Simpson, a woman he has known for several years. He is convicted and receives a seven-year sentence. At his sentencing, Carl is assigned to Blackacre State Prison, a maximum security facility. When Carl arrives at the prison, he receives a "Resident's Handbook" that explains the procedures and operations of the facility. Among these procedures, the handbook explains the prison's visiting policy:

> Visiting is conducted on Tuesday and Thursday between the hours of 6 P.M. and 9:30 P.M. and on Saturday and Sunday between 8 P.M. and 11 P.M. All residents are permitted 15 hours of visiting each month. A visiting room is provided for inmates and their guests. Limited physical contact is acceptable, subject to supervision by correctional officers in order to ensure the safety and security of the prison. Conjugal visits are not permitted. The introduction of contraband will result in permanent expulsion of a visitor.

Carl presently is 45; Diana is 39. Carl and Diana have often discussed the possibility of having children. However, they are worried about Diana's advancing age, which decreases the likelihood of conception and increases the likelihood of birth defects. They would like to have the opportunity to conceive a child before Carl is released from prison. Carl decides to join a number of other prisoners to challenge the no-conjugal-visit policy.

In the event such a challenge is unsuccessful, Carl and Diana decide to consider the possibility of artificial insemination. He and Diana both agree that Diana will attempt artificial insemination with a third-party donor. Diana consults a gynecologist who agrees to perform the procedure. Carl signs a written consent form. Diana undergoes the insemination, conceives, and gives birth to a little girl, Samantha. She raises the child herself for several years until Carl is released from prison.

Upon his release, Carl takes up residence with Diana and Samantha. Unfortunately, Carl has employment-related difficulties, and he and Diana have difficulty readjusting to each other. Also, Diana learns from Carl's probation officer that Carl was not incarcerated for armed robbery, as he told her. In fact, he was convicted of a felony murder—murder of a policeman during the robbery. Diana is so fed up with Carl generally and so incensed at Carl's deception that she decides to end their relationship. Because of her religious beliefs, she desires to secure an annulment rather than a divorce.

When Diana informs Carl that she has decided to end the marriage, he is furious. He tells her that he "won't give her or Samantha a dime!" Diana has no desire for spousal support for herself, but she does think that Carl should have to support Samantha. When she petitions for divorce and requests child support, Carl counters with the claim that Samantha is not his child, so he does not have to pay child support.

Part A. What constitutional arguments should Carl and the other prisoners raise about the prison's conjugal visiting policy?

Part B. What arguments should Diana raise in her attempt to annul her marriage to Carl?

Part C. What is the basis of Carl's claim refusing to support Samantha? What is the likelihood of his success?

Essay Exam Answers

SAMPLE ANSWER TO QUESTION 1:

Support during the marriage

First, Rachel inquires how she may require Samuel to provide support for her and the children at the present time (in the midst of the marital difficulties). Attorney Atwood should advise Rachel about the jurisdiction's rules on the duty of support. At common law, the husband had a duty to provide support for his dependents (i.e., his wife and children). The husband was required to furnish "necessaries" such as food, clothing, and shelter. In the event that the husband refused to pay, the law permitted indirect enforcement of the husband's duty by enabling a creditor to sue the husband for the costs of these items.

However, because a gender-based duty of support violates equal protection, jurisdictions have changed the common law. Rachel's likelihood of success depends on whether Blackacre follows the common law, has abolished the doctrine, extends liability to both spouses, or imposes primary liability on the serviced spouse. If the jurisdiction follows the common law, Samuel will incur liability for support of his dependents. If the jurisdiction extends liability to both spouses or imposes primary liability on the serviced spouse, Rachel will incur financial liability for the family expenses.

Rachel faces another problem with efforts to force Samuel to provide for her and the children in the midst of marital difficulties. She may be precluded from obtaining support by the doctrine of nonintervention. This doctrine, enunciated in *McGuire v. McGuire*, holds that a court will not interfere in an ongoing marriage. The doctrine is intended to promote family harmony, and to avoid adjudication of *de minimis* (trivial) issues. At the time Rachel first consults Attorney Atwood, her marriage is still intact, as she has not yet moved into the basement quarters. Thus, the court may refuse to adjudicate the matter.

Rachel can also attempt to obtain support from Samuel for her and the children by means of civil and criminal actions for nonsupport. Criminal remedies for nonsupport now exist by statute in all states with respect to children, and in many states with respect to spouses as well. However, Rachel faces an additional problem. Statutory remedies for spousal support dictate that relief is available only if the marital parties live apart. Because Rachel is still living with Samuel, she may not be able to benefit from these statutory remedies for her nonsupport.

Support upon divorce

Rachel will also attempt to obtain spousal support and child support from Samuel in the event she decides to seek divorce. At common law, a husband's duty to support his dependents extended to the duty to provide alimony in the event of a divorce. Spousal support was available to the party who was without fault. At common law, then, Samuel would have had a duty to pay Rachel alimony, especially given that she had not committed any fault-based act (unless a court interpreted her acts as desertion, see discussion *infra*).

However, *Orr v. Orr* declared that gender-based support requirements upon divorce are unconstitutional. In response to women's liberation and changing gender roles, modern courts take a much more restrictive approach than did the common law to spousal support following divorce. If Blackacre follows the Uniform Marriage and Divorce Act, for example, Rachel will probably be out of luck. UMDA provides that a spouse should receive maintenance only if that spouse lacks sufficient means to support himself or herself "through employment or because of child care responsibilities." Based on this provision, a court is unlikely to award Rachel spousal support because she is currently employed, has been the sole provider for the family for the last eight years, and is in good health. Her only hope would be to argue that she is unable to work because of her child care responsibilities to her infant son. This argument probably will fail because there is no evidence to support it. The infant is cared for at Rachel's place of employment.

Further, it is even possible, based on *Orr*'s invalidation of gender-based duties of support, that Rachel may have to pay Samuel spousal support in the event that they divorce. But, again, if Blackacre follows the UMDA approach, a court may decide against such an award to Samuel because he is able physically to support himself through employment (i.e., he could go out and get a job).

Rachel also desires child support from Samuel, in the event of divorce, for the couple's four children. At common law, the father was primarily liable for the support of his children. However, the modern trend is to consider both parents responsible for the support of their children. Traditionally, courts based the standard for child support on the needs of the children and the parents' ability to pay. Applying this standard, it seems likely that the court will order Samuel to provide support for his children based on his ability to pay (i.e., he is capable of gainful employment). Perhaps he could pay his support obligations from his book royalties, or else he would have to find employment.

Rachel's request for child support also depends on Blackacre's guidelines on child support. Federal legislation spearheaded the movement from discretion to guidelines. According to the Child Support Enforcement Amendments of 1984, the Family Support Act of 1988, and subsequent welfare reform legislation (Personal Responsibility and Work Opportunity Reconciliation Act), every state must establish guidelines for child support awards. Application of such guidelines by Blackacre would also support the imposition of liability on Samuel for child support. Because the federal law does not recommend any particular set of guidelines, the actual support ordered under Blackacre's guidelines will depend on which of the three models the jurisdiction has adopted: the income shares model (the most popular), the percentage of income model, or the Melson formula. Under any of these models, it is likely that Rachel will have to pay more toward support of the children than will Samuel, unless his income increases.

Attorney Atwood should also advise Rachel against any attempt by her to condition Samuel's visitation rights on his payment of child support. Most jurisdictions hold that a parent's right to visitation is not dependent on the duty to pay child support. Thus, Rachel may not withhold from Samuel the right to visit the children if Samuel does not pay child support. Atwood should advise Rachel that there are other methods available for the establishment and enforcement of child support awards, even in the event that she leaves Blackacre to reside with her parents. For example, legislation exists to establish child support obligations and to facilitate interstate enforcement of those obligations. All jurisdictions now have adopted the Uniform Interstate Family Support Act (UIFSA) to replace the Uniform Reciprocal Enforcement of Support Act (URESA) and the Revised Uniform Reciprocal Enforcement of Support Act (RURESA). In addition, once Rachel secures a support order, she may be able to resort to various enforcement remedies, such as contempt, income withholding, liens against Samuel's property, and suspension of his driver's license. Given that Samuel has little property, the most effective remedy might be to hold him in contempt (if he refuses to pay child support).

Grounds for divorce

Rachel also requests Attorney Atwood's advice about possible grounds for divorce. Rachel might face difficulties if she were seeking a divorce during the fault-based era or if Blackacre's statute specifies that a petitioner must resort to fault-based grounds in some situations, such as in case of a nonconsensual no-fault divorce or covenant marriage. Proof of the traditional grounds for divorce (i.e., adultery, cruelty, and desertion) presents problems for Rachel. Samuel has not committed adultery. Although mental as well as physical acts qualify as cruelty, it is questionable whether Samuel's refusal of support rises to the requisite level of cruelty (i.e., a course of conduct with adverse physical effects). And Samuel has not deserted Rachel. In some jurisdictions, Rachel might be able to rely on nonsupport as one of the miscellaneous fault-based grounds. In fact, Attorney Atwood should advise Rachel (if the jurisdiction retains fault-based grounds) that Samuel might secure a divorce based on Rachel's desertion (i.e., her moving into the basement, without justification, with the intent not to resume cohabitation).

Atwood should advise Rachel that all states today have some form of "no-fault divorce." Although no-fault is interpreted differently in different states, Rachel may not need to establish that Samuel has been guilty of a fault-based ground (unless, as discussed above, the jurisdiction requires fault-based grounds for nonconsensual no-fault divorces or covenant marriage). Instead, depending on Blackacre law, Rachel may be able to petition for divorce on the ground of "irreconcilable differences." Alternatively, depending on the jurisdiction, she may have to show that she and Samuel have been living "separate and apart" for a statutorily designated period of time. In the latter event, a question may arise as to whether Rachel's residence in the basement for the past six months constitutes sufficient "living separate and apart."

Rachel's chances of success depend on the jurisdiction's requirements for "living separate and apart." Her six months' residence in the basement may satisfy the requisite time period (which tends to vary in different jurisdictions from six months to two years). More importantly, the term "living separate and apart" refers to both the act of physical separation and the intention to dissolve the marriage. Courts differ as to the relevance of, and interpretation of, these two requirements. Some jurisdictions hold that the spouses have lived "separate and apart" even though they live in the same house (e.g., as Rachel and Samuel did in separate bedrooms). Other jurisdictions require that the spouses maintain separate residences. In terms of intention to dissolve the marriage, some restrictive jurisdictions require that the spouses live apart by mutual consent. Other jurisdictions require that if only *one* spouse forms an intent to dissolve the marriage, that spouse must clearly manifest this intent to the other. If Blackacre is one of these latter jurisdictions and if Rachel and Samuel are not in agreement about living separate and apart, Rachel would have to show that she communicated her intention to terminate the marriage to Samuel in order for the statutory period to begin to run.

Division of property

Attorney Atwood's advice to Rachel about the division of property will depend on which marital property regime Blackacre follows. At common law, jurisdictions traditionally followed the title method, according to which, property belonged to the party who has title. If Blackacre follows this approach (which is unlikely because all jurisdictions now have abandoned this approach), the family residence would belong to the spouse(s) whose name(s) appears on the deed. For example, the funds in the bank account, held in Samuel's name, would belong to Samuel.

More likely, the court will divide Rachel and Samuel's property based on equitable distribution principles. The most common marital property regime today is equitable distribution. The objective of this system is a fair distribution, under all the circumstances, of the spouses' property. Under this approach, a court considers a number of relevant statutory factors, such as the duration of the marriage, the age, health, and employment of the parties, etc. Although in some jurisdictions, a presumption exists that the most equitable division is an equal division, courts are free to deviate from that presumption if it would lead to a more equitable result.

Alternatively, Blackacre may be a community property jurisdiction. This system, in a minority of states, considers marriage as a partnership to which both parties have contributed equally. Even if Blackacre has adopted this approach, some statutory variations do exist in community property states. For example, whereas a few community property states require an equal division of the community property, others follow a regime of equitable distribution.

Depending on the applicable marital property regime, Rachel may or may not have a claim to certain assets in the division of property. Under equitable distribution, after taking into account the statutory factors (such as Rachel's major financial contributions to the family and Samuel's history of nonsupport), a court might decide to award Rachel a substantial fraction of the marital property. In contrast, in a community property state, based on partnership principles, Samuel might well have an equal right to the marital property. Depending on the jurisdiction, Rachel faces an additional problem in regard to Samuel's bank account: some jurisdictions regard property that was acquired by gift as the separate property of the recipient spouse.

Rachel also may have a claim to Samuel's "enhanced earning capacity" (i.e., profits he derives from his work as a linguistic scholar) to the extent that that earning capacity is attributable to her efforts. During marriage, one spouse may help the other obtain a license, degree, or some other means of enhanced earning capacity (e.g., the acquisition of celebrity status). Courts sometimes must determine whether the enhanced value of a spouse's career is an asset subject to distribution upon dissolution. In one case involving opera singer Frederica von Stade Elkus, the court determined that celebrity status constituted marital property subject to equitable distribution. However, the *Elkus* case is distinguishable because the opera singer's husband's contributions appear to have been greater than Rachel's. He served as voice coach and photographer, sacrificing his own career to advance hers. Rachel's best argument is that Samuel's new-found status is attributable to her efforts and contributions (financial and otherwise) in maintaining the household and rearing the children so that Samuel could devote his full-time effort to the project. Rachel faces the obstacle that a court might find that Samuel's enhanced earning capacity was personal to Samuel (i.e., attributable to his unique skill and efforts).

Rachel also might have a claim for reimbursement of her efforts involved in "putting hubby through" the Ph.D. program in linguistics. Unfortunately, if Blackacre follows the majority approach, Rachel's claim would not be successful. The majority of jurisdictions refuse to treat professional degrees that represent a spouse's enhanced earning capacity as marital property. If this is the case, Rachel's only hope is that Blackacre is one of the jurisdictions which, instead, attempt to achieve a fair result by taking the degree into account in an award of spousal support. Some courts award "reimbursement alimony" in cases in which one spouse has supported the other through a professional program during the marriage to recompense the supporting spouse for her contributions (monetary and nonmonetary) to the education and training of the other. Reimbursement alimony represents a compromise by courts and legislatures to the harshness of denying relief versus the difficulties of characterization and valuation of a professional degree or license as property.

Rachel might also hope that Blackacre follows the ALI *Principles'* innovative rationale of "loss compensation" to compensate her for her financial contribution to her husband's enhanced earning capacity. Under that approach, a recipient spouse would have to make "compensatory spousal payments" to the donor spouse to compensate for certain losses that the donor spouse experienced during the marriage. Examples of compensable losses include child care responsibilities and loss of a standard of living she experienced based on her child care and sacrifices to put Samuel through the Ph.D. program in linguistics.

SAMPLE ANSWER TO QUESTION 2:

Ellen's claims in the custody dispute

Ellen and Trenton entered into an agreement to share joint legal custody of Katie. They also agreed that Ellen would have physical custody of the girl. Trenton appears to be basing his claim for modification of the custody agreement on the ground that Ellen's cohabitation with Linda renders Ellen an unfit mother. Traditionally, a parent's cohabitation resulted in a denial of custody. However, according to the modern view, a parent's same-sex sexual conduct is only relevant if it has an adverse effect on the child. To succeed, Trenton must show that Ellen's cohabitation with Linda is having an adverse effect on Katie. Trenton may point to Katie being teased at school as harmful, but absent additional facts, it does not appear that this teasing meets the burden of the necessary degree of harm. Katie's present unhappiness with her life in Redacre is attributable primarily to the move. Being the subject of teasing as a new student is not sufficiently unusual or harmful for children that it would constitute an "adverse effect."

Ellen would also argue that Trenton is unable to meet the requisite standard for a custody modification. The parent seeking modification has the burden of proof. The standard for modification generally is higher than for an initial custody determination because of a judicial concern with avoiding the disruptive effect of changes in children's lives post-divorce. Different jurisdictions apply one of several standards for modification. Depending on Redacre's approach, Trenton may have to establish a material and/or substantial change of circumstances; show that the "best interests of the child" dictate a modification; or show that the modification is necessary because of the presence of serious endangerment of a child's physical, mental, moral, or emotional health. In the last case, if the jurisdiction follows UMDA ("serious endangerment") and Trenton cannot show endangerment, he would have to fulfill a two-year waiting period following the initial decree before he could petition for modification.

Trenton would argue that Ellen's cohabitation with Linda constitutes a "material and/or substantial" change of circumstance because now Ellen has less attention for Katie. Ellen would argue that Katie's life with her mother continues largely as before (i.e., when they left Trenton). She would argue that she still spends considerable time with Katie and does the same caretaking tasks for her as before.

Trenton could argue also that Katie is being seriously endangered, physically and emotionally, because of Linda's living with them. He might charge that the endangerment is moral because Ellen and Linda are lesbians living together without being married. Ellen would counter that no endangerment exists. She might even point to the benefits that have accrued to Katie from Linda's interest in the child. Ellen might also argue that, under *Lawrence v. Texas*, it is unconstitutional to deprive her of custody based on her same-sex relationship with Linda. In *Lawrence*, the U.S. Supreme Court held that state sodomy laws banning same-sex, but not opposite-sex, sodomy violate the individual's constitutionally protected liberty and that moral disapproval is not a legitimate interest to justify such differential treatment. However, Trenton might argue that Katie's best interest is a sufficiently compelling state interest to overcome *Lawrence*'s application to the custody context.

Trenton's best hope is that the jurisdiction follows the lowest standard for modification—merely that modification be in the best interests of the child regardless of any change in circumstances. Even so, Trenton would have difficulty meeting this standard because Katie appears to be adjusting to her new life in Redacre. She has been with her mother in Redacre for eight months. She is doing well in school and likes her new school. Modification, which would entail uprooting her at this time, would not be in her best interests.

Trenton might also argue that Ellen's relocation to Redacre where her parents reside and where she has employment constitutes grounds for modification. Jurisdictions employ different standards in relocation cases. According to the strictest standard, Ellen would have to show "exceptional circumstances" that justify the move. She probably would not be able to satisfy this burden unless she can show that she could not find employment in computer programming anywhere else. Ellen would have an easier time establishing the most liberal standard because that standard incorporates a presumption favoring the custodial parent's decision that relocation is in the child's best interests. However, most courts adopt the third approach (i.e., a balancing test that takes into account all relevant factors). If the court follows this approach, Ellen might have a difficult time because the relocation might negatively affect Trenton's ability to visit Katie. Thus, Ellen's claims for custody would depend on Redacre's standard for modification.

Ellen's claim as Trenton's common-law wife

Ellen's claim to share in Trenton's estate as his legal spouse rests on the argument that Ellen was Trenton's common-law wife. A common-law marriage, which is recognized by about a dozen states, requires no marriage ceremony. For a valid common-law marriage, the parties must presently *agree* to enter into a legal marital relationship, *cohabit*, and *hold themselves out* as husband and wife in the community.

To establish that she and Trenton had a valid common-law marriage, Ellen first must establish that she and Trenton agreed to enter into a marital relationship. Although no specific words are required, the couple's words must indicate a present agreement. Ellen would argue that Trenton's statement that she is "[his] wife in the eyes of God" and her response, "I'm as married to you as I ever could be," constitute the present agreement to marry.

Second, Ellen would argue that she and Trenton satisfied the cohabitation requirement. That is, she could show that they lived together in Redacre, a jurisdiction that recognizes common-law marriage. Statutory and case law fail to require a specific period of cohabitation. Ellen and Trenton's short visits to Redacre for purposes of Trenton's business and to visit her parents probably would suffice to establish this element.

Third, Ellen must show that she and Trenton held themselves out as husband and wife. Their conduct probably would satisfy this element. Their friends believed that they are married. And Ellen used Trenton's surname for all purposes. Having met the requisite elements to establish a common-law marriage, Ellen should be entitled to inheritance rights as Trenton's common-law spouse. Alternatively, Ellen might argue that she is justified in a share of Trenton's intestate estate because she was Trenton's "putative spouse." However, this argument would fail. A putative spouse is a marital partner who has a good-faith belief in the validity of the marriage. But Ellen knew that she was not validly married to Trenton because they had never undergone a marriage ceremony. Therefore, Ellen does not qualify as a putative spouse.

SAMPLE ANSWER TO QUESTION 3:

Part A.

Prisoners' arguments regarding prison's conjugal visiting policy

Carl and the other prisoners would argue, first, that Blackacre State Prison's policy of refusing the inmates conjugal visits violates their constitutional rights. First, the prisoners would argue that the policy infringes their *right to marry* because the right to marry includes a right to engage in sexual intercourse with one's spouse. In *Loving v. Virginia*, *Zablocki v. Redhail*, and *Turner v. Safley*, the U.S. Supreme Court recognized the constitutional right to marry. Those cases declared that the right to marry is a fundamental right. As such, it is subject to strict scrutiny. That is, to survive constitutional challenge, the restriction must be necessary to a compelling state interest (discussed *infra*).

Second, the prisoners would argue that the prison's restriction on conjugal visitation infringes on the *right to privacy*. The U.S. Supreme Court in *Griswold v. Connecticut* enunciated the constitutional right of privacy. In invalidating a Connecticut statute prohibiting the use of contraceptives by married couples, the Court held that the right to privacy protected intimate decision making by marital partners. Carl and the other prisoners would argue that the prison policy interferes with this right to privacy (i.e., by infringing on his right to marital intimacy with his wife). The prisoners would argue that this infringement, similar to the infringement on the right to marry, should call for strict scrutiny review (discussed *infra*). They would argue that, in *Griswold*, *Eisenstadt* (both regarding contraceptives), and *Roe v. Wade* and *Planned Parenthood v. Casey* (both regarding abortion), as broadly interpreted, the U.S. Supreme Court guaranteed a right to procreational freedom. The prisoners would argue that the right to procreation is meaningless if the prison bars access to the means to effectuate that right by banning conjugal visits.

The prisoners' first argument, based on the constitutional protection for the right to marry, would not prevail. The cited cases (*Loving*, *Zablocki*, and *Turner*) did, indeed, establish constitutional protection for the right to marry. However, those precedents concerned the right to *enter into* the marital state. The prison prohibition on conjugal visits does not interfere with a prisoner's right to marry. It prohibits, instead, sexual intimacy with one's spouse.

The prisoners' second argument, based on the alleged infringement with the right of privacy, would also be unsuccessful. The prison would argue that *Griswold* is distinguishable from the present situation. *Griswold* involved the right to intimate decision making, specifically, regarding contraception. The prison might argue that the prison policy does not interfere with couples' decision making regarding the use of contraceptives. Rather, the policy pertains, instead, to overnight spousal visitation, which implicates security concerns (discussed *infra*).

The prisoners' third argument is that the policy infringes on their privacy rights in terms of their interest in procreation, based on *Griswold*, *Eisenstadt*, *Roe v. Wade*, and *Casey*. Even if the prison were to agree that the ban on conjugal visitation violates the prisoners' procreational freedom, the prison would probably be able to justify the policy by showing that the ban survived constitutional scrutiny. *Roe v. Wade* held that an infringement on the individual's right to procreational freedom (technically, abortion) called for strict scrutiny. Yet, *Casey* held that not all restrictions on abortion call for strict scrutiny—only those that create an undue burden. Applying the *Casey* standard, the prison would argue that the prohibition on visitation does not create an undue burden. That is, the ban does not create a legal obstacle to a prisoner's procreational rights. Rather, the prison would argue that it only creates a delay (i.e., the prisoner may procreate upon release from prison). In other situations, the Supreme Court has upheld the constitutionality of restrictions which merely delay the exercise of constitutional rights (e.g., the waiting period in *Casey*, durational residency periods in *Sosna v. Iowa*). If the policy does not constitute an undue burden, then the prison need only justify the policy by showing that it is rationally related to a legitimate governmental interest.

The prison would have little difficulty meeting this standard. The prison would argue that the ban on conjugal visitation is justified by the legitimate governmental interest in maintaining internal security of the facility. That is, permitting spouses to stay overnight in private visits in the prison entails the serious risk that such persons would bring in weapons or drugs. A ban on conjugal visits serves to minimize this risk. Given that prisoners' rights are considerably circumscribed during incarceration (*Turner*), it is likely that this argument would succeed.

Finally, the prison would have a countervailing argument to the prisoners' argument that the right to procreation is meaningless if the prison bars access to the means to effectuate that right. The prison would find support for their counterargument in an analogy to the abortion funding cases. In *Harris v. McRae*, the Supreme Court held that, although the individual has a constitutional right to an abortion, the state does not have the responsibility to fund that right by the provision of federal Medicaid funds. By extension, the prison would argue that although the individual has a constitutionally protected right to procreate, the state does not have the responsibility of facilitating the exercise of that right. Thus, the prisoners would not prevail in their efforts to invalidate the ban on conjugal visits.

Part B.

Diana's request for an annulment on grounds of fraud

Diana wonders if she might be able to secure an annulment from Carl on the ground of fraud. Carl informed her that he was being imprisoned for armed bank robbery. Instead, she learns from the probation officer that his crime was more serious: felony murder. Diana would argue that Carl's misrepresentation gives her the requisite ground for an annulment of the marriage.

Most states provide that fraud furnishes grounds to annul a marriage. The existence of fraud vitiates the party's consent and makes the marriage voidable at the request of the injured party. Diana faces several problems in her efforts to have the marriage annulled. First, Diana would have to find out which test is used in her jurisdiction to establish fraud. If the jurisdiction relies on the strictest test, the fraud must go to the "essentials" of the marriage, especially if the marriage has been consummated. Other jurisdictions adopt a "material" test (similar to the materiality standard for ordinary contracts) or a "but for" test requiring that the plaintiff would not have married had she or he known of the misrepresentation.

Diana will have a tough time trying to satisfy any of these tests. First, Carl's fraud does not appear to go to the "essentials" of the marriage. Case law has interpreted that requirement as referring to sexual intercourse or procreation. Carl's misrepresentation only referred to the nature of his offense, not his ability to have sexual relations or to procreate. In addition, Diana may not be able to meet a "materiality" standard. It is not clear that Carl's statement induced the marriage or that she would have refrained from marrying Carl had she known of the true basis for his criminal conviction. Finally, Diana faces an added problem: misrepresentations of health, wealth, and status, generally, are not legally sufficient bases for annulment. A court might find that Carl's misrepresentation is analogous to a fraudulent representation about social standing. These types of statements are not sufficient to justify annulment of marriage.

Part C.

Carl's refusal to pay child support for Samantha

Carl will not be successful in his efforts to refuse child support for Samantha, the child conceived by Diana by means of artificial insemination with a third-party donor. A husband's consent to the artificial insemination of his wife gives rise to obligations of support for the ensuing child. Carl gave his consent to the insemination while he was in prison. By his consent, he impliedly agreed to support any ensuing child and to assume paternal obligations. Therefore, Carl may not assert Samantha's parentage as a defense to Diana's claim for child support.

Glossary of Terms

This glossary gives definitions for key terms and concepts used in this Outline.

Abortifacient: This herb, product, or implement is used to induce an abortion.

Abrogation: This procedure is the annulment of an adoption by adoptive parents. Despite a concern with the negative impact on the adoptee, courts permit abrogation in some cases (e.g., when the adoptive parents are victims of fraud, such as on the part of an agency).

Absolute divorce: English law, historically, distinguished between "absolute divorce" (our modern idea of divorce) and "divorce a mensa et thoro" (i.e., a legal separation which did not permit the parties to remarry). Absolute divorce was not granted in England until 1857. In contrast, by the nineteenth century in America, all the northern colonies granted judicial divorces.

Adoption: In this legal process, the adoptive parent(s) assume(s) all legal rights and obligations in relation to an adoptee and, thereby, terminates all rights and obligations of the biological parents. The process may also be used in many jurisdictions to adopt an adult (e.g., for inheritance purposes).

Adultery: Adultery, i.e., the act of engaging in sexual relations with someone other than one's legal spouse, is both a criminal act and a fault-based ground for divorce.

Affinity: Affinity (to be distinguished from "consanguinity," which refers to relationships by blood) involves a relationship created by law (e.g., step-relationships, in-law relationships). A marriage between persons who are related by affinity may be invalid depending on the jurisdiction. *See also consanguinity.*

Alienation of affections: This tort claim is based on a third party's intentional interference with the marital relationship.

Alimony: Alimony was the term formerly used to signify payments from one spouse (traditionally the husband) to the other for support either pending the divorce litigation ("alimony pendente lite") or following the divorce. Modern usage has replaced the term with the gender-neutral "spousal support" and "maintenance." Gender-based statutes prescribing that husbands shall pay wives alimony violate equal protection.

Annulment: This judicial declaration specifies that no marriage occurred because of the existence of some impediment. An annulment declares a marriage void ab initio, unlike a divorce, which terminates a valid marriage. Annulments were more common during the fault-based era when divorce was difficult to obtain.

Antenuptial agreement: *See premarital agreement.*

Anti-heartbalm legislation: These state statutes (sometimes confusingly called "heartbalm acts") abolished claims, such as breach of promise and alienation of affections, because of their sexist, outdated, and extortionate nature.

Anti-miscegenation statutes: These laws, which were declared unconstitutional in *Loving v. Virginia*, prohibited interracial marriages.

Antinepotism policies: These policies, which were originally enacted to prevent public officials from conferring employment on unqualified relatives, prevent a spouse's employer from employing the other spouse (hence, sometimes called "no-spousal employment" policies).

Arbitration: This dispute resolution process (commonly used in the labor context) is sometimes resorted to by marital parties to permit a third party, chosen by the parties, to serve as a decision maker.

Artificial insemination: This reproductive technique, originally used in humans to combat male infertility, results in the introduction of a man's sperm into a woman's uterus.

Assisted conception: This contemporary term refers to methods of new reproductive technology to combat infertility, such as in vitro fertilization, embryo transplants, and surrogacy.

Babyselling: This criminal offense punishes the payment or acceptance of money or other consideration in exchange for the adoption of a child. Some courts and commentators analogize surrogacy to this practice.

Battered child syndrome: This medical condition, discovered by radiologists in the 1960s, refers to injuries to children which are in various stages of healing and inflicted by parents who provide inconsistent causal explanations.

Battered woman's syndrome: This syndrome, discovered by psychologist Lenore Walker, describes the nature of the abuse suffered by long-term victims of battering. The modern trend is the acceptance of the admissibility of this evidence to establish a defense in intimate partner violence.

Best interests of the child: These criteria, based on a concern with child welfare, shape the subjective standard for custody and adoption decisions. Many factors (race, religion, sexual orientation, domestic violence, disability) enter into the determination of the child's best interests.

Bigamy: This criminal offense involves being married to more than one spouse at one time, i.e., contracting a second marriage without having legally terminated the prior marriage.

Bilateral divorce: This type of divorce proceeding, in which personal jurisdiction exists over *both* spouses, permits a court to settle property issues incident to the divorce (not just the marriage termination).

Breach of promise to marry: This cause of action, now abolished by most states, permits the imposition of tort liability for the violation of a promise by one person to marry the other.

Capacity: A marriage may be annulled for lack of capacity, i.e., the ability to understand and fulfill a marriage contract. Traditional statutory requirements for capacity include: the parties must be of opposite sexes; married to only one spouse at a time; not related; and above the statutorily defined age. These requirements are distinguished from "state of mind" restrictions, which require that the parties marry voluntarily, without fraud or duress.

Central registry: This database of reported cases of suspected child abuse, established by many states, was intended originally to ascertain the incidence and nature of abuse, to assist professionals to determine whether a child has been previously abused, and to keep track of persons suspected of abuse. Social services agencies also use these registries to preclude individuals with abusive propensities from working in child care.

Civil union: A civil union is a form of domestic partnership that recognizes a legal relationship between unmarried partners (same-sex and sometimes opposite-sex partners). Civil union legislation grants these partners many of the same legal rights and obligations as spouses.

Cohabitation: Cohabitation is the state of living together without being formally married, and is generally thought to include sexual intercourse. It is one of several requisite elements of a common-law marriage.

Collaborative law: Collaborative law involves an alternative dispute resolution process in divorce by which the parties and their respective lawyers agree to negotiate a settlement without judicial intervention. If either party decides to litigate subsequently, he or she must retain different counsel.

Collaborative reproduction: This form of assisted reproduction involves third parties, such as gamete donors and gestational surrogates.

Collusion: The presence of this defense, i.e., a spousal agreement to perpetrate a marital offense (feigned or actual) for the sole purpose of divorce, serves to preclude the plaintiff from securing a divorce.

Comity doctrine: Under this doctrine, an American court may exercise its discretion to recognize a judgment granted by a foreign nation, provided that that judgment was obtained after a fair hearing by a court with jurisdiction over one or both parties. Comity, often relied on to recognize foreign divorces, is distinct from the constitutional requirement of "full faith and credit."

Common-law marriage: This form of marriage, followed by approximately a dozen states, requires a couple to enter into a present agreement to be married, to cohabit for a period of time in a jurisdiction that recognizes common-law marriages (although the time may be quite brief), and to hold themselves out as spouses. Common-law marriage, since it is a valid marriage, must be dissolved by death or divorce before the parties may enter into a subsequent marriage with other parties.

Communal family: This family unit is a group of unrelated people who live together, often forming a single housekeeping unit, who may or may not be regarded as a "single family" for zoning purposes (depending on the jurisdiction). The Supreme Court, in *Boraas v. Belle Terre*, refused to accord this family unit constitutional protection.

Community property: Under this marital property regime based on a partnership model, the spouses who reside in a community property jurisdiction are regarded (as of the date of the marriage) as the respective owners of an undivided one-half interest in all property which is acquired following the marriage. Community property is distinct from "separate property." (*See separate property*.) Whereas a few community property states require an equal division of the community property, others follow a regime of equitable distribution. Further, statutes in some community property jurisdictions give their courts authority to include separate property in equitable distribution, whereas other community property states exclude separate property.

Comstock laws: These state and federal laws banned the circulation and importation of "obscene" materials through the national mail at the end of the nineteenth century. "Obscene" materials were defined to include articles for prevention of conception, producing abortion, or other immoral purposes.

Conciliation: This form of alternative dispute resolution consists of marital counseling that is entered into with the object of reconciliation. In the fault era, some states established court-connected conciliation services, which now provide mediation services.

Conditional gift: This present, often an engagement ring, is given by a donor on the condition that the donee will perform a future act (such as undergo a marriage). The theory underlying a conditional gift is that if the act upon which the gift is conditioned does not occur, then the donee must return the gift.

Condonation: According to this fault-based defense to divorce, the act of forgiveness by an innocent spouse for the guilty party's commission of a fault-based ground (such as by the resumption of sexual relations following infidelity) precludes the plaintiff from obtaining a divorce.

Confidential marriage: This procedural variation, permitted in some jurisdictions, similar to proxy or common-law marriage, permits a marriage to be entered into without the necessity of fulfilling all the usual requirements (e.g., dispensing with blood tests).

Connivance: This doctrine in the era of fault-based divorce (specifically a fault-based defense) bars a divorce when a spouse participates in or consents to the other's wrongful conduct.

Consanguinity: This term denotes a blood relationship between two persons, such as parent-child, brother-sister, uncle-niece, etc. It is distinguishable from affinity relationships (relations created by law). Almost all jurisdictions have incest statutes that provide criminal sanctions for marriage or sexual intercourse between persons related by consanguinity. In addition, civil restrictions prevent persons thus related from obtaining a marriage license.

Consortium: The cause of action for "loss of consortium" consists of a tortious interference by a third party with a spouse's rights to the services, companionship, affection, and sexual relations of the other spouse. The action was available first only to husbands, but later extended to wives.

Constitutionalization of family law: By this process the U.S. Supreme Court has applied constitutional doctrine to many areas of family law that were formerly the subject only of state regulation.

Constructive desertion: This fault-based ground for divorce (which is also a fault-based defense) consists of a "guilty" spouse's conduct which, without justification on the part of the "innocent" spouse, causes the innocent spouse to leave or justifies the innocent spouse's departure. Frequently, one spouse's charge of desertion is countered by the other's charge of constructive desertion (i.e., to show that the defendant's departure was justified by the plaintiff's behavior).

Consummation: This term signifies the act of sexual intercourse following a marriage. Consummation became significant in the fault-based era because a higher standard for fraud was required if consummation had occurred in order to annul a marriage (for the reason that the woman had been "sullied").

Contraceptive mandate: The Patient Protection and Affordable Care Act (PPACA, also called "Obamacare") requires employers of more than 50 employees to offer health care plans that cover contraceptive services without out-of-pocket costs to patients (known as the "contraceptive mandate"). Federal regulations offer exemptions to religious employers (such as churches) and accommodations to nonprofit employers with religious objections. The Trump Administration significantly broadened the exemptions to employers (both nonprofit and for-profit) who have religious objections *and* moral objections.

Covenant marriage: This type of marriage, recognized by statute in a small number of states, makes divorce more difficult to obtain by permitting the spouses to divorce only after a two-year separation or proof of fault. Covenant marriages stem from a reform movement aimed at countering the rising number of divorces and the negative effects of divorce on children.

Coverture: Under this common-law term (from the Norman French), the husband and wife became one legal entity upon marriage. The doctrine is also referred to as the "fiction of marital unity" or "merger." Coverture resulted in significant common-law disabilities for married women (regarding property, contracts, etc.), which were largely eliminated by the nineteenth century Married Women's Property Acts.

Criminal conversation: Under this common-law tort, a husband might seek damages against another man for the latter's interference with the marital relationship. Unlike the tort of alienation of affections, criminal conversation required proof of the tortfeasor's sexual intercourse with the wife.

Cruelty: This fault-based ground for divorce consists of a course of conduct that is so severe as to create an adverse effect on a plaintiff's physical or mental well-being. Although early courts required actual or threatened physical violence, courts subsequently permitted mental cruelty to suffice.

Cryopreservation: This mode of assisted conception, which involves the preservation of embryos by the freezing process, poses issues about the property rights which attach to genetic material.

Defense of Marriage Act (DOMA): This federal law defined marriage as occurring only between a man and a woman for purposes of federal benefits and permitted the states to exercise discretion to refuse to recognize same-sex marriages. The U.S. Supreme Court declared DOMA Section 3 (the definitional section) unconstitutional in *United States v. Windsor* and abrogated it entirely in *Obergefell v. Hodges.*

Degenderization of family law: This process, triggered by the women's movement, entails a shift away from traditional gender-specific family roles that characterized the woman as the caretaker of the home and children, and the father as the financial provider. The movement has significantly influenced the substance and terminology of family law.

Derivative citizenship: Rules governing citizenship by descent ("derivative citizenship") for foreign-born children of a U.S. citizen-parent depend on the citizen-parent's marital status and gender. The Supreme Court declared derivative citizenship laws based on a citizen-parent's marital status and gender unconstitutional as a violation of equal protection.

Desertion: This fault-based ground for divorce consists of conduct on the part of the defendant, which is without consent or justification by the plaintiff, by which the defendant voluntarily departs from the marital abode with intent not to resume cohabitation. *See also constructive desertion.*

Disability, common law: This signified married women's civil disabilities (or legal inabilities) to work in certain professions, sue or be sued without their husband's consent, execute a contract, make a will, etc. *See also coverture.*

Dispositional hearing: This second stage of a juvenile court proceeding, such as for abuse or neglect (following the first adjudicatory stage), determines the appropriate placement for the child (i.e., with a relative, foster care, return to the home).

Dissolution: The word "divorce," with its gender-based stereotypes and stigma, has been replaced with this more modern usage.

Divorce a mensa et thoro: *See absolute divorce.*

Domestic partnership legislation: This legislation, which has been enacted in a few jurisdictions, extends various degrees of legal protection to same-sex couples, and, occasionally, to some opposite-sex couples as well. It requires public registration of the partnership and formal dissolution of the partnership.

Domestic relations: The older terminology for the substantive field of family law.

Domicile: This legal concept is a prerequisite for the assertion of jurisdiction in many family law matters, such as marriage, divorce, custody, and adoption. At common law, a married woman acquired the domicile of her husband. Domicile includes physical presence plus intent to remain permanently. Although the term generally is distinguishable from "residence" (since a person has only one domicile but may have many temporary residences), some states' durational residency requirements for divorce often are construed so as to be indistinguishable from "domicile." *See also durational residency requirements.*

Dual representation: Some commentators and courts criticize this practice of having one attorney represent both spouses in a divorce proceeding as resulting in an inherent conflict of interest. The practice is also referred to as "multiple or joint representation."

Due process, procedural: According to this constitutional guarantee (under the Fourteenth Amendment), the government may infringe life, liberty, or property only if it does so by a procedure that provides adequate notice and an opportunity to be heard before the decision is rendered.

Due process, substantive: According to this constitutional guarantee (under the Fourteenth Amendment), the government may infringe certain fundamental rights (those rights inherent in the concept of "liberty") based only upon a strong justification that survives strict scrutiny.

Durational residency requirements: Durational residency requirements require a divorce petitioner to be a state resident for a specific period of time, varying from a minimum of six weeks to one year. Some states impose durational residency requirements either instead of, or in addition to, a domiciliary requirement. The Supreme Court in *Sosna v. Iowa* held that these state requirements are constitutional.

Ecclesiastical courts: These English courts, historically, asserted jurisdiction over church-related activities and rituals, including marriage and divorce. In the American colonies, marriage and divorce were regarded as secular matters.

Emancipation: This procedure releases a minor from parental care and control. Thus, it enables a child to acquire, for example, the right to retain earnings and to make decisions regarding medical care. Emancipation may occur expressly, such as by parental consent, or implicitly, such as by acts of parental abandonment. At common law, marriage or service in the armed forces resulted in emancipation. A minor may also secure emancipation judicially.

Embryo transplant: In this method of assisted conception, a fertilized embryo is implanted in the uterus of a woman who will bear the child.

Enoch Arden statutes: Named after the protagonist in a Tennyson poem, these statutes constitute a defense to a charge of bigamy. The statutes permit a spouse, who entertains a good-faith belief that her former spouse is dead, to remarry after a statutorily designated period (often five years).

Equal protection: This guarantee, under the Fourteenth Amendment, prohibits the government from denying equal protection under the law. This requirement has been interpreted as meaning that the government must treat alike those persons who are similarly situated.

Equal treatment/special treatment: These two theoretical approaches provide opposing rationales for maternity leave policies. The equal treatment approach signifies that women should be treated equally with men (which would result in "parental" leaves rather than "maternity" leaves, as exemplified in the Family and Medical Leave Act). The special treatment approach signifies that women should receive special protections.

Equitable adoption: By resort to this equitable remedy, courts effectuate an adoption (or effectuate the consequences of an adoption) in cases in which a legal adoption never occurred. The process is sometimes referred to as "virtual adoption." Many cases arise when a foster parent dies and the foster child seeks a determination of inheritance rights. Courts sometimes apply equitable adoption by resort to either contract theory or estoppel theory.

Estoppel: This doctrine was relevant in the fault-based era when many courts refused to recognize foreign divorces. Such divorces might be protected by means of the estoppel doctrine. That is, a spouse who goes to a foreign country and secures a foreign divorce could be estopped from denying its validity subsequently.

Ex parte divorce: In an ex parte or unilateral divorce, a court has jurisdiction over only one spouse. This enables the court to terminate the marriage but not to adjudicate the financial incidents of the marriage (i.e., property, spousal support).

Family and Medical Leave Act (FMLA): Congress enacted this legislation in order to provide employees with gender-neutral leave for reasons of childbirth, adoption, or illness. It provides for three months of unpaid leave to care for infants or seriously ill family members and applies to employers of over 50 employees.

Fault-based divorce: This doctrine permitted divorce to the "innocent" spouse, thereby placing blame for the marital breakdown on the "guilty" spouse who had committed a marital wrong. Traditional fault-based grounds for divorce included: cruelty, adultery, and desertion. Traditional fault-based defenses include: recrimination, connivance, and condonation. Prior to the late 1960s, when the movement for no-fault divorce emerged, fault-based divorce was the only type of divorce permitted in the United States.

Federalization of family law: This movement signifies the increasing importance of congressional legislation in matters of family law, such as child support, child custody, child abuse and neglect, paternity establishment, etc.

Fetal protection legislation: Federal and state legislatures have enacted laws that protect the fetus. These laws establish the crime of fetal homicide, restrict abortion based on the personhood of the fetus and its gestational age, restrict abortion based on the detection of a fetal heartbeat, and regulate the disposition of fetal remains.

Freedom of Access to Clinic Entrances (FACE) Act: Congress enacted this legislation in 1994 to penalize the use of force, threat of force, or physical obstruction to the entrance of abortion clinics. The legislation was enacted in response to violent protests at abortion clinics which reduced women's access to abortion.

Forum shopping: This practice (sometimes referred to as "migratory divorce"), by which a spouse sought to secure a divorce by establishing temporary residence in a jurisdiction with liberal divorce laws, was common during the fault-based era. The practice was also resorted to prior to legalization of abortion and by parents involved in custody disputes.

Free exercise clause: This First Amendment provision prohibits government from interfering with the individual's exercise of his or her religion (religious beliefs or religious conduct).

Full Faith and Credit Clause: This constitutional provision (Article IV, §1) provides that a state shall give full faith and credit to "the public acts, records and judicial proceedings" of other states. The doctrine was especially important, in the fault-based era, to give effect to divorce decrees granted by other states which had jurisdiction over at least one of the marital parties. The Clause is also important before the advent of marriage equality. *See* Defense of Marriage Act (DOMA).

Fundamental right: For equal protection purposes, fundamental rights are rights that are either explicitly or implicitly guaranteed by the Constitution. For substantive due process purposes, fundamental rights are those rights that are "deeply rooted in our history and traditions" (according to *Griswold v. Connecticut*), and may or may not be explicitly enumerated. They are subject to strict scrutiny review.

Gestational surrogacy: In this method of collaborative reproduction, a woman carries a child that was conceived using eggs and sperm from a couple or from donor eggs and sperm. In such a case, the carrying mother is not biologically related to the child. This method of conception contrasts with traditional surrogacy in which the carrying mother's own egg is used and combined with sperm through intrauterine insemination (IUI) or in vitro fertilization (IVF). In such a case, the carrying mother is biologically related to the child.

Get: This religious divorce follows Orthodox Jewish practices. The "Get" has been used as a type of spousal blackmail since, without a Get, a marital partner is stigmatized and unable to remarry another Jew, and future children are bastardized.

Goodwill: This constitutes the reputation of a business or profession which predictably will result in future earnings. Similar to other intangible marital assets, it is difficult to divide upon dissolution. Cases wrestle with how to characterize it as a property interest or as personal (i.e., the product of unique skills). Although a division of authority exists, the modern trend is to hold that enterprise goodwill constitutes a marital asset subject to distribution.

Guardian ad litem: This individual, who may or may not be an attorney (depending on the jurisdiction), represents a child in judicial proceedings

Hague Convention on Protection of Children and Co-operation in Respect of Intercountry Adoption: This Hague Convention is an international convention dealing with international adoption that attempts to secure the recognition in a member nation.

Hague Convention on the Civil Aspects of International Child Abduction: This Hague Convention is an international treaty that proposes guidelines on international child abduction and attempts to ensure the prompt return of children who have been abducted from their country of habitual residence or wrongfully retained in a contracting nation.

Heartbalm acts: *See anti-heartbalm legislation.*

Heartbalm suit: These causes of action provide tort liability for such claims as breach of promise to marry and alienation of affections. Many states have abolished or circumscribed recovery for these actions. *See anti-heartbalm legislation.*

Illegitimate: This term for a child who is born out of wedlock, i.e., to parents who are not married, has been replaced by the less stigmatizing term "nonmarital child."

Incest: Incest signifies marriage or sexual relations between persons who are related by consanguinity or affinity. Incest constitutes both a criminal offense and a civil restriction on marriage.

Incompatibility: This early no-fault ground for divorce eliminated proof of fault.

Independent adoption: This form of adoption is the placement of children with adoptive parents by private (i.e., not state) persons or agencies. Because of the unlicensed nature of the practice, it is the subject of public policy concerns.

Indian Child Welfare Act (ICWA): This federal legislation applies to Native-American children in adoption, custody, and child placement proceedings. It mandates a preference for placement of the child with tribal members, absent good cause.

Intermediate scrutiny: This middle-tier test is used by courts to review possibly unconstitutional legislative classifications. The test is used by the U.S. Supreme Court for gender-based classifications (among others), although some states use strict scrutiny for gender-based classifications.

Interspousal immunity: This common-law doctrine precluded one marital partner from recovering in tort from the other. The preclusion was based on the rationale that the partners constituted one legal entity and that judicial intervention would disturb marital harmony. The majority of courts have abolished the doctrine for intentional and negligent torts.

Interspousal wiretapping: This practice involves electronic surveillance by one spouse of the other within the marital home. Virtually all federal courts hold that liability attaches for interspousal wiretapping under Title III of the Omnibus Crime Control Act.

Intestate succession: An "intestate" is a person who dies without a will. Adopted children generally lose the right to inherit from a biological parent who dies intestate because the adoption terminates the child's former relationship with the biological parent(s). In addition, inheritance law, traditionally, also precluded nonmarital children from inheriting from their father (but not their mother) by intestate succession. The Supreme Court has declared this policy a violation of equal protection in some situations (e.g., *Trimble v. Gordon*).

In vitro fertilization (IVF): In this method of assisted conception, an ovum is removed surgically from a woman and subsequently placed in a laboratory medium with sperm. The resultant embryo is then implanted either in the ovum donor or another woman.

Irreconcilable differences: This no-fault ground for divorce (sometimes termed "irretrievable breakdown") specifies that the marriage is broken but does not place blame on either party.

Joint custody: Joint custody (technically joint legal custody) is a custody arrangement, based on the rationale that children need frequent and continuing contact with both parents following divorce, that confers legal responsibility upon both parents for major childrearing decisions regarding the child's upbringing, health, welfare, and education. "Joint legal custody" is distinguishable from "joint physical custody." That is, parents may share joint legal custody, although the children may reside primarily with one parent.

Judicial bypass: A judicial bypass is a judicial procedure that allows a minor to obtain an abortion without the notification or consent of her parents.

Learned helplessness: This aspect of the battered women's syndrome is characterized by Post-Traumatic Stress Syndrome resulting in depression which affects the victim so that she loses the ability to respond to the physical abuse. It is used to explain to juries why victims do not leave their abusers.

Level of scrutiny: This term refers to the appropriate test that courts use to evaluate laws or legislative classifications that burden constitutional rights. The three tests include: minimal scrutiny (the rational basis test), intermediate scrutiny (substantially related to an important governmental objective), or strict scrutiny (necessary to a compelling interest).

Lex loci: The rule of lex loci (Latin for "law of the place") holds that a marriage that is valid in the place where it was performed is valid everywhere. The major exception to the rule is when a marriage is contrary to public policy.

Licensure: Licensure is one of the formalities states require for entry into marriage. Specifically, states require that parties who desire to marry procure a marriage license, often by applying to a county clerk. The clerk may refuse to issue the license if the information provided by the parties reveals that they are ineligible to marry. *See also solemnization.*

Living separate and apart: This no-fault ground for divorce refers to a physical separation or intention to dissolve a marriage. Courts do not always require that the spouses actually reside in separate homes.

Long-arm statutes: These statutes confer personal jurisdiction over nonresidents who have contacts with the forum that are sufficient to meet the requisites of due process. Prior to the 1970s, many states permitted the assertion of jurisdiction over nonresidents in domestic relations cases by liberal interpretations of their long-arm statutes. Now, many states have revised their long-arm statutes to include specific provisions for the assertion of jurisdiction in claims for spousal support and child support. The U.S. Supreme Court delineated the scope of due process limitations in *Kulko v. Superior Court* and *Burnham v. Superior Court.*

Maiden name: This term describes a woman's surname at birth. Traditionally, by custom, a woman gave up her maiden name upon marriage and adopted her husband's surname. Modern social mores have resulted in more women retaining their maiden (or "birth") names.

Maintenance: This modern term, used to describe the financial support given by one spouse to the other following divorce, has replaced the former term "alimony."

Marital rape: This act, which was not recognized as a criminal offense until recently by several states, consists of a husband forcing his wife to have sexual intercourse against her will.

Marital unity: *See coverture.*

Marriage for a limited purpose: *See sham marriage.*

Married Women's Property Acts: This legislation, enacted in many jurisdictions in the mid- to late nineteenth century, eliminated many of the legal disabilities which married women faced at common law.

Maternity leave: This policy provides women with temporary leave from employment for the purposes of pregnancy or childbirth. *See equal treatment/special treatment; Family and Medical Leave Act; Pregnancy Discrimination Act.*

Matrimonial Causes Act: England did not permit judicial divorce until this legislation in 1857.

Mediation: Divorce mediation is a process by which the parties themselves, with the help of a third-party mediator, resolve their disputes. Unlike in arbitration, the parties do not cede their authority to a neutral third party to resolve their dispute, but rather make their own agreements with the mediator serving as a facilitator. Some jurisdictions make mediation mandatory (e.g., California for custody and visitation disputes).

Meretricious relationship: This form of relationship (signifying a "sham" marriage) often refers to unmarried opposite-sex couples living together.

Minimal scrutiny: This test is the lowest level of scrutiny that is used by courts to review legislative classifications. It requires only that the petitioner prove that the classification is not rationally related to any permissible governmental purpose. Almost any classification can survive minimal scrutiny on the theory that a legislature must have had a sound reason to enact a given law.

Miscegenation: This term refers to the "mixing" of blood of persons of different races. Prior to 1968, when the Supreme Court declared a state anti-miscegenation law unconstitutional, many states had statutes proscribing marriage or sexual intercourse between persons of different races. *See anti-miscegenation statutes.*

Necessaries: These items (e.g., food, shelter, medical care) are deemed by courts to be necessary for basic sustenance. At common law, a husband was responsible for the necessaries of his wife and children and could be charged for payment of necessaries even without his consent.

Ne exeat: This equitable writ restrains a person from leaving or removing property from the jurisdiction; it is often used to restrain a parent from removing a child from the jurisdiction.

No-fault divorce: This form of divorce largely eliminates the importance of finding one spouse at fault for the breakdown of the marriage. After first being enacted in California in 1968, it has now been adopted, in one form or another, by all jurisdictions. However, no-fault divorce does not have the same meaning in all jurisdictions: some states permit no-fault divorce only if both parties consent, whereas other states permit it even if only one party desires it. Further, some states define "no fault" to mean that the parties have "irreconcilable differences," but other states define it to signify a marital breakdown that results in the parties' physically living apart for a statutorily defined period of time.

Nonintervention, doctrine of: According to this doctrine, the courts should not interfere in an ongoing marriage to settle disputes between the marital parties. This doctrine, based on a desire to preserve family privacy and marital harmony, has come under severe criticism by law reformers in the context of domestic violence.

Nonmarital child: This modern term is used to describe a child whose parents are not married to each other. The term eliminates the stigma of such traditional terms as "illegitimate" or "out-of-wedlock."

No-spousal employment policies: *See antinepotism policies.*

Nuclear family: This traditional family was composed of husband and wife and their co-resident children. It is now decreasing in importance with the rising incidence of divorce and the growth of alternative family forms.

Open adoption: In this modern form of adoption, the biological parents of a child who is placed for adoption are aware of the identity of the adoptive parents. Similarly, the adopted child is aware of the identity of the biological parents. Occasionally, the biological and adoptive parents may enter into an agreement regarding the adoption such that the biological parent(s) continues to play some role (e.g., visitation) in the child's life.

Out-of-wedlock: *See illegitimate; nonmarital child.*

Palimony: This term refers to a lawsuit, award, or agreement by a member of an unmarried couple who seeks "quasi-spousal support," similar to alimony (hence the name "palimony"). Such claims became popular in the wake of *Marvin v. Marvin,* which held that unmarried couples may enter into express contracts (unless the consideration for these contracts rests on the exchange of sexual services) as well as implied contracts.

Parens patriae: This Latin term (literally "parent of the country") signifies that the state is responsible for the welfare of its vulnerable citizens (such as children). The concept is often invoked when courts assert jurisdiction over abused and neglected children.

Parental privilege to discipline: This right, based on constitutional principles derived from *Meyer v. Nebraska* and *Pierce v. Society of Sisters*, permits parents to discipline their children as part of their protected Fourteenth Amendment "liberty interest" in raising their children as they see fit. However, by statute in many jurisdictions, the force used to administer discipline must be reasonable and for purposes of correction.

Parenting time: The preferred term for "visitation" in some states based on the rationale that a parent spending time with his or her own child is really *parenting* the child and not merely visiting with the child.

Partial-birth abortion: This type of abortion occurs in the late stage of pregnancy (in or after the fifth month). Many states enacted prohibitions on partial-birth abortions. Congress successfully enacted a federal prohibition.

The Patient Protection and Affordable Care Act (PPACA) (known as Affordable Care Act or ACA) is a federal health care reform statute. The Act increases the affordability of health insurance coverage, covers preventive health care services, and includes a "contraceptive mandate."

Polygamy: This criminal offense involves having *more than two* spouses at one time, and is distinct from "bigamy," which means having two spouses at one time, and "monogamy," which means having only one spouse. Civil restrictions prevent an individual who is validly married from obtaining a license to marry (again) without terminating the prior marriage.

Post-majority support: This form of child support, after a child reaches the age of majority (18 in most jurisdictions), may be ordered by a court, for example, to require a noncustodial parent to pay for the child's college expenses.

Posthumously conceived child: This child is conceived through in vitro fertilization after the father's death.

Preemption: This doctrine holds that federal statutes preclude operation of state law on a given subject according to congressional intent.

Pregnancy Discrimination Act: This amendment to Title VII of the Civil Rights Act of 1964 was enacted by Congress in 1978 to address employment discrimination against pregnant employees. The act analogizes pregnancy to a disability by mandating that an employer shall provide the same benefits for pregnant employees as the employer provides to disabled employees. Feminists have criticized the act for its outmoded treatment of pregnancy as a disability.

Premarital agreement: This contract (also called an "antenuptial" agreement), which is executed by prospective spouses, establishes the parties' property rights in the event of death or dissolution.

Presumption of legitimacy: Courts often apply this presumption, which holds that the husband of a married woman is the biological father of any child to whom she gives birth at any time during the marriage. The presumption is based on a desire not to interfere with family harmony. The presumption raises potential problems in the surrogacy situation because the surrogate's husband may thereby acquire parental rights to the child; surrogacy agreements must overcome this presumption.

Primary caretaker presumption: This presumption would accord custody to the parent who has been the child's "primary caretaker" (i.e., performed the majority of caretaking tasks). Although it no longer operates as a presumption, many jurisdictions take primary caretaker status into account in the determination of the best interests of the child.

Private ordering: This principle signifies the ability of the divorcing parties to resolve matters of property and support themselves without judicial intervention. The practice has been on the increase since the 1960s, and was triggered by considerable dissatisfaction with traditional dispute resolution processes.

Pro se divorce: In this process, an individual represents himself or herself in a divorce proceeding. Although it makes divorce easier and less expensive, some legal commentators argue that it precludes the divorcing parties from obtaining adequate representation.

Proxy marriage: This procedural variation of the traditional marriage ceremony permits a third party to substitute for the bride or groom. The practice often is permitted in time of war or other conflict, especially to legitimize children.

Putative spouse doctrine: This doctrine protects the property rights upon death or dissolution of an "innocent" spouse by upholding the validity of a marriage provided that that spouse has a good-faith belief in the validity of the marriage. The doctrine is distinguishable from common-law marriage because, in the putative spouse situation, the parties have undergone a marriage ceremony which at least one spouse believes has resulted in a valid marriage.

Recordation: This aspect of the marriage procedure follows the solemnization of the marriage. The person who officiates at the wedding signs the marriage certificate and submits it to the county clerk. Recordation occurs when the county clerk registers the marriage so that it becomes part of the public record.

Recrimination: This defense to fault-based divorce barred a divorce when both spouses were found to be at fault. Rationales included: the clean hands doctrine; the availability of divorce only for an innocent spouse; preservation of marriage; and the need to provide economic protection to women by denying divorce so that husbands will continue to provide support. Commentators criticized the doctrine because it denies divorce in cases of marriages that merit termination.

Rehabilitation: Under this modern principle of dissolution, a spouse is awarded only enough spousal support to permit her to become self-supporting. Thus, a court may award a dependent wife enough funds to enable her to obtain education or training to begin a new career or take up a career that she abandoned upon the marriage.

Relation back doctrine: This doctrine has the effect of rendering a marriage that has been nullified judicially to be considered void from inception. As a result, the doctrine may result in reinstatement of a benefit, for example, that was lost because of the relationship.

Religious- (or racial-) matching provisions: These provisions, applicable to adoption, provide that the religion (or race) of the adoptive parents shall match that of the adopted child, whenever possible. The constitutionality of these provisions has been upheld.

Religious refusal laws: Also known as "conscious clauses," these state laws allow health care providers to refuse services and health care to individuals based on the providers' religious and sometimes moral objections.

"Right to Know" laws: Provisions in state laws that require health care providers to impart designated verbal and/or written information to women seeking abortion as well as information concerning any alternatives to abortion. Courts have upheld the constitutionality of these provisions.

Separate property: This term, as used in community property jurisdictions, signifies property that is acquired by a spouse prior to the marriage *and* property acquired after the marriage, by either spouse, by gift, devise, or bequest. Statutes in some community property jurisdictions give courts authority to include separate property in equitable distribution, whereas other community property jurisdictions exclude separate property. *See also community property.*

Separation agreement: This agreement, which is entered into by spouses who have decided to separate (and, usually, to terminate their marriage as well), addresses the financial incidents of the divorce (property, spousal support, etc). It is sometimes referred to as a "marital settlement agreement."

Settlement agreement: *See separation agreement.*

Solemnization: This is one of the formalities that states require for entry into marriage. All states require solemnization of marriage by an authorized person before witnesses (subject to some exceptions), although no specific form of ceremony is prescribed. *See also licensure.*

Sham marriage: This form of marriage is entered into solely for the convenience of the parties (i.e., not because of genuine affection between them). Cases of immigration fraud are sometimes considered "sham marriages" or "marriages for a limited purpose." That is, one person gives consent to marry the other for a limited purpose (e.g., to enable the other person to qualify for immigration entry status). Congressional legislation addresses immigration fraud.

Special relationship doctrine: Some courts recognized a federal civil rights cause of action (based on 42 U.S.C. §1983 that imposes liability on governmental officials for deprivation of a constitutional right under color of law) against law enforcement or municipalities for the failure to protect battered women. A cause of action will not arise for failure to provide a specific individual with police protection unless a "special relationship" exists between the governmental agency and the individual, such that the governmental agency assumes an affirmative duty to act on behalf of the injured party, has knowledge of the consequences of inaction, and incurs the injured party's justifiable reliance on the municipality's affirmative undertaking. The Supreme Court limited application of this doctrine in *DeShaney v. Winnebago.*

Spousal support: This modern term is used to describe the financial support provided by one spouse to the other following the termination of a marriage. Traditionally, it was referred to as "alimony."

Strict scrutiny: This level of scrutiny is the highest level of judicial examination that is used to determine the constitutionality of a regulation or act. The test requires that the regulation or act must be necessary to a compelling state interest in order to be upheld. This level of scrutiny is applied to racial qualifications and also to determine whether a fundamental constitutional right has been violated. The Supreme Court has not applied strict scrutiny to sex-based discrimination, although some state courts do so.

State-created danger doctrine: This doctrine, another exception to *DeShaney v. Winnebago*, provides that state actors (such as law enforcement officials) may be liable to private persons under §1983 if the state actors created or enhanced the danger of private violence.

Subsidized adoption: This policy provides state funds in order to facilitate the placement of children with special needs, i.e., those children who are hard to place owing to their age, race, or background.

Substantially related to an important governmental interest: This phrase describes the intermediate level of scrutiny, which the Supreme Court has determined (in *Craig v. Boren*) is applicable to review sex-based discrimination. Although higher than the rational basis test, this test is not as rigorous as the strict scrutiny test.

Summary dissolution: This divorce procedure, authorized by statute in many jurisdictions, permits termination of marriage in a relatively short period of time. It often obviates the need for an appearance. Some states provide for the procedure if both parties consent, have no children, have no real property, have few debts, and the marriage is of short duration.

Summary seizure: This disposition, which is sometimes ordered by courts in child abuse and neglect cases, provides for the removal of a child from an abusive home without notice to a parent or parents. Removal of the child, prior to a full hearing, is permitted based on the state's concern that the child is being endangered by immediate or threatened harm. Courts and commentators have expressed constitutional concerns about the vagueness of applicable statutes and the arbitrary nature of the practice.

Surrogate motherhood: This method of assisted conception consists of a contractual agreement that specifies that a woman agrees to be artificially inseminated with the semen of a man who is not her husband (or fertilized with an egg that is not her own), to carry the ensuing fetus to term, and to surrender the child at birth to the intended parent(s). Many jurisdictions have held such agreements to be violative of public policy. The most famous surrogacy case is *In re Baby M. See also gestational surrogacy.*

Telemedicine: Telemedicine serves as a substitute to physical presence (of health care provider and patient) because it allows the provision of remote services to patients (such as reproductive health services) through modern technology (e.g., video chat). The COVID-19 pandemic highlighted the importance of access to medication abortion through telemedicine because many states restricted access to abortion by health care facilities.

Tender years presumption: According to this presumption, which came into effect in the mid- to late nineteenth century, courts presume that a child of "tender years" (defined differently in various jurisdictions but generally includes preschool children) should be in the custody of the mother. Modern courts have held that the presumption violates equal protection.

Therapeutic abortion: This type of abortion is undertaken in order to safeguard the mother's mental or physical health. The liberalization of state abortion restrictions began in the 1960s, when many jurisdictions adopted the American Law Institute (ALI)'s Model Penal Code abortion provisions liberalizing abortion for pregnancies resulting from rape or incest, for those involving a deformed fetus, and when necessary to safeguard the mother's health.

Transracial adoption: This type of adoption, formerly known as "interracial adoption," refers to an adoption of a child by parents of a different race. Today, it is a highly controversial practice.

Trimester framework: These guidelines for abortion were established in *Roe v. Wade*. The Supreme Court held that, due to the constitutionally protected right to an abortion, the state may not interfere with the abortion decision during the first trimester. However, during the second trimester, the state may regulate abortion in the interest of maternal health. And, after viability, the state may regulate, and even proscribe, abortion in the interests of the protection of potential life. The trimester scheme was subsequently abandoned by the Court.

***Turner* Guidelines:** Federal reforms prompted by the U.S. Supreme Court's decision in *Turner v. Rogers*, 564 U.S. 431(2011), strengthened due process protections for child support obligors by providing states with guidance on the factors to consider when determining which cases should be referred for civil contempt, including a determination of the noncustodial parent's ability to pay, and prohibiting state enforcement programs from treating a parent's incarceration as voluntary unemployment, thereby, leading to possible reductions of child support obligations during periods of incarceration.

Undue burden: This standard, by which to evaluate state abortion restrictions, was announced by the U.S. Supreme Court in *Planned Parenthood v. Casey*. Only those regulations that impose an "undue burden" on the woman's abortion decision will be subject to strict scrutiny. The Court defines undue burden as the placement of a substantial obstacle in woman's path. The *Casey* Court determines that neither the informed consent requirement nor the 24-hour waiting period creates undue burdens, although spousal notification policies do.

Unilateral divorce: *See ex parte divorce.*

Vagueness: This shortcoming renders a classification unconstitutional because the classification fails to alert people as to the specific conduct that is prohibited. That is, it constitutes a violation of due process under the Fourteenth Amendment.

Void marriage: States have substantive requirements regarding capacity which determine marriage validity (restrictions about incest, bigamy, same-sex marriages, etc.). The presence of any of these substantive defects renders a marriage "void," i.e., invalid from its inception.

Voidable marriage: In addition to states' substantive restrictions regarding capacity, jurisdictions also have state of mind requirements for entry into a valid marriage. Unlike substantive defects, which render a marriage void, a defect concerning state of mind renders a marriage "voidable." For example, the existence of fraud or duress vitiates consent and makes the marriage voidable at the request of the injured party.

Waiting period: Many states impose a waiting period (often three to five days) between the time the applicants apply for the license and its issuance in order to deter hasty marriages.

Wrongful adoption: This doctrine enables an adoptive parent to recover tort damages (similar to an action for misrepresentation) from an adoption agency that fails to fully disclose information about a child's biological parents or prior history.

Table of Cases

References are to page numbers.

A-B-, Matter of. 84
Adkins v. Adkins 131
Adoptive Couple v. Baby Girl 277
Akron v. Akron Ctr. for Reprod. Health 225
Albertini v. Veal 80
Am. Acad. of Pediatrics v. Lungren 234
Am. Coll. Obstetricians & Gynecologists v. U.S.
    Food & Drug Admin. 232
Ammarell v. France 79
Ankenbrandt v. Richards 140, 141, 145
Astrue v. Capato. 239, 257

Baby M., In re 243, 320
Baehr v. Lewin 26
Baggett v. Baggett 138
B.C. v. Plumas Unified Sch. Dist. 262
Beal v. Doe. 228
Belle Terre, Village of v. Boraas. 98
Bellotti v. Baird 233, 237
Bender v. Bender 155
Bethany v. Jones. 201
Bethel v. Fraser. 261, 268
Biliouris v. Biliouris. 19
Bilowit v. Dolitsky 40
Blair v. Blair. 41
Bloomfield v. Bloomfield. 20
Blumenthal v. Brewer. 102, 105, 117
Board of Educ. v. Earls. 262
Boddie v. Connecticut 129
Bonds, In re Marriage of 19
Borough of Glassboro v. Vallorosi 98
Bostock v. Clayton County, Ga 31, 100
Box vs. Planned Parenthood of Indiana &
    Kentucky 236
Bowers v. Hardwick 26, 27, 219
Brackeen v. Bernhardt 277
Bradwell v. Illinois. 64
Braschi v. Stahl Assocs. 100
Braun, In re 131
Brown v. Entertainment Merchants Assn. . . . 260, 268
Brown v. Thomas 14
Buck v. Stankovic. 22
Burnham v. Superior Court 138, 139, 171
Burwell v. Hobby Lobby Stores, Inc 5, 222
Butler v. Wilson 24

Buzzanca, In re Marriage of. 244

Caban v. Mohammed 7, 108, 279, 293
C.A.C., In re. 240
Caldwell v. Holland of Texas, Inc. 73
Califano v. Jobst. 24
California Federal Savings & Loan Assn. v. Guerra 70
Callahan v. Parker 13
Campbell v. Robinson 14
Carabetta v. Carabetta 44
Carey v. Population Servs. Int'l 219, 220
Carney, In re Marriage of. 192
Castle Rock, Town of v. Gonzales 87
Catalano v. Catalano. 35
Cates v. Swain 105
Ceja v. Rudolph & Sletten, Inc. 47
Chatterjee v. King. 109
Chen v. Fisher. 82
Christopher, Ex parte 166
Ciesluk v. Ciesluk. 206
City of. *See name of city*
Clagett v. King. 140
Clark v. Jeter. 112, 115
Clark Sand Co. v. Kelly 101
Clay City Consolidated School Corp. v.
    Timberman 252
Cleveland Bd. of Educ. v. LaFleur 69
Cline v. Oklahoma Coalition for Reproductive
    Justice 232
Clippard v. Pfefferkorn. 13
Cochran v. Cochran . . . .
Collier v. Fox 32, 34
Committee to Defend Reproductive Rights v.
    Myers. 229, 234
Conduct of Balocca, In re. 132
Congdon v. Congdon 151
Connell v. Francisco. 132
Craig v. Boren 2, 7, 320
Crawford v. Washington. 87
Crews v. Crews. 18
Culliton v. Beth Israel Deaconess Med. Ctr. 244
Curtis v. Kline 166

Dalip Singh Bir's Estate, In re 33
Danielle A. v. Christopher P. 253

Danielson v. Board of Higher Educ. 72
Daubert v. Merrell Dow Pharms. 85
Davis v. Washington 88
DePasse, Estate of 44
DeShaney v. Winnebago 86, 87, 94
Devine v. Devine 187
DeVita v. DeVita 197
Dickens v. Ernesto 275
Dike v. School Board 71
Dillon v. Legg 101, 114
District of Columbia v. Heller 89
D.L., Matter of Welfare of 273
Dodd v. Burleson 200
Doe v. Bolton 224
Doe v. Dilling 81
Doe v. Renfrow 262
Doe v. State 111
Dove v. Dove 17

Edwards v. Edwards 201
EEOC v. Rath Packing Co. 65
Eisenstadt v. Baird 7, 28, 216–218
Elden v. Sheldon 101
Elkus v. Elkus 155
Elonis, United States v. 84
Epstein v. Epstein 77
Estate of. *See name of party*
Ex parte. *See name of party*

Faherty v. Faherty 142
Feinstein, Matter of Intestate Estate of 288
Feltmeier v. Feltmeier 82
Ferguson v. Ferguson 150
Ferguson v. McKiernan 240
Florida Dept. of Children & Families v.
    Adoption of X.X.G. 273
Ford, Estate of 287
Fox v. Gibson 80
Franco v. Franco 197
Friezo v. Friezo 18
Frye v. United States 85
Fulton v. City of Phila., ... 274

Gardiner, In re Estate of 30
Garges, Estate of 45
Garska v. McCoy 187
Gaulrapp v. Gaulrapp 149
Geduldig v. Aiello 69
General Electric v. Gilbert 69
Gerty v. Gerty 123

Ghassemi v. Ghassemi 51
Giles v. California 88
Ginsberg v. New York 260
Glazner v. Glazner 76
Gonzales v. Carhart 230, 237, 249
Goodridge v. Department of Public Health 27
Gordon v. Railroad Retirement Bd. 33
Graham v. Graham 16
Graves v. Estabrook 101
Griswold v. Connecticut 216, 304, 313
Groves v. Clark 286
Guardianship of Phillip B. Gutierrez, State v. 76

Hammon v. Indiana 88
Hanke v. Hanke 197
Hanson v. Hanson 198
Harris v. McRae 229
Harris, In re Marriage of 153
Hawkins v. Grese 240
Hazelwood Sch. Dist. v. Kuhlmeier 260
Henne v. Wright 63
Hess v. Johnson 14
Hewitt v. Hewitt 102
Hicks v. City of Tuscaloosa, Alabama 71
Hill v. Colorado 230
Hisquierdo v. Hisquierdo 156
Hodgson v. Minnesota 234
Holder v. Holder 189
Hollon v. Hollon 190
Holm; State v. 34
Howard v. Howard 158
Hurley v. Hurley 132

In re. *See name of party*
Iowa Supreme Court Attorney Disciplinary Bd.
    v. Morrison 132
Israel v. Allen 36, 284

J.D. v. Azar 235
Jersey Shore Med. Ctr. v. Estate of Baum 60
Jewish Child Care Assn. of N.Y., In re . . . .
J.F. v. D.B. 241
J.M.H. and Rouse, In re Marriage of 38
John B. v. Superior Court 81
Johnson v. Calvert 242
Jones v. Swanson 79
June Med. Servs. v. Russo 227

Kelly; State v. 85
Kimura, In re Marriage of 137

King v. King.............................. 129
Kirkpatrick v. Eighth Judicial Dist. Court 38
Kreigh v. Cogswell......................... 255
Kulko v. Superior Court 138, 171

Ladue, City of v. Horn 99
Lalli v. Lalli 167, 256
L.A.M. v. B.M............................ 191
Larson v. Dunn........................... 209
Lawrence v. Texas 7, 26, 27, 190, 195, 197, 219
Leary v. Leary 204
Lehr v. Robertson......................... 279
LeTellier v. LeTellier 173
Levy v. Louisiana......................... 167
Liberta; People v......................... 78
Lipscomb v. Simmons 97
Lister v. Lister 121
Little Sisters of the Poor v. Pa............... 222
Littlejohn v. Rose......................... 130
Lofton v. Secretary of Dept. of Children and
    Family Servs.......................... 273
Long v. Wiley............................ 287
Loving v. Virginia..................... 7, 23, 64

M, In re Adoption of........................ 36
Maher v. Roe 228
Mani v. Mani 161
Marquette S., In re 280
Marvin v. Marvin (Marvin I) 103–105
Marvin v. Marvin (Marvin II)................ 105
Marvin v. Marvin (Marvin III) 105
Mason v. Coleman 206
Masterpiece Cakeshop v. Colorado Civil Rts.
    Comm'n............................. 30
Mathews v. Eldridge........................ 174
Maynard v. Hill 58
M.C., In re 246
McCarty v. McCarty.................... 156, 159
McCullen v. Coakley 230
McGriff v. McGriff......................... 198
McGuire v. McGuire 110
McLaughlin v. Jones ....
McLaughlin v. Superior Court 211
McLeod v. Starnes 166
McMillen v. McMillen...................... 205
Melbourne v. Neal 62
Mennen v. Mennen........................ 170
Meyer v. Nebraska 258
Michael H. v. Gerald D..................... 108
Miles v. Miles........................... 178

Miller v. Miller............................ 61
M.J., In re............................... 189
Moe v. Dinkins........................
Moore v. East Cleveland...................... 97
Moreno, U.S. Dept. of Agric. v................ 96
Morone v. Morone 103
Morrison; United States v..................... 89
Morse v. Frederick 260
Muhammad v. Muhammad.................... 121
Mullane v. Central Hanover Bank & Trust Co. 137
Muth v. Frank............................ 37

Natale, Matter of 61
New Hope Fam. Servs., Inc. v. Poole........... 274
New Jersey v. T.L.O. 261, 268
Nicholson v. Scoppetta...................... 90
Noesen v. State Dept. of Regulation &
    Licensing, Pharmacy Examining Bd. 221
Nolan v. LaBree 244
North Dakota Fair Housing Council v. Peterson .. 101
North Ford, In re Estate of 287
Norton v. McOsker......................... 141

Obergefell v. Hodges 5, 27, 28
Okin v. Village of Cornwall-on-Hudson Police
    Dept. 87, 94
Olmstead v. Ziegler 169
Orr v. Orr 160

Painter v. Bannister 200
Palmore v. Sidoti 188
Parker v. Parker 122
Pavan v. Smith 63
Pennoyer v. Neff.......................... 137
Penobscot Area Housing Dev. Corp. v. City of
    Brewer............................. 99
People v. *See name of opposing party*
Peters-Riemers v. Riemers 191
Petrie, Matter of......................... 282
Phillip B., In re.......................... 265
Pickering v. Board of Ed..................... 106
Pierce v. Society of Sisters................... 317
P.K. v. R.K............................. 124
Planned Parenthood v. Danforth.......... 220, 233
Planned Parenthood Fed'n of Am. v. Heckler 220
Planned Parenthood of Greater Tex. Surgical
    Health Servs. v. Abbott 232
Planned Parenthood of Minnesota, North &
    South Dakota v. Rounds 226
Planned Parenthood of Southeastern ....

Pa. v. Casey 225, 226, 233, 234
Planned Parenthood Southwest Ohio Region v.
    Dewine. 232
Pryor v. Pryor 50

Quilloin v. Walcott . . . .

Ramadan, In re 140
Rankin v. Rankin 124
Raymond T. v. Samantha G 245
Rebecca B., In re 204
Reed v. Reed. 2, 7
Reid v. Reid 122
Reynolds v. United States. 32, 33
Richardson v. Richardson. 178
Rivkin v. Postal 12
Robbins; People v. 65
Robert Paul P., In re 290
Roe v. Wade 5, 215, 222, 223–226, 228, 233
Roger B., In re 289
Rooks, In re Marriage of 241
Ross, In re Matter of. 123
Russell v. Russell 205

Safford Unified School Dist. No. 1 v.
    Redding 263
Sagar v. Sagar. 189
Sail'er Inn v. Kirby. 2
Samantha I. ex rel. Emily K. v. Luis J. 83
Santa Barbara, City of v. Adamson 98
Santosky v. Kramer 7
Sargent v. Sargent. 123
Scarpetta v. Spence-Chapin Adoption Serv. 291
Schilling v. Bedford Cty. Mem. Hosp. 59
Scoggins v. Trevino 62
Segal v. Lynch 198
Sessions v. Morales-Santana 111
Shanks, In re Marriage of. 18
Sher v. Desmond 201
Sherrer v. Sherrer 137
Shields v. Gross 254
Sholes v. Sholes 129
Silicott v. Oglesby 209
Simeone v. Simeone. 18
Singh v. Singh 35
Sistare v. Sistare. 170
Skoien; United States v. 89
Smith v. Avanti. 100
Smith v. Fair Employment & Housing Comm'n . . 101
Smith v. Millville Rescue Squad 130

Sosna v. Iowa 135
Stanley v. Georgia 219
Stanley v. Illinois 108, 278, 293
Stanton v. Stanton. 38
Stark County Bar Assn. v. Hare 281
State v. See name of opposing party
State ex rel. See name of related party
Stenberg v. Carhart. 230
Stuart v. Bd. of Supervisors of Elections 60
Sumners, In re Marriage of 34

Taylor v. Taylor 198
Territory v. Manton 65
Texas Dept. of Family and Protective. 32
Thornley, In re Marriage of 153
Tinker v. Des Moines Indep. Community Sch.
    Dist. 259
T.J.S., In re 244
Town of. See name of town
Trammel v. United States 75, 76
Travis v. Murray 193
Treto v. Treto 168
Trimble v. Gordon 167, 256, 267
Trombley v. Trombley 169
Troxel v. Granville 200
Trump v. Pa. 222
Tshiani v. Tshiani. 45
Tsoutsouris, In re 133
Tummino v. Hamburg. 221
Tummino v. Torti 220
Turner v. Rogers. 174, 321
Turner v. Safley 24
Turner v. Turner 165, 196

Underwood, In re Estate of Kimberly M. 47
United States v. See name of opposing party

Vanderbilt v. Vanderbilt 170
Vargas, Estate of. 48
Vaughn v. Lawrenceburg Power System 64
Vernonia Sch. Dist. v. Acton 262
Village of. See name of village
Virginia; United States v. 2
V.L. v. E.L. 275

Wallis v. Smith. 221
Ward; State v. . . . .
Watkins, Matter of . . . .
Watt v. Watt 206
Weber v. Aetna Casualty and Surety Co. 167

Webster v. Reproductive Health Servs. 229

Whole Woman's Health v. Hellerstedt 227

Williams v. North Carolina
(Williams I) 135, 136, 143

Williams v. North Carolina
(Williams II) 135, 136, 143

Williams v. Ormsby 102

Windsor, United States v. 27, 311

Winfield v. Renfro 46

Wisconsin v. Yoder 7, 259

Wolfe v. Wolfe 40

Wolford v. Children's Home Soc'y of W. Va. 291

Yoder v. Yoder 139

Young v. United Parcel Service (UPS) 70

Younger v. Harris 140

Zablocki v. Redhail 7, 23, 64, 304

Table of Statutes

United States Constitution

Article IV, §1 . . . . 26, 135, 313
Amendment I 29, 30, 32, 33, 39, 64, 79,
      96, 99, 101, 116, 128, 188, 195, 197, 213, 216,
      225, 230, 251, 259, 260, 261, 267, 268, 274, 313
Amendment II 89
Amendment III. 216
Amendment IV. 217, 261, 262, 263, 267, 268
Amendment V 28, 111, 217, 277
Amendment VI. 88, 94, 174
Amendment IX. 216, 217
Amendment XIV 28, 30, 111, 116, 174,
            216, 217, 223, 230, 240, 249,
      251, 258, 259,261, 262, 292, 311, 317, 321

Federal Statutes

Abuse, Neglect and Custody
      Proceedings Act. 8, 204
Adoption and Safe Families Act (ASFA) 6, 283
42 U.S.C. §671(a). 283
42 U.S.C. §673b. 283
42 U.S.C. §675(5) 283

Adoption Assistance and Child Welfare
Act of 1980 (AACWA). 6, 282
42 U.S.C. §§620–628 282
42 U.S.C. §§670–679(a). 282

Bankruptcy Abuse Prevention and Consumer
      Protection Act of 2005 (BAPCPA) 157, 181
11 U.S.C. §523(a)(5) 157
11 U.S.C. §523(a)(15) 157
11 U.S.C. §1328(a)(2) 157

Bankruptcy Code 157
11 U.S.C. §362(b)(2) 157
11 U.S.C. §541. 157

Bankruptcy Reform Act (BRA) 157
11 U.S.C. §523(a)(15) 157

Child Abuse Prevention and Treatment Act of
      1974 (CAPTA). 7

Child Support and Establishment of Paternity
      Act of 1974 175
42 U.S.C. §659. 175

Child Support Enforcement Amendments of
      1984. . . . . 7, 164, 166, 175, 300
42 U.S.C. §651. 164
42 U.S.C. §666(a)(5)(A)(ii) 166

Child Support Recovery Act (CSRA). 175
18 U.S.C. §228(a). 175

Civil Rights Act of 1964,
      Title VII. 2, 7, 64, 69, 95, 100, 318
42 U.S.C. §1983. 86, 87, 319
42 U.S.C. §2000e-2(a)(1). 64

Deadbeat Parents Punishment Act 175
18 U.S.C. §228(a). 175

Defense of Marriage Act
      (DOMA) 26, 27, 28, 310, 311, 313
28 U.S.C. §1738(c). 27

Department of Defense Authorization Act 229
10 U.S.C. §1903(a). 229
10 U.S.C. §1903(b) 229
"Don't Ask, Don't Tell" (DADT). 107
10 U.S.C. §654. 107

Employee Retirement Income Security
      Act of 1974 156
29 U.S.C. §§1000 *et seq.* 156

Equality Act 107

Fair Housing Act 100
42 U.S.C. § 3602(k) 100

Fairness for Breastfeeding Mothers Act. 72

Fair Labor Standards Act 71
29 U.S.C. §207(r)(1)–(4) 71

Family and Medical Leave Act
      (FMLA). 7, 57, 71, 72, 73, 93, 312
29 U.S.C. §§2601 *et seq.* 72

Family Expense Acts 60

Family Law Act of 1969. 3

Family Support Act (FSA) of 1988 . . . 7, 8, 164, 172, 175
42 U.S.C. §667(a)–(b) 164
42 U.S.C. §1305 167

Federal Full Faith and Credit for Child Support
    Orders Act (FFCCSOA) 173

Forced Marriage Act of 2008 42

Foster Care Independence Act (FCIA) 7

Fostering Connections to Success and Increasing
    Adoptions Act (FCSIAA) of 2008 7

Freedom of Access to Clinic Entrances (FACE)
    Act 229
18 U.S.C. §248 229

Full Faith and Credit for Child Support Orders
    Act (FFCCSOA) 7, 172
28 U.S.C. §1738(B) 172
28 U.S.C. §1738B(e) 173
28 U.S.C. §1738B(g)(3) 173

Hague Convention on Protection of Children
    and Cooperation in Respect of Intercountry
    Adoption 283
42 U.S.C. §§14901–14954 283

Hyde Amendment of 1977 228

Illegal Immigration Reform and Immigration
    Responsibility Act of 1996 41
8 U.S.C. §1154(A)(iii)(1) 41
8 U.S.C. §1254(a)(3) 41

Immigration and Nationality Act (INA) 41
8 U.S.C. §1151(a) 41
8 U.S.C. §1151(b) 41

Indian Child Welfare Act (ICWA)
    of 1978 . . . . 7, 208, 275, 276, 293, 314
25 U.S.C. §§1901–1963 . . . . 208, 276
25 U.S.C. §1903(4) 276
25 U.S.C. §1911 276
25 U.S.C §1912(d) 276
25 U.S.C. §1915 276
25 U.S.C. §1915(a) 276

International Child Abduction Remedies Act
    (ICARA) 209
42 U.S.C. §§11601–11611 209

International Marriage Broker Regulation Act
    (IMBRA) 41
808(a)(2)(A) 41

International Parental Kidnapping Crime Act
    (IPKCA) 209
18 U.S.C. §1204 209

Magnitsky Act . . . .

Marriage Fraud Amendments Act 41
8 U.S.C. §1154(h) 41
8 U.S.C. §1255(e) 41

Married Women's Property Acts 58, 81, 316

Matrimonial Causes Act of 1857 120

Multi-Ethnic Placement Act (MEPA) 275
42 U.S.C. §1996b 274

Omnibus Crime Control Act, Title III 76, 93
18 U.S.C. §§2510–2520 76

Parental Kidnapping Prevention Act
    (PKPA) 7, 186, 208

Partial-Birth Abortion Ban Act (PBABA) 7, 230
18 U.S.C. §1531 230

Patient Protection and Affordable Care Act
    (PPACA) 5, 74, 221, 310, 317
29 U.S.C. §207(r)(1)–(4) 71

Personal Responsibility and Work
    Opportunity Reconciliation Act (PRWORA)
    of 1996 . . . . 109, 167, 172, 175
42 U.S.C. §312 175
42 U.S.C. §653(a) 175
42 U.S.C. §666 167
42 U.S.C. §666(f) 172

Pregnancy Discrimination Act
    (PDA) 7, 57, 69, 70, 74, 93, 318
42 U.S.C. §2000e(k) 69

Railroad Retirement Act (RRA) 33, 156
45 U.S.C. §231a(c)(4)(i–iii) 156

Religious Freedom Restoration Act 101, 221

Retirement Equity Act of 1984 (REA) 156

Social Security Act 239

Title XIX 228

Tax Cuts and Jobs Act 162, 179

Unborn Victims of Violence Act (UVVA) 7, 235

18 U.S.C. §1841 235

Uniformed Services Former Spouses Protection
 Act (USFSPA) 156
10 U.S.C. §1408 156

Violence Against Women Act of 1994 . . . . . . 7, 41, 83,
 8889, 111
42 U.S.C. §§14014 *et seq.* 89

Violence Against Women Act Reauthorization
 of 2013 . . . . 38, 41, 83, 111
122 U.S.C.A. §7104(j) 38
42 U.S.C.A. §13925(a)(39) 111
42 U.S.C.A. §13925(b)(13)(A) 111

Violence Against Women Reauthorization
 Act of 2020 . . . . 89, 112

Women's Health Protection Act (WHPA) 228

Federal Rules of Evidence
Rule 702 85

Uniform Acts . . . .
Revised Uniform Reciprocal Enforcement of
 Support Act (RURESA) 172, 300

Uniform Child Abduction Prevention Act
 (UCAPA) 8, 186, 209

Uniform Child Custody Jurisdiction Act
 (UCCJA) 208, 212

Uniform Child Custody Jurisdiction and
 Enforcement Act (UCCJEA) 8, 186, 208, 212

Uniform Collaborative Law Act (UCLA) 8

Uniform Deployed Parents Custody and
 Visitation Act 8

Uniform Interstate Enforcement of Domestic
 Violence Protection Orders Act (UIEDVPOA) . . . 8

Uniform Interstate Family Support Act (UIFSA)
 of 1992 . . . . 8, 172, 183, 300
§201 172
§205 172
§205(a) 172
§305(b) 172

Uniform Marital Property Act
 (UMPA) 8, 17, 20, 148

Uniform Marriage and Divorce
 Act (UMDA) 3, 8, 36, 44, 50, 51, 125,
 126, 135, 148, 149, 151, 161,
 164, 186, 189, 192, 203, 205
§204 44
§206(b) 44
§207 36
§207(c) 50
§302(a)(1) 135
§302(a)(2) 126
§307 . . . . 126, 149
§307(a) 148
§307(b) 148, 152
§308 126
§308(a) 161
§309 164
§316 168
§402 . . . . 186, 189
§402(2) 203
§402(5) 192
§409(a) 205
§409(b) 205

Uniform Marriage Evasion Act (UMEA) (1912) . . . 52

Uniform Nonparent Custody and Visitation Act
 (UNCVA) 8, 202

Uniform Parentage Act (UPA), (1973) 8, 109,
 167, 238, 239, 257
§4 167
§4(a)(4) 257
§4(4) 167
§5a 238
§5(b) 239

Uniform Parentage Act (UPA) (2000) 112

Uniform Parentage Act (UPA) (2002) 167
§5 167
§801(b) 242
§802 . . . . 242, 243

§803 242
§803(b) 242
§809 242

Uniform Parentage Act (UPA) (2017) 109, 110,
                                        201, 238, 239, 243
§204(a)(2) 110, 201, 202, 246
§609 202
§613 . . . . 109, 246
§708 239
§802 243
Article 9 238

Uniform Premarital Agreements Act
   (UPAA) 8, 17, 19
§2 17
§3(a) 17
§3(b) 17
§6(a)(2) 19

Uniform Premarital and Marital Agreements
   Act 8, 20

Uniform Probate Code 167
§2-117 167

Uniform Reciprocal Enforcement of Support Act
   (URESA) 172, 173, 300

Uniform Representation of Children in Abuse,
   Neglect, and Custody Proceedings Act 8, 204

Uniform Transfers to Minors Act
   (UTMA) 257, 258, 267

State Statutes
Alabama
Ala. Code §22-9A-19(d) 61
Ala. Code §30-1-9.1 44

Arkansas
Arkansas Stat. Ann. . . . .
§20-9-602(7) 264

California
California Civil Code
§1714.1 252
§1714.01 102

California Family Code
§306.5 61
§358 43
§500 45

§511 45
§1612(c) 19
§1830 210
§2310(a) 126
§2311 126
§2400 129
§2641(b)(1) 153
§3040(d) 245
§3080 192
§3173 142
§4323 169
§7500 255
§7541(b) 108
§7612(c) 245

California Health and Safety Code
§103425 61

California Probate Code
§6454 288

Colorado
Colorado Anti-Discrimination Act
Colorado Rev. Stat.
§14-10-124 191

Connecticut
Connecticut Gen. Stat.
§46b-150b 255

Florida
Florida Stat. Ann.
§63.213 241

Illinois
750 Ill. Comp. Stat. 47/1-47/75 244

Iowa
Iowa Code of Professional Responsibility
   for Lawyers
DR 1-102(A)(1) 132
DR 1-102(A)(6) 132
DR 5-101(A) 132

Massachusetts
Massachusetts Gen. Laws
c. 46, §1D 61
c. 272 218

Massachusetts Alimony Reform Act
Minnesota
Minnesota Stat.
§518.17(13) 192

New Mexico
New Mexico Stat. Ann.
§40-8-2 61

New York
New York Civil Rights Law
§81 13

New York Domestic Relations Law
§115-b(6)(d)(v) 291
§§121–123 241
§236B(5)(d)(7) 154
§236B(5)(h) 128
§236B(6)(d)(7) 154
§253 128
18 NYCRR Rule 421.3(d) 274
22 NYCRR §1200.0; Rule 1.8(j) 132

New York Codes, Rules and Regulations
North Carolina Gen. Stat. Ann.
§51-2.1 37

Texas
Texas Fam. Code Ann.
§153.0072 212

Utah
Utah Code Ann.
§30-1-9.1 34
§76-7-101 35
§76-7-101.5 34

Washington
Washington Rev. Code
§9A.40.060 198

ABA Model Act Governing Assisted
    Reproductive Technology Agencies (2019) 246

ABA Model Rules of Professional Conduct
Rule 1.6 131
Rule 1.7 . . . . 130, 133
Rule 1.8(j) 133
Rule 2.2 282
Rule 4.3 131

ALI Principles
§2.03(1)(b) 202

§2.03(1)(c) 202
§2.06(1)(a) 188, 194
§2.06(1)(b) 188, 194
§2.08(1) 188
§2.11(c) 191
§2.12(1)(a) 188
§2.12(1)(c) 189
§2.12(1)(d) 191
§2.17(1) 206
§2.20(4)(a) 206
§3.16 166
§4.07 154
§5.05 161
§5.12 154
§7.04(a) 20
§7.04(b) 20
§7.04(c) 20
§7.04(e) 20
§7.05 19

Human Fertilization and Embryology
    Authority 247

Restatements
Restatement (Second) of Conflict of
    Laws 11
§21 63
§21(1) 63
§70 135
§71 135
§72 135
§98 139
§283(1) 51

Restatement (Second) of Torts
§283A 251

Restatement (Third) of Conflict of Laws
§2.01(2) 52

Restatement (Third) of Restitution & Unjust
    Enrichment
§33 254

Restatement (Third) of Torts
§10 252
§10(b) 252
§10(c) 252

Subject Matter Index

ABA
Attorney and client relationship, 133
Collaborative law, 142, 212
Confidentiality, 131
Fertility agencies, 246
Joint representation, 130–131
Mediation, 210–211
Model Act Governing Assisted Reproductive
   Technology Agencies, 246
Model Rules of Professional Conduct, 130–131, 133

ABANDONMENT, 121, 126

ABORTION, 222–235
Admitting privileges requirement, hospitals, 227
Ambulatory surgical care requirements, 227
Background, 222–223
Buffer zones, 229
Clinic access, 229–230
Clinic violence, 229–230
Consent
   husband's consent, 232–233
   informed consent, 226
   parental consent for minor, 233–234
   "right to know" laws, 225–226
   spousal consent, 232–233
Fetal protection legislation, 235–237
   fetal homicide, 235
   fetal remains laws, 235–236
   gestational limits, 235
   heartbeat laws, 235
   personhood laws, 235
Freedom of Access to Clinic Entrances Act, 229–230
Funding, 228–229
Hospitalization requirements, 224–225
Husband's rights, 232–233
Hyde Amendment, 228–229
Informed consent laws, 226
Judicial bypass, 234
Late stage, 231
Medication abortions, 231–232
Mifepristone, 231
Military personnel, 229
Minors' rights, 220, 233–235
Parental involvement laws, 233–234
Partial-birth abortion, 230–231

Prosecuting women, 232
Prosecuting health care providers, 232
Religious refusal clauses ("conscience clauses"), 6,
   215, 221
Right to, 223–228
"Right to know" laws, 225–226
Roe v. Wade, 223–224
RU-486, 231
Spousal consent, 232–233
Spousal notification, 233
Targeted regulation of abortion providers (TRAP)
   laws, 226–228
Undocumented minors, right to, 234–235
Undue burden standard, 226
Viability, 224
Violence, 228
Waiting periods, 226

ABUSE. *See* INTIMATE PARTNER VIOLENCE

ADOPTION, 271–294
Abrogation, 291
Adult, 290
Agencies, 281
Baby selling, 281
Baby Veronica, 276–277
Background, 271–272
Best interests of child, 272, 285
Confidentiality, 289
Consent, 278–281
   father has no relationship opportunity, 279–280
   indicia of parenthood, 278–279
   noncustodial parent's consent, stepparent
      adoption, 280
   prebirth, 243
   revocation of, 290–291
   unmarried father, 278–280
Contract theory, 287
Custody and visitation issues, 285
Cutoff rule, 284
Decrees, interstate recognition of, 274
Defined, 271–272
Discrimination in placement, 273
Equitable, 286–288
Estoppel theory, 287
Failure of, 290–292

ADOPTION (*Cont.*)
Faith-based adoption agencies, 273–274
Full, Faith & Credit Clause, as applied to, 274–275
Home study, 281
Indian Child Welfare Act, 275, 276
Independent, 282
Independent placement, 281–282
Infertility as factor in selection of adoptive parent, 276
Inheritance, 284–285, 286–287
International, 283
Internet, influence of, 272, 289
Intestate succession, 284
Jurisdiction, 273
Legal consequences of, 284–285
Marriage, restrictions regarding, 284
Native American children, 275, 276
Open, 285–286
Origins, adoptee's right to know, 289
Paternity registries, 278
Placement procedure, 281–282
Pre-birth consent, 243
Race matching, 275
Relatives, preference for, 272–273
Religion as factor in selection of adoptive parent, 275
Same-sex couples, discrimination against, 290
Screening prospective adoptive parents, 281
Selection standards, 272–277
Sexual orientation, 273–275
Statistics, 272
Stepparents. *See* STEPPARENTS
Stranger-to-the-adoption rule, 284–285
Subsidized, 282–283
Wrongful, 281, 291

**ADOPTION AND SAFE FAMILIES ACT
          (ASFA)**, 6, 283

**ADOPTION ASSISTANCE AND CHILD
          WELFARE ACT (AACWA)**, 6, 282, 283

ADULT ADOPTION, 290

ADULTERY
Bigamy, 27
Child custody decisions and, 189
Grounds for divorce, 121, 150

AFFINITY, 36

AFFORDABLE CARE ACT (ACA), 6, 71, 83, 221

AGE
Factor in domestic violence, 82–83

Restrictions on right to marry, 37–40. *See also* CHILD
          MARRIAGE
     domestic laws, 38
     empirical data, 39
     international laws, 38

ALI. *See* ALI PRINCIPLES

ALIENATION OF AFFECTIONS, 78–80

ALIMONY. *See* SPOUSAL SUPPORT

ALI PRINCIPLES
Child support post-majority, 166
Contribution approach to property division, 150
Custodial and decisionmaking responsibility for
          children, 192
De facto parents, 202
Earning capacity, 154
Overview, 9
Parenting plan and parenting coordinators, 193–194
Premarital agreements, 20
Professional licenses and degrees, 152–154
Race or ethnicity, 188
Religion, 189
Relocation and child custody controversies, 206
Sexual conduct or orientation, 191
Spousal support, 161
Unmarried couples, dissolution of relationship, 106
Visitation, 202

ALTERNATIVE DISPUTE RESOLUTION
Child custody, 211–212
Divorce, 141–142

ALTERNATIVE FAMILIES. *See* FAMILIES

ALTERNATIVE REPRODUCTION. *See*
          ASSISTED REPRODUCTIVE
          TECHNOLOGIES

AMERICAN LAW INSTITUTE (ALI), 9
ALI Principles. *See* ALI PRINCIPLES

ANNULMENT, 49–50
Divorce compared, 49, 51, 141
Fraud and duress as grounds for, 50
Separation compared, 141

ANTENUPTIAL AGREEMENTS, 15. *See also*
          PREMARITAL AGREEMENTS

ANTI-FRATERNIZATION RULES, 65

ARBITRATION, 141–142

ARTIFICIAL INSEMINATION, 238

ASSISTED REPRODUCTIVE TECHNOLOGIES
    (ARTs), 6, 238–245. *See also*
    SURROGACY
Artificial insemination, 238
Access, problems of, 238
Baby M, 243
Birth certificates, 244
Definitions of parenthood, 6
Disputes about ownership of genetic material, 6
Embryo transfers, 240–241
Internet, influence of, 238
In vitro fertilization, 238–240
Legitimacy of children, 238
Regulation of health care personnel who
    provide, 6
Reproductive material, ownership of, 241
Rights of children conceived through ARTs, 6
Same-sex partners, 240
Sperm donors' rights, 238, 239
Surrogacy, 241–245

ATTORNEYS
Divorce, 131–133
Dual representation, 131
Ethics, 131–133
Independent adoptions and, 281
Mediators, 210–211
Premarital agreements, representation of
    parties, 20
Right to counsel
    children, 204
    divorce, 130–132
Role of as counsel to child, 204
Role of as counsel to child support, 174
Sexual relationships with clients, 132–133

ATTORNEY'S FEES
Divorce proceedings, 133
Guardianships, 256
Trusts, 257

"BABY DOMAs," 311

BABY M, 243

BABY SELLING, 281

BABY VERONICA, 276–277

BANKRUPTCY
Child support and, 157–158

Client representation, 132
Property division in divorce, 157–158
Spousal support and, 157–158, 162

BANKRUPTCY ABUSE PREVENTION AND
    CONSUMER PROTECTION ACT
    (BAPCPA), 157–158

BANKRUPTCY REFORM ACT (BRA), 157

BATTERED CHILD SYNDROME,

BATTERED WOMAN'S SYNDROME, 84–85

BATTERY. *See* INTIMATE PARTNER VIOLENCE

BEST INTERESTS OF CHILD, 188–192
Adoption, 272
Constitutional factors, 188–189
Fitness factors, 189–192

BIGAMY, 31–35
Annulment, as ground for, 50
Child bigamy laws, 34
Conflict of laws, 33
Post-marriage equality challenges to state
    bans, 31–32
Presumptions and burden of proof, 33–34

BILATERAL DIVORCE, 134

BIOLOGICAL PARENT PRESUMPTION,
    199–200, 240

BIRTH CERTIFICATES
Alternative reproduction, 244
Same-sex spouses' right to be listed on, 62–63
Surrogacy, 244

BREACH OF PROMISE TO
    MARRY, 11, 12–13

BREASTFEEDING DISCRIMINATION, 71–72

CALIFORNIA LAW, 108, 171

CAPACITY
Consent to medical care, 264
Contributory negligence of child, 252
Marriage, 25–31

CHILD ABDUCTION, 209–210

CHILD ABUSE AND NEGLECT, 6, 208

CHILD ABUSE PREVENTION AND
    TREATMENT ACT (CAPTA), 7

CHILD CUSTODY, 185–214
Background, 186
Best interests of child, 188–192
Biological parent presumption, 199–200
Change of custody, 198
Child's preference, 203–204
Collaborative law, 211–212
Custodial interference, 198
Custodial parent, standards for selecting, 187–194
Definition, 186
Disability as factor in selection of custodial
   parent, 192
Dispute resolution, 210–213
Domestic violence, 191–192, 206, 211
Enforcement of orders, 208–209
Ethics, 211
Existing Indian Family Exception, 276
Expert testimony, 204
Friendly-parent provisions, 192
Joint custody, 192–193
Jurisdiction, 191, 207–208
Modification of orders, 204–206
Native Americans, 208
Parental cooperation, 193
Parenting plans and parenting coordinators, 193–194
Pet custody, 193
Presumptions, 187–188
 natural parent, 188
 primary caretaker, 187–188
 tender years doctrine, 187
Race, 188
Religious disputes, 188–189
Relocation controversies, 205–206
Same-sex couples, 189–190
Sexual abuse, 196–197
Sexual conduct, 189–191
Sexual orientation, 190
Stepparents, 201
Tender years doctrine, 187
Third parties, rights of, 200–202
Travel rights, 206
Visitation. *See* VISITATION
Wealth, 191

CHILD MARRIAGE, restrictions, 38–39. *See also*
   MARRIAGE

CHILDREN AND MINORS
Abortion, 220, 233–235
Abuse and neglect. *See* CHILD ABUSE AND
   NEGLECT

Adult activities by, 252
Annulment, 50
Child support. *See* CHILD SUPPORT
Civil rights, 4
Consent to medical treatment, 264
Contraception rights, 219–221
Contract liability, 254–255
Counsel for in custody proceedings, 204
Custody. *See* CHILD CUSTODY
Earnings, 255
Education. *See* SCHOOLS AND EDUCATION
Emancipation, 255, 264
Emergency contraception, 220–221
Fetal protection legislation, 235–237
Firearms, 268
Free speech, First Amendment rights, 259–260
Gifts to, 257
Inheritance, 255–257
Marriage, 37–38
Names, 61–63
Necessaries, duty to furnish, 60
Nonmarital
 discrimination against, 167
 inheritance rights, 256–257
 legitimacy, 22
 presumption of legitimacy, surrogate
   births, 243
 support rights, 166–167, 112
Paternity establishment, 167
Political speech, First Amendment rights of
   minors, 259
Posthumous conception by artificial insemination,
   238–239
Pre-birth determination of parental status, 244
Property, 255–258
Right to counsel, 204
Searches and seizures, Fourth Amendment rights,
   261–262
Tort liability, 251–254

CHILD SUPPORT, 163–168
Artificial insemination, 238
Bankruptcy discharge, effect of, 157–158
Contempt, 174–175
Contraceptive use, misrepresentation of, 221
Criminal liability for nonpayment, 174
Discretion, 163
Enforcement, 170–176
Federal law, 164
Guidelines, 163–164
Income shares model, 164

Jurisdiction, 170–176
Melson formula, 164–165
Models for, 164–165
Modification of award, 168–170
Money judgments, 173
Nonmarital children, 166–167
Parental liability for, 163
Percentage of income model, 164
Posthumous support obligation, 238–239
Post-majority, 165–166
Same-sex couples, 168
Sperm donors' rights, 239
Standards for awarding, 163
Stepparents, liability of, 165
Tax consequences, 179
Turner guidelines, 175
Visitation, 196

CHILD SUPPORT AND ESTABLISHMENT OF PATERNITY ACT, 175

CHILD SUPPORT ENFORCEMENT AMENDMENTS, 7, 164, 166, 175

CHILD SUPPORT RECOVERY ACT (CSRA), 175

CITIZENSHIP BY DESCENT, 110–111

CIVIL RIGHTS ACT (TITLE VII)
Antinepotism policies, 65–65
Gender identity, 31, 100–101, 106–107
Pregnancy Discrimination Act. *See* PREGNANCY DISCRIMINATION ACT (PDA)
Sexual orientation, 31, 100–101, 106–107
Women's movement and, 2

CIVIL RIGHTS LEGISLATION (STATES), 65

CIVIL UNIONS, 27, 107

COHABITATION. *See* UNMARRIED COUPLES

COLLABORATIVE LAW
Custody disputes, 211–212
Divorce, 142
Ethical considerations, 211–212

COLLABORATIVE REPRODUCTION, 6

COLLUSION, 124

COMITY DOCTRINE, 139–140

COMMON-LAW DISABILITIES, 58, 63–64

COMMON-LAW MARRIAGE, 45–47. *See also* MARRIAGE

COMMON-LAW NECESSARIES DOCTRINE, 59–60

COMSTOCK LAW, 216, 222

CONCILIATION, 141–142

CONDONATION, 123–124

CONFIDENTIALITY. *See also* PRIVACY RIGHTS
Adoption, 289
Attorneys, 131
Mediation, 211

CONFIDENTIAL MARRIAGES, 45

CONFLICT OF LAWS
Bigamous marriages, 33
Breach of promise to marry, 13
Common-law marriages, 46
Domicile, married woman, 63
Marriage validity, 11, 51–52

CONFLICTS OF INTEREST
Attorneys, 130, 133
Employment policies, 64
Independent adoption, 281–282

CONNIVANCE, 123

CONSANGUINITY, 35

CONSENT
Abortion
    husband's consent, 232–233
    informed consent, 226
    parental consent for minor, 233–234
    spousal consent, 232–233
Adoption, 278–281
    father has no relationship opportunity, 279–280
    indicia of parenthood, 278–279
    noncustodial parent's consent, stepparent adoption, 280
    prebirth, 243
    revocation of consent, 290–291
    unmarried father, 278–280
Artificial insemination, 238
Health care
    minors, 264
    parental consent, 264–265
No-fault divorce, 126

CONSORTIUM, 78, 94

CONTEMPT
Interference with visitation rights, 198

CONTEMPT (*Cont.*)
Nonpayment of child support, 174–175
Violation of child custody orders, 209

CONTRACEPTION, 215–222
Access to, 215–216
Background, 216
Emergency contraception, 220–221
Expanded conscience rule, 222
Health care providers' rights and, 221
Health insurance coverage, 221–222
Married persons' rights, 216–217
Minors' rights, 219–221
Misrepresentation of use, 221
Pharmacists' rights and, 221
Police powers, 217
Religious refusal laws ("conscience clauses"), 221
Same-sex sexual couples' rights, 218–219
Unmarried persons' rights, 217–219

"CONTRACEPTIVE MANDATE," 6, 221–222

CONTRACTS
Alternative families, 102–106
Breach of promise to marry, 12
During marriage, 16
Illicit consideration, 102
Marriage as contract, 58
Minors, 254
Premarital agreement distinguished, 16
Restitution of benefits, 254
Unmarried couples, 102–106

CONTRACT THEORY OF ADOPTION, 287

CONTRIBUTORY NEGLIGENCE, 252

COVENANT MARRIAGES, 127

COVERTURE, 58

COVID-19, 232
Medication abortions, 232
Restricted access to abortion, 232

CRIMINAL CONVERSATION, 80

CRIMINAL LIABILITY, 74–92
Abortion, 223, 232
Adultery, 121
Battery, 85
Between spouses, 74–76
Bigamy, 31–32
Child custody orders, noncompliance with, 208–209

Child support nonpayment, 174
Criminal conversation, 80
Fetal homicide, 235
Incest, 35–37
Marital rape, 77–78
Medical care, failure to provide, 65
Sexual conduct, 99
Spousal property, 78
Testimonial privileges, 74–76

CRUELTY, 120–121

DEADBEAT PARENTS PUNISHMENT ACT, 175

DEATH AND DYING. *See also*
        INHERITANCE LAW
Posthumous child support, 238–239
Posthumous conception, 238–239
Property rights in spousal remains, 66

DEFENSE OF MARRIAGE ACT (DOMA), 27–28

DESERTION, 121–122

DISCLOSURE OF FINANCIAL STATUS, 17–18

DISCRIMINATION
Breastfeeding discrimination, 71–72
Divorce, based on, 129–130
Employment, 106–107
Family responsibilities, 70, 73
Gender, 2
Housing, 99–101
Pregnancy, 70–72
Sex, 2, 7, 69
Unmarried couples, 106–107

DISPUTE RESOLUTION, 4, 210–213

DISSOLUTION OF MARRIAGE. *See* DIVORCE

DIVISIBLE DIVORCE, 134, 170

DIVORCE, 119–145
Abandonment, 121
Access to, 128–129
Adultery, 121
Alternative dispute resolution, 141–142
Alternatives to, 141
Annulment. *See* ANNULMENT
Attorneys, role of, 131–133
Background, 120
Bilateral, 134
Child support. *See* CHILD SUPPORT
Collaborative law, 142

Conflict of laws, 52
Corroboration requirement, 121
Covenant marriages and, 127
Cruelty, 120–121
Defenses, 122–125
    collusion, 124
    condonation, 123–124
    connivance, 123
    insanity, 124
    recrimination, 122–123
Desertion, 121–122
Discrimination based on, 129–130
Divisible, 134
Division of property. *See* PROPERTY DIVISION,
    DIVORCE
Domicile, 134–135
Embryo disputes, 240–241
Estoppel, 140
Ex parte, 134
Fault-based, 120–124
Financial consequences of, 147–183. *See also*
    PROPERTY DIVISION,
    DIVORCE
Financial limitations and filing fees, 128–129
Foreign decrees, 139–140
Incompatibility, 125
Indigent plaintiffs, 128–129
Irreconcilable differences, 126
Irretrievable breakdown, 126
Jurisdictional issues, 126, 134–141
Long-arm statutes, 138–139
Mediation, 141–142
New York reforms, 154
No-fault, 125–128
Pro se, 129
Reform movement, 151
Religious limitations on, 128
Residency requirements, 135
Right to counsel, 129, 130–134
Spousal support. *See* SPOUSAL SUPPORT
Standard of living after, 3
Summary dissolution, 129
Surrogacy, during, 244
Trends, 3
Unilateral, 126

DIVORCE REVOLUTION **(WEITZMAN),** 3

DOCTRINE OF NONINTERVENTION, 59

DOMESTIC PARTNERSHIPS
Inheritance, 107
Legislation, 27
Post-marriage equality,

DOMESTIC VIOLENCE. *See* INTIMATE
    PARTNER VIOLENCE

DOMICILE, 63
Definitions, changing, 52
Divorce jurisdiction, 134–135
Marriage validity, 52

DON'T ASK, DON'T TELL POLICY, 107

DURESS, 41–42

EARNING CAPACITY, 154–155

EDUCATION. *See* SCHOOLS AND EDUCATION

EMPLOYERS AND EMPLOYMENT
Anti-fraternization rules, 65
Antinepotism rules, 64–65
Discrimination, 2, 4, 7, 106–107, 129–130
Family leave policies, 72–73
Married women, 63–65
Unemployment benefits, 73
Unmarried couples, discrimination
    against, 106–107

ENFORCEMENT
Child custody orders, 208–209
Child support awards, 170–176
Separation agreements, 178
Spousal support, 162

ENGAGEMENT RINGS. *See* GIFTS

ENOCH ARDEN STATUTES, 33

EQUALITY ACT, 107

EQUITABLE ADOPTION, 286–288

ERISA, 156

ESTOPPEL, 140

ESTOPPEL THEORY OF ADOPTION, 287

ETHICS. *See also* ATTORNEYS
Attorneys, 131–132
Child custody, 211
Collaborative law, 142, 211–212
Mediation, 211

EVIDENCE
Battered women's syndrome, 84–85
Confidential communications privilege, 75–76
Cohabitation, termination of, 169–170
Fraud, 40–41
Privilege. *See* PRIVILEGES
Spousal disqualification privilege, 75
Wiretapping, 76–77

EX PARTE DIVORCE, 134

FAIR HOUSING ACT (FHA), 100–101

FAMILIES, 95–118
Alternative/nontraditional, 95–118
Cohabitants. *See* UNMARRIED COUPLES
Communal, 97–99
Extended, 97
Functional definition, 96–97
Legal recognition, 96
Same-sex couples. *See* SAME-SEX MARRIAGE;
      UNMARRIED COUPLES
Unmarried cohabitants. *See* UNMARRIED COUPLES

FAMILY AND MEDICAL LEAVE ACT (FMLA),
      7, 71, 72–73

FAMILY EXPENSE ACTS, 60

FAMILY LAW
Constitutionalization, 1, 7–8
Defined, 1
Federalization, 1, 6–7
Generally, 1–2
Internet, influence of, 13, 238, 272, 289
Legal trends, 6–9
Societal influences, 2–6
Terminology, 5
Uniformity of state laws, 1, 8–9

FAMILY PRIVACY DOCTRINE, 59, 60

FAMILY RESPONSIBILITIES
      DISCRIMINATION, 70, 73

FAMILY SUPPORT ACT (FSA), 7, 164, 167, 175

FEDERALISM, 155–156

THE FEMININE MYSTIQUE **(FRIEDAN)**, 2

FIREARMS
Constitutional right to bear arms, 89
Domestic violence, 89
Minors, 268

FLUIDITY AMONG FAMILY FORMS, 4

FORCED MARRIAGE, 42. *See also* MARRIAGE
Domestic laws, 38
International laws, 38

FORMER SPOUSES' PROTECTION ACT, 159

FOSTER CARE, 6–7, 32, 72, 97, 208, 272–276,
      282–283

FOSTER CARE INDEPENDENCE ACT (FCIA), 7

FOSTERING CONNECTION TO SUCCESS AND
      INCREASING ADOPTIONS ACT
      (FCSIAA), 7

FRAUD, 40–41. *See also* MARRIAGE
Contraception, 221
Fertility fraud, 247
Marriage, 40–41

FREEDOM OF ACCESS TO CLINIC
      ENTRANCES (FACE) ACT, 229–230

FRIEDAN, BETTY, 2

FRIENDLY-PARENT PROVISIONS, 192

FULL FAITH AND CREDIT CLAUSE
Comity distinguished, 140
Divorce decrees, 135–137
Same-sex marriage, 26

FULL FAITH AND CREDIT FOR CHILD
      SUPPORT ORDERS ACT, 7, 172–173

GAY MARRIAGE. *See* SAME-SEX MARRIAGE

GESTATIONAL AGREEMENTS. *See*
      SURROGACY

GIFTS
In contemplation of marriage, 11, 13–14
To minors, 257
As nonmarital property, 148
Property transfers incident to divorce, 179

GOODWILL, 154

GRANDPARENTS AND VISITATION RIGHTS,
      200–201, 285

GUARDIANS AD LITEM, 204

GUARDIANSHIPS, 256

GUNS. *See* FIREARMS

HABEAS CORPUS, 209

HAGUE CONVENTION ON PROTECTION OF CHILDREN AND COOPERATION IN RESPECT OF INTERCOUNTRY ADOPTION, 283

HAGUE CONVENTION ON THE CIVIL ASPECTS OF INTERNATIONAL CHILD ABDUCTION, 209

HEALTH CARE
Affordable Care Act, 221
Duty to provide, 65–66
Employment-related health benefits, unmarried couples, 106–107
Minor's consent, 264
Parental consent, 264–265

HEALTH INSURANCE AND CONTRACEPTION, 221–222

HEARSAY, 88

HEART BALM ACTIONS, 12, 14, 78

HOMEMAKER SERVICES, VALUATION OF, 150

HOMOSEXUAL CONDUCT. *See* SEXUAL CONDUCT; SEXUAL ORIENTATION

HOUSING DISCRIMINATION, 99–101

HYDE AMENDMENT, 228–229

ILLEGAL IMMIGRATION REFORM AND IMMIGRATION RESPONSIBILITY ACT, 41

ILLEGITIMACY. *See* CHILDREN AND MINORS

IMMIGRATION FRAUD, 41

IMMUNITY
Interspousal, 80–81

INCEST, 35–37

INCOME SHARES MODEL, 164

INCOMPATIBILITY, 125

INDIAN CHILD WELFARE ACT (ICWA), 7, 208, 275, 276–277
Background, 276
Defined, 276
Constitutionality of, 277

INHERITANCE LAW
Adoption and, 284–285
Children, 255–257
Domestic partnerships, 107
Equitable adoption, 286–287
Frozen embryos and, 240–241
Nonmarital children, 256–257
Posthumously conceived children, 238–239, 257
Social Security Survivor Benefits, 239, 257
Stepparents, 284
Spousal benefits after voidable marriage, 42
Stranger-to-the-adoption rule, 284–285
Uniform Probate Code, 167
Unmarried couples, 107

INSANITY, 124

INTENT-BASED PARENTAGE, 242

INTENTIONAL INFLICTION OF EMOTIONAL DISTRESS, 81–82

INTERNATIONAL CHILD ABDUCTION REMEDIES ACT (ICARA), 209

INTERNATIONAL LAW
Adoptions, 283
Foreign divorce decrees, 139–140
International adoption, 283
International parental child abduction, 209
Parental leave policies, 73
Same-sex marriage, 30
Surrogacy, 245

INTERNATIONAL MARRIAGE BROKER REGULATION ACT (IMBRA), 41

INTERNATIONAL PARENTAL KIDNAPPING CRIME ACT (IPKCA), 209

INTERSPOUSAL WIRETAPPING, 76–77

INTIMATE PARTNER VIOLENCE, 82–90
Assault, 85
Battered women's syndrome, 84–85
Battery, 85
Children's exposure to, 89–90
Disability, 83
Elder abuse, 83
Factor in child custody decisions, 191–192, 211
Factor in visitation conditions, 196–198
Failure to protect, 86–87
Firearm restrictions, 89
Gender and, 83

INTIMATE PARTNER VIOLENCE (*Cont.*)
High lethality crimes, 84
Immigration and, 83–84
Lethality assessment, 84
Mandatory arrest, 88
Mediation, 211
Mutual, 191–192
Name changes, 61
No-drop policies, 88
Protection orders, 111
Race and, 83
Risk assessment, 83–84
Role of various factors generally, 84
Same-sex partners as victims, 83
Self-defense, 85, 88
Shelters, 89
Sexual orientation and, 83
State-created danger doctrine, 86–87
Teen dating violence, 82–83
Unmarried couples, 111–112

IN VITRO FERTILIZATION, 238–240

IRRECONCILABLE DIFFERENCES, 126

IRRETRIEVABLE BREAKDOWN, 126

JOINT CUSTODY, 192–193. *See also* CHILD
CUSTODY
ALI Terminology, 192
Criticisms of, 193
Defined, 192
Parental agreement, 193
Presumptions, 193
Rationale, 192
Reform movement, 193
State approaches, 193

JURISDICTION
Adoption, 273, 276
Child custody, 191, 207–208
Child support awards, 170–176
Divorce, 134–141
Domestic relations exemption to federal jurisdiction,
140–141
Domicile, 134–135
Lex loci, 23
Long-arm statutes, 171
Native American children, 208
Personal, 134, 137–139, 170–171
Residency requirements, 135

Subject matter, 134–137
Transitory presence, 139

LEGAL TRENDS, 6–9
Congressional role, 6–7
Constitutionalization, 7–8
Federalization, 6–7
State laws, 8–9

LICENSES. *See also* PROFESSIONAL LICENSES
AND DEGREES
Marriage, 43, 44
Suspension for failure to pay child support, 175

LIVING WILLS, 66

LONG-ARM STATUTES
Child support jurisdiction, 171
Divorce, 138–139

MARITAL STATUS DISCRIMINATION, 47, 62.
See also MARRIAGE

MARITAL RAPE, 77–78
Common-law rule, 77
Modern trend, 77–78
State approaches, 77

MARRIAGE, 11–94
Age restrictions, 37–40
Annulment. *See* ANNULMENT
Capacity to marry, 25–31
As civil status, 58
Common-law, 45–47
Confidential, 45
Conflict of laws, 11, 13
Consummation, 41
Contraception. *See* CONTRACEPTION
As contract, 16, 58
Covenant marriage, 127
Coverture, 58
Divorce. *See* DIVORCE
Domicile, 52
Forced marriage, 42
Fraud and duress, 40–42
Fraudulent, 37–38
Licenses, 43, 44
Minors, 37–38
Necessaries doctrine, 59–60
Persons related by adoption, 284
Premarital agreements. *See* PREMARITAL
AGREEMENTS

Preparation for, 11–55
Prisoners, 24
Procedural formalities, 17, 44
Procedural restrictions on, 43–49
Property rights in spousal gametes, postmortem, 6, 238, 245
Property rights in spousal remains, 66
Proxy, 44–45
Putative spouse doctrine, 47–49
Remarriage and modification of support awards, 169
Restrictions on, 22–49
    adoption, 284
    affinity, 36
    age, 37–39
    capacity, 25–31
    consanguinity, 35
    constitutional limitations, 22–25
    procedural, 43–49
    state of mind, 40–43
    substantive, 25–43
"Retreat from marriage," 3
Same-sex. *See* SAME-SEX COUPLES; SAME-SEX MARRIAGE
Separation agreements, 16
Spousal right to terminate life support, 66
Transgender persons, 30–31
Unmarried couples. *See* UNMARRIED COUPLES
Validity of, 6, 17–19
Void and voidable compared, 49–50

MARRIAGE EQUALITY, 4

MARRIAGE FRAUD AMENDMENTS ACT, 41

MARRIAGE LICENSES, 43
Abolition of, 44

MARRIED WOMEN'S PROPERTY ACTS, 58, 81

MASSACHUSETTS LAW, 162, 230, 252

MATERNITY. *See* PREGNANCY AND MATERNITY

MEDIATION
Child custody, 210–211
Divorce, 141–142
Ethics, 211

MEDIATORS, 210–211

MELSON FORMULA, 164–165

MERETRICIOUS RELATIONSHIPS, 5, 102, 106.
    See also UNMARRIED COUPLES

MILITARY
Abortion, military personnel, 229
Discharge, 107
Don't Ask, Don't Tell policy, 107
Retirement benefits, 156

MINORS. *See* CHILDREN AND MINORS; PARENT-CHILD RELATIONSHIP

MODIFICATION OF CHILD CUSTODY ORDERS, 204–206
Joint custody, 192–193
Relocation controversies, 205–206
Standard for, 204–205

MODIFICATION OF SUPPORT AWARDS, 168–170
Factors considered, 168–170
Standard, 168

MORALITY, 5
Increasing role in reproductive health restrictions, 5
Waning of beliefs about, 5

MULTI-ETHNIC PLACEMENT ACT (MEPA), 275

MULTIPLE PARENTS, 245–246
Landmark California legislation, 245–246
Modern approach, 245
State law reform, 245
Traditional approach, 245
UPA provisions, 246

NAMES
Change of, 60–61
Children's surnames, 61–63
Domestic violence, 61
Maiden name, 60–61
    resumption of, 61
    retention of, 60
Same-sex couples, 61
Transgender persons, 61

NATIVE AMERICANS, 208, 275

NECESSARIES DOCTRINE, 59–60

NEPOTISM, 64–65

NEW YORK LAW, 154

NONMARITAL CHILDREN, 256–257
Fathers' rights to, 257
Support rights of, 256
Uniform Parentage Act, 257

NONTRADITIONAL FAMILIES. *See* FAMILIES

NOTICE
Parental notification
   minor's abortion, 234
   minor's access to contraceptives, 220
Personal jurisdiction, 137–138

OBAMA ADMINISTRATION, 107, 234

"OBAMACARE." *See* AFFORDABLE CARE ACT

OPEN ADOPTION, 285–286

PARENTAL CONSENT
Abortion, 233–234
Adoption. *See* ADOPTION
Health care for minors, 264–265

**PARENTAL KIDNAPPING PREVENTION ACT
    (PKPA),** 7, 208

PARENTAL RIGHTS
Contrast with same-sex spouses, 110
Second parent, 240
Voluntary vs. involuntary termination, 272

PARENT-CHILD RELATIONSHIP
Consent to medical treatment, 264–265
Earnings of child, 255
Education of child. *See* SCHOOLS AND
      EDUCATION
Medical care, 264–265
Necessaries, duty to furnish, 60
Parental fitness factors, 189–192
Termination of parental rights. *See* PARENTAL
      RIGHTS, TERMINATION OF
Tort liability, 251–254

PARENT LOCATOR SERVICE, 167

PARENTING COORDINATORS, 193–194

PARENTING PLANS, 193–194

PARENTING TIME, 186

**PARTIAL-BIRTH ABORTION BAN ACT
    (PBABA),** 7, 230–231

**PASSPORT DENIAL FOR NONPAYMENT OF
    SUPPORT OBLIGATIONS,** 176

PATERNITY
Child support, 167
Extension of laws to same-sex couples, 109–110
Presumption of, 108

**PATIENT PROTECTION AND AFFORDABLE
    CARE ACT (PPACA),** 221

PENSIONS AND RETIREMENT BENEFITS,
    155–156

PERCENTAGE OF INCOME MODEL, 164

PERSONAL JURISDICTION, 134, 137–139,
    170–171

**PERSONAL RESPONSIBILITY AND WORK
    OPPORTUNITY RECONCILIATION
    ACT,** 167, 172, 175

PET CUSTODY, 193

POLICE AND LAW ENFORCEMENT, 217

**POLITICAL SPEECH, FIRST AMENDMENT
    RIGHTS OF MINORS,** 259

POSTHUMOUS CHILDREN, 238–239, 257

POSTHUMOUSLY CONCEIVED CHILDREN,
    238–239, 257

POVERTY
Abortion funding, 229
Restrictions on marriage, 23–24

PREGNANCY AND MATERNITY
Fetal protection legislation, 235–236
Maternity leave policies, 69
Parental and family leave policies, 72–73
Pregnancy accommodations, 70
Pregnancy discrimination, 69–70
State sanctions for abortion participants, 232
Unemployment benefits, 73
Work-family conflicts, 73

PREGNANCY DISCRIMINATION ACT (PDA),
    7, 69–71

PREMARITAL AGREEMENTS,
    11, 15–22, 178

PRENUPTIAL AGREEMENTS. *See*
    PREMARITAL AGREEMENTS

PRESUMPTIONS
Bigamy, 33–34
Legitimacy, 243
Natural parent, 188
Primary caretaker, 187–188
Tender years doctrine, 187

PRINCIPLES OF THE LAW OF FAMILY DISSOLUTION: ANALYSIS AND RECOMMENDATIONS. *See* ALI PRINCIPLES

PRISONS AND PRISONERS
Marriage, 24

PRIVACY RIGHTS
Abortion, 223–224, 233–234
Confidentiality
adoption, 289
attorneys, 131
mediation, 211
Contraception and, 215–222
Family privacy, 8, 59, 60, 258
Marital communications, 75
Same-sex sexual conduct, 26, 36, 218–219

PRIVILEGES
Confidential communications privilege, 75–76
Interspousal wiretapping, 76–77
Self-incrimination, 217
Spousal disqualification privilege, 75
Testimonial privileges, 74–76

PROCEDURAL FORMALITIES, MARRIAGE, 17, 44

PROCREATION, 215–250
Abortion. *See* ABORTION
Alternative reproduction. *See* ALTERNATIVE REPRODUCTION
Contraception. *See* CONTRACEPTION
Infertility and adoption, 276

PROFESSIONAL LICENSES AND DEGREES
As property, 153–154
Suspension of for failure to pay child support, 175

PROPERTY DIVISION, DIVORCE
Adultery, 150
Bankruptcy, 157–158
Child support. *See* CHILD SUPPORT
Common law, 148
Community property, 148, 150
Contribution approach, 150
Earning capacity, 154–155
Equitable distribution, 148–149
Fault, role of, 149, 150–151
Goodwill, 154
Homemaker services, valuation of, 150
New York approach, 154

Partnership model, 150
Pensions and retirement benefits, 155–156
Professional licenses and degrees, 152–154
Property acquired post-separation, 148
Property determination, 152–153
QDROs, 156
Rationales for, 149–151
Separate property, 149
Separation agreements. *See* SEPARATION AGREEMENTS
Spousal support. *See* SPOUSAL SUPPORT
Standards for, 147–168
Steps in dividing, 152
Tax consequences, 162

PROPERTY SETTLEMENT AGREEMENTS. *See* SEPARATION AGREEMENTS

PRO SE DIVORCE, 129

PROXY MARRIAGES, 44–45

PUTATIVE SPOUSE DOCTRINE, 47–49

QUALIFIED DOMESTIC RELATIONS ORDERS (QDROs), 156

RACE
Factor in adoption, 275
Factor in child custody decisions, 188
Racial restrictions on marriage, 23

RAILROAD EMPLOYEES' RETIREMENT BENEFITS, 156

RAILROAD RETIREMENT ACT (RRA), 156

RAPE, MARITAL, 77–78

RECRIMINATION, 122–123

REHABILITATIVE ALIMONY, 162

REIMBURSEMENT ALIMONY, 162

RELATION BACK DOCTRINE, 50

RELIGION
Conflict between religious liberty and equality principle. *See* RELIGIOUS ACCOMMODATION LAWS
Factor in adoption, 275
Factor in child custody decisions, 188–189, 197
Factor in divorce, 128
Visitation and, 197
Waxing and waning of religious beliefs, 5

RELIGIOUS ACCOMMODATION LAWS
Abortion, 223–224
Adoption, 273–274, 275
Conscience clauses, 5–6
Contraception, 221–222
Extension to moral objections, 5–6
Religious refusal clauses, 5–6
Same-sex marriage, 29–30

REPRODUCTIVE TECHNOLOGY, 6

**RESTATEMENT (SECOND) OF CONFLICT OF
        LAWS**, 11, 51–52, 63, 135, 139

**RESTATEMENT (THIRD) OF CONFLICT OF
        LAWS**, 11, 52, 93

**RESTATEMENT (THIRD) OF RESTITUTION
        AND UNJUST ENRICHMENT**,
        254, 266

RESTATEMENT (SECOND) OF TORTS, 81, 251

RESTATEMENT (THIRD) OF TORTS, 252, 266

RESTITUTION OF BENEFITS, 254

RETIREMENT EQUITY ACT (REA), 156

**REVISED UNIFORM RECIPROCAL
        ENFORCEMENT OF SUPPORT ACT
        (RURESA)**, 172

ROE v. WADE, 223–224

SAME-SEX (UNMARRIED) COUPLES. *See also*
        SAME-SEX MARRIAGE
Access to assisted reproductive technology, 240
Constitutional protection, 99
Custody and visitation rights, 189–190, 201–202
Domestic partnerships, 27
Employment discrimination, 106–107
Foster parents, 273
Housing discrimination, 99–101
Inheritance law, 107
Non-marital children of, 168
Parental rights, 110
Paternity laws extended to, 109–110
Tort law, 101–102
Support and property rights, 102–106

SAME-SEX MARRIAGE. *See also* SAME-SEX
        COUPLES
Access to assisted reproductive technology. 240
Adoption rights, 273–275, 290

Artificial insemination, use of, 240
Child custody and visitation, 189–190, 201–202
Cohabitation contracts, 105
Common-law marriage and, 46–47
Constitutional protection, 99
Contraception, 218–219
Custody and visitation rights, 201–202
Foster parents, 273
Health benefits; employment-related, 106–107
International law, 30
Legalization of, 4
Name changes, spouses, 61
Parental rights, 110
Paternity laws extended to, 109–110
Religious accommodation laws, 29–30
Right to be listed on birth certificates, 62–63
Surrogate parenting, 242

SCHOOLS AND EDUCATION, 258–263
Canine sniffing, 262
Drug testing, 262
Firearms, 268
Free speech, First Amendment rights of minors,
        259–260
Locker searches, 262
Parents' right to control upbringing of child, 258–259
Political speech, First Amendment rights of
        minors, 259
Searches and seizures, Fourth Amendment rights of
        minors, 261–262
Special needs doctrine, 263
Strip searches, 262–263

SEPARATION
Annulment distinguished, 141
Divorce distinguished, 141
Legal separation, 141
Living separate and apart as ground for no-fault
        divorce, 125

SEPARATION AGREEMENTS, 177–178
Antenuptial agreements distinguished, 16
Child support post-majority, 166
Enforcement, 178
Modification, 178
Premarital agreements distinguished, 16, 178

SEX DISCRIMINATION, 2, 7, 69

SEXUAL ABUSE
Child bigamy laws, 34
Role in visitation conditions, 196–197

SEXUAL CONDUCT
Contraception, 218–219
Criminal liability, 99
Role in custody, 189–191
Role in visitation rights, 197–198
Same-sex relationships, 189–190

SEXUAL ORIENTATION. *See also* SAME-SEX
    MARRIAGE
Adoption and, 273–275
ALI Principles, 191
Employment discrimination, 106
Factor in child custody case, 190, 191
Role in visitation rights, 201

SHARED CUSTODY, 192–193. *See also* CHILD
    CUSTODY

SOCIAL SECURITY SURVIVOR BENEFITS,
    239, 257

SOCIETAL INFLUENCES, 2–6
Adoption and, 5, 6
Alternative family forms, 4
Children's rights, 4
Curtailment of reproductive freedom, 5–6
Dispute resolution process, dissatisfaction with, 4
Divorce trends, 3
Gay rights, 4–5
Morality, decreasing influence of, 5
Reproductive technology, 6
Traditional family, dissatisfaction with, 4
Waxing and waning impact of morality and
    accommodation of religious beliefs, 5
Women's movement, 2–3

SPERM BANKS, LEGAL REGULATION,
    246–247
ABA Model Act Governing Assisted Reproductive
    Technology Agencies, 246
Disclosure of medical and identifying
    information, 246
Federal law, 246
Fertility fraud, 247
International regulation, 247
Model law, 246
State law, 247

SPERM DONORS, 238, 239

SPOUSAL SUPPORT, 160–163
Alimony reform movement, 161–162
Background, 160

Bankruptcy discharge, effect of, 162
Contempt, enforcement by, 162
Defined, 160
Duty of support, 160
Massachusetts Alimony Reform Act, 161
Modification of award, 168–170
No-fault divorce and, 160
Permanent, 162
Premarital agreements, 19–20
Property division distinguished, 162
Rationale for, 160–161
Rehabilitative alimony, 162
Reimbursement alimony, 162
Statutory obligations, 60
Tax consequences, 162, 178–179
Temporary, 162
Termination of award, 162
Types of, 162

SPOUSES, RIGHTS AND RESPONSIBILITIES
Abortion, 232–233
Annulment, 50
Common-law disabilities, 58
Domicile, 63
Employment issues, 63–65
Health care, duty to provide, 65–66
Name changes, 61
Support, duty of. *See* SPOUSAL SUPPORT
Upon death, 66

STATE-CREATED DANGER DOCTRINE, 86–87

STEPPARENTS
Adoption
    custody and visitation issues, 285
    inheritance law and, 284
    noncustodial parent's consent, 280
Child custody, 201, 285
Child support, 165
Visitation rights, 201, 285

STRANGER-TO-THE-ADOPTION RULE,
    284–285

SUBJECT MATTER JURISDICTION, 134–137

SUBSTANCE ABUSE
Visitation rights and, 198

SUMMARY DISSOLUTION, 129

SURROGACY, 241–245
Birth certificates, 244

SURROGACY (*Cont.*)
Defined, 241
Dispute resolution, 242–243
Divorce and, 244
Foreign legislation, 247
Gestational agreements, 242
Intent-based parentage, 242
International law, 245
Parental status, pre-birth determination of, 244
Presumption of legitimacy, 243
Public policy, 243
Same-sex couples, 242
Statutory violations, 243

TARGETED REGULATION OF ABORTION PROVIDERS (TRAP) LAWS, 226–228

TAX CONSEQUENCES, 178–180
Child support, 179
Spousal support, 162, 178–179
Transfers of property incident to divorce, 179

TAX CUTS AND JOBS ACT (TCJA), 179

TENDER YEARS DOCTRINE, 187

TESTIMONIAL PRIVILEGES, 74–76

TITLE VII. *See* CIVIL RIGHTS ACT

TORT LIABILITY, 74–92
Actions against third parties, 78–80
Alienation of affections, 78–80
Battery, 84–85
Child custody orders, failure to comply with, 198, 209
Children, 251–254
Cohabitants, rights of, 101–102
Contraceptive use, misrepresentation of, 221
Contributory negligence, 252
Intentional infliction of emotional distress, 81–82
Interference with visitation rights, 198
Interspousal immunity, 80–81
Loss of consortium, 80
Massachusetts Rule, 252
Parents' liability for children's torts, 251–254
Sexual torts, 81
Unmarried couples, 101–102

TRANSGENDER PERSONS, 30–31
Discrimination in child custody, 190–191
Discrimination in housing, 99–100
Discrimination in military, 107
Domestic violence, 83, 111–112

Employment discrimination, 107
Name change, 61
Right to marry, 30–31

TRUMP ADMINISTRATION, 30, 107, 222, 234–235, 274

TURNER **GUIDELINES**, 175. *See also* CHILD SUPPORT

UNBORN VICTIMS OF VIOLENCE ACT (UVVA), 7, 235

UNCONSCIONABILITY, 19

UNEMPLOYMENT BENEFITS, 73

UNIFORM CHILD ABDUCTION PREVENTION ACT, 8, 209

UNIFORM CHILD CUSTODY JURISDICTION ACT (UCCJA), 208

UNIFORM CHILD CUSTODY JURISDICTION AND ENFORCEMENT ACT (UCCJEA), 8, 208

UNIFORM COLLABORATIVE LAW ACT (UCLA), 8

UNIFORM DEPLOYED PARENTS CUSTODY AND VISITATION ACT, 8

UNIFORMED SERVICES FORMER SPOUSES PROTECTION ACT (USFSPA), 156

UNIFORM INTERSTATE ENFORCEMENT OF DOMESTIC VIOLENCE PROTECTION ORDERS ACT (UIEDVPOA), 8

UNIFORM INTERSTATE FAMILY SUPPORT ACT (UIFSA), 8, 172–173

UNIFORM LAW COMMISSION, 8, 20, 112, 125, 172, 202

UNIFORM MARITAL PROPERTY ACT (UMPA), 8, 17, 20

UNIFORM MARRIAGE AND DIVORCE ACT (UMDA), 3, 8, 125, 126, 148–149, 161, 168, 192
Child custody, 186
Child support guidelines, 164

UNIFORM MARRIAGE EVASION ACT, 52

UNIFORM NONPARENT CUSTODY AND VISITATION ACT (UNCVA), 8, 202

UNIFORM PARENTAGE ACT (UPA), 8, 112, 167, 257

UNIFORM PARENTAGE ACT (UPA) (2000, 2002), 242, 257

UNIFORM PARENTAGE ACT (UPA) (2017), 109, 112, 167, 238, 257
Application to unmarried parents, 110
Application to same-sex couples, 201–202
Assisted reproduction, 239
De facto parents, protection for, 201–202
Multiple parents, 246
Surrogacy provisions, 242–243

UNIFORM PREMARITAL AGREEMENT ACT (UPAA), 8, 17, 20

UNIFORM PREMARITAL AND MARITAL AGREEMENTS ACT (UPMAA), 8

UNIFORM PROBATE CODE (UPC), 167

UNIFORM RECIPROCAL ENFORCEMENT OF SUPPORT ACT (URESA), 172

UNIFORM REPRESENTATION OF CHILDREN IN ABUSE, NEGLECT, AND CUSTODY PROCEEDINGS ACT, 8, 204

UNIFORM STATE LAWS, 8–9

UNIFORM TRANSFERS TO MINORS ACT (UTMA), 257

UNILATERAL DIVORCE, 126

UNMARRIED COUPLES, 99–115
Citizenship by descent, 110–111
Common-law marriage, 46
Contraception rights, 217–219
Criminal sanctions for sexual conduct, 99
Dissolution, 106
Domestic partnerships. *See* DOMESTIC PARTNERSHIPS
Domestic violence, 111–112
Employment discrimination, 106–107
Fluidity among family forms, 4
Housing discrimination, 99–101
Immigration-related issues, 110–111
Increased rate of, 112

Inheritance law, 107
Same-sex couples. *See* SAME-SEX MARRIAGE
Same-sex partners (former) parentage rights, 109–110
Support and property rights, 102–106
Tort liability, 101–102
Unmarried fathers' parentage rights, 107–108, 278–280
Zoning ordinances, 99

UTAH LAW, 40

VESTED, DEFINED, 155

VIOLENCE AGAINST WOMEN ACT (VAWA), 7, 89
VAWA (1996), 41
Reauthorization Acts, 38, 41, 83, 89, 111–112

VISITATION, 196–198
Child support and, 196
Conditions on, 196–198
Denial of, 196
Domestic violence, 196
Grandparents, 200–201
Interference with rights, 198
Religion and, 197
Same-sex couples, 201–202
Sexual abuse, 196–197
Sexual conduct, 197–198
Sperm donor's rights, 238
Stepparents, 201
Substance abuse, 198
Third parties, rights of, 200–202

VOLUNTARY ACKNOWLEDGEMENTS OF PATERNITY, 167

WASHINGTON (STATE) LAW, 106, 200

WEITZMAN, LENORE, 3

"WIFE BEATING," 85

WIRETAPPING, INTERSPOUSAL, 76–77

WITNESSES
Expert witnesses, child custody determinations, 204
Privileges. *See* PRIVILEGES

WOMEN'S HEALTH PROTECTION ACT (WHPA), 228

WRONGFUL ADOPTION, 281

YEARNING FOR ZION RANCH RAID, 32